"We Return Fighting"

"We Return

MARK ROBERT SCHNEIDER

Fighting"

The Civil Rights Movement in the Jazz Age

Northeastern University Press

Boston

NORTHEASTERN UNIVERSITY PRESS

Library of Congress Cataloging-in-Publication Data

Schneider, Mark R. (Mark Robert), 1948–
    We return fighting : the civil rights movement in the jazz age / Mark Robert Schneider.
        p.   cm.
    Includes bibliographical references and index.
    ISBN 1–55553–490–2 (acid-free paper)
    1. African Americans—Civil rights—History—20th century. 2. National Association for the Advancement of Colored People—History. 3. Civil rights movements—United States—History—20th century. 4. African Americans—History—1877–1964. 5. United States—Race relations. I. Title.

E185.61 .S355   2001
973'.0496073—dc21   2001030836

Designed by Christopher Kuntze

Composed in Adobe Utopia by Coghill Composition Company in Richmond, Virginia. Printed and bound by Thomson-Shore, Inc., in Dexter, Michigan. The paper is Writers Offset, an acid-free sheet.

MANUFACTURED IN THE UNITED STATES OF AMERICA
06 05 04 03 02   5 4 3 2 1

For JUDITH

and

for BEN LIEBERSON

Contents

Illustrations

Acknowledgments

At the outset of this project, I had conversations with three distinguished scholars of African-American history, who encouraged me to proceed and helped to shape this book. August Meier and John Bracey convinced me to limit the research to the 1920s, and John Hope Franklin advised that the job could be done. Later, Gerald Gill, through critical remarks at a meeting of the New England Historical Association, helped me to rethink some of my assumptions. Herbert Hill provided valuable insights into some of the leading characters.

Along the way, I met or otherwise conversed with people in various cities who illuminated the places they knew. New Orleans has a particularly complicated history, and I am thankful to the late Joseph Logsdon and Raphael Cassimere Jr. for suggesting a way through its labyrinth. In Detroit, Elaine Driker led me to Norman McCrae and Bernard L. Coker, who know more about that city's African-American history than I could squeeze into this book. Other researchers with local expertise read relevant sections: Phyllis Vine on Detroit, Alfred Brophy on Oklahoma, Monte Akers on Kirvin, Texas, and Griffin Stockley on Arkansas. The errors are all mine.

And, of course, I got by with a little help from my friends—my generous hosts Joanna Berkmann in Washington and Brad Rudin in New York. Ann Sparanese and Bob Guild, general readers with an interest in this subject; Boston College law professor Mark Brodin; and *Boston Globe* book critic George Scialabba read early chapters of the book. My supervisors at my "day job" at Amtrak's Back Bay station—notably Pete Cleary and Gerry Flaherty—were more than understanding of my occasional special needs.

At Northeastern University Press, I am especially grateful to John Weingartner, who has continued to believe in my work, and to the two anonymous readers who critiqued it.

Most of the research for this book was done in the Boston Public Library microfilm reading room. Thanks are due to John Divine, Elise Oringer, Dawn Riley, Henry Scannell, Nancy Walsh, and Xiping Zhang.

But most of all, I couldn't have done this without you, Judith.

"We Return Fighting"

Introduction

Ask any American what image the words *civil rights movement* conjure up, and she or he will probably answer with a statement about Martin Luther King Jr. leading a march in the 1950s or 1960s. Then ask the same person about the Jazz Age, and you are likely to hear about gangsters, Prohibition, flappers, or maybe even Louis Armstrong. Few Americans connect the civil rights movement of the 1950s and 1960s to its historical antecedents in any period. When I mentioned the title of this book to friends, they typically responded, "The civil rights movement in the Jazz Age? I didn't know there was one."

The civil rights movement is as old as the first slave's resistance to an overseer. That struggle is at the heart of American history. It is as old as the importation of slaves to St. Augustine, Florida, in the sixteenth century and runs like a river, sometimes almost trickling out and sometimes flooding the banks, throughout American history. We know the river best when it runs strong; I hope this volume helps us to understand the drier seasons.

The problem of how to view the river becomes compounded in the 1920s. Most of our textbooks focus on the two new and dynamic African-American movements of the period, that of Marcus Garvey and the Harlem Renaissance. After the World War, white Americans dashed the hopes for democracy of black veterans and their communities. Some of our historical literature suggests that African Americans gave up the struggle against Jim Crow and affirmed their separate identity through black nationalism and cultural self-expression. This image is partially true, but we should not let it obscure the continuing saga of the civil rights movement.

It would be more accurate to give at least equal billing to that struggle. In 1919, the National Association for the Advancement of Colored People, America's only nationally organized civil rights group, celebrated its tenth birthday. The NAACP had survived a difficult childhood and adolescence and was about to enter young adulthood. During the 1920s, it fought and won important battles in the streets, courts, press, meeting halls, state legislatures, city governments, and Washington lobbies. Even the battles that civil rights activists lost, such as the fight for the Dyer antilynching bill, had positive effects on American life.

Yet the NAACP of this period is still shrouded in myth. One myth is that it was white-dominated. The NAACP was born of a fusion between white radicals and W. E. B. Du Bois's Niagara movement, and its board of directors was indeed one of the few integrated bodies in the United States. However, the ascension of James Weldon Johnson and Walter White to the secretariat of the Association in 1919–1920 marked the first time in American history that African Americans ran a nationally organized civil rights group. Along with Du Bois, editor of the Association's monthly magazine the *Crisis*, and other colleagues, they formed a team leadership that gave their movement internal stability and authority within African America.

The focus of this book, however, is to dispel a second myth about the NAACP, which is that it had no mass base. My central argument is this: to understand African America in the 1920s, we must get off the A train to Harlem and head out of Manhattan for points west and south. In the vast America beyond, three hundred to four hundred African-American branches of the NAACP fought for voting rights and education, against segregation and lynching, in a thousand battles both spectacular and quotidian. From Elaine, Arkansas, to Duluth; from Charleston, West Virginia, to El Paso and Detroit, NAACP members distributed the leaflets, campaigned for members, and raised the money that kept the movement alive.

Another myth about the 1920s NAACP is that its rival—the Garvey movement—represented a mass movement of the working class, while the NAACP was an isolated movement of the black middle class. It is true that NAACP branch leaderships were generally middle class in composition, but the rank and file usually listed their occupations on the branch charters as those menial jobs to which white America had consigned them. In some industrial cities, notably Detroit and Birmingham, the NAACP and other black leaders helped African-American workers to get jobs in the factories by cooperating with employers. However, the NAACP's long-term strategy was to fight for the rights of those workers on and off the job. The Garvey movement, in contrast, was thoroughly imbued with the commercial spirit of the age.

The notion sometimes persists that the NAACP was assimilationist in its goals and not authentically African-American. Evidence for this idea sometimes comes from the camaraderie of the NAACP leaders with white patrons of the Harlem Renaissance, and perhaps from the lighter skin color of many Association leaders. The reality is more complex. Johnson, Du Bois, White, and *Crisis* literary editor Jessie Redmon Fauset contributed to the literature of the Renaissance and, through the *Crisis*, presented the young writers of the literary movement to a wider public. Through their writing, the NAACP leaders affirmed their pride in their separate identity and contributed to the very creation of African America through a national literature.

Yet, there is a more important matter than the activities of the New York leaders in assessing the nature of the NAACP in the 1920s. The branch members were black people, assembling in African-American churches, singing a national anthem written by James Weldon Johnson, and associating mostly among themselves. Because of the false polarity scholars sometimes posit between the impulse of black nationalism and the goal of desegregation, we sometimes view them as opposites. In fact, the NAACP is itself best understood as a moderately "nationalist" institution of the African-American community.

I have not discussed as a separate issue in this narrative the relation of the NAACP to the African-American church, but readers who know about the modern civil rights movement may be struck by the absence of preachers among the activists of the 1920s. Johnson, White, and Du Bois each had a spiritual side, but none of them was drawn to organized religion. Rather, they were enthusiastically secular people, more in tune with literary modernists than with purveyors of Sunday morning hellfire and brimstone.

In considering the NAACP and its place in American history, we have sometimes overlooked the obvious. The NAACP has endured because it had the right strategy to promote a revolutionary goal: full civil and political equality for African Americans. Every aspect of its strategy was at some point contested, and rivals who sought to destroy it—inveterate localists (often newspaper publishers such as Boston's William Monroe Trotter or Pittsburgh's Robert L. Vann), Garvey, or in the 1930s the Communist Party—failed. The NAACP was nationally organized, democratically run, interracial but black-led, and focused on one multifaceted goal. As this story will show, the NAACP used a variety of tactics to implement this strategy, ranging from mass action to lobbying. Whatever the individual failings of NAACP leaders, they had crafted the appropriate instrument to win the civil rights agenda, at least through 1954.

The story of the NAACP in the 1920s also highlights the attenuated nature of white racial liberalism in the early twentieth century. The old abolitionist impulse, best represented by the Association's national president, Boston attorney Moorfield Storey, and board chairman Mary White Ovington, was giving out. Populist and progressive reformers, even socialists, from the 1890s on had largely turned their back on civil rights issues, regarding it as a lost cause. The whites on the NAACP's board of directors represented a fading older generation, and no younger generation came along to take up their banner. In the 1930s, whites who fought for civil rights were more likely to join the Communist Party.

There may be a tautological perception that because nothing fundamental changed in American race relations during the Jazz Age, nothing too important could have happened then. The present story suggests that the mostly defensive battles of the 1920s were part of the river that overflowed the banks at midcentury. I hope that when readers contemplate the stories here about Phillips County, Arkansas, they will make the connection between the Supreme Court decision in that case to the outcome of the Scottsboro case of the 1930s. The Association's defense of integrated education in Gary, Indiana, helped pave the way for *Brown v. Board of Education* in 1954. The El Paso–based *Nixon* case facilitated the Voting Rights Act, and the defense of the Sweet family in Detroit and its opposition to residential segregation presaged the end of the restrictive covenant.

I have had to be selective in choosing what to include here and what to exclude. The NAACP archive, even for the 1920s, is enormous. I have attempted to arrange the narrative chronologically while organizing the chapters thematically and paying attention to geographic inclusion. So, for example, because I have paid much attention to the Phillips County, Arkansas, case, I have omitted other Arkansas material, such as the challenge to the white primary, while including Richmond's white primary case. In the education chapter, I have omitted the Fisk student struggle but included Harvard because Tennessee is discussed in the Maurice Mays case, but New England otherwise would be absent.

This story is about people who continued the fight when victory was not on the horizon. NAACP activists of the 1920s furthered human rights for all Americans, even if they did not win most of their battles. As the people who upheld the validity of Reconstruction-era amendments to the Constitution, these leaders of the 1920s deserve their place in American history along with the founders of the Republic, whose noblest beliefs they upheld and expanded.

I offer a final introductory word on terminology. When the narrative voice is my own, I use the contemporary terms *African American* or *black*. When reprising the voices of historical actors, I use the words they would have used in the 1920s: *colored people* or *Negroes*.

1

Make Way for Democracy!

THE armistice was only seven weeks old, and America was just getting used to peace in January 1919. Millions of survivors looked forward to resuming their normal lives and enjoying the familiar rhythms of work and home. There would be no more trenches, shelling, machine guns, and no-man's-land; now it was back to the factory or farm. In April baseball would start, and in the summer there would be time for picnics and the beach.

For African Americans, the end of the war promised change, not a return to old ways. President Woodrow Wilson had called the conflict "a war to make the world safe for democracy" when he asked Congress to fight Germany in April 1917. Returning black veterans knew that there was little democracy for them in America. They had killed and died in the trenches just like white men, and now they wanted their rights at home.

James Weldon Johnson remembered the promises. He was there when New York's black regiment, the Buffalos, marched from Madison Square Garden up Fifth Avenue to receive their colors from the governor at the Union League Club. The orators spoke stirring and patriotic words, urging the men to bring the flag home in victory, and now they had done it.

Johnson was the field secretary of the National Association for the Advancement of Colored People (NAACP). In his capacity as traveling organizer, he had recruited thousands of new members and organized dozens of branches since joining the staff at the end of 1916. A native of Jacksonville, Florida, he had experienced his share of race prejudice, and he had left the South with his New York–born wife, Grace Nail, to get away from it. Now forty-seven, Johnson had enjoyed a remarkable career as youthful baseball pitcher, school principal, lawyer, Tin Pan Alley songwriter, U.S. consul in Venezuela and Nicaragua, poet, and columnist for New York's leading African-American weekly, the *New York Age*. A balding, mustachioed man with a sober mien but good sense of humor, James Weldon Johnson was a true Renaissance man.

Johnson had carefully honed his speaking skills as well. On January 6 he left his ailing mother in his sister's care and proceeded to Carnegie Hall, where the NAACP was holding a rally for African freedom. The building was packed. Still concerned about his mother, Johnson sat, distracted and blue, on the platform. When it came Johnson's turn to speak, he told of that day when the troops had marched off to war, bearing the American flag. His voice swelled with the memory of the day's emotions, and the audience interrupted with a storm of applause. The flag, Johnson declared, bore

> the stains of Disfranchisement, of Jim Crowism, and of Lynching. . . . The record of black men on the fields of France gives us the greater right to point to that flag and say to the nation: Those stains are still upon it; they dim its stars and soil its stripes; wash them out! wash them out!

The crowd cheered again, and Johnson recalled the speech as the most effective of his career.

The next morning his mother was dead.[1] The bewildering confusion of triumph and death, of hope and sorrow, and above all of unleashed emotion made that night in January a paradigm for the rest of the year. The year 1919 would be the most tumultuous in American peacetime history, and the leaders of the NAACP would be right in the center of the action.

Although Woodrow Wilson had promised to keep America out of war in the 1916 election, most Americans agreed that when Germany began unrestricted submarine warfare against American ships, the country had no choice but to declare war. Only a small handful of radicals claimed that the World War was a slaughterhouse in which poor men died senselessly. William Edward Burghardt Du Bois, the editor of the NAACP's monthly magazine the *Crisis*, sympathized with that view. Yet, when war was declared, he argued that black people could best defeat American racism by loyally joining the war effort rather than opposing it. At war's end, he prepared to place the question of black rights on the American agenda.

Du Bois reached his fifty-first birthday in February, a highly celebrated and yet isolated man. Born to an African-American mother and a mysterious, light-skinned Franco-Haitian father whom he never met, Du Bois grew up in the mostly white Berkshire village of Great Barrington, Massachusetts. A brilliant student, he graduated from the local high school and attended Fisk University, Harvard, and the University of Berlin. He was the first black man to earn a doctorate at Harvard. Du Bois taught at Wilberforce College in Ohio, did sociological research in Philadelphia, and then taught at Atlanta University. During this time he published his research in history and sociology and in 1903 a book of essays titled *The Souls of Black*

Folk. This best-seller in African America established him as the leading black intellectual in the country. He helped to found the NAACP in 1909 and came to New York to edit the *Crisis*. Du Bois built it into the most outstanding civil rights organ in the nation, and by 1919 it had one hundred thousand readers.

Controversy over the African American's role in the war centered at first on the creation of a separate training camp for colored officers in Des Moines, Iowa. When the army refused to integrate officer training, Joel E. Spingarn, chairman of the board of the NAACP and Du Bois's most trusted white friend, accepted the separate camp as a compromise. Greatly influenced by Spingarn, Du Bois did as well, in part because he saw the positive role of separate black institutions generally. At the same time, Spingarn, who became a military intelligence officer, arranged to offer Du Bois a commission, which he accepted. Du Bois then wrote an editorial for the July 1918 *Crisis*, urging African Americans to "Close Ranks" behind the war effort and "while this war lasts, forget our special grievances." Rival civil rights leaders, including some NAACPers, attacked Du Bois for this conciliatory stance. The army reconsidered, denied Du Bois his office, and shipped Spingarn to France as a major in a white regiment.[2] Meanwhile, over 367,000 African Americans signed up for the military, proportionately more than the number of whites. Of these, 200,000 went overseas, serving mostly as stevedores and laborers. Those who saw combat, like their forefathers in the Civil War, covered themselves in glory. Four infantry regiments fought bravely in French trenches. The 369th from New York fought longer than any other American regiment and reached the Rhine before any white troops did. Having put their lives on the line, as well as earned the respect of the French and the fear of the Germans, the veterans and their home communities now expected the government to pay them its debt.[3]

Du Bois especially felt this way. He had encouraged the war effort through the *Crisis*, and he felt responsible for the war's effect on civil rights. Du Bois's biographer David Levering Lewis showed the similarity between the editor's situation and that of President Woodrow Wilson at war's end. Both were idealistic historian-intellectuals who cast aside grave doubts regarding the efficacy of war, yet Wilson led a nation and Du Bois a race into one. Both therefore had high hopes for the peace. The irony was that Wilson, a Virginian, held traditional southern racial views and would deny to African Americans the same rights he posited for subject European peoples in his Fourteen Points.[4]

On Armistice Day, the NAACP board met and agreed to send Du Bois on a dual mission to France. Each of his tasks would be Herculean for a team of scholars or activists. The first was to prepare a multivolume history

Returning soldiers, 1919. Courtesy of Schomburg Center for Research in Black Culture, New York Public Library.

of the African-American troops in the war. Even before the guns had stopped, American military officials began a campaign of slander against the colored officers, and Du Bois aimed to investigate their charges. The second assignment was to represent the NAACP and the *Crisis* at the peace conference by calling a Pan-African Congress (PAC). This would gather delegates from Africa and its diaspora to prepare resolutions for the conference of victors at Versailles.

Du Bois sailed for France on December 1, on the official press boat for peace conference journalists. There he shared a room with Robert Russa Moton, the successor to Booker T. Washington at Tuskegee Institute. Despite their philosophical differences, the two men got along cordially and even lectured the white journalists aboard ship. Sometime in January Du Bois began his investigations at the front, only to be met with icy hostility by white officers, trailed by military intelligence, and kept as far as possible from unsupervised contact with the black soldiers.[5]

Despite these obstacles, Du Bois gathered shocking evidence that indicted the high command. African-American soldiers and French authorities both criticized white American officers. In the May *Crisis*, Du Bois published "Documents of the War," which included interviews with these men and official military communiqués. Headquarters for the 372nd Colored Infantry secretly sought, in its own blunt language, "replacement of colored officers by white officers." The French called on their men to respect southern white racial mores, which forbade treating black soldiers as equals. In this and subsequent articles, Du Bois exposed fraudulent charges of rape against colored soldiers and proved the heroism of black men in battle. Perhaps most embarrassing for the military was Du Bois's charge that black troops had deliberately been sent "over the top" of the trenches underequipped and insufficiently armed. He concluded that "white officers fought more valiantly against Negroes than they did against the Germans." Du Bois had too many responsibilities, and he never wrote the multivolume history.[6]

Back in New York, the city welcomed its colored veterans home with a ticker tape parade. On a cold, sunny Monday, February 17, 1919, twenty-nine hundred men of the old New York Fifteenth National Guard, now the 369th Infantry Regiment, paraded seven miles up Fifth Avenue from 23rd Street to 145th and Lenox Avenue. The men gathered at Madison Square Park near the statue of Lincoln's secretary of state William Seward, and just across from the imposing new skyscraper, the Flatiron Building. Dubbed "Hellfighters" by their German foes, they made an impressive sight for the hundreds of thousands of New Yorkers, black and white, who lined the avenue and showered them with applause and candy. Led by Big Jim Reese Europe's marching band, the men received the heroes' welcome they had earned in the Champagne trenches over 191 days.[7]

Two days later, Du Bois opened the Pan-African Congress in Paris. Fifty-seven delegates from sixteen nations met for three days of speeches at the Grand Hotel. Blaise Diagne, a Senegalese representative in the French Parliament, collaborated with Du Bois and served as president of the meeting. The State Department denied visas to would-be American delegates, but sixteen Americans attended anyway. Addie W. Hunton, an African-American YMCA worker who would later join the NAACP staff, spoke on the neglected role of women in the freedom movement.

Du Bois wrote the preliminary and final resolutions for the Pan-African Congress, which dramatized the central weakness of the meeting: only a handful of the delegates were in fact African or had even visited there. Most of Du Bois's proposals were directed at the fate of Africa's four German colonies, inhabited by twelve million people. The delegates insisted that these should not simply be divided among the victors as spoils of war. Instead, they wanted an international commission to supervise them, in which African and diaspora leaders would have the decisive voice. Their task would be to prepare these natives, and perhaps those of the Portuguese and Belgian colonies as well, for independence by education. Contrary to imperialist propaganda, Du Bois argued, Africa would not descend into "chaos" once freed. Furthermore, who were Europeans, who had just plunged their own continent into chaos, to judge their black brethren? The PAC delegates argued that the supervising bodies must hold land in trust for the natives, abolish forced labor, promulgate health and education, and respect local cultures.[8]

This program fell short of demanding immediate independence. It was transitional in nature, mixing generally democratic ideas with more radical notions that led in the direction of independence. Certainly, the vengeful European victors were more intent upon punishing Germany than propitiating a handful of colored people who had no real power. While the French press covered the Pan-African Congress respectfully, the diplomats at Versailles paid it little heed. This was not the fault of Du Bois and his colleagues, and on balance the congress represented a bold attempt to assert African rights and to recognize the common bonds among a black diaspora divided by language. These were advanced notions for African Americans in 1919, and for Africans it was a harbinger of the freedom movement to come. Du Bois was the NAACP's visionary, a dreamer who thought internationally and took big risks to assert grand principles.

The NAACP had its share of pragmatic activists who thought the Pan-African Congress was a waste of time and money. Among such critics was Archibald H. Grimké, nineteen years Du Bois's senior and president of the most important branch, Washington, D.C. Grimké had faint hopes for peace and even less interest in Africa. Earlier he had criticized Du Bois for wishing to accept an officer's commission and still edit the *Crisis*. At the February board meeting he urged the Association to focus on American problems and stormed out when his resolutions were rejected. Nevertheless, under his pressure the board turned down Du Bois's requests for more money.[9]

The editor returned to New York in mid-April and answered his critics in the May *Crisis*. This cover depicted a sturdy black soldier chiseling his record onto a shield: "Loyalty, Valor, Achievement." Defending the congress, Du Bois argued that Paris had become the headquarters of all nationalities seeking self-determination, and that the congress had now established a permanent presence there on behalf of the darker races. "And yet," the editor thundered in conclusion, "some American Negroes actually asked WHY I went to help represent the Negro world in Africa and America and the Islands of the Sea.''

Turning to the other part of his mission, Du Bois made new enemies for himself among men whom the Association was courting at that very moment. He suggested that his shipboard companion, Dr. Moton, had whitewashed military racism in his reports. While not questioning Moton's integrity, Du Bois wrote that the principal's activities in France consisted of delivering bland homilies to the angry and militant soldiers. Further, he testily criticized the investigation by Emmett J. Scott, head of the War Department's Negro Bureau and former secretary to Booker T. Washington. Black newspaper editors were often more friendly to Moton and Scott, both of whom the Association was imploring to speak at its antilynching meeting in New York. Distressed chairman Mary White Ovington reported to the board in May that Du Bois had failed to submit these controversial editorials to the NAACP *Crisis* committee.[10]

Certainly, Du Bois had been more honest than politic. His weapon was the rapier, and sometimes he wielded it without regard to the consequences. However, when it came to expressing the poetry of a political moment, Du Bois had no contemporary American equal. He was African America's Tom Paine, the stirring pamphleteer whose ringing words called a people to action. The passage he wrote for the May *Crisis* was among the most memorable of his ninety-five-year-long life:

> The faults of *our* country are *our* faults. Under similar circumstances, we would fight again. But by the god of heaven, we are cowards and jackasses if now that the war is over we do not marshal every ounce of our brain and brawn to fight a sterner, longer, more unbending battle against the forces of hell in our own land.
>
> We *return.*
> We *return from fighting.*
> We *return fighting.*
>
> Make way for democracy! We saved it in France, and by the Great Jehovah, we will save it in the United States of America, or know the reason why.[11]

While Du Bois was in France, his colleagues planned a broad conference that asserted the growing power of the Association on the national scene. This meeting, organized by Executive Secretary John Shillady in New York and President Moorfield Storey of Boston, addressed the problem of lynching in America. Its platform reflected the NAACP's origins as a project of white liberals who had connections both to powerful whites and to African Americans.

White mobs lynched African Americans with impunity in 1919. Northern racist violence tended to be urban, and the perpetrators generally understood that they were committing a crime. Southern lynching was increasingly a public act of ritualistic terror carried out in the town square. Southern elected officials and newspapers generally condoned lynching as just punishment for evildoers, but racial liberals in the South opposed the practice as an affront to law, order, and civilization. Sometimes the newspapers would advertise the time and place of a lynching in advance. Often the victims were entirely innocent of any crime, often they were teenagers, and sometimes they were women. Sometimes the mobs tortured their victims and burned them at the stake. In 1917, mobs killed thirty-six African Americans, in 1918 they took sixty lives, and in 1919 seventy-six.[12]

The Association had focused on racial violence throughout its ten-year existence because it blatantly violated American law and was so dramatically barbaric. White northern opinion, while finding lynching deplorable, regarded it as one of those unfortunate facts of life about which nothing could be done, just as it had regarded slavery before the Civil War. The NAACP leaders thought they could mobilize progressive opinion against lynching, but they had to focus attention on what seemed to be one of just many problems Americans faced before and during the World War.[13]

In the aftermath of the war, race reformers raised their expectations. Moorfield Storey believed that the time had come to act on the matter. The distinguished seventy-five-year-old Bostonian represented in his very persona the New England antislavery tradition. A Harvard graduate, then secretary to Massachusetts senator Charles Sumner during Reconstruction, conservative corporation counsel, former head of the American Bar Association (ABA), and leader of the anti-imperialist movement during the war against the Philippines, Storey combined shrewd pragmatism and strict moral probity in his character. Although occupied with his private law practice, he was much more than a figurehead president. As leading spirit of the Association's antilynching committee, Storey hosted a meeting in his Boston residence at 24 The Fenway in November 1918. The committee called for a large conference to be held in New York. In April, Shillady brought out an NAACP pamphlet titled *Thirty Years of Lynching* that documented America's sorry record of racial violence. Storey and Shillady sought endorsers and speakers from the moderate center.[14]

Although the NAACP initiated the meeting, it was not to be an official Association event. Storey was under no illusions about the new situation posed by the armistice, and he wanted forces more powerful than the

NAACP to speak. He wrote to Shillady that white southerners planned "to prevent the negroes from claiming any further consideration on account of their services in the war. The negroes will come back feeling like men, and not disposed to accept the treatment to which they have been subjected. . . . I forsee a serious crisis." To meet it, Storey wanted declarations against lynching from the wealthy philanthropists who were bankrolling southern Negro education. Therefore, Storey and Shillady were careful to keep militant African Americans off the program, for fear of offending the moderates. Boston's outspoken editor William Monroe Trotter was kept at arm's length, and even Du Bois, who was in France during the planning, did not address the meeting.[15]

Storey insisted that he wanted a nonpartisan and nonsectional meeting, and his proposed lineup for the Carnegie Hall meeting would have Supreme Court justice and 1916 Republican presidential candidate Charles Evans Hughes; Democratic attorney general A. Mitchell Palmer; former Alabama governor Emmett O'Neal; and suffragist Anna Howard Shaw. James Weldon Johnson pointed out to Shillady that there was no colored speaker on the list, and only then did Storey realize that Johnson should speak. Robert Russa Moton and Emmett J. Scott, both of whom Du Bois had just criticized in the *Crisis*, declined to speak, probably after conferring with philanthropist George Foster Peabody.[16]

The conference was moderately successful, certainly a step forward, but in some ways was bitterly disappointing to Storey. The masses came, twenty-five hundred of them, black and white, on a day when the thermometer hit a broiling eighty-six degrees, but the New York lawyers whose influence Storey coveted stayed away. Justice Hughes brought the Carnegie Hall crowd to its feet when he demanded that the principles of the League of Nations should apply also to the United States and that the nation owed the colored veterans an end to the barbarism. Former governor O'Neal argued that governors should remove sheriffs who countenanced lynching, and suffragist Shaw and Johnson made effective speeches. The Tuesday afternoon session at the Ethical Culture Society featured African-American leaders, among them Judge Robert H. Terrell of Washington, Esther Morton Smith of Philadelphia, and Dean William Pickens of Baltimore's Morgan State College.

The *New York Age* ran the story under a banner headline, and the meeting brought several African-American leaders closer to the Association. Even Trotter praised the conference; Madame C. J. Walker, the cosmetics millionaire, and businessman Scott Bond of Arkansas contributed five thousand dollars and one thousand dollars, respectively; William Pickens later joined the Association's staff, and Moton spoke at the Tuesday meeting. But the event got little coverage in the white press and was buried on page 15 of the *New York Times*.[17] Two years later Storey complained to former U.S. attorney general George W. Wickersham that the appeal later drafted by a conference committee was signed by many prominent lawyers, "but when the conference was held not one of them came. They would not even walk across the street from their offices."[18]

Johnson wrote that the conference "marked an era" in the fight against lynching, and in a sense it did. The failure of new white leaders to join the movement showed the apathy of whites toward "the national disgrace," as Johnson called lynching.[19] The May meeting would be the last one geared toward winning white moderates. Finally, it would help convince the NAACP that national legislation was needed to stop a problem that was not going away.

THE NAACP took a major step forward at its tenth annual convention in Cleveland during the last week of June. Here the overwhelmingly African-American delegates took charge of the proceedings, and the white officers and board members realized how profoundly the Association had been transformed. The members arrived full of enthusiasm and plans for the future. Delegates came from small southern towns and big northern cities. They were female and male, professionals and workers, representing a diverse constituency. They addressed tough questions regarding the Association's strategy in the workplace, at the polls, and in education.

The chief organizer of the Cleveland meeting was the unofficial mother of the NAACP, the fifty-four-year-old former settlement house worker from Brooklyn, Mary White Ovington. The daughter of an abolitionist family, as a child Ovington heard fierce denunciations of Daniel Webster and Henry Clay for compromising with slavery. She was a "happy, healthy child," she recalled, who went to private school and later Radcliffe College, and who turned her youthful reform impulses toward settlement work in Brooklyn's immigrant Greenpoint neighborhood. At twenty-five, in 1890, she heard Frederick Douglass lecture, but it seemed then that "the colored question" was fading out. Years later when Du Bois published *The Souls of Black Folk*, Ovington eagerly read it and decided to start a settlement for Negroes in Brooklyn. Her investigations brought her into contact with Du Bois's militant Niagara movement, and she became its only white member. She was thus the only founding member of the NAACP with real contacts in the black and white worlds. By 1919 she was chairman of the board of directors and volunteered her time as secretary of branch work, in which capacity she made the convention arrangements.[20]

The Cleveland meeting was the first NAACP convention after the armistice, and the delegates felt that they faced a situation similar to that which existed at the end of the Civil War. The theme of a second Reconstruction appeared in several speeches. As before, the nation had passed through a terrible trial, African Americans had contributed their blood and sweat, and now it was time for whites to live up to wartime rhetoric. Even Emmett J. Scott, whose integrity Du Bois questioned in the May *Crisis*, came to speak. His very presence suggested that the old divisions had ended and that an exciting new period was beginning. To the astonishment of his former adversaries, Scott criticized the army brass for its racism, called for a full division of Negro troops led by Negro officers, and warmly praised the Association's leaders. There were new figures on the platform, such as Morgan State College's dean William Pickens, who touched on the Reconstruction theme, and old friends such as African Methodist Episcopal (AME) bishop John Hurst.

The Association was growing faster than it could manage, Association secretary John Shillady reported. In January 1918 there were 80 branches with 9,200 members, and now it claimed 229 branches with 62,200 members. The preconvention press release announced they were "Organizing 100,000 for Negro Rights." Texas, with the largest number of members, had 5,300 people in 24 branches. When Silsbee asked for its charter, he said, the office staff had to look it up on a map, and now it had 58 members in a town whose total colored population was 158. Birmingham, Alabama, had gone from 80 to 650 members that year. And lest there be any doubt about whether the NAACP was to be for the middle class only, Shillady emphasized that "we want every element of the community." The Texas branches had "farmers, longshoremen, people who work at everything." Looking out over the sea of black faces, the pale Irishman attempted to reconcile the Association's past with its future. The national office "regards itself as an agent and expression of the will and purpose of the colored people of America." Why then, is its president, chairman, and secretary white? "I do not know except that the great majority of the membership is colored and they seem to like us." Nonetheless, he added, "But the white people in this movement are very, very few, after all, when you think we have none in the South."

The Cleveland convention belonged to the delegates from the grass roots, many of them new recruits drawing inspiration from the sheer energy and number of their colleagues. At the session on publicity, the New Orleans members offered their branch newspaper, the *Vindicator*, as a model for other large cities. Southern representatives wondered aloud at how quickly their cities seemed transformed by the movement's growth.

Charleston, South Carolina, now had 1,300 members; the Wilmington, North Carolina, branch had helped 200 to vote at the last election. At an NAACP meeting many would know of the riot there in 1898 to block African-American voters. Wilmington, Delaware, had banned the showing of the offensive movie *Birth of a Nation*. Delegates from Thomasville, Georgia; Selma, Alabama; and Pensacola, Florida, described how the NAACP branch was born in their city. Shreveport, Louisiana, recruited 1,300 members through the churches, and the Columbia, South Carolina, Civic League had reorganized itself as an NAACP branch. They were registering people to vote (2,200 so far) and won a $40,000 Negro school building. A Louisville, Kentucky, delegate frankly addressed the class question. Facing hints that the NAACP was for the upper class, the local leadership went to a northern-owned factory that employed black workers, told the manager they were missionaries, and went onto the factory floor to talk a little Jesus and a lot of civil rights. Atlanta, with 65,000 African Americans, had the largest black population in the South. Women NAACPers organized a combined voter registration and join-the-NAACP drive, with as many as 180 people at nightly meetings. At the end of the campaign they held a rally at the largest auditorium in Atlanta. Now they placed a challenge before the entire Association. All previous conventions had been held in the Northeast or Midwest. If the NAACP was going to fight for civil rights, it was time to hold the next convention in Atlanta.

There were also complicated issues to consider. Probably nothing was more vexing than African-American relations with labor and capital. The NAACP cooperated with a sister organization, the Urban League, which devoted itself to economic questions—work and housing, especially. At Cleveland, Urban League leader Eugene Kinckle Jones motivated a closer working alliance between his group, the NAACP, and the American Federation of Labor (AFL), still led by the old cigar maker Samuel Gompers. He began with the lack of leadership for black workers. The Big Four railroad brotherhoods, then the most powerful unions in the country, banned colored members, but they were negotiating a merger with the AFL, whose recent Atlantic City convention had passed an antidiscrimination resolution. This presented an opportunity for black workers to gain admittance to the brotherhoods or form their own unions with genuine collective bargaining rights. In a few years, the AFL promise would prove to be mere rhetoric, and the African-American railroad workers would organize their own Brotherhood of Sleeping Car Porters under the leadership of A. Philip Randolph. The NAACP and its allies saw the opportunities as early as 1919.

On the other hand, the present reality was that white workers were overwhelmingly hostile to black workers, who in turn hoped to get jobs in ex-panding industries by forging cordial relations with the employers. Many NAACP leaders favored this approach to race improvement. Lieutenant George L. Vaughn of St. Louis reported that in his city, colored former strikebreakers now held good, permanent jobs in a steel plant from which the whites had formerly barred them. Birmingham NAACP leader Dr. Charles A. McPherson also tilted toward an alliance with capital, since 75 percent of the workers in the coal mines and steel plants there were black. The Newport News, Virginia, shipyards employed 4,500 Negroes, said local leader William Anthony Aery, some of whom earned the unimaginable sum of one hundred dollars a week. The Association weighed its hopes for an alliance with labor against the reality of white working-class hostility throughout the 1920s.

Another difficult question for the Association was how to use the ballot. African Americans were not entirely disfranchised in the South, were just beginning to vote in numbers in the North, and were overwhelmingly Republican. Yet, some African-American leaders occasionally voted Democrat. For example, James Weldon Johnson had himself been a Republican appointee, but Du Bois voted for Democrat Woodrow Wilson in 1912. Could branches participate in local politics without splitting over electoral matters? To what extent should the Association be involved in electoral politics at all? This would vary from place to place, and gradually the NAACP worked out an informal set of principles for itself, but in 1919 these questions were hardly settled. Wilmington, Delaware's Alice Dunbar-Nelson urged that colored women should get out and vote with the coming of women's suffrage. She also argued that colored voters should vote for the man and not the party, a position that raised eyebrows among strict Republicans. Mordecai Johnson of Charleston, West Virginia, made the strongest case for political action and Republican loyalty. Three Negroes served in the West Virginia legislature, one representing a majority white district. They had ended Jim Crow seating of railroad passengers, won better funding for the schools—which included two Negro colleges—and had established a facility for the mentally ill. On the other hand, warned Butler Wilson of Boston, a rock-ribbed Republican himself, some branches, like his own, had to be wary of alienating possible Democratic friends.[21]

Years later Ovington reminisced about this period in a column for the *Baltimore Afro-American*. "I wish I could make my readers realize the tremendous courage and enthusiasm that all we NAACP workers felt after our two conferences were over. . . ."[22] Within three weeks they would understand how much they needed those qualities as white America exploded in a fury of rage against the assertive New Negroes who had come home from the war.

2

It Just Explodes

ONE factor that underlay the NAACP's rapid growth in 1919 was the raised expectations of the returning veterans. A second factor was the burgeoning migration out of the South to the North, where jobs and freedom beckoned. As African Americans moved, they became more urban, proletarianized, and sophisticated. The migration deepened racial tensions all over the country, and these exploded during the summer of 1919 as white fears and hates encountered the assertive New Negroes. James Weldon Johnson branded the summer of 1919 "the Red Summer." This chapter examines the relationship between the Great Migration, the Red Summer, and the NAACP.

THE NAACP's biggest challenge was to recruit new members from the migrants who moved to the cities and to the North. Starting in 1915, an African-American migration out of the South laid the groundwork for a renewed civil rights movement. By voting with their feet against Jim Crow, defending their own rights, and creating the threat of a black labor shortage in the South, the migrants helped shift the balance of power in the struggle for civil rights. The migrants infused new life and energy into many northern NAACP branches.

Historians continue to reinterpret the causes, course, and size of the migration, which was closely observed by contemporaries. A blues song explained the migration's causes:

> Boll weevil in de cotton
> Cut worm in de cotton
> Debil in de white man
> Wah's goin' on.

Some historians have emphasized the economic push factors of crop failure and the oppressive tenant farming system. Others point to the continuation of Jim Crow while national leaders talked of democracy. Still others stress the pull factor of high wages in northern industrial jobs. They all agree that the desire to be treated with respect was the main reason for the exodus.[1]

The chief organizer of the flight was the *Chicago Defender*, edited by Robert Abbott, a migrant to Chicago who built his newspaper into the largest selling African-American weekly in the country. The *Defender*'s paid circulation grew from ten thousand in 1916 to ninety-three thousand in 1918, and it was read by hundreds of thousands more. Abbott argued that African Americans should not put up with southern depredations and called for a great leave-taking during the week of May 15, 1917. Railroad men distributed the paper throughout the South, and readers wrote to it of their plans. "Twenty families want to leave 'this hard luck place.' . . ." wrote one woman, "we can't talk to you over the phone here we are afraid to. They don't want to hear one say that he or she want to leave here if we do we are apt to be killed." Said a Florida woman of the migrants: "Negroes are not so greatly disturbed about wages. They are tired of being treated as children; they want to be men."[2]

It is difficult to know precisely the size of the migration. Historian Florette Henri notes that contemporaries estimated that 300,000 to 1,000,000 blacks went north by 1920. She settles for a figure of about half a million. There is no doubt that many northern cities suddenly had growing black communities. A special U.S. Census report on Negro population (itself a testament to the migration) emphatically concluded that "the greatest change in the distribution of the Negro race within the United States since 1790 occurred in the decade 1920–1930." While there had been one previous out-migration, that of the "Exodusters" of 1879 to Kansas and Oklahoma, this popular movement was decidedly greater. The largest black urban center was New York, where the population grew from 91,709 in 1910 to 327,706 in 1930, increasing by 66 percent in the first decade and 115 percent between 1920 and 1930. Chicago went from 44,103 in 1910 to 233,903 in 1930, and Philadelphia grew from 84,459 to 219,599. By 1930 these cities were respectively 5, 7, and 11 percent African-American. Of all cities, Detroit, seventh in total black population, showed the steepest percent increase. Only 5,741 African Americans inhabited the city in 1910, but the promise of industrial jobs swelled the population to 120,066 by 1930, a 194 percent growth rate in the 1920–1930 years. Only Gary and Buffalo grew faster, but their black populations were very small in 1910.[3]

More than a movement to the North, however, the postwar migration was a movement to cities. During the 1920s, the United States first showed an urban majority; in those years an urban area had more than 2,500 residents. White Americans were making the same trek as blacks from farm to city. It is sometimes forgotten that southern cities were growing, too. By 1930, Baltimore had the fourth largest black population with 142,106 (up from 84,749 in 1910); Washington was fifth with 132,068 (up from 94,446); and New Orleans was sixth with 129,632 (up from 89,266). After Detroit, the next largest black populations were in Birmingham, Memphis, and St. Louis. An often-quoted poem about the migration was entitled "They're Leaving Memphis." *Some* were leaving Memphis, but others were arriving. Its black population was 52,441 in 1910 and 99,077 in 1930. The historian Earl Lewis found that between 1900 and 1920, more blacks migrated to southern cities than to northern cities. (This probably changed in the next decade.) Of the next ten largest black population centers, six were in southern cities and all grew from 1910 to 1930.[4]

Some contemporary observers stereotyped the migrants as share-croppers, and certainly many were. Others, however, had worked in manufacturing enterprises such as lumber mills, railroads, iron and steel production, or the construction trades. About half the migrants came from towns, according to a Labor Department survey. The promise of higher wage industrial work was a major pull factor for many migrants. African-American workers headed for the coal pits and steel plants of Birmingham; the docks of New Orleans; the shipyards of Norfolk; the steel mills of Pittsburgh, Gary, and Chicago; the auto plants of Detroit; and the more diverse industries of Cleveland, Philadelphia, and New York.[5]

The demographic change wrought by the Great Migration must be kept in perspective, however. By the time the depression of 1929 slowed the movement down, 78 percent of black people still lived in the South, 20 percent in the North, and the remainder in the West. Northern African Americans dwelled overwhelmingly in cities, but despite the increase in urbanization, most southern blacks lived in rural areas. Georgia, Mississippi, and Alabama had the largest black populations from 1910 to 1930, and in 1930 the next eight states in order were all southern. Georgia was home to 1,071,125 African Americans in 1930, and the state with the largest black population in the North, Pennsylvania, had only 431,257. Those eleven southern states accounted for 8,407,397 of the country's 11,891,143 African Americans in 1930. African Americans made up almost 10 percent of the national population. It was this people, still mainly southern and rural but increasingly northern and urban, that the NAACP represented during the 1920s.[6]

WHEN AFRICAN AMERICANS arrived in cities, they looked for jobs and housing. White workers looked at them as dangerous rivals, not as brother workers. In six places, whites instigated major race riots. In Charleston, South Carolina; Washington, D.C.; Chicago; Knoxville; Omaha; and Phillips County, Arkansas, whites characterized Negro migrants as criminals, strikebreakers, or in Arkansas, as revolutionaries. At least twenty-five smaller clashes took place. Meanwhile, the mostly southern practice of lynching produced seventy-six black victims in 1919, up from sixty the year before. The NAACP tried to head off violence where it could, to prosecute its perpetrators, and to expose the economic causes of white fears.

The Charleston riot was exceptional in that local whites stayed out of it. The aggressors were sailors from a naval training base, who killed an African American during an altercation. When police attempted to arrest the sailors, their comrades fought back and then marched on the black community. The city authorities called out the marines, and the mayor insisted that "the negroes of Charleston must be protected." Charleston, a city of one hundred thousand, was almost 50 percent African-American, the highest percentage of any major American city. The possibility for serious violence was very real if the authorities did not act. Charleston's black men shot back when the sailors attacked, and when the firing stopped, two were dead and seventeen wounded; the better-armed whites suffered eight wounded. The mayor argued that the navy should compensate Negroes who lost property, and the coroner's jury blamed the sailors for starting the violence. The Charleston NAACP branch demanded that the navy punish the offending sailors, and a navy board ultimately convicted six men at court-martial. In this, too, the Charleston riot was unusual. In this Deep South city, the intellectual capital of secession, the city administration took firm steps to quell an antiblack outbreak and punish the offenders.[7]

JAMES WELDON JOHNSON scarcely had a moment to reflect during that entire breathless year; his only chance to put events in order would come when he composed his weekly column for the *New York Age*. These articles displayed the wide range of Johnson's interests: international politics, music, literature, the theater, race relations, U.S. politics. Johnson worked in New York during the winter, corresponding with scores of NAACP branches, attending the weekly staff meetings and monthly board meetings of the Association, writing his column. Later in the spring, Johnson planned a tour of the West Coast branches for himself. He made an effective speech at the Association's antilynching meeting at Carnegie Hall in May, and then he headed west.

On the way, Johnson took one day off to see the Grand Canyon. He spoke in San Diego and recruited two judges and the chief of police; that same day he took the train north and spoke in Pasadena. At Oakland a large audience gathered in the city auditorium. By the time he reached the Northwest he was completely exhausted, but he veered off to Spokane and then doubled back to Seattle. There he was welcomed by Mayor Ole Hanson, who in February had broken a general strike. On June 6 Johnson took the ferry to Tacoma, dashing off a note to Ovington complaining that he had had "only three consecutive hours to myself since Los Angeles." Looking ahead to the NAACP convention at the end of the month, he implored, "If I am alive when I get to Cleveland, I hope I may be excused from speaking."[8]

The Washington riot lasted for five days in mid-July and drew national headlines. This was the first big city clash in which African Americans fought back with guns. Johnson praised them in his column and went there in the heat of the battle.

The District of Columbia had received few black migrants during the war because the Democratic Woodrow Wilson administration offered them few jobs. White southerners poured in, however, bringing their racial attitudes with them. Washington officials refused to allow a parade for its returning African-American veterans. When a black man was charged with committing sex crimes in July, the *Washington Post* whipped up a pogrom, to the point of advertising a mobilization site for white thugs. Washington NAACP leaders tried unsuccessfully to convince the white dailies to desist, but they all ran alarmist headlines. They implored Navy Secretary Josephus Daniels to restrain off-duty white sailors, but he did nothing. Part of the *Post*'s motivation was to force the resignation of the district's commissioners, and innocent African Americans paid for this cheap political ploy with their lives. So did whites. The police arrested about one hundred blacks and a few whites.[9]

On the train to Washington, Johnson sensed the apprehension of the trainmen, who knew him and urged him to be careful. He arrived on July 22, in the middle of the fighting. To his surprise, Johnson found the black community "calm and determined." Along with other local leaders, he urged the authorities to deputize colored men, but they turned a deaf ear to his idea. Three friendly senators agreed to promote congressional hearings, but most senators regarded the violence as a local problem. Then Johnson met with the editors who had stirred up the trouble, one of whom seemed "struck dumb" by all that had happened, Johnson wrote. Johnson was astonished when the newspaper printed his remarks, unattributed, the next day. After a return to New York, during which Chicago erupted in worse violence, Johnson went back to Capitol Hill to lobby again for an investigation. The branches must "bombard their representatives in Congress with telegrams and letters," he wrote Ovington.[10]

Then Johnson was back on the train for St. Louis and the National Negro Business League convention. There he made a speech and met among the delegates one M. H. Gassaway of Anderson, South Carolina. Gassaway was principal of the Negro school and president of the NAACP branch. The white newspaper was charging Gassaway with leading an organization that advocated "social equality" and asserted that he therefore should be run out of town. Hurrying next to Atlantic City, this time to address the fraternal lodges of the Knights of Pythias, Johnson found a letter from Ovington describing a similar situation in Austin, Texas. In this case, state officials had requisitioned the Association's books, threatening to declare the NAACP illegal throughout the state. Johnson, putting the two stories together, began to grow alarmed. "It would be disastrous just now to allow the colored people in the South to be so intimidated that they would be afraid to be identified with the Association," he wrote. John Shillady should go to Texas and South Carolina to stop the problem before it spread, he urged.

> In all these questions, the National Office must stand strongly behind the locals. It will not do to let them feel that it is *their fight and not ours.* It may be that the whole future of the organization in the South depends on what we do at this moment.

At Atlantic City, Johnson addressed the Pythians for an hour and twenty minutes and made a striking impression. The next day he spoke to the Court of Calanthe, the women's division, and the entire group endorsed the Association. "The Pythians have key men from all over the country," he wrote Ovington. Within a few months, a Little Rock, Arkansas, Knight would become the Association's lawyer in its most important case of the 1920s. But now Johnson, confident of Shillady's mission, set out for the Hampton Institute in Virginia and a few days' rest.[11]

THE ASSOCIATION's assistant secretary, whom Johnson had recruited from the Atlanta branch, was the serendipitously named Walter White, who could change his racial identity virtually at will. Light-skinned, blue-eyed, and blond-haired, he appeared to those who met him as a "white" man, but the trace of Negro blood in his parents' veins made him a colored boy in Atlanta, where he was born in 1893. Despite his appearance, White felt that he was "colored," a sentiment formed during the 1906 Atlanta pogrom when a mob menaced his house. He came to work for the Association in

February 1918, filled with brash exuberance. White proved to be fearless in the matter of infiltrating groups of white killers.

During 1919 he traveled relentlessly. In January he organized an NAACP branch in Nashville, Tennessee, convincing local rivals to put their differences aside. He had a similar success at Chattanooga, where he also urged the newly elected state attorney general to present an antilynching bill. In New Orleans, 1,200 people packed the NAACP headquarters at the Pythian Temple, and 102 new members joined. "I reached your class," he boasted to Johnson, "when I had to hold up my hand to stop the cheering. In other words, 'I done a Roscoe' on them."[12]

White next went to Tuscumbia, seat of Colbert County in Alabama's northwest corner, on the Tennessee River. There he met with NAACP secretary Shillady to attend an unusual trial of southern lynchers. The preceding November, Will Byrd of nearby Sheffield had celebrated the armistice by firing his revolver into the air. For this he was jailed, unfortunately next to two other African Americans who had shot a local policeman. When a lynch mob came for the latter two, they got Byrd by mistake and killed him. Later they realized their error and returned to the jail, finding one of the others, whom they also lynched. Governor Charles Henderson and the state attorney general then decided to prosecute eighteen of the perpetrators. At the trial, several African-American prisoners courageously testified that they saw the sheriff put up only token resistance, and identified the lynchers. In his conclusion, the prosecutor baldly spelled out the state's motivation in the case: if niggers are lynched, he argued, especially the wrong ones, northern business, like the local nitrate company, might decide that the situation was unstable and leave the state. Despite this appeal to business practicality, the first two defendants were found not guilty to rousing applause after twenty minutes of deliberation. All the locals knew they were guilty, White reported, and everyone knew they would be released.[13]

White returned to New York and promptly set out on another grueling journey. In March he was in Coatesville, Pennsylvania, scene of a notorious 1911 lynching. This time the police had run out of town laid-off African-American industrial workers. In justification, the police chief declared he had expelled unemployed whites, too, and that his police force was integrated. Then he went down the East Coast from Boston to Aiken, South Carolina, and after that to the Midwest to build the Cleveland convention. In Indianapolis he joined Du Bois at a meeting of 800 people; later the local branch sponsored a banquet for them at which 327 new members signed up. Even the governor came along, telling White he hoped "50,000 more colored come to Indiana." The Indianapolis branch had recruiting posters up on the streetcars. After the Cleveland convention, White left for Atlanta, finding the opposite mood from that of Indianapolis. In the wake of the Washington riot, Atlanta felt like a powder keg. Whites were buying guns in a frenzy but blacks could not. "The result [is] that everybody is afraid to talk," White found.[14]

The Chicago riot began on a sweltering July 27, when a white man threw stones at a group of young black bathers. One boy drowned and his companions ran for help. They had been swimming in a "no-man's-land" between segregated beaches. The youths found a black policeman and pointed out the culprit, but a white officer stopped the black one from making the arrest. As word spread along both beaches, anger and then shooting started. It lasted for five days, halted only by rain and the state militia. When it was over, 38 were dead, 23 of whom were African American, and 7 of these had been killed by police. Official reports counted 537 injured, 342 of whom were black.

As in Washington, blacks defended themselves with guns when attacked. The police tried to stop the fighting by massing their forces along neighborhood racial borders, but this left blacks working in white neighborhoods unprotected. Tough, mostly Irish gangs of hoodlums like the Ragen Colts, Hamburgers, and Aylwards could gang up on isolated individuals. Unlike Washington, however, African Americans in Chicago committed counterterror, firing on whites in retaliation.[15]

Arriving after the violence stopped, White met with the local NAACP leader, dentist Dr. Charles E. Bentley; T. Arnold Hill of the Urban League; and sociologist Robert E. Park, Urban League president and former speechwriter for Booker T. Washington. On August 7 he watched as three thousand black stockyard employees returned to work protected by machine-gun-wielding state troops. Later he attended a meeting of the Joint Emergency Committee, an interracial body of white liberals and mainstream black community groups, which Shillady had organized shortly before White arrived. White was put in charge of investigating the riot for this group. He found four broad areas (he enumerated them as eight in a *Crisis* article) that underlay the riot. But White ran up against the complex reality of Chicago race relations and black community politics, which the NAACP was never able to surmount during the 1920s.[16]

Chicago was the promised land of the Great Migration. Chicago meant jobs, especially in the packinghouse industry. However, the businessmen who encouraged the migration frequently used newly arrived black workers, some of them entirely unsophisticated regarding urban labor relations, as strikebreakers. For their part, the unions either barred African-American workers or failed to protect them if they admitted them. As historian Wil-

liam M. Tuttle Jr. argues, black packinghouse workers, despite belated efforts of union organizers, largely refused to join the union in the city's
largest industry. A labor upsurge in Chicago left these black workers "between the devil and the deep blue sea," White wrote.[17]

The situation was further complicated by the significant political power
African Americans already commanded. In effect, Republican mayor William H. "Big Bill" Thompson owed his election to black voters, who gave
him 24,000 of his 28,000 vote plurality. He in turn rewarded a select few
with patronage, and this base gave him continued loyalty. An outsider, the
headstrong White wanted to call Chicago officialdom to account while
local leaders were inclined to proceed more cautiously. They understood
that some Democratic politicians wanted to use the violence to separate
the black community from its alliance with Thompson.[18]

A third cause of the riot was lack of housing and consequent attempts
of middle-class black people to move into white neighborhoods. By 1920
the black population of Chicago had almost tripled from fifty thousand in
1915. Crowded into a Black Belt centered in the second and third wards,
wealthier African Americans attempted to buy homes in white areas. The
whites responded with a campaign organized by neighborhood associations, often backed by realtors attempting to "protect" property values.
In June, White infiltrated a meeting of the Kenwood–Hyde Park Property
Owners Association. There he heard plans to drive out new black home
owners. The whites schemed to fire blacks from their jobs and foreclose
their mortgages if they missed a payment. Ultimately, they turned to violence. Between January 1918 and August 1919 twenty black-owned proper-
ties were bombed in Chicago. There were no arrests.[19]

This led to the final cause of the riot and, to White's mind, the one most
demanding a response. During the riots, the police let white terrorists go
free while killing seven black men themselves. In one case, White thought
witnesses could identify policemen who escorted white thugs away from a
murder scene and freed them. He counted fifty Negroes charged with serious crimes, while whites were accused only of lesser ones. White thought
the committee should vigorously defend the accused Negroes.

Old factional rivalries blocked White's efforts. Conservative white reformers such as Park thought the only province of the committee was talk.
"I told him there was an immediate need of action," the frustrated White
reported to Ovington. Others, he felt, completely underestimated "the seriousness of the situation" and were disinclined to prosecute racist policemen. The same spirit infected the local NAACP, which was, more than
most branches, influenced by whites and conservative middle-class blacks
typified by dentist Charles Bentley. Militants hindered the work also. One

day White met attorney Ferdinand L. Barnett. White did not know he was married to Ida B. Wells, the fiercely independent antilynching crusader who regarded the NAACP as too white-influenced. Wells was there with her husband. "Had I known it I would not have gone," White lamented. "She launched into a tirade against every organization in Chicago because they have not come into her organization and allowed her to dictate to them."

On another occasion, on his way to visit a black-owned bank, the blond-haired White turned his head to discover a black man pointing a pistol at him from behind a tree. He jumped out of the way as the bullet missed him by inches. White left Chicago with a sense of its vast importance to black America and the NAACP and the difficulty of organizing it.[20]

THE RIOT at Longview, Texas, began with an interracial love affair. In June 1919 Lemuel Walters was discovered in the room of his lover, arrested, and charged with rape. Then Walters was dragged from his cell and through the streets of Longwood to a suburb, where he was riddled with bullets and his naked corpse left tied to a tree.

Longview was a cotton center about 150 miles east of Dallas, one-third of whose five thousand people were African American. A Negro Business-men's League, founded by Dr. C. P. Davis, was intent on winning farmers a fair price for their crop by eliminating white middlemen. One of Davis's colleagues, a high school teacher named Samuel L. Jones, reported the lynching of Walters for the *Chicago Defender*, which circulated widely in the South. The article declared that Walters was no rapist and that his grieving lover would have married him had state law not forbidden it. Jones's article was unsigned, but on July 11 a mob came for him as the probable author, beat him severely, and ordered him out of town. Then a larger crowd invaded the black community and burned down several homes and shops until they were driven off by armed defenders who wounded four whites. The governor called in the Texas Rangers, who ar-rested twenty-three whites and twenty blacks. These latter were sent hun-dreds of miles south to Austin, probably to prevent a storming of the jail.[21]

The Austin and San Antonio NAACP branches then appealed to Texas authorities to release the men, most of whom had not been charged. The state freed half of them after ten days, and the others, who allegedly had done the shooting, in August. They were let go on the condition that they not return to Longview. Jones and a few others escaped by train the night of the white invasion, mixing incognito with a group of black soldiers by passing themselves off as ignorant field hands. Dr. Davis evaded a pack of bloodhounds and drove north to Topeka, Kansas.[22]

The NAACP intervention on behalf of the Longview prisoners concerned Texas authorities. It fit into a pattern which hard-line whites in the state, county, and city governments began to put together. From small towns such as Greenville in the northeast corner of the state; to Cuero, southeast of San Antonio; and in most big cities, black people were joining the NAACP and demanding full citizenship rights. In Houston, a new and outspoken leadership grouped around Clifton F. Richardson, editor of the *Informer*, was replacing more conservative black leaders.[23]

Austin, state capital and seat of Travis County, also had a new NAACP branch. In late 1918 and early 1919, local activists signed up seventy-five charter members, thirty-four of whom were women. About twenty members were professionals—doctors, lawyers, ministers, teachers—and the rest were laborers, domestics, cooks, and other workers. Branch leaders met with the mayor and police chief to protest the beating of a Negro veteran by a gang of whites after he bumped into a youth in a store. The police arrested the seriously injured veteran and let the whites off. Branch president P. A. Williams wrote that the veterans "have returned to old homes but are not going to submit to old conditions." The Austin branch boycotted the store, the merchant lost his African-American customers, and the local people raised money for a defense fund.[24]

This was all too much for a gang of Negrophobes among the state, county, and municipal governments. Governor William P. Hobby ordered the Texas Rangers to investigate suspected Bolshevik propagandists among the Negro population. The authorities secured a copy of the *Crisis* and decided that the NAACP could be shut down for operating without a state charter. The attorney general demanded that Austin president Williams present the Association's books on August 9. This Williams did and, fearing prosecution, wrote to the national office for guidance.

Considering this letter in their office at 70 Fifth Avenue near Fourteenth Street in Manhattan, John R. Shillady and Mary White Ovington realized that the fate of the organization in the South might lay in the balance. They reckoned that the Association, a national membership organization incorporated in New York state, would have nothing to fear if taken to court. Further, the NAACP by now had a lot of clout: a U.S. Supreme Court justice had spoken at the Carnegie Hall antilynching meeting, and if the NAACP appealed its banning in Texas to a federal court, it would probably win. A visit by Shillady to the governor should impress upon him the Association's dedication to, rather than subversion of, law and order. Yet, Texas was a violent lynching state, and Shillady asked frankly, "Do you think there is any danger?" The Shilladys had lost two children, and Ovington knew that he and his wife were still grieving. John Shillady was a tall, prematurely greying Irishman from County Down who had left a career in social work to join the Association's staff. Ovington reminded him of his recent trouble-free trip to Memphis and suggested that Texas should be no worse.[25]

Shillady made the two-day train ride to Texas, arriving in Austin on the evening of August 20. The next day he met the Austin NAACP leaders, who reported that the authorities had disbanded the branch. Then he went to the capitol building to discover that the governor and attorney general were out of town. He did meet with an acting attorney general and the adjutant general in charge of the Rangers, W. D. Cope. Cope told him that his office had been investigating Negroes since the Longview riot, and he had concluded that by advocating "race equality," the NAACP was stirring up trouble. Shillady made his case for the law-abiding nature of the NAACP and left with the matter unresolved.

On his way out, he was tapped on the arm by a man who served him with a subpoena and led him immediately before a kangaroo "court of inquiry." There a gang of hard-faced, hostile interrogators sought to intimidate him, asking questions such as, "Would you want your daughter to marry a nigger?" They made it clear that they regarded him as an outside agitator who had better get out of town.[26]

Undeterred, Shillady met the following morning with the local NAACP-ers again to report what had happened. Upon his return to the Driskill Hotel, the same gang was waiting for him and another group pulled up in an automobile. County judge David J. Pickle accused Shillady of "inciting" the Negroes against the whites.

"You don't see my point of view," Shillady answered.

"I'll fix you so you can't see," Constable Charles Hamby replied and slugged him in the eye. Shillady, a pacifist, didn't have a chance, and three men beat him until his face was covered with blood. Shillady staggered into the hotel, got a doctor to sew his face back up, and went straight to the train station, boarding the 12:20 for St. Louis. The whole affair had taken place in broad daylight on a busy street, and when it was over Pickle told a reporter, "I whipped him and ordered him to leave because I thought it was for the best interests of Austin and the state." Pickle blandly gave the names of his associates, saying that they were acting in an unofficial capacity. Over the next two days, Association officials followed Shillady's progress home in the newspapers. The New York office protested to Governor Hobby, who returned a terse message: "Shillady was the only offender in connection with the matter."[27]

Johnson, Ovington, and Mrs. Shillady met him at Penn Station in New York. The NAACP had been recruiting the redcaps in the station, black men who worked mostly for tips, and encouraging their unionization. When the train arrived, Ovington recalled, the group "heard the cry of 'Shillady' as the train came in and I saw Red Caps, dozens upon dozens, tearing down the platform, crowding to meet the man who had suffered in their cause. It was a great demonstration."[28] Even after several days on the train, Shillady looked wounded when he got off. "His face and body were badly bruised," Johnson remembered, "moreover he was broken in spirit. I don't think he was ever able to realize how such a thing could happen in the United States to an American, free, white, and [over] twenty-one." Ovington, using the language of the day, thought he looked "like a shell-shocked soldier."[29]

Ovington and Johnson hoped to turn this lost battle into a victorious war. Surely, they reasoned, liberal opinion would force Texas officials to back down and prosecute the known perpetrators of a brazen assault. They thought the Texans had overplayed their hand, and the Association prepared to call their bluff. They urged Congress and the president to investigate, since the governor had abdicated responsibility. They would ask New York governor Al Smith to demand protection for New Yorkers traveling in Texas, and they would sue for damages. Finally, Johnson blasted conservative Austin Negroes, led by Reverend L. L. Campbell of the large Ebenezer Tabernacle, who had trivialized the incident.[30]

All these plans came to naught. Storey wrote to his legal friends in Texas, who recommended a San Antonio lawyer who might take the case. Yet one friend frankly advised that the case would be "very unpopular," and indeed, the NAACP, which at this point still relied on white lawyers in crucial cases, could not retain one attorney in Texas. The San Antonio branch did convince the mayor, sheriff, and *San Antonio Express* editor to speak out against lawless behavior, but it wasn't enough. As Shillady and Ovington had initially feared, the Texas branches crumbled under renewed local pressures. Historian Steven A. Reich concluded that "by the end of 1921 all but 7 of the 33 branches had disbanded."[31]

The effect on Shillady was no less traumatic. He continued to serve until June of 1920, but his colleagues could see that his spirit was broken. Arthur Spingarn, the head of the Legal Committee in New York, thought he had a kind of "nervous breakdown" and that he "was ashamed of himself" for what had happened in Austin. Ovington more charitably, and with greater insight, recalled that it was Shillady "who put our house in order," turning the Association into a smoothly functioning machine.[32]

THE September 28 Omaha riot was similar in some respects to Chicago's in that whites felt provoked by Negro migrants who unwittingly broke a strike. The triggering incident was an obscure charge of rape, the veracity of which remains questionable. Black people were a small minority in this meatpacking town: only ten thousand lived among two hundred thousand whites.

The Omaha NAACP was founded in 1918 after Mary White Ovington spoke there. Its members included a doctor and two ministers, but most of the charter members were working-class people: four waiters, three janitors, three housewives, three laborers, three domestics, and a smattering of tradesmen. The branch leaders, Reverend John A. Williams and attorney Harrison J. Pinkett, a Howard graduate and veteran of France, had opposed older Negro "bosses" who ran the vice rackets in the city's red-light district, the Midway. Williams and Pinkett worked throughout 1919 to alleviate racial tension and build a strong presence, holding weekly meetings in a church. When the *Omaha Bee* ran sensationalized stories on Negro crime, the NAACP organized a protest rally of six hundred. A police watchdog committee discovered that most of the newspaper stories were baseless. W. E. B. Du Bois spoke there in May 1919, and Mayor Edward P. Smith sat on the platform. The four hundred NAACPers joined an interracial committee that sponsored a "Welcome Home" picnic for returning veterans, and the festivities at Krug Park proceeded without incident.[33]

Earlier in 1919, meatpackers and teamsters went on strike, and African Americans took their jobs, having been blocked from the industry previously. This encouraged a groundswell of racial animosity. The *Bee* began its crime stories, and in September a white girl was raped, claiming her assailant was a black man. The police drove forty "suspects" out of town, and finally, on September 28, the police arrested William Brown. A mob gathered at the courthouse, Mayor Smith refused to turn Brown over, and the mob seized the mayor. Mayor Smith was beaten, a noose thrown around his neck, and he was about to be hung from a light pole when the police rescued him. Still the police refused to fire on the crowd, attacking it with fire hoses that were easily cut. The mob overwhelmed the lawmen, set fire to the court, and found Brown, whom they beat, hanged, and riddled with bullets. Then they set fire to the corpse. A front-page photograph in the *Chicago Defender* showed a crowd of forty celebratory white men standing over Brown's body. He had protested his innocence from the time of his arrest.

At last, federal troops under General Leonard Wood arrived, too late to save Brown but in time to prevent an attack on the black community.

Wood established an effective martial law, and civil authorities arrested fifty-nine whites on serious charges. Police testified against the ringleaders, and the final grand jury report blamed liquor and gambling interests as the instigators.

Nationally the NAACP issued a flood of press releases drawing the lessons of the Omaha riot and urged its congressional allies to investigate the riots. Smith had made a strong stand, and for this the NAACP congratulated him. Omaha NAACP leader Pinkett reported the sorry record of the *Bee*'s race-baiting stories. The NAACP denounced the murder of Brown, and showed also the threat that lynching posed to the entire social fabric.[34]

WHILE these shocking urban confrontations spilled over city streets, southerners continued their rural variant of lynching. The major difference in these cases was that southern civil authorities cooperated with mobs, covering themselves with the merest of fig leaves. Every month when the NAACP board of directors met in its New York office at four in the afternoon on the second Monday, the secretary would give the first report, which included a review of the month's lynchings and the action taken by the office. As the members assembled—usually a few staff executives, African-American ministers and white lawyers resident in New York, sometimes an out-of-town visitor—they must have greeted each other cordially and caught up on personal news. Then the grisly summary would begin. At the March 1919 meeting, for example, the board members listened as John Shillady recounted the horror culled from the black press and branch reports. On January 30, Sampson Smith was lynched at Monroe, Louisiana. The office sent a note of protest to the governor and mailed press releases to the newspapers. On February 6, John Daniels was taken from the New Bern, North Carolina, jail. The office protested again to the Louisiana governor when Will Faulkner was lynched at Bossie. A mob took Eugene Greene from the jail at Belzoni, Mississippi, and he disappeared. The notorious governor Theodore Bilbo did not reply to the NAACP telegram.[35]

In May and June 1919, the *New York Age* uncovered a story from Vicksburg, Mississippi, that encapsulated the typical lynching paradigm. The *Vicksburg Herald* reported on May 15 that Lloyd Clay, a "negro laborer," broke into the home of a nineteen-year-old white girl and tried to rape her. The girl screamed, the "negro" ran, and bloodhounds caught him, but the girl "was not certain as to his identity." A mob of between eight hundred and one thousand beat down the doors of the jail, seized Clay, set him on fire, hanged him from a tree, and fired into his body. Two weeks later an anonymous *Age* reader in Vicksburg reported a different story. Apparently, all Vicksburg knew that the man in the girl's room was her white lover, untimely discovered by the girl's father. Clay was the white man's chauffeur, and when the police came for the driver, they found his story entirely plausible and let him go. Both the girl and her father identified Clay as an innocent chauffeur. The mob seized Clay at his home, not at the jail. An unusual aspect to this story was that five hundred white citizens of Vicksburg signed a protest petition, but there were no prosecutions. Variants of the Vicksburg case were repeated month after month in the South and sometimes in the rest of the country. The southern code was the problem: if the word of a white man was always right against that of a black man, how could any white man who argued that a black was guilty, especially of rape, be found guilty himself? Lloyd Clay was one of many who paid the ultimate price for this system, and there was nothing that the NAACP could do about it in a place like Mississippi.[36]

Southern lynchings had yet another peculiar aspect: they were sometimes advertised. Such a case occurred in Ellisville, Mississippi, in the southeastern corner of the state. Late in June, John Hartsfield was accused of rape. A posse and bloodhounds tracked Hartsfield down and wounded him. The dying man was brought back to town and the impending lynching announced in the Jackson newspaper. Governor Bilbo declared that he was unable to intervene. Then the leading citizens of Ellisville tortured Hartsfield to death.[37]

The toll climbed still higher in 1919. A Birmingham, Alabama, case was of a different type: the one-on-one murder. A streetcar conductor shot and killed Sergeant Major Joe Green, who had the insolence to ask for his change. The conductor shot Green three times and wounded another man; the other passengers on the colored car fled for their lives. African-American veterans offered a $250 reward for the arrest of the conductor, but he was never charged. It is not clear whether the man knew Green was a veteran, but eight other black veterans were killed by southern whites in 1919. In Blakely, Georgia, in April, local thugs murdered Private William Little for walking around town in his uniform. The hoodlums had warned him to wear civilian clothes, but he didn't have any.[38]

James Weldon Johnson wrote: "One by one the idealistic war dreams are vanishing, and as they vanish the solid outlines of the old, pre-war conditions loom up clearer and clearer." In the aftermath of the Chicago riot, the editors of the *Chicago Defender* entitled their commentary "Reaping the Whirlwind." Noting the loyalty of the race's soldiers, citing their own promises that race relations would improve after the war, they now found their cup empty. How would the NAACP counteract the growing mood of despair?[39]

3

America's NAACP

THE NAACP that confronted the violence of the Red Summer was ten years old in 1919. At its founding, the Association was heir to a complex legacy of civil rights activity, and it by now had its own history. By 1919, it had developed its own organizational forms, leadership structure, and internal race relations. Before proceeding with the story of the Association in the Jazz Age, let us take some time to review what those were.

THE ORIGINS of the NAACP lie in the critique of Booker T. Washington. Washington, principal of Alabama's Tuskegee Institute, argued in an 1895 address at the Atlanta Exposition that colored people would forgo civil rights in the short term, in return for economic mutual cooperation. "Cast down your bucket among those people who have, without strikes and labor wars, tilled your fields, cleared your forests . . . ," he urged southern businessmen. In return, the Negro people would accept race relations as they were at present: "In all things that are purely social we can be as separate as the fingers, yet one as the hand in all things essential to mutual progress." White leaders, and most blacks, greeted Washington's speech enthusiastically, and philanthropists donated generously to Tuskegee. With this backing, Washington influenced much of the African-American press, controlled patronage appointments, and made or unmade careers through the operation of what W. E. B. Du Bois later called the Tuskegee Machine. Showing a deferential face to whites, the wily Washington tried to crush his pro–civil rights opponents, but secretly organized civil rights lawsuits himself. Washington's biographer concluded that he lived behind many masks. In a sense, so did every African American under Jim Crow law.[1]

African Americans at first viewed Washington with some ambivalence, but he became the most influential Negro leader from 1895 until his death in 1915. Throughout his career he addressed sizable audiences, North and South, and had millions of devoted supporters. Yet, a minority of critics chipped away at his argument as white supremacy gained ground. Whites attacked blacks attempting to vote in the Carolinas in 1898, and in 1900 the last African-American congressman lost his seat. President Theodore Roosevelt invited Washington to dinner at the White House, but when infuriated southern whites objected, he began a steady retreat on civil rights issues. In 1906 Roosevelt issued dishonorable discharges to black soldiers without due process after a trumped-up shooting incident at Brownsville, Texas. Atlanta whites shot up the black community in an orgy of violence, and the perpetrators went unpunished. The president, meanwhile, announced that lynching would stop only when black men stopped raping white women.[2]

These developments infuriated Washington's opponents, especially Boston's William Monroe Trotter, who launched the *Guardian* newspaper in 1901. He made common cause with Du Bois, then a professor at Atlanta University, and along with other activists they began a new organization. The Niagara movement, named after its first meeting place, remained small and isolated. It lacked money, white allies, organizational leadership, and mass black support. Trotter quarreled with Du Bois over trivial matters, maintained a separate organization, and generally hamstrung Niagara's progress.[3]

Whites who had fought for civil rights earlier in the nineteenth century devoted their energies to African-American education in later decades. Many of the aging abolitionists cooperated with Washington, although they mostly did not relinquish their long-term vision of full equality. These former activists became increasingly gloomy as race relations worsened, but were spurred to action by the 1908 Springfield, Illinois, racial attack that left eight blacks dead, more than fifty wounded, and thousands homeless. Springfield was the city of Abraham Lincoln, and the next year was the centennial of his birth; the symbolism was powerful. William English Walling, a Kentucky-born journalist, and his wife, Anna Strunsky, a Russian Jewish émigré, went to Springfield to investigate. Walling asked in the *Independent*, a progressive monthly: "What large and powerful body of citizens is ready to come to [the Negro's] aid?"[4]

This was a rhetorical question. There was no such organization.

Mary White Ovington read Walling's account intently. Years later, she wrote: "Here was the first person who had sent a challenge to white and colored to battle, as the abolitionists had battled, for the full rights of the Negro. Drums beat in my heart. I sat down and wrote to the author of the article."[5]

By 1920, Mary White Ovington was, along with Du Bois, the only founding leader of the movement active on a day-to-day basis. She was, and remains, unique in American history in two senses. Ovington played the central role in founding the NAACP and bringing together its leadership. In addition, as the only white female leader of the NAACP, she brought forward black women as leaders in the branches. Ovington deserves a place in the history of American reform equal to that of Susan B. Anthony and Elizabeth Cady Stanton.[6]

In every sense of the word, Ovington represented the constellation of reform impulses that had called the Association into being. First, she was an uncompromising (in 1920, this adjective was no cliché) fighter for civil rights. At the founding meeting, she urged the organization to stand for the full civil rights agenda, yet craft a leading committee that would not alienate the broader forces led by Booker T. Washington. Second, Ovington had a sound understanding of the proper relation between the civil rights movement and feminism. Within the movement, she insisted on the advancement of colored women as leaders, pushing forward the careers of Mary Talbert, Addie Hunton, Vernina Morton Jones, and countless others. She linked the NAACP to female board members with wider ties to progressive reform, such as Florence Kelley and Jane Addams. She brought suffrage activists such as Ella Rush Murray onto the board while maneuvering with feminists who would ignore civil rights. Finally, as a socialist who had worked with the poor of both races, she would fight against the lily-white trade unionists as she did with the feminists. She learned to keep economic conservatives like Moorfield Storey and labor-oriented socialists like Walling and Charles Edward Russell on the same team. As historian Daniel Walter Cryder has suggested, Ovington "was the conciliator, the keeper of the peace,"[7] but she certainly had her own vision of the Association's proper role. She and Du Bois were probably the only indispensable people during the NAACP's first decade. Effectively, she brought Oswald Garrison Villard and Du Bois under the same roof, and functioned as the support beam of the entire structure until Johnson came along. It was altogether appropriate that she chaired the board of directors during the transition to an African-American secretariat and during the decade of the country's best team leadership in the civil rights movement.

Walling, Ovington, and Henry Moskowitz, another social worker, met at Walling's apartment to call a new organization into being. For the next ten years, Mary White Ovington worked at the center of action at NAACP headquarters. At first only white people ran the office, and some of them were women: Mary Blascoer and then May Childs Nerney. The top positions went to white men: Oswald Garrison Villard and later Joel E. Spingarn

Mary White Ovington, Chairman of the NAACP Board.
Courtesy of Library of Congress.

were the first board chairmen. The national secretaries were Royal Nash and then John Shillady. Ovington served as secretary, acting secretary, and acting board chairman as these people came and went. By 1919, all were out of day-to-day activity, and Ovington, who had worked behind the scenes for a decade, was chosen as chairman of the board.

The founders included Charles Edward Russell, a colleague of Walling's; Oswald Garrison Villard, grandson of William Lloyd Garrison and publisher of the *New York Evening Post*; two African-American ministers— Bishop Alexander Walters and Reverend William Henry Brooks; and social workers Florence Kelley and Lillian Wald. The group, based in part on Walling's contacts in the Liberal Club, continued to expand; and on Lincoln's centennial, sixty activists of both races issued a call for a national conference. It was penned by Villard, the most prominent of the founders and a longtime friend of Booker Washington.

The conference convened on May 31 and June 1. About three hundred interracial participants attended sessions that were mostly scientific in nature, designed to refute racialist theories of Negro inferiority. The National

Negro Conference, as it was called, determined to form a permanent organization and assigned a Committee of Forty to carry forward the work. The
wider forces around Booker T. Washington stayed away, and his acolytes
downplayed the meeting. Trotter and his allies contested the composition
of the Committee of Forty, and the final list omitted him. The thirty-eight
members included fourteen African-American men, two African-American
women, eight white women, and fourteen white men. Probably no reform
group was as diverse by race and gender as these initial NAACP leaders. All
were middle class and most were easterners.[8]

The Association showed its determination to press for the full civil rights
agenda by assigning Du Bois as director of publicity and research. After
moving from Atlanta to New York, Du Bois decided to publish a monthly
magazine, the *Crisis*. On his first day at the office, Villard told Du Bois that
the magazine's financial future would be bleak. The first number came out
in November 1910, and in December Du Bois doubled the press run to
twenty-five hundred. By 1919 they were printing one hundred thousand
copies. The *Crisis* was a stimulating, by turns intellectual, poetic, artistic,
and journalistic success; there has not been anything like it in American
life since Du Bois resigned in 1934. The editor wrote monthly features on
race relations and developments within black America, celebrating black
achievement. He wrote an "Opinion" column that ranged over national
and international politics. These "opinions" were decidedly radical on a
range of questions upon which the NAACP itself expressed no opinion. In
politics, he assailed Republican orthodoxy at a time when African-
American voters were loyalists. On economic matters he applauded the
working class and socialism while condemning the racism of white workers. He attacked all forms of discrimination, including anti-Semitism, and
vigorously backed women's rights. Du Bois condemned imperialism and
questioned the European war before America entered it.

At its second annual meeting in New York in May 1910, the National
Negro Committee adopted its new name. Some disliked it for its cumber-
some length, and a few whites objected that it suggested a race-based
membership, but it stuck. The National Association for the Advancement
of Colored People chose a leading Committee of Forty, which in turn
elected officers. The Association at first had many generals and few soldiers, but it gradually developed branches in Boston, New York, Philadelphia, Baltimore, Washington, Chicago, and St. Louis. The most important
problem of the first six years was the almost constant internal bickering
among the leaders, often about how much editorial control the board of
directors should exercise over the *Crisis*. Villard served as chairman of the
board or treasurer during the first decade. Du Bois's radicalism and nas-

cent black nationalism rankled him. Du Bois chafed at Villard's imperious manner and paternalism. Villard, for example, wanted to publish a list of black crimes alongside the *Crisis*'s lynching record. "I resented this," Du Bois wrote, "not only because it was logically silly, but because it was interfering with my business."[9] The *Crisis* was the NAACP's magazine, but board members realized that bureaucratic oversight would convert it into a stale house organ. Villard's resignation from the chairmanship in 1916, as well as the accession of Du Bois's allies Joel Spingarn and later Mary White Ovington, resolved these conflicts in Du Bois's favor.[10]

Despite internal discord, the Association quickly made a name for itself as the authoritative national civil rights organization. When President Woodrow Wilson segregated the federal departments in Washington, the Association protested in the press, meeting halls, and streets. Association leaders convinced South Carolina's governor to commute the death sentence of Pink Franklin, a sharecropper who shot a plainclothes sheriff who had burst into his house unannounced. From this case a permanent legal committee evolved. The Association challenged residential segregation in Baltimore and other cities, publicized discriminatory funding of Negro education in the South, and defended the rights of black students and intellectuals in the North. All over the country, NAACP branches protested the showing of D. W. Griffith's cinematic portrayal of Reconstruction, *The Birth of a Nation*. Local branches took up local issues—segregated theaters in New York, discrimination at the YMCA in Boston, or lily-white hiring policies in Washington—and these efforts won the Association respect.[11]

When Booker Washington died in November 1915, the NAACP leaders realized that the civil rights movement now had an opportunity to reach into his milieu. It professed to be an integrated civil rights organization, and its board of directors was indeed carefully balanced racially. The membership was probably 90 percent African-American, but the New York office staff remained mostly white. Du Bois was the Association's most prominent African-American leader, but he was an editor, not an organizer. His personal rivalry with Booker Washington had thus far made a committment to the NAACP a difficult matter for African Americans who coveted a job that Washington influenced.[12]

Now the Wizard was gone. Du Bois, Joel Spingarn, and some others recognized that the Association must someday hire a colored leader. Du Bois himself was not the man for that job, and he knew it. He was, however, a fair man who could work well with the rare colleague who shared his breadth of vision. Around the time that Booker Washington died, the NAACP began to court James Weldon Johnson. Du Bois nominated him for membership in Sigma Pi Phi, an elite academic fraternity. Villard had

connections to the Woodrow Wilson administration and, at Du Bois's suggestion, proposed Johnson as minister to Haiti.[13]

The following summer, Joel Spingarn invited black leaders with differing points of view to a conference at his Catskill mountain home, Trout-
beck, in Amenia in upstate New York. There Johnson joined about fifty
black activists from diverse professions. The NAACP leaders were impressed with Johnson and he with them. In the fall Spingarn asked him to
work full-time for the Association as field secretary. Du Bois entered the
debate he expected was taking place in Johnson's mind. "I am inclined to
think that contact with human beings will be an incentive rather than a
drawback to your literary work," he wrote. He urged Johnson to consider
the mutual benefits of their collaboration on the *Crisis* and reminded him
of their common fraternity bond. Finally, as a member of the board of
directors himself, Du Bois expressed confidence that they would easily ap-
prove his hiring. In December, Johnson came aboard.[14]

Johnson's coming to the NAACP in 1916 was a vital link in the chain that
led to the end of *de jure* segregation in the United States. He changed the
Association's character immediately. In January of 1917 he set out on a tour
of the South, in which the NAACP then had just three branches. He met
privately with local leaders from Richmond to Tampa and convinced them
to organize public NAACP meetings. On the return trip he spoke at those
meetings and left 13 NAACP branches with seven hundred total members
behind him. These were based in more tolerant cities such as Richmond
and Norfolk, Virginia; Greensboro, Raleigh, and Durham, North Carolina;
and Atlanta, Augusta, and Savannah, Georgia. By the end of 1919, 131 of the
Association's 310 branches were located in fourteen southern states. It
does not detract from the status of Du Bois to point out that he could not
have brought this about. Du Bois was the prophet, Johnson the organizer.[15]

Johnson traveled extensively through the country in 1918 and 1919. He
served as acting secretary when Joel Spingarn was in the army during the
World War. He visited Wilson in the White House, leading a delegation that
presented petitions on behalf of the imprisoned Houston soldiers. Johnson
personally investigated two lynchings, that of Ell Persons near Memphis,
and Mary Turner at Quitman, Georgia. He did contribute articles to the
Crisis, but there was no time for literature. Du Bois had been right about
one thing, though: his experiences would provide the inspiration for future
work. While on one speaking tour, he witnessed a preacher exhort a congregation with a magnificent extemporaneous sermon, and seven years
later turned it into the poem *God's Trombones*, a Negro rendition of the
Creation story.[16]

The developing unity in African America came just in time. Tension brought on by the migration and World War led to two explosive riots which would have long-lasting effects on the Association's work. At East St. Louis, Illinois, white workingmen attacked the black section of town on July 2, 1917. This industrial center was home to railroad yards, stockyards, and meatpacking plants, and when labor strife developed, the employers hired African-American strikebreakers. Rumors of "Negro crime" and Republican manipulation circulated through white slums near the plants, and when the bloodshed was over, forty African Americans were dead. The militia and other lawmen in some cases aided the marauders. In the aftermath, ten African Americans but only four whites were convicted of murder.

The NAACP sent Du Bois and Martha Gruening to investigate the riot and initiate defense work. The Chicago and St. Louis branches joined the effort, and organized a volunteer committee of twenty-five to take testimony. Charles Nagel, a former secretary of commerce, led the defense effort, and the Association initiated a special fund. In New York, Villard proposed a silent protest parade against the East St. Louis violence and against lynchings at Waco, Texas, and Memphis, Tennessee. On July 28 thousands of marchers silently paraded downtown from Fifth Avenue and Firty-sixth Street to the beat of muffled drums. Schoolchildren dressed in white, and the marchers carried appropriate banners. The organizing meetings for the parade brought a new layer of community activists closer to the NAACP: this was probably the first street protest against lynching in American history.[17]

Less than a month later, a riot of a different sort broke out in Houston, Texas, on August 23. After several incidents of police brutality, men of the Twenty-fourth Infantry marched into town and began attacking police officers and white citizens, killing seventeen. The army's retribution was swift and severe. Military prosecutors ultimately charged 110 men and hanged 19. Long prison terms were meted out at three trials. The NAACP waged a petition campaign to defend the Houston prisoners, an effort that lasted into the 1920s.[18]

Besides taking to the streets and meeting halls, the Association fought against segregation and disfranchisement in the courts. During its first decade, the NAACP won two limited but significant victories in the Supreme Court, one against residential segregation and the other against the white primary. Whites, however, were easily able to devise more defensible strategies, and these practices continued for many years.

In 1910, Oklahoma amended its constitution to exempt the descendants of registered voters from ballot requirements. Whites were effectively "grandfathered" onto the voting rolls, while blacks would have to pass a test. Moorfield Storey convinced the solicitor general that the Oklahoma measure violated the national Fifteenth Amendment. The Justice Department challenged the "grandfather clause," and Storey filed a friend of the court brief on the NAACP's behalf. In the case of *Guinn v. the United States*, the Supreme Court invalidated the Oklahoma amendment, and the Association had its first Supreme Court victory.[19]

In 1910 Baltimore passed a municipal segregation ordinance. The local NAACP branch defeated this law and another in the courts. A decision on a third Baltimore ordinance was put off pending a Louisville, Kentucky, case. This was an NAACP challenge as well, and the Association sent Joel Spingarn and William Pickens to strengthen the divided Louisville branch. The Association arranged for William Warley, branch president, to contract with a sympathetic white realtor to buy property in a white neighborhood. Warley then broke the contract, citing the municipal segregation ordinance. The realtor sued. The NAACP thus cleverly placed a white property owner before the bar, demanding the enforcement of his contract, which he claimed superseded the social engineering of segregation. Local NAACP attorneys lost the case in the Kentucky Court of Appeals, but in November 1917 Moorfield Storey won a unanimous verdict in the U.S. Supreme Court.[20]

Johnson took over as acting secretary after Shillady's resignation in June 1920; at the November meeting the board made his appointment permanent. The appointment of James Weldon Johnson as the first African-American national secretary marked a major turning point in the history of the Association and the history of African America. The minutes of the board during the 1920s suggest that Johnson and White shifted the locus of power in the organization to themselves simply by their sheer energy and leadership abilities. For the first time in American history, African Americans commanded a nationally organized, powerful civil rights organization.

THE APPOINTMENT of Johnson as national secretary did not stop nationalist critics of the Association, such as Marcus Garvey, from arguing that the NAACP was controlled by whites. The impression has lasted until the present. How valid was this charge in the 1920s?

The NAACP was not legally incorporated until it had functioned for two years. Its bylaws, drawn up by Boston attorney Albert E. Pillsbury, established a board of directors, later expanded to forty in size. The board elected officers from within its ranks: a chairman, president and vice presidents, secretary, and treasurer. Further, it assigned a director of publicity and research (Du Bois) and established legal, financial, and membership committees. In 1923, a Committee of Executives, the full-time staff members and officers, began to meet between board meetings. The board held an annual meeting in January and met monthly to consider reports from its standing committees and paid staff members. It assigned a nominations committee to make proposals for three-year terms of membership on the board. Du Bois was the only board member who was also a paid staff officer as editor of the *Crisis*.[21]

Nothing in the NAACP constitution stipulated anything about the racial composition of the board or staff. The board worked out for itself an unwritten goal of achieving racial balance. By 1920 only thirty-five seats were filled by nineteen blacks and sixteen whites. Six members were female, four of them white: social workers Jane Addams, Florence Kelley, Mary White Ovington, and Lillian Wald. The white members more heavily represented New York and were chosen for legal expertise (Charles Nagel, Arthur B. Spingarn, Moorfield Storey, and Charles Studin) or connection to other professions or reform efforts (Kansas senator Arthur Capper, John Haynes Holmes, Paul Kennaday, William Loud, John Milholland, Charles E. Russell, Joel Spingarn, William English Walling). African-American members reflected geographic and professional representation of the membership. They were lawyers (E. Burton Ceruti, Harry Davis, Archibald Grimké, William Sinclair, Butler Wilson), ministers (Hutchens C. Bishop, John Hurst, Garnett Waller), educators (George Cook, George Crawford, Du Bois, Neville Thomas), and dentists (J. Max Barber and Charles Bentley). One politician (Robert Church Jr.), one businessman (Harry Pace), and one soldier (Charles Young) broadened the Association's connections with other fields of endeavor. The most important imbalance on the board was that there were only two black women: Mary Talbert and Dr. Vernina Morton Jones. Geographically these board members heavily represented East Coast cities, and those outside New York rarely attended monthly meetings.[22]

By 1929 the board was little changed. Nineteen of thirty-seven members were African-American; seven members were female, only two of whom were African-American—Nannie H. Burroughs and Maggie Walker. Beyond the racial and gender composition of the board, the important thing that the minutes and secretary's and branch secretary's reports show is that the African-American staff led the work. Usually about eight board members attended meetings. They contributed most as legal advisors, financial donors, or conduits to other power centers. Little debate took place on the board, and it never broke down along racial lines.

Central to this transformation was the relation among the staff members. Johnson, White, and Du Bois formed a leadership triumvirate whose abilities and authority collectively exceeded the two previous one-person leaders after Emancipation, Frederick Douglass and Washington. Their strengths meshed together so as to diminish each individual's weaknesses. Johnson possessed the vision, strength of character, and interpersonal skills both to lead the board of directors and to inspire a mass membership. White showed boundless energy as an organizer and as the link between the branches and the Legal Committee. He demonstrated remarkable courage as an investigator of lynchings. Together they made it possible for Du Bois to focus on the *Crisis* and his own speech making, which enhanced the Association's prestige.

The next most important people on the staff were the traveling organizers, who will be more fully introduced in the next chapter. Robert Bagnall served as branch secretary and William Pickens as field organizer. Mary Talbert and Addie Hunton also did field work, but the former died and the latter retired midway through the decade and were not replaced until Daisy Lampkin joined the staff in 1929. Richetta Randolph anchored the office staff throughout the 1920s. Catherine Lealtad also handled much correspondence from the branches as Bagnall's secretary. The lone white staff member was Herbert J. Seligmann, who issued the Association's news releases.

Tensions existed among all these people, to be sure. Du Bois angered the board in 1921 when he became enmeshed in an obscure scandal that never reached the public. Pickens threatened to resign over his low salary on several occasions; Du Bois had to counsel him avuncularly when he antagonized the Cincinnati branch on a visit. When Johnson retired in 1929, the weaknesses of Du Bois and White came to the surface. Both had imperial leadership styles, and the two men could not get along without Johnson's steadying influence. Despite these and other problems, the NAACP leadership commanded great respect in the three to four hundred black communities in which it had branches.[23]

The staff was ably assisted by a first-rate Legal Committee. Walter White sifted requests for advice and financial aid from the branches and placed the material before Chairman Arthur B. Spingarn. Spingarn, forty-two in 1920, litigated his first civil rights case in 1905 after graduating from the Columbia Law School. Born into a secular German-Jewish immigrant family, he is eclipsed in civil rights historiography by his older brother Joel, who was an NAACP founder. Arthur was probably more important to the movement as chief legal counsel until the mid-1930s. He served with African-American troops during the World War and became a bibliophile with a special interest in Africa.[24] The committee included Moorfield Storey, Spingarn's law partner Charles Studin, Herbert K. Stockton, Louis

Arthur B. Springarn, Chairman of the Legal Committee,
NAACP. Courtesy of Library of Congress.

Marshall, and Washington, D.C., attorney James Cobb, the first African American in this group. Later William T. Andrews, also African-American, joined the staff as the first full-time legal coordinator, taking on much of Walter White's work.

The Association's treasurer in the 1920s was Joel E. Spingarn, a former professor of literature at Columbia University and Du Bois's best white friend. Spingarn and the members of the board from time to time appealed to their friends on the Association's behalf, usually to contribute to special funds dedicated to a single goal. The early historiography of the Association stresses the role of white contributors. In fact, the branches contributed substantially to the general fund, the operating budget of the movement, whose debit side included salaries, rent, postage, travel, telephones, and other expenses. In 1930, Bagnall reported the branches' contributions over a ten-year period. In 1919 they contributed $34,366; in 1929, $40,797; and the figure fluctuated over the years from a low of $25,698 in 1920 to a high of $66,301 in 1925. Each year the branches conducted a financial campaign along with the annual membership drive. Bagnall's letters in the 1920s are replete with frustration and outrage as he cajoled the local leaders to carry out this most tedious yet necessary of tasks. White contributions to the NAACP were very helpful, but the branches provided the bedrock of the operating budget.[25]

Among the handful of whites in the Association were a disproportionate number of Jews. These included the brothers Spingarn, Louis Marshall, who chaired the American Jewish committee, and publicity man Seligmann. Jews such as Julius Rosenwald, Jacob Schiff, and Herbert Lehmann gave generous financial contributions. In the branches, rabbis sometimes joined African-American ministers as speakers. Robert Bagnall noted in a report on "work among whites" that Jews were prominent among Kansas City contributors and that Temple Gymel Daleth in Minneapolis had resolved to make common cause with the Association. As Hasia Diner and others have argued, many immigrant Jews and their children recognized the oppression of black Americans as the image of their own suffering in Europe.[26]

The NAACP held two annual meetings that brought the organization together to set policy, inspire the membership, and project itself before the public. The formal annual meeting of the board convened each January in New York. These were typically routine business meetings, but they were accompanied by a rally at the Harlem Casino that projected the Association's campaigns. Conventions met annually during the summer for five days; these were characterized by political harmony as the leadership fired up the troops. Thousands of civil rights activists came together to form a national community at these meetings. A highlight of each convention was the presentation of the Spingarn Medal, donated by Joel, for achievement in any field by an African American. Winners, beginning in 1919, were Archibald Grimké (law and diplomacy), Du Bois (civil rights), Charles S. Gilpin (drama), Mary B. Talbert (service to women), George Washington Carver (science), Roland Hayes (music), James Weldon Johnson (civil rights), Carter G. Woodson (history), Anthony Overton (business), Charles W. Chesnutt (literature), and Mordecai Johnson (academic administration). Later in the decade, African-American cosmetics heiress A'Lelia Walker contributed scholarship awards to branches and branch leaders for building the Association.

The accusation of white control over the NAACP rings false. The board of directors was interracial but usually majority-black. Votes among this body never broke down along racial lines in the 1920s. The real leadership lay in an almost all-black staff, which initiated policy and communicated it to the branches. African Americans made up almost all the active members. The NAACP celebrated black pride and achievement through the *Crisis* magazine and its Spingarn awards. Board, staff, and branch activists collaborated with white financial contributors and legal advisors.

Three points about the branches deserve mention here. First, although women were very poorly represented on the local boards, they were the real leaders of the branches. While men held the key offices and made the speeches, women ran the organization. They organized the recruitment drives, directed the fund raising, led the junior branches, corresponded with the national office, and helped set policy on local boards. As the narrative unfolds, many of these characters will emerge as the local heroines they were.

Second, throughout the decade, the Association claimed in its press releases to have about one hundred thousand members in three hundred to four hundred branches. Local activists conducted annual membership drives by going door-to-door in the black community. The only qualification for membership was to pay one dollar to join. Thus, the membership existed mostly on paper. Most branches had some period in which they went into deep recess. If a branch did not meet its financial quota to sustain the national office for a period of time, the board could revoke its charter, and each year a dozen or twenty branches disappeared as new ones were chartered. Almost every branch issued some cry of distress to New York as the inevitable year or two of apathy dragged on. However, the important point about the branches is that they existed at all. No mass organization can consistently bring its membership out to monthly meetings for a long period of time. Typically, branches mobilized in crisis or to attend speeches by national officers on tour.

Finally, the successful branches usually appeared where there was something to fight about. In the Northeast and South, the terms of race relations were pretty well settled. Black New Yorkers expected to vote without any trouble, and black Georgians outside Atlanta knew that voting rights was not on the agenda. The civil rights battles of the 1920s were fought along an undefined racial border, neither Deep South nor Yankee. This border ran from Texas north to Minnesota, and from Philadelphia west to Los Angeles. This elusive borderline extended far into the North, as new black communities developed in cities that previously had few African-American residents, especially in the Midwest. It was along this border—in the nonseceding slave states, Delaware, Maryland, Kentucky, and Missouri; in the nonslaveholding sections of the Upper South, such as West Virginia and eastern Tennessee; and in the West that bordered the South, such as Texas and Oklahoma—that the NAACP could exploit the contradiction between the promise of the amended Constitution and the reality of race discrimination. Into that sometimes dangerous territory the NAACP organizers went, and we shall meet four of them in the next chapter.

On the Road

URING the chilly February of 1919, an obscure Detroit minister traveled through the new black communities of Ohio, speaking on behalf of the NAACP. "I was in Columbus last Friday and spoke to 1,200 people," he reported to James Weldon Johnson. Many new members signed up, and the NAACP developed some clout at the state capital. The Ohio branches held a state conference to lobby for a civil rights bill, introduced into the legislature by an African-American representative from Cincinnati, former branch president A. Lee Beaty. The Ohio bill failed after intense pressure by hotel and restaurant interests, but the branches (fourteen in 1918) had made a good fight.[1]

The organizer was thirty-five-year-old Robert Wellington Bagnall, born to an Episcopal priest and his wife. Robert followed in his father's footsteps and served congregations in Pennsylvania, Maryland, and Ohio. In his ministerial high collar Bagnall looked like a sensitive soul, coffee-colored and wide-eyed with almost imperceptible eyebrows. He married the spirited Lilian Anderson of Baltimore in 1906, and five years later Bagnall became minister at St. Matthew's Episcopal in Detroit. There he urged his middle-class parishioners to help struggling migrants from the South to get jobs and homes. Bagnall soon affiliated with the NAACP. The Detroit branch encouraged Ford Motor Company to hire more African-American workers, helped defeat a segregated school proposal in Ypsilanti, and worked against police brutality. Impressed by Bagnall's organizing ability, the national office in 1918 made him the Great Lakes district organizer and put him on the road.[2]

Bagnall had big plans for the NAACP. He thought it would get so big that the district organization approach of linking branches regionally would not work—they would need smaller state organizations with a director for each state. Money was important, too. "Our people must be educated to the idea of paying for their freedom as well as fighting for it," he wrote, and soon the NAACP was selling blue and gold certificates to the members. To build the Association, they must have two annual drives, one for members in the spring and one for money in the fall. They needed a button and a song: "Our audiences don't sing 'America' with any ardor." The NAACP was his passion. As he wrote to Mary White Ovington, "[T]he Association has so gripped me that I am ever thinking of it."[3]

Later in the month the minister was back in Michigan, building branches in Kalamazoo, Ypsilanti, and Jackson, where a Reverend Crider, "an energetic young Methodist minister," was the new president. By June, Bagnall had founded more branches in Flint, Grand Rapids, Bay City, Benton Harbor, and Lansing. At tiny Benton Harbor, in the southwest corner of the state on Lake Michigan, seventy-nine members selected a chiropodist as president. Three hundred came to the NAACP banquet in Kalamazoo, and a good crowd came out at Flint. Saginaw, located in the space below the thumb and forefinger of the Michigan mitten shape, was a growing industrial center with six hundred to seven hundred Negroes, "many of whom are migrants," Bagnall reported. The Reverend Mr. Marks, a Methodist, was the new president, the vice president a waiter, the secretary a housewife, and the treasurer a janitor and father of a *croix de guerre* winner. At Muskegon, almost halfway up the Lake Michigan coast, most of the four hundred Negroes came from the South also, and now worked at the Continental Motors shops. Bagnall gave his speech there on a hot August night. "A street car riot occurred the night of the meeting and the car barns being directly opposite the hall, I had the unpleasant competition of the shouting of the mob and the smashing and burning of cars." Undeterred, Bagnall started a branch that night.[4]

Many of the new members came from these burgeoning factory towns of the Midwest. Only twenty African Americans lived in Elkhart, Indiana, before the migration, but now several hundred worked in the railroad shops. The branch president was Mr. Tantsi, a Zulu. At Beloit, Wisconsin, the NAACPers were migrants working at the Fairbanks Manufacturing Company. In Ohio, the Elyria members toiled in factories also; Bagnall revived a dormant branch there in December. He visited tiny Wellsville, on the Ohio River bordering West Virginia. That night the thermometer registered below zero, but the people came out. "An amusing feature of its meetings is that the various officers sit behind raised stands at the four sides of the walls as is done in Masonic meetings. This branch is almost entirely male, and I succeeded in getting their promise of an active canvass for women members." Revived branches appeared in the southwestern part of the state, at Springfield and Dayton. In 1921, the board assigned Bagnall as national branch secretary, and for the next twelve years he

Robert Bagnall, Director of Branches, NAACP. Courtesy of Library of Congress.

would correspond with and travel to hundreds of cities, encouraging, ca-
joling, and soothing the wounded egos of local activists.[5]

IN MOST PARTS of the South, NAACP activity was conducted with a view
to insuring the safety of the members. Therefore, Mary Talbert traveled for

the NAACP under the guise of the National Association of Colored Women's Clubs (NACW), of which she was president. Talbert would turn fifty-three in 1919. She grew up in Oberlin, Ohio, whose college was open to women and Negroes in the 1830s. Her parents ran the barbershop and restaurant that catered to students. Mary Burnett attended the Congregational Church and graduated from Oberlin. Then she went to Little Rock as a teacher and became principal of the Union High School. As a rare female principal, she earned a national reputation in African America. An attractive, snub-nosed woman who wore her hair in a modest Afro, she married William Talbert in 1891 and moved with him to his native Buffalo. He was president of the Colored Republican Club and a confidant of Booker T. Washington, but the couple also befriended W. E. B. Du Bois. Mary Talbert hosted the preliminary meetings of the Niagara movement in her home.

Talbert committed herself to the women's club movement. She helped initiate the Phillis Wheatley club in Buffalo in 1899, which established a settlement house. In 1916 she was elected president of the NACW, a post she held until 1921. In this capacity she toured the South, urging that communities build institutions to protect Negro children: schools, recreation facilities, reformatories. During the World War she went on tour again, selling liberty bonds. A charismatic orator and capable organizer, she built the NACW into a strong group as its president. In 1918 the NAACP asked her to speak in Texas on its behalf. This job was too risky for a man to do in the open; but hopefully white southerners would ignore a woman, who could be talking, presumably, only about domestic matters.[6]

That fall Mary Talbert traveled for three months in East Texas and parts of Louisiana, covering 7,162 miles to give fifty-seven lectures to thirty-five thousand people. She started nine new branches: Galveston, Silsbee, Orange, Austin, Corsicana, Alexandria, Marshall, Texarkana, and Gonzalez. She worked on membership drives in San Antonio, Dallas, Fort Worth, Beaumont, and at Shreveport and New Orleans in Louisiana. "The harvest now is plentiful if the Association only had the laborers to go in and reap," she reported to John R. Shillady.[7]

Of these thousands of new members, many were workers and farmers. Historian Steven A. Reich, after studying the charters and files of East Texas branches, concluded that "the Black working class likely constituted the core of the membership."[8] Unionized longshoremen started the Galveston branch. San Antonio, which grew from fifty-two in March 1918 to over seventeen hundred by the summer of 1919, included a variety of workers. In the rural town of Silsbee, railroad men took the lead: the president was a switchman and the vice president a brakeman. At Leggett, Mumford, and Wharton, farmers made up a big portion of the membership.

Reich also found that a significant percentage of East Texas NAACPers were women. After surveying the charters of thirty-two branches, he learned that seven branches were over 40 percent female, five over 30 percent, and eight over 20 percent. The San Antonio group fought for the interests of African-American women, getting one hundred of them jobs at Fort Sam Houston. Talbert, as a dynamic speaker, inspired women with the self-confidence that they too could play public roles. While the women rarely occupied titled positions, they did much of the work.

The NAACP recruited a cadre of returning soldiers as well. Lieutenant C. C. Taylor was a leader of the Wharton branch, and two veterans inspired the Corsicana group. These militants campaigned, in some cases successfully, to ban the racist movie *Birth of a Nation* and to rid army bases of antiblack propaganda. Some branches conducted voter registration drives. At San Antonio, the NAACP won a $250 settlement for a black woman assaulted by a store clerk. Texas NAACPers convinced Governor W. P. Hobby (the same governor who later justified the attack on John Shillady) to introduce an antilynching bill into the state legislature. Hobby recognized that growing black assertiveness threatened his political power, and later in 1919 he moved to quash the NAACP. After the assault on Shillady, many of the Texas branches succumbed to fear. A few years later Talbert saw that much of her work had been undone and was reluctant to return. "Jim Crow travel is not only hard but hazardous in that part of Hell," she wrote Bagnall and volunteered to go somewhere else.[9]

Mary Talbert returned to her home at 521 Michigan Avenue in Buffalo in late December. In May she sailed to France on another mission, this time for the YWCA. By June she reached the cemetery of the vast killing field at Verdun, her motherly face welcome to thousands of black men still in uniform, now digging graves. With three coworkers, her picture appeared on the front page of the *New York Age* in October, stout, smiling, dressed in a white smock and cap behind a table of soup and sandwiches, a harbinger of home for the sons and brothers of her new NAACP recruits in Silsbee or Gonzalez, Texas.[10]

FOR ADDIE D. WAITES HUNTON, the road to the NAACP led through embattled France. She was one of the first three female African-American YWCA workers assigned to the black soldiers overseas, and with a colleague she wrote a book about the experience. This remarkable memoir of war, *Two Colored Women with the American Expeditionary Forces*, is preceded in African-American literature only by Susie King Taylor's account of her Civil War experiences with the First South Carolina Volunteers, *Reminiscences of My Life in Camp*. Hunton and her coauthor, Kathryn M. Johnson, recorded the contradictory experiences of black people in a white-led army during World War I.[11]

Hunton was born in Norfolk, Virginia, in 1875 to Jesse and Adelina Waites. Her father owned an oyster company and a shipping enterprise, and was a leader in his church and lodge. Her mother died when Addie was young, and she was sent to Boston to live with an aunt. Addie graduated from the prestigious Girls Latin School, and then from the Spencerian College of Commerce in Philadelphia. As a young adult, she started a career as a teacher in Portsmouth, Virginia, where she married William Alpheus Hunton, one of the first African-American YMCA workers. Mary White Ovington described her as being "deep brown in color with a finely molded mouth, and large unfathomable eyes . . . a nobly beautiful woman."

After six years of marriage, they moved to Atlanta, where Addie worked at Clark College. They arrived about the time of a horrific lynching, that of Sam Hose in the spring of 1899. The Atlanta riot of 1906 may also have contributed to Hunton's interest in civil rights. Hunton did some YWCA work on her own, touring the South and Midwest in 1907–1908. She contributed articles to the *Crisis* in 1911 and 1912. When William died in 1916, Addie Hunton became a widow with adult children in a world at war.[12]

American entry into the conflict opened new possibilities to women, who raised money at home and served abroad. African-American women had a similarly liberating experience and determined to use their new self-confidence afterward. Alice Dunbar-Nelson, later a leader of the NAACP's Wilmington, Delaware, branch, recalled in a chapter of Emmett J. Scott's *Official History of the American Negro in the World War*: "Into this maelstrom of war activity the women of the Negro race hurled themselves joyously. They asked no odds, remembered no grudges, solicited no favors, pleaded for no privileges."[13] Hunton volunteered to go abroad right away.

With Kathryn M. Johnson, Hunton sailed in the summer of 1918 on the French liner *Espagne*, a crowded troop ship, and arrived at Bordeaux. In the port city they got their first visual shock, the sight of armed Negro soldiers guarding German prisoners. The women saw African-American troops working as stevedores, depot guards, front line combat troops, and postwar grave diggers. She saw the dockworkers unloading cargo transports, handling the cold steel in winter without gloves and without complaint. The combat troops of the New York "Old Fifteenth" regiment "adopted" her as their mother.[14]

Hunton and Johnson endured the devilishness of Jim Crow, now thrown into the starkest relief. Johnson recalled an incident in which a Negro band was called to play for white soldiers. When black soldiers tried to join the fun, the whites ejected them from their recreation tent. But the white bandleader refused to play under such circumstances, and the musicians walked out. Hunton saw the gratitude of the French toward the colored troops and remembered the people of Laon kissing their hands as they walked the streets. She recounted the testimony of the French mayors regarding the soldiers' heroism. Then there was the great victory parade in Paris in late summer 1919—when all the white troops paraded, the black soldiers were kept out by a spiteful, southern-dominated officer corps.

Hunton and Johnson worked at a variety of tasks, but their most valuable assignment was simply to be there. They set up libraries, taught literacy, arranged shows and movies, wrote letters home for the illiterate, and served coffee. Hunton worked for several months at St. Nazaire in the Loire Valley, and at Romagne amongst the grave diggers on the Meuse-Argonne battlefield. A picture of her ran in the *New York Age*, showing a determined woman in a greatcoat, in rugged snow-covered terrain alongside a young soldier. Just before Armistice Day, at Pontanezen near Brest, the main debarkation point, she caught influenza. Luckily she recovered, and in time to speak at the Pan-African Congress on the role of women in the struggle for racial democracy. Later, in the summer of 1919, another group of "Y" service workers came over. Among them was Mary Talbert, then only a few months removed from her work in Texas. "We felt deeply honored in having her a member of our overseas group," Hunton wrote.[15]

The presence of Talbert and Du Bois may have rekindled Hunton's earlier interest in the NAACP. Her colleague Kathryn Johnson had been an NAACP field organizer herself, but she had not been happy in her work. Johnson spoke her mind as she stumped the country, and she wanted the Association to have an all-black leadership. For her candor, she was fired in 1916, and she may well have communicated the negative fallout from this experience to Hunton, the former *Crisis* woman's columnist.[16]

Addie Hunton was something of a celebrity in African America by the time she returned. Tens of thousands of black veterans would have known her name. The *New York Age* reported that five hundred women held a reception for her at the Brooklyn Academy of Music in October 1919. The veterans adored her. In 1921, now a full-time NAACP worker, she met former soldier Rudy McEnglish at the Detroit NAACP convention. He wrote her afterward. "As you perhaps know, you were the most widely talked of, the most dearly loved woman in the AEF . . . I can never forget those wonderful days at Camp Orl, St. Nazaire, France." Hunton's meetings with the troops "kept our hearts warm with memories of our own firesides and mothers."[17]

Hunton worked for the Association as a field organizer in the early 1920s. She helped build Brooklyn into a successful branch, but Baltimore, her other long-term project, was the NAACP's most conspicuous failure. Assigned to work with Baltimore in June 1920, she helped the branch sign up two thousand new members that fall. The key problem there was a lack of leadership. Without a team of people who made the NAACP their top priority, the members would slip away. Hunton was particularly sensitive to feminist issues, and she called the case of a young girl, hired out to work for a white man who abused her, to the branch's attention. Apparently no one pursued the case, and without a cause, the membership dropped. Returning to Baltimore in January 1923, she built another mass meeting, despite heavy snow, at which she and AME Bishop John Hurst spoke. "As I spoke, questioned, and observed in Baltimore," she noted, I was asking myself . . . what can be done to maintain the membership in our branches generally? Where did 2,000 members signed up in 1920 go? . . . People are interested everywhere. We fall down on the field for want of a sustained leadership."[18]

In five months of 1923, Hunton traveled throughout the South, rebuilding dozens of branches that lapsed into inactivity. She had visited forty-three cities in nine states, giving forty-nine speeches. In North Carolina, she found a mixture of relatively benign race relations, for the South, and a fear of rocking the boat. She held a large public meeting at Raleigh, but not at Durham, the insurance capital of African America. There she met the employees of the Mutual Insurance Company, who pledged to recruit a hundred new members, but Hunton doubted their resolve. At Greensboro and Winston-Salem she again saw great potential but little leadership. Things looked better in Florida, where she visited Pensacola, Tallahassee, St. Augustine, Jacksonville, and Tampa, holding her best meeting at Bethel Baptist Church in Jacksonville. She had kick-started many dormant branches, but found that leadership was still the main problem. "So many men are selling their birthright for a mess of pottage," she mourned.[19]

William Pickens's maternal grandmother "could thread her own needles when she was eighty," but for half those years she walked with a crooked back. She had been a temperamental house slave and once received a beating that broke her spine. Her daughter Fannie gave birth to William, the sixth of ten children, in 1881. William's father, Jacob, was an ebony-hued man with European features. They lived in Pendleton, South Carolina, in the northwest corner of the state.[20]

Hoping to improve the family's circumstances after Fannie's death, Jacob moved to Arkansas when William was seven. After a year of tenant farming, he fell deeper in debt, and the family ran away to North Little Rock. There William attended a nine-month school for the first time and fell in love with education. He worked his way through grammar school and then the Union High School. Young Pickens earned forty cents a day by rowing a ferry boat across the Arkansas River, conjugating Latin verbs as he pulled on the oars. He graduated high school in 1899 as valedictorian.[21]

Pickens got a teacher's license, and he could have earned a living as a local instructor, but he set his eye on higher learning. To earn tuition money, the valedictorian joined his father at a remote railway camp, working with rough laborers to lay track. After a month he set off on the five-hundred-mile journey for Talladega College in Alabama. Pickens passed the math and Latin test, handed the gratified college president three ten-dollar bills as tuition, and began his college career.[22]

Talladega was a Congregational haven, a "monument of unselfishness," Pickens called it. He excelled there as he had in high school. From Talladega he transferred to Yale, earning money while working summers at a Chicago ironworks. Pickens earned outstanding grades at Yale, graduating Phi Beta Kappa.[23]

After college Pickens returned to Talladega as a teacher and worked there for the next ten years. He married Minnie Cooper McAlpine, also a teacher, and they had three children. Gradually radicalizing, Pickens attended the founding meeting of Du Bois's Niagara movement and wrote for the militant magazine *Voice of the Negro*. After Talladega he taught at Wiley College in Marshall, Texas, and then at Morgan State in Baltimore. There he was made dean, and the title stuck for life.[24]

Now closer to the major political centers, Pickens spoke more often for the NAACP, which he had joined as a founding member. In 1914 he accompanied Joel E. Spingarn to help the Louisville branch prepare for the residential segregation case. When America entered the World War, Pickens agreed with Spingarn and Du Bois that black Americans should accept the controversial separate officers' camp. He spoke at the May 1919 anti-lynching meeting, and James Weldon Johnson praised his "power to satirize race prejudice" in his weekly *New York Age* column. In 1920 he became a contributing editor for the Associated Negro Press, and for the next twenty years he wrote columns that appeared in over one hundred newspapers. In February that year Pickens joined the NAACP staff as field secretary and moved his family to New York.[25]

Throughout the 1920s, Pickens maintained a frenetic speaking schedule. In April of 1923, for example, he spoke in southern Ohio and then Johns-

William Pickens, NAACP Field Organizer. Courtesy of Library of Congress.

town, Pennsylvania. On the sixth, he was at the Bethel AME Church in Baltimore, and five hundred people came to hear him at Philadelphia's Varick Temple on the eighth. The following week he spoke in Brooklyn and Harlem, and then was off to Pittsburgh. At the end of the month he visited Clarksburg, West Virginia, speaking to congregations at the AME, Methodist Episcopal, and Baptist churches on one Sunday. In May he was at Parkersburg, West Virginia, and then Charleston, where fifteen hundred came out at First Baptist. In Beckley, four hundred came to hear him at the city hall, and two hundred showed up at Bluefield, Graham, and Huntingdon each. The crowds were even bigger in Kentucky at Georgetown, Frankfort, Maysville, Lexington, and Louisville, where three hundred came to the Quinn Chapel meeting. For twenty years, Pickens kept up a breakneck pace that would have exhausted almost anyone else.[26]

Perhaps because of his modest upbringing, Pickens always dressed immaculately, priding himself on a pair of fancy kid gloves and his expensive luggage. One day he got off the train at a lonely stop in the South and found himself confronted by a gang of rednecks. Pickens's dress and demeanor represented everything they hated. "Whose bags are these, boy?" one of them demanded. Not wanting to take a beating and unwilling to lie, Pickens drew himself up to his full height and announced, "Why, *those* are *Mr. Pickens's* bags," implying that they had better not interfere with the mighty potentate whom he served.[27]

Few activists in American history logged as many railroad miles and delivered as many speeches as Pickens did; he was on the road for six or seven months a year from 1920 until 1942. The historian Sheldon Avery concluded that "Pickens came into more direct contact with the Negro masses than any other black leader of his time."[28] His public speeches combined erudition with the wit and wisdom gained in the hard school of ferry boatmen, track laborers, and ironworkers. Pickens could refer to Shakespeare without pretension or tell a revealing anecdote with conviction. He maintained some distance from the national office, however, which made him at once more difficult and more valuable. A looser cannon, he was drawn to Garveyism and Communism briefly, and perhaps not accidentally. Pickens was the most dark complexioned of a decidedly light-skinned staff and the only man in the leadership who had worked hard with his hands and back. In this sense he brought a wide experience of life into the sometimes rarefied offices of the NAACP.

5

"There Is No Justice in Phylips County"

J UST a few days after the Omaha lynching of William Brown, the front pages of the newspapers carried another story of a racial clash, this time from the Mississippi Delta region of eastern Arkansas. On October 2, 1919, dailies from Boston to Birmingham reported that one thousand to fifteen hundred armed Negroes had gathered near Elaine in Phillips County and that they had battled whites in the streets of the town. The whites evacuated women and children by train to the county seat at Helena, twenty miles northeast. The Negroes even fired on the train. It sounded like a full-scale race war—something more ominous than anything yet during the long Red Summer of that year.

The trouble started Tuesday night September 30, when lawmen set out to find a bootlegger. Stopping by a Negro church near the settlement of Hoop Spur to fix a flat tire, they were shot at from ambush. The gunmen killed W. A. Adkins, a railroad detective, and wounded Charles W. Pratt, a sheriff's deputy. The Negro driver, a "trustee" accompanying the whites, escaped and telephoned the authorities. As dawn broke, white men from all the surrounding counties poured into Helena. They organized posses to find the guilty parties and encountered armed bands. One colored man killed Orly Lilly, a Helena alderman, but the posses gunned down the man and his three brothers.

That night, federal troops from Camp Pike near Little Rock boarded a train for the one-hundred-mile journey east to Helena. They arrived Thursday morning, accompanied by Governor Charles H. Brough. The Negroes shot at the governor's automobile, but he narrowly escaped. As the fighting continued, one soldier was killed and another wounded, and a fourth white man, Clinton Lee, was killed. Nevertheless the rebels soon surrendered to federal troops by the hundreds, and the soldiers locked them up in various public buildings at Helena.

A disturbing aspect of the affair was the involvement of white men, variously reported as socialist or Industrial Workers of the World (IWW) agitators. One posse arrested O. S. Bratton at the Ratio plantation, three miles south of Hoop Spur, and charged him in the death of Adkins. He was the son of a Little Rock attorney named U. S. Bratton, whose very initials suggested parental approval of Yankee general and president Ulysses S. Grant. The senior Bratton had been an assistant federal attorney, and in that capacity had represented Delta Negroes before, winning peonage convictions against white planters. Posses discovered a stack of incriminating literature in his firm's Helena office. Further, Ed Hicks, one of the Negro prisoners, identified O. S. Bratton as an instigator of the trouble. Bratton claimed that he knew nothing of the seditious literature, and that his son was at the Ratio plantation securing evidence and collecting legal fees for another lawsuit. The Ratio tenant farmers wanted only a fair accounting for their crops and the supplies the planters furnished them, Bratton insisted.[1]

This astonishing story was front-page news on October 2 and 3 all over the country. By Monday, October 6, reporters had the full story, and again it ran under bold headlines. "Negroes Plan Slaughter of Whites" the *Birmingham Age-Herald* announced across its front page. "Wholesale Murder of White People in Arkansas May Be Part of Plot against South" it continued; "Fifty Thousand Rounds of Ammunition Found in Normal School." The following day the *New Orleans Times-Picayune* said that a young Negro, Robert L. Hill, was behind the riot, that he had collected union membership fees from local people, organized an uprising, and encouraged Negroes to buy high-powered rifles. Monday was the day of the planned uprising, and the Negroes were to shoot all whites on sight. Five whites and over twenty Negroes had been killed.

Helena's leading white citizens formed a Committee of Seven investigators, headed by E. M. Allen. After interviewing hundreds of prisoners, Allen revealed that the Negroes planned to "demand a settlement" on their crops. Then, on Monday, October 6, they would assassinate twenty-one specific white men. This would be the signal for a broader insurrection. Hill, the ringleader, told his ignorant supporters that an army would come from his town of Winchester, and, backed by the U.S. government, the Negroes would get the land of the white planters. An extensive network of runners called the "Paul Reveres" would function as the communications system, and "We've just begun" was the password. Luckily, the Hoop Spur incident had set off the revolt prematurely before the Negroes could gain the element of surprise.

The organizing headquarters of the rebellion was the Progressive Farmers and Household Union, which supposedly had an office in Washington, D.C. Hill identified himself in the union literature as a "U.S. and foreign

Roundup of Phillips County, Arkansas, sharecroppers, October 1919. Courtesy of Arkansas History Commission.

detective" and implied that he was somehow connected to the federal government. According to Allen, Hill was simply a swindler. He had started the fake union in April, charging men $1.50 and women $.50 to join. He sold shares at $10.00 each for a proposed building in Winchester that never was built. For $50.00, a man could get a badge, handcuffs, and a certificate saying that he, too, was a "U.S. and foreign detective." Hill preyed upon a "race of children," Allen declared, for the purpose of getting their money. But the scheme had a sinister side as well. A huge cache of arms and ammunition had been discovered at a Negro school fifty miles west of Elaine at Pine Bluff, possibly the arsenal for Hill's army. Yet, when the fighting started, Hill disappeared with a large sum of cash, his fleeced victims now dead or in jail.

Bizarre as this story sounded, and despite its prominence, many readers may have overlooked it because everything else in the country was falling apart as well. During early October President Woodrow Wilson was still incapacitated by a stroke, and his physician announced that he was "gravely ill." Meanwhile, a hot fight continued in the Senate over the president's peace treaty with its League of Nations. Steel strikers rioted at Gary,

Indiana, and a Senate committee grilled William Z. Foster, their leader, on his connections to radicalism. At Weirton, West Virginia, American Legionnaires rounded up 150 Finnish radicals and forced them to kneel and kiss the American flag.[2]

In the midst of this distressing news, white Americans still had baseball to remind them of their common nationality. On the day the fighting started in Arkansas, the World Series opened at Redlands Field in Cincinnati. The American League Champion Chicago White Sox were favored to beat Pat Moran's Reds in the best of nine game playoffs. To the sporting world's amazement, the Reds jumped out to a lead as the White Sox inexplicably struck out and booted plays. The Reds won the Series. Baseball, with its rules and regularity, its reassuring rural feeling in an increasingly urban nation, stood like a cultural signpost of the nation's common culture and endurance. The trouble in Arkansas must have seemed like a faraway, baffling event, while baseball showed America to itself as it truly was.

THERE WAS MUCH about the Arkansas story that did not smell right to the NAACP leadership in New York. The idea of a planned Negro insurrection would have seemed preposterous to them. Almost predictably, Assistant Secretary Walter White implored his superior, John Shillady, to dispatch him to the scene. White wrote that he was "exceedingly anxious to make the investigation personally and I . . . am assuming complete responsibility for any personal consequences which may . . . arise." He had just finished a tough assignment in Chicago after the violence there. The Association raised White's fare and sent him on the first train. Meanwhile he had arranged through the Chicago NAACP to secure press credentials from the *Daily News*, and he represented himself in Arkansas as a reporter.[3]

Before leaving for Arkansas, White checked with his southern sources about the situation there. These included Robert Church Jr., who replied that the idea of a Negro insurrection was "ridiculous" and that the charge against the union was "camouflage" to mask exploitation of the tenants. White had visited Little Rock in 1918, but apparently did not contact the local branch this time, perhaps to conceal his identity. Only a year old, its leaders included Thomas J. Price, an attorney with offices in the Mosaic Temple Building, J. H. McConico, and a group of physicians, teachers, ministers, and their wives. A catchall African-American labor union/benevolent society also wrote to New York and may have affiliated with the more middle-class NAACPers. White wrote to the branch in October 1918, congratulating them as a "splendid group."[4]

He arrived in Memphis on October 9 and spent the evening with Church. The son of a wealthy African-American businessman and political boss, the younger Church was an NAACP board member, but did little to build the Association himself. He was active in the national Republican machine and was a valuable source of political information. The next day White arrived in Little Rock and met with U. S. Bratton, whose son was still in jail at Helena. Bratton explained the conditions in Arkansas agriculture, how his son had been arrested at the Ratio plantation, and the absurdity of the "planned insurrection" story. This interview provided the basis of articles White wrote later.[5]

Using his press credentials, White also met with Governor Brough. A balding man with hard, birdlike features, Brough laid the trouble at the feet of outside publications such as the *Crisis* and the *Chicago Defender*. Born in Mississippi, Brough was a Johns Hopkins–trained economist and a graduate of the University of Mississippi Law School. Many regarded him as a New South progressive, but he was also a typical paternalist who believed in white supremacy. He was not a race-baiter, however, saving his rhetorical fire for "reds" who scarcely existed in Arkansas.[6] A few days before White's interview, the governor's private secretary wrote a letter that revealed the mind-set in the governor's office. "If he [the governor] had not gone there when he did, no doubt the negroes would have wiped out three or four of those little towns down in the southern end of Phillips County. But they were able to quiet the situation with only a few additional deaths . . . I think that this will be a lesson to the negroes in the Black Belt. . . ."[7] The at least twenty African-American dead did not really exist for the secretary except for instructional purposes. Brough, taking White for a sympathetic northern reporter, furnished him with a letter of introduction for use in Phillips County.[8]

White also spoke with an African-American attorney who was destined to take over the legal cases growing out of the Elaine confrontation. This was the fifty-six-year-old Scipio Africanus Jones, son of a slave mother and a white father. Jones warned White that it would be dangerous for Helena Negroes to talk with him. White did meet some refugees from the area in Little Rock, and even they were reluctant to speak. Nevertheless, White hoped to interview the prisoners at Helena, and the governor's letter probably helped convince Sheriff F. F. Kitchens to meet White at the jail. "As I walked down West Cherry Street, which ran parallel to the railroad track, a Negro overtook me," White recalled in his autobiography. Furtively, the man told him, "I don't know what you are down here for, but I just heard them talking about you—I mean the white folks—and they say they are going to get you. The way I figured it out is that if the white folks are so against you, you must be a friend of ours."

While in Little Rock, White had telegrammed James Weldon Johnson on a minor matter, using his middle name, Francis, as a signature. Possibly, this telegram tipped off the Helena mob. The next train was leaving in a few minutes, and White caught it just in time. A practiced raconteur, White retold the story of what happened next throughout his life. The conductor told him that the train would be delayed and that he was about to miss some fun. "There's a damned yellow nigger down here passing for white and the boys are going to get him." With a characteristic gesture, White impatiently consulted his watch, protesting that he had important business in Memphis. His story continued:

> "What'll they do with him?" I asked.
>
> Shifting his cud of tobacco, he shook his head grimly and assured me, "When they get through with him he won't pass for white no more."
>
> No matter what the distance, I shall never take as long a train ride as that one seemed to be.[9]

Walter White's longest train ride ended in New York by October 17, and he published articles in the *Chicago Daily News*, the *Nation*, the *Crisis*, and other places that told a very different story from what America had heard so far about Phillips County. He rooted it in the economic struggle of the tenant farmers to get an honest accounting for their crops. Throughout the Red Summer, newspapers had portrayed national racial violence as caused by two aspects of African-American behavior: the Negro as rapist (Washington, D.C., Knoxville, and Omaha) and the Negro as scab (Chicago and Omaha). In Walter White's account, Phillips County was about poor people sticking up for their rights by building a union.

Phillips County was home to 44,530 people in 1919, 32,929 of whom were African-American. Farmers there owned nine million dollars' worth of property in 1920, two-thirds of it planted in cotton. Negro tenants raised most of the cotton, but their white landlords reaped the profits. At the last census in 1910, 587 African Americans in the county owned their own farms, but 3,598 were tenants. They raised twenty-five thousand of the thirty thousand bales of cotton harvested in 1919, but whites owned most of it. A bale of cotton weighs five hundred pounds, and in 1919 cotton sold on the market at forty-three cents per pound, plus fifteen dollars per bale for seed.

The landowner furnished the tenant with farm and household supplies from a central commissary. For this he charged high prices, paid on installments at phenomenal interest rates ranging from 25 to 50 percent. In 1904, cotton had been only nine cents a pound, but wartime demand brought prices up to twenty-eight cents in 1917 and forty-three cents in 1919. If marketed fairly, the steep rise in price would have freed many tenants from debt and allowed others to buy land. As examples, the NAACP later estimated that the twelve main defendants in the Phillips County cases should have been fairly paid eighty-six thousand dollars on their cotton crop in 1919. Recognizing this, the landlords generally refused to give a reckoning of their tenants' accounts and sent them away at harvest time with unitemized bills. Many in the Delta region were not paid for their 1918 crop until July 1919.[10]

Under these conditions, black farmers turned to the twin strategies of organization and legal redress. The obscure Robert Hill incorporated his Progressive Farmers and Household Union in 1918 and by April of 1919 was active in Phillips County. During the summer the union held meetings at Ratio, Elaine, Hoop Spur, Old Town, Ferguson, Mellwood, and other places. Modeled on the Masonic lodges, the union had special passwords and secret grips. Its literature appealed to biblical authority, the solidarity of the poor, and the improvement of civic virtue. With their cash flow at a high point in the summer of 1919, the farmers approached Bratton's law firm, and he agreed to represent sixty-eight plaintiffs for fifty dollars plus a percentage of the settlement. As part of the struggle, African-American women refused to join the cotton harvest as wage workers—in effect, striking. For purposes of self-defense, the farmers purchased guns. They anticipated violence from the whites and refused to be intimidated.[11]

The landowners became alarmed. White did not know that Sebastian Straub, a Helena merchant, had gone to Chicago and hired a Negro detective to investigate the union. The detective mailed a report to Joseph Meyers, a Helena businessman. This report, or Meyers's interpretation of it, warned of the so-called uprising and assassination plot. The whites prepared to nip this horror in the bud. They discussed the situation with some Helena black leaders and warned the telephone operator at Elaine. The speed with which the posses formed after the Hoop Spur shooting suggests these were prearranged.[12]

The Sunday before the violence, a Helena white man showed up in Elaine drunk on "white mule" and started threatening to shoot local Negroes. Blacks protested to the sheriff's office at Helena, but the man was not arrested. This may have been the pretext for the Tuesday expedition to Hoop Spur. According to White's *Nation* article, the lawmen tried to enter the church, were denied admittance, and opened fire. The defenders shot back, but ran for their lives. After the trustee called for help, word spread like wildfire, and by the next morning Helena was an armed camp.[13]

Walter White's version of the events at Hoop Spur became the basis of the two best accounts of the Phillips County affair. These are several chapters in a thoughtful analysis of all the race riots of 1919 by historian Arthur Waskow, and an excellent monograph focused on the legal issues by political scientist Richard C. Cortner.[14] The problem, however, with Walter White's story is that it makes no sense. The Committee of Seven's story makes even less sense. Their account was further undermined by evidence that the prisoners at Helena were tortured into making incriminating statements, and by affidavits offered later by two repentant white posse members. The trials themselves never inquired about the outbreak of the violence or how the African Americans were killed.

The question arises: why would the planters, intent on crushing what they later claimed to be a serious insurrection complete with an organized army, dispatch a railroad detective, a sheriff's deputy, and an African-American driver against it? Or, if this trio really was in search of a bootlegger, why would they fire into a church filled with farmers who were conceivably armed?

In June of 1920, the NAACP received a curious, handwritten letter from a Topeka, Kansas, African American named S. H. Tarbet relating one possible explanation of the Hoop Spur incident. Tarbet was in touch with the mother of Robert Hill, the union leader. Hill's mother, in turn, got her information from the colored mistress of a white man at the Ratio plantation known as "Dug." In this version, a gang of about thirty white men from Ratio went over to Hoop Spur and fired on the union meeting in the darkness, causing a panicked flight. Tarbet wrote that "all colored people run. [W]hile they were there on scene up drove an automobile colored driver. [T]hey thought them colored men returning to church. [S]o they blazed away . . . killed agent and . . . wounded deputy sheriff."[15]

This story's weakness is that it is thirdhand, and its original source is an interested party. However, it may best explain the events at Hoop Spur. During the Supreme Court case, the defense submitted an affidavit by another railroad detective who arrived at Hoop Spur just before dawn. He found the church a bullet-strewn shambles. It was later burned down, he averred, to hide the evidence. The next day he "heard some planters and from their conversation I understood that a number of white men had gone to Hoop Spur church house the night before for the purpose of breaking up the meeting." Another planter boasted " 'I told my negroes about two months ago that if they joined that blankety-blank union I would kill every one of them.' "[16] Given the national and local events of 1919, the likelihood is that the planters decided to make good on this threat. Tarbet concluded his letter: "[T]here is no justice in Phylips County Arkansas Investigate and do not print my name."[17]

The roots of white determination to put down the tenants' union ran even deeper. Greenfield Quarles, a white Helena attorney, explained the local history to Professor David Y. Thomas of Fayetteville in a 1920 letter. Quarles fully accepted the white version of events, extolling local race and labor relations and the work of the Committee of Seven. To Quarles, "[t]his unfortunate affair came as a clap of thunder in a clear sky." But, he reminded Thomas, "Under Reconstruction this county was placed entirely under Negro rule, the sheriff, county clerk . . . constable and policemen were negroes. This condition of affairs continued for ten years," until 1878.[18] White and black descendants of the Reconstruction era, in a majority African-American region, carried deep-seated resentments about this past experience: African Americans at having their rights stripped away, whites fearing the return of equality. In 1919 these long-simmering tensions exploded as rising African-American expectations smashed against white resistance.

Walter White never arrived at an estimate of how many African Americans were killed in the violence. Five whites were killed, but the governor, the newspapers, and all of official white society could care less about how many African Americans died. The newspapers reported the African-American dead in the twenties. White's 1919 articles said that as few as twenty-five or as many as one hundred perished. Later the NAACP claimed that as many as two hundred may have been killed. The low figure would be as many as were killed at Chicago; the high figure would be twice as many as were killed in the aftermath of Nat Turner's 1831 insurrection.[19] The death toll alone makes the general neglect of the Phillips County affair by historians lamentable.

Evidence on behalf of the high figure was offered by George Washington Davis of Pine City, Arkansas, grand secretary of the Pythian and Masonic lodges. He declared on November 30, 1920, that his lodge paid on 103 burial claims and that 73 others "that we knew personally" died. His own three sons were killed at Elaine. However, Davis also claimed that an equal number of whites died, which is certainly false.[20] While this weakens Davis's credibility, it does not prove him wrong about the number of black victims, about which he was in a position to know something. Later, H. F. Smiddy, a posse member who gave evidence on behalf of the accused, swore, "I do not know how many negroes were killed in all but I do know that there were between two hundred and three hundred negroes killed that I saw with my own eyes."[21]

The ferocity of the combined posse and military assault is undeniable. The *Memphis Press* reported on October 4 that a score of Negroes were killed, but this probably represented what the reporter could verify. "Dead bodies were lying in the road a few miles outside the city," he recorded. "Enraged citizens fired at the dead bodies of the negroes, as they rode out of Helena toward Elaine. When the troops rounded up the negroes, hardly any had guns or ammunition. . . . The soldiers used their machine guns on one group of negroes. . . . Two negroes were killed outright and the rest threw up their arms and surrendered."[22] Colonel Isaac Jenks, commander of the Camp Pike soldiers, tried to disarm the whites, but they had had a full day to wreak their vengeance unchecked. Jenks found "the town [Helena] in a great state of excitement. Hundreds of white men all carrying firearms on the streets." When they moved out, "one of the first things we saw was a Negro woman on her doorstep, barely alive . . . she died soon after."[23] In 1921, Walter White wrote to an inquirer that "the number of Negroes killed during the riot is unknown and probably never will be known. . . . A number of colored people took refuge in the canebrakes, many of them wounded and a number died there." Other bodies rotted unburied on riverbanks and other isolated areas, White wrote.[24]

His unsigned *Crisis* article told how the four Johnson brothers were killed. These sons of a Presbyterian minister included a dentist, a doctor, and a veteran of Chateau-Thierry. On October 1, they were out hunting and had no idea of the growing conflict. They ran into a group of white acquaintances. These men warned them of the danger and urged them to stack their arms and take a train home. This they did, but a posse stopped the train and seized them. The brothers had been deceived and suspected they were about to be lynched. The dentist grabbed the gun of Orly Lilly, the Helena alderman, and shot him dead. Lilly's companions raked all four brothers with gunfire, leaving hideously destroyed corpses.[25] White revealed no source for this story, but it could only have come from a white participant.

The anonymity and unreliability of many of the sources regarding the Phillips County affair suggest that White was right about one thing: the total number of dead may never be known. However, the quality of the October 1 affair should be clear. There was a hugely disproportionate number of African-American deaths. As we shall see in a subsequent chapter, all of the white deaths except Lilly's may have been caused by whites. There was no insurrection. Instead, there was a massacre with scattered African-American resistance. The whites gathered together, driven by a "Great Fear" similar to that which gripped the French countryside in 1789 as peasants mobilized against imagined "brigands."[26] Phillips County showed the Great Fear at the heart of the white American nightmare: that the African-American working poor, cheated out of their just deserts, would rise up in arms and take what they thought was theirs.

Walter White never got into the Helena jail to see its prisoners. While he made his escape by train, the Helena Committee of Seven, with authorization from the governor, was busy interrogating them. This privatization of law enforcement procedures by itself suggested how weak and arbitrary was the regular state and county prosecutorial apparatus. To a large extent, the interrogation involved planters vouching for their tenants. Hundreds for whom whites would speak were released. The prisoners were, after all, "their negroes," whose labor was the source of their income. Black farmers who owned their own land, however, could expect no such protection. A grand jury, drawn from whites only, indicted 122 African Americans, charging 73 with murder.

County judge J. M. Jackson opened the trial of the first six defendants on November 2. The prosecutor charged Frank Hicks with killing Clinton Lee, a posse member, and accused Frank Moore and four others as accessories. Court-appointed white lawyers represented the defendants. After perfunctory testimony, including that of two African-American prisoners, the state rested. The defense challenged nothing. Outside, an angry mob patrolled the streets. An all-white jury took eight minutes to convict Hicks and seven minutes for the other five. Two days later another five were convicted under similar circumstances. A week after that, Judge Jackson sentenced all eleven to death in the electric chair, the sentence to be carried out between December 27 and January 2, 1920. One more man, Ed Ware, the secretary of the union, was captured at New Orleans, returned to Helena, and condemned to die with the others. Of the remaining prisoners, another sixty-seven pled guilty to lesser charges and received sentences of from one to twenty years.[27]

Through U. S. Bratton, the NAACP organized a legal defense for the accused. Bratton came to New York and met with its board of directors on November 10. The Association decided from the outset to hide its role in the defense, fearing that local antipathy to an interracial organization headquartered in New York would freeze Arkansas authorities into an intransigent posture. Bratton thereupon met discreetly with NAACP supporters in New York and Boston to initiate a defense fund. Then he accompanied White to Washington, and the two men met with Justice Department officials and friendly senators. At the Justice Department, White and Bratton convinced one administrator to order an investigation of the Phillips County matter. White reported to the NAACP board that the Justice Department found no evidence of a planned massacre of whites. On Capitol Hill, Republican senator Charles Curtis of Kansas invited Bratton to testify at his hearings on the race riots during mid-January. Bratton did this, but the hearings generated much less publicity than the NAACP hoped, partly because Attorney General A. Mitchell Palmer captured the headlines with a series of spectacular raids on the offices of alien radicals.[28]

Back in Little Rock, Bratton secured counsel to handle the appeals. As a radical, he himself would have been an inappropriate defense attorney. In addition, his son had been imprisoned and nearly lynched in the affair. (O. S. Bratton was quietly released after a month, having no knowledge of any of the events until after the fact.) The lawyer of record would be Colonel George W. Murphy, a prominent criminal attorney and, equally important, a wounded Civil War veteran. Murphy had served as state attorney general from 1901 to 1905, and even ran for governor in 1912 as a Progressive. The NAACP antilynching committee, based in Boston, approved the choice, and the board of directors agreed to pay Murphy three thousand dollars to handle the appeals to the state level. The Association anticipated that the cases would go to the Supreme Court and therefore aimed to raise a fund of twenty-five thousand to fifty thousand dollars.[29]

The Association paid a high price, however, for its decision to keep its role secret. At the simplest level, the secrecy made fund raising very difficult. As Mary White Ovington wrote to a potential contributor, "It would queer the case if a northern organization was known to be financing it." The Association asked the larger branches to contribute twenty-five dollars each, and the smaller ones ten dollars. The New York office sought out wealthy individuals or foundations privately. Julius Rosenwald of Sears and Roebuck agreed to contribute five hundred dollars for every forty-five hundred dollars the Association raised. Bostonians contributed over five hundred dollars, and the New York Foundation was another big contributor. By January, the NAACP counted over six thousand dollars in the defense fund.[30]

A second problem was that the NAACP could not promote a campaign of mass pressure, either through letter writing to the governor or by holding mass meetings in the North. It did try to influence public opinion through White's articles in the northern press and by responding to articles that accepted the official version of events. In New York, the Association joined with the Socialist Party–backed Committee for Justice to the Negro. This ad hoc formation staged a protest meeting at the Harlem Casino, and the NAACP participated enthusiastically. "We are approving of everything that they do," Ovington wrote to an NAACP leader in New York, but maintained the necessity of continued discretion. The Association, however, might have sponsored a broad public defense campaign, asking less controversial liberals to speak out publicly or appeal to Arkansas officials, while they stayed in the background. The decision to keep the campaign secret probably hurt the Arkansas defendants more than it helped them.[31]

The more profound problem was that the Association's cautious posture toward Arkansas authorities extended to the local African-American community. The first response of black leaders was to reassure the state's white rulers that they opposed violence, and that they were willing to work with the governor to preserve law and order and improve interracial communication. Several black church, academic, and legal figures sent a letter to Governor Brough, commending his establishment of an interracial commission. Among the signers was Scipio Jones. The new race commission had nine white and eight African-American members. They urged that the appeal of the cases should be heard by the state supreme court. They motivated this rebuke of the first trial by arguing that the honor of the state needed to be defended in the face of northern editorial attack. Privately, the black commission members, unaware of the NAACP's initiative, organized their own defense efforts. Like the NAACP, they believed the accused to be innocent as well. In late November, Thomas J. Price wrote to White, appealing for funds on behalf of his own efforts and those of Scipio Jones. Suspicious of the local lawyers, whom they feared might be incompetent gold diggers with their eyes on the Association's fund-raising abilities, White and Johnson evaded the Arkansans' request.

At the suggestion of Monroe Work, a Tuskegee sociologist, the Arkansas leaders set up the Citizens Defense Fund Commission to raise money publicly. The secretary of this group was J. H. McConico, the Little Rock NAACP president, yet the national office kept him in the dark as well. While the legal battle continued in Arkansas over the next two years, the local leaders raised more money than the NAACP did nationally. In their relationship with the local leaders, White and the other staff members showed a mixture of distrust and elitism that weakened the defense efforts.[32]

Despite the tension between the local and national activists, Scipio Jones, the ex-slave, and Colonel Murphy, the Confederate veteran, worked together on the appeals. Governor Brough stayed the executions, and within sixty days, on December 18, they filed their motion in the circuit court. Jones and Murphy challenged every aspect of the trial: the mob in the court and on the street had created an atmosphere in which a not-guilty verdict was impossible; the defendants were denied due process because they had inadequate time to consult their attorneys; and the exclusion of blacks from the juries denied them equal protection of the law guaranteed by the Fourteenth Amendment. Finally, they presented affidavits of two defendants, Alf Banks Jr. and Will Wordlow, who declared that they had been tortured with whips, electric shocks, and strangling drugs. The state docketed the cases in two sets of six, *Ed Ware et al.* and *Frank Moore et al.*

The state supreme court heard the cases on March 22. Murphy now added a new argument. During the original *Ware* trials, the jury had not declared whether the defendants were guilty of first or second degree murder. In one of the cases in the second group, Judge Jackson corrected this omission by writing it in himself. The supreme court upheld Murphy's argument on this point in the *Ware* cases but not in the *Moore* cases. The former group could be granted a new trial on this technicality. In the *Moore* cases, the judges ruled that the trial judge had properly corrected the omission in the verdict and, ominously for the *Ware* defendants, held that the rest of the trial had been fairly conducted. From this point on, the cases of the two groups of six took differing routes through the courts. The *Ware* six went back to Helena for a new trial, while the latter group remained on death row in Little Rock, pending appeal to the U.S. Supreme Court. In May 1920, Murphy filed for a review by the nation's highest court.

Back in Helena, Murphy and Jones fought every issue during the second *Ware* trial, which began May 3 before the original judge. They sought and failed to win a transfer to the federal courts due to the exclusion of blacks from the juries. They tried to get a change of venue, again without any luck. This time, however, defendants John Martin and Will Wordlow described how they were tortured before the first trial. Unfortunately for the defense, the seventy-nine-year-old Murphy became critically ill. Jones had to continue on his own. Helena was hostile territory, and he had to sleep at the home of a different black family every night. Within a few days, the defense rested and the verdicts came back: all guilty. Judge Jackson condemned the six to death for the second time.[33]

The men now rejoined their comrades on death row in Little Rock. The *Arkansas Gazette* reported that the prisoners maintained their innocence throughout. "We also think that the Lord will never let us die, for we are innocent," Ed Ware declared. "All we can do is read the scriptures, pray to the Lord and sing, and time passes on." The *Ware* defendants could still appeal to the Arkansas Supreme Court, and they did. Again the governor stayed their executions. After nine months in the courts, however, the outlook for the twelve defendants was grim indeed.[34]

IN 1919, Topeka, Kansas, had fifty thousand people, forty-eight miles of electric street railway, seventy-eight churches, no saloons, and an active NAACP chapter. The president of the NAACP was U.S. senator Arthur Capper, who owned a string of newspapers headquartered at the Capper Building at Eighth and Jackson, overlooking the state capitol. The Topeka NAACP, an integrated branch founded in 1913, accomplished much during its early years. It blocked the showing of the inflammatory movie *Birth of a Nation* and won admission for African-American children to the Orpheum Theater's educational movies. The NAACP fought efforts by the Kansas state legislature to segregate public schools in big cities. During this campaign, the NAACP called a mass meeting on February 22, 1919, asking "Will the War for Democracy Be Applied Here?" Thirty-five years later the Supreme Court answered Topeka's question in the affirmative, ruling that Linda Brown must be admitted to a white school because segregated education was inherently unequal. The 1954 *Brown* decision was the Court's most important ruling of the century. The road to that decision lay through the Topeka NAACP, and the next episode in the Arkansas cases played an important part in that branch's history.[35]

In January 1920, Robert Hill, the leader of the Arkansas tenants' union, was arrested in Kansas City, Kansas, on charges of murder and night riding in Arkansas. Hill had run away from the Ratio plantation when he saw the posse approach. He made his way to the all-black town of Boley, Oklahoma, then to South Dakota, and finally to Kansas, where fellow Masons hid him. From there he wrote to a man in Arkansas, asking him to convey his wife and child to Kansas. The man did this but betrayed Hill to Arkansas authorities. On January 21, James H. Guy, the vice president of the Topeka branch and a leading African-American attorney, was summoned to the city jail to represent Hill. There he found Hill's wife and child, whom the authorities released.[36]

A few days later, U.S. attorneys in Arkansas indicted Hill for impersonating a federal officer and for conspiring to do so. These charges referred to Hill's presentation of himself as a "U.S. and foreign detective." If not for the fact that Hill's life hung in the balance, the charges amounted to a comic parody of the law; there were, after all, at least dozens of dead black Arkansans whose deaths had gone uninvestigated. The federal charges were meant to get Hill back to Arkansas even if the governor of Kansas refused to extradite him on state charges. To handle these complicated affairs, attorneys Elisha Scott and A. M. Thomas joined Guy on Hill's defense team.

The NAACP national headquarters had been secretly aware of Hill's whereabouts since December. In late November and early December, Hill contacted the Association through attorneys Thomas Price and U. S. Bratton. He gave his version of the events at the Ratio plantation the morning Bratton's son had been arrested, mentioning the same "Dug" as one of the posse ringleaders. All the union's intentions had been peaceful, Hill emphasized. There were unions in twenty-five or thirty other counties, he wrote, and if they were going to initiate violence, they would have done it everywhere at once.[37]

Unlike the Arkansas situation, the NAACP could proceed openly in Kansas. Topeka had an active branch, and Kansas a liberal governor and Senator Capper, who sat on the Association's board of directors. In Kansas the NAACP ran a public campaign of mass pressure, through which it exposed the realities of Arkansas justice.

John R. Shillady immediately telegrammed Governor Henry J. Allen and urged him to deny Arkansas's request for extradition. Through Senator Capper, the Association added a white attorney, Hugh Fisher, to the legal team. In doing this, the NAACP was only recognizing the racial realities of the day. During the 1920s, white authorities showed contempt for African-American lawyers. Only a few were admitted to northern law schools; most learned their craft through apprenticeship. Good black law schools did not yet exist. The simple fact was that a black lawyer was not allowed to beat a white one.[38]

Fisher, the Shawnee County prosecutor, threw himself enthusiastically into the case. Using his political connections to the governor, he arranged to hold the state hearings before the federal officers could proceed against Hill. The idea was to gain time and keep Hill out of Arkansas. Governor Allen agreed to postpone Hill's hearing, all the while reassuring the Arkansas lawman who had arrived to take Hill home. However, large numbers of Topeka African Americans attended the preliminary hearing and harassed the Arkansas envoy, while Capper's newspaper blasted away at Arkansas justice. Disgruntled, the southerner went home without his man. Hill's lawyers had won the first round. Fisher wrote to Colonel Murphy, requesting information on the torture of the Arkansas prisoners, and to Shillady, informing him that Governor Allen was a partisan of land reform. The letters suggested that the governor would not look favorably upon the torture and murder of land reformers.[39]

Then disaster struck. Three black members of the Arkansas Race Commission, AME bishop J. M. Conner, Philander Smith College president J. M. Cox, and Arkansas Baptist College president J. A. Booker wrote to Governor Allen urging him to extradite Hill. They joined Helena white leaders in praising Arkansas governor Brough and the state's judicial procedures. "If true," Fisher telegrammed Shillady, "cripples us. Please investigate."[40]

The Association began a multipronged counterattack to this potentially fatal blow. Shillady sent a circular letter to the branches, urging them to write the Kansas governor. They should point out that Arkansas colored leaders would be under pressure to put their state in the best light. The best proof of Arkansas's record was its farcical trials and death sentences for the men already imprisoned. Next, the Association directly lobbied Allen. U. S. Bratton traveled from Little Rock and met privately with him. James Weldon Johnson later met Allen in Chicago, and the governor assured him that if Hill could establish his nonviolent intentions, there would be no extradition.[41]

Finally, the NAACP tried to negotiate with the Arkansas black leaders. William Pickens, who had grown up in Arkansas and was a former college administrator, wrote exploratory letters to college presidents Booker and Cox. His purpose was to keep open the lines of communication and urge cooperation wherever possible. There was a complex range of opinion among the Little Rock black elite, but their shared framework was the sort of accommodation advocated by Booker T. Washington. The Arkansas letter placed the NAACP in a delicate situation. The northern black press denounced Cox, Conner, and Booker, but they were among the founders of the local defense committee. In his reply to Pickens, Cox argued that Hill's testimony would further the cause of the Arkansas inmates, that the state would ultimately free the prisoners, and that only two local leaders disapproved of their letter. Attorneys Scipio Jones and Thomas Price concurred with their request, he wrote.[42]

The Arkansas civil rights movement, it should be remembered, had essentially gone underground. There had just been a massacre of black citizens, a judicial lynching was impending, and the black community had exactly two white allies: Murphy, who would die in one month, and Bratton, who would shortly flee the state. In the following year, the Ku Klux Klan (KKK) would emerge as a serious political force. The Little Rock NAACP probably did not function in this period; its correspondence file is virtually blank in the early 1920s. The defense work was based in the secret Masonic lodges, in whose building Jones had his office. The NAACP thus had to keep Conner, Cox, and Booker as allies in Arkansas while opposing them in Kansas. When the March issue of the *Crisis* ran a brief challenge to them, the Association could only hope that the Arkansans would see their point of view.[43]

It is not clear if Cox correctly stated Jones's position. Later in February, J. H. McConico of the local NAACP suggested that Jones represent Hill on the federal charges. Jones in turn supplied Hill's Topeka lawyers with useful depositions for the Kansas extradition hearing. Jones did indeed fight the federal charges. It is possible that the two unnamed Little Rock opponents of the extradition letter were McConico and Jones. The only Arkansas leaders to oppose extradition publicly were the Fort Smith NAACPers, but they were far away in the western part of the state. In a 1921 letter to Walter White, they charged that the Arkansas black leaders were paid off for their cooperation.[44]

Back in Topeka, African Americans organized a mass meeting in defense of Hill on the eve of his March 22 extradition hearing. They packed the hearing room with concerned black citizens, too. Arkansas was represented by its attorney general, John D. Arbuckle, a portly, moon-faced man with a walrus mustache who referred to black people as "niggahs" during the proceedings. This drew angry murmuring from the crowd. In this hostile atmosphere, unused to dealing with African-American attorneys on terms of equality, Arbuckle grew flustered and bungled his presentation. Hill, in contrast, testified capably that he had been miles away from Hoop Spur, had neither participated in nor advocated violence, and had fled only to save his life. The following day Governor Allen announced that Hill would not be extradited. This was the first NAACP victory in the Arkansas cases. It came on the same day that the Arkansas blacks lost in the state supreme court.[45]

Hill's freedom was not yet assured. He still faced the trumped-up federal charges of impersonating a U.S. official and conspiring to do so. The conspiracy count of the indictment was defeated after Scipio Jones won a directed not-guilty verdict for Hill's alleged co-conspirator in Arkansas. That left the impersonation charge itself, and this the Association blocked by filing affidavits with the Justice Department in Washington. Walter White laid the case before Assistant Attorney General William C. Herron. He brought with him affidavits by the three Kansas African-American attorneys regarding Hill's intentions and his chance for a fair trial in Arkansas. Another affidavit by Bratton related his son's imprisonment on false charges and near-lynching. Herron found this statement convincing. By the end of July, the Kansas federal judge released Hill on bail, and in October freed him on the second and last federal count.[46]

Topeka African Americans celebrated their victory, and Vice President Thomas R. Marshall denounced it before a cheering crowd of three thousand at Hot Springs, Arkansas. The state's white supremacists sent Governor Allen a load of hate mail.[47] NAACP leaders felt they had exposed the initial Arkansas story as a tissue of lies, but the larger battle for the freedom of the twelve death row and sixty-seven long-term convicts lay ahead.

Meanwhile, Americans were discovering that another national drama had also been misrepresented to them. Little by little in 1920, the story developed that the Chicago White Sox had thrown the 1919 World Series, taking payoffs from a notorious gangster. Many Americans know this latter story, and a popular Hollywood movie has been made about it. The events of Phillips County, Arkansas, in 1919 remain all too obscure.

6

Land of His Ancestors

N late July of 1915, a revolution threatened to topple the regime of Haitian strongman Vilbrun Guillaume Sam. As supporters of insurgent Rosalvo Bobo neared Port-au-Prince, Sam fled to the French legation. He was still holding in prison about two hundred hostages, many drawn from the upper classes. Sam sent a message to the warden, telling him to proceed as he thought best. When the revolutionaries finally broke into the jail, they found 167 bodies, including those of former president Oreste Zamor, and three sons of an opposing general.[1]

News of the massacre quickly spread among the capital's elite. They mobbed the French embassy, broke into a bathroom where Sam was hiding, and butchered him in front of his family. Outside the embassy gates, the crowd dismembered Sam's corpse and carried away the pieces. From aboard the USS *Washington*, anchored in the harbor, Rear Admiral William B. Caperton watched the bloody end of the brief Sam regime.

The next day, Caperton ordered 330 sailors and marines ashore. Their mission was to end the anarchy and take control of Haiti. Only two of his men were killed during the fighting, probably by friendly fire, but these deaths provided a rationale for sending more troops. Within a few weeks marines held all the government buildings, but no one at Washington seemed to be able to explain the rationale, purpose, or projected length of the Occupation. Meanwhile, Bobo's revolutionaries were frustrated in their goal of taking power. These "Caco" rebels took to the hills and cut off the city's food supply. The United States might have acted against this, but Secretary of the Navy Josephus Daniels cautioned President Woodrow Wilson. "It is very dangerous to begin to supply provisions because the Haitians are like Negroes in the South after the [Civil] War and would quit work entirely, deserting plantations if our government had undertaken to feed them." This was an analogy the Virginia-born president could appreciate, so Port-au-Prince went hungry. Besides being inhumane, Daniels's observation was also absurd: most Haitians were small farmers who owned their own land and had nothing to do with plantations.[2]

Admiral Caperton was now in charge, but he needed to find a Haitian president. The United States had had a difficult relation with Sam, part of whose backing came from a tiny German-Haitian community. After three candidates rejected the admiral's offer, Sudre Dartiguenave agreed. In return, he consented to allow the United States to build a naval station at the port of Mole St. Nicolas and agreed to pay claims made by the U.S.-owned National Railway. Protected by U.S. Marines, the new president assumed office on August 12. Not all Haitians were pleased by the installation of this handpicked leader, and many protested. Admiral Caperton declared martial law and tried offending Haitians in American military courts. The edict provided for newspaper censorship as well. By February of 1916, the U.S. Senate ratified a treaty with Haiti that gave the United States effective power to act as the nation's financial receiver, and to organize its police and public works departments.

Meanwhile, the rebels, barefoot and armed with machetes and old rifles, carried out an irregular campaign of opposition in the wild and mountainous north. Within six months, the marines easily wiped them out. At Fort Riviere, Marine General Smedley Butler wrote that his men "hunted the cacos like pigs" and killed seventy-five of them while suffering no casualties. At the capital, Colonel Littleton W. T. Waller had taken over for Caperton and was disgusted by the Haitians he met. "These people are niggers in spite of the thin varnish of education and refinement," he wrote to his friend Colonel John A. Lejeune.[3]

The American people heard little about Haiti for the next five years. The World War was raging in Europe, and no one cared about this small French- and Creole-speaking black nation occupying half a Caribbean island. Over the next five years, the Occupation forces would boast that they had pacified the island, built a road from the capital to the northern port of Cap-Haïtien, and improved public health. The road, however, was built by means of conscripted labor. When marines began pulling peasants off their farms and forcing them into work gangs, they revolted. A new leader of this Caco rebellion emerged in the person of the presciently named Charlemagne Peralte.[4]

Charlemagne, a handsome and educated political leader, resisted the road gangs and was tried by an American court-martial on charges of aiding the rebels. He was convicted and sentenced to five years on the chain gang himself. While working on the streets of the northern town of Cap-Haïtien, he escaped and organized a guerrilla band. He eluded capture until 1919, when two marines entered his camp by means of a ruse and shot him dead from ambush. American magazines glorified their bravery. The Occupation circulated a photograph of Charlemagne's corpse. Nude except for a loincloth, bound upright to a board by a rope across his chest, the dead body was the image of a black Christ after the Crucifixion. The contemporary viewer is immediately reminded of the photograph of the Argentine revolutionary Che Guevara after his 1968 assassination in Bolivia. Charlemagne became a martyr, but his disorganized forces were easily routed by the marines. By their own count, the marines killed 1,861 "bandits" in 1919 alone.[5]

From their office in New York, NAACP leaders viewed the developments in Haiti with growing alarm. Here were American soldiers, many of them picked from Louisiana regiments because they might speak French, gunning down black people in a foreign land. The United States had landed marines in other Caribbean countries during the ten years of the NAACP's existence, but Mexico and Nicaragua were not inhabited by people of African descent. For reasons of racial solidarity then, the NAACP decided in 1918 to send an investigating team there. Not until 1920 did the money become available for such a journey, and late in March James Weldon Johnson and publicity director Herbert J. Seligmann sailed for Port-au-Prince.[6]

For Johnson, the last few months had been exceedingly busy. In December 1919 he conferred with congressmen regarding the feasibility of a federal antilynching bill. Back in the office he prepared a report for the January annual meeting, conferred with his colleagues on a Harlem candidate for state assembly, and protested the dismissal of an African-American postal clerk. On January 2 Attorney General A. Mitchell Palmer rounded up thousands of suspected alien communists for deportation, and an antisedition act was introduced in Congress. Fearing its use against colored people, Johnson traveled again to Washington to testify against it. Next he spent a week in Chicago, where terrorists had bombed Negro homes and the community was in an uproar. Johnson spoke to a meeting of twenty-five hundred people. By coincidence, the governor of Kansas was in town, and Johnson appealed to him on behalf of Robert Hill, who was facing extradition to Arkansas in the Phillips County affair. A few days later he met with William C. Graves, the assistant to philanthropist Julius Rosenwald, who had contributed previously to the Arkansas defense. Next he was off to Minneapolis for a speech, and finally home for a board meeting. After this, the trip to Haiti must have seemed like a vacation. Nonetheless his mission carried profound personal overtones: he bore a personal grudge against President Woodrow Wilson, whose State Department had discharged him from diplomatic service. More importantly, he was going for the first time to the land of his ancestors. James Weldon Johnson's own story, as he told it, began in Haiti.[7]

"In 1802 Etienne Dillet, a French Army officer in Haiti, placed Hester Argo, a native Haitian woman, together with her three children aboard a schooner bound for Cuba."[8] This is the opening sentence of one of the most remarkable American autobiographies ever written. James Weldon Johnson's *Along This Way* is the absorbing story of a true Renaissance man: he was by turns an eager baseball pitcher, student, school principal, hit songwriter, lawyer, poet, novelist and essayist, diplomat, newspaper editor, and civil rights leader. His story reads seamlessly, as though written at a single setting or told orally over a drink. Johnson's eye for the nuance of American race relations is as sharp as that of any writer before or since. Perhaps because Johnson was involved directly in no violent confrontations, got along splendidly with his parents and with almost everyone untouched by prejudice who met him, his story is virtually unknown to all but close students of African-American history.

JOHNSON was an experienced Caribbean voyager when he first saw Port-au-Prince from his ship, but its beauty surprised even him. He did not anticipate the magnificent Haitian mountains, nor the impressive French colonial buildings and squares of the capital city. Herbert J. Seligmann accompanied Johnson until illness forced his return to New York. Johnson boarded at the Hotel Bellevue, the most attractive in the city, and began sending his letters of introduction to prominent Haitian leaders and writers. Publicly he was discreet about his business, which was to gather information for the NAACP and write a series of articles for the *Nation*, the most important liberal weekly in America. He soon found that the country was divided between an upper-class Francophone mulatto elite based in Port-au-Prince and a black peasant Creole-speaking majority. The former adhered to a Liberal Party that at first cooperated with the American Occupation, and the latter often belonged to the Nationalists. A more loosely organized grouping of National Progressives attracted the more independent thinkers whom Johnson found more congenial.[9]

By 1920, even the mulatto upper class was disgusted with the arrogance and brutality of the Occupation. Johnson dined with President Sudre Dartiguenave at the national palace on April 13. "I believed he was a patriot at heart, but he was in a delicate position and was extremely guarded in what he said to me," Johnson recalled in his autobiography. He seemed to be speaking in innuendos, Johnson thought. In his *Nation* article, however, he judged the president to be "bitterly rebellious at heart," a puppet whose

James Weldon Johnson. Courtesy of Library of Congress.

masters ignored his recommendations. Equally cautious was Louis Borno, the former foreign secretary, who succeeded Dartiguenave as president. Borno was another man of the mulatto elite, and Johnson respected his accomplishments as poet, linguist, and statesman, but he, too, bridled under the Americans. By the end of the year, Johnson wrote to him hopefully about prospects for independence.[10]

Johnson found the dissidents more forthcoming. Chief among these was the mulatto lawyer and man of letters Georges Sylvain. The two men must have recognized each other as analogues: Sylvain, too, was a poet and essayist. A shy, diminutive man, he had been warmly received at the Sorbonne and the French Academy. He was the founder of a "Union Patriotique" to oppose the Occupation, which, at Johnson's suggestion, was turned into an NAACP-like organization at a mass meeting in the capital. H. Pauleus Sannon, a bulky and imposing figure, had written a biography of Toussaint L'Ouverture, leader of the Haitian Revolution. Jean Price-Mars, a gentle scholar, had served as ambassador to France during Sam's overthrow. Along with like-minded leaders such as Dr. Arthur C. Holly, a student of voodoo and activist among the National Progressives; and Perceval Thoby and Stenio Vincent, later the president, they sought to overcome the divisions based on skin color and class that plagued Haiti. Now they were united on at least one issue: the Americans should go home and Haiti should determine its own affairs.[11]

Johnson spoke to American marine officers as well. To his own amazement, some would drop all inhibitions after a few drinks of *la goutte d'or* (drop of gold), and address him as though he were a fellow white racist. "The trouble with Haiti is that these niggers down here with a little money and education think they are as good as we are," one of them told Johnson. Another marine frankly described the massacre of gamblers at a cockfight that had been passed off as a battle.[12]

Johnson added a two-week vacation to the end of his trip, arranged by Lemuel Livingstone, the American consul at the northern city of Cap-Haïtien and a Jacksonville native. Livingstone told him how to get to Christophe's citadel, the vast military fortress built into the side of a mountain by a black general during the war for independence. Johnson approached the site first by automobile, and then by an arduous mule-trek. The imposing walls, cannon, and turrets of the towering structure took Johnson's breath away. The edifice is the most vivid testimony to African engineering skills in the New World. Upon his return to America, Johnson lectured on Haiti, and his talks revived interest in the black republic among African Americans.[13]

The field secretary returned to the United States in time to attend the

Association's Atlanta convention and then the Republican national convention in Chicago. During the summer he made two visits to Marion, Ohio, and convinced candidate Warren G. Harding that the Haitian issue might be used as grist for his campaign mill. Harding "looked upon the Haitian matter as a gift right off the Christmas tree," Johnson remembered. The senator sat in a swivel chair, alternately smoking cigarettes and chewing tobacco. Later in the campaign, Democratic vice presidential candidate Franklin Delano Roosevelt boasted of writing the Haitian constitution, and Harding hit him with a blast of bombast supplied by the NAACP. He charged that the marines had jammed the constitution "down their [the Haitians'] throats at the point of bayonets." In further declarations from his front porch, he reiterated Johnson's charges to him that thousands of Haitians had been slaughtered needlessly.[14] The issue fit the Republican campaign theme of opposition to international commitment in general and the League of Nations in particular. This matched the growing popular mood of disillusion with all things foreign. The Woodrow Wilson administration responded to Harding's charges by sending a team of military officials to investigate the situation. For the first time in its brief history, the NAACP had spoken on a matter of foreign relations, and the United States had been forced to act.

During the summer Johnson worked on his *Nation* articles. Herbert Seligmann fired the first salvo in the July 10 issue, beginning with this arresting parallel: "To Belgium's Congo, to Germany's Belgium, to England's India and Egypt, the United States has added a perfect miniature in Haiti." His indictment included testimony of torture, theft, arson, and murder, as told by victims, perpetrators, and observers. The motives for the original takeover remained undefined, Seligmann argued, and the continued occupation could no longer be justified by strategic concerns. Beneath Wilsonian rhetoric, Seligmann charged, lay pure imperialistic goals: Americans were buying up land, a practice sanctioned by the new constitution (one company alone owned fifty thousand acres), and establishing profitable sugar mills and lighting plants.[15]

Johnson's articles ran from late August to September, and he developed Seligmann's themes into a convincing case. His very first paragraph began with an indictment of New York's First National Bank, whose vice president R. L. Farnham functioned as "virtually the representative of the State Department." Without taking sides among the various Haitian factions, he showed how their division opened the door to American control. The new constitution and their military dominance gave the United States effective control over the Haitian economy and politics. "Deserving Democrats" had followed the marines and were taking over various bureaucratic posts as spoilsmen. These were invariably Louisiana or Mississippi racists, and Johnson lay bare their cupidity with analytic precision. They occupied luxurious villas, employed squadrons of servants, and commandeered automobiles, while the president of Haiti himself had none of these things. Johnson blamed his old antagonist, President Woodrow Wilson. "The originator of 'open covenants openly arrived at' . . . has enforced by the bayonet a covenant whose secret has been well guarded by a rigid censorship."[16]

A second article belittled American accomplishments on the island. The road, the hospital, the public health measures were pretty small beer when balanced against three thousand dead Haitians. The following week he offered a sophisticated economic analysis of the Occupation. He showed how the Haitian middle and upper classes had been forced by hard times to sell their government bonds to Americans, who snapped them up at low prices. Then they reorganized the Haitian National Bank and dictated that it redeem the bonds at par. The national budget and the value of the currency itself were similarly subject to the decisions of Farnham and his cohorts. In the final installment, Johnson challenged the stereotyped image of independent Haiti as a poverty-ridden republic of the indolent. Johnson saw instead an industrious, literate people whose leadership was cultured and worldly. He compared its notorious political instability favorably to that of Mexico and reminded his readers that the American South was more lawless than Haiti had ever been. The four articles formed a stern indictment of the Occupation in prose that was by turns ironic, analytical, and moving.[17]

The NAACP complemented the series with a press release by Johnson that many black and some white newspapers carried. In its statement, the Association took credit for the Navy Department investigation, but labeled its result a whitewash. Johnson hit especially at the continuing censorship of news from Haiti. "We need direct and open communication, openly arrived at, between the Haitian people and the American people. Then it will appear who were the bandits in Haiti." He thus turned Wilsonian rhetoric upon the president. It was impossible, Johnson insisted, for Marine Commandant Lejeune and Admiral Knapp to write a fair-minded account of their own Occupation.[18]

Secretary of State Bainbridge Colby himself attempted to refute Johnson's charges without naming him. He reiterated the country's "benevolent purpose" in bringing peace to Haiti and invoked the usual rhetoric about "chronic disorder," the demands of Haiti's European creditors, and the importance of the Monroe Doctrine. He argued that the First National Bank did not influence the administration, but said nothing about the censorship. So effective had the Occupation been, Colby wrote, that its work was "nearing completion." (In fact, American troops would remain in Haiti until 1934.) The next day the *New York Times* picked up where Colby had left off, accusing Senator Harding of making a "hysterical" charge regarding the three thousand deaths. These had been merely defensive sallies against "banditti" who were "the tools of cowardly politicians in Port-au-Prince." Later investigations would confirm the death toll that Johnson reported.[19]

For its part, the NAACP tried to raise its own profile on the domestic front. Walter White wrote to *Washington Bee* editor W. C. Chase that American Negroes must "unite with their brothers in Haiti." Johnson's articles were creating a "furor," he declared. As often happened, the exuberant assistant secretary was overstating the case. A few days before the Haiti articles appeared, terrorists set off a bomb on Wall Street that killed over thirty people and wounded hundreds more. The only "furor" in New York was directed against the probably anarchist perpetrators of this deed, who never were caught. Meanwhile, Johnson importuned Harding and Republican campaign official Coleman DuPont to keep up the pressure.[20]

Among Johnson's Haitian friends, the articles did indeed create a furor. The Haitians wholly overestimated his importance in the United States, regarding him as a powerful advisor to a future president. In his autobiography, Johnson writes that he tried to disabuse his admirers of this notion, but at the time he himself was swept away by the moment's possibilities. "The expose made through the articles in *The Nation* has attracted the attention of the entire American press and people," he enthused to Etienne Mathon in September. Two days after Harding won the election, Johnson assured Louis Borno that a new naval investigation would lead to congressional action against the Occupation. The Haitians took this at face value. After the *Nation* series began, lawyer Alfred Henriquez remarked upon the sensation caused among the Haitian elite. "Your name runs on all lips," he reported. Dr. Arthur Holly wrote he was "likened to that of a second Toussaint L'Ouverture, to that of a messiah." At other times, Johnson advised his Haitian contacts that they must count on America for nothing, put aside their differences, and rely on their own resources to restore Haiti's sovereignty.[21]

In New York, the NAACP was cooperating with a broader group of anti-imperialist reformers. The link between anti-imperialism and antiracism had been forged twenty years earlier, during the opposition to the American war against the Philippine independence fighters (one might go back further to the opposition to the Mexican War of 1848). NAACP president Moorfield Storey had spoken against the Philippine War, and the current activists added his name to their letterhead. Now the headquarters of the Friends of Haitian Freedom was located, naturally enough, at the *Nation*'s offices at 20 Vesey Street in Manhattan. Ernest Gruening, the magazine's managing editor, and publisher Oswald Garrison Villard were among its guiding spirits. This body met with Haitians living in New York, and in October they drafted a document calling for a joint Haitian-U.S. congressional commission to report on the Occupation. None of them trusted a new naval commission to do a proper job.[22]

One week later all the activists were amazed to read in the newspapers that the latest military report on Haiti by Marine Commandant George Barnett largely verified Johnson's charges. The *New York Times*, formerly supportive of the Occupation, now printed reports of massacres and atrocities in much the same language Johnson had used. The NAACP, through its various contacts, urged the Republicans to step up their use of Haiti as a campaign theme. A week before the election, Johnson wrote to Harding that he had addressed a mass meeting in Washington on the Haiti issue and that a State Department official had quietly solicited his advice. Shortly after Harding won the election, the NAACP board met and decided that Johnson might make another trip if the money could be raised. With Republican majorities in both houses, a congressional investigation now seemed likely.[23]

Johnson urged his Haitian correspondents to form a representative commission to come to Washington and lobby the Congress. Haitians in New York flocked to the NAACP office as "Muslims to Mecca," Johnson wrote to Emmett J. Scott. In March of 1921 the Union Patriotique delegation finally arrived. The NAACP hosted dinners and other social functions for H. Pauleus Sannon, Perceval Thoby, and Stenio Vincent. Then they told friendly Republican congressmen about human rights abuses, including unprovoked killings and torture, financial mismanagement by the Dartiguenave regime, and the illegal nature by which the Haitian constitution had been adopted. The new document gave foreigners the right to buy land, which was being gobbled up by American interests. Johnson himself reprised the anti-American sentiment he had heard in Haiti.[24]

In autumn 1921 the Senate began an investigation, headed by NAACP ally Senator Medill McCormick. The senator sent Ernest Gruening to Haiti to organize hearings held there. Despite the heightened military presence, the Union Patriotique demonstrated against the Occupation when the senators arrived. Representatives of the Haitian elite and dark-skinned Haitian peasants all had their say before the committee. The Republicans, however, proved to be only slightly less disappointing than the Democrats. The McCormick committee issued a several-thousand-page report that argued for reform of the Occupation rather than its end. It echoed Johnson's charges against the abuses during the Wilson administration, but saw much merit in the public health measures, road building, and economic oversight of which Johnson had been skeptical. In effect, the National City Bank's Roger Farnham and Carl Kelsey, a sociologist who had written a pro-Occupation report, carried the day.[25]

During the following summer, isolationist prairie senators supported an amendment by Utah Democrat William H. King to end the Occupation. The NAACP organized a letter-writing campaign on its behalf, but it came to naught. The NAACP had too busy a domestic agenda for the rest of the decade, and Haiti dropped down on its list of priorities. The white activists transformed their committee into one that dealt with Santo Domingo, the Spanish-speaking half of the island as well, and the NAACP let them take the lead. Ironically, the Democratic president elected in 1932 was Franklin Delano Roosevelt, who as vice presidential candidate in 1920 had boasted of writing the Haitian constitution. Shortly after his election, he announced a Good Neighbor policy toward Latin America, and by 1934, American marines were gone from Haiti.[26]

The NAACP could justly claim some credit for this development. In 1920, James Weldon Johnson surfaced the submerged issue of Haitian independence. The Association mobilized African-American opinion by journalistic exposés, mass meetings, and political pressure. Johnson worked with wider forces on a foreign policy issue and argued the Association's case before a future president and influential senators. In Haiti itself, Johnson's visit helped convince the competing factions to bury their differences and unite around the issue of restored sovereignty. For James Weldon Johnson personally, his trip to Haiti presented an opportunity to repay his ancestral debt to Etienne Dillet and Hester Argo. The withdrawal of American troops must have provided him with a moment of deep, abiding, and very private satisfaction.

7

Hope and Terror in the South

WHILE James Weldon Johnson was away in Haiti, several incidents transpired in the South that showed the unpredictability of Dixie's race relations. Almost 80 percent of all African Americans still lived in the South in 1920, and as the year began, the NAACP claimed 42,588 southern members, more than the 38,420 in the North (western and foreign branches brought the total to 91,203 in 310 branches).[1] One of the key questions confronting the movement was whether the Association could sustain its southern branches. This was a vast and complicated region, with very different political, economic, and social conditions prevailing depending upon the place. Events in early 1920 suggested that the Association might thrive in Upper South places such as Lexington, Kentucky; in industrial cities such as Anniston, Alabama; or in commercial centers such as Atlanta. Mississippi showed that Deep South race relations in rural areas were hopelessly stable.

ON TUESDAY, February 2, the body of Geneva Hardman, a ten-year-old white girl, was found in a cornfield outside Lexington, Kentucky. The girl's skull had been crushed with a stone. That night the police arrested Will Lockett, an African American, at the home of a friend six miles away and charged him with the murder. Lockett confessed. He was a war veteran who had been institutionalized for mental illness or retardation, and today would probably be recognized as criminally insane. Lockett was indicted and removed to the state capital at Frankfort, about twenty miles west, to prevent trouble.

The court ordered Lockett's trial to begin immediately on the following Monday. Republican governor Edwin P. Morrow called up a National Guard unit to protect the prisoner, and the guard commander warned people to stay away from the court. Morrow had just taken office in December, and his party held a majority in the lower house, an unusual situation even for the Upper South. He had spoken favorably of equal political rights for colored citizens in his inaugural address. Morrow told his guard commander to shoot to kill if a mob attacked the Fayette County court on Monday.

The Lexington police and National Guard roped off the sidewalk in front of the court house, but a mob of four thousand formed in the chill, grey morning nonetheless. Lockett was brought back by special train and was smuggled past the crowd without incident. Gradually the street filled with people so that the men in the front line, pressing against the rope barricade, threatened to surge forward and assault the building. A cameraman shouted for the men to "shake your fists and yell" for his photograph. A brawny farmer, holding a noose, called for an advance. The guard commander struck one agitator with his gun butt, shouted a warning, and fired into the air. A photograph of the scene shows an officer in a greatcoat, pistol pointed skyward with his finger on the trigger, confronting an emotional throng. The police and troops were outnumbered, and probably most of the mob knew that white men did not kill their brothers in defense of a colored man. The crowd surged forward.

The National Guard adjutant general gave the order to fire. In an instant, the dead and injured lay on the ground, and the horde dispersed through the adjoining streets. When it was over, six had been killed and about fifty wounded. This was the first time in the South that lawmen fired into a lynch mob. Black America could hardly believe it. "Bullets Halt Mob," screamed a banner headline in the *Chicago Defender*, followed by "Cowards Flee as Militia Shoots." Hardly anyone noticed or cared that inside the courtroom Will Lockett had been speedily convicted and sentenced to death.[2]

This story made the New York newspapers by afternoon, so the twelve people assembled for the monthly NAACP board meeting had the news. The board resolved to congratulate Governor Morrow and send out a press release. Claiming four thousand members in Kentucky, the NAACP expressed its "keen admiration for the energy with which you have vindicated the laws of Kentucky. . . ."[3]

By 1920, Kentucky ranked fourteenth in black population with almost 236,000 black residents, about 10 percent of the total. Kentucky was a battleground state for the NAACP. The Association won the greatest victory of its first decade when it overturned Louisville's residential segregation ordinance in the Supreme Court. It had a strong branch at Louisville and a new one chartered at Lexington in the same month that Morrow became governor. Its unofficial but real leader was Lizzie B. Fouse, who was also a leader in the women's club movement. In the decade to come, Kentucky

Kentucky militiamen defending Will Lockett from lynch mob, Lexington, Kentucky.
Courtesy of Special Collections, Transylvania University Library.

NAACPers would fight a number of skirmishes that kept the civil rights dream alive in a state where race relations were actively contested.[4]

"The Second Battle of Lexington," as some newspapers dubbed it, probably gave future lynchers pause. Three major Kentucky newspapers backed up Morrow, and the legislature passed an antilynching law. A grand jury investigated the ringleaders but returned no indictments. While lynching would continue during the decade, Governor Morrow's bold order contributed to its decline.

ON THE CHRISTMAS EVE that followed Armistice Day, the Reverend R. R. Williams of Anniston, Alabama, sat down to write by hand an anguished letter to the NAACP in New York. "We have a serious case here that is being rushed through the courts for fear of mob violence and I am sure that under conditions the man cannot get a fair trial the passion is so huge." The case was that of Sergeant Edgar Caldwell, an active-duty soldier who made the mistake of sitting in the white-only section of the Oxford Line streetcar. In addition to this indiscretion, he had quarreled about paying his fare. The motorman and conductor struck him and physically threw him off. Then Sergeant Caldwell withdrew a pistol and fired, killing the former and wounding the latter.[5]

Like Lexington, Anniston was an unusual city. Located sixty miles east of Birmingham near the Georgia border, it was built from the ground up as an industrial center by an enterprising Englishman and a Connecticut Yankee. They started an iron foundry and textile mill, and imported workers from Europe in the 1880s. Anniston's founders reinvested their profits and built parks, schools, and neat cottages on symmetrical streets. Black workers labored in the foundries, and by 1899 they developed a separate town called Hobson City, which they governed themselves. Anniston-Hobson boasted the largest black-owned drugstore in America, and black people owned groceries, clothing stores, and repair shops, too. Henry Grady, the post-Reconstruction editor of the *Atlanta Constitution* and prophet of an industrial "New South," praised Anniston as a model in his editorial columns.[6]

The NAACP rejected more cases than it took up, and at first glance, the Caldwell case might have fallen into the first category. The case of a black man shooting two unarmed whites, regardless of the provocation, did not seem promising to Association secretary John Shillady. He advised Williams that the NAACP usually worked through its local branches and that there was none in Anniston. He had consulted with the NAACP Legal Committee, which suggested simply that they get the sergeant a good lawyer. Shillady wrote to the Montgomery branch about the matter, but told Williams frankly that an intervention by New York might do the defendant more harm than good.[7]

Williams saw Shillady's point. He replied that the local people had hired one E. M. Allen of Birmingham to represent Caldwell. The soldier had been indicted in ninety minutes and was facing trial at a special court session on January 17. However, Williams insisted, there was a principle involved in this affair. As a soldier, Caldwell was entitled to a trial by a military court, where he had a chance for clemency, rather than a state court, in which execution was certain. Williams felt that this was "a test case of what is coming [to] us after the war." He had written to Emmett J. Scott, in charge of Negro Affairs at the War Department, to see if jurisdiction might be denied the civilian authorities.[8]

Shillady was still skeptical. Yet he wrote the Washington, D.C., branch and had them take the matter up with Scott as well, but he didn't think it would help. He was right. Williams wrote him back the day of the trial. After a few hours in court, an all-white jury found Caldwell "gilty of murder in the first digree [*sic*]." This didn't seem right to Williams. Caldwell was a military man, he should not have been tried by an Alabama court, and the War Department should have helped him. Although Caldwell was "a stranger in this city," the local people had raised one thousand dollars for his legal defense and weren't ready to quit.[9]

The NAACP heard little more about the matter until shortly after its conference in May 1919. Williams wrote that Caldwell's appeal would come before the state supreme court on June 2. Could the NAACP now try to get the U.S. attorney to look into the case? Shillady wrote to Attorney General A. Mitchell Palmer and urged the Montgomery branch to help out with fund raising.[10]

This didn't satisfy the Reverend Williams, so he appealed directly to Moorfield Storey. He wanted the national body to pressure the federal government to intervene, and he believed that President Woodrow Wilson had already told his attorney general to inquire into the case. For his part, the Reverend Williams was throwing himself body and soul—quite literally— into saving Caldwell's life. He organized his colleagues into an Anniston-Hobson chapter of the NAACP and promised to get one hundred members for it. In addition, he wrote, "I have broken my rule on the Lord's Day [in writing a letter] but the matter is so important I feel that I am clear."[11] Reverend Williams apparently believed that His eye was on the sparrow, as the old spiritual went, and, in the words of the song, "I know He's watching me."

Shillady, with Williams's letter to Storey in hand, wrote to Washington, D.C., NAACP president Archibald Grimké, now taking the reverend's side. Williams might have a point about federal action saving Caldwell's life after the Alabama appeals were exhausted. To no one's surprise, the Alabama Supreme Court rejected the sergeant's plea on July 7 and sentenced him to hang on August 15. Williams wrote that Caldwell's wife was prostrate with grief.[12]

The New York office, meanwhile, buzzed with new problems regarding the Red Summer, making the Caldwell case just one issue among many. Then, in mid-July, Williams and the new Anniston NAACP leaders finally sent a letter that clarified the murky incident itself. Before throwing the sergeant off the car, conductor Cecil Linton and motorman Kelsie Morrison had punched him twice in the face. They literally threw him off the car, and Caldwell landed face down. Morrison kicked him in the stomach as he lay prone, and Caldwell, as he had been trained, rolled over and fired while being kicked. In their opinion, this might be murder, but not in the first degree. Caldwell had fired in self-defense and without premeditation. Beside this information, there was other news: President Wilson *had* written the governor to block Caldwell's execution pending a federal investigation. Charles D. Kline, Caldwell's appeal attorney and a state senator, would go to Washington to argue his cause.[13]

With renewed concern, Walter White asked James A. Cobb, the head of the Washington branch Legal Committee, to meet him at Union Station one hot night as he was changing trains on a trip south.[14] Cobb got right on the case and, in the midst of the Washington riot, reported his opinion to Johnson. The law, Cobb said, gave the War Department the discretion to turn a soldier over to civilian authority. If it did, however, it was obligated to see that he received a fair trial, which Caldwell clearly had not received. At most, he should have been charged with manslaughter. The all-white jury was chosen by illegally barring blacks from the rolls. Further, there was a lynch-mob atmosphere at the trial, and the minority opinion in the Leo Frank decision might now prevail in this case: every citizen had Fourteenth Amendment rights that no state could deny. If Caldwell were hanged, it would be "judicial murder."[15]

A few days later, on August 2, while the Chicago riot was in full swing, Johnson wrote to Cobb with more news from Anniston. Emmett J. Scott had discussed Caldwell's case with President Wilson's secretary, Joseph P. Tumulty. This cleared the way for the NAACP to present Caldwell's side to the attorney general. Cobb arranged a meeting with Assistant Attorney General Harry Stewart, bringing with him Emmett J. Scott, Caldwell's attorney Kline, Washington NAACP leader Lafayette Hershaw, and a man named Houston (probably attorney William Houston, whose son Charles Hamilton would later found the full-time NAACP legal department). This high-powered delegation argued that Caldwell merited federal protection in the state court, that he was overcharged in the state court, that he should have had an army lawyer by his side, and that he should have been dressed in uniform. Stewart gave the men a sympathetic hearing but remained noncommittal about federal intervention.[16]

Meanwhile, the Alabama Supreme Court declined to rehear the case, and Caldwell was condemned to hang on December 5. Now the only hope was for Attorney General Palmer to apply for a writ of error at the U.S. Supreme Court. In the interim, Cobb met with Secretary of War Newton D. Baker and an aide. Emmett J. Scott and Kline went along on Cobb's side. This time Cobb played what he hoped would be his trump: a precedent involving a white Kentucky soldier charged with murder who had not been turned over to civilian authorities. Baker listened and agreed to meet the next morning. But this time the aide appeared with hostile assistants, and little was accomplished.[17]

Cobb and Scott now proceeded to the White House for a meeting with

Joseph Tumulty, secretary to President Wilson. Tumulty listened sympathetically and agreed to write a memo for the president. After a few days,
Tumulty informed Cobb that the attorney general had instructed an *amicus* brief on Caldwell's behalf.[18]

Two days before Caldwell was to hang, a federal judge issued a certifi-
cation of reasonable doubt, entitling Caldwell to appeal to the Supreme
Court. Caldwell was removed from the prison at Anniston and transported
to Birmingham pending the appeal. Three months later, Cobb learned of
an ominous backroom maneuver. Alabama prosecutors had convinced Attorney General A. Mitchell Palmer to remove R. P. Stewart from the *amicus*
brief. Palmer, having just captured the headlines for his roundup of alien
Communists, was in the hunt for the presidential nomination and was
susceptible to southern pressure. "This is what political influence has
done to defeat justice," the indefatigable Reverend Williams wrote in the
margin of Stewart's letter. The federal interest was turned over to the solicitor general's office, where an unfriendly Georgia attorney was now handling matters. To Cobb's surprise, this man prepared a competent brief as
friend of the court.[19]

On March 4 and 5, Cobb and his associates argued before the U.S. Supreme Court on Caldwell's behalf. The appeal rested on a technicality, but
the sergeant seemed to have the law on his side. The armistice was only a
cease-fire and did not end the state of war between the United States and
Germany. Therefore, Caldwell was subject to existing wartime regulations,
which had explicitly been changed to name a court-martial as the only
agency empowered to try a soldier. "And if this be so," Cobb implored,
"no civil authority may for the time being lay hand upon him. . . ." Cobb
thought the justices were deeply interested. Stewart and the solicitor general told him that the case was indeed important.

The length and authorship of the Court's ruling suggest that this was so.
The nine-page opinion by Chief Justice Edward Douglass White was
among the longest written at the October 1919 term. White was a Louisiana
veteran of the Civil War; every year on the anniversary of the Battle of
Antietam he presented Union veteran Justice Oliver Wendell Holmes with
a rose. The Court's lengthy decision traced the evolution of the Articles of
War from revolutionary times to the present, and made a distinction where
Cobb had seen none. Although the nation was at war, the crime had been
committed "within the jurisdiction of a State where hostilities are not present and where martial law has not been proclaimed." Therefore, the Court
ruled, the intent of the law was not "to bring about as a mere result of a
declaration of war, the complete destruction of state authority." The Alabama decision would stand. Cobb thought that White's opinion intimated

that the case might have had a different outcome if it had gone directly to the court-martial, as it should have.[20]

This legal postmortem could provide no comfort to Sergeant Caldwell. The *Crisis* ran a picture of him in uniform, showing an earnest young man at parade rest, wearing the doughboy's standard broad-brimmed hat and white leggings. Before the Supreme Court decision, he wrote to James Weldon Johnson from his Birmingham jail. In a wavering hand he told the NAACP leader that he was "asking God to go into president Woodrow Wilson's head and give me another chance here on earth." After the Court decision, Wilson did appeal to Governor Thomas E. Kilby for a commutation of Caldwell's death sentence, but southern governors simply did not spare black men convicted of killing whites.[21]

On July 30, 1920, a crowd of twenty-five hundred people gathered before the Calhoun County prison. Sergeant Caldwell was permitted to address them. He read the Twenty-third Psalm, sang two songs, and prayed that his listeners would abjure vice and racial hatred, and accept Christianity. Many in the crowd wept. The *Crisis* recorded these militant last words: "I am but one of the many victims among my people who are paying the price of America's mockery of law and dishonesty in the profession of a world democracy." An eyewitness reported that "Caldwell went to the scaffold with a nerve seldom exhibited by a man being put to death."[22]

What did Sergeant Edgar Caldwell's story tell the NAACP about race relations in the South? Without segregation Sergeant Caldwell would never have noticed the conductor on the Oxford Line car. He was overcharged for his crime and denied justice by all the courts that heard his case. Du Bois was especially bitter, calling the execution "a legal lynching." He felt that Caldwell was justified in shooting his assailant and that "[n]o red-blooded person would have done otherwise."[23] Yet, in its perverse, horrific fashion, the disposition of the case represented the same kind of progress as that shown in the case of Will Lockett. The Supreme Court considered Caldwell's plea, and the president had urged mercy for him. He had died a dignified death at the hands of the law.

The NAACP also learned something about the temper of the colored Americans it hoped to advance. When there was trouble, those people looked to them for leadership. If they faltered, the people would go on ahead and rouse them to their duty. The NAACP's Alabama branches at Anniston, Montgomery, Birmingham, Selma, and Tuscaloosa had all raised money to fight for Caldwell. Behind the scenes, they got the American Legion, some white women, and even the dead man's wife to plead for Caldwell's life.[24] Was there not some reason for hope even with this tragic outcome?

THE Reverend E. R. Franklin was "a man of property and standing" in Jackson, Mississippi, when his sister died in April of 1920. He would have to settle her estate, and so on a Sunday after her death, he boarded a Yazoo and Mississippi train for the sixty-mile trip north to Tchula. To occupy himself during the journey, he took along a copy of the *Crisis*, fifty copies of which he sold in Jackson each month.[25]

Mississippi had the most rigid caste system of race relations in the United States. Even other Deep South states had some complicating social situation that served as a crack in the iron curtain of caste. In Georgia, the New South pretensions of Atlanta industrialists, or in Alabama the class tensions engendered by heavy industry, provided some small opening wedge for proponents of racial uplift. In Louisiana, the presence of Francophone Catholics suggested a language for toleration, and New Orleans had a cosmopolitan culture, as port cities inevitably do. Mississippi had none of that: little industry, no religious or ethnic differences among whites, little education, no interstate commercial centers. Within Mississippi, the Delta region, stretching downriver from Memphis to Vicksburg and forty miles east, was even more unbending than the rest of the state. Here cotton was still king, whites owned all the land, and redneck farmers were represented by racist populists such as James K. Vardaman or Theodore Bilbo, the most vicious demagogues in American politics. Historian James C. Cobb called the Delta "the most southern place on earth." Tchula lay at its southeastern tip.[26]

During his journey, Franklin gave a fellow passenger a copy of his magazine. The conductor grew curious and asked to see it. Franklin thought nothing of it. The conductor said nothing.

When the train pulled into Tchula station, Franklin saw a menacing crowd of white men gathered along the tracks and was horrified to discover that they had come for him. The conductor must have signaled ahead that the train carried a trouble-making Negro. Minister Franklin was flogged with a whip. The leader sneered to the man of God that "he would meet him in hell," but Franklin survived. At dusk he staggered out of town down the lonely railroad tracks from whence he had come.

As night fell, Franklin heard the mob come back to finish him off. He waded into a swamp and threw his coat over his head, hoping to pass for a tree stump while flashlights splayed over the area. The next morning the exhausted minister stumbled upon a white man who took him back to town. There the justice of the peace had an affidavit sworn against him for distributing the *Crisis*. He sentenced Franklin to six months of labor on the county farm and a fine of five hundred dollars, the maximum allowed by the law. Franklin learned that he had violated a new state law. It was now a crime in Mississippi to "circulate printed or published appeals . . . favoring social equality or marriage between the white and negro races."

In Jackson, Franklin's friends raised his bail and sent a lawyer to Tchula. The same mob met the lawyer and threatened to whip him as well. The justice of the peace declined to accept the bond and told the lawyer that Franklin would be lynched if released on bond. Sidney D. Redmond, an African-American lawyer of Jackson, wrote to W. E. B. Du Bois at this juncture: "Under such conditions we hardly know what to do." Redmond enclosed two dollars for a subscription to the *Crisis*. One could no longer purchase it in Jackson.[27]

The NAACP's standard operating procedure in such circumstances was to appeal to higher authority. John Shillady addressed a telegram to Governor Lee M. Russell, asking him to confirm the facts and protect Franklin's lawyer. The acting governor replied that the facts were wrong: Franklin had gotten only five months on the county farm and a four hundred dollar fine, but "the mildness of his sentence was because of his ignorance. If the editors of this sheet would visit Mississippi we would make an example of them that would be of lasting benefit to the colored people of the South. . . ."[28]

How could anyone reply to a telegram like this? Shillady ignored it and sent another, like the first, to the governor. Then he sent out a press release with the contents of the exchange, which the African-American press covered and the white-owned press ignored. "Would He String up Shillady, Johnson, Pickens, and Du Bois?" asked the *Boston Chronicle* in a large headline. The *Brooklyn Eagle* and *New York Age* ran big articles as well. After a few days, Governor Russell wired back. Russell was a clone of his mentor, former governor Theodore Bilbo. "This party got out very light," the governor replied. "I fully endorse the telegram of Acting Governor [H. H.] Casteel." Nevertheless, he suggested that all parties would be protected but repeated that "the less agitation there is about this matter the better it would be for all."[29]

The Association leadership now had to consider its strategy. Shillady consulted with the Legal Committee and advised Redmond in Jackson that New York saw this as a very important case. If the Mississippi law, a clear violation of the First Amendment, went unchallenged, other southern states might copy it, and the NAACP could disappear from the South.[30] Meanwhile, the Association took other steps to secure Franklin's freedom. Shillady had earlier wired Robert Church Jr. in Memphis, urging him to contact fellow Republican leader Perry Howard in Mississippi. It is not clear what this exchange produced, but a few weeks later Franklin showed up, a free man, in Jackson.[31]

Redmond met with him right away, and he could see that Franklin still bore scars. Franklin had had enough and wanted the NAACP to back out. He was going to leave for Chicago. However, Redmond wrote, there was a note of poetic justice in the affair: the mob leader who had vowed to meet the minister in hell had already bought his own one-way ticket. The very same railroad train that carried Franklin to Tchula had run him over.[32]

For African Americans, Mississippi remained a special circle of hell. The day after Franklin returned to Jackson, an African-American waiter named George Washington was taken from his home and whipped, allegedly for talking back to a white female waitress. Redmond met him, as he had Franklin, and saw that he was "one continuous mass of sores." Washington knew his tormentors, but nothing was done to arrest them. The story was even covered in the *Jackson Clarion-Ledger*, which treated the whipping as a joke. Redmond explained the real story. There had been a labor dispute at the restaurant, and the colored men could not join the striking women waitresses. The men who flogged Washington told him to quit and take the other employees with him. Shortly afterward, twenty-five of them left en masse, without their paychecks, for Chicago.[33]

Thus Mississippi whipped the appropriately named Franklin and Washington in April 1920. In September, Redmond came to New York, and the national office urged him to go back to Mississippi to challenge the anti–free speech law. Franklin was due to return to the state for trial that month, but he begged the NAACP, "for the sake of my life," to forget about making a test case. The NAACP respected his wishes, and the *Crisis* magazine ceased to circulate in Mississippi.[34]

"WE GO to Atlanta in May," wrote W. E. B. Du Bois in that month's issue of the *Crisis*. "We do not go truculently or with braggadocio, not as irrational extremists or firebrands, but simply to say to the South plainly and earnestly, without pretense or equivocation: we want to vote. We want lynching stopped. We want schools. We want 'Jim Crow' cars abolished. We want labor peonage ended. We want decent conditions of wages and labor and a cessation of insult and slander."[35]

The subtext of this editorial was addressed to northern NAACPers who questioned whether it was wise to go to Atlanta in May or any other month. At its 1919 convention, Atlanta delegates had pushed for this bold venture, and in a spirit of enthusiasm it had been adopted. Then the rioting of the Red Summer broke out, and John Shillady was beaten in broad daylight on a busy Austin street. In the fall of 1919, a wave of lynching swept over rural Georgia. To the more sober heads, or timid souls, in the group, holding an

NAACP convention in Atlanta now seemed like waving a red flag in front of a bull. The Boston branch executive committee urged the board of directors to reconsider. At its December meeting, on a motion by Arthur B. Spingarn, the board resolved to go ahead with its first national convention in the South.[36] Why did they take the risk?

Atlanta and Georgia were crucial to the aspirations of the NAACP. The city harbored hopes for a progressive future in which the excesses of race hatred would be curbed. After the Civil War, the city rose from the ashes to become the railroad and commercial center of a "New South." However, in 1906, the city erupted in a race riot that left over two dozen African Americans dead. The heirs to the New South tradition organized the Atlanta Civic League to encourage interracial cooperation. In their view, modernization depended upon checking the instability brought on by racist eruptions. They had no thought of ending segregation or allowing significant numbers of blacks to vote, but they did not want mobs burning sections of the city and creating a national scandal. In 1920, Governor Hugh Dorsey and Mayor James L. Key represented this business-oriented tradition. Toward the end of his term, in 1921, Governor Dorsey issued a report that enumerated 135 hate crimes during his tenure, and the list was not meant to be exhaustive. "The Dorsey statement stunned Georgia," historian John Dittmer wrote. The NAACP circulated Dorsey's report around the country. Local NAACPers arranged for white liberals to invite the national body to Atlanta for its convention.[37]

Most white Georgians hated everything the NAACP stood for. They too, had a long political tradition, producing such demagogues as Hoke Smith and Tom Watson. On the NAACP's thirty-year lynching map (1889–1918), Georgia ranked first with 386 victims. Almost all these victims were African-American, but when Georgia lynched a Jew in 1915, it became national news. Leo Frank, the manager of a pencil factory, was accused in 1913 of murdering a fourteen-year-old girl employee. The evidence against Frank was shoddy, but an armed mob shouted threats from the courtroom pews, and Frank was convicted. His attorneys appealed the case to the Supreme Court, and Justice Oliver Wendell Holmes Jr. issued a famous dissent that would have thrown out the verdict. When the governor commuted Frank's death sentence, a mob broke into the state prison and hanged him. The chief prosecutor in the case used it to win the next election for governor. He was the same Hugh Dorsey who invited the NAACP to Atlanta. Three months later a group of Georgians marched to the summit of Stone Mountain and reincarnated the Ku Klux Klan, making Atlanta their headquarters.[38]

Georgia lynching continued even during the World War. In May 1918,

Brooks County whites killed eleven African Americans after a notoriously brutal white farmer was found dead. Among the victims was Hayes Turner. His widow, Mary, eight months pregnant, asserted his innocence and vowed to prosecute his killers. The mob hung her upside down from a tree, slit open her belly and squashed her infant, and then burned her to death. Walter White investigated this for the NAACP, and local black leaders bravely cooperated in bringing the facts to light. They supplied Governor Dorsey with the names of fourteen lynchers, but no one was prosecuted.[39] One year later, Telfair County NAACPers publicized the story of Berry Washington, a Milan Negro who killed a white man who was raping a black woman. Washington turned himself in, expecting a fair trial, but he was killed. NAACP exposure of this outrage led to the indictment of two lawmen who facilitated the lynching, but they were acquitted. In the year after the NAACP's 1919 convention, fifteen more Georgia black men were lynched.[40] That was Georgia: the headquarters of the Klan and the capital of lynching.

More important to the NAACP, Atlanta was, arguably, the capital of African America. Since 1870, Georgia had had the largest black population in the country. In 1920, over 1,206,000 African Americans lived there, about one-tenth of the total national population. Over 63,000 of these lived in Atlanta, making the state and the city about one-third black. Atlanta ranked eleventh in total black population, but only Birmingham and Memphis had a higher black percentage than Atlanta in the top ten cities.[41]

Black Atlantans lived along a narrow corridor running through the center of the city with large communities at either end, "stretched like a giant dumb-bell," as W. E. B. Du Bois once wrote. African Americans inhabited the entire city, often living in alleys behind the homes of whites for whom they worked as domestic servants.[42] Auburn Avenue, running from the downtown Five Points area to Inman Park, served as a fashionable main drag. People gathered at the Yates and Milton drugstore for soda and gossip. Men purchased fine neckties and banded hats at the Curry and Hill haberdashery. They got their hair cut at Alonzo F. Herndon's barbershop, a commodious enterprise with modern adjustable seats. Nearby was the NAACP office. Crowning the community's prestige were its churches, the mighty "Big Bethel" AME Church and Ebenezer Baptist, completed in 1922.[43] Typical of the community's residents were Mike King, who worked in a tire factory, and Alberta Williams, who met in 1920. Her father, Reverend A. D. Williams of Ebenezer Baptist, was the president of the Atlanta NAACP in 1920, and their son, born in 1929, became Reverend Martin Luther King Jr.[44]

The Atlanta NAACP branch sprang from a fertile professional milieu of businessmen, academics, ministers, doctors, and lawyers. In 1917, Walter White and Harry Pace, at Atlanta Mutual, mailed invitations to an organizational meeting attended by seventy-five people. The academics included John Hope and George Towns from Atlanta University. Benjamin J. Davis Sr., a leading attorney and publisher of the weekly *Atlanta Independent*, and Henry "Linc" Johnson, a Republican party stalwart, came along. Physicians William F. Penn and Louis T. Wright also attended.[45]

These civic leaders protested when funds for the Negro seventh grade were cut off, and after a two-year struggle they won approval for the Booker T. Washington High School. In 1919 they packed the Big Bethel Church to protest new cuts for Negro education. The NAACP organized a voter registration and membership drive. By election time 1,723 Negroes registered to vote, making up 11 percent of the total, twice the percentage of the year before. At the 1919 convention, President Williams reported that women activists had divided the community into districts and were signing up new members by going door-to-door. The women spoke at regular drive meetings—a first in male-dominated Atlanta.[46]

Meanwhile, the NAACP spread across Georgia to the important cities of Savannah, Augusta, Athens, and Macon. Even smaller towns with easy access to rural areas developed branches: Albany, Americus, Brunswick, Cordele, Columbus, Dublin, Hawkinsville, Milledgeville, Rome, Thomasville, Valdosta, Waycross. Thomasville, scene of the Mary Turner lynching, recruited three hundred members, and whites threatened to kill the branch president. Under this sort of pressure, the branch collapsed. Even in Atlanta, two white men killed an NAACP member, although not in connection with political activity. If the national leadership had backed down, the same fate might await many other such branches. In *Along This Way*, Johnson remembered, "I had been one of those at the national office who had most loudly proclaimed the conference should not be postponed or transferred to some other city; that it should be held in Atlanta, despite any risks."[47]

Harry Pace came to New York to plan the convention. A few days before the meeting, the Association announced its plans in a press release titled "New Epoch in Race Relations," touting their invitation from the city fathers.[48] Despite this overstated claim, some conferees found the atmosphere tense. One of them was Edward L. Bernays, a public relations man hired for the occasion. The city was already jumpy. The Socialist Party had just met at Atlanta to nominate Eugene V. Debs for president. America's most famous antiwar activist was then a prisoner at the federal penitentiary in the city. When Bernays arrived, he heard menacing comments from white bellhops and taxi drivers. "I feel as if I were sitting on a volcano," one delegate told his assistant.[49] Black Atlantans probably felt emboldened. Johnson arrived by train with Arthur Spingarn, and he felt a surge of pride when the redcap ushered them, together, through the white-only main entrance.[50]

At last, the delegates (227 representing ninety-two branches) and guests (the press release claimed fifteen thousand total at four mass meetings, but these might be the same four thousand or so coming repeatedly) packed the Big Bethel AME Church for an unusual interracial meeting in the American South. Mayor Key welcomed the delegates, and new Atlanta branch president Reverend R. H. Singleton introduced the speakers. Arthur B. Spingarn, the rotund, bespectacled chairman of the Legal Committee, gave an upbeat speech. Spingarn praised the legacy of Henry Grady, placing him in the civil rights tradition. He portrayed an advancing black America, developing its farm, business, and home ownership, and educating its youth—a "bring us all together speech." To James Weldon Johnson fell the more somber task of analyzing the lynching statistics of the past thirty years, during which 2,472 Negroes had been killed by mobs.[51]

On the following day, a panel addressed the problem that most concerned the South's commercial leaders: the Negro migration out of the region. Dr. Plato Durham, a dean at Emory College, presented a new plan of interracial cooperation, dubbed "the Atlanta Plan," which would promote understanding across racial lines in the South but not challenge segregation or white political leadership. Throughout the decade and after, the Commission on Interracial Cooperation (CIC) pursued this moderate plan. Led by Will Alexander, a former Methodist minister, the group would pose a southern-based alternative to the NAACP. At the convention's final panel, a long list of speakers discussed the Atlanta Plan and the issue of migration.[52]

Later that day the Association honored its educator-in-chief by bestowing the coveted Spingarn Medal upon Dr. W. E. B. Du Bois for his work in organizing the 1919 Pan-African Congress. Among others, John Hope and Mary White Ovington praised him as teacher, writer, activist, and colleague. For Du Bois, it must have been a deeply satisfying moment. Atlanta was where he had made his mark for the ten years from 1899 to 1909, and this day celebrated his homecoming and his efforts to link the African diaspora.[53]

The Atlanta convention missed one opportunity. The Association failed to devote a session to the pending passage of the Nineteenth Amendment. Women speakers were better represented at this meeting than at previous conventions, but the prospect of African-American women voting for the first time merited focused attention. Florence Kelley, Mrs. W. Spencer

Murray, and Mary White Ovington addressed the issue in their speeches, but the NAACP could have used the convention to urge its branches to mobilize women voters. These three women were all white. African-American women were just beginning to emerge as leaders in the 1920s.

On other matters, the convention did what Du Bois promised it would. The NAACP program called for the right to vote, federal suppression of lynching, federal aid to education, federal legislation against the Jim Crow car in interstate travel, an end to segregation in Washington, and the independence of Haiti. The *Atlanta Constitution* covered the convention fairly, placing two stories on its front page and three on inside pages. Despite the tense atmosphere, there was no trouble and even a relaxation of the Jim Crow laws. James Weldon Johnson later declared in his *New York Age* column that the Atlanta conference was the "most important gathering ever held by our organization." By going to Atlanta, the NAACP "made it possible and safe for anybody to speak the truth on the race problem and do it in the South."[54]

The Atlanta convention constituted a significant accomplishment for the Association and a validation of the new leadership team. Yet, Atlanta represented the flaring of a brief candle. The financial report by Joel Spingarn had noted one disturbing trend. In 1919, only 10 branches had failed to forward their membership dues, but this year 135 were derelict, and the majority of these were in the South.[55] In the decade to follow, most southern branches would spring to life only during a crisis. The simple fact was that the white South presented a solid bloc in favor of Jim Crow. Even the handful of white southerners who had dared to attend the NAACP convention accepted white supremacy. Without the possibility of a winnable battle, the ranks of a volunteer army go home.

This would be the fate of the Atlanta branch itself, and its problems were emblematic of all branches in tolerant southern cities where naked repression was not used. Atlanta stayed active for about another two years. The Atlanta NAACP protected many refugees from work farms during this period, organizing what it called an underground railroad. Atlanta boasted 950 active members that year, and 3,500 dues payers.[56]

When this campaign ended, apathy set in. In January 1925, Robert Bagnall wrote to E. Franklin Frazier, a Morehouse College sociologist: "We have been a bit troubled about the Atlanta branch. It should be much stronger. Our president is a very fine man, but he has his hands too full to give attention to the work." A frustrated Frazier agreed, decrying the complacency of the city's Negro leaders.[57] Unable to budge white Atlanta, black leaders instead built community institutions, which had their own fund drives, board meetings, and publications. Amid these competing claims for resources, many southern NAACP branches foundered where they were permitted to exist during the 1920s.

Yet, as historian W. Fitzhugh Brundage concluded in a study of lynching in Virginia and Georgia, "[T]he impact of the NAACP was greater than most historians have recognized."[58] The Association contributed to the decline of lynching in Georgia during the 1920s. Its very existence prompted liberal whites at least to meet them partway on some issues and encouraged the formation of the CIC. The wonder of these years was not that the Association was so weak in the South, but that it existed at all.

8

Election Day in Florida

THE summer and fall of 1920 promised African Americans a chance to throw the Democrats out of Washington and replace them with Republicans. Black voters, including women, flocked to the polls to make their votes count, and their leaders tried to remind the politicians that they were still supposed to be the Party of Lincoln. They demanded that Lincoln's heirs speak out at the beginning of the campaign, when three innocent youths were lynched in Duluth, Minnesota, and at the end when would-be voters were slaughtered in Ocoee, Florida.

There was not much to do in Duluth, and when the John Robinson traveling circus pitched its tent on Monday, June 14, families and teenagers eagerly came out to see the wild animals, trapeze artists, strongmen, and clowns. Irene Tusken, eighteen, set out for the big top just west of the iron ore docks on Lake Superior. There she met her boyfriend, James T. Sullivan, and, according to his account, they were watching the roustabouts lock up the wild animals when about five Negro circus hands approached. One placed a gun to Sullivan's head and forced the couple to a ravine where several of them raped Irene, who fainted. Finally the Negroes fled, and the white couple took a streetcar home. Irene did not tell her parents about the harrowing experience. Sullivan stayed home for a few hours and then went to his job at the ore docks on the midnight shift. His father worked there, and James told him what had happened. The elder Sullivan called the girl's father, and then somebody called the police.

The authorities caught up with the circus train at the Canadian Northern Yards, with the couple in tow. They mustered 150 Negro workers off the train and lined them up. Irene identified 6 of them, who were brought back to the station and interrogated. They were all southern youths, with little education, and they were terrified. Under questioning, 2 of them said they had heard something vague about a white girl, and they volunteered more names. The police returned to the train and brought back 11 more suspects. From this lineup, Tusken and Sullivan identified Max Mason as the gunman and one other as a participant, and the police held them all at headquarters.

Duluth was a port and industrial city of about one hundred thousand, tucked into the southwestern corner of Lake Superior about 150 miles north of Minneapolis–St. Paul. News of the Tusken rape appeared in the newspapers and traveled quickly through the bars and pool halls of the city's working-class west side. The next afternoon, the police ignored an anonymous tip that a lynch mob was forming, but by seven in the evening, a gang of toughs drove an open truck around police headquarters on Superior Street, twirling a noose in the air and inviting passersby to "help get the niggers." Within a few hours, a mob of five thousand filled the street, screaming for revenge. Fire trucks arrived and trained their hoses on the mob, but the people cut the lines. They hurled rocks at the jail, shattering the windows. The police put up only token resistance, and hundreds of men shoved past their perimeter into the jail. There they found three of the terrified Negro prisoners, and they cut through the bars with saws and a battering ram. They staged a quick kangaroo trial and hauled their captives into the street, pummeling the youths as they dragged them to the Shriners' Auditorium on First Street. A Catholic priest pleaded for the mob to desist in the name of God, but he was hooted down. Then they hung Isaac McGhee from a lamppost, but the rope broke and they had to repeat the procedure. Elmer Jackson was next, and when he was dead, his body was lowered near the ground and stripped naked. Ellis Clayton cried and begged for mercy, but as he dangled from his rope, still twisting, a man shinnied up the pole and kicked him in the face. The crowd, which included women and children, cheered.[1] This was more exciting than the circus, and one did not even need a ticket.

James Weldon Johnson read about these events in the *New York Times* the next day. He immediately telegrammed the Minneapolis and St. Paul branches, seeking more information and instructing them to protect the surviving prisoners. Fewer than nine thousand African Americans lived in Minnesota, less than half a percent of the total population, yet the NAACP had an unusual advantage in the state. Governor J. A. Burnquist, a Republican progressive, served as the titular president of the St. Paul branch, and he sent the National Guard to Duluth right away. By letter, Mary White Ovington encouraged him to save the other prisoners in this tense situation. Meanwhile, the Twin Cities branches sent an investigator to Duluth and demanded prosecution of the lynchers. Charles Sumner Smith, president of the Minneapolis branch, went to Duluth the next Sunday and organized a branch that elected George B. Kelley as its president.[2]

As Johnson wrote in his *New York Age* column, it would not "take a

Sherlock Holmes" to see that the case against any of the Negroes was absurd. As for the young man's tale, "the natural conclusion . . . would be that the girl was not forced and Sullivan made up this version of the story after thinking the thing over," he wrote Kelley. The girl could not possibly have taken a streetcar home without attracting attention, told her mother nothing, and claimed no memory of a rape if it had ever taken place. Nor was it likely that a circus ground could provide the setting for a Negro to pull a gun. The Duluth lynchings infuriated Johnson. After Kentucky authorities had shot into a mob, it seemed incredible that lynchers should succeed in Minnesota.[3]

Middle-class, respectable Duluth was sickened, too. Both Duluth newspapers demanded justice. The *Duluth Herald* wanted the mob leaders punished. The *News-Tribune* called the lynchers "murderers," concluding that "[n]ow the penalty of the law must be paid." The Kiwanis Club confessed that "Duluth has been disgraced before the world and every decent citizen has been made to hang his head in shame." The assistant county attorney told a meeting of Duluth African Americans that he would indict the ringleaders. He also led the American Legion post, and reported that he had volunteered his men as deputies against the mob and had been rebuffed. Charles Sumner Smith wrote Johnson that "the best elements of whites are fearful for their own safety." The Duluth lynchings polarized white society, setting the middle class against lawless populist elements.[4]

Within the tiny Duluth black community, class tensions emerged as well. Not everyone was satisfied with the leadership of George Kelley. Two branch members complained to New York that Kelley "is a keeper of a 'dive' of low repute" in which illegal gambling was conducted. The "better class" of colored people were staying away. Johnson set his own inquiries on foot by contacting his brother Rosamond, then on a musical tour at the St. Paul Orpheum Theater. Rosamond found some doubters, but other Twin Cities NAACPers, including William T. Francis, vouched for Kelley's integrity.[5] Francis was "an elegant young lawyer with fair skin and features. He parted his hair in the middle, wore high white wing collars, soft silk ties, and a red rose in his lapel," remembered Roy Wilkins, who grew up there. Kelley may have had the support of a clear majority by the time the branch charter was issued. The sixty-nine signers were no aristocrats. The most common occupations listed were seventeen laborers and nine porters, and most others worked with their hands.[6] During the next six months, Kelley and his colleagues toiled diligently to see that justice was done in Minnesota.

Their first problem was to raise money and secure attorneys for the thirteen youths remaining in jail. The new Duluth branch set up a defense fund, and the other Minnesota branches held public meetings to help contribute. The money came mostly in one-, two-, and five-dollar amounts, but ultimately they raised thirteen hundred dollars. They hired Chicago attorney Ferdinand Barnett and Minnesota attorneys R. C. McCullough of Duluth and Charles W. Scrutchins from Bemidji, a town several hundred miles west. Scrutchins went to Duluth in June and decided that the defendants were clearly innocent. He wrote to Francis that the youths, all southerners, "were strangers in a strange land" and that he would work on the case for free.[7]

Meanwhile, the St. Paul branch sent an investigator to Duluth. His report showed that young Sullivan's story was a tissue of lies. The man was "a wild, vicious character" who had been arrested for vandalism, and Irene Tusken was a woman of "loose morals." Despite her claim to have fainted during the alleged ordeal, it was she who picked the men out of a lineup. The examining physician had seen no evidence that she had been raped. Sullivan's father would not talk. The girl's mother admitted that she might have inadvertently provoked the lynching. When asked after the alleged rape how her daughter was, she mumbled, "In bed," and her auditors heard, "She's dead." The case against the remaining Duluth prisoners was bound to collapse, Minnesota leaders confidently advised.[8]

A minor legal complication developed when the father of one of the lynching victims decided to sue Duluth officials while the charges were still pending against the fourteen prisoners. Smith and Kelley thought this suit premature and tried to discourage it. In mid-July the grand jury indicted seven prisoners and freed the rest.[9] They had to wait until January to have their day in court, when all the charges were dropped except those against Max Mason, who was convicted. In his affidavit, Mason swore he was working in the big top between nine and ten o'clock, but he was sentenced to thirty years for a crime that probably never occurred. The jurors most likely felt that they had to convict someone. If they freed Mason, it would have meant that Irene Tusken and Sullivan were lying all along. After a few years, NAACP attorneys secured his release.[10]

The NAACP rightly claimed the outcome of these cases as a victory won by hard work, financial resourcefulness, and good publicity. Nevertheless, three men had been lynched, one had been imprisoned for several years, and the others had languished in jail for half a year. The New York office got a reminder of the disproportionate punishment of Negroes when a Duluth sympathizer observed the case of a white man accused of rape. No spectators came to court, and the newspapers allotted it only a tiny article.[11]

Still remaining was the matter of punishing the perpetrators. Given the small size of the state's African-American population and the inherently political nature of such a prosecution, it was not likely that the guilty would be convicted. Governor Burnquist, however, probably brought some pressure to bear on the side of justice. Early in July, Burnquist wrote to Ovington that twelve lynchers had been indicted for first degree murder. Minneapolis branch president Charles Sumner Smith (whose own name reflected the Republican legacy) thought Burnquist had arranged to have the special grand jury impaneled. Later eighteen more were indicted on various counts. Duluth branch president Kelley doubted there would be any convictions. "The police have the support of labor, and capital is unwilling to force the issue," he wrote Johnson in October. "None of the real ringleaders of the mob have been convicted. Only some without friends or money."[12] The lynchers organized a public defense committee of their own, whose literature identified two-thirds of the indictees as veterans and appealed for support on that basis. Meanwhile, the chief of police, who had been absent during the riot, resigned under pressure. The commissioner of public safety defended his decision not to shoot because women and children were present, but the grand jury report blamed the lynching squarely on this man.[13]

The Duluth matter had one more long-term result. It changed the life of an African-American journalism major at the University of Minnesota. "I was just short of nineteen the night the bodies of McGhee, Jackson, and Clayton swung from a light pole in Duluth," Roy Wilkins wrote in his autobiography. "I read the stories in the newspapers and put them down feeling sick, scared and angry all at the same time. . . . I found myself thinking of black people as a very vulnerable *us*—and white people as an unpredictable, violent *them*."[14] Wilkins would later come to New York to work on the *Crisis*, and from 1955 until his death in 1981 he would lead the Association as executive secretary.

IN JUNE, the same month as the Duluth lynching, the party of Lincoln gathered in Chicago for its quadrennial convention. The Republicans sensed that November would bring them victory as the national mood shifted toward a desire for calm, order, and economic stability. The prospect of an easy win, however, produced too many eager aspirants for the nomination. The convention floor coliseum buzzed with news of each delegation's favorite: General Leonard Wood, Illinois governor Frank O. Lowden, and progressive senator Hiram Johnson of California were the frontrunners. The last idea in the minds of its thousands of delegates was the matter of civil rights for African Americans.[15]

James Weldon Johnson went to Chicago with few expectations. He was among five African-American advisors to the platform committee. Earlier in the year, Du Bois had sent seventeen presidential aspirants a questionnaire regarding their stand on civil rights matters. Only three had bothered to reply, and they had evaded the issues. At the platform committee, the black delegates made little progress again. They wanted the Grand Old Party to include planks on the ballot, lynching, equal distribution of education funds, elimination of the Jim Crow car in interstate travel, segregation in Washington, and an end to lily-whitism in the southern Republican Party. They did not even contemplate seeking an end to segregation in the South. The Republicans incorporated only the antilynching plank, its traditional salute to the fading Lincoln legacy.[16]

In addition to this disappointment, Johnson perceived a strengthening of lily-whitism in the convention. Throughout the South, African-American Republican clubs (called "black and tan") competed with white Republicans for federal patronage and representation on national bodies. Only a few African-American delegates attended the convention, and when Massachusetts senator Henry Cabot Lodge called the roll, a thundering "No!" greeted the name of Henry "Linc" Johnson, the leader of the black Republicans. Northern party bigwigs seated him anyway, but the moment registered a growing white backlash. Further, women in the Tennessee delegation blocked the credentials of Bob Church, claiming that white southern women would reject the party if a Negro was seated. In their hope of breaking the solid Democratic South, white Republicans were ready to throw the Negro overboard, Johnson alleged. "In the final analysis," Johnson wrote, "it was the Negro that caused the Republican Party to be brought into existence. It was his cause that furnished the party its chief inspiration." Johnson came away from the convention tired and discouraged. "Chicago knocked me out," he confided to Church, and he remembered his service there as "an empty honor."[17]

Black Republican loyalists saw more to cheer about. The *New York Age* ran a banner headline celebrating the nomination of dark horse Ohio senator Warren G. Harding for president and Massachusetts governor Calvin Coolidge for vice president. The Republicans had at least accepted the antilynching plank, which urged Congress to act against the "terrible blot on American citizenship."[18]

Then, too, Negro Republican loyalists felt that they had real villains to run against—a party based on unregenerate southern racists and lily-white northern labor. Johnson instructed San Francisco branch president Walter Butler to attend the Democratic national convention that nominated Ohio governor James M. Cox and New York's Franklin Delano Roosevelt. This was merely a formality to show nonpartisanship, and Butler came away with no promises, as expected. Bagnall attended the Chicago convention of the Farmer-Labor Party and the Committee of Forty-eight, remnants of the old Progressive movement, whose main body was now safely back in the Republican mainstream. Bagnall was warmly received, but the progressives chose obscure candidates and ran a weak campaign.[19]

A few weeks later, on July 22, candidate Harding surprised African Americans with an acceptance speech that mentioned the antilynching plank. Further, Harding declared, "I believe the Negro citizens of America should be guaranteed the enjoyment of all their rights," and cited their wartime service as credit in the account of national sympathy.[20] Johnson was enough impressed that he stepped up his effort to meet with the candidate. The next day he wrote to Harding, seeking an audience at his home in Marion, from which the candidate was running a "front porch" campaign. Within a few days, George B. Christian, Harding's secretary, replied that the senator "would feel honored" to meet him.[21]

Johnson was not the only African-American representative Senator Harding wished to meet. The paradigm for all ethnic political activity was the patron-client relationship in which underbosses delivered votes in exchange for jobs. However, African-American politics was necessarily more complicated than that of other ethnic groups because the national black community was fighting for radical change. Practical politics did not contemplate ending segregation, and Harding's general pitch for "normalcy" flew in the face of the civil rights crusade. Negro Republican leaders accepted these boundaries. Georgia's Henry "Linc" Johnson worked with Cleveland's Thomas W. Fleming to plan a Colored Voters Day at Marion, similar to pilgrimages organized for Irish voters or traveling salesmen. William Pickens was in Cleveland during late July, and he urged Johnson to meet with Harding before the "big feed" that Fleming was arranging. "It is the opinion of non-politicians among colored people that Harding needs instruction on the race question," he wrote. Colored Voters Day, which the irrepressible Pickens dubbed a "thanking and non-spanking" affair, would leave Harding feeling that he had the Negro vote wrapped up. Johnson and Cleveland NAACP leader Harry E. Davis thereupon arranged a meeting with the candidate before Colored Voters Day. This was the conversation in which Harding expressed interest in utilizing the Haiti issue as campaign fodder. On other matters he was less forthcoming.[22]

Johnson viewed this meeting as the beginning of a dialogue. Later in the month he wrote to Harding, asking him to address the issues that he had deferred. Johnson praised the senator's acceptance speech but urged him to speak on equal federal aid to education, the vote, segregation in the federal departments, Negro officers in the National Guard, and Jim Crow interstate travel practices. In short, he pushed the senator to go considerably beyond his party platform. Negro voters, Johnson argued, would not be persuaded by general statements. During their meeting, Harding had expressed agreement with the NAACP agenda, but said that practical politics dictated his silence on them. This was an error, Johnson advised, especially since hundreds of thousands of new Negro voters could tip the balance in states such as West Virginia, Kentucky, Maryland, or Indiana. In fact, the NAACP had not publicized their meeting because it thought colored voters would be disappointed by the dearth of Harding's promises.[23]

Meanwhile, Henry "Linc" Johnson was churning out propaganda, contrasting Harding's lofty but vague pronouncements to the hate speech of Democratic demagogues such as South Carolina's Ben Tillman (who had died in 1918) and the silence of Cox and Roosevelt. "Linc" also had to deal with potential problems at the September 10 Colored Voters Day. Marion, a southwest Ohio crossroads town, did not serve black people in its hotels or restaurants. Cleveland African Americans therefore refused to attend. To smooth over this difficulty, "Linc" Johnson's committee brought in trainloads of Negro Baptists and Methodists from their conventions nearby. At two o'clock, "Linc" Johnson and his colleagues made speeches of greeting, the brass bands played, and General John J. Pershing addressed the crowd along with Harding himself. The Marion AME Church fed the guests, and by nightfall they were hustled safely out of town. Harding considered the day a fine success.[24]

The NAACP stayed away. It was publicly nonpartisan, and this was not the sort of event it could endorse. Its policy was not to back candidates unless a clear civil rights issue was at stake. Harding offered only electoral hoopla, and the NAACP, whose membership probably voted solidly Republican, could not offend northern white Democrats who might prove friendly. Furthermore, Colored Voters Day had exactly the effect upon Harding that Pickens predicted it would. The candidate rejected the arguments of Johnson's letter. He would not "make the specific declarations that you require," his secretary George Christian replied, nor would he "appeal to classes." He implied that the Negro vote was assured and no more need be said on the matter. From the standpoint of practical politics, Christian was probably right, as the Republican victory would show.[25]

Harding not only had the Negro vote under control but also felt he might steal a victory in the contested state of Oklahoma. Forsaking his front porch, Harding journeyed to the Sooner State and replied to the questions of the *Daily Oklahoman* with something for everyone. "I believe in race equality before the law. You can't give one right to a white man and deny it to a black man. But I want you to know that I do not mean that white people and black people shall be forced to associate together in accepting their equal rights at the hands of the nation." This small part of the speech went unreported in the North but reassured white Oklahomans that a Republican victory would not overthrow Jim Crow. Northern Negroes would have to decide if their glass was half empty or half full. Most African-American newspapers were pleased.[26]

On the eve of the election, the *New York Age* ran a banner headline calling for a straight Republican vote. Johnson held a more nuanced position, fueled, no doubt, by his anger at the Duluth lynchings and another atrocity at Paris, Texas, in which two brothers were killed. Johnson wondered how a Republican presidential candidate could say nothing about these lynchings that formed so reprehensible a part of the national fabric. The political situation seemed confounding. The Negro's vote, Johnson mourned, "is conceded to one of these parties, and the other . . . *says expressly that it does not want it.*" There was no alternative but to vote for the lesser of two evils, and, Johnson concluded in capital letters, "THE POWER OF THE SOUTH MUST BE DESTROYED."[27]

No American political campaign is complete without its element of farce, and the 1920 race provided that as well. Sensing the coming Republican landslide, Ohio Democrats played the race card. They charged Harding not only with supporting race mixing but also with being a Negro himself. A Wooster, Ohio, college professor concocted a Harding family tree full of ancestors labeled "Black" and "Mulatto." Just before the election, Harding's elderly father and a friend ran into a Democratic judge at a Marion cigar store. A shouting match ensued, and Dr. Harding's companion slugged the magistrate in the head because of the "Negro" slurs. This was the level of racial politics in the 1920 election.[28]

On election day, the Republicans rolled up a spectacular 60 percent of the popular vote, their highest margin ever, and won majorities in the House and Senate. Harding even carried Tennessee and Oklahoma. African-American Republicans were elected as state representatives in New York, West Virginia, Ohio, and Pennsylvania, and for the first time ever in New Jersey and Missouri. The African-American press greeted this outcome enthusiastically. Johnson rejoiced that the southern despoilers had been driven from the temple, but cautioned that the Negro would have to achieve freedom on his own. He wrote to Harry Davis, now a state representative himself, that it was a "glorious victory for Harding," and that "we have put the rebels out of Washington. . . ."[29]

It was hard not to be swept up by the excitement of the Republican victory, but W. E. B. Du Bois managed this feat with ease. The saturnine editor saw little difference between the Democratic race-baiters and the Republican hypocrites. Years ago, Frederick Douglass had uttered a famous nautical metaphor, saying that in politics, the Republican Party was the ship and all else was the sea. "Well for God's sake," Du Bois declared in the September *Crisis,* "give us the sea." In the following issue, the editor ran an article that called for political independence. Du Bois summed up the result in December. Parties counted for nothing, he wrote. Only individual candidates mattered, and the victories of colored Republicans such as Harry Davis and a few white friends were positive signs. But not even the minor parties had said anything about civil rights. "And so the great farce ends," Du Bois concluded. "The people have spoken and said nothing."[30]

Du Bois's disgust reflected the central political difficulty that African Americans faced since the end of Reconstruction. The Republican Party, born of the antislavery impulse, was by 1877 also the party of big capital. As late as 1920, this meant that African Americans were the friends of labor's enemy. White workingmen voted Democratic and kept their unions lily white. After twenty years of progressivism, the Negro still had precious few white friends. Socialist Eugene Debs polled almost a million votes from his Atlanta cell, but even the socialists said nothing about African-American rights, which they saw as simply part of the labor problem. The Farmer-Labor candidate, whose convention Bagnall had attended, drew only twenty-six thousand votes, and they were no better than the socialists. Probably the *Nation* magazine spoke best for the NAACP's few prominent white members, those on the board of directors. The *Nation* bemoaned Harding's victory as a triumph of big business and popular disillusionment. Thus, white progressives and black activists shared no common ground in the American politics of the 1920s, and Du Bois's cynicism was rooted in this harsh reality.[31]

Yet, somewhere between Johnson's guarded optimism and Du Bois's cold realism lay a fair assessment of the new situation. Clearly, Harding had neither a mandate nor the inclination to do anything about civil rights. Nevertheless, the sweeping Republican victory did change the landscape for civil rights activists and suggested new opportunities. Over the next two years, the NAACP's attention would turn increasingly to Washington, D.C., and the new relation of party forces. They now had the ear of the president, some new friends in Congress and several state houses, and the chance, perhaps, to pass antilynching legislation at the state and national level. The Republican victory of 1920 laid the groundwork for a proactive campaign that would focus the Association's attention for the next two years.

AFRICAN AMERICANS were not the only oppressed group fighting for their rights at the end of the World War. Women, too, hoped to turn their home-front support for the war effort into suffrage rights. At the nexus of these separate struggles were African-American women, whose very identities offered a rebuke to Wilsonian pretensions that the United States had entered the war to make the world safe for democracy.

African-American women had already built their own organizations. Local black women's clubs sponsored an 1895 conference arranged by Josephine St. Pierre Ruffin, the widow of Massachusetts' first black judge. Influenced by Lucy Stone, the Boston women brought together such diverse figures as antilynching crusader Ida B. Wells and Margaret Murray Washington, wife of Booker T. Washington. The following year they founded the National Association of Colored Women's Clubs (NACW), choosing Washington, D.C., educator Mary Church Terrell as their first president. White feminists kept their colored sisters at a distance. As feminism gained strength among southern women, they motivated suffrage on the basis that it would reinforce white supremacy. Suffrage leaders realized that some southern states would have to ratify a constitutional amendment, and they conciliated white southern women.

The National American Woman Suffrage Association (NAWSA), seeking the vote on a state-by-state basis, had won few victories by 1913, and these were all in western states desperate for female migrants. Discontent with this stalemate, a sober Quaker activist named Alice Paul urged the NAWSA to adopt the more militant tactics she had learned from British suffragists. Paul organized a suffrage parade at Woodrow Wilson's inauguration in 1913. Hostile men attacked the marchers, generating the kind of publicity that only confrontation brings. More conservative NAWSA leaders were unhappy, and President Anna Howard Shaw attacked Paul in no uncertain terms. NAWSA sought to win by persuasion, not by confrontation. Paul's strategy was to hold the party in power responsible for women's disfranchisement. Paul soon found herself outside NAWSA, and in 1917 she and her colleagues founded the National Woman's Party (NWP).[32]

Meanwhile, the more cautious NAWSA women, now led by Carrie Chapman Catt, won approval of women's suffrage in the House of Representatives for the first time on January 10, 1918. Later in the year, President Woodrow Wilson reversed course and came out for the Nineteenth Amendment, appealing directly to the Senate for passage. In February of 1919, the Senate barely failed to give the measure the necessary two-thirds majority. Southern Democrats counted heavily among the "nays," using the "state's rights" argument. In frustration, Alice Paul sought to mollify southerners by telling the newspapers that it was "nonsense" to think that the Nineteenth Amendment would guarantee colored women the vote.[33]

Mary White Ovington read this in the *New York Times* and hit the roof. She demanded that Paul retract the statement, but the feminist leader slyly responded that she had been misquoted. Lurking behind this contretemps was a potentially serious effort to insert state's rights language into the Anthony amendment (as some suffragists called it) by chairman of the Senate suffrage committee, New Mexico's A. A. Jones. Ovington was sure the language was aimed at barring potential black women voters. "I feel intensely on this matter," she wrote Woman's Party member Vida Milholland, daughter of NAACP founding member John Milholland. Ovington pledged that the NAACP would fight against a suffrage amendment so construed. Despite feminist protestations that the Jones amendment was a smokescreen, the NAWSA voted at its March national convention to accept such a rewording on a motion by Kentucky delegate Laura Clay.[34]

The suffrage amendment passed the House of Representatives again in May 1919, and this time passed the Senate in June. Thirty-six of the forty-eight states had to ratify it, and after a year only one more state was lacking. Tennessee became the battleground state, and a tough coalition of liquor interests, railroad barons, and female "anti's" vowed to smite the amendment dead. The "anti's" cast their campaign as a "battle to save southern civilization" by keeping woman on her exalted pedestal. Both NAWSA and NWP activists lobbied state legislators, and the vote came down to a tie. Alice Paul even asked the NAACP for help, and Tennessee branches approached their representatives. The day was finally saved when a young member changed his vote at his mother's behest. That one vote turned the Nineteenth Amendment into law.[35]

As soon as the ink was dry on the amendment, southern African-American women came forward to register. There were no "anti's" among them. White southern women, however, were divided on the question. In several locales, therefore, black women appeared to register in greater numbers than whites. "Negro Women in South Rushing to Register," a *New York Times* headline announced in September. At Richmond, African-American women signed up while whites stayed home. Now reversing roles, the Democratic city leader declared that "it is the duty of every woman who regards the dominion of the white race as essential" to pay her poll tax and register.[36]

A similar story unfolded at Columbia, South Carolina. Palmetto State African Americans made up a majority of the population, and at the capital they made up one-third of the people. If black South Carolina women voted, and this in turn opened the door to black male voters, white supremacy would be threatened. On the first day of registration, African-American women showed up with tax receipts in hand. The astonished registrars had no contingency plan for such an emergency and simply kept the African-American women waiting until the whites were registered. The black women waited for hours, and some succeeded in entering their names. The next day, the registrars showed a new determination to drive the women away by snarling insults and posing ridiculous "test" questions such as "Explain a *mandamus.*" Then the sheriff came in and threatened them all with buckshot. After a week of this determined struggle, twenty educated, tax-paying African-American women swore out affidavits against the registrars. At the end of the year, the NAACP presented these to a congressional committee.[37]

Black women made more substantial gains in other parts of the country. According to historian Rosalyn Terborg-Penn, "black women registered in large numbers throughout the South, especially in Georgia and Louisiana." NAACP branches started citizenship classes for women in eleven states. James Weldon Johnson encouraged these classes in his *New York Age* column, urging local leaders to make them specific to the laws of each state. In Jacksonville, black women turned out to vote in greater numbers than white women.[38]

In the North, African-American women had more success. The Republicans wanted their votes and appointed Mary Church Terrell, a Washington educator and NACW leader, to get them. "However much the white women of the country need suffrage," she wrote to local suffrage leaders, "colored women need it more." During the campaign she addressed colored women's clubs, almost getting arrested for her efforts at Dover, Delaware. In Cleveland, NAACP activists reported "intense interest taken in politics by women. Meetings and classes are held all over the city where white and black women go to be taught how to vote."[39]

Despite this enthusiasm, in more places than not, African-American southern women were turned away by racist registrars. Mary White Ovington wanted the white women to stand up for their colored sisters and decided to press the issue at the February 1921 meeting of the National Woman's Party. The NWP failed to invite a single black speaker to its upcoming convention in the heavily black nation's capital. Ovington, not a party member herself, worked through intermediaries Florence Kelley and Harriot Stanton Blatch to place Mary Talbert on the program.[40]

Kelley, head of the National Consumer's League and an NAACP board member, met with Alice Paul. Paul wanted to know what specific feminist legislation the NACW was backing, and Kelley replied, "Antilynching." This was not good enough for Paul, but Kelley pointed out that it was just as valid as consumer's rights. Moreover, the NACW was working on a voting rights enforcement bill for colored women. Then Paul came to the point: "She was of the opinion that the appearance of Mrs. Talbert on the program talking about lynching would inflame the Southerners." More prompting, however, got the New York branch of the NWP to press for the inclusion of an African-American speaker.[41]

By this point, Mary Talbert was thoroughly disgusted by the influence of southern racists in the women's movement. After her Texas NAACP work and 1919 war relief effort in France, she had toured the Midwest, West, and New England for the Association. Then in August she sailed again for Europe to represent the NACW at the September International Council of Women meeting in Norway. "We had scarcely left the shores of America before some of the Southern women . . . commenced their race hatred propaganda." In Paris the YWCA refused to serve her until a lone white colleague spoke up. The courageous civil rights veteran cried at this humiliation. She went on to Norway, presented a resolution to the meeting, and educated the European press on American race relations. After this experience she was reluctant to face any more American feminists and begged off Ovington's proposed trip to the NWP convention.[42]

The assignment now fell to Addie Hunton, who had been busy organizing for the Association in Brooklyn and Baltimore. In February, Hunton and Mary Church Terrell led a delegation of sixty African-American women to the NWP convention. Ovington warned the NWP to heed their protest and chastised them for commissioning a statue of only white suffrage heroines. Paul received the black women coldly. Further, the NWP turned down a resolution presented by Ella Rush Murray, soon to be an NAACP board member, demanding that Congress look into the disfranchisement of black women. Hunton reported, "Although we did not picket the Woman's Party we harassed them very thoroughly and succeeded in bringing our issue to the floor of the convention." Female NAACPers took seriously the notion that white women had a responsibility to their colored sisters and tried to hold them to account.[43]

Two days after the Republican victory on election day, NAACP leaders in New York found a startling front-page story in the *New York Times*, headlined "Kill Two Whites and Six Negroes in Florida Riot." This conflict broke out at Ocoee, twelve miles from Orlando, when Jules Perry was turned away from the polls allegedly for failing to pay his tax. Perry claimed he had paid his tax and returned after dark with a shotgun and some allies, determined to do his duty as a citizen. A posse of armed whites, however, dispersed Perry and his men and pursued them to the Negro settlement at the edge of town. They surrounded Perry's house, but he shot dead two intruders when they advanced onto his property. The whites set fire to the house, killing a woman, an infant, and several others. Perry himself was captured and lynched. "Armed whites were reported patrolling the region and closing in on Negroes who fled to the woods," said the newspaper. Whites burned over twenty buildings in the Negro community, effectively destroying it. After this article appeared, the story dropped out of the news.[44]

A few days later a slender, twenty-seven-year-old man with blue eyes and golden hair, standing five feet seven inches and weighing 135 pounds, came to Ocoee. The stranger had recently applied to join the Ku Klux Klan (on his application he listed his size, hair and eye color, and Congregational religion, but left blank the space asking if he believed in white supremacy) and told people at Ocoee that he wanted to buy an orange grove. The man was Walter White, whose Klan application and agricultural interests were a ruse to gain information. The NAACP had been following events in Florida just before the election because the Klan had openly vowed to prevent black Floridians from voting.[45]

The Klan had been active all over the state, staging a coordinated series of parades and acts of terror. At Jacksonville they marched one thousand strong in full hooded regalia on the Saturday night before the election. Black residents were not intimidated. They made up half the city's ninety thousand people and came to the parade in force. One woman shouted, "We weren't afraid of the Germans and we're not afraid of you." On election day they proved it. Ten thousand African Americans had registered to vote in Duval County, and most of them showed up at the polls. Almost half were turned away, many after waiting in deliberately understaffed lines all day. The registrars simply stalled at the segregated voting places. Harding received only five thousand votes in the county, and almost all the black voters were registered Republican. Black community leaders had the names of thousands of these voters and were prepared to present them to Congress. The Klan paraded at Orlando, too, and threatened to tar and feather any Negroes who tried to vote. White got this story from eight African-American and four white leaders in the two cities, including a white Republican county chairman.

When White got to Ocoee, the first thing he saw was the last black family leaving town. Their worldly possessions were piled atop a flatbed truck, and six frightened children huddled in the back as a gang of white thugs jeered at them. From his Florida informants, White surmised that the Ocoee death toll ranged from twenty-five to thirty-five. The entire colored district had been burned to the ground. Before election day, the Klan had warned colored voters to stay away. Perry and Mose Norman had been the wealthiest black men in town, having made their money in orange grow-ing. Norman, too, had gone to vote and had been beaten up. In the after-math of the massacre, Perry, his arm shot off, was turned over to the mob by jailers in Orlando. Souvenir hunters took bones from the embers, and one participant boasted to White that he had killed seventeen himself and that the true death toll was in the fifties. An eleven-year-old girl told White about the "fun we had when some niggers were burned up."[46]

This story was underreported in both the white and black press until a visiting northern survivor of the massacre gave a story to the *New York Age*. Mrs. Hattie Smith of Youngstown, Ohio, told how she escaped the fires and shootings of that terrifying night. She was awakened around midnight by gunfire, and when the house began to burn, she ran out into the darkness and hid while her relatives perished in the blaze. Four days later a sympa-thetic white man found her, dazed and hungry, and put her on a train for Jacksonville. If not for the middle-aged and respectable Hattie Smith, this story would have been missed. In proportion to population for the riots of 1919, the disaster that befell Ocoee was far worse, more like the 1890 massa-cre of the Indian community at Wounded Knee. As in Elaine, Arkansas, the tribulations of rural southern Negroes were of small concern to northern dailies and deliberately misrepresented by southern ones. By 1920, a land boom was under way in Florida, and realtors had reason to hush up any signs of instability.[47]

The NAACP would not let the matter rest. At the end of December, John-son, White, Pickens, Archibald H. Grimké, and James Cobb testified before the House Committee on the Census. They were joined by Dr. W. S. Ste-vens of Quincy, Florida. The black leaders sent southern congressmen into an uproar as they presented evidence showing how Florida and South Car-olina kept potential Negro voters away from the polls. In addition to the evidence from Jacksonville and Ocoee, White reported the case of the Jones brothers from Live Oak, who were severely beaten by the Klan. The NAACP leaders called for a congressional investigation of the Florida events. They called attention to section 19, chapter 3 of the Federal Crimi-nal Code, which made it a felony to conspire to deny citizens the right to vote. In addition, they urged Congress to reduce the representation of states that disfranchised citizens, in accordance with the Fourteenth Amendment. The Association prepared careful charts, showing that a South Carolina congressman represented only 8,269 voters, while a New Jersey congressman represented 64,567. These cases were typical for the North and South.

Representatives Mulligan of Missouri, Larson of Georgia, and Bee of Texas had probably never before been rebuked to their faces by colored men, and they angrily interrupted the NAACP speakers. "Knowing what we have done in upbuilding the Negro race," Carlos Bee broke in, "I cannot sit silent under a statement made by a witness from New York." Ironically, the NAACPers were all southern-born. The congressmen's indignation boiled over when a press photographer arrived. The galleries were filled with African Americans, and it was unthinkable for a southern congressman to appear in a photograph with Negroes acting as citizens. Representative James S. Aswell of Louisiana declared that he "wasn't going to have his picture taken with a bunch of niggers," and the committee went into executive session.[48]

The southern congressmen counterattacked. Florida's Frank Clark called the NAACP "meddling, fussing persons working on the ignorant negroes of the South." He presented a telegram from Jacksonville's mayor asserting that colored people could vote. According to the mayor, black leader J. Seth Hills, one of White's informants, declared that he himself had voted. Dr. Stevens now denied that he had been beaten, and Florida newspapers reported that the Jones brothers had not been roughed up at Live Oak in Sunapee County. "The Association has secured more publicity on the hearings than on any other matter it has handled," Johnson told the board. At its annual public meeting, held at Harlem's Palace Casino on 135th Street, two thousand people turned out to hear the NAACP leaders denounce the Klan and the southern press.[49]

As these stories appeared in the Florida newspapers early in January, the NAACP received a new stream of mail validating its original presentation and adducing further evidence of a concerted Klan campaign. Jacksonville's African-American weekly reminded its readers that Hills's vote did not prove that thousands of others had been denied. The Jones brothers had been beaten, but not in Sunapee County. The substance, if not all the facts, of White's testimony was accurate. African-American Floridians added further horror stories. At Palmetto, Lake Butler, Quay, and St. Lucie, carloads of armed whites had patroled the colored voting places. In Dade County ten African Americans swore out affidavits against white registrars. Then the bound and sandbagged body of a black man turned up in the Ocklockonee River, bearing gunshot wounds.[50]

The lame-duck Congress did nothing about any of it. The new Republican president would have hefty majorities in both houses of Congress. On the Census Committee the NAACP made two new allies in Chairman Siegal and George H. Tinkham of Boston. The experience of coming to Washington, telling the truth about southern "democracy," and watching its apologists squirm was suggestive and empowering for NAACP leaders. The idea gradually dawned upon them that the big Republican majorities might now be receptive to a real antilynching bill.[51] Yet, all the while, they had been observing an unexpected phenomenon that swept Harlem like a tropical tidal wave: the mass enthusiasm for a Jamaican immigrant and his plan to establish a black-owned fleet of ships.

9

The Emperor of Harlem

O N August 2, 1920, one week before James Weldon Johnson was to
confer with candidate Warren G. Harding, and a few months after
the Duluth lynchings, a hurricane of excitement blew over Harlem. At the center of the storm was a determined and intense man of supreme self-confidence, a portly Jamaican immigrant named Marcus
Garvey. He had come to the United States as an obscure young man in
March of 1916, but as August 1920 approached, Garvey was organizing the
largest political rally in African-American history.

Excited crowds greeted thousands of uniformed members of Garvey's
Universal Negro Improvement Association (UNIA) as they paraded down
Lenox Avenue. Men of the African Legion, attired in crisp blue uniforms,
marched in military order at the head of the file. They were followed by
Black Cross nurses in white uniforms, ranks of singers, bands, and children
organized in their own clubs. Garvey himself, a handsome man with ebony
skin, was resplendent in academic robes, sporting a tasseled mortarboard
on his head and bearing an imperial-looking walking stick. That night
twenty-five thousand black people packed Madison Square Garden to hear
their leader speak. The spectacle was unforgettable. No one had seen anything like this meeting because nothing like it had ever happened before.
On the stage sat robed African tribal leaders under red, black, and green
tricolor banners, and chorales and bands that performed for two hours.
Finally Garvey stepped forward to speak. He began by pledging the solidarity of the world's four hundred million Negroes to the cause of Irish
independence. This startling opening unveiled his movement as internationalist in vision, nationalist in sentiment, racially proud but not racially
blind. Just as Ireland should belong to the Irish, so should Africa belong to
the Africans, not their European conquerors, Garvey declared. For the next
month, delegates to this first UNIA convention would sound this theme,
enshrining African independence into a "Declaration of the Rights of the
Negro Peoples of the World." Garvey drew toward his movement tens of

thousands of poor black people previously unmoved by any other would-be spokesmen. He attracted new leaders as well, such as Philadelphia's Reverend James W. H. Eason, the actress Henrietta Vinton Davis, columnist John E. Bruce, and even Emmett J. Scott, Booker T. Washington's erstwhile chief aide. Garvey had emerged, seemingly out of nowhere, to become the most powerful Negro leader in the world virtually overnight. He was only thirty-three years old.[1]

THE YOUNGEST of eleven children, Garvey was born in a Jamaican village to a humble stonemason and his religious wife. He had to leave school at age fourteen to learn the printer's trade, and three years later he made his way to Kingston, the capital. Soon he was a foreman at one of the island's largest print shops. When the workers walked out on strike, Garvey was the only supervisor to join them. The owners fired him and kept him out of the industry. Thrown back on his own resources, Garvey, who had been an avid reader from childhood, launched several newspapers of his own. These did not last, but the experience afforded Garvey the chance to travel about the Caribbean, studying the conditions of Negro workers on the islands and in Latin America.

At age twenty-five he set off for London, where he spent two years mixing among African students and exiles, exploring his fascination with the Mother Continent. There he discovered as well Booker T. Washington's *Up from Slavery*, which so forcefully impressed him that he returned to Jamaica determined to establish his own version of the Tuskegee Institute. He founded the UNIA, designated himself president, and set out to launch his school. No one was interested. He had imported a race-conscious American model to an overwhelmingly black island whose residents rarely interacted with whites and who thought, consequently, little about race. Garvey decided he could raise more money for his school in America, and Booker T. Washington himself agreed to meet him. Unfortunately the Wizard of Tuskegee died before Garvey departed. His follower sailed for Harlem instead.[2]

Harlem was fast on the way to becoming the largest Negro metropolis in the world. The 1920 census would count 152,467 Negro New Yorkers, surpassing Washington, D.C., for largest total black population. By 1930, that figure would more than double. In that year, more Negroes lived in New York than in Birmingham, Memphis, and St. Louis combined. Migrants came from all over, but the largest plurality, 54,754, came from the West Indies. Most other migrants came from the southeastern states, with 44,471 Virginians heading the list.

Fully two-thirds of Negro Manhattan (one of five city boroughs) lived in Harlem in 1920. Harlem lies in northern Manhattan, stretching from 120th Street to 155th and beyond, bounded by Eighth Avenue on the west and the Harlem River on the east. By 1930, much of the neighborhood was over 90 percent West Indian and African-American.[3]

Unlike many African-American neighborhoods in urban America, this was no run-down slum where black people lived in alleys. Harlem was a relatively new and beautiful community where the housing stock was superb. The planned extension of the Lenox Avenue subway line led to a building boom around the turn of the century. Realtors estimated that property values would treble as New Yorkers flocked to Harlem. Despite attempts by white residents to keep them out, African-American migrants moved in. Negro middlemen took out long-term leases and rented out housing units themselves. Later, black churches bought real estate in big chunks, and Harlem's population mushroomed. By 1914, rents soared to an average of over twenty-three dollars a month, but the promise of jobs lured more and more migrants to the city.[4]

New Harlemites brought with them their churches, clubs, and other institutions. Most high-toned among the churches was St. Philip's Protestant Episcopal, founded in the Five Points in 1809 and later transplanted to the Tenderloin. In 1911, St. Philip's opened a new building, designed by Negro architects, in Harlem and then transacted the largest real estate purchase by Negroes in New York history, buying $640,000 worth of apartment houses. The pastor of the church was Reverend Hutchens C. Bishop, originally from Charleston, South Carolina, a tall Negro with light skin and a bald pate. Bishop also served on the NAACP board of directors; he was just the sort of Negro leader that Marcus Garvey hated. The Reverend Dr. Adam Clayton Powell moved his Abyssinian Baptist to Harlem around the same time. Reverend F. A. Cullen, another NAACP loyalist and foster father to the poet Countee Cullen, moved the Salem Memorial Methodist Episcopal uptown, as did dozens of others. Negro fraternal lodges followed suit. The *New York Age* moved its office, and two new weeklies appeared, the *Amsterdam News* and the *New York News*.[5]

James Weldon Johnson's love affair with New York had begun with his childhood visits to Brooklyn. His 1930 book, *Black Manhattan*, reprised the island's troubled racial history, which had been scarred by the nation's worst pogrom ever against black people during the Civil War. But Johnson emphasized Manhattan's thriving black cultural life, in which he and his brother Rosamond had participated as Tin Pan Alley songwriters, in reverential tones:

> Throughout coloured America Harlem is the recognized
> Negro capital. Indeed, it is Mecca for the sightseer, the plea-
> sure-seeker, the curious, the adventurous, the enterprising, the
> ambitious, and the talented of the entire Negro world; for the
> lure of it has reached down to every island of the Carib Sea and
> penetrated even into Africa.[6]

In his own way, Marcus Garvey was as much a creature of booming Jazz
Age Harlem as the fictional Jay Gatsby was a creature of the Wall Street
bull market. Like Gatsby, Garvey was a self-made man who came to the
big city from the frontier, a man of mystery who dazzled his followers and
brought tragedy upon himself. For a little while, Harlem was like the fictional West Egg, a place where all things were possible and jazz played all
the time. To the new migrant from Virginia or Carolina, Harlem represented hope, and for a while much of that hope was directed toward Marcus Garvey.

WITHIN little more than a month after his arrival, Garvey was entreating
W. E. B. Du Bois to introduce him as a public speaker before a Harlem
audience. The presumption shown by his approach to Du Bois is revealing;
Du Bois, who was out of town, later gave Garvey's meeting favorable notice
in the *Crisis*. After his speech, Garvey was off to see America, visiting thirty-
eight cities and conferring with Negro leaders. Back in Harlem, Garvey
tried without much success to solicit money for his school from the same
sort of wealthy white men who contributed to Tuskegee. At the same time
he circulated among various competing Harlem radicals, including Hubert
Harrison, a nationalist intellectual from St. Croix. Later he spoke at meetings organized by the socialists Asa Philip Randolph and Chandler Owen.
His plan was to build his own movement, and by late 1917 the American
version of the UNIA was under way.

Somewhere in this period, Garvey decided to make New York his headquarters. After a few infights with Harlem rivals, Garvey toured the country
again, building branches in new cities. Then, on October 14, 1919, a former
employee, enraged over an alleged twenty-five dollar debt he claimed Garvey owed him, walked into the leader's office on 135th Street and shot him
twice. The unarmed Garvey and his secretary, Amy Ashwood, drove the
attacker into the street, where police caught him. The gunman jumped to
his death while in custody, and Garvey's legend began to spread. He called
a meeting at Madison Square Garden two weeks later, an act of political
risk taking that matched his physical courage. New York's African-Ameri-

can activists typically held their events uptown in Harlem and would not dare to try to fill the vast building downtown on 34th Street. On Christmas Day, Garvey and Ashwood married, and the story was on everyone's lips. New recruits streamed into UNIA headquarters at Liberty Hall on 138th Street.[7]

It took more than luck and courage, however, to attract the following that Garvey commanded by 1920. Garvey masterfully synthesized diverse elements of African-American and diaspora yearnings, and filtered them through the prism of his life experience. He succeeded because he said what millions of black Americans thought and acted boldly on his words.

Above all, Garvey was a race-proud black nationalist who preached self-reliance. Negroes would free themselves from oppression not by appealing to the dubious better natures of white people, or to the supposedly inclusive principles of the American founding documents, but by doing for the race first. In contrast to NAACP leaders, ministers, and political spoilsmen, Garvey told his listeners that they had their own traditions and could build their own institutions. This notion was deeply rooted in African-American history. Whenever black aspirations for inclusion were dashed, the nationalist impulse asserted itself more forcefully. Black abolitionists, including even Frederick Douglass, showed this sentiment especially in the 1850s, when the Fugitive Slave Act, Kansas-Nebraska Act, and Dred Scott decision extended the slavocracy's grasp. After the failure of Reconstruction, the Exodusters set off to establish all-black towns in the West. With the emergence of a full-blown Jim Crow system, Booker T. Washington's accommodationist nationalism seemed to many to be the only sensible recourse. After World War I, white America turned against black expectations with murderous fury. Garvey expressed a feeling that must have beat, at least sometime, in the breast of every Negro: *To hell with these white people, all of them*. Even his preferred term for his people—*Negro*—implied a distinction between the races that the word *colored* downplayed. The former suggested a people, a nationality; the latter a mere skin color, a physical designator like short or tall.

Garvey's nationalism was sophisticated and internationalist in scope. Like Jewish Zionists, he imagined that diaspora blacks would lead the regeneration of the ancestral homeland, now possessed by interlopers. This notion went as far back as Paul Cuffee, an early nineteenth-century Massachusetts ship captain who settled a small group of ex-slaves along the African coast. Its best expression in Garvey's world was the African nation of Liberia, founded in the 1830s as a haven for former slaves. Garvey's message struck deep chords of longing among millions of people who felt themselves to be a lost tribe among strangers. Nonetheless, Garvey never undertook to lead a mass migration, and his "Back to Africa" rhetoric was relegated to a mystical future.

Garvey's appeal had a further advantage in that it corresponded with a nationalist upsurge taking place among many peoples of the world from Asia to Europe. In India, Mohandas Gandhi led a movement for independence. White Americans themselves were going back to Europe in unprecedented numbers as their homelands were liberated from the collapsed Russian, German, and Austro-Hungarian empires. As they returned to newly created nations such as Czechoslovakia or Poland, they set a certain tone in America, especially in New York. Their fellows who stayed behind fought for a free Ireland, the granting of Fiume to Italy, a Jewish homeland, or an independent Poland. Why should black people not campaign for a free Africa or dream of touching an ancestral shore?

Garvey spoke of race consciousness, but he represented a thoroughly American class consciousness as well. His own career served as a case in point. He was a poor immigrant who by courage and determination had recreated himself in America. Garvey's natural constituency was an uprooted people from the American South and the Caribbean who identified with his model. This was no socialist appeal but the old vision of America as a land of opportunity. When Garvey thundered, "Up you mighty race, you may do as you will," black Americans believed that this injunction might be true. Just as many white Americans respected self-made immigrant millionaires like Andrew Carnegie, so did Negroes respect Garvey's accumulation of wealth.

Garvey's real success lay in deeds rather than words. He resolved to launch a fleet of ships—the Black Star Line (BSL). Along with four colleagues, each holding forty shares of stock at $5 a share, they proposed to sell a total of one hundred thousand shares and buy boats with that capital. Garvey announced his venture in May 1919, and by September he had put down $16,500, 10 percent of the purchase price of the SS *Yarmouth*, an ungainly freighter as old as Garvey himself. When the ship appeared at Harlem's 135th Street pier, five thousand enthusiastic Negroes paid $1 each just to walk on board. Its maiden voyage was delayed because of a lack of insurance, but the sight of this black-owned and captained vessel, proudly flying the red, black, and green flag, inspired all who saw it. Soon enough the ship was on its way to the West Indies, and the Black Star board of directors authorized purchase of two more boats.[8]

The ships were a perfect symbolic choice, and for the purpose of selling stock, he could not have started a better business. As physical objects they were visible, movable symbols of wealth. Every nation calculated its power in terms of ships, and the Black Star Line suggested that Negro America possessed its own merchant fleet. In a very real sense they promised to link the peoples of the African diaspora. Garvey's fleet created a sensation from Harlem to the Caribbean. Finally, the ships rekindled memories of an almost forgotten African-American past. Free black men of the new American nation had been sailors themselves, until driven from the sea by southern politicians and northern workmen.[9] Now they would be seamen, navigators, captains, and owners.

Garvey made it possible for everyone to be an owner. He promised each five-dollar stockholder a dividend. Here Garvey really caught the spirit of the moment, as the postwar economic chaos gave way to the bull market of the Roaring Twenties. Garvey transmitted his own self-confidence to potential stock purchasers, and thousands of people proudly invested their money in the Black Star Line. The company may not have had a track record, but everyone could see for themselves that the ships were real. White Americans by the thousands were at the same time buying stock from an Italian immigrant of Boston named Charles Ponzi, and this swindler's Florida land offerings did not even exist. Black Americans who bought Garvey's stock could see for themselves that the BSL's capital was real.

Underpinning Garvey's nationalist philosophy and business zeal was his sheer style. Despite his dignified bearing and academic pretensions, the man was a born showman, "our black Barnum," as W. A. Domingo, a former colleague turned opponent, once wrote. "No Living Negro Can Afford to Miss Seeing the Great International Demonstration," cajoled a flyer for Garvey's 1922 convention in true circus tradition.[10] He projected enormous charisma, dressing himself for grand parades in flamboyant military outfits with epaulets, braids and tricornered plumed hats, or academic robes. The *Negro World*, his weekly newspaper, sold for only five cents and covered his own doings in banner headlines, so that his readers could follow his career as if he were one of those new phenomena, a movie star. In short, Garvey advertised himself as that ultimate modern commodity of the 1920s, a celebrity. He was to African Americans in the Jazz Age what Charles Lindbergh was to whites.

Garvey invented his celebrity status from a mixture of exoticism and commonality. On the one hand he was the obscure common man who had arrived in New York, like a million others, with nothing but his dreams. With bravado and bombast he sold these dreams to the masses and made himself the talk of the town. In true celebrity fashion, he made a public marriage with his secretary, Amy Ashwood, on Christmas Day, and almost as quickly divorced her to marry Amy Jacques. Moreover, he was unique as a Jamaican who spoke the King's English with an island lilt. A lifetime

Marcus Garvey. Courtesy of Library of Congress.

spent in the British Empire suggested to him the power of monarchy as a unifying symbol, so he created that, too, appointing ranks of nobles in grandiose medieval ceremonies. Intellectuals might scoff at these affairs, but they gave his followers a sense of belonging to something communal and purposeful. The pomp and pageantry mirrored the ceremonies that made Englishmen proud of their sceptered isle and Americans, in good Tocquevillian fashion, proud to be Masons or Ku Klux Klan members.

Garvey's Jamaican origins provided one more element to his success. During the Great Migration of southern African Americans to the North, Jamaicans and other Caribbean natives journeyed to America, especially to New York. By 1930, over fifty-four thousand of them were New Yorkers, a figure ten times greater than that of any other American city. This meant that by 1930, one in six black New Yorkers was West Indian. They had typically immigrant entrepreneurial ambitions, and Garvey spoke especially for them. They formed the core of Garvey's supporters and gave him a unique ethnic base.[11]

Two metaphors come to the mind of any writer considering Marcus Garvey. The first is natural: the man blazed like a meteor in the sky above Harlem and flamed out in the friction of the American atmosphere, his movement falling to earth in pieces. The second is literary: Marcus Garvey lived as a tragic hero, "unable to explain his spectacular rise and fall even to himself," as the astute editor of his papers, Robert Hill, noted.[12] Garvey, a great man who left a lasting imprint on American history, had classic flaws to match his abilities. Against each of Garvey's strengths lined up an obverse weakness.

Garvey was a visionary in business and a master salesman, but he had no practical abilities in managing a company. He wrecked the Black Star Line as quickly as he built it up. In the first place, he knew absolutely nothing about ships and lacked the temperament to learn. Each one he bought was an overpriced, damaged hulk. The flagship *Yarmouth* set the pattern for several ships that followed. Its boilers were so weak that it could hardly proceed against ocean currents, and on its first voyage it ran aground near the Bahamas. On a subsequent trip the captain had to jettison its cargo of liquor. The Black Star Line had to pay $30,000 in repairs after its purchase and then was forced to sell it off for $1,625. The *Yarmouth* lost over $190,000. Similarly, Garvey paid $60,000 for the *Kanawha* as a Hudson River excursion boat and wound up spending another $134,000 on repairs. The ship returned $1,207 in income. Even the company's name proved to be ironic: the "Black Star Line" was patterned after the "White

Star Line''—owner of the *Titanic*. Garvey's bookkeeping methods were as bad as his business decisions. Money from the BSL and UNIA were mixed together indiscriminately and accounted for haphazardly.[13]

Complicating this problem was another—Garvey made enemies easily. He was impulsive, egotistical, and imperial, and could not abide strong people among his inner circle. Traditional Negro leaders expressed their hostility openly. Robert Abbott, editor of the nation's most popular black newsweekly, the *Chicago Defender*, drove Garvey out of town. Fred Moore, editor of the *New York Age*, called Garvey "a mountebank, a money grubber and a discredited but cunning schemer."[14]

The NAACP observed his rise from a distance. The Association never discussed Garvey at a board meeting, except once when he threatened to sue them for libel. Du Bois wrote in the *Crisis* that the *Yarmouth* had a wooden hull, and he had to retract his error under pressure. These two great leaders regarded each other warily in a relationship that quickly degenerated into mutual contempt. Garvey developed a "pathological" hatred for Du Bois, his first biographer wrote. Du Bois limited his memory of Garvey to three terse paragraphs in his final autobiography.[15]

In 1919 Garvey associated with the socialists A. Philip Randolph and Chandler Owen, and he attacked Du Bois from the left, as they did. Du Bois "was never elected by any one except by the capitalist class," he declared with typically abstract bombast. He argued that Du Bois's African program failed to call for the immediate withdrawal of the colonial powers. During Du Bois's first Pan-African Congress in Paris, he obstructed the work of a UNIA emissary, Garvey complained before a Harlem mass meeting. Du Bois later retorted that he had never heard of the man.[16]

Yet, in 1920, Garvey invited Du Bois to place his name in nomination before the UNIA convention as leader of American Negroes. Perhaps this was his way of showing he was the more powerful man. During the convention each negatively assessed the other in interviews with a journalist. Garvey charged that Du Bois "has obligated himself to the white folks," and Du Bois characterized Garvey as "a demagogue," a West Indian who did not understand American conditions. However, Du Bois allowed, American Negroes were getting more radical, and he would not stand in Garvey's way.[17]

Du Bois reserved extended comment in the *Crisis* until December 1920 and January 1921, when he wrote two balanced and thoughtful articles that fairly assessed Garvey's abilities. Du Bois was a partisan of black entrepreneurship, too, and he defended Garvey against character assassins as "an honest and sincere man with a tremendous vision, great dynamic force, stubborn determination and unselfish desire to serve." The editor also saw

Garvey's vanity, suspicious nature, and "domineering" style. Most significantly, Du Bois subjected Garvey's mystifying financial statements to rigorous analysis and warned of future collapse. Yet he maintained a tone of careful encouragement, urging Garvey's followers that they "insist that he get down to business and make income and expense balance," and stop his reckless attacks against critics. Other leaders are not jealous, Du Bois added (referring most likely to himself), "but they are afraid of his failure, for his failure would be theirs." Du Bois and his colleagues expected that Garvey would self-destruct, and they did not want the blame for the implosion.[18]

Garvey's African adventure met the same obstacles as his business plans. Having named himself provisional president of Africa at his 1920 convention, he faced the dilemma of dealing with actual African government. Garvey had never been to Africa and would never set foot there during his entire life. In 1920, Liberia was the only free African coastal country. This American-founded nation was dominated by descendants of repatriated former slaves. President C. D. B. King was dependent upon American loans and could not antagonize the United States. Garvey, flushed with his early business success, set out to replace the American government as Liberia's banker. He proposed UNIA loans and technical assistance to the struggling nation. The Liberians received Garvey's emissaries cordially but remained noncommittal. Garvey publicized the former response and complained privately about the latter.[19]

The Liberian elite occupied a precarious position even without having to contend with Garvey. At home they were afraid of their own people, and in international affairs they did not wish to alienate British and French imperialism. They would naturally view Garvey as a schemer who planned to replace them. In June 1921 Du Bois ran an "Open Letter from the President of Liberia" in the *Crisis*. The unnamed Marcus Garvey was clearly the subject of the missive. President King declared that Liberia could not absorb a migration from the United States and would not be used as a military base against its neighbors. This was a message for Garvey to keep out.[20]

Three years later, President King cut off a UNIA colonization project at the same time that Liberia granted a concession to the Firestone Rubber Company. This marked the end of Garvey's African plans, which never sent anyone "Back to Africa" to stay. Du Bois had represented the United States at King's recent inauguration, and Garvey wrongly blamed Du Bois for turning the president against him. The Liberians had reasons of their own to distrust Garvey.[21]

If Garvey antagonized Du Bois, he fared better with William Pickens.

Pickens wrote a weekly syndicated column for the Associated Negro Press. In the spring of 1921 he defended Garvey against those who charged that his West Indian nationality disqualified him from American leadership. He defended Garvey in the *Nation*, and by the end of the year he was addressing him in the *Negro World* as "Puissaint Leader." As late as June 1922, he boasted to a Louisiana NAACP official that Garvey had offered him a ten thousand dollar salary. Stealing Pickens away would have been a major coup for Garvey.[22]

In the summer of 1922, Garvey made a spectacular turn that revealed the ultimate direction of his politics. This move was rooted in a secret development beginning one year earlier. During the spring and summer of 1921, Garvey made an extended trip to the Caribbean, selling stock to thousands of investors from Costa Rica to Cuba. Meanwhile he feuded with the officers of the ship *Kanawha*, broken down yet again. Garvey complained about them to the American consul at Kingston, who sided with Garvey's antagonists. The State Department became interested in Garvey's visa and blocked his reentry into the country. According to Robert A. Hill, the editor of Garvey's papers, Garvey's attorney had to bribe corrupt officials in the State Department through the Negro politician Henry "Linc" Johnson. "Whatever the cause of the abrupt change in the government's policy of exclusion, the impact on Garvey's political course was immediate," Hill concluded. After July of 1921, Garvey eliminated antiwhite rhetoric and began stressing the importance of racial purity for both races.[23]

At Garvey's second annual convention in 1921, he drove out of his movement critics on the right and left. Noah Thompson, the Los Angeles leader, had enough business sense to be alarmed by the BSL's financial situation, and he demanded a strict accounting of the money. On the left, Cyril Briggs, a leader of the African Blood Brotherhood, wanted Garvey to support the labor radicalism developing in the West Indies. By removing these critics, Garvey banished both his business caution and his social conscience. The men left around him learned that one got ahead in the UNIA by toadying to the leader. Thompson took the West Coast Garveyites out of the movement, and Briggs opened a propaganda war against Garvey that resulted in libel litigation.

Lurking not far below the surface of Garvey's ideology was the notion that miscegenation was a crime against Negroes. This idea was linked to Garvey's class resentments. In Jamaica, where very few whites lived, social class distinctions were coded in skin pigmentation. A mulatto elite (as in Haiti) occupied the social service, professional, and business sectors from which the aspiring Garvey had been proscribed. To Garvey, light skin signified that a person was "a white man's Negro." With the white-looking Briggs blasting away at him in the *Crusader* newspaper, this idea was reinforced in Garvey's imagination.[24]

Garvey saw the leaders of the NAACP in the same light. In the fall of 1921, he attacked Du Bois as an integrationist. By contrast, he wrote, "[The UNIA] believes that both races have separate and distinct social destinies, that each and every race should develop on its own social lines, and that any attempt to bring about the amalgamation of any two opposite races is a crime against nature." James Weldon Johnson replied in his *New York Age* column that this line echoed racist politicians like Mississippi's James K. Vardaman. By attacking "social equality" as well, the UNIA leader admitted that segregation was a good thing, Johnson continued. In response, Garvey conceded Johnson's point. For now, Negroes had no interest in riding in railroad cars or going to school with whites, and blacks should stop seeking their company. Waverers between the two camps could now begin to see how large were the stakes in this struggle of ideas.[25]

In January 1922, federal agents arrested Garvey and three associates on various counts of mail fraud. Cyril Briggs had been alleging that this was exactly what Garvey was doing: selling stock in and tickets for two ships that he did not own and advertising for them under the names with which he planned to christen them. In other words, Garvey's boats *Antonio Maceo* and *Phillis Wheatley* did not exist. When some Black Star shareholders complained that they had been swindled, federal prosecutors easily won indictments at the end of the month. Garvey blamed "certain organizations calling themselves Negro Advancement Associations," charging them with sabotage, and flailed out against unnamed Bolshevik agents. Johnson demanded that Garvey retract this baseless accusation, but Garvey refused. Nonetheless, the BSL was compelled to shut down its operations.[26]

Out on bail, Garvey turned to a new market for stock selling: the American South. On his southern tour, Garvey openly embraced Jim Crow practices. Segregation was good for black business, he declared in Raleigh, North Carolina. "This is a white man's country," he announced in New Orleans. "I'm not vexed with the white man of the South for Jim Crowing me." Then on June 25, 1922, Garvey met with Ku Klux Klan leader Edward Clarke in Atlanta. Back in New York, Garvey lamely defended this meeting by repeating Klan propaganda that it was pro-white, not antiblack. In truth, as Johnson had pointed out a year earlier, Garvey's ideology matched that of southern racists.[27]

This defense of the Klan took place in a climate of continued lynching and mob violence. It was the straw that broke the camel's back for African-

American fence-sitters, Pickens among them. Pickens, who had been invited to join Garvey's "cabinet" at the upcoming convention, now lashed out at him. Once your rank and file realize what you have done, Pickens accused Garvey directly, you are through. You propose a deal with the Klan—we'll give up America if you let us go back to Africa, Pickens summarized Garvey's dialogue with the Klan wizard. But the Klan can't give you Africa, Pickens pointed out; this is a deal as stupid as the one you made with white men for broken-down boats. The scales were falling from Pickens's eyes, and he began to realize what a colossal blunder he had almost made.[28]

Pickens now joined with *Messenger* editors A. Philip Randolph, Chandler Owen, and NAACP colleague Robert Bagnall in a "Garvey Must Go!" campaign. During the UNIA's 1922 convention, each critic spoke against the movement's leader on successive Sundays at Harlem's Shuffle Inn on 131st Street. One by one they took up Garvey's apologies for the Klan, his irresponsible waste of investors' money, and the absurdity of going "Back to Africa." Johnson joined the chorus in his *New York Age* column. During the UNIA convention, Garvey staged a royal night at Liberty Hall, investing his leading supporters with African fiefdoms as they knelt before His Supreme Highness the Provisional President of Africa. The NAACP leader, thoroughly revolted by this caricature of Negro tomfoolery straight out of a racist cartoon, deplored Garvey's recreation of the worst aspects of ranked, monarchical society.[29]

A new theme of Garvey's antagonists was his growing propensity for violence. Hecklers tried to break up the Harlem meetings, and fistfights broke out. When Pickens reported Garvey's threats to "do away" with him, the tumult grew so intense that the police had to restore order. Two years earlier Garveyites had fought with members of Adam Clayton Powell's Abyssinian Baptist Church, but that seemed then to be an isolated incident. Now Garveyites attacked meetings of critics around the country. At the UNIA convention, leader William Sherrill vowed, "Black folk as well as white who tamper with the UNIA are going to die."[30]

A few weeks later, A. Philip Randolph received a suspicious-looking package in the mail, sent from New Orleans without a return address. He called the bomb squad, who discovered that the package contained a human hand, that of a white man. Enclosed was a letter signed "K.K.K." that said, "If you are not in favor with your own race movement you can't be with ours. . . . Now let me see your name in your nigger improvement association as a member. . . ." Randolph charged, as seemed obvious, that the threat came from the Klan on behalf of Garvey. The UNIA leader told a reporter that the recipients had cooked it up as a publicity stunt. This crass lie in defense of a horrible crime terrified everyone who had crossed Garvey.[31]

A more ominous development was to follow. While enemies from without assailed the UNIA, Reverend James W. H. Eason, Garvey's Leader of American Negroes, declared at the 1922 convention that the movement should play down its African plans and focus on American possibilities. Eason and Garvey had a shoving match on the platform at Liberty Hall, and Garvey expelled his rival from the movement. Eason then launched his own version of the UNIA, as the Los Angeles leader had done the year before on the West Coast. On New Year's Day, 1923, Eason was shot from ambush after giving a speech at New Orleans. Eason's associates identified three Garveyites as the killers. Two of them were Jamaican members of Garvey's "police force." They were found guilty, but their convictions were overturned on appeal because of a technicality. One of the shooters gloated that Eason had got what he deserved, and few African-American activists doubted that Garvey had at least encouraged the assassination.[32]

Shortly after Eason's murder, eight African-American leaders wrote U.S. Attorney General Harry M. Daugherty urging that he prosecute Garvey vigorously on the still-pending mail fraud charges. In addition to the four orators of the previous summer, the signers included Harry Pace, president of the Black Swan Phonograph Corporation; Harlem realtor John E. Nail; New York City alderman George W. Harris; and Robert S. Abbott of the *Chicago Defender*. The letter detailed Garvey's long history of violence against his opponents, including recent attacks on anti-Garveyites in Baltimore, New York, Pittsburgh, and Toronto, Canada. "We advocate that the Attorney General use his full influence to completely extirpate this vicious movement, and that he . . . push the Government's case against Marcus Garvey for using the mails to defraud." While the eight signers affixed their names as individuals, the letter had strong backing from individual NAACPers. In addition to Pickens and Bagnall, Pace served on the Association's board of directors, and Nail was Johnson's father-in-law.[33]

A second theme running through the anti-Garvey campaign was the notion that he and his movement represented a foreign threat that African Americans rejected. The *Messenger* denounced Garvey as "A Supreme Negro Jamaican Jackass." Reverend Bagnall's litany of abuse called him a "Jamaican Negro of unmixed stock" and likened his features to those of a dog and a pig. In one way or another, the *Messenger* editors especially insinuated that the source of Garvey's errors lay in his Jamaican origins. This offended Garvey's West Indian critics, such as W. A. Domingo, a former Garveyite who protested against the magazine's appeals to American chauvinism and the growing calls for Garvey's deportation. To their credit, official NAACP spokesmen steered away from this kind of rhetoric. Domingo pointed out to the *Messenger*'s editors that Du Bois pointedly included the contributions of foreign-born Negroes to American life in his magazine. Johnson assured Domingo that he opposed Garvey's deportation, and Pickens earlier expressed himself against "a coward's advantage" as well.[34]

Ad hominem attacks mystify rather than clarify ideas, and offered in heat they poorly served Garvey's opponents. Yet, as Randolph later told his own biographer, it was impossible to understand the Garvey movement without taking into account its Jamaican origins.[35] Garvey did carry the baggage of his life experience with him to American shores. First and most important, his antipathy to light-skinned Negroes defied African-American political experience. True, a form of Caribbean style color-coded class distinction had long existed in African-American life. However, all African Americans were oppressed regardless of their hue, and black American leaders strove to unify the race. "One drop of blood" was all you needed to be lynched in America. No one better illustrated this than Walter White, almost the victim of a Georgia lynch mob at age thirteen. Who, anti-Garveyites thought, was the immigrant Garvey to read light-skinned Negroes as not authentically black?

A second aspect of the Garvey movement that reflected its Jamaican roots was its entrepreneurial emphasis. Garvey's encouragement of black enterprise grew out of the immigrant experience and the historic differences between Jamaican slavery and America's peculiar institution. In a mainly black country, slaves were permitted to engage in a wider range of economic activities than in America, where the relatively high white-to-black population ratio limited slaves mostly to plantation agriculture and produced in the whites a pronounced sense of racial consciousness. Moreover, immigrants from anywhere to America tended to be the most risk-taking portion of the population. Jamaicans moving into Harlem often impressed their American cousins as "pushy" or "the Jews of the race." Indeed, they quickly acquired many of the small stores in Harlem. Garvey spoke for these people above all.[36]

The stereotype regarding Garvey and the NAACP is that Garvey's followers were the poor, and the NAACP represented a middle-class and professional elite. In terms of their programs and in part their following, this stereotype deserves to be reversed. The NAACP's local leaderships surely represented middle-class African America, but the rank and file who signed the branch charters listed their occupations time and again as laborers, janitors, porters, laundresses, and domestic helpers. In its program and activities, the NAACP committed itself to the defense of sharecroppers, workers, students, soldiers, and most of all, victims of white violence. The American anti-Garveyites might have been wrong to hold Garvey's Jamaican origins against him, but his public defense of Jim Crow and the Klan really could not have passed the lips of an American-born black leader in 1922. Randolph, Bagnall, and the others could not help but notice the link between Garvey's origins and his program.

Finally, the assassination of Garvey's former American leader by Jamaican agents raises the question of how rooted Garveyism was in African-American life. The photographs of the spectacular Garvey parades, the meetings at Madison Square Garden, and Garvey's own claims of two or four million members have reinforced the notion that Garvey led a mass movement, while the NAACP represented a tiny fraction of the urban Talented Tenth. This picture deserves to be rethought as well. Garvey kept spotty records of his membership, so there is no way for sure to know how many paid-up UNIA members there were in a given year, how quickly they turned over, or what their occupations were. In January 1923, Du Bois, basing his estimate on rough figures supplied by W. A. Domingo, concluded that the UNIA had only ten thousand to twenty thousand paid-up members at the height of the movement. The lion's share of these were in New York, where West Indian immigrants provided the base of his supporters.[37]

As the historian Judith Stein shows in a chapter on four midwestern UNIA branches, these were sometimes West Indian–led, kept low political profiles, and were unable to elaborate a program meaningful to their city. While she asserts that the Detroit and Cincinnati branches were large, she can give no membership figures for those cities and guesses the Gary branch to have 185 members. In Detroit and Gary, the UNIA supported Klan-backed mayoral candidates in 1924.[38] It is easy to see, therefore, why Garveyism collapsed so abruptly. The likelihood is that Garveyism never sank roots in African-American soil. Like the Nation of Islam leader Louis Farrakhan in the late twentieth century, Garvey drew the large crowds, but his organizational backing was shallow. The ultimate evidence for this conclusion lies in the overall contrast between the record left by the Papers of the NAACP and those of the UNIA. The former contains hundreds of boxes showing that hundreds of branches carried out varied activities during the 1920s directly related to important developments in their communities. The Garvey papers are devoted almost entirely to the speeches and letters of the leader.

The beginning of Garvey's end came with his trial in May 1923 for conspiring to use the mails to defraud. Garvey and three colleagues were well represented in court, but Garvey impulsively fired his attorney to speak on his own behalf. He alienated the presiding judge, Julian Mack, by asking that he disqualify himself because he was an NAACP member. Mack stayed on the case, and even the *Negro World* conceded that Mack handled the proceedings fairly. The government easily proved that the Black Star Line was mismanaged, bringing thirty disgruntled former employees and stock-holders to the stand. It introduced Garvey's dubious stock promotional liter-ature as evidence that he misrepresented his company's prospects. Business incompetence, however, is not a crime, and Garvey's three co-defendants were acquitted. Garvey, whose abrasive courtroom antics proved the adage that "he who defends himself in court has a fool for a lawyer," was con-victed and sentenced to five years. The conviction was absurd on its face: the charge was conspiracy to use the mails to defraud, so he must have been a conspiracy of one. Judge Mack remanded Garvey to the Tombs Prison, where he sat until bailed out in September.[39]

The resilient leader turned his persecution to advantage. He had to can-cel the usual August convention, but when he left prison, the crowds turned out to hear him celebrate at Liberty Hall. With new energy, he launched a second shipping line and purchased his largest vessel yet, christened the *Booker T. Washington*. But this faulty ship made only a one-way trip to the Caribbean, losing thousands of dollars. In 1924 Garvey turned the UNIA toward American politics, enthusiastically backing Calvin Coolidge and two Klan-endorsed candidates in northern cities.[40]

Throughout his brief career, Garvey blamed his failures on ideological opponents. Chief among these was Du Bois, for whom his envy was in-tense. In his speeches and in his writing, Garvey laid every personal set-back at the door of the NAACP. He accused the NAACP of sabotaging his ships and charged that its president, Moorfield Storey, had urged Judge Mack to sentence him harshly. By contrast, Du Bois's appraisals of Garvey were moderate in tone until Garvey endorsed the Ku Klux Klan. When Du Bois returned from Africa in April 1924, his colleagues had to arrange police protection for him at the pier because of Garveyite threats. In the next issue of the *Crisis*, Du Bois finally hit back without restraint. "A Lunatic or a Traitor," he titled his editorial. Garvey had no one to blame for his fail-ures but himself, Du Bois wrote. He had had a fair trial, and rival leaders were glad to see him in jail because he had killed one of them, not because they were jealous. "This open ally of the Ku Klux Klan should be locked up or sent home," Du Bois vowed. As the political scientist Manning Marable pointed out, Du Bois cautiously watched Garvey's career without getting in his way. Only when his crimes against the movement were palpable and threatened to continue did Du Bois try to bring him down.[41]

Time finally ran out on Garvey's appeals and in February 1925 the doors

of Atlanta's federal penitentiary closed behind him. In a farewell message
he urged his followers to have faith in his vision:

> If I die in Atlanta my work shall then only begin but I shall live,
> in the physical or spiritual to see the day of Africa's glory. When
> I am dead wrap the mantle of the Red, Black and Green around
> me, for in the new life I shall rise with God's grace and blessing
> to lead the millions up the heights of triumph with the colors
> that you well know. Look for me in the whirlwind or the storm,
> look for me all around you. . . .

The man who had once launched a fleet of ships now languished behind
bars, scrubbing pots in the kitchen. His biographer concludes that "Garvey
was still a towering force in Negro life and thought, and never was his great
gift of persuasive power and vivid imagery turned toward more effective
use than in his farewell address from Atlanta."[42]

This conclusion is doubtful. Another reading of this hyperbolic rhetoric
is that Garvey, with his enormous ego, convinced himself that he was a
biblical Christ/Messiah. Like many cult figures, he himself was the whole
show, and once he was gone, his followers fell out among themselves and
the movement vanished into air. He had squandered about half a million
dollars of his investors' money. In effect, he had transferred a small fortune
from the hands of aspiring African Americans into the pockets of white
swindlers, buying a coterie of hangers-on with a portion of the funds.
Meanwhile he vilified the civil rights movement, wasting money that could
have gone to defend the Arkansas sharecroppers, the Ocoee victims, or the
Duluth defendants.

In 1927, President Calvin Coolidge commuted Garvey's sentence, and,
as a noncitizen felon, he was deported from New Orleans to Panama. He
never returned to America, and he died in London in 1940, a forgotten man
in the United States. He was quintessentially a man of the Roaring Twenties, and he had nothing to say to the radical depression years of the 1930s.
There was no Garveyism without Garvey, and his movement collapsed
without him.

Garvey was a unique figure in African-American history, but every culture has had a heroic figure like him. As a self-made man from an island
off the mainland, who speaks the native tongue with an accent and rises
to lead his people after their revolutionary hopes have been dashed, Garvey may be usefully compared to Napoleon. In American politics, his ana-
logue might be James Michael Curley, the four-time mayor of Boston who
dramatized his own lowly origins, demonized the city's Yankee upper class,
and appealed to Irish-American ethnic pride. But the best comparison may

be to his contemporary, Benito Mussolini. Like Garvey, Mussolini began his political career as a radical, shifting to capitalist economic plans after the World War. Both men appealed to themes of nationalist unity, created a cult of personality through bombastic rhetoric, and used violence against their opponents. Like Bertolt Brecht, who captured all this about the Italian fascist in his play *The Resistible Rise of Arturo Ui*, Eugene O'Neill saw all these contradictions in Garvey. Brought to life by the actors Charles Gilpin and later Paul Robeson in *The Emperor Jones*, an African American becomes king of an African tribe when he is washed ashore after a shipwreck, but his own overreaching brings him low. So it was with Marcus Garvey, for a while the Emperor of Harlem.

10

The Horror

F AR from Harlem, three incidents in the first half of 1921 dramatized the horror of American caste oppression at its worst. African Americans stared into the face of Hell as black victims were killed by fire, water, and conflagration that season. An Arkansas lynching, a mass murder in Georgia, and the Tulsa racial pogrom showed civil rights activists that they must stand their ground and fight.

On January 27, 1921, the *New York Times* reported on its first page the burning alive of an Arkansas Negro. The intoxicated Henry Lowry, forty, had shot and killed a white planter and his daughter while they stood on the porch of their home. Lowry ran away and was captured in El Paso, Texas. As Arkansas lawmen escorted him home for trial, their train was intercepted by a gang in Sardis, Mississippi. When the train pulled into the station, heavily armed men accosted the deputies and absconded with Lowry. They drove him some seventy miles to the scene of his crime on the Craig plantation in Nodena, Arkansas, just above Memphis. By the light of torches, Lowry confessed to his crime before a crowd of five hundred in a natural amphitheater with the Mississippi River at its back. Then the ringleaders fed Lowry a last meal, chained him to a log, brought his wife and child before him, and roasted him slowly to death. His ordeal lasted almost an hour.[1]

The *Times* wondered about this tragedy on its editorial page under the headline "They Fed Before They Killed." Why? What explained this last act of charity by a mob intent on killing a helpless prisoner? Probably, the writer speculated, the people wished to observe the tradition in state executions of granting the condemned man a last meal, thereby distinguishing themselves from uncivilized barbarians acting out of passion and thus conferring an air of legitimacy on their enterprise. At any rate, the bizarre proceeding was ultimately a matter for students of mob psychology.[2]

The philosophical tone of this rumination perfectly captured the attitude of educated northerners toward lynching. Lynching was not a matter about which one could do something. It was a bad thing that happened, like hurricanes or floods, and sometimes it made news and sometimes it didn't. The *Boston Globe*, for example, placed the Lowry story on page 6, next to a longer one regarding a speech given to the Boot and Shoe Club Ladies Night.[3]

The Lowry lynching horrified James Weldon Johnson. Sixty African Americans had been lynched in 1920, but the Lowry case combined every possible variant of illegality and barbarism. Unknown to the public, it also intimately involved the NAACP. The NAACP had extracted a promise of safety for Lowry from the Arkansas governor, which had now been abrogated in the most violent manner imaginable. How had this happened? The NAACP office dispatched William Pickens to the scene, and two months later he published a comprehensible version of the Lowry lynching in the liberal weekly the *Nation*.[4]

Henry Lowry, it turned out, was not a drunken criminal but a hardworking tenant farmer on the plantation of O. T. Craig. Craig and his two sons ruled their plantation with an iron hand. Shortly before Christmas Day, 1920, Lowry approached Craig and asked for a settlement of his account, which indicated that Lowry wanted the money owed to him so he could leave the plantation. Craig wouldn't allow that, and he drove Lowry off with a blow and told him that there wouldn't be any settlement. On Christmas Day Lowry returned, this time with a gun. According to Pickens's sources, Craig's son shot and wounded Lowry, who then fired at the assembled Craig family standing on the porch, killing two.[5]

With the help of his comrades in an Odd Fellows lodge, Lowry escaped to El Paso, Texas. From there he wrote to his wife, but Craig's son, the local postmaster, intercepted the letter. Lowry was arrested at his rooming house on 1201 East Third Street. Pickens omitted what happened next, perhaps to protect Lowry's landlady. The landlady went straight to the local NAACP leaders, who hired attorney Frederick Knollenberg to defend him. Branch president L. W. Washington, Knollenberg, a local minister, and Dr. L. A. Nixon (who would later challenge the state's "white primary" law) visited Lowry in jail. He agreed not to fight extradition efforts if the Arkansas governor would guarantee his safety. Governor Thomas McCrae promised this by wire, and a few days later Lowry surrendered to two Arkansas deputies.[6]

Significantly, Lowry was seized on a train in Sardis, Mississippi, which lies east of Arkansas. The shortest distance by train from El Paso to Little Rock runs through Dallas. Lowry's train originated in New Orleans, hundreds of miles out of the way for a trip from El Paso to Little Rock. The men who captured Lowry arrived in six cars half an hour before the train arrived and made no secret of their intentions at the station. There could be only one explanation for this sequence of events: the deputies had wired ahead to Memphis in collusion with the lynchers.[7]

Nodena formed part of Memphis's cotton hinterland. Memphis was the largest inland cotton port in the world, and the city's prosperity depended in large part on the stability of its agricultural commerce. Memphis was 40 percent Negro in 1920, and Republican boss Edward Hull Crump relied on Negro votes. In the next few years, the *Memphis Commercial Appeal* would wage a relentless campaign against the Ku Klux Klan that would win it a Pulitzer Prize.[8]

The lynching party felt so righteous that they telegrammed a Memphis newspaper that they planned to parade their captive down the main street of the city before killing him. This might have embarrassed local authorities, however, and the plan was abandoned. The *Memphis News-Scimitar* announced in a banner headline: "NEGRO TO PAY MOB'S PENALTY FOR CRIME / AVENGERS SET SIX O'CLOCK AS LYNCHING HOUR." Ralph Roddy, a reporter for the *Memphis Press*, was there and recorded the scene in all its grisly detail. Lowry apparently met his end with incredible courage and held his tongue so as to shield his family from his agony.

Johnson wrote one of his most impassioned columns in the aftermath. "In the whole history of lynching in the United States, there is not a more revolting chapter than the one written last week in the state of Arkansas." He quoted extensively from the Memphis report so his readers could imagine the depravity of the affair. Governor McCrae had wired the local county sheriff and would have sent the National Guard to stop it, but the sheriff never answered the wire, explaining that everyone in the county approved of what had been done. "It is sickening," Johnson concluded. "It is maddening. It is sufficient to make Negro citizens of this country hysterical, either with the quakings of fear or the desires of vengeance." And if America allowed this to continue, Johnson predicted, the country would go straight to hell and damnation.[9]

The Lowry case would later become the NAACP's poster atrocity that showed why the United States needed federal antilynching legislation. The Association published a pamphlet titled *An American Lynching*, and circulated it internationally. They placed the Lowry pamphlet on the desk of every U.S. congressman, but none of them spoke out. The *New York World*, the *Buffalo Express*, and the *El Paso Times* all condemned the lynchers, but there was no sustained outcry. Lowry was typical in that he was an honest tenant farmer, and most cases of lynching derived from exactly this sort of confrontation between a tenant and a landlord. Also, Lowry's crime was committed in self-defense, and had the racial roles been reversed in the shooting, a white man would never have been prosecuted. Further, some of the Memphis newspapers had whipped up blood lust to sell newspapers, another common feature of lynchings. Most important, the Lowry affair demonstrated the common collusion between local officials with lynchers. Governor McCrae had acted in good faith with the El Paso NAACPers who advised Lowry. Later he condemned the crime vigorously, and the NAACP praised him for it. Yet, the sheriff foiled him, and no one was prosecuted for a lynching that had been advertised in advance.[10]

William Pickens titled his article "The American Congo—Burning of Henry Lowry." For the Yale-educated Pickens, this was truly a journey back to an evil Conradian heart of whiteness, where Christian morality served as a thin cover for pagan blood sacrifice. In the Ell Persons lynching four years earlier, the victim's head was displayed in Memphis, like the skulls surrounding Kurtz's villa in Conrad's *Heart of Darkness.* Pickens rallied the black community and spoke to a thousand people at a meeting arranged by Robert Church Jr. But in the hinterland, he reported, black people were terrified: one man he questioned jumped up and ran away when Pickens raised the subject. Those people still worked for landlords like O. T. Craig, and for them the horror was real.[11]

SIX WEEKS AFTER the burning of Henry Lowry, a white boy in Newton County, Georgia, was playing on the banks of the Yellow River when he observed a human foot in the water. He ran for help, and by the end of the day, county officials had dragged two Negro bodies from the river. Ten days later the *Atlanta Constitution* reported the chilling result of an investigation into what the coroner ruled as murder. John S. Williams, a plantation owner in neighboring Jasper County, and his Negro straw boss, Clyde Manning, were arrested and charged with killing eleven workers held as debtors on the Williams farm.[12]

Rural Jasper County lay about forty miles southeast of Atlanta in flat cotton country. Williams, a tall, physically imposing figure with a bristling mustache and piercing eyes, owned two thousand acres there. He was fifty-four years old, the father of twelve children. Three sons owned farms nearby, another was a doctor, and a cousin was a county official. During the World War, four sons served in the army. Cotton prices were high and labor costs dear. Williams, like many other farmers in the region, added to his workforce by bailing out Negro convicts from prisons in Macon or Atlanta. He brought them back to his farm, locked them up in a bunkhouse at night, and armed several trusted Negro overseers like Manning with pistols. Legally, his convict laborers were bound to him until they worked off their bail, but these terms were never committed to paper. Once they arrived on the Williams farm, the law stopped. To enforce the work pace, Williams or his sons would whip them.

Probably as early as 1911, Williams committed his first murders, shooting three workers for arbitrary reasons. When his sons returned from the war, the killing began again. In early 1920, the three Williams sons killed a total of four rebellious prisoners. In one case, a man who had been whipped said he'd as soon be dead as treated like that, and one of the Williams men shot him on the spot. Inevitably, some of the convicts tried to run away. Those who were caught suffered hellacious beatings, but on Thanksgiving Day 1920, prisoners escaped from the farm and reported their experiences to federal authorities.[13]

In mid-January 1921, the United States attorney's office for the northern district of Georgia announced that it would file suits against three white farmers of Heard and Troup Counties for holding men against their will as peons. What initiated this proceeding is not entirely clear, but on October 2, 1920, Walter White had met with two officials of the Justice Department and lay before them the results of his own research on the peonage conditions in Arkansas that prompted the conflict there. The two officials promised to look into the matter. Some combination of the reports by the escaped workers, White's allegations, and perhaps the Republican victory in November caused U.S. District Attorney Hooper Alexander to launch a statewide investigation into forced labor conditions in rural Georgia.[14]

A month later, two federal agents arrived at the Williams farm to inquire about Gus Chapman, one of the runaways from the previous fall. There they found Manning, who denied any knowledge of Chapman. However, when John Williams returned to the farm, he freely admitted to the agents that he had once caught Chapman attempting to run away. Chapman had told the agents that Williams severely whipped him, and Williams must have known that. Williams inquired if he had broken any laws, and one agent replied that if he "worked the nigger against his will," he would be guilty of peonage. Manning later testified that Williams told him, after the agents left: "Clyde, we have got to do away with these Negroes, or they are going up to Atlanta and break me and my boys's necks."[15]

Sometime after that, he ordered Manning to kill one convict laborer with an ax, and when Manning seemed reluctant, Williams demanded the ax himself. Manning believed that his boss would use it to kill him, and so he did as he was ordered. Next two men were seized, bound, and thrown off a bridge into the Alcovy River. Three more were killed with an ax. Along with a second trustee, Manning and Williams overpowered three more convict laborers, placed them in chains, and drove them to the Allen

Bridge over the Yellow River. The two overseers threw two of them off as they begged for their lives and the third victim watched in terror. They drove him to another bridge, and knowing his fate, he pleaded only to be allowed to jump. "Lord have mercy," he said, and plunged to his death. In all, eleven men were killed in the 1921 murder spree. The bodies found in Newton County near the Allen Bridge were those of Lindsey Peterson and Will Preston. Their identities probably led the law to the Williams farm, and on March 24 Manning confessed to Newton County investigators. Then he led them to the buried bodies, with newsmen tagging along. For the next three weeks, the story dominated the front page of the *Atlanta Constitution* and made headlines all over the United States.[16]

Williams remained impassive in the face of these developments. He assured reporters that he knew nothing about the murders, which he attributed to a frame-up perpetrated by hostile neighbors. Manning, he declared, was lying. Williams did not have to say it, but everyone knew that when the word of a white man was set only against the word of a black man, a Georgia jury would not need much time to make up its mind. In fact, Williams was the first white man in the South to be indicted for first degree murder of a black man since 1877, the last year of Reconstruction. His arrest was extraordinary, but the pattern of southern jurisprudence weighed heavily in Williams's favor, and he knew it.

To expedite the prosecution and help resolve jurisdictional problems between neighboring counties, Governor Hugh M. Dorsey assigned two special prosecutors to the case. Although Williams and Manning were indicted together, they were tried separately. Newton County tried Williams first for the murder of Lindsey Peterson, one of the men thrown off the Allen Bridge. Before the trial began, a Jasper County grand jury heard evidence regarding some of the other murders. Survivors of the Williams farm testified, and prosecutors leaked their testimony of brutal beatings. In reply, Dr. Gus Williams, a nonimplicated son of the patriarch, told the press that the criminal employees incurred their wounds before arriving in Jasper County.

The "murder farm" trial, as the newspapers dubbed it, opened at Covington in Newton County on April 5 before Judge John B. Hutcheson. Williams must have taken heart as a jury of seven farmers and five merchants was impaneled. The courtroom was tightly packed with reporters and spectators. The two federal agents testified about the conditions they found on the Williams farm, but on cross-examination they admitted that the Justice Department had not yet brought peonage charges against the Williamses. Then Clyde Manning, "soot black" and "impassive" according to Rowland Thomas in the *New York World*, took the stand. He testified for six hours during which one "could not hear a breath" drawn in the tense atmosphere. Manning told his story in a direct, unemotional tone of voice, his hands folded before him and his feet still, his eyes staring ahead. He told how Lindsey Peterson and Willie Preston were "tied together by the necks and hands with a trace chain and some wire and a sack of rocks that weighed maybe a hundred pounds. . . . On the bridge Mr. Johnny stopped the car and said 'Get out boys.' " Turning to Manning, Williams said, "It's their neck or yours."[17]

Earlier Manning had confessed his motive to reporters. "Why did I do it? Because the boss said . . . that if I didn't make 'em disappear, he'd kill me. And I knew he meant what he said." Manning was twenty-nine years old, illiterate, and unaware of his birthplace. "When I first remember myself I was in Jasper County," he testified, and said that he often wanted to run away but had never left the farm and wouldn't know where to go. The defense objected to testimony by Manning about the other murders, but the prosecutors pointed out that in the Leo Frank case, the judge had admitted collateral testimony. Manning then recounted the whole story, including one case in which a victim was struck with an ax and buried without ascertaining if he was dead.[18]

The next day a confident Williams took the stand in his own defense. He explained that after the federal agents came, he "told any niggers who wanted to leave that they could go, even if they owed me money." He even paid the three men found in the Yellow River five dollars each and told Manning to take them to the train station. Two weeks later, Williams said, "I heard from an old nigger that the three niggers had turned up dead." The implication was that Manning had robbed and killed them. Williams was the only witness for the defense. The only direct testimony against him had come from an illiterate black farmhand. The jury stayed out for nine hours, which indicated a serious debate in a case that might have been thrown out in minutes. The next day Williams faced his jurors. A photograph showed him standing erect, sporting a colorful tie but looking with grim visage out of the corner of his eyes with, the *Constitution* reported in hindsight, "a glance that bore defiance to the words he knew would make him a striped felon for the rest of his days." The jury found him guilty but recommended mercy. Eight had wanted hanging and four acquittal, and this was their compromise. He was sentenced to life in prison. No southern white man would meet the same fate for killing a black man until 1966.[19]

The NAACP office in New York was electrified by the "murder farm" news story. Since the autumn of 1919, they had been working diligently behind the scenes to defend the twelve Arkansas sharecroppers condemned to death. Hoping to win the support of white progressives, they had painted that case as an economic struggle rooted in the oppressive labor conditions of the rural South. The Lowry story shared the same features, but because in both those affairs there were dead white people, all that whites could see were the white corpses. Here was a case that derived from the same conditions but did not have that distraction. Williams held captive labor, ran his farm like a prison camp, and had committed mass murder. The NAACP hoped to use the Williams case to illuminate the wider problem of peonage in the South.

Peonage was hard to define. In the 1920s, it was a dirty secret about which no one spoke. Pete Daniel, in his careful study *The Shadow of Slavery: Peonage in the South 1901–1969*, showed it as an outgrowth of the antebellum slave system. Sharecroppers were advanced food, farm supplies, and fertilizer against a portion of the harvest. Theoretically, the sharecropper would show a profit at harvest time and could use his payment to purchase land. In some cases, this was the way the system worked. But a sharecropper could easily turn into a debt peon if a cheating landlord refused to give the farmer an account of what had been advanced to him, or paid far below market price on the cotton. Without recourse to the courts, cowed by the overwhelming political and physical weight of white authority, the sharecropper slipped into debt peonage. He became little more than a slave, except that he did not work in a gang driven by an overseer. Others found themselves working as forced laborers like the convicts on the Williams farm. Extensive southern laws against vagrancy could land any law-abiding black male into such a situation. One of the runaways from the Williams farm had been arrested for sitting down at the Macon station. Still others were leased out of jail on road or construction projects or as farm laborers. Some states, such as Georgia, had had a convict-lease system but abolished it for the bailout system under which Williams and his neighbors in Jasper County operated.[20]

How widespread was peonage in the South? Daniel concluded, "Because peonage was frequently isolated in the backcountry, no clear estimate of its extent is possible." He cited a Justice Department investigator who in 1907 calculated that one-third of all medium and large farms in Georgia, Alabama, and Mississippi held workers against their will. Daniel's study is replete with cases suggesting the large scale of the practice, and he shows how illiteracy, corrupt law enforcement, white economic interest, and racism combined to create a "vortex of peonage" that probably left most of it unreported. In its national press releases, the NAACP insisted that the practice was general throughout the South, but federal investigators usually said there were only pockets of it.[21]

The issue of peonage was particularly attractive to the NAACP for a variety of reasons. The Association understood that it affected hundreds of thousands of African Americans, and that it contributed mightily to the ignorance, poverty, and violence to which its victims were condemned. Most important, peonage was prohibited by federal law, and authorities had occasionally enforced it. This was true of no other form of racial oppression. During Reconstruction, the United States prohibited peonage in the territory of New Mexico. To accomplish this, Congress had to write federal statutes. The relevant sections of the federal code would punish its practitioners with up to five years in jail, a five thousand dollar fine, or both. The Supreme Court upheld these laws in a 1905 case called *Clyatt v. United States.* Attorney General William H. Moody himself argued the case before the court. The problem, of course, was that Justice Department enforcement of the law was rare. Federal attorneys are appointed on the recommendation of local politicians, who were interested in keeping the issue forgotten.[22]

James Weldon Johnson dispatched a series of telegrams designed to sound an alarm. He wired President Harding, Attorney General Harry M. Daugherty, and Governor Dorsey, insisting that the Williams case was "not an isolated one but is indicative of similar conditions." He wrote to twelve African-American state legislators in nine states, urging them to introduce resolutions calling for a full federal investigation of peonage and prosecution of violators. The Ohio legislature passed the resolution, and it was introduced in several other states. Johnson wrote to ten labor leaders, seeking similar resolutions from labor councils or federations. The Pennsylvania state chairman assured Johnson that his state convention would condemn "this worse than chattel form of slavery." They sent a circular letter to northern branches, encouraging them to hold protest meetings: "[T]he big thing to be accomplished is to arouse public sentiment," the letter declared. Buffalo and Washington, D.C., held such meetings. They furnished information to editorial writers, issued press releases every few days, and sent Press Secretary Herbert J. Seligmann to Atlanta. Johnson even met with Governor Dorsey when he visited New York in April.[23]

The success of this campaign was limited. There was a national hue and cry against the murderer Williams but a subdued reaction against peonage itself. The drama of the murders and trial "rivals a Bluebeard romance" the *Atlanta Constitution* noted, and naturally that story overwhelmed consideration of the underlying social problem. The southern press registered its revulsion at the murders just as unequivocally as the northern press. "Georgia Peonage Horror Rivals Turk Atrocities" read a headline in the *Knoxville Sentinel* even before the verdict was in. Other southern papers agreed. None of the papers suggested that Williams might be innocent. On the other hand, they generally presented Williams as an isolated case and his punishment a sign of the region's rectitude. Few if any southern papers addressed the framework in which his crime gestated.[24]

The northern papers ran large articles and expressed shock at the story. The *New York Times* called attention to the peonage issue, which "dies hard because the community is not horrified enough to make an end of such atrocious practices." A second editorial cited an NAACP press release, and the *Times* backed its demand for a full investigation. The *Chicago Herald and Examiner* ran illustrations of a booted Williams, outfitted like an African explorer, beating his farmhands. A *Buffalo Express* editorial compared Williams to Simon Legree, the evil slave driver of the novel *Uncle Tom's Cabin*, and the *Hartford Courant* praised Georgia for convicting Williams.[25]

Within Georgia, editorials sounded two interrelated themes: Williams was guilty, and the northern press should not throw stones. The NAACP collected not one editorial alleging that Williams was innocent and Manning guilty, as might be expected. The *Atlanta Constitution* ran one article taking up the connection between the murders and the penal labor problem. The *Zebulon Journal* and the *Sylvania Telephone* made this connection as well. The *Constitution* noted editorially the charge to the grand jury by Judge James B. Park, who observed that "unless the spirit of lawlessness is checked by our courts . . . we will be shunned by the best class of people, and capital will refuse to come among us to develop our natural, our agricultural, manufacturing and commercial enterprises." The *Atlanta Journal* deplored the crimes, as did the *Macon Telegraph*. Even before the trial, the *Telegraph* insisted that Manning must be telling the truth because in the South, white planters knew what was happening on their farms.

Some Georgia editorialists bristled at northern condemnation of southern affairs. The *Macon Telegraph* attacked the NAACP for sending its message to Governor Dorsey, writing that the northern-based Association "has virtually outlawed itself in the South." The *Savannah News* deplored the crime but also regretted that northern reformers felt "that they are better qualified to look after the welfare of the Negro in the South than is the white man of the South, who knows him best." The *Dublin Herald* wrote that there were more murders in the North every day, as did the *Searchlight*, the Atlanta-based newspaper of the Ku Klux Klan.[26]

If the Georgia press showed ambivalent feelings regarding the exposure of the Williams murders, Atlanta NAACP leaders felt vindicated. They had been grappling with the peonage problem for some time. In June they reported to the NAACP national convention in Detroit that they had established an underground railroad "for the benefit of people fleeing from the cruelty and oppression of rural communities." They had almost one thousand active members and thirty-five hundred total members, and they raised $1,493 in June to help defend and resettle escaped peons. Crawford Landers of Tennille ran away after being beaten by his boss. He hid in the swamps for three days before reaching Atlanta. Addison Fuller of McDuffie County told his story to Herbert J. Seligmann, the Association's publicity man, and it was published in the *Nation* magazine. Fuller also submitted an affidavit to the United States attorney that his debt was "entirely fictitious" and that he had been whipped while two men held him down. "In at least a dozen other cases, the Association has taken charge of whole families, provided homes for them and sustained them until work could be secured," the Atlanta branch reported.[27]

Immediately after the Williams trial, Governor Hugh M. Dorsey threw a bombshell into the state's political life. He issued a report, prepared with the help of the Commission on Interracial Cooperation, that documented 135 cases of lynching and peonage in Georgia's recent past. The commission reflected liberal, religiously based sentiment that lynching had to be stopped, although it kept more divisive issues such as voting rights and segregation off its agenda. Dorsey's pamphlet, *The Negro in Georgia*, pulled no punches. "In some counties the negro is being driven out as though he were a wild beast, in others he is being held a slave, in others no negroes remain," Dorsey declared. He backed this indictment with the stories of these depredations, keeping the locales anonymous. The pamphlet concluded with two sets of proposals. In civic life, he urged that Georgians admit and confront their problems. Sunday schools should teach mercy and justice; education should be mandatory for both races; and committees on race relations should meet separately by race and, when necessary, together. He urged the state to strengthen the governor's hand to act against lynching: a state constabulary should be established; counties that allowed a lynching should be fined; the governor should be empowered to appoint investigative boards and special grand juries. The Dorsey pamphlet, James Weldon Johnson wrote, "constitutes one of the strongest indictments of the South for injustice, cruelty and brutality against the Negro ever yet made." The Association reprinted it.[28]

The Williams case helped put the drivers of convict labor on their guard in the short term. The U.S. attorney's office did prosecute some holders of peons, and lynching declined in the state during the 1920s, but both these practices continued up until the time of the modern civil rights movement. Clyde Manning was tried twice for his crimes, was sentenced to life on the chain gang, and died in prison. Williams's three sons later turned themselves in but were never tried for their crimes and lived out their lives as gas station owners in Florida. Ironically, John Williams was made a "trustee" in prison, just as Clyde Manning had been for him. One day there was a prison break, and John Williams died a violent death trying to stop it.[29]

THE ONLY integrated public conveyance in Jim Crow America was the elevator. They were just too expensive to build and the ride too short to bother with. For a brief few moments then, black and white Americans, male and female, might be sequestered alone together in a public space.

On May 30, 1921, a nineteen-year-old African-American bootblack in Tulsa, Oklahoma, entered the Drexel Building on Main Street to use the bathroom on the fourth floor. Some jostling of the machine caused Dick Rowland, by all accounts a responsible and polite young man, to step on the foot of the elevator operator, a seventeen-year-old white woman named Sarah Page. She stumbled against him, and he reached out to keep her from falling. Sarah Page believed she was being attacked and ran screaming from the elevator. The next day the *Tulsa Tribune* reported that Rowland had been arrested for assaulting her.[30]

The word *assault* had two meanings in the 1920s, and readers determined which was appropriate by the context in which it was used. If two men were brawling, an "assault" meant a punch. But if a man "assaulted" a woman, it meant he raped her. Newspapers did not print the word *rape* in the 1920s.

Tulsa, Oklahoma, in 1921 was a boomtown, capital of the country's oil industry. Indian territory, home to the Five Civilized Nations driven from the Southeast, did not become a state until 1907. Blacks and Indians lived easily together and coexisted with white settlers. In 1910, only eighteen thousand people lived around Tulsa. With the oil boom, whites and blacks poured in, the whites driving Indians off valuable land. By 1921, between seventy-two thousand and ninety thousand people lived there. About eleven thousand African Americans inhabited the Greenwood District in the northeast part of the city. Greenwood shared the prosperity of the city as a whole. Black inhabitants built a thriving commercial district, homes, church buildings, two schools, theaters, restaurants, and a library. Whites located the vice district nearby, as they did in most American cities. Mainly, Greenwood was home to hardworking service sector employees. It was also home to some rich African Americans—real estate dealers and a professional class that boasted Dr. A. C. Jackson, among the leading black surgeons in the country.[31]

Tulsa's rapid growth brought with it a host of social tensions that were settled by vigilantism. The radical Industrial Workers of the World (IWW) set out to organize the oil field workers in 1917. When the home of an oil baron was bombed, the police arrested twelve IWWs and charged them with vagrancy. The *Tulsa World* ran an editorial titled "Get Out the Hemp," inviting Tulsans to lynch the prisoners. A posse of hooded men captured the Wobblies in transit, then whipped them and poured hot tar on their wounds. Two years later, three black men were charged with shooting a white. Black Tulsans did not want a repeat of the IWW affair; two hundred of them showed up outside the prison to make sure there was no lynching, and there wasn't. The next year a white man accused of killing a cabdriver was hanged by a mob. Fifty masked men broke into the courthouse and lynched Roy Belton before a crowd of thousands. The police helped direct traffic at the scene. Dick Rowland, the bootblack, was now held in the same courthouse jail in which Belton had been imprisoned.[32]

Although no edition of the *Tulsa Tribune* for May 31 survives, black Tulsans remember its headline reading "To Lynch Negro Tonight." In the Greenwood District, men vowed that this would not happen. Hundreds of them were war veterans, and many of them had guns. Meanwhile, a rumor spread that the whites were already gathering near the jail. A few black men were on the Tulsa police force, and by telephone they volunteered the services of black defenders to help guard the prison. Apparently the sheriff gave conflicting answers to different callers, and so twenty-five men headed downtown. A mob of four hundred whites was there, but they were not attacking. The sheriff had disabled the jail elevator and had stationed a heavily armed guard at the top of the stairs where Rowland was kept. The black men returned to Greenwood to report. Then a second rumor began to circulate, and this time fifty to seventy-five black men returned. The crowd had now grown to fifteen hundred or two thousand. When a white man tried to disarm one of the blacks, a gunfight broke out, and perhaps ten whites and two African Americans were killed in this initial exchange. Outnumbered, they retreated to Greenwood.[33]

The Tulsa police responded by deputizing and arming white men. Meanwhile, Oklahoma officials lost valuable hours before mobilizing the National Guard. The whites looted gun shops, and at daybreak the mob surged into the Greenwood District, firing from automobiles into the commercial area, looting, burning, and killing. Blacks shot back, but the white numbers were overwhelming. During the battle, police and deputies rounded up thousands of African Americans and herded them into internment centers at the ballpark, fairgrounds, and convention center. Black people were marched through the streets, hands held up, under the watch-

Tulsa, Oklahoma, June 1920. Courtesy of Library of Congress.

ful eyes of rifle-toting whites. The rioters put Greenwood to the torch, burning churches, lodge buildings, and everything in their path. Photographers captured scenes of whites emerging from handsome frame houses with booty, and then burning the homes. An elderly couple was murdered in their home, and Dr. Jackson was gunned down in cold blood. Airplanes buzzed overhead, and some black Tulsans believed they bombed the neighborhood.

The nightmare ended when there was almost nothing left to destroy. Property damage was over $1.5 million. Walter White estimated that 50 whites and perhaps 150 to 200 black people were killed. Scott Ellsworth, author of a 1982 book on the riot, estimated that 75 died. Thousands lost their homes and everything they owned, and had to spend the winter of 1921–1922 in Red Cross tents. Forty-four blocks were razed. In terms of total destruction, Tulsa, the last of the World War I–era race riots that had begun in East St. Louis, Illinois, in 1917, was the worst.[34]

One of the victims was Buck Colbert Franklin, a lawyer who had moved to Tulsa in February. Franklin had tried to cool passions before the fighting broke out and by his own account foiled a plan to set preemptive fires in the white neighborhoods. Like thousands of others, Franklin was arrested and placed in detention. He returned to find his office "in ashes. . . . As far as one could see, not a Negro dwelling-house or place of business stood."[35]

Greenwood found a way to rebuild. Tulsa assigned an emergency committee headed by a former mayor, who frankly expressed the shame felt by many of the city's "best citizens," a term that usually meant its ruling class. "Tulsa weeps at this unspeakable crime and will make good the damage . . . to the last penny," he pledged. Most aid from whites flowed through the Red Cross, which provided tent shelters, food, and medical care in the emergency. Yet, white-led relief groups turned away several outside offers of financial support, claiming that Tulsa could handle the problem itself. The black community established its own relief fund, and NAACP branches contributed about two thousand dollars. As Scott Ellsworth concluded, black Tulsans rebuilt Greenwood through their own self-sacrifice.[36]

However, before Greenwood could be resurrected, Tulsa African Americans had to reverse a nefarious attempt by Tulsa's "best" white citizens to take over their land. Greenwood lay close enough to the downtown area that some city fathers coveted the district as the site of a new railroad station and industrial area. The city commission passed a fire ordinance one week after the riot, mandating a financially prohibitive building code that would force property owners to sell rather than rebuild. Buck Colbert Franklin and his law partners challenged this ordinance while working out of a tent. The court voided it, and over the next decade, Greenwood rose like a phoenix from the ashes.[37]

Although a grand jury returned indictments in twenty-seven riot-related cases, only one person, a black man, ever went to jail. The police chief was suspended and found guilty of two crimes but did not serve time. White Tulsa burned black Tulsa to the ground and suffered no legal penalty. And, of course, the whole episode had been about nothing. Sarah Page dropped her charges against Dick Rowland.[38]

"There is a lesson in the Tulsa affair for every American who fatuously believes that Negroes will always be the meek and submissive creatures that circumstances have forced them to be during the past three hundred years," Walter White concluded in an article for the *Nation*. "Dick Rowland was only an ordinary bootblack with no standing in the community. But when his life was threatened by a mob of whites, every one of the 15,000 Negroes in Tulsa . . . was willing to die to protect Dick Rowland. Perhaps America is waiting for a nationwide Tulsa to wake her. Who knows?" Black

Tulsa paid the highest price for its courage, but this battle marked a turning point. From now on, white mobs could invade the black section of an American city only at their peril.[39]

Five years later W. E. B. Du Bois came to Tulsa to address a meeting of eight hundred African-American teachers. He was deeply moved by Tulsa's resurrection, and in the *Crisis* he noted that the reconstruction had been accomplished despite the insurance companies' failure to compensate their policyholders. In the crowd was an eleven year-old boy, who stared up at the speaker with wonder. "He was wearing a full dress suit with a sash across it, and medals he had gotten from Liberia. I had never seen a black man looking like that," the son of lawyer Buck Colbert Franklin remembered seventy years later. Perhaps that event was a turning point for John Hope Franklin, who would grow up to become the leading historian of African America in the twentieth century.[40]

11

The Prophet of Pan-Africa

THE cover photo of the November 1921 *Crisis* magazine depicted a Sphinx-like, veiled Egyptian statue—a reposed figure of Africa, typifying Science. Situated in the Palais Mondial of Brussels, the monument bore this inscription: "I am the one that was, that is, and that shall be. No mortal may unveil my face." To a certain extent, this somber representation suggested the complicated person of the magazine's editor. Dr. W. E. B. Du Bois had just returned from the Pan-African Congress held in London, Brussels, and Paris, which he himself had organized. The statue must have struck a chord within him. For Du Bois, too, was a man of Africa and a man of science; like the statue his roots were in the Dark Continent but his location fixed in Western civilization; and like the eyes of the mythical figure, his own gazed straight ahead and far off into the future. As an essayist he had crafted a compelling literary image of his people, rich in spirit and wisdom but hidden behind a veil, unknowable to westerners who projected upon it images of their own making.

Du Bois, as the architect of the Pan-African Congress, editor of the *Crisis*, and one of the most brilliant and prolific American writers of his day, at age fifty-three stood at the peak of a long and distinguished career. The Second Pan-African Congress registered a significant, if limited, achievement. After two years of organizing, Du Bois brought together over one hundred delegates from twenty-five nations for two weeks of meetings. Representing much of the African diaspora, they learned about each other's diverse cultures and pondered their common problems. Their meetings attracted considerable notice in the European press, and at the end, they laid their concerns before the League of Nations in a formal presentation. While the Pan-African Congress achieved no immediate result, it adopted a document written by Du Bois that helped lay the intellectual groundwork for the liberation of Africa after the Second World War.

For the American delegates, the congress was a powerful personal experience that broadened each participant's world view. Yet, these internationally minded leaders remained unheralded prophets in their own land. Most African-American newspapers ignored it, except to distinguish its proceedings from those of the Marcus Garvey movement. Unlike his rival, whose acolytes elected him "Provisional President of Africa," Du Bois tried to build genuine cooperation among the intelligentsia of diaspora peoples. Some writers have labeled him an elitist for his concentration on a "Talented Tenth" of educated people, but this accusation overstates the case.[1] Du Bois did have elitist tendencies, but he was no egotist hogging a spotlight, and he knew the need for organization and teamwork to get a political job done. His effort to bring together leaders from Africa and its diaspora transcended the goals of the NAACP, showed his own abilities as a leader, and presaged such movements as the international antiapartheid campaigns of the late twentieth century.

BLACK AMERICA was neither enthusiastic about nor opposed to the Pan-African Congress. The experience of the Garvey movement informs this point: with all his rhetoric about going "Back to Africa," almost no African Americans even visited there. Black Americans had neither the means nor the inclination to do so, even if many were curious about Africa and resented its colonial status. NAACPers were most of all concerned about race relations in their own city. Du Bois's visionary project would have to appeal to the hard-pressed domestics, mailmen, Pullman porters, and schoolteachers who made up the NAACP rank and file.

Shortly before the November 1920 board meeting, he circulated a memo to the members, seeking their input regarding the two tasks he began in 1919—compiling the history of Negro troops during the war and organizing the Pan-African Congress. While he was in France during 1919, Du Bois reminded the board, they had voted that the *Crisis* should fund half of the first project itself, a burden that the editor felt was "unfair." On the second matter, he wrote, "The question is now how far the Board wishes to go in promoting the Second Congress." Although the *Crisis* could not contribute to it, the Association should, Du Bois argued. "The time is propitious. The Negroes of the world are aroused and thinking and acting as never before. No local Negro problem like ours or Haiti . . . can be solved without reference to Africa." Du Bois estimated that organizing costs would run only from one thousand to two thousand dollars until August, and after the congress a self-sustaining international organization would be set up. Most of the board members who responded showed lukewarm support for this appeal, and some called attention to other pressing financial tasks, but no one opposed it.[2]

Ten points were on the agenda at the November meeting, including the decision to hire James Weldon Johnson as the permanent secretary. Du Bois's report was heard after others on the Arkansas case, the membership drive, and new nominations to the board. After some discussion, the board agreed to meet the expenses of the conference even though no budget was prepared, and it assigned a four-person committee to oversee the project. Ultimately, Du Bois would do all the preparatory work. Next month the board agreed to fund three thousand dollars of the conference expenses. In short, the conference was entirely underwritten by the NAACP, even though many different organizations attended.[3]

How exactly the money would be raised remained an open question. Du Bois worked steadily through the spring, corresponding with diaspora leaders, American government officials, and prospective American delegates. Meanwhile the Association expended its money on the understanding that it would be refunded by special appeal. In March, Du Bois and Blaise Diagne of Senegal, respectively secretary and president of the congress, announced the representation formula for organizations: one delegate for groups with under one thousand members, two delegates for groups under five thousand members, and so forth. They proposed a modest ten-dollar per delegate contribution from attending organizations. London, Brussels, and Paris, capitals of three leading colonial powers, would be the conference sites. In April the Association reported that twenty-five nations would send representatives, and it released a list of American delegates. Yet, as late as July, Du Bois had spent twenty-six hundred dollars, and the Association had not raised any money to cover the expenditures. That month the board voted to raise the money by appeals to branches and individuals. It further resolved that while proud of its leading role, in the future the Association would "not assume sole financial responsibility" for the congress.[4]

Early in August, Du Bois, Walter White, and Jessie Fauset, literary editor of the *Crisis*, sailed for Plymouth, England, over a smooth sea. White debarked at port while Du Bois and Fauset continued on to France to make arrangements for the Paris meeting. For the next few weeks, White conferred with English liberals and Labor Party representatives for the purpose of establishing an English antilynching committee. Du Bois and Fauset returned to London, and on August 25, the Second Pan-African Congress opened in Central Hall of Westminster Abbey. Fauset chronicled the events of the next two weeks in articles for the *Crisis*.[5]

Opening day was tremendously exciting. Just the sight of each other entering the hall, dressed in distinctive national garb and conversing in various languages, fired the delegates with a sense of possibility. From Af-

rica came Nigerians, Gold Coasters, Sierra Leoneans, and South Africans.
There were Afro-Caribbeans from several countries, African expatriates
resident in Europe, and most of all, Americans. Du Bois had gathered thirty
of them from fraternal orders, church groups, the YMCA, and teachers'
federations. White, Du Bois, and board members Florence Kelley and Arthur Spingarn represented the NAACP, while Fauset attended on behalf of
Delta Sigma, a college honors sorority.

The delegates listened attentively to the Africans especially, getting a
sense of how complicated the continent was and how different the problems were from one region to another. The Nigerian delegate urged that
the black diaspora should help finance projects in Liberia, the only free
West African country. East African delegates discussed the intricacies of
native and East Indian–immigrant relations in their countries.

At the conclusion of the meeting, Du Bois read out a noble manifesto
entitled "To the World," putting forward a gradualist program of emancipation from colonialism in reasonable but ringing tones. This far-seeing
document asserted first principles that profoundly challenged the intellectual framework of Western imperialism. The manifesto was to Pan-African
ideology what the founding documents of Western democracy were to En-
lightenment thought: a synthesis of vanguard thinking stated in elegant
prose. "The absolute equality of races—physical, political and social—is
the founding stone of world peace and human advancement," Du Bois
began. He thereby rendered explicit Jefferson's opening line in the Declaration of Independence, whose "all men are created equal" was meant by
the American founders to include only whites.

Du Bois attacked the "dishonorable propaganda" that postulated permanent white supremacy in biological terms. He demanded local autonomy for non-Western colonies. In forceful language, the manifesto
denounced the commercial rapacity with which Europe conscripted colored labor to work its African mines, mills, and ports, "enslaving labor . . .
so that the favored Few may luxuriate in the toil of the tortured Many."
White labor, whose parliamentary representatives supported the whole
scheme, acted in "*particeps criminis* with white capital" in this evil
scheme, while the Western intelligentsia pretended not to notice. Then the
document appraised the records of the colonial nations country by country, condemning the greed and hypocrisy that characterized the imperial
mind-set. The manifesto concluded with eight general programmatic
points that called for racial uplift and pointed toward self-determination.
Perhaps most controversial was point six, calling for "[t]he ancient common ownership of the land and its natural fruits and defense against the
unrestrained greed of invested capital." Points seven and eight asked the

League of Nations to consider these aspirations through organized commissions. It concluded:

> To our aid we call all men of the Earth who love Justice and Mercy. Out of the depths we have cried unto the deaf and dumb masters of the world. Out of the depths we cry to our own sleeping souls.
>
> The answer is written in the stars.[6]

A second group assembled for the next sessions at Brussels, as some delegates departed and representatives of the Belgian Congo, Abyssinia, Senegal, and others arrived. Belgium was in the contradictory position of being at once the formerly invaded victim of German militarism in the World War and the most brutal of European colonists in Africa. Hundreds of suspicious whites packed the galleries at the Palais Mondial in Cinquantenaire Park, creating a hostile atmosphere for the delegates. Tiny Belgium owed much of its wealth to the Congo. It displayed its African trophies at a Congo museum whose treasures showed how much mineral and artistic booty the Low Country had extracted from Africa. On the program, colonial officials put the best possible face on Belgium's atrocious colonial record.[7]

In this effort they were joined by Mfume Paul Panda, the nephew of an African chief who collaborated with Belgium. A colonial official had brought the five-year-old Panda with him to Belgium, where he was lovingly raised by the official's sister. Panda was sent to university, later visited the Congo, and became the leader of Belgium's African community. Loyal to the imperial project, he favored administrative reform and colonial education, but could not imagine struggle against the regime from below. The Pan-African Congress found him uncomfortably caught in the cross fire between Du Boisian radicals and colonial bosses.[8]

"We sensed the Fear about us," Du Bois later wrote. When he read aloud the challenging anticolonial London resolutions, a wave of "consternation" swept the hall, Du Bois thought. Panda registered the dismay of the white Belgians, and the radical Americans let him put through a moderate resolution in its place. The Americans wisely prevented a split in the movement by this tactical retreat. The resolutions had little effect in the real world anyway, and the point was to keep talking and build unity. "But we left Belgium in a thoughtful and puzzled mood," Fauset remembered.[9]

The Paris sessions reflected the balance of forces between the radical and moderate representatives. Here the audience was almost entirely black, and the atmosphere of republican France felt refreshing after monarchical Belgium, Fauset observed. Again, the Francophone delegates (with the exception of the Haitian Dantes Bellegarde, who worked with the American NAACP) sang the praises of French civilization. The Americans reiterated their positions but did not force a showdown.

At Paris, Blaise Diagne played the same role as Panda did in Belgium. Born to a poor Senegalese family in 1872, Diagne became a customs official and later was elected to the Chamber of Deputies. During France's moment of crisis in the World War, Diagne raised hundreds of thousands of African troops to fight against Germany. Prime Minister Georges Clemenceau acknowledged his debt to Diagne and could not refuse his request to hold the 1919 congress in Paris. Diagne was much better connected in France than Du Bois was in America; the Pan-African movement would be narrow without him. By the same token, Diagne posed a formidable obstacle to the fashioning of radical declarations against French imperialism. Walter White remembered that Diagne "occupied as large and imposing an office . . . as Clemenceau" and recalled that "he threatened to withdraw from the Congress and denounce it if there were any condemnation of France." White noted that the French writer Andre Gide was publishing a magazine series exposing French atrocities in Africa during the congress, and he thought that the articles helped keep Diagne in line.[10]

The final gesture was to send a delegation to Geneva, headquarters of the League of Nations. By persistent diplomacy, the Pan-Africanists presented their main resolution to Sir Eric Drummond, secretary of the league. Du Bois conferred with international officials and received attentive hearings. Perhaps because the United States had no representative at the league, the Haitian Dantes Bellegarde reported the resolution before the Mandates Commission. Thus, an idea born in Du Bois's mind made its way before what passed for the conscience of the Western world.[11]

In addition to this propaganda coup, the congress drew considerable coverage in the European press, much more than the previous meeting. Most of this reportage was respectful, but some commentary showed that the empire builders were alarmed, contemptuous, or paternalistic. Jessie Fauset reviewed this reaction in the December 1923 *Crisis*, accenting the positive.

If the organizers could draw some satisfaction from the European press, American reporting of the congress was disappointing, especially that by the African-American press. America had no African empire, and the congress seemed too remote to provincial Americans, regardless of race. Claude E. Barnett of the Associated Negro Press wrote to White that only six of one hundred subscribers had signed up for syndicated articles on the congress. Even the *New York Age* ignored it. The *Chicago Defender* sent Dr. Wilberforce Williams, its health editor, who wrote a lengthy page 1 article on the American delegation at the London meeting. Nonetheless, most African Americans probably never heard of the Pan-African Congress, and many who did confused it with Garvey's movement. Before the meetings, Du Bois had to issue a statement clarifying the differences between the two projects.[12]

With the headquarters for the Pan-African Congress located in Paris, Diagne retained an undue influence over the movement as it prepared for its next meeting. The NAACP no longer bankrolled the PAC, and so organizing was further restricted by a lack of funds. As with all new movements, enthusiasm faded once the exciting beginning stage was over, and European domination of its black colonies showed no sign of diminishing in the short term.

Meeting under these conditions in early November 1923 in London and in early December in Lisbon, the Third Pan-African Congress kept open the channels of communication among diaspora activists. The London meeting benefited as well from the participation of the English Labor Party activists who had been organized into a committee by White during his 1921 London sojourn. American representatives included future historian Rayford Logan, Mrs. Ida Gibbs Hunt, and a Bishop Vernon of the AME Church. This meeting adopted a resolution that started with the specific needs of the colonized, rather than an indictment of the colonizers. It briefly reprised the situation of the black colonies, free diaspora nations, and American Negroes, reiterating demands for land reform, civil equality, and education. It insisted upon better policing of the colonial regimes by the League of Nations and black representation on its relevant commissions. Eleven nations sent delegates to the Lisbon meeting. Portugal's vast African empire ranked second only to Belgium's for brutality, and the Lisbon locale helped focus attention on the plight of its often-forgotten colonies.[13]

SHORTLY after the Third Pan-African Congress, new President Calvin Coolidge appointed Du Bois as American representative to the inauguration of Charles King as president of Liberia. Coolidge consulted with loyal Republicans William Henry Lewis and Emmett J. Scott about the envoy; the approval of the former Bookerites suggests that the old split in African-American politics was gone by 1924. After his trip Du Bois wrote a lyrical remembrance for the *Crisis*, showing his enchantment with the flora, fauna, and people, a Puritan son of New England home at last in the jungle. He noted "the riotous, unbridled bursting life of leaf and limb," and he recalled the cries of monkeys, leopards, and exotic birds. "And the people! Last night I went to Kru-town and saw a Christmas masque. There were young women and men of the color of warm ripe horse chestnuts, clothed in white robes and turbaned." Du Bois was deeply moved and rendered his feelings in prose that read like poetry.[14]

That was for the *Crisis*. It was all true, but only part of the story. While in Africa, he visited Sierra Leone and Senegal, which opened windows on English and French colonialism. For an elite white audience, he penned a more analytical piece in *Foreign Affairs*, then a new journal. Disarmingly titled "The Negro Mind Reaches Out," Du Bois's article might well have been headed "The Rape of Africa." Thirty to fifty years ahead of his time, Du Bois laid bare the legacy of imperialism and looked forward to a postcolonial world. He showed remarkable foresight merely by raising a subject that few American writers, black or white, were prepared to address. He demonstrated an impressive scope as well; few American intellectuals could write from personal experience of Europe and Africa, and Europeans were too blinded by nationalist loyalties to view colonialism clearly. Du Bois saw how the contradictions opened by the World War might explode. He sketched the relation between Marxism and Third World liberation that would dominate world politics during the cold war. As an organizing principle, he compared and contrasted the functioning of the European empires in Africa, and concluded by showing how the whole network might come apart.

The aspect of colonial race relations that most struck Du Bois was how different colonizers erected color caste lines and how they administered their satrapies. He did not visit a Portuguese colony, but while in Lisbon he met the mulatto representative of São Tomé to the parliament and observed African university students mixing with the Portuguese. Here was the same pattern he detected in France and Senegal. The offspring of interracial mating were accepted by the French as legitimate while shunned as bastards by the English. This "flaunting of the white fetish," he pointed out, "explains the deep-seated resentment against France on the part of England and America." Moreover, France had been saved by 845,000 African soldiers during the World War, and therefore "a tremendous wave of sentiment toward black folk welled up in the French heart."

He was not, however, willing to turn a blind eye to the underlying economic arrangement between the center and the colonies. "As I looked more narrowly, what seemed to be happening was this: the white Frenchmen were exploiting black Africans in practically the same way as white Englishmen, but they had not yet erected . . . caste lines." France had recruited a black bourgeoisie as fellow exploiters in Africa, but ultimately the extractive industries of the French Congo were no different from those of the Belgian Congo.

Toward the British model, Du Bois showed unwavering dismay. He was sharply interrogated upon disembarking at Sierra Leone. Here he found clear caste lines, similar to those of the United States but enforced with subtlety rather than American-style barbarism. The English kept Africans out of their colonial officer corps and skimped on education. Meanwhile they extracted seventy-two thousand tons of cocoa for the chocolate industry from the Gold Coast, returning nothing to the local economy. All of this was justified by the new hero of the empire, Jan Smuts, the Boer spokesman for white supremacy and loyalty to the Crown. The British empire had evolved a haphazard set of political relations with its dominions, ranging from sovereign commonwealth states (the former white colonies) to royally governed dependencies, with varying degrees of autonomy in the black nations. Smuts stood for white control over the colored peoples, spelling out the threat to white dominance posed by liberalism in any corner of the empire.

The exploitation of African workers posed a challenge to the European labor and socialist parties. Moreover, the new example of Soviet Russia raised the moral stakes, for "Russia has been seeking a *rapprochement* with colored labor," Du Bois averred. The West Indian poet Claude McKay had been traveling in Russia; McKay testified to the Third International's support for anti-imperialist struggles. The problem of the color line and the problems of Western labor were now inextricably intertwined in the new world market.

Ultimately Africa and the West had much to learn from each other, and Du Bois saw the American Negro as the natural leader of the inevitable coming together of these disparate civilizations. Of late there had been significant changes in American race relations. The New Negro now spoke for himself; the old paternalistic relationship was finished. Through political struggle by the NAACP, lynching had dramatically declined to only one per month from earlier highs of one to five a week. American restrictions against European immigration would strengthen the hand of black workers in America. They were now bidding to unite the African diaspora. Liberia, the African coast's lone free country, "represents to me the world," Du Bois concluded. "Liberia, that is a little thing set upon a Hill," he ruminated, using the same image as John Winthrop had in describing Boston. Here lay the Afro-Puritan Du Bois's hope for the future.

In general terms, Du Bois proved to be prophetic, seeing far ahead like the veiled African figure of Science. African liberation would come only after a second world war, and the specter of communism did indeed haunt that continent, too. He misread only the relation between the contrasting colonial styles and the process of emancipation. It was the British who understood that the sun was setting on their empire, and newly elected Labor ran the Union Jack down from India to Ghana without firing a shot. English-speaking whites would have to separate from the empire, as they did in Rhodesia and South Africa to fend off majority rule. The French would cling tenaciously to Algeria and Indochina, and would be driven out only by long and bloody wars. The Portuguese, French, and Belgian colonies would be wracked by bloody revolutionary and then internal wars as rival groups struggled for control of the riches, and perhaps most tragically, the same process would unfold even in Liberia.

Du Bois was not able to build a lasting Pan-African organization. He hoped to call a fourth meeting in Africa, but the colonial powers blocked it, and his relations with the Francophone leaders became strained at best. The next and last meeting was not held until 1927 in New York. It was called by ten women of the Circle for Peace and Foreign Relations of New York City, really a group of Du Bois's NAACP friends. There was no sign of an organization called the Pan-African Congress. Two hundred delegates attended, more than the number at the European meetings, but the Francophones were conspicuously absent and the final declaration a mere repetition of what had gone before. Although it was covered by the *New York Times* and the *Brooklyn Eagle*, the meeting generated little enthusiasm.[15]

The idea of Pan-Africanism was ahead of its time in the 1920s. Du Bois's work influenced the leaders of African independence in the 1950s, such as Ghana's Kwame Nkrumah and Kenya's Jomo Kenyatta. West Indian anti-imperialists such as Walter Rodney and C. L. R. James also owed something to Du Bois's movement. In the United States, internationally minded radicals such as Malcolm X and Kwame Touré (earlier known as Stokely Carmichael) conceptualized the African-American struggle in its world perspective. A series of Pan-African demonstrations took place in the United States in the 1970s, and the struggle against South African apartheid derived much from Du Bois's pioneering work as well. Ultimately Du Bois himself would flee a hostile United States to die in Ghana. The bloody tribal and political conflicts that wrack Africa in the twenty-first century stand as a horrific rebuke to his dream of African unity.

For the NAACP, the Pan-African Congress tested the limits of its avowed purpose. The Association was a civil rights organization, and fighting European imperialism was not on its agenda. It might speak out against American depredations against Haitians, but further than that it could not reasonably go. At the simplest level, African Americans were not willing to pay for such a venture in the 1920s. Only a handful of radicals have tried to launch similar efforts since then, despite widespread cultural identification by African Americans with the Mother Continent. Du Bois's voice in the international debate on Africa remains more prophetic than realized.

12

The Antilynching Bill

THE lynching issue stood at the top of the NAACP's agenda because it was so horrible to contemplate. The threat of terrorism underlay all the other forms of black oppression. Poverty, illiteracy, segregation, disfranchisement—these were chronic conditions that remained invisible to white Americans. Lynching, by contrast, was highly visible. Vast crowds attended these ghastly executions, sometimes in a festive spirit as the victim was put to death. Many NAACPers hoped that by focusing on lynching, the Association could also call attention to the underlying racial caste system.

For the first ten years of its history, the NAACP tried to educate the public about this national disgrace. It argued that lynching deprived the victim of due process, terrorized a whole class of the population, undercut law and order, and barbarized society as a whole. After U.S. entry into the World War, it became increasingly clear that negative publicity would not convince southern state governments to put down mobs. Joel E. Spingarn, who was serving as an army intelligence officer, promoted a wartime emergency antilynching bill, but skeptical congressmen throttled it in the House Judiciary Committee.[1]

The May 1919 New York conference chaired by Moorfield Storey was the last great propaganda effort of the NAACP's antilynching committee. While that conference brought together a broad array of prominent speakers and was well attended by African Americans, few whites paid it any notice, and it produced no new legislation in the states. Individually, leading NAACPers began to question whether it might be possible to pass a law making lynching a federal offense. Storey, however, was not convinced that such a law would be constitutional, since it would extend federal power into areas traditionally reserved for the states.

Despite Storey's hesitations, several Republican congressmen, less aware of the constitutional minefield that lay before them, had already introduced their own legislation. Leonidas Dyer of St. Louis represented the industrial south side of his city. He was sincerely outraged by the 1917 East St. Louis riot, and his growing black constituency made an antilynching bill politically expedient as well. In 1918 he introduced a bill based on an earlier effort crafted by Albert E. Pillsbury, a Boston NAACP founder. Dyer's bill (H.R. 11279) would protect U.S. citizens from lynching. It defined a lynching mob as three or more persons who killed a citizen when state officials failed to protect him. Lynchers would be prosecuted in federal court for murder. Heirs of lynching victims could recover up to ten thousand dollars from counties that permitted lynchings. Officials who failed to act against lynchings could face five years in prison and five thousand dollar fines. People who took part in mob attacks could be banned from jury duty. The bill used race-neutral language and was based on the Fourteenth Amendment's guarantee of equal rights under the law.[2]

The violence of 1919 encouraged greater enthusiasm in the NAACP for Dyer's bill. Texas's failure to prosecute the lawmen who beat John Shillady helped change Storey's mind. In November he telegrammed Shillady that he now favored passing the bill even if the Supreme Court might later rule against it. In late January 1920, the Association sent a strong delegation to testify for the Dyer bill before the House Judiciary Committee. Washington, D.C., branch leaders, NAACP Legal Committee chairman Arthur B. Spingarn, and Boston's William Monroe Trotter argued that Congress should pass the measure and leave the question of its constitutionality to the courts. Johnson presented a detailed review of lynching statistics and introduced antilynching sentiments by prominent Republicans William Howard Taft, Elihu Root, and Charles Evans Hughes. None of the witnesses could satisfy the congressmen, who closely questioned them on constitutional matters, and the bill died in committee.[3]

In November, the Republicans won their smashing victory at the polls. If an antilynching bill was going to pass, now was the time. The issue was becoming hot. In December the Brooklyn branch sponsored an antilynching meeting at the Academy of Music and raised the astonishing sum of three thousand dollars from a packed house. News of the Ocoee massacre spread in the black press. When NAACP leaders testified about that before the House, the Association received a great deal of national publicity.[4]

Within the NAACP, the change in the leadership also contributed to a stronger orientation toward seeking federal remedies. At the November 1920 board meeting, Johnson was voted permanent secretary. He had always seen the Dyer bill as a political battle worth fighting, rather than as a legal dilemma worth solving. On January 15 he met with the president-elect and came away impressed with Harding's possibilities but cognizant of his limitations. Johnson always respected Storey's opinion, but he did not defer to it as completely as Shillady had. With Johnson as the new Association secretary and Harding as the new president, the chances for an antilynching victory seemed much stronger.

Storey tried to convince former attorney general George B. Wickersham of his stronger opinion. He argued that even if the bill failed in the courts, it might retard lynching anyway. "On the matter of constitutionality," he wrote, "I have felt that we might sustain the law upon the ground that the citizens of the United States are entitled to protection from the United States against the denial of protection against injustice by the states. The Fourteenth Amendment creates the citizenship of the United States and it has been recognized in the various cases." The Dyer bill would be "an experiment worth trying," he concluded. When Wickersham responded with a list of Supreme Court rulings that the Fourteenth Amendment applied only to state action (not state *inaction* and not action by private citizens), Storey held his ground. He was aware of the difficulties posed by those decisions. Now he argued that lynching should be regarded as something more than simple murder. "So far as the Negroes are concerned, there is in the southern states no republican form of government." He reminded Wickersham that the federal acts that suppressed the Ku Klux Klan during Reconstruction had not been challenged, and that an antilynching law would be analogous to those. "It is a doubtful question," he conceded, "but we are face to face with a necessity which needs a law, and I do not like to admit that the U.S. is powerless to protect its own people." This was a different man from the cautious lawyer of 1918.[5]

Eleven days after Storey wrote this, Henry Lowry was burned at the stake near Memphis. Johnson was sickened. He felt "towering but impotent rage to utter dejection." The day the Lowry lynching appeared in the newspapers, Johnson was meeting New Jersey Negro leaders at the home of Dr. George Cannon, president of the Jersey City branch and leader of the state's colored Republicans. An African American had just been elected to the state assembly, and he was preparing a Dyer-like bill for New Jersey. The confluence of the Lowry lynching and Johnson's deepening ties to Negro Republicans pushed the federal orientation further along. In April the Association delivered a copy of *An American Lynching* to every member of Congress.[6]

Late in March, Johnson visited Kansas senators Arthur Capper and Charles Curtis. Capper had introduced a bill calling for an investigation of lynching, a standard NAACP response to every such atrocity. He asked if the NAACP now wished to abandon that approach in favor of Dyer's bill. The senator did not think Dyer's bill could pass, and an investigation would at least be a start. Johnson gave an indefinite answer but tilted toward the Dyer bill. On April 4, he met with President Harding at the White House. Johnson gave the president a seven-point memo on the NAACP's wish list, and an antilynching bill was at the top. Next was a proposal to form an interracial commission to investigate race relations in general. Harding approved of this plan, but the necessary legislation was killed in Congress. Johnson came away feeling that this meeting with Harding was "very satisfactory."[7]

A week later, President Harding did just as Johnson asked. In his April 12 address to Congress, he requested an antilynching bill using language very close to that of Johnson's memo. The NAACP now seemed to have the president's support, and the Association abandoned any thought of a mere congressional investigation. Johnson was set upon the Dyer bill. Dyer introduced it the day before Harding's speech, and it was assigned the unlucky number thirteen. "We joked a bit about it, but neither Mr. Dyer nor I was dismayed . . . ," Johnson recalled.[8]

The House Judiciary Committee, with fifteen Republicans and six Democrats, heard debate on the Dyer bill on June 18. The latest version expanded protection to "all persons" rather than to citizens; it now contained fifteen sections. The first witness for the bill was Indiana's Merrill Moores, who had introduced an antilynching bill at an earlier session. The Democrats, predictably, focused their attack on constitutional issues. They noted that the bill would initiate federal action if states failed to act against lynching. The Fourteenth Amendment, section 1, prohibited state action that would "deny to any person within its jurisdiction the equal protection of the laws." Southerners insisted that the Dyer bill did not conform to this language. Further, they argued, the logic of the bill would expand federal police power to crimes such as bootlegging that were not equally enforced by states. Moores agreed, and the southerners scored a point among Republican strict constructionists.[9]

The bill received new impetus when Assistant Attorney General Guy Goff appeared on its behalf—the first time that the administration had come forward in Congress on the issue. When southern congressmen posed hypothetical lynching cases in which Dyer sanctions might be activated, he, too, volunteered expansive interpretations. In August, Attorney General Harry Daugherty backed his assistant in a personal memo to the Judiciary Committee. NAACP ally Louis Marshall, the attorney who had defended Leo Frank, warned Johnson that Goff's testimony postulated a broader federal police power than the Constitution warranted. As the historian Robert L. Zangrando has noted, 1920s notions of federal power were much more limited than they would be after the New Deal, and the Dyer bill challenged the assumptions of the time.[10]

On October 20, the Judiciary Committee reported the bill favorably to the full House. Chairman Andrew Volstead reduced the Dyer bill to seven sections, narrowing its purview. The new version eliminated certain categories of action that would trigger federal policing and raised a mob's size to five. The bill still retained stiff penalties for negligent law officers, lynchers, and lynching counties. Johnson regarded these modifications as minor and determined to fight for the bill.[11]

Dyer was willing to let the bill proceed through normal congressional channels, leaving months before a vote. Alarmed by the possibility of death by inaction, Johnson hastened to Washington and met with all the top Republican leaders. "I tramped the corridors of the capitol . . . so constantly that toward the end, I could, I think, have been able to find my way about blindfolded," he remembered. Meanwhile the Association contacted twenty-seven branches, urging them to institute letter-writing campaigns. The Association also sent letters to eighty-four representatives.[12]

On October 26, President Harding spoke on race relations in Birmingham, Alabama, to a crowd of several thousand. A presidential address on this subject in the South was unprecedented and was in itself a sign of progress. Harding began by reprising Booker Washington's formula of social separation but economic cooperation between the races. He broke new ground when he declared, "I would say let the black man vote when he is fit to vote." He called for "equal educational opportunity" but denounced "social equality" and "racial amalgamation." Predictably, southern Democrats blasted the call for Negro suffrage. African-American newspapers were generally favorable. "President Harding Speaks Up for Justice to Negro Race," read the *New York Age* headline. Johnson, in his column, offered a more nuanced appraisal. He commended Harding's stand on the Negro vote but questioned his statement about social equality. The NAACP needed the president on its side and had to accent the positive, as Johnson did. "We shall watch," he promised. Action would be the real test, not words.[13]

Unexpectedly, two southern African-American Republicans tried to emasculate the bill. These were Henry "Linc" Johnson of Georgia and Perry Howard of Mississippi, old-line Booker Washington–style politicians who did not want to put southern Republicans, few as they were, on the spot. They viewed the NAACP as a threatening rival and Du Bois, in particular, as a dangerous radical. They proposed restricting the bill only to cases where the victim was already in custody, which were a small minority of lynching situations. Concerned by this development, James Weldon Johnson hurried again to Washington, where he found Dyer inclined to accept the compromise. He told Dyer and other Republican leaders it was "better a good bill fails than a bad bill passes." The constitutional issue, he insisted, was "a mere pretext" for blocking the bill, and that they should just pass it and let the courts worry about the consequences. No changes were made.[14]

After the holiday break, Johnson sent a new letter to House members, along with two NAACP antilynching pamphlets. This time he took up the argument that lynching was just murder, a local crime to be adjudicated locally. "Lynching *is* murder, but it is also *more* than murder," he wrote. Because lynchers arrogated to themselves the judicial powers of the state, it was a form of anarchy, "anarchy which the states have proven themselves powerless to cope with." He asked rhetorically what the United States would do if a U.S. citizen was murdered abroad and the foreign country did not prosecute the known killer. Congressmen knew that ultimately such an incident could serve as a *causus belli*.[15]

Republican leaders still dragged their feet. Martin Madden and Majority Leader Frank Mondell of Wyoming told Johnson to expect a long delay before the bill came to the floor. Madden, whose South Side Chicago district had a fast-growing Negro population, buckled under Johnson's prompting first. "Mondell remains the great stone to be moved," Johnson wrote to his New York colleagues. "Have the Cincinnati branch and Kansas pressure Longworth and Campbell. . . . The method is still tact and diplomacy and fair but friendly pressure." Dyer was out of this loop, "happy as a child and just about as innocent of what was going on in the 'inner circle,'" Johnson wrote. The message must have gotten through. The next day Mondell won a 184–86 vote to bring the bill to the floor with seventy-seven others "paired" in favor. Johnson prepared for the floor debate, which continued over two weeks.[16]

In the 1920s, speeches on the House floor were reported in local newspapers. Southern representatives now downplayed the constitutional issues and turned to the more popular line: defense of lynching based on race hatred. Thomas Sisson of Mississippi said he "would rather the whole black race of the world were lynched than for one of the fair daughters of the South to be ravished and torn by these brutes." Another branded H.R. 13 "a bill to encourage rape," and a Georgian asked northerners to "quit howling about lynchings and begin preaching against rape." This went on and on, speech after speech. Some sounded the themes aired in committee—H.R. 13 was a violation of state's rights, it was a sectional bill aimed at the South—but the main line was a defense of lynching, not an apology for it.[17]

Northern Republicans took contrasting tacks in favor of the bill. Dyer himself denied that H.R. 13 was sectionally motivated and said that lynching was a national problem that needed a national remedy. Most others echoed this defense. Hamilton Fish of New York and a few others frankly blamed the southern states for flouting their own laws. Johnson reminded his supporters that only 17 percent of victims were even accused of rape and that some victims were women. As historian Claudine L. Ferrell observed, the general level of the floor debate was so low that little attention was paid to the complex issues the bill did raise.[18]

On January 26, the final day of debate, African-American Washingtonians packed the galleries by the hundreds. As Johnson recalled:

> The news that the Anti-Lynching Bill was being debated jammed the galleries on the following day; the majority of the crowd being Negroes. There was intense excitement. At a point in one of the speeches, the Negroes in the galleries broke the rules and rose and cheered. A voice from the floor shouted, "Sit down, you niggers!" And a voice from the galleries shouted back "You're a liar! We're not niggers." The speaker announced that he would have the galleries closed if there was any further applause. At three o'clock the bill went to a vote, and at three-thirty the speaker declared it passed by a vote of 230–119.

The votes in favor included eight northern Democrats and one southern Republican, a Texas German American. Of the opponents, seventeen Republicans broke ranks and fifty-six stayed away. The NAACP, in the February *Crisis*, vowed to punish the defecting Republicans it could hurt in scattered northern states. For the first time, the NAACP invoked an electoral strategy, moving away from its generally nonpartisan stance. Now as the fight moved to the Senate, the Association would confront the constitutional question raised by more formidable opponents.[19]

JOHNSON set immediately to work on the Senate Judiciary Committee. The Association had two good friends in the upper chamber in the Kansans Capper and Curtis, but their influence was slight. On the Judiciary Committee, no member came from a state with a significant voting black population, which diminished the Association's clout. Johnson had no interested party like Dyer to help him. He could only hope that a powerful Republican such as the president, Majority Leader Henry Cabot Lodge of Massachussetts, or William Borah of Idaho would lead the fight for the bill.[20]

Borah was the first disappointment. He was one of three Republicans on the five-person judiciary subcommittee assigned to the bill. He was a progressive, an old lion of the Senate whose antipathy to Lodge and the eastern establishment went back many years. He coveted Lodge's seat as chairman of the Foreign Relations Committee and was a possible contender for the 1924 presidential nomination. Borah told Johnson "that he would do anything in his power, as a Senator, to save the life of a single Negro from a lynching mob," but he would not support the bill if he thought it unconstitutional. "Once when I saw him he looked at me squarely from under his shaggy eyebrows, but with that expressive characteristic of his, which makes you uncertain as to whether he is in earnest or laughing at you," Johnson wrote. Borah fancied himself a constitutional authority, in part because he had a college degree in a chamber full of apprentice-system-trained lawyers. He suggested to Johnson that the Association forget the bill and try to amend the Constitution instead. If Johnson wanted to convince him, he needed a constitutional argument—not horror stories or statistics about lynching.[21]

To allay Borah's concerns, Moorfield Storey prepared a brief. In effect, he reprised his own earlier doubts and answered them. Storey now could not accept that the federal government was powerless to act. Each court interpreted the Constitution as it read it; the court was influenced but not bound by past rulings. Along with Storey, African-American attorneys Butler Wilson and William Henry Lewis of Boston, and James Cobb of Washington, began work on their own arguments. In correspondence with Storey, Borah, like Wickersham earlier, was unimpressed and cited the Supreme Court rulings that restricted the Fourteenth Amendment's applicability only to positive action by states.[22]

Meanwhile, the Association did what it could to mobilize public opinion. During its annual meeting at Harlem's Palace Casino, NAACP leaders, this time including Mordecai Johnson of Charleston, West Virginia, all addressed the lynching issue. The Association circulated to prominent Americans a petition on behalf of the bill, and twenty-one governors, twenty-eight mayors, and like numbers of church, academic, journalistic, and legal leaders affixed their names. On March 1, they sponsored a meeting at New York's Town Hall, where Dyer, Wickersham, and Storey spoke. Johnson gave speeches in several other cities, and in April he testified at an American Bar Association (ABA) committee meeting. The full ABA convention endorsed the bill in August. In June, the Association sponsored a Harlem parade for the bill, and four thousand people started downtown to Fifty-ninth Street, but a rainstorm scattered the marchers. In Baltimore, two thousand people packed the Bethel Church to hear NAACP branch president Reverend Monroe Davis introduce Dyer. A year later five thousand Washingtonians marched down Pennsylvania Avenue past the White House to the Capitol to show their feelings. This was no legalistic, top-down campaign, but a sustained battle for public opinion.[23]

Meanwhile Borah remained unmoved, but he had not yet cast a committee vote and declared that he remained open to persuasion. When Johnson spoke late in April at Boston's Twentieth Century Club, Butler Wilson convinced Johnson that the Association should work through Massachusetts senator Henry Cabot Lodge. Wilson was the main African-American leader of the Association's whitest branch, an attorney, and a Republican loyalist. He knew that Lodge was facing a tough reelection campaign in the fall, and he hoped that African-American Bay Staters could leverage their small numbers in return for Lodge's action on the bill. Moorfield Storey could be of no use in this matter, for as a liberal "mugwump" Republican in the 1880s, he had opposed party regular Lodge, and the two men had scarcely spoken since then.[24]

Lodge is remembered in American history as an imperialist, a backer of immigration restriction, and the man who sank American entry into the League of Nations. However, in 1890, at the beginning of his congressional career, he had introduced a federal elections bill that would protect the black vote in the South. He told NAACP leaders that he supported the Dyer bill. Now he was senate majority leader, and, ironically, this rock of the eastern establishment became the NAACP's best hope against the anti-imperialist Borah, who opposed the occupation of Haiti. Familiar politics thus stood on its head.[25]

After a week of trying to contact Lodge, the Association arranged a meeting between him and a committee of Johnson, Butler Wilson, and Archibald Grimké. Lodge was impressed by the many signers of the NAACP petition and promised to present it to the Senate. "The committee felt decidedly encouraged after their visit to the capitol," Johnson reported to the board.[26]

A few days later came horrific news that confirmed the urgency of their mission.

ON THURSDAY, MAY 4, the same day that James Weldon Johnson was discussing constitutional matters with Henry Cabot Lodge, a seventeen-year-old girl named Eula Awsley was riding her horse home from school in Kirvin, Texas. This was a rural farming town of five hundred residents, lying eighty miles southeast of Dallas. When Eula did not come home, the sheriff summoned volunteers for a search party, and that night Eula's body was discovered bearing twenty-three stab wounds.

Eula's parents were both deceased, and she had been living with her grandfather, rancher J. T. King. She was a popular girl, and the small town was naturally horrified by the crime. According to the *Dallas Morning News*, suspicion fell upon a Negro, "Snap" Curry, who had participated in the search but dropped out when he learned that bloodhounds would be brought in. The sheriff visited Curry's home, where his wife said that he had blood on his clothes the night of the murder. Curry was locked up in a bank building in Wortham. According to the newspaper, he confessed that he had plotted the crime months earlier with two other hands on the King ranch, J. H. Varney and Mose Jones.

The next day a mob of five hundred men surrounded the bank. The sheriff tried to hustle Curry away in an automobile, but as he must have expected, the crowd blocked the vehicle and seized Curry along with the keys to Freestone County Prison. Varney and Jones were abducted from the jail, and all three suspects were transported to the Kirvin town square. Curry reportedly repeated his confession, but the other two denied any involvement in the crime, even under torture. The three men were "mutilated," the newspaper said, which probably meant that their genitals were cut off. At dawn each was burned at the stake, one at a time. The last victim died singing a church hymn. According to the newspaper, the girl's grandfather was present and gave his consent to the burnings.[27]

The Kirvin story was reported on the front page of the Sunday, May 7, *New York Times*. Underneath it appeared a tiny article saying that two white men had been detained at nearby Teague in relation to the murder and had been released. James Weldon Johnson was very suspicious and deeply upset about the Kirvin burnings. The next day he reported his activities on behalf of the Dyer bill to the board of directors. Regarding Kirvin he said, "This we believe is the most atrocious case of burning in the whole history of lynching." He postulated that two of the men were probably innocent and most likely the third was as well. He sent telegrams to the *Houston Post* and *San Antonio Express*, both of which had editorially deplored the lynching. Johnson wanted more information on the culpability of the victims, but neither paper ventured a hypothesis.[28]

The Kirvin lynching disappeared from the *Times* after the initial story. There was nothing to report: no one expected any investigation of the lynching, and of course there was none. But Johnson would not let the matter drop. Had the men been clearly guilty of the murder, the manner of their execution would still have been profoundly evil and a horrible justification for all his efforts of the past year. But the story did not add up.

Very little black-on-white crime occurred in America, and what little there might be was usually either impulsive or committed in self-defense. That three black men in Texas would conspire to murder a white girl, for no apparent reason, seemed highly unlikely to Johnson. Every Negro in America knew what the outcome of such a crime would be. He wrote a letter to President Harding to this effect, enclosing the *Times* article.[29]

Johnson also wrote to Dan Kelly of Waco and asked him to find out more. Kelly was a rare southern white liberal who had worked with the NAACP. He had helped to investigate the 1916 Waco burning case and afterward moved to New York for a few years, probably for his own safety, before returning home. He was well connected in Texas and had even gone to high school with the reporters who covered the Kirvin story. He, too, had doubts about the way it was reported. Kelly promised to go to Kirvin and later to visit Governor Pat Neff, who happened also to be from Waco and a friend of Kelly's family. Within a few weeks Kelly had his story. It ran in the Sunday *New York World*. Kelly came up to the Newark NAACP convention and told the story in more detail.[30]

Kirvin, it seemed, was a typical backwoods East Texas town. A few whites owned the land, and the Negroes worked it as tenants. Few of its residents had even left the country. Like many such places, it was marked by a clan feud.

Two years earlier, there had been a bad cattle deal between the King and Prowell families. Afterward, some Prowells knifed King's son, leaving him permanently scarred. The Kings then drove some Prowells out of the county. Therefore, when Eula Awsley did not come home from school, her grandfather knew something was very wrong and immediately contacted the sheriff.

According to Kelly, King told the sheriff he did not want any innocent Negroes killed. When two Prowell boys disappeared right after the slaying, King knew that they had done it. There were even tracks from the murder scene to the Prowell home, and the two men detained at Teague were in fact Prowells. They explained the tracks away by saying they had been making bran mash in a thicket earlier in the day.

Snap Curry's wife, Kelly averred, hated her husband, but he swore that the blood on his clothing came from killing rabbits. Curry never confessed and gave up two other names only under torture, saying, "[T]hey are as guilty as I am." It was unclear whether or not King was at the Kirvin town square the morning of the burnings. Kelly reported that "[o]ld man King was devastated" by the entire sequence of events.

Seventy-seven years after the Kirvin burnings, a dogged local researcher, dissatisfied with both accounts of the original story, pursued the descendants of the participants to see if better sense might be made of these crimes of rage and retribution. In *Flames after Midnight*, Monte Akers surmised that Snap Curry had been lured to the scene by the Prowells to stop Eula Awsley's horse, and was then smeared with the girl's blood by the perpetrators. However the original crime may have transpired, its emotional effects have been passed down through several generations of Texans, African-American and white, who have lived with its bitter memories in private.[31]

In 1922 the most important part of the story lay in Kelly's appraisal of the town's mood. "The people of that community are utterly unaware that they have done any deed for which they should be ashamed," he told the NAACP convention. Governor Neff said only that the lynchers should have been tried, but in another county. Kelly went home to Waco just in time to learn of two more lynchings in the area. In one case, the corpse of the victim was dragged behind a car. There was no hope that Texas was going to solve a lynching problem that it did not acknowledge. As for the federal government, the Justice Department wrote to Johnson that there was nothing it could do either: "[T]here is no federal statute covering such offenses."[32]

The Kirvin events sickened Johnson but made little impact on the implacable Borah, who was still awaiting the completion of forthcoming NAACP constitutional briefs. Later in May came an unanticipated development, similar to the intervention by Henry "Linc" Johnson and Perry Howard one year earlier, this time from a militant. William Monroe Trotter of Boston wrote in his *Guardian* newspaper that the Association was permitting the bill to languish while prompt action was necessary. He brought his own delegation to see Lodge at his Beacon Street office and urged that he work to report the bill out at once. Lodge instructed Borah to do just that, and Johnson hastened again to Washington to prevent a prematurely negative report. He spent an anxious few days at the capital, delivering to Borah briefs in varying stages of completion. Borah told Johnson that since Lodge wanted the report out now, it would have to be adverse. With the subcommittee meeting in executive session, Johnson and James A. Cobb frantically lobbied the White House, Republican National Committee Chairman John T. Adams, and senatorial allies. Johnson was furious, angry that Trotter might have undone fourteen months of work. "Trotter gummed the case up by his action," Johnson complained to a colleague. "He wanted the publicity for getting the bill reported out when the NAACP had failed to get it done." The Association issued a diplomatically worded press release rebuking Trotter. "It is unnecessary to point out that [Trotter's] delegation did secure prompt action, but in the wrong direction,"

Johnson told his board of directors. Meanwhile, the inept Dyer further complicated matters by telling a Boston audience that Negro voters should punish Lodge in November if he failed to get the bill passed. Borah issued a negative report, thus hurting the bill and Lodge, whose defeat by a Democrat would serve his own narrow interests.[33]

In the Senate lobby, Johnson fired more legal ammunition in the form of a brief by New York attorney Herbert K. Stockton. Arthur B. Spingarn felt that Stockton's argument on behalf of the bill was the most clearly argued of all, and sixty years later historian Claudine L. Ferrell, who carefully reviewed the constitutional questions, concurred. Stockton came to the Association from out of nowhere, asking White in April if he could help on the matter. Incorporating the criticisms of Louis Marshall, who did not support the bill, Stockton developed a new line of argument focused on the Constitution's defense of the rights of state, rather than national citizens. This led him to deny the relevance of the precedents that Borah thought so significant, and toward other cases. Stockton's precedents supported federal policing of state failure to enforce all laws equally. This meant that H.R. 13 would not overthrow the rulings that Borah so valued. Stockton and Marshall agreed that the Constitution sanctioned federal prosecution of a sheriff who relinquished a prisoner to a mob, but Marshall did not agree that a federal law could be passed to prosecute the mob members, as Dyer's bill would. Stockton introduced new precedents showing that federal law had been invoked against conspirators with corrupt local officials. He held that lynchers stood in an analogous relation to the local government, and he suggested a refinement of the bill's language to reflect this.[34]

This argument carried the day within the Judiciary Committee. Albert Cummins of Ohio sharpened the bill's fourth section so that it stipulated the conditions for indicting state officers who failed to act. At the end of June, the committee voted 8–6 to bring the bill to the floor, with Borah the lone Republican defector. However, the majority could not agree among themselves on the reason for their conclusions, with most members holding reservations about the constitutionality of one or another section. Only new California senator Samuel R. Shortridge fully believed the whole measure to be constitutional, and it fell to this unknown to introduce the measure to the Senate.[35]

WHILE the Senate Judiciary Committee considered the Dyer bill, three thousand African Americans opened the annual NAACP convention at Newark on Sunday, June 18, with a silent parade from Lincoln Park to the city hall. A group of teenagers marched behind a banner that declared "We Are Fifteen Years Old. A Boy Our Age Was Roasted Alive Recently." This referred to a lynching on May 15 in Davisville, Georgia. The whole convention reflected the tense emotions signified by this banner.

Moorfield Storey told a rally at the Newark Armory that if the United States could punish Russia for human rights abuses, it could do the same thing to lynchers on its own soil. Tuesday was Women's Day, and for the first time ever the Association awarded the Spingarn Medal to a woman, Mary Talbert. At this convention Talbert launched the Anti-Lynching Crusaders, which conducted a special women's campaign for the Dyer bill. Dan Kelly raised the convention's emotions with a gripping account of the Kirvin burnings. There was also time for a little fun, with a boat excursion up the Hudson.

The Newark convention registered a significant shift in the Association's strategy regarding electoral politics. This was always a difficult matter for individual branches, whose members inevitably had clashing relationships with local politicians. Now the Association was fighting for a bill of transcendent importance, and it decided to support its friends and oppose its enemies at the polls. Boston's Butler Wilson, once a Republican regular, declared, "If the Republican Party does not keep the faith, it ought to be wiped out of office." T. G. Nutter of the Charleston, West Virginia, branch gave a presentation on "What a Branch May or May Not Do in Politics." The West Virginia branches confronted candidates on civil rights issues during the primaries. Their aggressive approach yielded a state antilynching law, integrated seating on railroads, and good funding for Negro schools and institutions. There were principles to follow: branches should support men and measures, not parties; politicians should not be branch presidents; branch leaders should not take gifts from politicians. This upset Jersey City branch president, NAACP board member, and Republican official George Cannon, and a Kansas City delegate who thought it best to stay out of elections altogether. James Weldon Johnson backed Nutter. The national Association would remain nonpartisan, but branches should endorse candidates when a real principle was at stake.

Johnson developed this theme in his keynote address, one of the most impassioned of his career. He was thoroughly fed up with the constitutional debate, which he ridiculed as "bunkum," a "pretext" to allow lynching to continue. Other bills had been passed and ruled unconstitutional; why not find out with this one?

> The task is Power! Power! That is the thing. It is a new thing to us. . . . We are not a weak people. There are twelve million of

> us. . . . A right is not a thing issued on a silver tray . . . not a thing you can put in your pocket like a gold piece. You have to fight to keep it. That is the mission of this organization. The great job before this organization is to awaken the American Negro, work him up. . . . Therefore it takes mass action.

He pointed to Jewish self-organization as a model, citing a case in which a Jewish naval cadet at Annapolis was baited, and Jewish organizations got the Senate to stop such incidents. Patience is a virtue, he continued, but not the one Negroes needed now. All the anger and frustration of the past year poured out in eloquent language designed to inspire action. The 1922 Newark NAACP convention marked the first significant break with strict Republican loyalty by post-Emancipation African Americans, and pointed toward the first black majority vote for a Democratic presidential candidate in 1936.[36]

In three states especially the conventioneers went forward with the new marching orders. NAACPers in Delaware and New Jersey helped to defeat anti-Dyer Republicans in a general election. In Michigan they backed a pro-Dyer Republican, who won in the primary against an "anti." Because the Dyer bill was only one issue, it is difficult to draw conclusions about Negro voting power from the results. At the very least, the 1922 elections raised the African-American profile in national politics.

One of the sharpest fights was waged in the smallest state, Delaware. Alice Dunbar-Nelson, the New Orleans–born former wife of the poet Paul Laurence Dunbar, led the Wilmington branch and edited the black community newspaper the *Advocate*. A light-skinned woman with straight hair and a snub nose, she could "pass" for white but became a spirited campaigner for civil rights. She published poetry and fiction, and worked as a journalist and social worker.[37]

When Republican congressman Caleb R. Layton voted against the Dyer bill in 1921 and ran for Senate the next year, Dunbar-Nelson went on the warpath. The white Republicans expected Negro loyalty and were dumbfounded when the poverty-stricken editor turned down their offer of a job. "Rags are royal raiment when worn for virtue's sake," poet Dunbar-Nelson reminded fellow poet Johnson. She was challenging the Du Pont family machine on behalf of a Democrat who promised to vote for the Dyer bill. Dunbar-Nelson spoke all over the tiny state. At Bridgeville, Negro workers at a canning factory quit work to hear her. She held meetings at Milford where "the people [Negroes] are peculiar, belonging to an offshoot of the Moors." Walter White came down to speak at Wilmington, and he wrote an article for the *New York Times* about it later. African Americans campaigning against Republicans made news. Dunbar-Nelson naively believed that Dyer himself should break party ranks and was disappointed when party regulars brought him over to speak for Layton. She did not build the NAACP branch through this campaign, but when Layton lost by a narrow margin, the Association boasted that Negro voters had shown their muscle.[38]

A second victory was registered in New Jersey, where the Association campaigned in the Ninth Congressional District against anti-Dyer Republican E. Wayne Parker. The Association wounded a possible friend when Addie Hunton denounced Senator Frelinghuysen for being absent when they needed his vote. She was right of course, but this antagonized George Cannon of the Jersey City branch. He insisted that Frelinghuysen was a sure vote for the bill on the floor, that the Democrat was a racist, and that the Association must correct its error. The national office sent a mailing to this effect to its numerous New Jersey branches, many of them clustered in the New York metropolitan area. When Frelinghuysen lost along with Parker, the Association's news release mentioned only the latter candidate.[39]

The Association fought its most extensive campaign in Michigan. Here the Association had sixteen branches, and forty-three thousand potential Negro voters might hold the balance of power. In 1922, anti-Dyer Republican Patrick H. Kelley challenged pro-Dyer incumbent Charles Townsend in the senatorial primary. Bay City NAACP leader Oscar Baker served as Townsend's Negro coordinator. Baker led a statewide Negro registration effort, and Townsend beat Kelly by twenty-five thousand votes. Townsend attributed his victory to the Association's efforts, and the NAACP announced this as evidence of Negro voting power. But this power was limited; Townsend lost the general election.[40]

NAACPers worked in three other state elections to forward the Dyer bill. In West Virginia, thirty thousand Negro voters contributed to the primary victory of a pro-Dyer candidate. In Missouri, the Association vigorously backed Dyer in his St. Louis district. Milwaukee activists backed socialist Victor Berger, who credited black voters with his victory.[41]

ALONG with this electoral strategy, African-American women organized a publicity and fund-raising campaign around the issue. Black women had long ago seen that they had a special role to play on the lynching question. The white South justified lynching on the lie that black men raped white women. Black women knew that white men could rape them with impunity. Black women knew that they, too, were lynched. This argument had been advanced as early as 1892 by Ida B. Wells. She was the young editor of a Memphis black community newspaper when whites killed three African-American store owners. Wells urged the new African-American women's clubs to take up this issue, and many of them did.[42]

During the women's suffrage movement, few white women called attention to the connection between gender and lynching. After the 1920 victory, however, some white southern suffragists joined the Commission on Interracial Cooperation (CIC) and spoke out. The CIC accepted second-class citizenship for blacks but denounced lynching, urging southern states themselves to end the practice. The most prominent female white southern antilynching activist was Jessie Daniel Ames. A widow from the Texas Hill country, she brought a gendered antilynching argument to white southern women, and her speeches were reported in the African-American press.[43]

At the Newark NAACP convention, Mary B. Talbert decided to revive the women's campaign. She gathered a core group of sixteen women, chaired by Mary E. Jackson of Providence, who planned to circulate a women's antilynching petition. The Anti-Lynching Crusaders were organized separately from the NAACP, but Talbert reported its activities to the board of directors. Some NAACP branches had women's auxiliaries, and the Crusaders functioned in a like capacity. The Crusaders pledged to secure one dollar from a million women, who would raise the sum by abstinence and motivate themselves by prayer.[44]

This ambitious goal proved wildly unrealistic, but the Crusaders ultimately netted about seven thousand dollars for the campaign. Talbert established a national headquarters at her home on Clinton Street in Buffalo. She spoke in key northern cities, and the Crusaders distributed one hundred thousand pieces of literature. The campaign reached several thousand white women who might have avoided an NAACP appeal. Mary Talbert wanted to keep the organization alive permanently, but Nannie H. Burroughs, a Washington, D.C., member of the NAACP Board, argued that this would be counterproductive.

During this campaign, the National Association of Colored Women's Clubs (NACW) completed the restoration of the Frederick Douglass home in Anacostia, Maryland. Talbert had initiated this project while serving as the NACW president, and it was for this work that she received the Spingarn Medal. Late in the fall of 1922 she fell ill, and in October of 1923 she died. It was as though her work was done, and it was time to pass on. A gracious and courageous woman, she deserves to be remembered as a heroic pioneer of the civil rights movement.[45]

UNDER the stress of his activity, James Weldon Johnson fell ill after the Newark convention and spent much of August recovering his energy. At his Atlantic City retreat, he learned from New York's senator William Calder that the Dyer bill would sink to the bottom of the Republican agenda without prompt action. Johnson entrained yet again for Washington and after a round of hectic meetings convinced the Republican steering committee to get the bill onto the floor.[46]

He was nervous about Senator Shortridge's low standing. "My heart sank as I thought of the gap between a Borah and a Shortridge," Johnson recalled. "I judged that Daniel Webster was his model, for in speaking he employed the Websterian tone, and even wore his right hand in the bosom of his long coat." As the day for the bill's presentation neared, Johnson urged the branches to write their senators. On September 21, Shortridge took the floor. The inexperienced Californian yielded to a Democrat out of politeness, and the Democrats launched a filibuster. After a few hours, Shortridge regained the floor and made "a very strong" speech, Johnson wrote, but when he was done there was no longer a quorum sitting. Ten Republicans were among the missing, including Lodge and several Judiciary Committee members. The bill was automatically put over until the next session.[47]

This was a significant setback. Storey had warned Johnson during the summer that the Republicans might keep the bill alive until after the November elections and then kill it: "Unless they use their power and keep their promise, they are not our friends." Johnson clung to the hope that they were not yet beaten; he had seen the fight over many obstacles so far and was ready to battle to the end. Shortridge felt disillusioned, too. He wrote an angry letter to Lodge, who made a lame excuse for missing the quorum call.[48]

The NAACP had one more arrow left in its quiver. Since September it had been preparing a full-page advertisement to appear in selected national newspapers at a key moment. The concept was developed by Edward L. Bernays, the public relations man, and Arthur Spingarn. The Association applied to the American Fund for Public Service, on whose board Johnson sat, for an emergency ten thousand dollar loan to pay for the ads. The Association had already expended forty thousand dollars over the last seven years on the issue, and the American Fund delivered twenty-five hundred dollars toward a matching fund. The ad appeared in nine major daily newspapers with a combined readership of two million on November 22 and 23, 1922. "THE SHAME OF AMERICA" included headlines of the worst lynching stories, listed prominent endorsers of the Dyer bill, and urged readers to write their senators at once. "The ad is great," Johnson wrote White from Washington. "It has made a sensation here among our people." The advertisement represented the boldest attempt to shape national opinion in the Association's history to that date.[49]

It did not succeed. When Congress convened on November 20, the Democrats filibustered again, tying up all business in the Senate. Senator Oscar Underwood of Alabama told the Republicans they would have to withdraw the bill for the whole term of the Sixty-seventh Congress, which would mean starting over in the next Congress. "Once or twice during the fight, I caught a glance from Senator Borah," Johnson remembered. "This time I felt sure that he was laughing at me, and somewhat maliciously."[50]

The Republicans considered their response at a caucus on Saturday night, December 2. Before the meeting, Lodge and two colleagues had assured Johnson that the bill would not be abandoned on southern terms. But the Republicans agreed to lay the bill aside, leaving the door open to further action that term, with only nine Republicans dissenting. Johnson was helpless. He read about it in the newspapers the next morning. He sent an anxious telegram to the president, asking him to keep the bill alive, otherwise, he warned, there "will be a terrible blow to the colored people of the country, and [it] will have an incalculable political effect on them." Harding did nothing, and the next day Lodge announced the party's complete surrender. The Dyer bill was dead.[51]

Every defeat raises the question of whom to blame. Johnson lashed out in his *Age* column at both parties, but since the Democrats were beneath his contempt, he reserved most of his scorn for the Republicans, especially Lodge. In private correspondence he confronted the senator with his failure, and Lodge replied defensively that he had not promised what Johnson thought he had. Johnson wrote also to Harding's secretary, lamenting that the Republicans had exerted little effort, letting their opponents kill the bill and then blaming them. For his part, Du Bois wrote a scathing editorial for the *Crisis*; the first sentence of the first draft read "The Republicans did not intend to pass the Dyer bill." Johnson had to edit it down.[52]

The national secretary felt bitter himself. Over the next eight days in December, mobs lynched four more victims. One of these was tortured in public and burned at the stake. Later in the month, forty North Carolina Klansmen in full regalia seized a state employee and whipped him for speaking up on the Dyer bill. What, Johnson demanded to know, did the United States Senate propose to do about this, now that the Dyer bill was dead?[53]

There were other recriminations as well. The Association accused Negro Republican Perry Howard, now working in the Justice Department, of treachery. Before the vote, Howard wrote to Delaware congressman Cole-

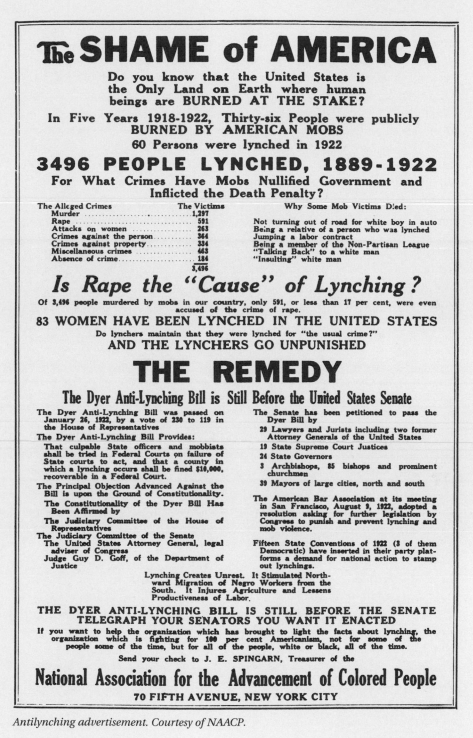

The SHAME of AMERICA

Do you know that the United States is the Only Land on Earth where human beings are BURNED AT THE STAKE?

In Five Years 1918-1922, Thirty-six People were publicly BURNED BY AMERICAN MOBS

60 Persons were lynched in 1922

3496 PEOPLE LYNCHED, 1889-1922

For What Crimes Have Mobs Nullified Government and Inflicted the Death Penalty?

The Alleged Crimes	The Victims
Murder	1,297
Rape	591
Attacks on women	263
Crimes against the person	364
Crimes against property	334
Miscellaneous crimes	463
Absence of crime	184
	3,496

Why Some Mob Victims Died:

Not turning out of road for white boy in auto
Being a relative of a person who was lynched
Jumping a labor contract
Being a member of the Non-Partisan League
"Talking Back" to a white man
"Insulting" white man

Is Rape the "Cause" of Lynching?

Of 3,496 people murdered by mobs in our country, only 591, or less than 17 per cent, were even accused of the crime of rape.

83 WOMEN HAVE BEEN LYNCHED IN THE UNITED STATES

Do lynchers maintain that they were lynched for "the usual crime?"

AND THE LYNCHERS GO UNPUNISHED

THE REMEDY

The Dyer Anti-Lynching Bill is Still Before the United States Senate

The Dyer Anti-Lynching Bill was passed on January 26, 1922, by a vote of 230 to 119 in the House of Representatives

The Dyer Anti-Lynching Bill Provides:

That culpable State officers and mobbists shall be tried in Federal Courts on failure of State courts to act, and that a county in which a lynching occurs shall be fined $10,000, recoverable in a Federal Court.

The Principal Objection Advanced Against the Bill is upon the Ground of Constitutionality.

The Constitutionality of the Dyer Bill Has Been Affirmed by

The Judiciary Committee of the House of Representatives
The Judiciary Committee of the Senate
The United States Attorney General, legal adviser of Congress
Judge Guy D. Goff, of the Department of Justice

The Senate has been petitioned to pass the Dyer Bill by

29 Lawyers and Jurists including two former Attorney Generals of the United States

19 State Supreme Court Justices

24 State Governors

3 Archbishops, 85 bishops and prominent churchmen

39 Mayors of large cities, north and south

The American Bar Association at its meeting in San Francisco, August 9, 1922, adopted a resolution asking for further legislation by Congress to punish and prevent lynching and mob violence.

Fifteen State Conventions of 1922 (3 of them Democratic) have inserted in their party platforms a demand for national action to stamp out lynchings.

Lynching Creates Unrest. It Stimulated Northward Migration of Negro Workers from the South. It Injures Agriculture and Lessens Productiveness of Labor.

THE DYER ANTI-LYNCHING BILL IS STILL BEFORE THE SENATE TELEGRAPH YOUR SENATORS YOU WANT IT ENACTED

If you want to help the organization which has brought to light the facts about lynching, the organization which is fighting for 100 per cent Americanism, not for some of the people some of the time, but for all of the people, white or black, all of the time.

Send your check to J. E. SPINGARN, Treasurer of the

National Association for the Advancement of Colored People

70 FIFTH AVENUE, NEW YORK CITY

Antilynching advertisement. Courtesy of NAACP.

man Du Pont, charging that the NAACP had become a Democratic front to which the Republicans owed nothing. They had squandered Negro money on "luxurious salaries" paid to the staff, so that Johnson could eat duck on his junkets to Washington while Du Bois stayed in New York, "stroking his Chesterfieldian beard." The newspaper ads had been a waste, too, and, he concluded, "these political bolsheviks should be annihilated as the basest of ingrates." Howard stuck to his earlier defense of a bill applicable only to prisoners in custody. The Association blamed Howard for giving the Republicans a cover to desert them.[54]

The Party of Lincoln was now dead to the Negro vanguard. The brief Johnson-Harding collaboration was essentially finished, and the president himself would be dead by August also. New president Calvin Coolidge appointed C. Bascomb Slemp, a Virginia segregationist, as his secretary. Johnson had an awkward interview with the new president, "but it was clear that Mr. Coolidge knew absolutely nothing about the colored people. . . . I was relieved when the brief audience was over, and I suppose Mr. Coolidge was, too." African America began a gradual process of reorientation to the northern liberal wing of the Democratic Party.[55]

The more significant development was the decline of lynching that began in 1923. During the 1920s, the number of black people lynched decreased from seventy-six in 1919 to seven in 1929. In 1922, fifty-one were lynched, then twenty-nine in 1923, and sixteen the following year. Several factors contributed to this major change in the American landscape. First was the newfound stability of the economy, which recovered after the 1921–1922 recession. The economic tensions that gave rise to lynching eased. There were probably far fewer of the landlord-tenant confrontations that produced many lynchings. A sign of the primacy of the economic factor is that lynching rose again during the depression, although not to 1917–1922 levels. The continued migration out of the South, which struck fear of a labor shortage into the hearts of local ruling groups, also contributed to lynching's decline. Closely connected to this was the fear of a mass retaliation on the ground, along the lines of what had occurred in Tulsa. Finally and just as important was the rise of mass media, such as radio and talking movies. The sheer boredom and isolation of rural life was transformed by the new technology, which generated a culture of celebrity heroes upon whom Americans could project their hopes and fears. Lynching became a throwback to an earlier, pre-electricity time as new entertainments expanded the horizons of a younger generation and turned their thoughts to baseball, movie stars, and radio melodramas.[56]

The NAACP could take its share of credit, too. As Johnson noted in a letter to Joel Spingarn two weeks after the Dyer bill's defeat, the most important aspect of the campaign was the fight itself, not the legislative outcome.[57] The white South had won a battle, but only narrowly, and it was put on warning. By fighting along a broad front for public awareness, the NAACP played a central role in ending the lynching epidemic.

13

Follow the North Star

OF the twelve million African Americans living in the United States in the 1920s, few remembered being a slave, but many had heard of that experience from their parents or grandparents. The Emancipation Proclamation was only fifty-seven years old in 1920. Some of the new writers of the Harlem Renaissance captured the poignancy of this generational transformation in their stories. In "Jonah's Gourd Vine," Zora Neale Hurston tells of a young man who escapes an abusive stepfather, a former slave. The young man, representing the new consciousness that is being born, symbolically crosses a river to begin his adult life.[1]

Flight from slavery by crossing the river—this was the Old Testament theme of rebirth that infused the narratives of the lucky few who escaped slavery by wit and courage. In these stories the hero would be resurrected in a new life by following the North Star. Buffalo or Detroit—the only major cities on the Canadian border, or Canada itself—were the places where many of these real-life stories ended. Escape stories continued after Emancipation, but in the 1920s the flight was from lynching or the sheriff. Even a guilty man could sometimes escape the clutches of southern law if a northern judge or governor decided that a prisoner might be lynched upon his return to the South. During the 1920s, NAACP branches blocked the extradition of a few dozen escapees from the South. Three stories from the early 1920s illustrate some of the variants of these tales.

MATTHEW BULLOCK'S nightmare began when detectives in Hamilton, Ontario, arrested him on January 11, 1922. A tall, handsome man, he worked as a laborer under the pseudonym of John Jones. Bullock made no attempt to protest that he was the wrong man. A Canadian newspaper reported that he was "almost paralyzed with fear" when he was locked in his cell. "They won't give me a fair trial," he said despairingly. "Those folks in the

South will string me up at the first telegraph pole. . . . Niggers in that county don't get a fair trial . . . they are just hanged."[2]

"That county" was Warren County in northern North Carolina, specifically the town of Norlina, which lay just south of the Virginia border and forty-five miles northeast of Raleigh. Bullock was not speaking rhetorically. One year ago his brother Plummer had protested when a white store clerk sold him rotten apples after he had paid for the good ones. Not knowing one's place was a crime in this town of seven hundred. Plummer Bullock's father, a respected minister, asked the sheriff to lock his son in jail for protection. A lynch mob formed anyway, but black men armed themselves and headed for the jail also. The two groups met and a gunfight broke out. Six whites and three blacks were wounded, some seriously but none fatally. Matthew Bullock was among the men defending his brother. Thinking they had driven the attackers off, the black men disbanded. The white mob returned and kidnapped Plummer Bullock and another man. The second man had not committed the unspeakable offense of demanding fresh apples instead of rotten ones, but they killed both men anyway.

Matthew Bullock ran away to Hamilton, Ontario, a medium-sized inland port tucked into the western corner of Lake Ontario, about forty miles from Buffalo. A number of black people lived in Hamilton, some of them the descendants of escaped slaves. One day a visiting North Carolinian, probably on a spying mission, spotted Matthew Bullock. He contacted North Carolina officials, who notified the Hamilton police. Matthew Bullock was wanted on charges of inciting to riot and shooting a white man. Canadian immigration officials began deportation proceedings against Bullock, on the grounds that he had entered the country illegally.[3]

The Hamilton black comunity knew its duty. They secured an attorney, and Reverend J. D. Howell telegrammed the NAACP in New York. Three nights later they held a protest meeting. "The church was packed to the doors," a participant wrote to her niece in Buffalo. "The whole city is stirred up . . . Oh, Violet, I just wish you could hear the white people speak in his behalf," wrote "Aunt Ab."[4]

Indeed, black and white Canadians were determined to give the American lynchers a lesson in civilization. The Canadian newspapers generally supported Bullock. "This country would feel that it had not given Matthew Bullock a square deal if he were to be sent back to North Carolina under an extradition order only to meet a fate like that of his brother," the *Toronto Globe* editorialized. Although the local officials ruled routinely that Bullock must be deported, the Canadian Department of Immigration ordered Hamilton to hold Bullock unless U.S. authorities could present a genuine charge against him.[5]

The Buffalo NAACP took up the case also. In 1920, black people lived downtown on a cluster of streets named for fruits, called the "fruit belt." Black men worked in the nearby Lackawanna steel mills and women worked as domestics. Southern migrants swelled the industrial ranks, and they joined the NAACP as well. This was the branch founded by Mary B. Talbert, and its president now was Amelia G. Anderson. Learning of Bullock's plight, she asked the national office to send help, and the next day Walter White came to town.[6]

If Bullock were deported, he would have to pass through Buffalo on his way to North Carolina. White and Buffalo NAACP leaders plotted with the chief of police to have Bullock arrested on a phony charge if he entered the city. North Carolina officials would then have to extradite Bullock again. The New York state NAACP branches were notified to send letters to the governor in this eventuality. White addressed several meetings in the Buffalo black community to explain the plan. At the end of January, the Immigration Commission at Ottawa heard an appeal of Bullock's case and reversed its lower office. Bullock was set free.[7]

Whites in Norlina would not let the matter rest. A Negro had shot a white man and got away with it, and then a foreign country had rebuked their justice system. This was an intolerable situation. The *Durham Sun* called Bullock "a nigger who has killed him a white man." North Carolina officials filed papers with the U.S. State Department, refining its legal charge against Bullock to attempted murder. Another of the African-American defenders at Norlina had been convicted on the same charge and sentenced to eight years. North Carolina felt that this legal proceeding strengthened its case. Canada rearrested Bullock in mid-February.[8]

Walter White was not worried. "I heard confidentially that the State Department [does not] want any more publicity," he advised a Canadian ally, and therefore would not press the case for extradition. The *New York Times* warned against pursuing the Bullock case in an editorial titled "This Case is Full of Difficulties," which compared it to the Dred Scott case of the 1850s.[9]

Bullock was assigned to a Judge Snider of Canada's Immigration Board, sitting at Hamilton. Late in February Snider gave North Carolina one week to send its witnesses to Canada. During that week, North Carolina NAACP branches sent White clippings from the newspapers showing the atmosphere of the state and the results of proceedings against other Norlina blacks in the shooting incident. Seven men had gotten six months to a year of hard labor on the road gangs. The *Greensboro Daily News*, an anti-lynching paper, doubted that the governor could save Bullock from lynching. The governor refused to take the Canadians seriously. Canada's de-

mand for witnesses was not "regular," he protested. He told the State Department that it should refuse to extradite Canadian criminals in reprisal.
On March 3, Judge Snider ruled against North Carolina, and Bullock was
free again. Ontario's Reverend Howell wrote Walter White that the NAACP
had won "undying fame in these parts."[10]

By standing up for Bullock, the Buffalo NAACP learned how to defend
other victims of injustice. In the summer of 1922, a white man raped a
nine-year-old black girl. The NAACP circulated petitions calling for the
prosecution of the perpetrator. The girl's parents were recent migrants
from the South and were afraid of the courts and reluctant to testify. The
NAACP convinced them to come forward, and the perpetrator was convicted. White Americans rarely paid for crimes against African Americans,
but Buffalo had the advantage of close proximity to a nation ruled by law.[11]

EVERY FUGITIVE lives with the apprehension of a fateful knock on the
door. For Thomas Ray it came on a Sunday, September 5, 1920, when two
Detroit detectives, the Wilkinson County, Georgia, sheriff and a fourth man
burst through his door with revolvers drawn. The fourth man was the
brother of DeWitt Faulkner, whom Ray had shot and killed the previous
June in Milledgeville, Georgia. The Milledgeville newspaper reported on
the day after the shooting that Ray would never be tried if the posse caught
up with him. Any reasonable observer of American race relations would
have to conclude that Ray was already a dead man.[12]

Ray had been a common farmhand, a day laborer. After four days of
work for Faulkner, Ray asked for his pay. Faulkner was a notorious Negro
hater, and he told Ray to go away. Infuriated by his hand's temerity, Faulkner proceeded to Ray's house and shot into it while Mrs. Ray and her children were at home. A few days later, Faulkner tracked Ray down at another
farm, drew his gun, and got off two wild shots before Ray shot him. A fellow
farmworker who had witnessed the shooting as an innocent bystander was
arrested and had to be moved twice for security reasons. Ray ran away to
Canada and after a while crossed the border back to Detroit, where he was
apprehended.[13]

The Detroit NAACP hired a trio of African-American attorneys, led by W.
Hayes McKinney, to represent Ray. The branch organized a fund-raising
campaign and circulated a petition against Ray's extradition, securing two
thousand signatures. Ray told his story to Governor Albert E. Sleeper at an
extradition hearing in Lansing on October 6. Ray's lawyers were up against
an unusual problem—Georgia was then governed by its first racial liberal.
Governor Thomas Dorsey promised Sleeper he would protect Ray and

change the venue of his trial to another county. Sleeper signed the extradition order.

McKinney's remaining procedural gambit was to seek a writ of *habeas
corpus*, which was granted. Meanwhile, a Georgia grand jury issued a new
indictment of Ray, and on this basis Sleeper scheduled a second hearing
for October 20. Ray awaited his fate at the Wayne County Courthouse
downtown on St. Antoine Street, and one night a rumor spread in the black
community that a white mob was gathering there. "Detroit is sitting on a
powder keg tonight," Walter White wrote to James Weldon Johnson from
the scene. A tense squad of black men stood by in the courthouse corridors, and when the blond-haired, blue-eyed White brushed against one
defender, the man squared for a fight. "I wish these crackers would start
something," White blurted to the puzzled man, explaining himself. "My
heart resumed its normal functions," White's account continued.[14]

There was no riot that night, but Ray lost at his second hearing, too.
Walter White testified that Governor Dorsey had told him that it was impossible to suppress lynching in Georgia. White displayed a map of the
state, placing a red star over every town in which there had been a lynching, and the map showed a blur of crimson. But Sleeper had essentially the
same evidence as he had earlier, and he ruled against Ray again. The governor might have known better, because in a previous case he had sent a
man back to Kentucky who was lynched within twelve hours of his arrival
in the state. Next Ray appealed to the Michigan Supreme Court, which
would buy more time. After a year's delay, Ray lost that appeal, too.[15]

In the interim, Michigan elected a new governor. Attorney McKinney
argued that he had new evidence regarding Georgia's ability to protect
Ray. The new governor, Alex J. Groesbeck, agreed to hear this evidence in
June 1921. After Ray's second appeal failed, a Georgia lynch mob met the
train that was supposed to be carrying him. Georgia officials in Michigan,
it turned out, had telegrammed their friends back home but neglected to
correct their message when NAACP attorneys appealed again. Georgia officials were acting in bad faith, McKinney argued. At the hearing this time,
Groesbeck decided that Ray had killed Faulkner in self-defense. Moreover,
the Georgia grand jury did not hear the testimony of the eyewitness to the
shooting, the other farmhand. "Ray's act was justifiable," Groesbeck
found. "His indictment . . . is unwarranted and illegal in both state and
federal law." Thomas Ray was a very rare African American: he had killed
a white man in Georgia and lived to tell about it.[16]

The liberal *Atlanta Constitution* was philosophical about the outcome.
While criticizing Groesbeck's decision, the editor admitted, "Just so long
as Georgia continues to head the list of states in lynching, it may expect

from time to time to be subject to this sort of humiliation—often unjustly, as it was no doubt in this instance."[17] The NAACP could take satisfaction not only in saving Ray but also in humbling Georgia.

ED KNOX was spared the trauma of a fateful knock on the door. He was arrested as he left the Alhambra Theater on January 31, 1921, in Charleston, West Virginia. At the end of September 1919, he had killed a white man during a dice game in Wartburg, about thirty miles west of Knoxville, Tennessee. Like Thomas Ray, Knox had acted in self-defense; he was shot during the fight. Knox hopped a northbound boxcar and got off in Charleston. There he lived for sixteen months without incident. After his arrest, Knox asked for the NAACP's help. If the gambler Knox's luck had run out in Tennessee, he hit a jackpot in West Virginia. He had run away to an NAACP stronghold.[18]

During the 1920s, African Americans organized eleven NAACP branches in southern West Virginia coal mining towns. The Charleston branch was the first and most spirited. Its founding members united the respectable middle class and tradespeople; among them were a molder, a carpenter, an ax forger, and a house painter. Of fifty-six founders twenty-five were women, mostly teachers and housewives.[19]

The other West Virginia branches were largely working class in composition, many of the rank and file being coal miners and their wives. As the historian Joe William Trotter has demonstrated, these branches advanced the political rights of black coal miners with remarkable success. They passed a state law banning racially divisive films and curtailed race-baiting in newspaper crime stories. They defended black men accused of several crimes, winning reductions of sentences in a few cases. In 1925, the Gary and Bluefield branches helped Payne Boyd, who ultimately proved he was not guilty of killing a white man. Most important, the branches got an antilynching bill passed in the state legislature in 1921, after a white man had been lynched. West Virginia civil rights activists won a 1919 state supreme court decision insuring that African Americans would be called for jury service. The state allocated better funding for segregated institutions for the handicapped and for black colleges.[20]

The Charleston branch was the most dynamic in the state. After a confusing start, with different factions vying for its leadership, a young Baptist minister named Mordecai Johnson was elected its president. Johnson was the son of an elderly ex-slave father who worked in a planing mill during the week and preached on Sunday. His doting mother inspired him to get an education. This Mordecai Johnson did, earning a degree at Morehouse

College and then joining its faculty in economics. When his mother died, Johnson resolved to give his life over to community service, and he entered Rochester Theological Seminary, where he studied with the liberal thinker Walter Rauschenbusch. After graduation and some YMCA work, Johnson became a minister at First Baptist Church in Charleston. Mary White Ovington remembered him as "dignified, serious, but full of energy and swift to understand conditions."[21]

Johnson made the NAACP a project of his ministry, the civil arm of a spiritual crusade. Black miners would join the NAACP "if they once got the vision of the Association as an arm of God." Besides helping to build other branches, Johnson and his successor, attorney T. G. Nutter, turned the Charleston branch into the pride of the parent body. By 1925, it had a thousand members, and it consistently met high financial quotas during fund drives. Like the other branches, they defended accused criminals, with Nutter heading the Legal Committee. The branch won admittance of African-American plumbers into the union, an unusual occurrence in the construction trades. Mass meetings were held at First Baptist, and the people came out one thousand strong for an October 1919 antilynching meeting. By 1921 the branch had seven standing committees, including an education committee, which taught black history to high schoolers. The great educator and historian Carter G. Woodson taught at Institute, West Virginia, and he put his stamp on young leaders of the NAACP in the state. While Ed Knox's case was pending in February 1921, W. E. B. Du Bois and Woodson spoke to NAACP meetings within ten days of each other. West Virginia was a powerful center of NAACP activism.[22]

Like most branches, Charleston had its own problems to sort out. In January 1921, R. C. McIver, a railroad baggage agent, complained to the national office that the membership drive was directed at only one denomination (presumably the Baptists). Mordecai Johnson replied that all denominations were welcome in the branch, but Baptists predominated because the ten Baptist churches outnumbered their rivals. Besides, why complain about a membership base of 1,142 people? McIver's dissatisfaction may have been class-based as well, as historian Joe William Trotter suggests, for middle-class people held the leading positions in the branch. However, McIver quarreled with coal miner NAACPers later, and Mordecai Johnson may have been an educated minister, but he was the son of a sawmill operative himself.[23]

A self-consciously middle-class leadership might have turned its back on a fugitive who killed a white man in a dice game. The Charleston NAACP came straight to Knox's defense. Working through the national office and the Knoxville branch, they learned that a man thought to be Knox had been lynched a few days after the gunfight. Attorney Nutter presented his evidence to a state judge, and on February 14 Charleston telegrammed the national office that Knox would not be extradited to Tennessee. The branch celebration was held at First Baptist.[24]

THESE latter two cases generated only local publicity, as did the several dozen similar cases northern NAACP branches conducted in the 1920s. The Bullock case became an international incident and was exceptional in that regard. All three cases showed several aspects of NAACP activity in the 1920s. First, the branches carried out unspectacular grassroots legal work that earned them respect in their communities. If an African American was in trouble with the law, the NAACP was the place to go. Second, the branches were not afraid to stand up for poor, even disreputable men who defended themselves with guns. Third, they would cross their political friends—such as Georgia's governor Thomas Dorsey—when the life of a black man was at stake. The NAACP's work in defense of fugitives from southern justice cuts across its image as a white-oriented, middle-class group.

14

"The Cornerstone of the Temple"

I N the summer of 1920, two groups of six Arkansas convicts waited for execution in the state prison at Little Rock. They were the condemned men of the October 1919 Phillips County massacre. Their original trials had been so brief that the jury failed to indicate whether the accused men were guilty of first or second degree murder. One jury had convicted Frank Moore and five others of killing Clinton Lee, and in their case the judge affixed the words "in the first degree" to the verdict. Ed Ware and three others were convicted of the murder of W. A. Adkins, the man killed at the Hoop Spur church; and Albert Giles and Joe Fox were found culpable in the death of posse member James A. Tappan. These last six, whose appeals were docketed together as *Ware et al.*, won a new trial on the technicality that the degree of their offense was indicated by neither jury nor judge. The *Ware* defendants lost a retrial of their case before the original trial judge. Their attorneys appealed the decision to the Arkansas Supreme Court. In addition to these convicts, sixty-seven others had been sentenced to long terms in prison for their alleged roles in the Phillips County conflict of 1919.

African-American Arkansans organized a Citizens Defense Fund Commission on behalf of the accused men and chose their best attorney to handle the appeals. Over the next five years, Scipio Africanus Jones would fight these cases through every possible state court. When the *Moore* case went to the U.S. Supreme Court, NAACP president Moorfield Storey argued the case and won. The two constituencies represented by these attorneys—African-American Arkansas and the national civil rights community—joined in a difficult alliance to win one of the most important and most overlooked civil rights victories of the twentieth century.

SCIPIO AFRICANUS JONES was born in 1863 to a slave mother and an unknown father, probably a white man. He went to school at Tulip in Dallas

County, chopping cotton to earn money. As a young man he graduated from Shorter College in 1885. He taught in the public schools while he studied law with three white Little Rock lawyers. Jones passed the bar in 1899, and with Thomas Price he established a partnership in 1908. Jones managed the insurance program of the Mosaic Templars, a fraternal organization. By 1924 the Templars had two thousand lodges with eighty thousand members. Headquartered in Little Rock, the Templars were the most important African-American organization in the city, and Jones became one of the best-known African-American attorneys in the state. He represented indigent African Americans *pro bono*, showing little interest in enriching himself as a lawyer. Jones did have an entrepreneurial side, and he launched a real estate venture with six colleagues.

Jones participated actively in the state's Republican Party. He fought a losing battle for over two decades against the party's lily-white faction, which kept blacks from holding federal appointive offices. In 1902, Jones lost a campaign for Little Rock school board by a vote of 2,202 to 181, which showed the extent of black disfranchisement. In 1920, while Jones was working on the Phillips County cases, white Republicans tried to exclude African Americans from the Pulaski County Convention. They retaliated by holding a convention of their own and nominated the principal of Negro schools in Helena for governor. Black Arkansans, including Scipio Jones, went to the Republican National Convention, which recognized the white delegates but passed a resolution encouraging unified county conventions.

Despite Jones's high profile in the black community, he maintained positive relations with Arkansas whites. According to historian Tom Dillard, he possessed a "courtly and gentlemanly manner." His contemporaries described him as "reserved" and "unpretentious." In other words, Jones showed deference to white attorneys and was careful not to offend them. There was no other choice for an African-American lawyer in the 1920s South.[1]

When the Phillips County trials began, Jones sat at the nexus of black organizational power. He had ties to the legal, political, business, and fraternal worlds. His colleagues moved in the religious and academic communities. They formed the Citizens Defense Fund Commission that united the whole community to represent the accused men. The NAACP was ill suited as a local defense organization on three counts: it was integrated, northern-based, and militant. Little Rock African Americans who built a vigorous NAACP chapter later in the decade never pushed to make that organization the public face of the Phillips County cases.

For its part, the NAACP in New York groped its way toward an accommodation with Arkansas black leaders. The *Crisis* had criticized Arkansans

Scipio Africanus Jones. Courtesy of Arkansas History Commission.

who supported the extradition of Robert Hill, alleged leader of the share-croppers' union, from Kansas to Arkansas. The Association raised money for the defense from its branches and wealthy white contributors, but for strategic reasons kept its hand hidden in the early stages of the case. Later, when its legal clout was necessary at the federal level, the Association assumed a more public role. Although the NAACP initially distrusted the local leaders, it gradually came to appreciate the dogged legal work and fund raising of the activists on the scene.

AN important part of that work was to foster divisions among white Arkansans over the execution of the imprisoned farmers. In February of 1921, E. L. McHaney, the white attorney of record in the case, addressed a meeting at Second Presbyterian Church in Little Rock. The meeting appointed a committee of prominent whites to lobby Governor Thomas C. McRae to delay the execution of the *Moore* prisoners until the *Ware* case was adjudicated. Further, the defenders introduced a bill into the state legislature to make a change of venue mandatory in capital cases. The defense committee hoped that an acquittal in the *Ware* case would create a situation in which the "[g]overnor will be forced by public sentiment and a sense of fairness to pardon the rest of the convicted men," Jones wrote. Finally, the defense committee paid a detective $125 a week to pursue leads in the case. In the spring of 1921, the NAACP took over much of the fund raising as local sources ran out. "[Y]our money will be matched, even if I have to pay every dollar of it myself," Jones vowed. "These men have lived in the shadow of the electric chair long enough." Ominously, Governor McRae set June 10 as an execution date in the *Moore* case. Meanwhile the *Ware* defendants won a change of venue to Lee County, near Phillips. This was too close for Jones's preference, but "any place is better than Helena," he wrote.[2]

As June 10 neared, Arkansas civil rights activists pressured Governor McRae to grant clemency. Bishop J. M. Conner led a delegation of prominent African-American citizens to see the governor, presenting him with a petition on the prisoners' behalf. Jones and McHaney later gave the governor evidence that torture had been used to extract confessions from the men. The NAACP urged that telegrams be sent in support of the petition, and branches and individuals responded. From Pine Bluff a ministerial alliance visited McRae, and the Jubilee Chorus of Arkansas Baptist College joined the prisoners in a prayer service. The plea that garnered the most attention for the case came from Robert T. Kerlin, an English teacher at Virginia Military Institute. He was the lone white southerner to speak out for the defendants, and his appeal was published in the northern liberal press and vilified in the South. He urged McRae to heed "the still small voice . . . that bids you stand for the eternal right."[3]

White Arkansans, especially at Helena, pushed just as hard for execution. They got Kerlin fired for breaking the code of white solidarity. They held a public meeting on June 7, demanding the death penalty. The American Legion, the Lions Club, and all the solid citizens of the town joined the outcry. They sent a delegation to visit the governor, too. Governor McRae had earlier solicited a report from John Miller, the Phillips County prosecutor. As expected, he recapitulated the prosecution case and recommended that the executions be carried out. The governor therefore refused to intervene. Time had now run out, and the prison warden had six caskets built.[4]

One last chance remained. Jones and McHaney had planned to file a *habeas corpus* appeal in the federal court before Judge Jacob Trieber. A rare Jew in Arkansas, Trieber had shown sympathy for African-American aspirations in the intra–Republican Party debate. Unfortunately, he was serving out of town. Jones and McHaney took their plea before John E. Martineau of the county chancery (real estate) court. To everyone's astonishment, Martineau ordered E. H. Dempsey, the state prison warden, to appear before him and show why the men should be executed. The state attorney general promptly challenged Martineau's ruling in the Arkansas Supreme Court. The attorney general won, but the court granted a new hearing, postponing the executions.[5]

A debate then opened between Little Rock's two leading newspapers, the *Arkansas Democrat* and the *Arkansas Gazette.* The former protested that the *Ware* and *Moore* cases were inextricably linked and that a resolution as final as capital punishment should wait until all twelve cases were adjudicated. This was the line that McHaney had urged before the Presbyterians. Citing unfavorable northern opinion against Arkansas should the executions be carried out, the *Democrat* counseled delay. The *Gazette* reflected white Helena's opinion that each case stood on its own merit, that the Negroes had killed the whites and should therefore be executed. The *Gazette* never printed the allegations of torture until the case came to the supreme court.

On June 20 the state supreme court heard the arguments. African Americans and whites packed a tense courtroom. Predictably, the supreme court found that a chancery court could not rule on a criminal proceeding. Yet the governor did not set a new date for execution. In the interim, Jones and McHaney appealed to the U.S. Supreme Court for a writ of error, thus forestalling a new date for execution.[6]

Two months later, McHaney secured dramatic new evidence showing that the sharecroppers' account of the 1919 events was accurate. For reasons that remain obscure, railroad detectives T. K. Jones and H. F. Smiddy swore out affidavits that destroyed the state's case against all twelve men. Their testimony may have been generated by Scipio Jones's detective. T. K. Jones, a supervisor, was among the first to learn of the shooting at Hoop Spur. He had driven to the church before daybreak, finding Adkins's body. The next day he overheard a planter describing how he threatened his "niggers" with death if they joined the union. T. K. Jones himself had interrogated prisoners and whipped them, helping to beat confessions out of two now-convicted men. He testified that "no man could have . . . voted for acquittal and remained in Helena afterward."

Smiddy backed up Jones's story, adding that the church was full of personal items, which suggested that the people inside had fled in haste. The building had been shot into and later was burned down, he thought, to destroy evidence of that. Smiddy had also taken part in the massacre of October 1. He rode with a posse of fifty men, who ruthlessly gunned down black men trying to surrender. "I do not know how many negroes were killed in all, but I do know that there were between two hundred and three hundred negroes that I saw with my own eyes," he stated. Smiddy had been standing next to James Tappan, a white victim, and swore that men from his own posse had inadvertently shot him. Like Jones, Smiddy had whipped the prisoners until they confessed.[7]

Unfortunately for the convicted men, on August 4 the Arkansas Supreme Court turned down their appeal for a writ of error without considering this new evidence. Governor McRae set September 23 as the new execution date, and with forty-eight hours remaining, he denied a postponement for the second time. Scipio Jones now filed for a writ of *habeas corpus* in the United States District Court. For the first time he could tell the whole story of the Phillips County affair, this time with inside information from whites.

Jones began with a retelling of the socioeconomic relations created by the sharecropping system. He insisted that whites began the shooting at Hoop Spur and that there was no plan for a Negro insurrection. The defendants had not fired at Clinton Lee, whom all six men were accused of killing. The original trial had been unjust. Jones detailed the torture of the prisoners and averred that all the defendants still bore the marks of it on their bodies. He noted that the defense attorneys did not meet with their clients, called no witnesses, and allowed the trial to conclude in less than an hour. Outside, a lynch mob was pacified only by assurances of speedy electrocutions.

The petition called special attention to the hostile racial climate of the proceedings. All the jurors were white, yet Negroes outnumbered whites by five to one there, and many were literate landholders. They had been intentionally excluded from the juries at all levels.[8]

Filing this petition stopped the executions, but, as political scientist Richard C. Cortner concluded in his study of the case, "the outlook was not promising." However, the Arkansas attorney general merely filed a demurrer to the petitioners' claim. In effect, this granted the truth of the *Moore* defendants' charges, but dismissed them as insufficient to stop the execution. The court upheld the demurrer but decided that an appeal to the U.S. Supreme Court was in order.[9]

At this critical juncture, E. L. McHaney and his firm demanded from the Association an additional seventy-five hundred dollars in legal fees. Rather than conduct the *Ware* appeal in Lee County themselves, they insisted upon hiring a new firm to do that, claiming that they had fulfilled their obligation to the NAACP. At its September 1921 meeting, the board of directors emphatically rejected this demand, and Johnson replied to McHaney by reviewing the Association's contractual agreement with him. This stipulated that McHaney would complete all litigation up to a Supreme Court appeal for five thousand dollars, which his firm had received. McHaney then withdrew from the case. The NAACP thought that his intentions had been merely pecuniary from the outset, and now that he had his money, he was through.

Scipio Jones now became the lead attorney in both cases. James Weldon Johnson wrote to Jones, decrying McHaney's perfidy. "[N]ot for a moment do we think that you will do anything else but stand by these men until the very last resource is exhausted. The Arkansas cases are no longer mere legal cases—they constitute a fight for common justice and humanity and those who are aiding in the fight are doing a great public service." Jones agreed that McHaney's "requirements are so unreasonable, I am sure that no one will attempt to comply with them." For his part, Jones vowed "to live up to my contract with the Association." The board angrily refused to accept McHaney's resignation (a futile gesture) and forwarded five hundred dollars to Jones at once.[10]

The *Ware* defendants would still need Lee County attorneys, and Jones secured the best possible firm. They wanted ten thousand dollars, an exorbitant fee. "[T]hey cannot be very deeply interested in the case," White protested to Jones, if they insisted on full payment in advance. In New York, the financial situation was difficult. The cases had continued for a long time and generated little publicity, which made fund raising difficult. Incredibly, Jones raised six thousand dollars in Arkansas within a week. "We have a fighting chance to acquit some of the defendants in Lee County," Jones wrote. A victory there might tip the scales in the *Moore* cases. When the trial began on October 10, the prosecution won a continuance until the 1922 spring term. This was a tacit admission that they had no case, Jones informed Arthur B. Spingarn in New York.[11]

The NAACP's recognition of Jones as its lead attorney in Arkansas marked a new departure for the Association and a turning point in African-American legal history. All legal decisions in Arkansas now were cleared with Jones alone. His unfailing optimism and tenacity prepared the way for an appeal to the U.S. Supreme Court. Scipio Jones represented the first step toward the black-led full-time Legal Committee that emerged in the 1930s under Charles Hamilton Houston and Thurgood Marshall.

With the prosecution postponing the *Ware* case, the main problem in the following year became the appeal to the Supreme Court in *Moore.* The Association had always turned to its president in these situations. Moorfield Storey was now in his late seventies, trying to wind down his legal practice and retire. Mary White Ovington and Walter White cajoled the veteran attorney into making one last appearance before the Court in what would surely be the Association's most important case. Storey begged off, pleading an older man's prerogative. He was out of touch with developments in the case, he wrote, and he suggested that the Association secure U. S. Bratton, whose name he could not even remember. In addition, Storey had one major doubt about the case and feared he might lose.[12]

The controlling precedent in the *Moore* plea would be the case of Leo Frank. Frank was the Jewish factory manager convicted of murdering a teenage girl employee in his Georgia pencil factory. His trial had been conducted in a mob-dominated courtroom in which armed spectators shouted threats against the judge. The case was appealed three times to the Georgia Supreme Court, and an appeal to the U.S. high court failed as well. Louis Marshall, president of the American Jewish Committee and a respected constitutional lawyer, argued before the Court that Frank had been denied his rights under the due process clause of the Fourteenth Amendment. Marshall stressed the atmosphere of the trial, which was so poisoned that the trial judge recommended that Frank not attend the reading of the verdict. The judge feared that Frank would be lynched if found innocent. Marshall argued that the federal courts should have granted a writ of *habeas corpus* in Frank's case to protect him from Georgia's violation of his due process rights. However, the Supreme Court ruled that Frank had had a fair appeal. Oliver Wendell Holmes wrote a stirring dissent in this case, earning him the sobriquet of the Great Dissenter. The governor of Georgia commuted Frank's sentence to life in prison, and in 1915 a mob abducted him from his cell and lynched him.[13]

Would not this precedent be cited in the Arkansas case? Storey gradually came to believe that the problem posed by *Frank* could be overcome, just as he had convinced himself of the Dyer bill's constitutionality. He would show the differences between the two cases and not attack the precedent.[14]

Storey still wanted U. S. Bratton, a white southerner, by his side. Bratton agreed to come for a nominal fee, "and that only because I lost so much in leaving Arkansas." Scipio Jones thought Bratton would be an asset at the Court, but feared the reaction in Arkansas should his name be publicly associated with the case again. Bratton was hated by Arkansas racists, and Jones believed that they would punish the defendants if only to repay Bratton. If they won at the Supreme Court, Arkansas might still retry the men, or a reduced sentence might be arranged. Jones wanted to make the political situation easier for the governor by keeping Bratton out. Ultimately, Bratton did argue orally, but his name was omitted from the written brief.[15]

The first section of Storey's brief followed that written by Jones in the federal district court. He reviewed the events of 1919 just as Jones did. He stressed that the state attorney general had merely demurred in the Arkansas high court, which amounted to an admission of the facts as presented by the appellants. Storey contrasted the legal proceeding in *Moore* with that of the *Frank* case. In Arkansas, defendants and witnesses had been tortured, there had been no real defense attorneys, and the trial had lasted less than an hour. Frank had been represented by a leading attorney during a three-week trial and made no claim of witness tampering. The only similarity was the mob atmosphere. "[T]he record of the whole case shows what, if consummated, is only judicial murder," Storey wrote. Therefore the Arkansas defendants deserved the relief denied to Frank. "This is in fact the extreme case which the minority of this court used as an illustration in the *Frank* case," Storey concluded.[16]

On January 9, 1923, Storey and Bratton argued before the Supreme Court. Oliver Wendell Holmes showed his sympathy toward the appellants throughout. He asked friendly, leading questions during Storey's presentation. When the Arkansas attorney general spoke, Holmes interrupted him to ask, "Do you mean that if the judge and jury literally and figuratively had a pistol pressed to their breasts it was still a fair trial?" Chief Justice William Howard Taft reminded the Arkansas prosecutor that the state had admitted the appellants' version of the facts by merely issuing a demurrer. Bratton wrote White that the only negative remark came from Justice James C. McReynolds, "who suggested that the negroes got a rotten deal but that it might not be in the court's power to grant relief." In his argument Bratton emphasized the enormous disproportionality in the violence and prosecution. Two hundred Negroes were dead and no whites indicted; twelve Negroes were accused of killing a handful of whites. The treatment of his son, O. S. Bratton, falsely imprisoned for a trumped-up crime and released in secret to prevent his lynching, showed the inflamed temper of the local community.[17]

Six weeks later the court issued its ruling. This time Holmes wrote for a 7–2 majority. The different verdict from that of the *Frank* case owed not only to the procedural failings of *Moore* but also to a liberalization in the composition of the Court over eight years. Holmes found that the Court had to accept the appellants' version of events, given the state's demurrer at the Arkansas Supreme Court. Leaving aside the guilt or innocence of the men, Holmes agreed that their constitutional rights had been violated. He reviewed the story of O. S. Bratton, which showed how the mob spirit dominated Helena. He adduced the inflammatory newspaper articles and the demands of prominent Helena citizens for the death penalty. He gave full credit to the affidavits of the tortured prisoners and the railroad detectives. He noted the absence of Negroes from the juries. Finally, he endorsed Storey's analysis of the *Frank* decision. The Supreme Court reversed the verdict and returned the case to the district court.[18]

Only four months after this remarkable victory, Jones and the expensive Lee County firm won a second triumph in the *Ware* case. The prosecution failed to proceed yet again. Arkansas law granted prisoners the right to seek release if their trials were continued against the protests of their attorneys over two consecutive terms. In April Jones sought the discharge of the six *Ware* prisoners under this statute, and on June 25 the Arkansas Supreme Court granted it. The sheriff transported the men by train to Little Rock, where Jones and a colleague met them. After a comical midnight interlude outside the walls of the state prison, where bickering officials argued about jurisdiction over the release, they were set free. The Little Rock black community took them in, free at last after four years of imprisonment for a crime they did not commit.[19]

The Association was still left with a complicated problem regarding the *Moore* prisoners. They might seek a *habeas corpus* hearing in Arkansas and gamble upon forcing the state to release the men. They might lose this, especially if the two railroad detectives (who had fled Arkansas) refused to testify. Jones entered into a complex discussion with NAACP attorneys Herbert Stockton, Arthur Spingarn, and Storey regarding the best procedure.

The northerners decided that the final decision should rest with Jones, but they recommended compromising with Arkansas officials. The state had its own reasons for wishing to avoid a new trial, not the least of which was the threat of adverse national publicity. John E. Miller, the original prosecutor, wrote to Jones that the state might prefer a deal to a new trial. Acting as an intermediary, a white Little Rock attorney named George B. Rose helped Jones negotiate the final act in the Phillips County drama. For a one thousand dollar retainer, a Phillips County attorney would petition the governor for a commutation of the death sentences to twelve-year terms, of which the men would serve one year. That way the deal would be palatable to the governor, who could appear to be acceding to the wishes of Phillips County whites. The convictions would stand, but the men would go free. Governor McRae, in one of his last acts, announced the commutation in November 1924, and in January he granted indefinite furloughs to the six prisoners. During this time, Jones arranged furloughs for the sixty-seven long-term prisoners also. On January 14, 1925, the final six men walked out of prison, ending the longest and most significant case in the Association's history to that date.[20]

Political scientist Richard C. Cortner, author of a careful legal study of the Arkansas trials, concluded that Holmes's finding in *Moore* marked a significant departure from that of the *Frank* decision. Although Storey had stressed the distinctions between the cases in order to win, Cortner averred, Holmes's ruling "was the first of a series of decisions in this century to liberalize the rules determining whether a state conviction may be collaterally attacked via the federal writ of *habeas corpus* because of alleged violations of the federal constitutional rights of the defendant."[21] Louis Marshall thought this true of Holmes's decision as well. "The stone the builders rejected has now become the cornerstone of the temple," he wrote. The *Moore* decision was "a great achievement in constitutional law." Cortner showed how in 1932 the high Court overturned an Alabama decision in the celebrated Scottsboro case by referring to the language of the *Moore* decision. Henceforth, federal courts could demand that states provide the reality, not merely the formality, of due process of law.[22]

Just as the NAACP nationally decided to conceal its hand in the Phillips County cases, the Little Rock branch of the NAACP played no public role in the defense effort. This was almost certainly because of the hostility felt toward the Association by the prominent whites with whom Jones would have to deal. The relation of forces between whites and blacks restricted the public role of the NAACP in the Phillips County cases. Merely communicating with African Americans who advocated "social equality" was the kiss of death for any southern politician. Moreover, Walter White had thrown a hand grenade into a tense situation at the very beginning of the case when he "passed" as a white man and deceived the governor.

Black Arkansans had to conduct their defense in enemy territory and on the enemy's terms. For such a campaign, the Mosaic Templars, a secret society, became the network through which the Arkansas fund raising was conducted. Arkansas African Americans raised sixteen thousand dollars over the five years of the case, a significant sum considering the economic limitations of the region. However, the Arkansas leadership took no steps to project a public campaign of mass rallies for the defendants. The NAACP in New York recognized that the relationship of forces in the state precluded such a course. By contrast, the NAACP campaigned vigorously on behalf of Ossian Sweet and his co-defendants in Detroit immediately afterward. The Association changed its defense strategies according to region and the wishes of the people on the scene, using legalistic and mass action approaches as appropriate.

These objective circumstances notwithstanding, the NAACP strategy in the Arkansas cases displayed weaknesses that may have delayed the victory they won. Throughout, Arkansas authorities showed that they did respond to publicity and pressures within the state. The two leading Arkansas newspapers split over the case, and the Presbyterian church group pleaded for mercy, at least. Ultimately, the state failed at certain key junctures to press its case against the condemned men. These points included the presentation of a mere demurrer at the state supreme court in the *Moore* case, the failure to prosecute the *Ware* case, the decision of Judge Martineau to order Warden Dempsey to show cause for the executions, and the concluding compromise in the *Moore* case. At some level, all the figures who might have brought the trials to a pitiless end showed that they harbored doubts about doing so.

The NAACP might have diplomatically pushed harder at these officials. The Kerlin letter showed the possibilities and limitations of public pressure. Arkansas hard-liners succeeded in getting Kerlin fired, but the moderates who ultimately settled the case indicated that they feared such public exposures. In addition, more discreet forms of pressure might have been exerted within the South by forces such as the Commission on Interracial Cooperation in Atlanta or antilynching southern journalists, to suggest that a compromise would have been the best solution.

More problematic still was the silence within African America regarding the Phillips County affair. The black press covered the story only sporadically. The original battle of 1919 was front-page headline news in black weeklies and white dailies, North and South. After 1919, it dropped out of the news. Arkansas was far from any newspaper center, and Phillips County was a rural backwater. Reporters from African-American newspapers rarely traveled out of state in the 1920s. Outside of Arkansas the story faded away. While the NAACP issued press releases about the case at crucial junctures, these were picked up unevenly by African-American newspapers, which always had more sensational local morsels to vend: the usual mix of crime and sex stories dominated the headlines. Neither the *New York Age* nor the *Chicago Defender* covered the *Moore* case at the Supreme Court, and the *Baltimore Afro-American*, which was quite friendly to the NAACP, ran only a small page 1 story. The *Defender* noticed the 1925 release of the last prisoners, but the other two did not.[23]

Scipio Africanus Jones, the courtly and reserved Little Rock lawyer, did far more to defeat Jim Crow than historians have recognized. Even the

NAACP underestimated him. At the *Crisis*, Du Bois paid the case far less attention than it deserved. The NAACP's annual report for 1920 counted the Arkansas case as "our outstanding work of the year," but the *Crisis* never featured it in a central fashion. The magazine was gradually becoming a cultural journal. Its covers never focused on national political issues such as the Dyer bill or Arkansas defense. Even the final victory was reported only in a routinely positioned article two months after the victory. Jones spoke at the 1925 NAACP convention in Denver, but the *Crisis* mentioned him only in passing. The NAACP tried too weakly to call attention to a case that might have been a *cause célèbre*, at least within Arkansas.[24]

The low publicity strategy also hindered fund raising. The cost of defending the Phillips County prisoners was daunting by the standards of 1920s African America. Over thirty thousand dollars was raised for the defense, a major achievement for that time and place. Arkansas African Americans carried the main load in the first year and a half, raising almost eleven thousand dollars by early 1921. In April of that year, the *Crisis* ran a brief, buried notice showing the disbursement of that fund to Arkansas attorneys. The *Crisis* played down tensions between the local leaders and New York over who should get credit for the work. When the McHaney law firm broke its contract with the NAACP later that year, Jones raised an additional six thousand dollars in a week. A large sum raised quickly probably came from a core of prosperous key donors such as the Mosaic Templars, who volunteered savings or accepted liens on property. There does not seem to have been a grassroots campaign around the state to fund the defense effort.[25]

The NAACP nationally raised a similar sum, but its low profile hurt the cause. The Association sent out a fund appeal within six weeks of the massacre and mass arrests. Mary White Ovington's circular letter to the branches sought only twenty-five dollars from the larger branches and ten dollars from the smaller ones. "Our name for obvious reasons must not be used," she insisted. At each turning point some similar appeal was sent out, and the returns were correspondingly small. An October 1921 appeal netted ten dollars each from Tuscaloosa, Alabama; Johnstown, Pennsylvania; Beloit, Wisconsin; Elkhart, Indiana; and dozens of other branches. The 1921–1922 *Crisis* appeal netted "one dollar each from every colored man in our town" of Tonopah, Nevada—a total of twenty dollars; and a Kansas City meatpacker collected sixteen dollars and thirty-five cents from the workers at the Armour packinghouse. There was more like this. But where was Harlem, Chicago, Washington, and Atlanta? Mass meetings in these cities would have more easily paid for the defense effort and put more courage in the hearts of Arkansas activists.

Instead the Association relied upon wealthy white (and predominantly Jewish) private philanthropists such as Leo J. Weissberg and Julius Rosenwald of Chicago, and Edward Lasker and William A. Fuerst of the New York Foundation, some of whom contributed five hundred dollars or more.[26]

The money went almost entirely for legal fees, mostly to Bratton, Murphy, McHaney, and Jones. The Topeka lawyers received less than one thousand dollars. But the NAACP national contribution must be measured also by the *pro bono* work done by Storey and Legal Committee chairman Arthur B. Spingarn, who closely advised the board of directors. Significantly, only about one hundred dollars was allocated to printing three thousand copies of a twenty-four-page pamphlet—another indicator of the lack of publicity.[27]

Little Rock NAACPers also failed to project the case as a statewide concern, probably sensing that the strategy might backfire. Jones's law partner Thomas J. Price helped to launch the Little Rock branch in 1917, but Jones never presented himself as a member. J. H. McConico, a leader of the Citizens Defense Fund Commission, served as president of the NAACP branch also. W. A. Singfield, the next branch president, worked with Jones on the independent black campaign for governor in 1920. Like most southern branches in the 1920s, Little Rock worked in fits and starts. It defended a man charged with "assault" on a white woman, gathered signatures for national petition campaigns, and survived embezzlement by their treasurer. Despite the strength of the Ku Klux Klan in Arkansas in the early 1920s, the branch won 264 new members in 1921.[28]

After the *Moore* decision, and around the time of the Klan's decline, the Little Rock branch became one of the few active southern chapters. It found its real leader in Carrie L. Shepperson, who served as branch secretary from 1924 until her death in 1927. Born in 1872, Carrie Lena Fambro was the daughter of a Spanish father and an African-American and Choctaw mother. She was educated at Atlanta University and taught English at the segregated Mifflin W. Gibbs High School. She had a son by her first marriage who grew up to become the leading African-American classical composer of his day, William Grant Still.[29]

In 1924 she took it upon herself to breathe new life into the NAACP branch. Using her influence as a high school teacher, she organized a junior branch. Then she sent the young people into the churches to preach the civic gospel in the sacred temples. This was a risky business for a schoolteacher who served at the pleasure of lily-white school boards. The African-American principal who ran for governor in 1920 was fired for his daring. The undaunted Shepperson spoke out at a meeting of the state's African-American teachers, urging them to initiate NAACP branches in their towns. "I lambasted the men," she wrote NAACP branch secretary Robert Bagnall, for being "spineless."[30]

She rejuvenated the branch, turning the junior division into an activist bastion. In 1924 Little Rock sent six hundred dollars to the national office, six times its agreed fund pledge. In the fall she organized an enthusiastic meeting for Bagnall, which pledged an additional twelve hundred dollars to the Association. The Women's Auxiliary raised more money through a "most beautiful baby" photo contest. The following year she was awarded the Madame C. J. Walker gold medal for branch-building work, and after that the branch won a one hundred dollar scholarship in Walker's name for a student chosen by the branch. Shepperson died in 1927, "a tower of strength in the service of her people," Robert Bagnall wrote. "If we had someone like her in every city we'd have millions of members and solve the race problem."[31]

Arkansas had been a dangerous place for African Americans until the Supreme Court victory. The Ku Klux Klan had a strong following throughout the state. From its downtown Little Rock office on Main and Fourth Street, above the Economy drugstore, Klan Number One directed statewide activities. By 1924 it felt strong enough to contest the governorship in the Democratic primary. Its candidate lost mainly because of the dictatorial methods of the main Klan leader. Not surprisingly, the Klan candidate carried Phillips County. He finished second statewide, but after this foray into state politics, the Arkansas Klan declined.[32]

During the Phillips County trials, a series of lynchings showed the impunity with which racist terrorists acted in Arkansas. In November 1921, in Helena, Will Turner was accused of attacking a white woman. A mob seized him from a sheriff's posse, shot him, and burned the corpse in a public park before a crowd of thousands. A week later Robert Hicks was lynched along a public highway near Lake Village because of a note he wrote to a young white woman. In February 1922 a Malvern Negro named John Harris was taken from police officers by twenty masked men and shot, and in August in Hot Springs an accused armed robber was hung in front of the Como Hotel in the downtown center. "No official action against the lynchers is expected," recorded the *New York Times*.[33]

The situation in the state improved later in the decade, as it did nationally. For its own internal reasons, the Klan declined. No doubt, the victory in the *Moore* and *Ware* cases strengthened the position of black Arkansans, but few people outside the state noticed. "Not only do the colored people of Arkansas but all the people of Arkansas owe to Judge Jones a debt of gratitude," the *Arkansas Survey*, the state's African-American newspaper, noted in an editorial titled "We Are Proud of Him." Jones "went down

there and gathered the data for his case when Helena was a seething caul-
dron of hate, when the least indiscretion meant death." The significance
of Jones's work went unnoticed outside the state.[34]

In separate postmortems, Du Bois and Walter White summarized the
significance of the Arkansas cases for the civil rights struggle. Du Bois
pointed out that the victory showed that the colored farmers did not organize an uprising, and that such an argument could not be so easily concocted in the future. He noted that it struck a blow against peonage in
general and averred that the decision reversed that of the *Frank* case.
White reiterated these points and called it "an achievement that is as important as any event since the signing of the Emancipation Proclamation."
This assessment was not far off the mark. The Arkansas victory owed to
the first strained, but later productive, collaboration between Little Rock's
African-American community and the NAACP.[35]

15

Clemency

O N the night of August 23, 1917, about one hundred African-American soldiers at Camp Logan in Houston mutinied, marched into town, killed sixteen whites and seriously wounded eleven others, and left four of their own ranks dead. There had been no event like this in American history except for Nat Turner's slave revolt in 1831, and nothing like it has happened since. The rampage was followed by the largest court-martial in American history and perhaps the largest mass execution—thirteen men were hanged on December 11 and six more the following year. Almost as remarkable as the events themselves was the NAACP campaign for clemency that resulted in reductions of sentence for sixty-three other prisoners condemned to long terms.

Perhaps what is most astonishing about this affair is how thoroughly it has been forgotten. It does not fit into the narrative of the African American as victim. Houston was not a matter of African Americans fighting back in defense of their rights, as the Nat Turner revolt was. The Houston mutiny was a collective lashing out in anger by black soldiers against an abusive police force, but it largely missed its target. Most African Americans recognized in the aftermath that the perpetrators must be punished. The NAACP insisted that justice be applied fairly in this case. After appealing with minor success for clemency to Presidents Woodrow Wilson and Warren G. Harding, the Association in the fall of 1923 organized a substantial petition drive on behalf of the imprisoned soldiers. The contrast to the Phillips County case is stark, especially when one considers that the Arkansas defendants injured no one.

THE UNITED STATES ARMY had only two colored infantry and two colored cavalry regiments when it declared war on Germany. These were created during the Civil War, and they were stationed where white Americans would be least likely to see them: in the West, where the "buffalo soldiers" fought Indians and Mexicans; and in the new American empire of Cuba and the Philippines. As the army prepared for European war, the Twenty-fourth Colored Infantry was divided into four battalions. The third battalion—Companies I, L, K, and M—about four hundred men, was dispatched to Houston in July 1917 to guard the construction of Camp Logan.

Southern whites opposed stationing African-American troops in their section. African-American soldiers were wary of such duty. The problem was simple. A black man in uniform, disciplined, tough, and armed, contradicted the racist image of the Negro as less than a man. How was a black soldier to guard a construction site—challenging trespassers to halt and be recognized—when no southern white would respond to a black man in authority? How could an African-American soldier take bayonet practice by day and submit to the racist insults of streetcar conductors while off duty? An African-American soldier undermined the Jim Crow system just by wearing his uniform. A series of confrontations between the men of the Twenty-fourth and Houston construction workers and streetcar conductors broke out as soon as the men took up their assignments.[1]

Problems multiplied as the Houston police clashed repeatedly with the unarmed African-American military police who attempted to mediate conflicts between the soldiers and white Houstonians. Among the most notorious police miscreants were Lee Sparks and Rufus Daniels, who harassed African Americans in the San Felipe District. On August 23 Sparks pursued a young dice thrower into the home of Mrs. Sarah Travers. True to his form, Sparks slapped Mrs. Travers, dragged her into the street half-dressed and called for a paddy wagon. A crowd of angry black citizens gathered to protest, among them Private Alonzo Edwards, who offered to pay any fine Mrs. Travers might have incurred. Sparks pistol-whipped Edwards and threw him in jail. A few hours later, provost guard Corporal Charles Baltimore, highly respected by his men, asked Sparks his version of the confrontation with Edwards. The policeman beat the unarmed Baltimore, fired his pistol at him when he fled, and locked him up in jail. A rumor spread among the soldiers that Corporal Baltimore had been killed. Enraged by this news, they began expelling white civilians from the base at gunpoint and plotted reprisals in their tents. When Baltimore returned from jail, his comrades were relieved to see him alive but were furious at his treatment by Sparks.[2]

As night fell, Sergeant Vida Henry informed a white major that trouble was imminent. The major summoned his officers and had them assemble the men in the company street, their arms to be stacked at a supply tent. The officers promised the men that Sparks would be punished, but the soldiers angrily expressed their disbelief. Some men, already determined to take their own revenge, did not muster or return their weapons. Perhaps by prearrangement, a cry of "Here comes the mob!" went up and shots rang out. Hearing the shouts and gunfire, men of the other companies rushed for their rifles and fired into the gloom. In the confusion, several men ordered their unarmed officers to disband, threatening to shoot them if they disobeyed. The officers ran ineffectually for help. When the firing stopped, Sergeant Henry barked out orders to fall in, and the men obeyed him, their superior officer. He formed them into a column and posted loyal allies at the rear with orders to shoot any runaways. As he marched the column toward town, it broke into smaller units. Another revolt broke out at the Lower A guard post and headed toward Houston also. Robert V. Haynes, author of a careful study of the incident, believes that Henry probably planned his every move, starting with his remark to the major, which he knew would precipitate confusion. The mutiny of August 23 was partially a planned punitive expedition against the police, partially a defensive action by confused soldiers who believed they were under attack by armed whites, and partially an act of obedience by privates following the order of their sergeant. Henry's personal motivation went with him to the grave, for he killed himself a few hours later.[3]

For the next two hours, separate columns of soldiers marched and shot their way through Houston's white Brunner District. They fired at anyone who tried to stop them but did not shoot indiscriminately at whites. They killed five policemen (including Rufus Daniels), two soldiers, and nine civilians. They wounded eleven other innocent victims. Undoubtedly, many others would have been killed had the National Guard not been mobilized in full battle dress. This regiment blocked armed white mobs, to whom the police had distributed guns, from engaging the soldiers in a widespread urban war. The soldiers killed two of their own men accidentally and one deliberately when he attempted to defect. Finally the men either returned to their base, hoping to avoid detection, or hid in the black community. The latter were tracked down in house-to-house searches.[4]

The next day the army placed all black soldiers under guard. Houston authorities demanded jurisdiction over the prosecution, but the army insisted on its prerogative to court-martial its own soldiers. White Houston cried for revenge, and African-American leaders in Houston could appeal only for calm in the vindictive atmosphere. Policeman Sparks took his personal tribute, killing a black civilian, a crime for which he was tried and found not guilty in one minute. Another policeman did the same, civilians lynched a third man, and black Houstonians fled by the thousands.[5]

The army was now faced with the intricate legal problem of prosecuting the perpetrators. No whites could identify any soldiers as shooters. The men themselves, now removed to New Mexico, would not cooperate. Ultimately the investigators separated out 156 men whose names had not appeared on muster rolls taken during the mutiny and shipped this group to Fort Bliss at El Paso. These suspects were told they could be hung for failing to name names. Enough men talked in exchange for immunity so that 63 men could be brought to trial.[6]

On November 1 the trial opened before a thirteen-judge panel at Fort Sam Houston in San Antonio. Known as the case of Sergeant *William A. Nesbit et al.*, the men were charged with violating four articles of war: willful disobedience of orders, mutiny, murder, and armed assault. All the men pleaded not guilty. The defense argued that the list of accused was compiled haphazardly, that nine of the men had never left camp, and that seven did so only under duress. Many acted in what they believed was self-defense or were merely following Sergeant Henry's orders. However, 169 witnesses testified for the prosecution, including the white officers. After one day of deliberation, the court on November 28 found fifty-four men guilty on all four counts, four on one count, and five not guilty. Of the most culpable, thirteen were sentenced to hang and the others sentenced to life terms at hard labor. Among the condemned was Corporal Baltimore. All requested to be shot by firing squad. At dawn on December 11, the thirteen men were marched to the banks of the Salado Creek, where they saw to their dismay that a mass gallows had been erected. The army did not notify President Wilson in advance, so there was no presidential review. The execution was conducted in secret and the public notified afterward.[7]

A second court-martial of fifteen men assigned to the Lower A guard post began six days later. The defendants in the *Corporal John Washington et al.* case were accused of quitting their posts, threatening civilians, and killing one. At this trial, one soldier testified that five of his comrades had fired at the victim; these men were all sentenced to hang. The other ten received lesser terms of seven to ten years. The executions in this case were delayed until a final trial of a third group was concluded.

The third trial of 40 soldiers began on February 18 and was known as the case of *Corporal Robert Tillman et al.* This group faced the same four charges as those of the first defendants. The evidence rested almost entirely on the testimony of fellow soldiers granted immunity. On March 26, the court found 23 guilty of all charges, acquitted 2, and found the rest guilty of some but not all charges. Of the most culpable, 11 were sentenced to hang and 12 sentenced to life in prison; the others got lesser terms. The combined outcome of the three cases was: 118 men charged, 110 convicted, and 8 acquitted or found incompetent. Of those convicted, 29 were sentenced to death, 53 to life in prison, and the others to lesser

Court martial of Houston soldiers. Courtesy of Schomburg Center for Research in Black Culture, New York Public Library.

terms. Ninety-seven men survived, hoping their sentences might be mitigated by clemency.[8]

THE NAACP at first reacted cautiously to the Houston violence. Du Bois's initial comment appeared in the October 1917 *Crisis*. With pithy eloquence, he expressed the mixed emotions shared by many African Americans: sorrow for the deaths and coming retribution, anger that whites would never understand the cause, and an irrepressible satisfaction that this time whites were learning how Negroes felt. He had to concede that the soldiers were guilty. "We ask no mitigation of their punishment. They broke the law. They must suffer."[9]

In the *New York Age*, James Weldon Johnson emphasized the causes of the attack, which he took as a "symptom" of a wider problem. This was the implacable hostility of the white South to the black man in uniform. The federal government must not back down to this intimidation, he insisted. On this point, the African-American press was divided. The *Age* editorial in that issue blamed the War Department for sending the men to

Texas in the first place. A similar split appeared in the pages of the *Balti-more Afro-American.*[10]

The NAACP also sent Martha Gruening to Houston. A liberal white journalist, she had just returned from East St. Louis where she and Du Bois had uncovered the collusion of the authorities with white terrorists. In Houston her job was much more difficult and her article in the *Crisis* much less informative than the East St. Louis one. She could not talk with the soldiers, and people in the black community were reticent; only Mrs. Travers shed any light on the triggering incident. Like Du Bois, Gruening called attention to the causes of the riot but concluded that "the soldiers should be severely punished."[11]

African-American reaction to the mass executions was also mixed. Most editors of black community weeklies supported the U.S. war effort and did not want to crusade on this issue. Du Bois penned a subdued editorial, "Thirteen," which he buried in the midst of others. "They broke the law," he reiterated. "Against their punishment, if it was legal, we cannot protest." But he did note the double standard of justice that allowed white killers of Negroes to go unpunished. Some voices in the black community sounded a more bitter note. While recognizing the soldiers' guilt, the *Baltimore Afro-American* thought that "the country stands aghast at these severe and summary sentences meted out to them." It ran a somber front-page picture of the defendants assembled in court. In the *Crisis*, Du Bois quoted writers angrier than himself. "[T]here are many black people in the country today who will hold that these thirteen soldiers gave their lives for liberty and democracy," just like soldiers in Europe, wrote a correspondent in the *St. Louis Post-Dispatch.*[12]

THE NAACP launched a campaign for clemency for the remaining prisoners. During December and January, the NAACP conducted a petition drive on behalf of the convicted men. In response, letters and telegrams poured into the White House and War Department. On February 19, 1918, Johnson led a small delegation of New York NAACP leaders to present over twelve thousand signatures to President Wilson, urging him to review the cases. The thirteen executed men had had this denied them, as was the army's prerogative in wartime. Yet, further harsh punishment, Johnson argued, "Would to the colored people of the country savor of vengeance rather than justice." To Johnson's surprise, Wilson listened with genuine interest. "I realized that the official air had been dropped," Johnson recalled, "and that he was, as we say, very human. . . . When I came out, it was with my hostility toward Mr. Wilson greatly shaken; however I could not rid myself of the conviction that at bottom there was something hypocritical about him."[13]

After a few weeks, the third and final court-martial began. Wilson put off action on the previous cases until the third was concluded; now he had sixteen death sentences to review. An army report on the cases found that five men did not kill anyone, and it recommended commuting those sentences to life in prison. Secretary of War Newton Baker added five more to that list. His report to the president took into account the loyal service of black army troops in the World War. Wilson, in approving these ten commutations on August 24, hoped that the show of mercy would be "an inspiration to the people of that race, to further zeal and service to their country." Next month the final six executions were carried out.[14]

In the aftermath of the Houston events, two separate groups applied for recognition as the Houston branch of the NAACP. One was the Civic Betterment League (CBL), formed after the August events. Led by older, generally conservative men, the CBL claimed 230 members. It had worked on issues such as transportation segregation and was tied to the Republican Party. E. O. Smith, the CBL's secretary, at first would not cooperate with the rival group led by Clifton R. Richardson. Richardson was editor of the *Houston Observer*; his group was younger and more confrontational. They pressed for the prosecution of policemen who shot African Americans after the mutiny. Richardson vowed, "We are going to endeavor to convict these murderers." Despite the differences between the two groups, the national office convinced them to collaborate. The new branch had about 300 members, and its charter showed that they were mostly male, of varying occupations including professionals, railroad clerks, and messengers. Richardson was maneuvered out of authority a year later and resigned; he edited another newspaper that did not cover the NAACP's activities.[15]

Interest in the Houston cases waned by the spring of 1918, and after the final executions, it seemed that little more could be done for the prisoners. The prisoners themselves would not give up. Some of them, especially those who believed they had been under attack by a white mob, wrote to the Association and urged it to take up their case anew. "I have bullets of three different kinds that were fired into the camp," one lifer notified the Association. Impressed by this letter, Walter White recommended that the Association open a new campaign for reduction of sentences. Later another man wrote an arresting letter to board member John Haynes Holmes. "I did not participate in the disorder in any way," he insisted. "I was convicted only on testimony of a witness who 'thought' he saw me at the riot." Holmes passed this letter on to Du Bois. "I think we ought to start something," Du Bois advised Johnson.[16]

The election of Warren G. Harding to the presidency opened new possibilities. Ten days after Harding was sworn in, the board of directors resolved to seek pardons for the remaining sixty-three prisoners. The branches took their petitions to the black community and by September had gathered fifty thousand signatures. Johnson brought a broadly representative delegation of thirty to the White House on September 28, 1921. Besides several prominent NAACP loyalists, this group included Robert Moton and Emmett J. Scott. Kansas senators Arthur Capper and Charles Curtis also appealed for clemency.[17]

President Harding promised to have the War Department review the cases again. Kansas congressman Daniel R. Anthony formally requested a War Department inquiry. At the beginning of December, Secretary of War John W. Weeks sent an adverse report to Anthony's colleagues on the Military Affairs Committee. Weeks reviewed the status of all 110 convictions in the Houston cases. He reported that nineteen men had been executed, one had been pardoned for his testimony, six had died in confinement, fifteen had served short terms and returned to duty, and six others had been granted reductions or released. Of the remaining sixty-three prisoners, fifty-eight were serving life terms and five were serving fifteen years. There had been 2,172 pages of trial records and careful reviews of the sentences already. A psychiatric report found that "practically all of these prisoners deny participation in the mutiny. . . . It seems to us that the conspiracy continues among these men." At this point, the War Department was inclined to do nothing more.[18]

The Leavenworth prisoners were bitterly disappointed but pressed the NAACP not to give up. While Weeks's report was negative, it did not preclude the president from acting affirmatively. Meanwhile Washington, D.C., attorney James A. Cobb informed White that Emmett J. Scott had met with two officers in the War Department. He learned that Colonel John A. Hull, acting judge advocate general of the army, was impressed by the excellent record of the men as prisoners. The prison warden thought morale would improve if good behavior was rewarded by some show of clemency. On the other hand, the War Department was sensitive to pressure from Texas congressmen who naturally opposed such a move. After a careful review, Hull proposed that six more lifers have their sentences reduced to twenty years. These were men who, he believed, had left the base but returned before the shooting started. All federal prisoners could apply for parole after serving one-third of their time; men serving life terms would be eligible after fifteen years. President Harding announced these reductions in December.[19]

The prisoners had hoped for more and felt disappointed by this review. "If we had started the trouble, or if our records were bad, we could not ask the good people to back us, but such is not the case," George Hobbes wrote. John Geter, one of the six granted clemency, was not satisfied either. "Had I been guilty . . . then I would smile," he wrote. "My name is among the first to appear on a check list, taken by an officer, to show who remained in camp. . . . The evidence against me was gotten from self-confessed participants who received immunity, and who perjured at will." These men praised the NAACP for its efforts and complained that they had not gotten the support from the African-American press and clergy that they deserved.[20]

The NAACP was encouraged by the pardons but felt overwhelmed by other tasks. The leadership wanted to do more but was too deeply involved with the campaign for the Dyer bill, the Arkansas defendants, and its own fund raising. In the spring it would turn its attention to Ku Klux Klan attacks on the black staff at the Tuskegee Veterans' Hospital. By the summer of 1923 the Association was ready to do more. Its 1923 convention was scheduled for Kansas City, twenty miles from Leavenworth Penitentiary.[21]

The border region in America had no typical pattern of race relations. Young Roy Wilkins arrived in Kansas City as a cub reporter for the *Kansas City Call* just before the opening of the NAACP convention. He was startled by the contrast to his native St. Paul, Minnesota. The *Call*'s office was situated at the heart of the bustling African-American business district near Eighteenth Street and Vine. Over thirty thousand black residents made up one-tenth of the total population, who lived mostly in the central east side. Black baseball fans sat in a segregated section when whites were playing ball, but whites sat among the black fans to cheer on the Kansas City Monarchs of the Negro National League. The streetcars had no Jim Crow section but everything else did. The police department under the corrupt but anti-Klan Pendergast family machine ignored crime when blacks were victims. African-American schools were grossly underfunded; several of the grammar schools still had outhouses. Black Kansas City mobilized by the thousands when the NAACP came to town.

Delegates from twenty-nine states paraded through the streets to Convention Hall for the opening rally. Over ten thousand black people crowded the building for the Association's largest meeting ever. Missouri governor Arthur M. Hyde's representative made a patronizing speech, telling a story about an "old darky," and was drowned out by a storm of opprobrium that lasted six minutes until Arthur B. Spingarn restored order. Then the unfortunate orator read a letter from the governor counseling patience and decrying "so-called equality." As Roy Wilkins recalled, James Weldon Johnson rose in reply:

> Facing the governor's man squarely, he pounded his hand down upon the table before him and said, "We are here to serve notice that we are in a fight to the death for the rights guaranteed us as American citizens by the Constitution." Ten thousand black people rose to their feet. They cheered and clapped until their voices were hoarse and their hands stinging with pain.[22]

This dramatic confrontation showed the resolve of a mass movement full of aspiration for the future. The Kansas City convention marked a high point of NAACP activity in the 1920s.

For some, the most emotional moment would come at a "pilgrimage" to Leavenworth Penitentiary to visit the "Houston martyrs." Five hundred delegates met in the chapel with the prisoners to pray and hear inspirational speeches by James Weldon Johnson, Addie Hunton, AME bishops John Hurst and W. T. Vernon, and Arthur B. Spingarn. Even Warden W. I. Biddle spoke, saying, "These men are not murderers. They are not criminals. I know them." The NAACP repeated these words in all its future press releases during the campaign. Johnson reviewed the progress made as the result of the two petition drives. Blacks and whites had signed on the men's behalf, Johnson said, and "all of them believed . . . you were innocent." Urging them to continue their good behavior, he concluded, "[T]his chance to look into your faces and to know what it means to you . . . will cause us to go away from here with a new determination."[23]

Thus, the NAACP completely recast its earliest response to the Houston "riot." Time had wrought a great change from the night of August 23, 1917. There had been nineteen executions, the violence was now six years old, and the war was concluded. The Association felt that the remaining men had suffered enough and was now willing to portray all of them as innocent. No doubt, some of them were and some were not. African America was ready to forgive any among them who may have fired a shot in momentary anger or fear. By making a "pilgrimage" to the "martyrs" through prayers in the chapel under the guidance of the bishops, the NAACP helped transform the image of the men.

The new petition would seek one hundred thousand signers for full pardon including restoration of citizenship rights. The NAACP pledged to take the campaign to every colored newspaper, lodge, women's club, and church. They would encourage NAACP branches to hold mass meetings on Armistice Day in honor of the Houston martyrs. This was a vigorous project, opposite in strategy to that undertaken in the Arkansas case. The main difference between the two situations was the opponent. The NAACP thought the federal government was amenable to public pressure and the Negro vote, while Arkansas officialdom was immune to those pressures and liable to react negatively. The Association's leaders may also have learned from the weaknesses of the Arkansas defense. A certain irony was attached to this situation, for the Arkansas defendants certainly were martyrs whose fellows had been gunned down, they themselves tortured and nearly executed. Most of the Houston men had mutinied, their colleagues had killed innocent civilians, and they would become in 1923 the *cause célèbre* that the Arkansas prisoners should have been.

The success of this petition drive astonished the NAACP. Every conceivable type of African-American organization, in the most remote or repressive part of the country, circulated petitions. A black American Legion post in Atlantic City, the Delaware State Federation of Colored Women's Clubs, the Oklahoma Baptist Convention, the Methodist Episcopal Church in four southern states, the Indiana Knights of Pythias, the Tuskegee-based colored musicians' union, and a man in Guntersville, Alabama, were among hundreds of groups and individuals who circulated petitions. By the end of the year, there were over one hundred thousand signatures at the NAACP office. The branches made the drive a focus of their work: Philadelphia turned in nine thousand, Newark seven thousand, Chicago and New York five thousand each, and Denver, Jersey City, and Kansas City three thousand each. In November Johnson reported to the board that "[t]he Association has never undertaken any cause which has been entered into with such whole-hearted enthusiasm." Another twenty thousand signatures were added in January 1924.[24]

In Houston itself, the campaign met with two sorts of opposition. Naturally enough, victims of the riot and white newspapers brought pressure to bear against pardon for the men. Even anti-Klan white liberals thought it wiser to abandon the issue. A district judge who chaired Houston's investigatory panel warned the Association, "The pardon of these men would be very damaging to the best interests of the colored people in the South." He argued that the clemency campaign only fueled the rabid Klan group that was always seeking to sharpen racial antagonism. A self-described "friend of the Negro," the judge added that the better element of Houston Negroes shared his views. He may have been referring, oddly enough, to Clifton Richardson's group. Richardson now edited the *Houston Informer*, which abstained from the pardon campaign. Although Houston NAACP leaders feared they were being spied upon by racists, they vowed to continue anyway.[25]

Johnson next began the work of assembling a prominent delegation to present the petitions to President Calvin Coolidge. In December and January representatives of Alpha Phi Alpha fraternity, the AME Church, the National Baptist Convention, Associated Negro Press, Odd Fellows, Knights of Pythias, National Association of Colored Women's Clubs, and Friends of Negro Freedom agreed to come. Almost on cue, Boston's William Monroe Trotter, who had been collecting signatures on his own petition, demanded to be represented in the delegation and make his own speech to the president. Disagreements over these arrangements flared up in the African-American press, and after mutual complaining about each other's behavior, Johnson relented, and Trotter brought his allies to the meeting. Influential African-American editors Robert Abbott of the *Chicago Defender*, Robert L. Vann of the *Pittsburgh Courier*, Carl Murphy of the *Baltimore Afro-American*, and Cyril Briggs of the *Crusader* news service came with Johnson.[26]

President Coolidge received the delegation cordially and, like his predecessor, ordered a new review but made no promises. Johnson and Trotter each spoke for their respective delegations, stressing the Negro contribution to the war effort. Through Negro Republicans Harry Davis and William Henry Lewis, the Association tried to deliver a more political message: the president was going to lose Texas anyway in 1924, but could win a big Negro vote if he did the right thing. The New York City dailies gave small notices of the presidential audience, and the African-American weeklies ran larger articles. Some ran a *Pittsburgh Courier* cartoon showing the ghosts of the hanged men pointing to Leavenworth and urging the reader to remember the prisoners. These papers sounded an optimistic note about the meeting, as did the *Crisis*.[27]

Secretary of War John W. Weeks reported to Johnson that he had appointed a two-man board to review the cases of all military prisoners, not just the Houston men. The NAACP kept the issue before the public while the panel worked. When New York congressman Hamilton Fish spoke out for clemency, the Association circulated his plea to the African-American press, which ran the story widely. Johnson encouraged African-American papers to run editorials on the subject. In March the Association sponsored a Harlem rally.[28]

The first news from the review board was disappointing. Johnson learned of the decisions only from the morning newspapers in mid-April. Seventeen men would have their sentences reduced to thirty years, but there was no report on the other fifty-four men. The dissatisfied Johnson hastened to the War Department, where he met with the officers conducting the review. They promised a full report in May, but warned Johnson that there was more political pressure against clemency than for it.[29]

Nevertheless, the review board released a favorable report on May 13. The board reduced the sentences of all thirty lifers. Under these conditions, ten would be eligible for parole in 1925, sixteen in 1927, and four in 1928. The other twenty-four would be eligible in 1925. Although the NAACP had pressed for full and immediate pardons, its press release announced that "there is cause for rejoicing." African-American newspapers generally shared this view. Carl Murphy of the *Baltimore Afro-American* congratulated Johnson on winning "a great victory" and featured the release prominently.[30]

The NAACP had led the wider black community to a significant triumph for racial healing. The victory was not based on new evidence; it was purely a political campaign for mercy. No prisoner (except one who had tried to escape) spent more than eleven years in prison. Despite the provocations the soldiers had faced, they had still participated in a crime of political passion that left many dead and wounded in what remains the worst violence committed by free blacks against whites in American history. The Association might have heeded the advice of liberal white friends and desisted from this campaign, but it did not. They won the victory in the year before thousands of Ku Klux Klansmen paraded through the streets of Washington. This was a sign that African America was neither intimidated nor in retreat during the 1920s.

16

The Hooded Order

THE Ku Klux Klan attracted a vast following among Protestants because many of them felt that immigration and modernity threatened their values. Cloaking itself in the rhetoric of patriotism or the Lost Cause, Christianity, temperance, and marital fidelity, the Klan sought to stem the tide of Al Capone's America. The Klan appeared to be familiar, like the Masons or the Methodists, and yet exotic enough to command attention. The hooded order languished in obscurity after its founding in 1915, burst onto the national scene in 1921, reached a high point with a big parade through the streets of Washington, D.C., in 1925, and faded as quickly as it grew in the late 1920s.

While the Klan prospered through its appeal to traditional American values, it also attracted recruits because it expressed American hates and fears. The turmoil of 1919 and the Red Scare of 1920 lent credibility to the Klan's fear mongering. The Second Klan suspected immigrants of disloyalty, reprising the nativist concerns of the Know-Nothing or American Party in the 1850s. The Klan threatened Catholics, who it portrayed as beholden to the Pope before their country. Jewish financiers gouged the workingman and their internationalism fueled communism, the Klan averred with contradictory logic. These un-American groups corrupted the social fabric by introducing labor strife, bootlegging, fornication, and divorce into American life, and the Klan took vigorous action to suppress these evils.

The Klan spread especially in urban areas, for in the city the forces of modernity and tradition collided. The historian Kenneth T. Jackson, in *The Ku Klux Klan in the City, 1915–1930*, showed that Klan chapters (Klaverns) thrived throughout the country but that urban centers led the villages. Over half of all Klansmen lived in metropolitan areas. Although the Second Klan began in the South, its strongest branches developed in states such as Indiana, Ohio, Texas, Pennsylvania, and Illinois. Only rare centers of diversity, such as New York City, or of Catholicity, such as Boston, were immune.[1]

Many joined the Second Klan because it advocated white supremacy. The outlandish hooded costumes, fiery crosses, mass silent marches, and floggings were meant to terrorize African Americans, and in some parts of the South the Klan inspired real fear. White Southern migrants to the North carried race hatred with them and spewed segregationist venom in Detroit and Indiana while hiding under their hoods. Yet there were plenty of anti-Klan white supremacists throughout the country, and its occasional championing of the Confederacy did not sell well in the North.

African Americans never doubted that the Klan menaced them. The NAACP sounded the anti-Klan alarm before Catholic, Jewish, immigrant, or labor groups did, playing its part in bringing the Klan to ruin. Walter White helped bring about a newspaper exposé in the *New York World* and a congressional investigation of it. When the Klan threatened the Negro Veterans' Hospital in Tuskegee, Alabama, the NAACP helped beat it back. In Indiana the NAACP mobilized the black community to fight it in the streets and ballot boxes. The Association struck another blow against the Klan by holding its 1925 convention in Denver and rallying anti-Klan fighters. In the *Crisis*, W. E. B. Du Bois waged war on the ideological underpinnings of white supremacy that flourished in academia and lent respectability to racism.

SIX FORMER Confederate officers from Pulaski, Tennessee, launched the first Klan. They formed a club to suppress black rights and overthrow the Reconstruction government. They took the Greek word for circle, *kuklos*, as their title, and the name evolved into an Americanized alliteration. The Knights of the Klan chose former Confederate general Nathan Bedford Forrest as Grand Wizard and created a host of offices with similarly bizarre titles. Klansmen whipped and murdered black politicians and successful farmers; they burned schools and churches throughout the South. Ultimately the Ku Klux Klan Act of 1871 led to the prosecution of thousands of Klansmen, but although the Klan disappeared, its principles triumphed with the defeat of Reconstruction.[2]

No particular crisis produced the Second Klan. This was the brainchild of William Joseph Simmons, an Alabama-born fraternal organizer and failed Methodist preacher. Simmons grew up in the post-Reconstruction South and nurtured romantic fantasies about the Klan just as children of the slavocracy absorbed medieval romances. The appearance of David Wark Griffith's movie *Birth of a Nation* in 1915 lent Simmons's dreams new energy. On Thanksgiving Day he led sixteen followers to the top of Atlanta's Stone Mountain, where they burned a cross and swore a solemn oath to the Invisible Empire of the Ku Klux Klan. Simmons, however, possessed no leadership ability, and for the next six years his movement languished. Moreover, as America fought a war in Europe, the government campaigned for the unity of all citizens. The Klan was divisive, and its message fell on deaf ears.[3]

Under the impact of the bombings, riots, and strikes of 1919–1921, the national atmosphere changed. Hoping to capitalize on new possibilities, two enterprising promoters offered their services to Simmons. Edward Young Clarke and Mrs. Elizabeth Tyler contracted with Simmons in June 1920 to conduct recruiting operations. They would retain $2.50 of every $10.00 initiation fee they collected, and set in motion a pyramid scheme in which lesser promoters would take a cut as well. They stepped up the racial and ethnic hatred themes. Fear and self-interest harnessed together proved a salable commodity, and in eighteen months membership soared from a few thousand in Georgia and Alabama to one hundred thousand nationally. Clarke and Mrs. Tyler got rich on membership fees, just like Mark Twain's the Duke and the Count in *Huckleberry Finn*, a pair of hypocrites harvesting suckers up and down the Mississippi River.[4]

THE NAACP first encountered the Klan during the 1920 election in Florida. There the Klan had paraded through Jacksonville's streets and conducted an armed terror campaign designed to keep African-American voters from the polls. The Association began to informally monitor its progress. Around September 1920, White initiated a correspondence with Edward Young Clarke, identifying himself as a native Georgian who lived in New York and had an interest in the Klan. Through this correspondence, White learned of other Klan contacts in the New York area. The correspondence stopped when Clarke discovered White's true identity. White received a stream of anonymous threats warning him not to reveal what he had learned.[5]

The Association sounded the alarm against this growing menace early in 1921. Its January annual meeting focused on the born-again Klan. The Association issued a pamphlet and printed sample anti-Klan resolutions for civic groups. White wrote an article for the liberal *Forum* magazine. In March the Association issued a press release calling on the Klan to open its books and publish an annual report, as the NAACP did. The Association proudly noted that the Klan branded it as their chief opponent. White and Johnson denounced Klan violence, such as the tarring and feathering of a white woman in Tenoka, Texas. The NAACP counseled, among others, an Ohio railroad fireman on how to get an anti-Klan resolution passed at his union convention; a Brooklyn Catholic newspaper editor on the Klan's ideology; and a New Jersey civic activist on how to form an interracial anti-Klan committee.[6]

The NAACP encouraged politicians, many of whom were fence-sitting on the Klan issue, to speak out. NAACP branches secured anti-Klan statements from the mayors of Cincinnati and Cleveland. In the fall the Association solicited statements from members of Congress, hoping to start an anti-Klan groundswell in the North. The New York office released samples from the almost one hundred replies it received, but the cautious phrasing of many letters showed that most politicians feared the Klan's power at the polls. Only seven senators and fourteen congressmen denounced the Klan; most declarations were evasive. When an African-American delegation visited President Harding seeking clemency for the Houston soldiers, the president remarked that the Klan this time was "not after the colored people." Washington, D.C., NAACP leader L. M. Hershaw advised Johnson that the president's mistaken assumption was common to most white Americans. Neither Harding nor Coolidge made a clear anti-Klan statement during their years in office.[7]

In New York City, the Association worked for official suppression of the Klan. The Klan was so strong nationally that the legal question of whether to ban it never surfaced. The NAACP encouraged the New York police department and the Federal Bureau of Investigation (FBI) to follow just such a course. Board chairman Mary White Ovington wrote to a Syracuse correspondent that "[t]he Association is doing everything in its power . . . to prohibit the operation of the KKK." The Association wanted to shut the Klan down as a criminal conspiracy, but it was weak in relation to an organization that had over a million members during the 1920s.[8]

The Association claimed a great deal of credit for the spectacular exposé of the Klan written by Rowland Thomas for the *New York World* in September 1921. Thomas spoke with Walter White, who turned the Association's files over to him. Thomas's articles detailed four Klan murders, forty-one floggings, and numerous instances of tarring and feathering. Most of these incidents took place in Texas. In Houston, the Klan flogged a lawyer for taking Negro clients. Beaumont Klansmen gave the same treatment to a doctor who performed abortions. In Dallas, a dentist named Hiram Wesley Evans was probably responsible for scarring an African-American bellhop with acid. Louisiana, Oklahoma, and Arkansas joined Texas as centers of Klan terrorism.[9]

The *World* articles led to a congressional investigation of the Klan. In

October, the House Rules Committee fished for evidence that the Klan defrauded its members or committed violence. Simmons himself testified, but the committee handled him with kid gloves. The Grand Wizard used the national spotlight to win new sympathy for the Klan. He represented himself as a courtly gentleman and the Klan as a benevolent society, dissociating it from any violence perpetrated by vigilantes. Claiming illness, Simmons passed out after making a dramatic declaration of the Klan's loyalty to law and order. James Weldon Johnson believed that the *World* articles had brought the Klan to "the verge of destruction."[10] He could not have been more wrong. The negative publicity of September was offset by Simmons's performance in Congress, which brought the Klan perhaps a hundred thousand new members and renewed confidence.

After the congressional investigation, the Klan spread rapidly across the country. Its growth was facilitated by a coup against Simmons, Clarke, and Mrs. Tyler. All three were drinkers, and the latter two, not married to each other, had been caught in a compromising sexual situation. Seizing the opportunity, Hiram Wesley Evans, the Dallas dentist, forced the trio from power. Evans moved the Klan toward electoral politics, but he also turned a blind eye to its violence. Politics in several states devolved into struggles between Klan and anti-Klan factions, and the prospect of power rekindled the Klan's growth.[11]

THE NAACP and Alabama African Americans won a bizarre campaign against Tuskegee whites and the local Klan in the celebrated case of the Tuskegee Negro Veterans' Hospital. Tuskegee whites created an ironic situation when they fought to retain control and staffing of a hospital for Negro veterans. Alabama law specifically prohibited white medical personnel from treating Negro patients, but the Klan fought to do exactly that. The Tuskegee Institute leadership, the NAACP, and African-American doctors combined to convince the Veterans' Administration (VA) to let African Americans control and staff the facility.

The Veterans' Administration stood out as a particularly corrupt department in a scandal-ridden presidency. Its first director, Charles R. Forbes, lived like a prince on a bureaucrat's salary; he demanded bribes from government contractors until his racket was discovered. Forbes's department decided to locate the lone hospital for African-American veterans in Tuskegee. The NAACP and the National Medical Association (the African-American medical association) opposed building such a hospital in the segregated South, but Tuskegee principal Robert Russa Moton sold the Veterans' Administration 316 of its 3,368 acres for one dollar. In exchange the

VA promised to build a six hundred bed hospital for Negro veterans. Most important, the seventy-five thousand dollar monthly payroll would go to a Negro director and staff.[12]

The Treasury Department, however, which was charged with building the hospital, promised the same patronage to Tuskegee whites. The whites planned to designate Negro nurses as "nurse maids," have them do all the work, and pay them menial salaries. They wanted the money, but there was more to it than that. An African-American medical staff, much of it northern-born or educated, not dependent on southerners for a livelihood, would pose a threat. As one white Alabaman put it, "We do not want any niggers in this state who we cannot control."[13]

The double-dealing of the headless Harding administration put Moton in a bind when he discovered in January 1923 the plans for a white staff. When the VA announced that the hospital director would be a southern white man "who thoroughly understands the Negro," Moton protested to President Harding. They both would be "justly criticized" for siting the hospital in Tuskegee and staffing it with cynical time servers, Moton wrote. He sought at least a compromise, urging that half of the thirty to forty doctors and sixty to seventy nurses be colored. Harding met with Moton on February 23 and agreed to hire a colored staff. Presidential secretary George B. Christian restrained the VA from hiring more whites and insisted upon finding colored personnel.[14]

Warren G. Harding has been remembered as a well-intentioned but weak president whose appointees betrayed him. The VA fit this pattern perfectly. The southern clique in its leadership simply refused to locate qualified Negro employees. Acting director Colonel George E. Ijams, the Tuskegee Hospital director, and the Alabama American Legion commander connived to foil Harding's directive. The latter two men were Klan loyalists, and the former tolerated their actions. This situation changed only when Harding appointed Frank Hines as permanent director of the Veterans' Bureau.[15]

Moton, his secretary, Albon Holsey, and aide Melvin Chisum feared that Harding's promise would be broken and that they would be ridiculed by the northern Negro press. Like their mentor Booker T. Washington, they showed whites a deferential face but worked in secret to build Negro institutions. Unlike him, they kept NAACP officials informed of developments, marking their letters "very confidential." Meanwhile, two other old Bookerites, Republican stalwarts Henry "Linc" Johnson of Georgia and Perry Howard of Mississippi, tried to get control of the hospital patronage for themselves. After some maneuvering, new VA director Hines rebuffed them. By early May, the Department of Civil Service began hiring Negro doctors, working through Dr. George E. Cannon, an NAACP board member and head of the National Medical Association. The NAACP sent out a press release celebrating the victory. The Association now had a working relationship with Tuskegee and had isolated two rivals.[16]

Alabama whites did not take this defeat lying down. They sent a delegation to lobby the president and organized a mass rally to protest the developing colored staff. The NAACP board urged Harding to replace the Klan-allied hospital director. Since whites would not permit an integrated staff, the Association held out for an all-black staff. In a letter to the president, Johnson wrote that the colored doctors and nurses would show the country their worth. For both sides, the stakes became higher than jobs and patronage—now the dispute was over power and pride.[17]

In this changed situation, Alabama whites turned to what they knew best: terror. They threatened the chief medical officer at Tuskegee Institute, and he left the city. Moton departed next, ostensibly on business but fearing for his life. Newspaper articles in the nearby *Montgomery Advertiser* (an anti-Klan daily) noted more Klan threats against Tuskegee itself. Holsey wrote that the whole town seemed to be sitting on a volcano.[18]

On July 3, John H. Calhoun, a Negro accountant, came to Tuskegee to take up clerical duties at the hospital, replacing a white woman. The hospital director handed him an unstamped envelope, which contained a threat from the "K.K.K." That night the Klan burned a forty-foot-high cross near Tuskegee and paraded seven hundred strong through the streets, dressed in full regalia and maintaining an ominous silence. Afterward a Klan squad entered the hospital with the collusion of the guards, looking for Calhoun. Not finding their prey, they dined on hospital food served by a white employee. The NAACP charged that the very sheets worn by the Klansmen were furnished by the hospital staff. If not for the presence of armed Tuskegee graduates from nearby Alabama towns defending the Tuskegee Institute, it, too, might have been invaded. The entire sequence of events showed that the Klan had access to every level of the hospital, from the director to the commissary.[19]

The Klan had now attacked a federal building, and the NAACP deluged the administration with calls for action. Johnson dispatched a series of telegrams to President Harding, who was traveling to the fateful Alaska vacation on which he would die within a month. The NAACP urged that army troops be sent to protect the hospital, preferably the Twenty-fourth Colored Infantry. Walter White went immediately to Washington, where FBI agent John Edgar Hoover told him that he was powerless to act. At the Justice Department a sympathetic official told White that Hoover was "playing politics with the Klan"; he dictated a letter to Hoover telling him to investigate possible criminal action against a federal building. The Association issued a stern news release. "If President Harding has a backbone the size of a toothpick, he will call that [Klan] bluff, and that will be the end of the present disgraceful situation."[20]

Neither Harding nor Coolidge called the Klan's bluff, but both stood firm on the question of the black staff. VA director Hines met with Tuskegee whites two days after the Klan parade and worked out a temporary compromise that saved face for these local leaders. A board of trustees would be established for the hospital with a white majority. The chief surgeon and two assistants would be white, but the rest of the workforce would be Negro. The Association opposed this deal. Hines forced the director out of office, and by July 1924 the hospital had an African-American director and staff. The white-dominated board of trustees was abolished, too.[21]

The Klan lost this battle because its position was too contradictory. It allowed local desire for patronage and control to trump the greater principle of segregation. Although both houses of the Alabama legislature voted unanimously to maintain a white medical staff, several southern newspapers doubted the wisdom of this position. The *Jackson Daily News* wondered whether white women should be working in such close proximity to black men. The *Birmingham Age-Herald* and *New Orleans Item* criticized the Klan march and viewed the segregated hospital as the proper southern way.[22]

The NAACP and the Tuskegee leaders won this round, and their cooperation moved the two sides closer together. An ill-phrased article by Du Bois and a similarly cold appraisal of Moton's role in the NAACP's 1923 annual report left relations more strained than necessary. Walter White remembered an interview with Moton during the affair and painted the principal as a gun-toting militant ready to die for Tuskegee. In truth, the NAACP and the former Bookerites had fought a good fight side by side, and over the long term, relations between the two improved.[23]

If the Klan lost this battle, it won the wider war in Alabama. The state was a Klan stronghold and remained a bastion of white supremacist violence through the 1960s. Birmingham's Robert E. Lee Klavern staged a mass meeting of sixty thousand in September 1923 to induct two thousand new members at a city park. The Klan won half the city's votes in the 1920s and dominated the entire law enforcement apparatus. Throughout the state, blacks and whites who violated Klan principles were flogged with impunity. Vagrancy laws, brutal police, and a harsh convict-lease system synchronized to produce thousands of prison laborers on the state's farms and roads. Alabama had the third highest illiteracy rate in the United

States in the 1920s. Black Belt counties spent $17.35 on each white student and $.90 on each African American. Rural land values were low, and child labor among rural blacks was the rule.[24]

The Klan did have powerful opponents among whites as well as blacks in Alabama. Senator Oscar Underwood, the *Birmingham Age-Herald*, the *Montgomery Advertiser*, and Montgomery politicians spoke out against Klan violence and attempts to muzzle the press. The attorney general won convictions for flogging, which hastened the Klan's decline.[25]

Nonetheless, white power crushed the Alabama NAACP branches or drove them underground. After World War I, local activists launched thirteen NAACP branches in Alabama. The three strongest were in Birmingham, Montgomery, and Mobile, but branches also developed in Uniontown, Blocton, Anniston, Florence, Selma, and other towns. The Birmingham branch claimed one thousand members after the World War. It grew out of a Colored Citizens League, and like most NAACP branches, it had a middle-class leadership and a working-class base. Birmingham African Americans made up 55 percent of the region's coal miners and 65 percent of its ironworkers and steelworkers. These workers shopped at black-owned stores and received services from black professionals. Despite its protests, the NAACP could not dent a Klan-dominated Jim Crow system in which everything was segregated and blacks were disfranchised. Dangerous jobs and poor medical care left the city's African Americans with high tuberculosis rates.[26]

To the consternation of national NAACP leaders, the Birmingham branch never cohered. Branch leader Dr. Charles McPherson told the national office that "a reign of terror" led to the branch's lapse into inactivity. In December 1921, Director of Branches Robert Bagnall visited the city and bemoaned "cringing servile Negro leaders who are a menace here." Bagnall saw sixty-five thousand black workers and wrote, "Five thousand members in a united branch would change largely the situation." Against the wishes of a conservative branch leadership, he met with women and student groups from which he recruited people. In 1923, with the growth of the Klan, the situation looked worse when Addie Hunton visited. She noted "a state of fear bordering on panic" in the spring of 1923. "I had no idea of the apprehension for my safety until I left," Hunton wrote. The waning of the Klan lessened, but did not end, repression against African Americans. In 1928 businessman Joseph Stone was gunned down by police without any provocation, and an investigation ruled this homicide justifiable.

Hunton spoke for the NAACP under the auspices of the National Association of Colored Women's Clubs, a precaution that suggests that the movement functioned in a semi-underground fashion. Also, women could act as organizers because they were less likely to lose jobs or be subject to violence. "The salvation of the branch is in the women there," Hunton advised New York. In 1926, one thousand women led by Elizabeth Little tried to register to vote.[27]

The Klan wielded less influence in Montgomery, first capital of the Confederacy. The NAACP attained a membership of six hundred, but rival factions based at the state normal college and in the business community frustrated organizing efforts. On her 1923 trip, Addie Hunton spoke under the auspices of the Women's Clubs; the NAACP leaders complained privately to her of the more conservative approach of the city's ministers. William G. Porter served as branch president later in the decade and tried to hold the branch together, but he became increasingly concerned that he would be assassinated, and the branch languished.[28]

Although the Mobile Klavern included twenty-five hundred members, it did not intimidate the NAACP chapter. John L. Le Flore, a young postal worker, rebuilt the branch in 1926, and many of his fellow workers participated. Hunton had her best results in 1923 at Selma, where black students came out to hear her speak at the Negro college. In Uniontown, 75 percent of the town's eighteen hundred inhabitants were African-American. This was "one of the few places that has given me a real hearty invitation to visit it," Hunton wrote of her well-organized public meeting.[29]

The NAACP branches in Alabama lived fitfully under Klan pressure. In Birmingham, the key city in the state and second most important city in the South after Atlanta, the Klan kept the NAACP on the defensive. In other cities, the main problem was that Jim Crow seemed intractable and activists became demoralized. Dorothy Autrey, who studied the NAACP in Alabama, saw the importance of the NAACP's continuity into the 1950s. She viewed its local leaders as courageous activists who risked their lives in the face of Klan and white supremacist pressures.[30]

FROM A POLITICAL STANDPOINT, the most important development in 1920s race relations took place in Indiana. There the Ku Klux Klan captured the Republican Party, elected its candidate governor in 1924, and won the Indianapolis mayoralty in 1925. In response, the NAACP and other black leaders campaigned for the Democratic candidate. This marked a major turning point for African Americans in northern state politics—and it presaged the African-American majority vote for Franklin D. Roosevelt in 1936. The Indiana Klan self-destructed in a spectacular scandal in 1925, which foreshadowed the Klan's demise nationally.

The Klan was stronger in Indiana cities than in rural areas. Historian Kenneth T. Jackson found that Indianapolis was the most important Klan center in the Midwest. Behind the Hoosier Klan's spectacular growth was a Texas-born army veteran named David C. Stephenson, "the most dynamic and colorful Klan leader in the United States," Jackson wrote. Stephenson outmaneuvered local rivals to become the state's Grand Dragon and director of recruitment in the North. He converted this position into personal wealth, including ownership of a mansion and a yacht. He built a private army as well, using a superannuated law to make his men deputies of the Horse Thief Detective Association. An admirer of Mussolini before his compact with the Vatican, Stephenson could orate like Il Duce. Stephenson aspired to be president of the United States.[31]

Klan membership in Indianapolis grew to twenty-eight thousand by 1923. A local weekly, the *Fiery Cross*, spread the Klan gospel throughout the nation. The Indianapolis Klan won significant support from blue-collar, nonunion workingmen, but it also had the backing of small businessmen and even a few bankers. The Klan contributed to churches, and much of the Protestant ministry backed it. On July 4, 1923 (the day after the Klan parade in Tuskegee), the Indiana Klan mobilized between one hundred thousand and two hundred thousand supporters at a state rally in Kokomo. Stephenson arrived by airplane, dressed in a purple and orange robe, and held the crowd spellbound.[32]

Beyond the Klan's rhetorical appeal lay the promise of power and patronage. In several Indiana city governments, the Klan dispensed jobs behind the scenes. In 1925, politicians such as Indianapolis mayor John Duvall agreed to vet law enforcement appointments through Stephenson. The Dragon controlled public works contracts as well, raking off his share like any big city boss. Many people joined the Klan because they wanted a job.[33]

At Dallas headquarters, Imperial Wizard Hiram Wesley Evans began to fear Stephenson's power. The rivals differed over strategy, too: Evans permitted a great deal of local autonomy, but Stephenson wanted a grand national political plan. Stephenson reveled in the grand gesture and promoted American nationalism. By contrast, Evans was the quintessential petit-bourgeois, a dentist with localist loyalties. Evans set his spies to work and confirmed what some insiders knew: Stephenson's erotic and alcoholic tastes matched his overweening political ambitions. The Indiana Dragon arranged elaborate drunken orgies at his mansion, casting himself as a whip-brandishing Lothario among a professional harem. At the Imperial Wizard's instigation, Stephenson's home Klavern at Evansville expelled him.[34]

Women of the Indiana Ku Klux Klan. Courtesy of W. A. Swift Collection, Archives and Special Collections, Ball State University.

Now Stephenson was free to go his own way. He set out to capture the Republican Party in the 1924 gubernatorial election. Contending for real power, he refashioned Klan rhetoric to northern sensibilities, blasting southern nostalgia for the Old Confederacy. In May Stephenson's forces packed the Republican State Convention and won control of the party. The Klan candidate, Ed Jackson, defeated his rival in the primary by 224,000 to 94,000. At the close of the state convention, 75,000 Indianapolis residents gathered to watch a victorious Klan parade.[35]

In New York, the NAACP observed the Indiana Klan's victory with alarm. It immediately issued a press release urging Negro voters to defeat the Klan candidate. James Weldon Johnson warned temporizing Republican politicians to denounce the Klan or face Negro opposition at the polls. In several states African-American voters might determine a close race. Johnson issued a second warning to the United States Senate, which had assigned Indiana senator James Watson to investigate charges against fellow Klan sympathizer Earl B. Mayfield of Texas. Meanwhile, Johnson consulted F. B. Ransom, the attorney for Madame C. J. Walker's cosmetics company, which had been founded in Indianapolis. Ransom replied, "The Negro and the Republican Party have come to the parting of the way, in fact there is no Republican Party in Indiana. It has been taken over, body and soul, by the KKK." He sent along concurring editorials in the Negro press. That was enough for Johnson, who issued a challenge to President Coolidge, asking him to take a clear stand on the Klan.[36]

Indiana had a small but growing black population. In 1930 the state's 112,000 African Americans made up only 3 percent of the total population, but the state ranked eleventh in black population growth. Indianapolis's African-American population doubled from 1910 to 1930, reaching 44,000. The NAACP was relatively well established around the state, with branches in Indianapolis, Gary, Fort Wayne, Evansville, Marion, Terre Haute, Anderson, and French Lick.[37]

Women founded the Indianapolis branch in 1913. Its first executive committee was wholly female. After a period of inactivity, the branch claimed five hundred members in 1921 when Addie Hunton arrived late in the year. The school board was planning to build a separate high school, and the black community mobilized against this idea. NAACP leaders Alberta Dent, Dr. Oscar W. Langston, Robert L. Bailey, and Louis H. Berry criticized the segregation plan. The branch protested a lynching, which it suspected was Klan-inspired, in 1922, and defended a man it believed was wrongly accused of murder. Two years later the branch merged with the Better Indianapolis League. Three hundred members made voluntary contributions above their dues, and the branch could contact fifteen hundred people in an hour through twelve clubs. While the branch had periods of inactivity, by 1924 branch leaders noted "great enthusiasm" among the rank and file.[38]

As the November election approached, Indiana Republicans campaigned for the African-American vote. Stephenson funneled thirteen hundred dollars to the publisher of a Negro weekly in return for positive coverage of Ed Jackson's campaign. In October, party stalwarts Henry "Linc" Johnson and Perry Howard stumped the state's black communities. But candidate Jackson had to live down the Klan's separate campaign propaganda for white supremacy and school segregation. The word on the street in the community became "Abe Lincoln Isn't Running This Year."[39]

African Americans waged a vigorous campaign against the Republicans. The NAACP sent William Pickens and Robert Bagnall to the Hoosier State. Boston's William Henry Lewis, former U.S. assistant attorney general, joined them to speak at Evansville, Terre Haute, and Gary. In Indianapolis an integrated crowd turned out for an anti-Klan parade. NAACP leader Dr. Oscar W. Langston chaired a rally that heard from Lewis, F. B. Ransom, New York Democratic leader Ferdinand B. Morton, and a Tulsa man who told how the Klan had tortured his brother in Oklahoma. Black Hoosiers predicted segregation of schools and parks, and white nepotism in govern-ment hiring if the Klan won.[40]

Candidate Jackson never mentioned the Klan, but the Klan rallied all over the state for him. Emphasizing his support for Prohibition, Jackson swamped his opponent. The Klan dominated the state legislature as well. The rival Klan factions had united behind the Republicans. In Indianapo-lis, a big majority of African Americans voted Democratic for the first time in a major city.[41]

With his man in power, Stephenson began to declare that "I am the law in Indiana." His private behavior grew increasingly reckless. Four months after the Klan's most significant electoral victory, the Dragon brought the whole edifice crashing down around his head. On March 15 he kidnapped a state house employee he had been dating. Accompanied by his body-guards, he sequestered the woman in a Pullman compartment, where he raped her, leaving tooth marks all over her flesh. The distraught victim took poison and made a deathbed accusation against Stephenson. Marion County prosecutors convicted the rapist of second degree murder. Ste-phenson felt confident that Governor Jackson would pardon him, but, fearing adverse publicity, the governor refused. The Grand Dragon retali-ated by opening a "little black box" of files revealing a network of corrup-tion and illegal deals, which led to the indictment of twenty Indiana Republicans. The scandal hastened the disintegration of the Indiana Klan, and a ripple effect spread throughout the country.[42]

THE KLAN attracted few followers in the West because few Catholics, Jews, or African Americans lived there. A few western cities with Mexican-American or Asian-American minorities did produce more Klaverns. In Denver, the western city most like the Midwest demographically, the Klan took control of the city government. With only 256,000 people, its 35,000 Catholics, 11,000 Jews, and 7,000 African Americans provided enough of a "different" presence to deliver tens of thousands to a local demagogue named John Galen Locke.

Locke's thugs threatened the NAACP president and warned a black building superintendent to stop associating with white women. An anti-Klan city attorney vowed to halt this sort of activity. The city polarized, with the anti-Klan forces lining up behind the city attorney, the Republican mayor, and an outspoken juvenile court judge named Ben Lindsey. The Klan backed Democrat Benjamin F. Stapleton for mayor in 1923; Stapleton coyly criticized them but cooperated with the Klan once elected. When he appointed a Klan police chief, he was threatened by a recall campaign.

This time Stapleton crushed his opposition by a 2-1 majority, and in 1924, Klan-backed candidates swept the state elections.[43]

The NAACP placed its weight on the liberal side by holding its 1925 convention in Denver. The Denver NAACP was well organized, and it helped inspire smaller branches in Canon City, Colorado Springs, Pueblo, and Trinidad. To the amazement of NAACP delegates, white Denverites joined their public meetings, "despite the fact that all around and about them was the shadow of the Ku Klux Klan," Du Bois wrote in the *Crisis*. "It was a thrilling bit of courage." The former governor, William E. Sweet, spoke with Johnson at a mass meeting in the downtown auditorium. Churches, white and black, opened their pulpits to NAACP speakers on Sunday morning. Juvenile court judge Ben Lindsey joined William Pickens and a Catholic priest on a panel devoted to the Klan. On the final night, the NAACP bestowed the Spingarn Medal on James Weldon Johnson.[44]

Like the national Klan movement, the Denver Klavern faded under the combined weight of internal corruption charges and external opposition. The Klan lost statewide elections in 1926, and Mayor Stapleton turned against his erstwhile allies. After 1926 the movement declined steadily. While wider forces ultimately dissolved the Denver Klan, the NAACP, by daring to hold its Denver convention in a Klan stronghold, showed that African Americans would stand up to the bigots and join forces with white friends when they appeared.[45]

Two years later, the Association repeated its Denver performance in Indianapolis. Mrs. Olivia Taylor became the first female branch president to host a national convention. Just as the NAACP had predicted in 1924, white Indiana began a movement to segregate its public schools, Klan or no Klan. But a sign of the Klan's fall from political favor was that Governor Ed Jackson, former Klan front man, agreed to speak at the meeting.[46]

SURPRISINGLY, the *Crisis* magazine almost never mentioned the Ku Klux Klan. The hooded order lay beneath the contempt of editor W. E. B. Du Bois. Writing in 1926, he remarked that "until last year I was of those mildly amused by the Ku Klux Klan."[47] Just as professors of geography did not debate representatives of the Flat Earth Society, Du Bois would not dignify the Klan by attacking it in his magazine.

In effect, every issue of the *Crisis* repudiated racial stereotyping of African Americans. The magazine devoted far more space to the Negro as college student than to the Negro as sharecropper, even though the latter far outnumbered the former. The *Crisis* ran an annual education issue featuring pictures of graduates, articles about faculty and administrators, or the financial situation of Negro colleges. Du Bois's articles were meant not only to uplift individuals but also to allow all his readers to reflect on black achievement and see how mean-spirited the stereotypes were.

Du Bois did publish at least one article on the Klan in another journal, the *New American Review*. He saw the 1920s Klan as less of a threat to African Americans than the Reconstruction version. He argued that the Klan could best be defeated by chipping away at the wider public sentiment that shared its views. First, biblical fundamentalism, so proudly on display at the trial of Tennessee science teacher John T. Scopes, provided a framework of irrationalism in which racist notions might flourish. Second, Du Bois pointed to the violence of the Klan, whose animus had also been directed against poor whites. In a widely publicized incident at Mer Rouge, Louisiana, Klansmen murdered alleged bootleggers and were found innocent.[48]

Du Bois and his colleagues debunked the notion that distinct "races" with fixed characteristics existed. The *Crisis* printed a speech by Herbert Adolphus Miller at the Association's 1925 Denver convention. Miller claimed that the social sciences were still in their infancy and were far from achieving scientific validity for any hypothesis. Before the 1920s, Du Bois, like most social scientists, had tended to accept the notion that each "race" had unique characteristics. However, the research of cultural relativists such as anthropologist Franz Boas suggested to him that making "culture" was a permeable human trait that could not be assigned to racial groups using neat categories. As Nordic supremacists such as Lothrop Stoddard argued that northern Europeans produced all technology, Du Bois became less interested in assigning special gifts to distinct groups.[49]

If Du Bois showed some ambivalence over his long career regarding "racial characteristics," he consistently dismissed the new science of educational testing as a false measure of inherent capability. Educational psychologists typically concluded that African Americans scored lower than whites on intelligence tests because they had lower intelligence. Du Bois pointed out that these "scientists" failed to account for the inferior educational system to which his people were consigned. When a Columbia University professor concluded that the test scores showed that Negroes should be trained only for menial work, Du Bois wondered how a major university could employ someone who produced such "utter rot." In 1924 the *Crisis* published a speech by Lincoln University's Horace Mann Bond. His college found a great divergence between northern and southern Negro students when they entered Lincoln, and discovered that by the time the students graduated, their abilities had evened out. Du Bois later took to task a Dr. N. M. Hirsh, who contrasted the scores of Tennessee

Negroes and Massachusetts whites and drew biological conclusions from his results. Du Bois reminded his readers that the Bay State spent seven times more per capita on each student than the Volunteer State.[50]

Beyond the claims of educational psychology lay the policy prescriptions raised by Nordic supremacists such as Lothrop Stoddard. In March 1929, Du Bois debated the author of *The Rising Tide of Color* before an audience of four thousand at the Chicago Coliseum. Stoddard's ideas held sway in academia and influenced the government to pass the immigration restriction legislation of the 1920s. Stoddard and the Klan advocated anti-intermarriage bills and justified meager education for Negroes based on the racial inferiority theory. In their dramatic Chicago debate, Du Bois reminded his opponent that Nordics had "spread their bastards over every corner of land and sea"; and urged him, if he was worried about miscegenation, to preach to the guilty. Du Bois made an uncharacteristic personal reference in his debate with Stoddard to make the same point more humorously. Referring to his mixed African and European ancestry, he noted, "Whenever it seems necessary to deny me any privilege, then I am a Negro, and whenever I do anything that is worth doing, suddenly I become preponderantly white." There was nothing wrong with miscegenation, Du Bois insisted, but, he scornfully demanded, "Who in hell asked to marry your daughters?" Drawing a picture of contemporary Mississippi, Du Bois asked if this "civilization" was worth defending. With a grand rhetorical flourish showing the influence of Marxism and Pan-Africanism, Du Bois predicted the end of colonialism and Jim Crow. His voice, crying in the wilderness of 1929 America, sounds righteously prophetic after the end of white supremacy throughout the world.[51]

SOMEWHERE between its electoral victories in 1924 and its August 1925 Washington, D.C., parade, the Klan reached the zenith of its power. The Klan parade was a show of strength rather than a political demonstration with a demand. No particular event inspired the march. The only issue on the Klan's national agenda was to keep the country out of the World Court, hardly a rallying cry. Nonetheless, forty thousand Klansmen and women paraded in unhooded costume to the jubilant sound of brass bands, fife and drum corps, and bagpipes. When the Imperial Wizard staged a repeat of this event in 1926, fewer than half the previous year's participants showed up. By 1929 the Klan was moribund. Why?

Part of the reason lay in the Klan's very success. The Congress passed anti-immigration bills into law in 1922 and 1924 that greatly restricted immigration from non-Protestant eastern and southern Europe. Roman Catholics did not threaten to take over the United States, although Al Smith's 1928 presidential campaign breathed new life into some Klaverns. Basically, the Klan sold fear of social change, and the fears proved groundless.

The seductions of modern urban life also undercut the enthusiasm of the average Klansman. In the late 1920s, Americans went wild over movie stars, baseball players, boxers, aviators, and celebrities of any sort. They were buying automobiles, stocks, radios, and washing machines. After a man had donned his Klan robes perhaps a dozen times by 1925, did it still make sense to go to another cross burning when he might go to a talking picture show?

Many Klansmen were not extremists. These men, who joined for fraternal or opportunist reasons, the same way they had joined the Elks or Masons, really believed in law and order rather than vigilante justice. Violent Klansmen perpetrated thousands of outrages that ultimately discouraged more ordinary joiners. The Mer Rouge, Louisiana, murders or Stephenson's crime against an innocent young woman convinced many wavering members to resign.

The NAACP played a small but important role in bringing down the Ku Klux Klan. The Klan was more important to the NAACP than it was to the Klan. In contrast to the NAACP, Marcus Garvey met with Klan leader Edward Young Clarke in 1922 and endorsed segregation. This was the most important cause of Garvey's downfall, while the NAACP's anti-Klan stand was a source of its strength. Klan themes of racial purity would be brought to their logical conclusion by European fascism in the next decade, and this development put the final nail in the Klan's coffin. More persistently than any other group, the NAACP called on Americans to stand against bigotry and intolerance. As we shall see in the next chapter, the failure of Republicans and southern Democrats to do so in the 1924 election underlay African-American discontent with these politicians and their search for new political alternatives.

17

The Ship and the Sea

FROM the Civil War until 1924, African-American political strategy appeared to be simple. Frederick Douglass described it with a nautical metaphor: "The Republican Party is the ship, all else is the sea." Lincoln had fought the Civil War and issued the Emancipation Proclamation; Ulysses S. Grant, Charles Sumner, and Thaddeus Stevens had reconstructed the South and added the Fourteenth and Fifteenth Amendments. Democrats led the slavocracy, organized secession, and gave birth to the Ku Klux Klan. While a few dissenters such as Timothy Thomas Fortune or William Monroe Trotter advocated political independence, they remained outside the mainstream. Frederick Douglass saw this; Booker T. Washington saw this; it was simple.[1]

African Americans had felt optimistic about the 1920 Republican victory. Harding's rhetoric had been friendly to the idea of uplift and fairness, and he opened his door to black leaders. His Justice Department prosecuted some white holders of peons, he set in motion clemency for the men of the Twenty-fourth Infantry, and he staffed the Tuskegee Veterans' Hospital with Negro medical personnel. Yet, these measures fell far short of African Americans' raised expectations after the World War. Harding and the Republican majority failed to pass the Dyer bill, they kept U.S. troops in Haiti, and they continued the segregation of the federal departments. This might have been overlooked, however, until the Ku Klux Klan takeover of several state Republican parties. When new president Calvin Coolidge refused to take a clear moral stand on this evil, African-American leaders began to wonder whether there might be another ship on the sea.

As the 1924 presidential election approached, NAACP leaders considered boarding newly designed political vessels. They noted that silent Calvin Coolidge said nothing about the Klan in his party. However, Catholics and liberal Protestants and even some white supremacists opposed the Klan within the Democratic camp. A third party led by Wisconsin senator Robert "Fighting Bob" La Follette promised serious economic reform, and his liberal backers courted the NAACP. A new paradigm promised to emerge but did not. At the national level, no party was ready to consider the revolutionary changes that African Americans wanted.

On the local level, important new developments began to take shape. Political scientist Martin Kilson has shown that before the Great Migration, local African-American politicians delivered votes for white party bosses in exchange for jobs and patronage, as did white ethnic politicians.[2] As northern black communities grew, more assertive politicians, relying on their own base, strained against the bounds of the old "patron-client" relationship. In Chicago, Cleveland, and New York, NAACP leaders participated in this transformation of local black politics.

THE KLAN infection of the Republican Party spread way beyond Indiana. In many other states, Klansmen contended for nomination from top to bottom of the Republican ticket. As in Indiana, Klan-backed Republicans won races in Kansas, Colorado, Oklahoma, and Iowa. Klan-backed Republicans won nominations but lost elections in other states. Of the three Klan targets in the North—Catholics, Jews, and African Americans—only the latter traditionally voted Republican. African Americans treated the rise of the Klan in the Grand Old Party (GOP) as a major turning point for them. They demanded that Republicans repudiate Klan support.

This test the Republicans failed almost completely. The chief responsibility for this moral collapse lay with the new president and leader of his party. Massachusetts governor Calvin Coolidge had had virtually no contact with African Americans before coming to the presidency. The state's abolitionist heritage had touched him not a whit. In 1921 he spoke in Atlanta and told an African-American audience to appreciate what their best friend, the southern white man, had done for them. "Vice President-Elect Given a Cold Greeting," read the headline in the *Baltimore Afro-American*. As president, his choice of Virginia's lily-white C. Bascomb Slemp as his secretary alienated Negro Republicans.[3]

As Klan power grew in the Republican Party, the NAACP insisted that the president lead on what it considered a great moral issue. Johnson sent Coolidge a letter asking for an "unequivocal statement" against the Klan; he released it to the press after the Klan-backed candidate won the Indiana gubernatorial nomination. The Association reiterated its demand when the GOP assembled for its convention in Cleveland. At Johnson's urging, the handful of Negro Republicans and their white allies tried to raise the matter at the convention. Sixty Klansmen were there, too, hoping to get their man nominated vice president. The convention bosses swept the matter under a rug of silence. Most northern Klansmen probably voted Republican; billboards went up in a few northern states reading "Keep Kool with Koolidge." Silent Cal kept his lip buttoned.[4]

The Democratic Party, by contrast, divided dramatically over the Klan issue. Its raucous convention in New York's Madison Square Garden put very strange fellows in bed. Leading contender for the nomination was William Gibbs McAdoo, former secretary of the treasury and administrator of the nationalized railroads during the World War. Georgia-born but now representing California, he had the backing of Wilsonian liberals such as Bernard Baruch, the railroad brotherhoods, and the Ku Klux Klan. His chief antagonist was New York governor Al Smith, a "wet" (anti-Prohibition) and a Catholic. The anti-Klan forces tried to pass a resolution denouncing the hooded order by name; this failed by one vote in favor of a general resolution condemning bigotry. The intense battle over this resolution finished the chances of McAdoo and Smith; John W. Davis emerged as the compromise candidate. Unlike Coolidge, Davis attacked the Klan vigorously throughout the campaign. Although not a single African-American delegate attended the convention, civil rights leaders were confronted by a role reversal between the two major parties.[5]

While the Democrats fell into disharmony at Madison Square Garden, the NAACP held its convention amid the sound of music in Philadelphia. The composer Carl Diton led several choral presentations, the young contralto Marian Anderson gave a recital, and tenor Roland Hayes received the Spingarn Medal in absentia. Politics dominated this meeting, too, but the NAACP leaders were singing a different tune from that of 1920. At the opening meeting Congressman Leonidas Dyer urged the members to vote against Klan-backed Republicans and opponents of his antilynching bill. A meeting on "The Political Future of the Negro" drew five thousand people to the Metropolitan Opera House. Board member John Haynes Holmes declared, "The party of Abraham Lincoln is one thing, and the party of Calvin Coolidge is another thing entirely." When Johnson called on colored voters in Indiana to oppose the Klan-backed Republican, the audience cheered wildly.

To drive this point home more emphatically, the Association passed a resolution expressing hope that the Progressive Party would announce civil rights goals. "Nothing will more quickly bring the old parties to a clear realization of their obligation to us and the nation than a vigorous third party movement. Such a movement may save us from a choice between half-hearted friends and half-concealed enemies." This was a declaration of independence. Johnson held a ceremony at the Liberty Bell to suggest the revolutionary changes taking place within African America.[6]

According to the historian Page Smith, the Progressive convention was "one of those classic gatherings of enthusiasts from the margins of American political life. . . . It was as though all the buried hopes and defeated dreams of a generation of political have-nots rallied for one more battle against Wall Street and the Eastern capitalists." While an assortment of oddballs, vegetarians, and single taxers did come bearing offbeat schemes, the Conference for Progressive Political Action (CPPA) ultimately rallied more substantial forces. Leading the charge were the railroad brotherhoods, disappointed that McAdoo had lost the Democratic nomination and unreconciled to Davis, who seemed to be just a Wall Street lawyer. The garment workers of New York, mostly Jewish and socialist, joined them. Later, American Federation of Labor (AFL) president Samuel Gompers threw his unions' support to the Progressives. Disgruntled midwestern farmers seeking price supports formed a second contingent. Eastern liberals such as New York congressman Fiorello La Guardia, philosopher John Dewey, Harold Ickes, Helen Keller, and Felix Frankfurter formed a third influential force. Viewed one way, the convention looked like the last comic gasp of Populism-Progressivism; more charitably it represented the future New Deal: labor, farmers, and urban liberals.[7]

This should have been the natural home of the NAACP and African America as well. Founder Oswald Garrison Villard and board members Jane Addams, Charles Edward Russell, and William English Walling all backed Progressive candidate Robert La Follette. The NAACP sent an official observer, William Pickens, and he turned out to be the only black man in the hall. Amid cries of "Let him speak," Pickens boldly strode to the rostrum and called on the delegates to make the full civil rights agenda their own, taking up the Klan, lynching, Haiti, and discrimination by trade unions. He had a grand moment, for his left-wing partisans cheered lustily, but the railroad men blocked any action on his proposals. "The brotherhoods, the unbrotherly brotherhoods were master," Pickens lamented to Johnson. Having observed the blowup at the Democratic convention, the Progressive leaders wanted no divisive issues on the floor. The socialist caucus condemned the Klan, but the full convention heard nothing of it.[8]

Had the Progressives adopted a civil rights platform, the NAACP might have backed them in the presidential race despite the Association's nonpartisan tradition. During the campaign, Johnson explained the Association's policy this way: "[T]he National Office does not endorse any candidate for office. The National Office urges . . . its branches to act independently and to vote for men and measures but does not attempt to dictate to them by placing any official endorsement upon any individual candidate."[9] Despite the limitations set by the Association's board and tradition, the sentiments expressed by leaders acting individually, the *Crisis* editorials, and the speeches at national conventions sent signals to the branches reflecting the thinking in New York.

The NAACP showed it would hold the Progressive Party to the same standard it held Coolidge and Davis. Abstract words would not do. La Follette would have to address the Klan issue, and, since his campaign was so heavily influenced by rail labor, it would have to speak against discrimination by the unions also. The Association issued a public letter to La Follette and a separate challenge to the AFL along these lines. La Follette spoke against the Klan, but neither he nor the unions did anything against lily-white union policies. Their failure to forge a relationship with the NAACP marked another historic moment in which white workers chose racial solidarity over class solidarity.[10]

The Progressives courted the NAACP but, like the major parties, did nothing to win the confidence of African-American voters. They assigned G. Victor Cools of Chicago, the only black member of the American Economic Association, as its Negro vote coordinator. Cools took the NAACP's Philadelphia resolution to mean that the Association was already in its camp. He issued a news release to this effect, touting La Follette's support for the Dyer bill and his opposition to the Klan. Walter White immediately protested that La Follette had not backed the Dyer bill in the Republican caucus when it counted. White wanted to join a "Fighting Bob" who fought for civil rights and felt frustrated when this candidate never appeared. "The platform of the CPPA at Cleveland did not go nearly as far as the Republican platform," he complained. He put the point more baldly to an editor at the *Nation*: "The time is ripe for a revolt of amazing proportions on the part of colored people from bondage to the Republican Party. Yet, when we extended an opening to the liberals, they evaded in a cowardly fashion."[11]

African America had no candidate in the presidential race. Johnson elaborated on the Philadelphia resolution in the October *Crisis*. In "The Gentlemen's Agreement and the Negro Vote," he wrote that Negro loyalty to the Republicans meant that neither party would act for them. Southern Democrats would bait them, and northern Republicans would take them for granted. Southern Republicans were not trying to win elections; they existed only to collect federal patronage, and they did not want competition from Negroes. That was why they acquiesced in Negro disfranchisement. Some northern Democrats were courting the Negro vote, and it made sense to vote for them but not commit to their party. Harlem, for example, had sent a Negro Democrat to the state legislature and another to the city board of aldermen. The thing to do now was to break the "Gentlemen's Agreement" between the two parties by not promising the Negro vote in advance to one of them. James Weldon Johnson had jumped the Republican ship, foreshadowing the coming turn of Negroes to the New Deal coalition.[12]

Many NAACP branch leaders had ties to their local Republican Party and stayed in the fold but showed diminishing enthusiasm. Edward H. Morris of Chicago, William T. Francis of St. Paul, and Harry E. Davis of Cleveland responded to a *Crisis* symposium by noting their party platform as the best of a bad lot or by dismissing La Follette's chances of victory. Board members George E. Cannon of Jersey City and Robert Church Jr. of Memphis remained loyal Republicans. Cannon quit the Association in a huff after the election, hurling charges of political betrayal at the Association against what he claimed was a new electoral policy. Most African-American weeklies, including the *New York Age*, *Chicago Defender*, and *Pittsburgh Courier*, counseled party loyalty.[13]

The Negro Democratic vote was a new development. In Delaware, Alice Dunbar-Nelson worked for the Democrats. Her family newspaper ran a humorous cartoon showing a carload of fat Republicans whizzing past a bewildered Negro stalwart manning an air pump. "Sorry we haven't room for you but we only need you when we have a flat tire," they call out. In Texas, African-American voters helped elect Democrat "Ma" Ferguson, who defeated a Klan Republican. Harlem returned a majority for Al Smith, running for governor. Indianapolis blacks went Democratic in the governor's race also.[14]

African-American support for La Follette was muted. Among NAACPers, Pickens campaigned for him, but his article in the *Crisis* on the Progressive convention was clear-eyed regarding its failures. The Progressives never addressed civil rights issues, and the railroad brotherhoods stayed lily white. Oswald Garrison Villard stumped Nebraska for La Follette, but a black Progressive in Omaha complained to the national office that the local branch was timidly Republican. Kansas presented a unique case. There the Republican editor of the *Emporia Gazette*, William Allen White, ran as an independent when his party's candidate for governor accepted Klan support. The president of the Negro Republican Women's Clubs worked for the Republican, but a Parsons, Kansas, NAACP activist, Mrs. A. Dorsey Clayton, backed White. White lost but contributed to the demise of the Kansas Klan.[15]

Du Bois estimated that over two million Negro voters gave half their votes to Coolidge and divided the rest evenly between Davis and La Follette.[16] The likelihood is that White and Johnson voted for Davis while Pickens and Du Bois voted for La Follette, all feeling disgusted. Thus the 1924 election laid the groundwork for the historic change of the 1930s.

ONE REASON for African-American loyalty to the Republican Party could be seen in the nation's second largest "Black Metropolis," as the sociologists St. Clair Drake and Horace R. Cayton dubbed it : Chicago. In 1928, it would send Oscar De Priest to Congress, the first African American to sit there since 1900. By 1930, Chicago's African-American population doubled in ten years, reaching 233,903, almost 7 percent of the population. The heart of this population stretched over an expansive trapezoid-shaped district just east of the stockyards. The "hog butcher to the world," as Carl Sandburg put it in his famous poem, was likely to be a Negro migrant to the South Side. Yet in this busy, hardworking city, the NAACP struggled for many years before sinking roots in the community.[17]

Only two important NAACP branches had white leaderships that were a meaningful factor in their development. In Boston, descendants of the abolitionists worked to build an active branch among a small black community. In Chicago, white progressives, despite their good intentions, retarded for many years the growth of an activist black leadership, isolating the branch from the community. It was no accident that these two cities produced militant black civil rights leaders who essentially shared the NAACP's perspectives but kept their followers out of it: William Monroe Trotter in Boston and Ida B. Wells-Barnett in Chicago.

The Chicago NAACP faltered because it developed an elitist leadership whose key figure was Dr. Charles E. Bentley, a prominent African-American dentist. Bentley had been a colleague of Du Bois from the Niagara movement days, and he typified the Talented Tenth leader who disdained popular activism. A number of white Chicago progressives rallied to the NAACP. They included social workers Jane Addams and Mary McDowell, Judge Edward O. Brown, Rabbi Emil G. Hirsch, and Unitarian ministers Celia Woolley and Jenkin Lloyd Jones. Early in the 1920s, future New Deal cabinet member Harold Ickes served as branch president.[18]

African-American Chicagoans developed institutions that lay along various points of the ideological spectrum. Among the newspapers, Robert Abbott built the *Chicago Defender* into the most widely read weekly in black America. He ran sensational stories under screaming headlines and distributed a national edition through squads of Pullman porters working out of Union Station. Besides the *Defender*, Chicago boasted two other weeklies, the *Whip* and the *Broad Ax*. Under the leadership of T. Arnold Hill, the Urban League helped many southern migrants to find apart-

ments, jobs, and social services. White liberals joined the boards of both
the Urban League and the NAACP. Julius Rosenwald of Sears Roebuck,
probably the most consistent financial backer of both groups, worked
closely with the Urban League and responded to NAACP appeals. Suspicious of all these enterprises was the feisty Ida B. Wells-Barnett, antilynching crusader and feminist. She distrusted white paternalists and
African-American male chauvinists with equal ardor. In the early 1920s,
Chicago also claimed a vigorous chapter of Marcus Garvey's Universal
Negro Improvement Association.[19]

The Chicago NAACP had a lot of competition for a hardworking migrant's free time, but the chief obstacle to its progress was its own conservative leadership. Chicago gave Robert Bagnall fits. He saw both its
potential and how it was squandered. Bagnall quickly identified Morris
Lewis, an energetic young man with some college education but no professional calling, as the best NAACP activist. Lewis wanted a career in politics
and community service, but he lost campaigns for state representative in
1920 and 1922. Working downtown in a clerical position, he devoted himself
to recruiting for the NAACP after hours, and he built the branch up to
almost two thousand members by 1921. Bentley and his white colleagues
frittered away every opportunity to consolidate an activist layer from this
membership. Divided by social class and living place, they could not even
agree on where the executive committee should meet.[20]

Bagnall saw it all clearly. "The Chicago branch is dead," he reported to
Johnson. "For a branch to work in Chicago, it must have Negro officers
who are acceptable to the people." An advisory council with white members might be appropriate, but real authority must rest with the real leaders, as it did in other branches. When terrorists bombed Negro homes and
buildings in 1921 and 1922, Lewis worked with a Citizens Defense Committee to pressure the police department to find the perpetrators. The NAACP
had no dedicated cadre to take the lead. Lewis worked with rising politician Oscar De Priest and banker Jesse Binga, but it does not appear that
the NAACP branch mobilized in the face of this threat. The branch had no
president because Bentley was seeking a wealthy white man for the job.
When Du Bois spoke at Wendell Phillips High School in April 1922, the
auditorium was packed. "We could have easily taken up $1,000 in member-
ships," Lewis moaned to Bagnall, "but no blanks were at hand, and no
organization provided for."[21]

Yet, Chicago was so important that the board of directors assigned
Lewis as a full-time organizer and underwrote his salary. Lewis worked
diligently, but he could not by himself fix the main problem, and the struggle progressed unevenly. When a movie theater's ushers roughly handled

THE SHIP AND THE SEA 257

an African American who objected to being segregated, Ickes hesitated to sue. Ida B. Wells-Barnett kept up a "spirit of bitter hostility" toward the branch, and ministers cooperated only irregularly. A benefit performance of the musical *Shuffle Along* raised seven hundred dollars, but only one member of the branch executive committee attended the performance. Lewis scored a success when three thousand people came to hear Congressman Dyer speak in May 1923. He used this burst of enthusiasm to hire a special train from Chicago to the 1923 Kansas City convention. Inspired, the membership gathered five thousand signatures on petitions for the Leavenworth soldier-prisoners. The energy proved difficult to sustain in 1924. "On the whole, the colored people are working, are making good money and are likewise having a good time," a frustrated Lewis concluded. "The intolerable conditions existing in Georgia, Mississippi, and Alabama now seem far away. . . ."[22]

Chicago realized its potential when the old leadership of Bentley and Ickes retired from NAACP activity. The branch elected Dr. Carl Roberts as its first black president and chose an African-American executive committee with only one white member. In a telling letter, Bagnall advised the new president of racial realities:

> The Association in Chicago has so long been regarded as an organization dominated by whites and a few colored individuals, that it will take some time to educate public opinion to the realization that it is an organization of the people. In the early days, the general plan of the organization in most of our cities, was to gather a group of influential whites and a group of influential Negroes and have the two . . . form an interracial committee. . . . Later the Association evolved into a mass organization, but a few places, Chicago and Boston notably, retained the old viewpoint with the resultant handicap. Since the World War there has been a revolutionary change in the psychology of the Negro. He now will work with white people . . . but he resents it when they work for him, he being their ward.[23]

Roberts resigned after eight months, but the branch found the leader who would guide its activity for the next seven years in Dr. Herbert A. Turner, a surgeon. Turner and Lewis mobilized the excluded rank and file. They broadened the Association's connections with other community leaders. The branch established a vigorous legal aid committee under the direction of Edward H. Morris, the most prominent African-American attorney in the city. Women, long marginalized in Chicago's affairs, stepped forward when Nannie Reed, a women's club activist, joined the leadership.

A group of postal workers, the Phalanx Forum, led by Archie L. Weaver, lent its support. "You can't realize what a new wave of enthusiasm has come over the NAACP in Chicago," Lewis reported shortly after Turner's election. In 1927, Weaver's group forced the post office to hire black supervisors for the first time. A meeting for Johnson raised fourteen hundred dollars, and the branch pledged five thousand dollars.[24]

Capitalizing on this improved situation, the NAACP held its 1926 convention in Chicago late in June. The branch now enjoyed better cooperation with the city's ministers, and public meetings were held at Bethesda Baptist, Ebenezer Baptist, and the Pilgrim Baptist Church. The Association scheduled speeches by Morehouse College president John Hope, Chicago judge Albert F. George, Congressman Martin Madden, Illinois state senator Adelbert H. Roberts, Oscar De Priest, and AME bishop Archibald Carey. At one meeting businessman/philanthropist Julius Rosenwald and labor organizer A. Philip Randolph spoke from the same platform in a show of civil rights unity. Historian Carter G. Woodson was awarded the Spingarn Medal. The high point of the convention occurred when James Weldon Johnson and famed Chicago attorney Clarence Darrow addressed a filled auditorium theater. Most Chicago dailies reported the events satisfactorily, and the the Chicago NAACP finally achieved the prominence the national leaders always hoped it would.[25]

Although the branch's activity ebbed and flowed in the years following the convention, part of its success lay in the upswing of African-American morale that accompanied the election to Congress of Oscar De Priest in 1928. De Priest had been at odds with the old branch leadership but was welcomed by the Turner regime. He had worked with Morris Lewis over the years, and Lewis now accompanied him to Washington as an aide. De Priest had helped bring the NAACP convention to Chicago, and Mrs. De Priest had organized a "flying squad" of female branch activists. The new congressman credited the NAACP with helping gain his victory.[26]

De Priest became a spokesman for African America in Congress, as well as a representative of his district. He began his term as a Hoover Republican in economic policy, opposing welfare programs, but he gradually adopted more progressive views. He did not toe the party line and opposed the nomination of lily-white John Parker to the Supreme Court. De Priest rekindled African-American confidence in political action, and he spoke in many states during his six years in Congress. He was unique in his own time: in 1934 he was defeated by African-American Democrat Arthur Mitchell as black people flocked to the New Deal.[27]

THE best example of an NAACP leader who transcended the old style patron-client relationship in politics was Cleveland's Harry E. Davis. The Cleveland branch functioned consistently throughout the 1920s and developed a team leadership with little factionalism. Cleveland deserved its reputation as a relatively liberal city, but bigots tried to marginalize African Americans throughout the Jazz Age. The Cleveland NAACP fought them, usually successfully, at every turn.

Cleveland's African-American population more than doubled from 1920 to 1930. In 1920, its 34,451 black residents formed 4.3 percent of the population, and by 1930 almost 72,000 black Clevelanders made up 8 percent of the people. Cleveland had the twelfth largest African-American population in the country by 1930, most of whom lived in an urban ghetto running along Central Avenue and bisected by East Fifty-fifth Street.[28]

Political leader Thomas W. Fleming might serve as a textbook example of the client in Martin Kilson's paradigm of black urban politics before 1920. Born into poverty in 1874, Fleming worked as a barber. He saw himself as a disciple of Booker T. Washington—a black man getting ahead by hard work and cooperation with whites. Fleming founded a Negro Republican club in 1903, but progressive Democratic mayor Tom Johnson limited Republican progress. Fleming allied with Republican boss Maurice Maschke, and in 1909 he was elected Cleveland's first black city councilman, a post he held on and off for the next twenty years.[29]

In contrast to Fleming, Harry E. Davis was born in Cleveland in 1882, coming into young manhood after Booker Washington's decline. He graduated from Western Reserve Law School in 1908, joined a Masonic lodge, and served in the state legislature from 1920 to 1928. While he, too, cooperated with the Maschke machine, unlike Fleming he advanced a civil rights agenda in the legislature and helped lead the NAACP.[30]

The Cleveland branch struggled through its first decade, but the 1919 national convention raised morale. By 1922 Clevelanders crafted a team leadership that rotated through responsible positions. Clayborne George and Charles W. White led the branch during the 1920s; Davis divided his time between his duties at Columbus and home, but he kept a careful eye on the needs of his constituency and the branch. Unlike the Chicago situation, only a handful of local whites joined the NAACP, and these, such as Russell Jelliffe, played only an advisory role. The Cleveland NAACP campaigned aggressively to recruit factory workers. In 1920, Davis wrote that they wanted to have one representative of the industrial working class on their local executive board and a "key man" in ten to fifteen factories. Its branch bulletin urged members to keep their factory jobs. Membership reached a high of three thousand but dropped off to a consistent sixteen hundred by 1922. For a while the branch maintained two offices, one in the community on East Fifty-fifth Street and another downtown. Cleveland inspired the growth of thirty-two Ohio chapters by 1924.[31]

Cleveland's organizational strength flowed from its political militance. Ohio forbade segregation in public accommodations, and when Cleveland proprietors flouted the law, the NAACP intervened. In 1924 the branch won two of five cases against restaurant owners. It convinced managers of theaters, a drugstore, a swimming pool, and a department store to treat African Americans equally. When the Erie Railroad shops tried to segregate its black employeees, the Association halted that as well with a letter to the railroad's central office.[32]

The Cleveland NAACP took up two cases of residential segregation that showed its determination to defend black home buyers. In 1924, Mr. and Mrs. Arthur Hill bought a home in Garfield Heights, a suburb. When a crowd of two hundred whites menaced them, they fled, and returned to find a warning to clear out permanently. Garfield Heights authorities refused to aid the Hills, and Harry Davis demanded that the governor remove the mayor and send in the National Guard. NAACPers gathered eight hundred signatures on a protest petition and held a mass protest meeting. James Weldon Johnson took up the issue in a speech at Springfield, Ohio, sent the governor his own angry letter, and blasted him in a press release when he did not reply. The Hill family moved out anyway.[33]

Cleveland racists challenged a tougher opponent when they tried to use the same tactics against Dr. Charles Garvin, who built a home within the city limits near Cleveland Heights. First they threatened violence against the workmen, then they used it against the Garvins after they moved in. One day the Garvins awoke to find "KKK" painted on the house. Early in 1926 a dynamite bomb shattered the windows. Unlike those in Garfield Heights, Cleveland authorities posted a guard around the home. Yet in July Garvin found another bomb, this time with a defective fuse. When the chief of police detonated the infernal device in a lake, it shot up an eighty-foot-high geyser and the story became front-page news. The police reposted their guard, the Garvins stayed, and there were no more incidents. The NAACP held up the Cleveland police response as a national model.[34]

Like many NAACP branches, Cleveland aided victims of the criminal justice system. In 1922, Harry Davis blocked the extradition of a South Carolina man who had simply run away from his creditors. Although he was a member of the UNIA in Cleveland, the Garveyites did nothing on his behalf, a lapse that the NAACP used for propaganda purposes. Early in 1926, a drunken railroad detective in Stark County fired his gun at African-American youths on the tracks, wounding one. In self-defense, one of the boys shot back and unluckily killed the man. Despite the boy's age and the unclarity of his intention in firing, he was found guilty and sentenced to death. Ohio African Americans thought the youth was wrongly charged and harshly punished; NAACP branches helped gather sixteen thousand signatures on petitions urging clemency in his case.[35]

Throughout the decade the Cleveland NAACP held regular public meetings for national speakers, kept up its financial obligation to the national office, and cooperated with the city's African-American ministers. Using Harry Davis's influence in the state legislature, the branch advanced its agenda on a variety of issues. In 1928, three African Americans won election to the city council, among them Clayborne George, who ran as an independent.[36] The NAACP's early participation in Cleveland politics helped pave the way for the first African-American mayor of a major American city, Carl Stokes, who became Cleveland's mayor in the 1960s.

THE RELATIONSHIP between the NAACP and Negro politicians was more limited in New York than in Chicago or Cleveland. Because the city was more Democratic than most northern cities, African-American New Yorkers were splitting their votes by the early 1920s. Another local peculiarity entered the equation with more force: the NAACP did not build an autonomous Manhattan branch.

New York's African-American Republicans exercised more power than those of any other city except Chicago in the 1920s. Their unquestioned leader was Charles W. Anderson, a Booker T. Washington protégé who served in some party capacity from 1890 until 1934. Anderson, like Fleming in Cleveland, functioned as the Negro cog in the Republican machine—a dispenser of patronage granted by white bosses. President Theodore Roosevelt appointed Anderson the internal revenue collector for the Wall Street District in 1905, and he in turn recommended prospective chauffeurs, stenographers, postal employees, policemen, and even assistant attorneys general. After Booker T. Washington's death, Anderson probably controlled more Negro appointments than any other African American.[37]

What made New York different was that it also had a Negro Democratic machine whose operations went back to an 1897 alliance with Tammany Hall. By 1915 its leader was Ferdinand Q. Morton. During the 1920s, Democrats John F. Hylan and Jimmy Walker held the mayor's office, and they dispensed patronage through Morton. Morton served as chairman of the Municipal Civil Service Commission, and so even jobs awarded on merit fell under his purview.

Despite the potential power generated by a population of three hundred thousand people, New York African Americans did not send one of their own to Congress until 1944, when Adam Clayton Powell Jr. was elected. The Harlem congressional and assembly districts were gerrymandered to dilute the black vote among majority-white districts. Harlemites sent the first African American, Edward Austin Johnson, a Republican, to Albany in 1917. Five more African Americans, including one Democrat, won assembly seats in the 1920s from the two districts. Charles Roberts, another Republican, became the first African American to serve on the board of aldermen in 1919, ten years after Fleming in Cleveland and four years after De Priest in Chicago.[38]

Roberts ran for Congress in 1924 and Johnson ran in 1928. The NAACP showed contrasting attitudes toward the two candidates. Roberts, a respected dentist, did not campaign in the white districts and refused to speak on any important issues. Du Bois gave him scant publicity in the *Crisis.* It seemed to him that the Republican bosses had conceded the seat to their Democratic rivals and chose Roberts as their candidate merely to keep black voters in the fold. Harlem politicos knew that NAACP field secretary William Pickens had considered running as a Progressive, and Negro Republicans took Du Bois's silence on Roberts as disloyalty. After Roberts lost, they accused the NAACP of treachery. Du Bois replied in the *Crisis* that he himself had voted for Roberts, but a candidate had to be more than a black face for the *Crisis* to advertise him. NAACP board member George E. Cannon of Jersey City resigned over the matter—he essentially wanted the NAACP to strike a false nonpartisan pose but back Negro Republicans without question.[39]

By contrast, the *Crisis* allowed Edward Austin Johnson to summarize his congressional campaign in its pages, but only after he lost. Johnson, a North Carolinian, had been a colleague of George Henry White, the last African American to sit in Congress. After the Tar Heel State effectively disfranchised black voters, Johnson came to New York and won election to the assembly in 1917. Within a year he wrote and helped pass a new civil rights law that expanded the list of public places that could not discriminate. He had a state employment office opened in Harlem. Unlike Roberts, Johnson campaigned energetically in black and white districts with the object of winning in 1928. He mobilized 350 workers to go door-to-door. Harlem voted for him by margins of 6–1 and 8–1, and he even carried some white neighborhoods. However, whites fought just as hard, and Johnson lost the race. His campaign increased the black vote and raised the profile of Harlem in state politics.[40]

In November 1921 the board of directors dissolved the Manhattan branch and placed a new one under the control of the national office. The motivation for this decision is not entirely clear from the record. Financial considerations were probably uppermost in the directors' minds. The branches and the national office could both appeal to their supporters for funds, and Manhattan was too lucrative to leave to a branch. The problem of dividing funds raised locally became contentious now and then, and by placing Manhattan under national direction the Association could reap the harvest of wealthy contributors without competition from an autonomous branch.

The timing of this move was probably also driven by a real estate problem. The lease was running out on the Association's downtown office, and the directors, at the same meeting, considered moving to Harlem. After a poll of the full body (those living outside New York rarely attended), the Association stayed downtown and later moved across Fifth Avenue to number 69. Pickens and later Addie Hunton were put in charge of the reorganized Harlem branch, which located its own office at 139 West 135th Street.[41]

Until 1921, the "New York" branch (there was one in Brooklyn and another in Queens) functioned like any other. More than most places, clerics figured prominently in its leadership: Frank M. Hyder of St. James Presbyterian, F. A. Cullen of Salem Methodist Episcopal, Hutchens C. Bishop of St. Philip's Episcopal, and Adam Clayton Powell Sr. of Abyssinian Baptist were among the branch's leaders and contacts. When NAACP leaders made recruiting speeches in churches on Sunday, it was likely to be in an upper-crust setting like these churches.

The NAACP campaigned for a mass following in Harlem but never achieved one. In the spring of 1921, Harlem leaders set out on a door-to-door recruiting campaign. The Association held successful membership meetings at Harlem churches. One thousand people came out to hear Johnson at "Mother Zion" Methodist Episcopal, Congressman Martin Ansorge spoke for the Association at Rush Memorial, and Eugene Kinkle Jones of the Urban League joined Robert Bagnall at Salem Methodist Episcopal. The branch grew but did not function in New York politics the way other branches did in their cities.[42]

Moreover, the face of the NAACP looked more *café au lait* and its accent sounded more refined in New York than in other places. Reverend Hutchens C. Bishop, an NAACP board member, exemplified this organizational persona. A native of Charleston, South Carolina, he was a "tall, thin and almost bald man who easily passed for white." On behalf of his church he bought and sold Harlem real estate with such perspicacity that by 1911, St. Philip's had purchased ten new apartment buildings for $640,000. Another upper-class New York leader was James Weldon Johnson's father-in-law, John E. Nail, one of the most prosperous African-American real estate dealers in Harlem. Harry Pace, a founder of the Atlanta branch, moved to New York, initiated the Black Swan recording label, and became another source of funds for NAACP projects. The national office feared that a locally controlled branch could squander financial and political relations with such important donors and leaders.[43]

ON THE NATIONAL LEVEL, the NAACP chafed against the constraints of Republican timidity. It began the decade with high hopes for the Harding administration and the Republican congressional majority. The Association cajoled the fledgling Progressive movement into fighting for civil rights and got nowhere. The simple fact was that no white politician of national stature would stick out his neck on a civil rights issue, and the NAACP learned this through bitter experience.

In local politics, the NAACP challenged old-style Republican clients of white patrons. In no city did the Association subjugate itself to an old-style party patronage machine, but it did work with and publicize the candidacies of principled civil rights advocates on the local level. The Association helped lead African-American politics away from men such as Perry Howard and Charles Anderson, and toward politicians such as Oscar De Priest, Harry E. Davis, and Edward Austin Johnson.

18

Dr. Nixon Goes to the Polls

O N a hot July afternoon in 1924, Dr. Lawrence A. Nixon waited in line to cast his Democratic primary ballot at the East El Paso fire station on Texas Street. Nixon, a tall, slender black man, forty-one years old, held his receipt for the $1.75 poll tax in his hand. He had lived in Texas all his life and voted in the last municipal election in May. Yet, when it came his turn, the election official said, "You know we can't allow you to vote." A 1923 Texas law prohibited Negroes from voting in Democratic primaries. "I know you can't," Nixon replied, "but I've got to try."[1]

By trying, Nixon helped set in motion a train of events that would significantly weaken the Jim Crow laws. Ultimately the NAACP would contest five cases in the Supreme Court before Texas African Americans could vote in Democratic primaries. The final two decisions, *Smith v. Allwright* (1944) and *Terry v. Adams* (1953), provided legal underpinning to the 1954 *Brown* decision and the 1965 Voting Rights Act. In Oklahoma, the Association pressured the Justice Department to compel registrars to sign up prospective Negro voters. As in Texas, the Richmond, Virginia, NAACP sued for the right to participate in Democratic primaries.

Yet, in all these places African-American activists had no white political friends. Almost every white politician in the South correctly calculated that the best strategy was to distance himself publicly from prospective Negro voters. Because most African Americans who could vote were Republicans, the failure of that party to support them facilitated their drift toward the Democrats. Simply by trying to vote, however, African Americans challenged the structure of white caste rule. If some could vote, others would demand the same right. With enough black voters, some form of black political power might reemerge as it had during Reconstruction. Far-sighted people—white supremacists and civil rights activists alike—could see into this future, the former with trepidation and the latter with hope.

By the 1920s, Texas had the most diverse population and economy in the South. The Lone Star State exported oil, cattle, and cotton from the Galveston docks or the Dallas railroad yards. European immigrants, especially Germans, still formed distinct communities, and much of South and West Texas still felt like Mexico. It had the the fifth largest African-American population nationally in 1930. Concentrated in East Texas, 854,964 African Americans made up 15 percent of the state's population.[2]

By the 1920s, the Texas Republican Party had virtually collapsed while the Democratic Party dominated local politics and played a disproportionate role in national politics. The Democratic Party was riven by factions over the issues of Prohibition and the Ku Klux Klan. In the heated 1922 Senate race, Klan member Earl B. Mayfield defeated James E. Ferguson, a colorful former governor who had been impeached for corrupt dealings with the state's brewers. In 1924, his wife, Mrs. Miriam A. "Ma" Ferguson, defeated a Klan-endorsed candidate for governor. The only real elections were the Democratic primaries. If Texas African Americans wanted to participate in politics, the Democratic Party was the only arena.[3]

As in the rest of the South, neither party openly courted black voters. To choke off even this possibility, Texas in 1905 made it illegal to pay someone else's poll tax and allowed county party executive committees to determine who might join a party. Thereafter, some county party organizations made membership dependent upon swearing an oath that began, "I am a white qualified voter. . . ." This device worked in a patchwork fashion to keep African Americans away from the polls on primary day.[4]

Houston Democrats allowed blacks to vote until the February 9, 1921, primary. The city was almost 25 percent African-American by 1920, with 33,960 black residents; by 1930 it would be thirteenth in total black population. Its segregated character facilitated the growth of a middle class that owned thirty restaurants and forty stores; the liberal professions were also well developed. Houston African Americans sought an injunction against this white primary. Charles N. Love, editor of the *Texas Freeman*, and W. L. Davis, editor of the *Western Star*, challenged the chairman of the Harris County Democratic Committee in court. The county court and state appeals court turned them down. The latter court found that since the election was over, the decision would be moot anyway. Attorney R. D. Evans, a black Yale Law graduate from Waco, assisted by James A. Cobb, carried the case to the Supreme Court. The Supreme Court agreed that the case was moot but admitted that a serious question would be raised if a properly prepared case came before it.[5]

Black activists in San Antonio forced the issue to the state level. San Antonio was a unique city at the border of the South and the West, and between America and Mexico. Its liberal German population gave the city an unusual political orientation in Texas. Besides the Germans, African Americans and Mexicans voted, too. The African-American community was led in politics by Charles Bellinger, a gambler and real estate man, who delivered the black vote to the Democratic machine in return for municipal services. Its NAACP branch got off to a good start in the postwar upsurge but later collapsed, not to recover until the late 1920s when J. R. Morriss, principal of the segregated Brackenridge School, became branch president. During a close primary race for county district attorney, one candidate appealed for black votes, and his victorious rival decided to prevent this from reoccurring. He had his legislative allies prepare a new law that included the clause "in no event shall a Negro be eligible to participate in a Democratic party primary election held in the State of Texas." The bill passed the house by a vote of 93–10, and the senate by 24–0, and became law in 1923. At the next election, Hurley C. Chandler, a San Antonio African American, sought an injunction against enforcement of the statute. Chandler contended that the new law violated the Fourteenth and Fifteenth Amendments, but the Federal District Court refused to uphold his claim. The court relied on a 1921 Supreme Court decision, *Newberry v. United States.* In this case, Justice McReynolds ruled that primaries are not elections under the purview of the constitution, but private matters, and that the Court could grant no relief because the election was over.[6]

El Paso NAACP branch president L. W. Washington thought he could craft a better challenge. At the 1923 NAACP convention in Kansas City, Washington discussed an idea with William Pickens, who encouraged him to proceed. The idea was to sue for damages rather than seek an injunction. El Paso might be a good place to launch the suit. This western town on the Mexican border had only a small black community of 1,562 people. Like many small black communities, it was tightly knit, and the NAACP branch was respected. The mayor was an anti-Klan, pro-labor Democrat. Finally, Washington thought he had a man who could represent the race.[7]

Washington's candidate to challenge the law was Dr. Lawrence A. Nixon. Nixon was born in Marshall, Texas, the son of a railroad car steward. At fourteen he went to work as an apprentice cabinetmaker in the Pullman railroad shops. Later he attended Meharry Medical College in Nashville, working his way through school as a Pullman porter. Nixon began his practice in Cameron, fifty miles southeast of Waco, but after a black man was lynched there, Nixon moved to El Paso. He joined the Methodist Church, the NAACP, and the Democratic Party. He paid his poll tax and voted in all the elections. As a doctor, he relied only on the black community for economic support. Nixon was an even-tempered man, and when election officials C. C. Herndon and Charles Porras turned him away from the polls, they did so respectfully.[8]

The El Paso NAACP also had a rare white friend in attorney Fred C. Knollenberg. Knollenberg had already advised the branch in the case of Henry Lowry. Born in Illinois, he carried his large frame with jovial good cheer. Along with branch president Washington, Knollenberg thought it best to seek damages for Nixon, choosing five thousand dollars as an appropriate figure. His goal was not to collect but only to get the case properly before the Supreme Court. Shortly after the July 1924 election, he filed a brief saying that the Texas law violated the Fifteenth Amendment and related federal statutes. The brief postulated that if Texas could exclude Negroes from its primaries, any state could exclude any class of people from its primary. Further, Knollenberg asserted that the primary was the only real election. The defendants' reply followed the Texas *Chandler* decision, reiterating that primary elections were distinct from general elections. On December 4, 1924, as Knollenberg expected, Judge Du Val West dismissed his suit without ruling on its merits. In February West granted a writ of error, allowing the case to proceed directly to the U.S. Supreme Court.[9]

The NAACP Legal Committee observed this case carefully. James A. Cobb, Arthur Spingarn, and Moorfield Storey realized its importance. The Legal Committee recommended that the board of directors guarantee half of Knollenberg's twenty-five hundred dollar fee, and the El Paso branch agreed to raise the rest in Texas. In February 1925 the board approved the plan and offered Knollenberg a contract stipulating its right to direct the case to the Supreme Court.[10]

The NAACP used the white primary case to raise the organization's profile in Texas. The El Paso branch held a rally in late March to raise funds. In New York, the Association sent out a press statement claiming that "the decision in this case will profoundly affect the Negro in America." The NAACP promised that the white primary case "will constitute the opening of a general attack upon the disfranchisement of colored people in the South," a promise that proved to be true. In response, the African-American weekly *Dallas Express* wrote a ringing editorial, calling on black Texans to revive the flagging NAACP. The Texas NAACP was still reeling from the repression of 1919. Only eight branches were still functioning—Yoakum, San Antonio, Texarkana, Mayfield, Houston, Galveston, Corpus Christi, and Corsicana. The New York office urged them to help out financially.[11]

AS PART OF THIS PROCESS, the NAACP grouped three major cases together and established a Legal Defense Fund to solicit money for them jointly. These cases were the the Texas white primary; the Washington and New Orleans residential segregation cases; and the defense of Detroit doctor Ossian Sweet, charged with murder after someone in his house killed a man in an attacking mob. The Association sought $50,000 to pay for these cases. This bold venture was facilitated by Johnson's position as the lone African-American member of the board of the American Fund for Public Service (AFPS). The AFPS was launched by Charles Garland, a recent Harvard graduate who donated his large inheritance to progressive causes. The Garland Fund pledged $5,000 to the Legal Defense Fund, and another $15,000 if the Association raised $30,000. Julius Rosenwald, the Chicago philanthropist, contributed $2,000 to the NAACP's share, but the rest of the money came from black communities donating through NAACP branches. By the end of 1925, Philadelphia had pledged $2,300, Cleveland $1,000, and Washington $880, and the national goal was met.[12]

A fund-raising project of this scope attracted the attention of rival bidders for financial support within the civil rights community. As the Association campaigned for matching funds, the *Pittsburgh Courier* ran a front-page article by Floyd Calvin questioning the Association's access to and disposal of the money. "NAACP Slush Fund Aired" the *Courier* headline announced on October 9, 1926. Calvin charged, among other things, that money sent to the Legal Defense Fund was used to pay for "the upkeep of a few Fifth Avenue barons who might otherwise find such fat salaries somewhat difficult to draw."[13]

The editor of the *Courier* was Robert L. Vann, a self-made man who worked his way through law school as a waiter. In 1914 Vann became the *Courier*'s editor. Over the next ten years, he built the weekly into one of the most widely read African-American newspapers in the country. The *Courier* campaigned for civil rights and covered the NAACP sympathetically. But Vann's original model had been Booker T. Washington, and the editor owed his personal success to hard work and self-denial. Moreover, Vann was a Republican loyalist at a time when the NAACP counseled political independence. Finally, Vann honestly believed that the NAACP leaders were overpaid and that contributions were better directed elsewhere.

The *Courier* issued a four-count indictment of the NAACP. It argued that Johnson had a conflict of interest as member of the board of the Garland Fund and secretary of the NAACP. Using his position on the board, Johnson was funneling money to an organization that paid his salary. Vann also objected to the Garland Fund's appropriation of five thousand dollars to Du Bois for a study of Negro education in South Carolina. Next Vann protested that money pledged to the Legal Defense Fund was being shunted

into the NAACP General Fund without any public accounting. Finally there
was the matter of the staff salaries.

Vann might have raised these concerns in a spirit of collegial criticism,
but the article constituted a frontal attack meant to destroy the reputations
of the officers. The allegations amounted to a charge of embezzlement and
could not be ignored. Johnson, White, and Du Bois felt that Vann had
stabbed them in the back while they were arrayed on the battlefield against
formidable white opponents. Johnson immediately issued a stinging rebuttal. He replied that as the lone Negro voice on the Garland Fund board,
he did not control the dispersal of funds to black groups. If he was guilty
of Vann's charges on this score, so were his white colleagues. The grant to
Du Bois was to study Negro education throughout the South, not just
South Carolina, and it was money well spent. Money contributed to the
Legal Defense Fund stayed there; the NAACP published the annual audit
of its income and expenditures and anyone could read its budget. The final
paragraphs pulled no punches, calling Vann "a poisonous gossip monger,"
liar, and in effect, a traitor to the race for assailing the NAACP. Johnson
even traveled to Pittsburgh to repeat his charges in the black community,
and at one meeting he lost his temper, a rare occurrence for the former
diplomat. Walter White, who had been writing a column for the *Courier*,
angrily gave it up. Joel Spingarn, the Association's treasurer, defended his
own probity and the NAACP's record of rigorous accounting.

Vann retorted that Johnson had not adequately answered his charges.
Most of the black press lined up on one side or the other. The *Chicago
Whip*, *Detroit Owl*, and *Cleveland Gazette* took Vann's part; the Charleston,
South Carolina, *Messenger*, *Philadelphia Tribune*, *Chicago Bee*, *Baltimore
Afro-American*, and *Richmond Pilot* backed the NAACP. Ultimately the
NAACP was vindicated by Vann himself, who dropped his charges in 1929
and claimed disingenuously that he had not read Calvin's initial article.
The *Courier* and the *Crisis* published Vann's retraction and statements by
Johnson and Du Bois accepting Vann's honesty.[14]

Vann's charges reflected a cynical view of reform efforts that was probably held by a small section of the black community. Vann was partially
right on the conflict-of-interest score. Johnson's service as the only African
American on the Garland board probably was inappropriate, and a neutral
figure such as Kelly Miller might have been more objective. But the allega-
tion that the NAACP created a surreptitious "slush fund" was bogus. The
Association did publish its annual audit. NAACP salaries may have seemed
too high to many potential African-American working-class contributors.
The Association's projected operating budget in 1927 showed $56,290 in
expenditures. Johnson was paid $5,600 while White, Bagnall, and Pickens

earned $4,000 each.[15] Some of Vann's readers might have regarded these as princely sums.

Yet, Vann missed the wider point. He postulated a zero-sum game for the civil rights movement. By contrast, Robert Bagnall advanced a more expansive conception of fund raising. He would say that a million black families could easily afford a dollar a year for the NAACP and a few dollars more for church, lodge, and YMCA, too. The job of the movement was to inspire mass participation, confidence, and optimism. The NAACP was building a mass movement; Vann was tearing one down.

The *Courier* may have been a factor in the weakness of the Pittsburgh branch during the 1920s. The Association found capable leaders during the decade in Reverend J. C. Austin of Ebenezer Baptist Church and attorneys Frank Steward and Homer S. Brown. All these men were overcommitted, as often happened to NAACP branch presidents. Bagnall patiently explained to Austin in a telling letter about branch leadership that one key person had to block out time to put the branch first. A swirl of activity took place around the time of the fight with Vann, when Pickens addressed a packed house at the Elmore Theater in December 1924. But the branch did not really get organized until 1929, when a talented group of female leaders stepped forward. Daisy Lampkin, Jeanne S. Scott, and Bessie H. Kennedy organized over eleven hundred members, collected thousands of dollars, and aggressively demanded the prosecution of policemen for brutality against black citizens. Their energy may have contributed to Vann's retraction of his charges against the NAACP.[16]

THE SUPREME COURT heard the Texas case on January 4, 1927. Knollenberg, making his first appearance at the Supreme Court, was joined by NAACP Legal Committee chairman Arthur B. Spingarn. Knollenberg took a rough grilling from Justices Pierce Butler and James C. McReynolds, but three others seemed favorable. Cobb felt that the El Paso attorney was not quite up to his task and had not properly explained the implications of the previous Texas decisions before the Court. Yet, he noted that Knollenberg "is tractable and easy to work with." Spingarn confined his remarks to the *Newberry* case. The brief filed by the defendants added nothing new, and it does not seem that they sent an attorney on their behalf.[17]

By chance, Texas attorney general and governor-elect Dan Moody was at the Court on another matter. The youthful prosecutor abruptly asked to answer the NAACP brief in writing. The Court allowed him thirty days and gave the Association another two weeks to respond. Despite Moody's intervention at the Court, the state's written brief presented no new arguments either.[18]

Louis Marshall agreed to write the NAACP's response. He was now just as prominent as Moorfield Storey. When he reached his seventieth birthday on December 14, 1926, eight thousand representatives of progressive organizations saluted him for a lifetime devoted to good causes. Born to poor German-Jewish immigrants in Syracuse, Marshall attended public schools and the Columbia Law School. By 1926 he had argued 150 cases at the appellate level in New York and more cases at the U.S. Supreme Court than any of his contemporaries. He had probably struck down more unconstitutional laws than any other living lawyer. Marshall came to the NAACP late in life. He was an observant Jew, serving as president of the American Jewish Committee from 1912 until his death in 1929. He was probably most well known to the general public as the attorney for Leo Frank, and shortly after Storey won the *Moore v. Dempsey* case, which effectively overturned the *Frank* decision, Marshall joined the NAACP Legal Committee. He admirably represented the Jewish interest in civil rights that flowered during the 1920s.[19]

Marshall hit hard at Texas politics. He showed that nomination in the primary guaranteed election. The general election, he declared, was "a tragic joke." In 1926, 703,766 people had voted in the August primary, but only 89,263 Democratic voters were necessary to elect Moody governor in November. Invoking the Fourteenth Amendment, Marshall argued that the white primary deprived Negroes of the equal protection of the law. Moreover, he wrote, the Fifteenth Amendment guaranteed citizens the right to vote regardless of race, and Texas was now barring Negroes from the polls in its only real election.[20]

Justice Oliver Wendell Holmes wrote for a unanimous Court that the Texas law did indeed violate the Constitution. "Color cannot be made the basis of a statutory classification affecting the rights set up in this case," Holmes concluded. The ruling gave the NAACP a dramatic victory but left Texas plenty of wiggle room to continue the same policy in practice. Holmes explicitly left the Fifteenth Amendment part of the argument aside, probably because not all the justices agreed that primaries were protected by it. The primary system was a late nineteenth-century development not contemplated by the Fifteenth Amendment. By omitting it, the Court gave Texas room to bar Negroes by other means. Nonetheless, with typical exuberance, Walter White telegrammed Johnson from Washington that the "decision [was] creating [a] sensation" and that it was "generally agreed that it nullifies ruling in Newberry case and rules that primaries an integral part of elections." In fact, the decision did not, as keener legal minds observed.[21]

If the outcome was not the sweeping victory that White took it to be, it certainly blew some political wind into the Association's sails. The NAACP announced the decision as "one of the most important won for the Negro since the adoption of the Civil War amendments . . . a rebuke to the persistent violation of the Fourteenth and Fifteenth amendments in the southern states." The African-American press gave the Association full credit for a significant victory. White newspapers reported the decision as well, including the *New York Times*, which called it a "judicial landmark." Its editorial declared that "[t]his . . . is the first time that the Supreme Court has pronounced on the clear issue of the rights of black men, as compared with whites, under the constitutional amendments adopted after the Civil War."[22]

Back in El Paso, Dr. Nixon wrote to Johnson that "Negroes are elated." The small El Paso black community had raised its share of the legal fees, but Nixon noted that wealthy African Americans around the state had not contributed. He hoped that the decision would help revive other NAACP branches, for the fight was clearly not over. The *El Paso Herald*, a Republican paper, called the ruling "the greatest reproach the Texas Democratic Party has ever received" and observed that the party leaders were not about to accept it lying down. The last celebratory act of the *Herndon* decision was Nixon's return to the state court, which awarded him one dollar in damages.[23]

White Texas politicians next passed a more precisely crafted law that abandoned the race- and party-specific language of the first measure. Governor Moody proposed a new bill that was overwhelmingly approved by the house and revised by the senate. Article 1 included the phrase "Every political party in this state, through its state executive committee shall have the power to prescribe the qualifications of its own members and shall in its own way determine who shall be qualified to vote. . . ." With the new law in place, the Democratic state executive committee resolved that only white Democrats could vote. The Republicans had not mustered enough votes at the last general election to warrant a primary. Thus the discriminatory power was transferred from the state to (in Texas's theory) private citizens. The progression of the legislation matched the way that residential segregation failed at the Supreme Court when mandated by a government, but succeeded when the state enforced a restrictive covenant among private citizens.[24]

Black Texans prepared different challenges to the new law in different cities. In Houston, NAACP branch president O. P. De Walt and J. B. Grigsby sought another injunction allowing them to vote. A San Antonio activist made a similar application. Both were denied. Nixon returned to the same polling place on Texas Street, where election judges turned him away under the new law.[25]

The NAACP Legal Committee now had to decide two questions. The first was whether to continue with Nixon as the main plaintiff. Marshall easily persuaded Houston and San Antonio that the strategy of seeking injunctive relief was bound to fail a second time. However, the Legal Committee and Knollenberg disagreed over whom to name as defendants in Nixon's second suit. Nixon had sent letters of protest to all thirty-one state Democratic committee members, and Knollenberg wanted to name them, along with the election officials, in the suit. Marshall feared that the broader target would obscure the role of the state in passing the enabling legislation and turning Nixon away. Moreover, if they lost, they might have to pay legal fees for all defendants. Knollenberg remained unconvinced but deferred to Marshall's authority. The NAACP argued the case at the state level and after five years appealed to the Supreme Court, where it won a 5-4 decision on narrow grounds. The Court ruled in *Nixon v. Condon* that the state could not lodge discriminatory power in the party executive committees, but left open the question of whether party conventions could bar Negro members. It would take three more Supreme Court decisions to strike down the white primary.[26]

The fight for voting rights in Texas helped revive the state NAACP after its decline in the early 1920s. Nixon and Knollenberg spoke on the case in other cities, winning new members. In later years, this activity would lead to new challenges to segregation. After World War II, an African-American prospective University of Texas Law School student won admission on the basis that a separate education would be inherently unequal. *Sweatt v. Painter* set the stage for the 1954 decision ending segregation in public education, and it owed much to the growth of the NAACP through its fight to eliminate the white primary.[27]

A FEW MONTHS after Dr. Nixon was first refused a vote in El Paso, African-American Oklahomans struggled to defend their hard-won voting rights also. There white supremacists utilized a different strategy to keep the ballot closed. Following the U.S. Supreme Court's invalidation of the grandfather clause in 1915, Oklahoma passed a 1916 "registration law" that guaranteed the vote to those already registered (whites), but limited new registrations to a brief preelection period. In 1924, African-American Oklahomans won a partial victory against this system. By doing so, they helped set back the Ku Klux Klan and, ironically, began to move toward the Demo-cratic Party.

When the federal government opened territorial land to settlers in 1889, between 5,000 and 10,000 African Americans joined the land rush. Many of them founded all-black towns clustered in the east central portion of the state in what became Okfusgee, Okmulgee, Muskogee, and Wagoner Counties. By 1920 there were about twenty such towns, such as Langston, Boley, Red Bird, Taft, and Coweta. Segregated black communities devel-oped in Oklahoma City, Tulsa, and Muskogee. The state's African-Ameri-can population was fairly dispersed, but by 1930 172,198 black people lived there, making up 7.2 percent of the population. Black pioneers in Okla-homa showed the same enterprising spirit as whites who moved there to farm or work in the oil fields. The black towns were self-governing and often had their own newspapers, and by the 1920s Oklahoma hosted over twenty NAACP chapters.[28]

Dr. A. Baxter Whitby, a dentist, launched the Oklahoma City branch, which received a charter in 1918. Its founding members were mostly mid-dle-class professionals. Joining him later was Roscoe Dungee, editor of the *Oklahoma City Black Dispatch*. Dungee united the branches into a state conference and became the most outstanding civil rights leader in the state. Whitby helped initiate branches in the black towns and in cities with black minorities.

These rural branches included a high proportion of farmers, who proba-bly owned their own land. At Boley, Caesar F. Simmons led the most im-portant of these branches, whose 1919 charter listed eighteen farmers. Simmons, born in 1890, was a Tougaloo graduate, a Methodist minister and temperance man, and a lifelong Democrat. When the state conference of NAACP branches met in Boley in 1921, fifteen sent representatives to hear a speech by the touring W. E. B. Du Bois. At Guthrie, one thousand people came out to hear him. At Rusk, all fifty-one charter members listed their occupation as farmers. In 1924, when whites tried to run black farmers off their land near Chickasaw, an NAACP appeal to the acting governor helped stop the evictions. Although the Oklahoma branches came together only in crisis, they suggested what black farmers in other states might have been able to organize without fear of white violence.[29]

The 1916 registration law was, in effect, a grandfather clause without the grandfathers. Those ineligible to vote in 1914 (African Americans) could register only during a two-week period. The registrars simply failed to show up in black townships. Over the next few years, African-American registration dropped to ninety out of seventeen hundred eligible in Okfusgee County, a handful in Wagoner and Muskogee Counties, and six out of four hundred in the town of Eufaula.[30]

In Oklahoma City, however, some white Republicans looked upon the NAACP with favor. They feared the anarchy of lynching, and when a white Tulsan and African-American Oklahoma City man were lynched within a few days of each other in 1920, they became more concerned. Whitby advised Walter White in January 1921 that "I have helped register colored women and have the support of white Republican leaders."[31]

However, by 1924 most black Oklahomans wanted to vote for former Democratic governor Jack Walton in his race for U.S. Senate against Republican W. B. Pine. As governor Walton had waged war against the Ku Klux Klan; he was the only governor to do so during the 1920s. After a brief flirtation with the Klan, Walton turned against them when he realized how completely the Klan took the law into its hands. In one case an Oklahoma City cabdriver was flogged for fornication; a Klan defector identified the state's Grand Dragon as a ringleader in this incident, but county prosecutors did nothing. Three days later Klansmen flogged policeman John K. Smitherman, a leading Tulsa African American, and cut off his ear. They accused him of attempting to register black voters in the Democratic primary. When Walton won the primary, Klansmen bolted the party and voted Republican, but Walton won a close race. While Walton was governor, Klan floggings caused Walton to send National Guardsmen into Okmulgee County and declare martial law. After Klansmen whipped a Jewish man accused of bootlegging in Tulsa, Walton did the same thing there. He tried with little luck to prosecute the perpetrators, but overt Klan violence came to an end. Walton's forceful actions turned most whites against him, and after ten months in office he was impeached.[32]

Walton was down but not out. He sought the Democratic nomination for U.S. Senate in 1924. Two Klansmen opposed him, but Grand Dragon N. Clay Jewett muddied the political waters regarding which Klansman to support, probably because he was secretly backing the Republican. Walton won the nomination but lost the general election in a landslide. Black voters mostly hoped to vote for Walton when they sought out the elusive registrars in 1924. Even Oklahoma City's A. Baxter Whitby, a Republican loyalist, wrote during the governor's anti-Klan campaign that "Governor Walton is every bit a man, and we even fear for his personal security, however, nothing daunts him." Whitby noted that only three of three hundred Klan attacks had been directed against African Americans. In the aftermath of the election, Klansmen fell to fighting among themselves and the group declined.[33]

During the election, the Muskogee branch insisted on registering black

Ku Klux Klan induction ceremony, Hobart, Oklahoma. Courtesy of Western History Collections, University of Oklahoma.

voters. Muskogee had a white majority, and the registrars made a mockery of their responsibilities. The NAACP was led by W. H. Twine, editor of the *Muskogee Cimeter* and a veteran of civil rights struggles going back to pre-statehood days. Twine organized a group of prospective black voters to appear before U.S. attorney Frank Lee. They swore out affidavits regarding their futile efforts to register. Also, they claimed that five thousand of their fellows had been disfranchised, citing especially the Negro towns of Red Bird, Boley, and Tullahassee. The registrars "hid, dodged, and lied," a Muskogee correspondent informed Walter White. James Weldon Johnson wired Attorney General Harlan Stone, demanding he take action. Frank Lee later indicted ten registrars, but they were released by a political ally for a supposed lack of evidence against them. The arrests frightened other election officials into performing their duties, and a few hundred African Americans in Muskogee and other places cast ballots in the 1924 general election.[34]

The real issue for African Americans had always been to maintain their rights at the ballot box and to wring concessions from politicians as the price of their support. As part of this struggle, they convinced a federal judge to inquire into Okfuskee County election procedures. When two officials refused to cooperate, he held them in contempt of court. The state senate responded by voting twenty-five hundred dollars for their defense. Twine urged Johnson to contact the Justice Department; he wanted Washington to appoint a special prosecutor to match the senate's hired lawyers. Later in June, hundreds of would-be black voters appeared before a federal judge, ready to testify before a grand jury against delinquent registrars. Apparently no convictions came of these investigations. African-American Oklahomans voted irregularly throughout the 1920s in the black towns and smaller cities such as Muskogee, but there were fewer impediments in Oklahoma City and Tulsa. In 1934, Red Bird mayor I. W. Lane overturned the registration law at the Supreme Court.[35]

The irony of the fight against disfranchisement in Oklahoma is that it gradually moved African Americans toward the Democratic Party. In one way, this process unfolded as it had in Texas: an anti-Klan Democrat and weak Republicans made the Democrats seem the better choice. In Oklahoma City, Roscoe Dungee's editorials counseled support for the national Republican Party, but he noted the drift of the state organization toward lily-whitism. Most black political leaders, such as Twine in Muskogee, followed Dungee's lead. In Tulsa, a different situation evolved. Perhaps because the Republicans were strongest there, some Democratic politicians appealed for the African-American vote. Andrew Jackson Smitherman (brother of the policeman, and whose unusual name suggests Democratically oriented parents), editor of the weekly *Tulsa Star*, turned Democratic in 1918 after the previous Republican administration instituted residential segregation. The Democrats barely won the election with black help, and in return they hired African-American policemen, increased funding for the segregated library and medical facility, and let blacks control their ward organization. Historian Jimmy Lee Franklin concluded that the drift toward the Democratic Party in the state was already under way in the early 1920s.[36]

Oklahoma African Americans had a much stronger hand to play than their Texas cousins. Oklahoma had not undergone the experience of Reconstruction and the collapse of Populism, both of which made white racism general throughout the South. The black towns gave the state's African Americans a sense of confidence. A strong Socialist Party had earlier helped block a threatened literacy test. A viable Republican Party made it difficult for the legislature to mandate white primaries. The 1915 *Guinn* decision made it harder to disfranchise African-American Oklahomans. The Sooner State maintained segregation but could not keep black citizens from voting.

AFRICAN-AMERICAN communities in Virginia, Florida, and Arkansas also challenged white primary laws in the 1920s. Legally, Richmond activists won the most important outcome, overturning a state white primary on Fourteenth and Fifteenth Amendment grounds. In Pensacola, Florida, the

NAACP branch mobilized the black community to register in a 1928 primary election, but established no new legal precedent, and an Arkansas legal challenge failed. Of the three challenges, Richmond's most merits attention.

With 53,000 black residents in 1930, Richmond ranked fifteenth in black population in 1930. Virginia's 650,000 black residents ranked it eighth among the states. Virginia passed strict requirements for voting that left most of its population disinterested and disfranchised at the beginning of the twentieth century. Voters had to show long residency in their county, pay a poll tax, or own a certain amount of property. Veterans and their descendants were exempt from some provisions. According to political scientist J. Morgan Kousser, state employees cast about one-third of the vote in many Virginia elections during the first half of the twentieth century. As in Texas, Virginia African Americans could vote in the general election, but few bothered in a one-party state. Virginia made sure they would not vote in the primaries by passing a new law in 1912. Virginia gave the Democratic Party the power to establish its own rules for membership. Like Texas, the state still paid for the primary election. In 1924, the Virginia Democratic Party decided that only white qualified voters could vote in its primary.

After the first NAACP victory in Texas, Richmond African American James O. West tried to vote in the city's mayoral primary on April 3, 1928. The election officials turned him and his colleagues away. The Richmond NAACP hired African-American attorney Joseph R. Pollard and a white lawyer, Alfred E. Cohen, on West's behalf. They sued election judge A. C. Bliley for five thousand dollars in damages.[37]

The Virginia NAACP branches followed a pattern seen in other ex-Confederate states. During and after the World War, rising African-American aspirations spurred the formation of branches in several cities. Johnson's 1917 southern tour encouraged the first two branches at Richmond and Norfolk. By 1921 NAACP growth spread to sixteen more towns, a truly impressive achievement. Their inability to change race relations caused many to decline, but Lynchburg, Roanoke, Richmond, Norfolk, and Portsmouth survived despite temporary collapses and reorganizations.

Black protest in the Upper South often took the form of cooperation with the political descendants of the old Whig aristocracy. These were business-oriented men who wanted good commercial relations with the North and benign but segregated race relations. Virginia had only six lynchings during the 1920s, compared with thirty-six in Georgia. The Commission on Interracial Cooperation barely got off the ground in Virginia, perhaps because race relations were so nonconfrontational. The NAACP, as a militant, northern-based organization, formed a hostile presence in this bastion of paternalism. As historian W. Fitzhugh Brundage observed, the Virginia NAACP was characterized by a "mixture of caution and activism." After the lynching of Leonard Woods in November 1927, the liberal editor of the *Norfolk Virginian Pilot* ran a series of antilynching editorials that won him a Pulitzer Prize. More important for African Americans, Governor Harry F. Byrd signed an antilynching law in March 1928 that helped state lawmen act against vigilantism.[38] This probably encouraged James O. West to try to vote in the Richmond primary less than a month after the antilynching law passed.

Working through William T. Andrews, the newly designated coordinator of legal work among the branches, Louis Marshall sharpened the formulation of the Richmond brief. He stressed that Virginia's underwriting of the primary made it a state function, akin to a general election. The state, therefore, was paying for an election open to whites only, a clear violation of the Fourteenth and Fifteenth Amendments. Marshall became impatient at the slow response from the Virginia lawyers, but on June 5, 1929, they won the case. A federal judge agreed with Marshall's argument, making his a broader ruling than the Supreme Court decision, which accepted only Fourteenth Amendment grounds to overturn the Texas law. The decision was upheld on appeal to the circuit court one year later, and the white primary in Virginia was dead.[39]

Virginia African Americans could not capitalize on this legal victory in politics. Both Texas and Oklahoma had anti-Klan factions in the Democratic Party, which promised tolerance if not an end to white supremacy. Virginia Democrats might oppose lynching with a good law, but further than that they did not go. The Republican Party had authority only through federal appointments, which it doled out only to southern whites. Only one hundred African Americans voted in the next Richmond Democratic primary. NAACP activist Dr. Leon A. Reid complained to Walter White that black Virginians "really think it is a joke that Negroes should want to vote as a Democrat."[40]

As Andrew Buni concluded in *The Negro in Virginia Politics, 1902–1965*, "resentment against the Democratic Party died hard." The Klan did attack Governor Byrd, but Virginia's anti-Klan Democrats were not the equals of the Fergusons in Texas or Jack Walton in Oklahoma. The 1928 Al Smith presidential campaign did split off some African Americans, including the influential newspapers the *Norfolk Journal and Guide* and the *Newport News Star*. Buni accepted an estimate of only 5,000 Negro votes cast in the 1928 election (out of a population of 650,000!) and thought most of them went to Hoover, who carried the state. Winning a vote in the Richmond Democratic primary meant less than it did in Oklahoma City or El Paso.[41]

The Richmond NAACP benefited, at least, from a reorganization. Shortly before the white primary challenge, black Richmond had protested a residential segregation law. A timid NAACP leadership had left that fight to ministers and Dr. Reid, who then was not an NAACP leader. Liberal whites spoke against the law only on the condition that the NAACP, which they saw as too radical, be kept out. On a visit to Richmond in 1929, Walter White agreed that the NAACP might keep a low profile on this issue, but he wanted a strong branch there. He met with Reid and Maggie L. Walker, who agreed to build a new leadership team.[42]

Maggie Walker was a central leader of the Richmond black community, an unusual role for an African-American woman of her time. Born in 1867 to freedpeople, Walker rose to become the first female bank president in the United States. She worked as a teacher, club woman, and community activist, founding a school, sanitarium, and other black community institutions. She became the Richmond NAACP vice president and joined the national board of directors in 1929. As one of the few female directors, she paved the way for other women to advance in the NAACP.[43]

IN GENERAL, millions of southern potential African-American voters were effectively disfranchised during the 1920s by the poll tax, violence or threats, literacy clauses, residence or property requirements, and the white primary. Black activists working through the NAACP attacked the white primary during the 1920s from the geographical fringes. Dr. Lawrence Nixon's personal journey dramatized this: he had to move from Marshall, in the East Texas cotton belt, to El Paso in West Texas. There he found a more tolerant atmosphere, a tightly knit small black community, and an NAACP branch, which provided the conditions for an attack on the Texas law. Oklahoma had never been part of the Confederacy. Its white people were southerners accustomed to Jim Crow, but they could not find a formula to keep blacks away from the ballot box. Richmond was an urban center of the Upper South with paternalistic race relations, relatively little lynching, and a black community confident and well organized enough to sue for its rights. Black voters won a little more space for themselves through the lawsuits brought by the NAACP in these three cases. Their real significance lay in the long term. Without these initial steps, there would have been no groundwork for the 1965 Voting Rights Act. In addition, the strategy of attacking segregation from the West, rather than from the heart of Dixie, could be seen in outline in these cases. Legal challenges to segregation from Texas, Oklahoma, and Kansas would eventually undermine Jim Crow in the 1950s and 1960s.

The campaign against the white primary further reveals that African American loyalty to the Republican Party was beginning to crumble in the early 1920s. The 1924 election first showed this tendency, but it is also clear that some African Americans turned toward the Democratic Party at the state level because anti-Klan Democrats promised some progress.

19

The Capitol, the Canal Street Shaft, the Statue of Liberty

THE single most explosive issue of 1920s American race relations was the effort by whites to keep blacks out of "their" neighborhoods. In the northern cities, black workers found industrial jobs and a housing shortage. They were crowded into slum areas, and poor whites who lived among them moved out so that racial ghettos formed. Some middle-class African Americans had the means to live in more expensive, better-served, and integrated neighborhoods. A combination of greedy realtors and Klan types, backed by almost universal white opinion, aimed to keep them out. Segregationists employed three different methods to achieve their goal: restrictive covenant, municipal ordinance, and violence.

The NAACP fought three major court cases over this issue during the 1920s. In Washington, D.C., a white property owners' group defeated an NAACP challenge to their "right" to enforce restrictive covenants. New Orleans lost its bid to dictate residential patterns by ordinance. Both these cases went to the Supreme Court. The most dramatic struggle in American history over the right of African Americans to defend their homes took place in Detroit. The story of the Ossian Sweet family will be considered in the following chapter, but here we will see how the NAACP defended a postman who bought a home on Staten Island, New York.

THE FOUNDERS of the United States made a sectional compromise to choose the area around Georgetown, Virginia, as the site of the nation's capital. In exchange for support of northern business aims, southerners had the capital located closer to their section than Philadelphia was. Washington, D.C., was born of the attempt to reconcile two different Americas, a house divided under one roof. The governance of the District of Columbia would become a battleground between the free labor, industrial North and the slave labor, plantation South.

Pierre Charles L'Enfant, a Frenchman, and Benjamin Banneker, a free Negro, surveyed the area for development. Slaves from Baltimore laid the stones of the Capitol Building. Not far from this monument to freedom white men built a slave market where they bought and sold slaves. Abolitionists petitioned the Congress to end this practice; the southern-dominated body refused even to receive the petitions for years. Not until the Compromise of 1850 was slave trading ended, but slaveholding continued.

By 1920, African-American Washingtonians lived in a totally segregated city except for the streetcars, libraries, and baseball park. They ate in separate restaurants, sent their children to separate schools, and worked in separate rooms in federal offices. African-American tourists stayed at separate hotels and viewed government buildings in separate groups. Nothing symbolized the triumph of segregation more profoundly than the dedication of William Chester French's monument to Abraham Lincoln on Memorial Day, 1922. When the invited African-American guests arrived, they discovered that a separate section had been reserved for them in the rear, and many of them left in disgust.

Washington, D.C., was the fifth largest city in African-America in 1930, and race relations there held great symbolic value for black people. Of the four cities with larger black populations—New York, Chicago, Philadelphia, and Baltimore—Washington had the highest African-American percentage of population. The District was 27 percent African-American while New York was 5 percent black and Chicago 7 percent, but the rate of growth had been much more spectacular in those cities. This was because no administration opened new opportunities for black workers in the government, the biggest employer of African Americans. The industrial centers attracted black people like magnets attracted iron, and Washington had little industry.

Yet, the capital still offered good opportunities to black workers with professional and clerical skills. By 1928, 51,882 of them worked at a variety of government jobs, earning over sixty-four million dollars. Most worked at menial positions as laborers, janitors, and messengers. At higher levels they toiled in the post office, in printing trades, and in libraries. The separate public schools employed several hundred teachers. The faculty at Howard University and an expanded professional group of doctors, lawyers, and ministers gave Washington a big black middle class.[1] Three factors especially shaped the capital's race relations. Black Washingtonians were more middle class than other African Americans; they made up a

Dedication of the Lincoln Memorial, a segregated event, Memorial Day, Washington, D.C., 1922. Courtesy of National Archives.

higher proportion of the population; and whites felt more threatened by them.

Washington's population of clerical workers and professionals formed the basis of the NAACP's largest and most important branch in the 1920s. Entirely black from the start, by 1915 its fifteen hundred members made up about one-sixth the total national membership. The branch's first decade was troubled by a factional dispute pitting its president, Reverend John Milton Waldron, against the leadership group that prevailed during the 1920s. Waldron had been an early opponent of Booker T. Washington. He helped to found the Association and wielded great authority among middle-class churchgoers. When he tried to convert this authority into a job in the Wilson administration, he antagonized a diverse group of opponents. Some of them had been Bookerites, such as Judge Robert H. Terrell, super-intendent of Negro schools Roscoe Conkling Bruce, and Mrs. Carrie W. Clifford. Within the NAACP his foes included Nannie H. Burroughs, founder of a prominent school for girls; Lafayette M. Hershaw, a government employee and old ally of Du Bois; and Neval Thomas, history teacher at the Dunbar High School. They coalesced around Archibald H. Grimké, an older civil rights veteran, and elected him president in 1914, a post he held until 1925.[2]

Beside Du Bois, Grimké was the most important African-American leader of the Association until Johnson joined in 1916. He had been born a slave, the son of one of Charleston's most prominent planters. During the Civil War, he escaped and attended Lincoln University in Pennsylvania. He left to meet his famous Boston aunts, the abolitionists Angelina and Charlotte Grimké. There he became a lawyer, journalist, and participant in the ideological struggle between Bookerites and militants. After serving as U.S. consul in Santo Domingo, he moved to Washington, where his brother Francis ministered at Fifteenth Street Presbyterian Church.

Grimké and Du Bois had a difficult relationship, possibly because they were so similar in temperament. Both were brilliant, multifaceted, and overly sensitive; both could be alternately diplomatic and acerbic. As the older man, Grimké may have felt himself entitled to a certain deference from the *Crisis* editor. He disagreed with Du Bois's "Close Ranks" editorial of 1917. After the Houston soldiers were hanged, Grimké wrote a poem in their memory, which Du Bois refused to publish for fear of wartime censorship; Grimké wrongly took this as a personal affront. He had little use for the Pan-African Congresses, which he saw as a waste of time. Although he fared better with James Weldon Johnson, Grimké's touchiness distanced him from the national office. The problem between Washington and New York would grow worse when his successor assumed the presidency.[3]

As Washington's black population grew, whites, who largely had southern sympathies, became frightened. The capital had been the scene of one of the worst riots of the Red Summer. Many white people banded together in neighborhood associations and formed compacts with each other to sell their homes only to other whites.

Irene Hand Corrigan, who lived on the 1700 block of S Street, signed such a restrictive covenant with her neighbors, and on June 1, 1921, they filed the document with the recorder of deeds. Fifteen months later, Mrs. Corrigan agreed to sell her home to Helen Curtis and her physician husband. When it became known that the Curtises were Negroes, John J. Buckley, a signatory to the covenant, won an injunction blocking the sale.[4]

Mrs. Curtis turned to the NAACP for representation in a case that became known as *Corrigan v. Buckley*. James A. Cobb, chairman of the NAACP Legal Committee, appealed the ruling to the District of Columbia Court of Appeals, and the national office contributed two hundred dollars to the defense. Here was a challenge, the Association believed, to the principle of the 1917 Louisville *Buchanan v. Warley* case: governments could not tell Americans to whom they might sell their property. The Association realized that the stakes were high in this case. Another injunction had been issued against a sale to Emmett J. Scott, former director of Negro affairs in the War Department. The NAACP correctly forecast that residential segregation would be legalized if these injunctions were allowed to stand. Residential segregation ordinances were proliferating in other cities, and Washington's white home owners' associations took credit for that.[5]

James A. Cobb was a graduate of the Howard University Law School. A lifelong bachelor and Republican, he had worked in the Justice Department and served as associate counsel in the NAACP's 1917 Supreme Court victory against the Kentucky residential segregation law. Cobb told a courtroom full of concerned Negro spectators that if the covenant was enforced, the court would wrongly restrain a citizen's right to sell his property. The covenant violated public policy and all three Reconstruction-era amendments. It would, among other things, degrade American citizenship, retard the progress of a group of citizens, deprive the treasury of taxes, and stimulate racial antipathy, Cobb declared. The three-judge panel was not persuaded. In June 1924 it upheld the injunction. The judges swept aside Cobb's numerous contentions by citing several well-known cases that had narrowed the scope of the Fourteenth Amendment: *U.S. v. Cruikshank, Virginia v. Rives, U.S. v. Harris, Civil Rights Cases,* and *Plessy v. Ferguson.* The court ruled that Negroes were free to buy whatever property they wanted but that they could not compel the court to order someone to sell to them. Cobb announced that he would appeal to the U.S. Supreme Court.[6]

The NAACP turned this appeal over to its most prominent lawyers. Cobb, who remained the attorney of record, would be joined by Louis Marshall, Moorfield Storey, former assistant U.S. attorney general William Henry Lewis, and Henry E. Davis of Washington. Marshall quickly identified the difference between the Curtis case and the Louisville case: in Washington private citizens initiated the discriminatory action. Therefore the central argument had to be that the covenant violated public policy, he wrote Johnson. It might also violate three specific sections of the U.S. Revised Statutes, but the constitutional appeal to the Supreme Court was weak. Marshall was further concerned by Cobb's failure to file a writ of certiorari with the appeal. This would have mandated that the record be forwarded to the higher court, and now the deadline for that had passed. The Association would have to emphasize that by enforcing the covenant, the lower court had acted with the force of the state, and in that sense the Louisville decision applied to the restrictive covenant.[7]

Emboldened by its victory in the District's court, segregationists launched an ambitious organizing drive to keep their neighborhoods lily white. They published a bulletin, *The North Capitol Citizen*, which reported the progress of new restrictive covenants created around the city. For example, the Bloomingdale Owners Association advertised their neighborhood's low prices; access to transportation, schools, and parks; and lack of "undesirable" residents. The segregationist newsletter had nothing against individual Negroes, it averred with classic hypocrisy, but it did act in "self defense" against "invaders" motivated by a false sense of "social equality." Throughout the year, restrictive covenants sprouted like mushrooms in Washington and around the nation, some of them barring Jews as well as Negroes.[8]

The NAACP kept up its own propaganda offensive. In the spring of 1925, newly elected branch president Neville Thomas organized a membership drive, billing the Association as the champion of the antisegregation campaign. Du Bois gave a speech at the Metropolitan AME Church. The branch sent out mailings to teachers, fraternal lodges, and women's groups, encouraging them to join the Association. In late October, Cobb attended a big NAACP dance and discovered that "every one whom I talked with was red hot on the segregation cases." The next day they flocked to a rally at the John Wesley AME Zion Church to hear Walter White and Sam Browne, whose Staten Island home had been attacked by whites. Cobb later spoke to an African-American convention on the subject and joined its delegation in an audience with President Coolidge. The famously reticent president assured his petitioners that he deplored segregation, but declined to speak publicly on the issue.[9]

The argument was finally heard before the Court in January 1926. Marshall damned the restrictive covenant as the "entering wedge of the KKK program of elimination." Should the lower court decision stand, Marshall declared, Negroes would be forced into distinct ghettos. Whites could even be enjoined from allowing Negro servants to live on their property. Storey fielded questions from the justices, who, the NAACP attorneys mournfully concluded, were hostile. Cobb was "greatly disappointed" by his side's performance. Only Marshall and Storey spoke, and Cobb felt they had not been aggressive enough in rebuttal.[10]

Meanwhile the Washington branch leadership engaged in a nasty dispute with the national office over minor issues. New president Neville Thomas seemed to possess his predecessor's strengths and weaknesses in magnified form. He battled indefatigably against segregation but sought also to buttress his own reputation. He saw himself as the real national leader of the NAACP. In an egocentric spirit he developed a clique that was loyal to him personally, and he disparaged work done by others.[11]

At the same time, the NAACP women's auxiliary launched a campaign for the Association's Legal Defense Fund on their own initiative. The women organized a round of church meetings, rummage sales, raffles, and a benefit performance of a local stage hit, *Moochin' Along*. They held a big meeting for Ossian Sweet's attorney, Arthur Garfield Hays. The program also featured Nannie H. Burroughs, director of the National Training School for Women and Girls. All together the women raised $1,753 for the defense campaign. Flushed with success, they advertised another meeting for January 7, 1926, hoping to bring the Sweets, now released from prison, to the capital.[12]

The national office canceled the Sweets' meeting in Pittsburgh to accommodate the Washington request. Then for petty reasons, Neville Thomas pulled the rug out from under the Washington event. Laura Glenn, president of the Washington Council of Social Workers, who had been the driving force behind the campaign, told Mary White Ovington what had transpired. Jennie McGuire, leader of the women's auxiliary, had polled her board to get sponsorship of the meeting. All were enthusiastic, but after the arrangements were made, she called another meeting and insisted that the Sweets not be invited. "One felt an undercurrent which never came to the surface," Glenn wrote Ovington. "Something had happened." She implied that Thomas had instructed McGuire to cancel the speech and then hid behind her. When Ovington called Thomas to account, his invective-filled letter insisted that the women were in charge of everything and that the branch did not cancel the meeting. He accused Johnson of trying to run the Washington branch and of giving Cobb credit for the work that he, Thomas, was doing. Johnson came to Washington in February to repair the damage but made little headway with Thomas. The testy history teacher furnished Johnson with a memo full of recrimination over minor organizational details, to which Johnson painstakingly replied.[13]

On May 24, the Supreme Court finally handed down its decision in the Curtis case. Justice Edward T. Sanford wrote that the Court rejected the NAACP appeal for want of jurisdiction, an outcome that Marshall had feared all along. The Court ruled that the appeal "does not present . . . a Constitutional or statutory question substantial in character." The lower courts had merely enforced a private contract and had violated the rights of neither the prospective buyer nor the seller. In disallowing the constitutional and statutory claim, the Court did not rule on the public policy argument. Marshall concluded from this that the appeal had been too broadly framed, allowing the Court to uphold the restrictive covenant without considering what Marshall thought to be the central point. He vowed, therefore, that "we have just begun to fight," and the Association put the best face possible on a disappointing ruling.[14]

The Association carefully studied five more similar cases in Washington, representing some of the claimants, but could not carry any more to the Supreme Court. For the next twenty years, restrictive covenants became a standard feature of real estate deeds in many communities, and they greatly facilitated residential segregation. Washington developed segregated housing patterns, but ironically the 1700 block of S Street became all African-American as the covenanters sold out, probably because the surrounding neighborhood was changing. Historian Constance McLaughlin Green concluded, "Housing in actuality would be the last category of discrimination in Washington to yield to the enlightened pressure of the 1960's." Not until 1948 would the Supreme Court overturn the restrictive covenant, in the case of *Shelley v. Kramer*.[15]

WASHINGTON had been especially important to the NAACP ever since Woodrow Wilson permitted his cabinet members to segregate their departments. The federal offices remained segregated through the next three Republican administrations. The humiliating lower caste role to which black workers were assigned showed the country that white America regarded Negroes as an inferior race; it meant that segregation was the American way, and that integration was a curious northern custom.

While the branch fought for justice in local enforcement matters, it focused mainly on the question of segregation in the federal departments. At the Treasury, officials finally agreed that Negro tourists could join white groups. When the War Department built segregated golf courses for the District, Thomas and women's leader Mary Church Terrell objected. The NAACP won a meaningful victory at the Pension Office of the Interior Department. There forty-two clerks had been removed to a segregated file room and assigned a lower pay grade. In February 1927, Thomas and his colleagues met with President Coolidge to protest on behalf of the clerks. The president promised to investigate, but half a year later, nothing had been done. With another delegation Thomas visited Interior Secretary Hubert Work, who blandly declared that the employees were happy where they were. The NAACP and other organizations held a protest rally, and by the end of the year, the Interior Department restored the clerks to their former positions. Civil rights activists won another victory in 1928 when Thomas confronted Commerce Secretary Herbert Hoover. Hoover was campaigning for the Republican presidential nomination, and after a few weeks of avoiding the fiery Thomas, he desegregated his department. These victories paved the way for the quiet desegregation of all the departments during the New Deal.[16]

During his presidency, Thomas played a complex role within the Washington branch and in wider District and African-American politics. On one hand, he was a builder. Immediately upon assuming the presidency, he began a recruitment drive that netted six hundred new members, bringing the total up to twenty-five hundred, making it the largest branch. The branch met regularly, upheld its financial obligations, maintained an office on U Street, and held public meetings. Behind the scenes, however, Thomas conducted a whispering campaign against local board members that gradually spilled over to public attacks against the Association. The first indication of this was his subversion of the meeting for the Sweets. For the next few years, he kept up a veneer of civility, even recommending Walter White for a Guggenheim Fellowship. Then in the fall of 1927, the local leaders refused to host public meetings for the national officers, as all the other branches did routinely. In a unique organizational move, the branch voted to recommend that Thomas be reelected to his seat on the board of directors, a measure taken by no other branch for its president. The following month, the branch demanded that the national office do more to help Washington with the campaign against segregation.[17]

Meanwhile, Thomas openly criticized his local colleagues. At a public meeting celebrating the victory at the Interior Department, Thomas blasted Cobb, George William Cook, and L. M. Hershaw for doing nothing during the fight. These three were closely connected to the national staff, and the blow was clearly aimed at New York. Later Thomas spoke at meetings in Boston sponsored by William Monroe Trotter, with whose Washington colleagues he had been working. In the spring of 1928, Thomas enjoyed a testimonial banquet on his own behalf. Among the guests were such traditionally conservative figures as Republican leader Perry Howard, Emmett J. Scott, and Howard University's Kelly Miller. Making a toast, Howard urged the Association to name Thomas its next national president. When the African-American press noted that national NAACP leaders were conspicuously absent, William Pickens replied in his column that they had not been invited. He charged that the Association had been set up for embarrassment not by Thomas, whom he regarded as a friend, but by the Association's rivals.[18]

The NAACP board tried to control the damage but could not. At its April 1928 meeting, it sent Thomas a congratulatory telegram for the "splendid victory" at the Commerce Department. Later the Association announced that he would receive the A'Lelia Walker Medal for branch work at its up-coming Los Angeles convention. Unfortunately, Thomas was spinning out of control in a manic spree of self-absorption that defied conciliation. Hoping to find an ally in Pickens, whose article had been diplomatically phrased not to offend him, Thomas dashed off a letter to the field secre-tary, calling Du Bois a "parasite" and Johnson a publicity hog. "I am the center, the leader," in the segregation fight, he brayed. He apparently sent similar letters, which loyal members turned over to headquarters.[19]

The board decided that it had had enough. Washington had more na-tional board members than any city other than New York, and the board probably felt that it had to act before it lost the branch or Thomas spread his discontent to other cities. At the 1928 Los Angeles convention, Mary White Ovington convened an informal board meeting to consider what to do about Thomas. The board branded his charges disloyal acts and de-manded that he put them in writing and present them to the whole board; it condemned him for failing to cooperate with the national office. At the next formal meeting, this resolution carried. For the next six months, the national staff and board wasted an enormous amount of time contending with Thomas's ever-shifting charges.[20]

Thomas finally appeared at the November board meeting. He spoke for fifty minutes in probably the stormiest meeting of that body during the 1920s. Thomas insisted that the board expunge from its minutes the charges made against him. He complained that Johnson had failed to take up the segregation issue at Washington and had instead tried to disrupt the local branch. Johnson wrongly took credit for NAACP successes by at-taching his name to its press releases. Further, the national office had failed to build a New York branch. It wasted money by paying the transpor-tation of staff workers to national conventions. Johnson packed the board with his cronies. Du Bois, Thomas continued, refused to cover the desegre-gation fight in the *Crisis*. The editor was responsible for the drop-off in circulation of the magazine. Finally, he recycled the ten-year-old charge that Du Bois had bartered civil rights for a potential officer's commission during the World War. After some discussion, the board resolved that "Mr. Thomas had not substantiated the charges" and demanded an apology. Surprisingly, Thomas did apologize, but when board member Paul Kenna-day moved a vote of confidence in the board, Thomas voted no.[21]

Matters dragged on through one more bitter month. Two weeks after the November board meeting, Thomas sent Johnson a typically angry mis-sive, protesting "the disgraceful bedlam" of the last meeting and promis-ing to rally those board members not in attendance to his side. Then the *Baltimore Afro-American* ran a story detailing the events of the November meeting under the headline "NAACP Smoothes Out Neville Thomas Complaint." Board meetings were conducted in confidence, and so Johnson was compelled to inquire of the five Washington members if they had leaked the story. Thomas, Charles Edward Russell, Burroughs, Cook, and Cobb all denied speaking with the newspaper, but Thomas couched his denials evasively. In their replies, only Russell came to Thomas's defense. The board at its December meeting passed another resolution expressing approval of the branch's work but "regret" over Thomas's course of action.[22]

At this critical juncture, an offstage character stopped what might have been a disaster for the Association's largest branch. Nannie Burroughs, one of the few African-American women on the board, came to the December meeting and probably put through the diplomatic resolution whose wording aimed to separate Thomas from the branch rank and file. Besides her NAACP activity, Burroughs participated in the National Association of Colored Women's Clubs, the National Association of Wage Earners, and the Association for the Study of Negro Life and History. She held strong Baptist religious sentiments and did not fear controversy. "We were so glad to have you at the last Board meeting," Ovington wrote her with relief. Back in Washington, Burroughs convinced the branch to invite the New York leaders to meet with them. Thomas wrote her a nasty letter, but the meeting came off as scheduled. Du Bois, White, Ovington, and Johnson came to Washington to argue the national office's cause. Despite a negative article in the *Baltimore Afro-American*, Johnson wrote branch secretary A. S. Pinkett that the meeting had been a "splendid one in every respect." Some level of respect for the national body had been restored.[23]

Thomas dropped his whispering campaign after this head-on challenge by the national leadership. The board and staff had acted carefully before interfering with a local branch, waiting until it felt that an internal problem might become a public scandal. The board not only gave Thomas a hearing but also had to force his private slander campaign into the open and examine it for substantive charges. In fact, Thomas proposed no philosophical or strategic counterorientation for the movement. His charges amounted merely to personal vilification. Further, Thomas had targeted the independent role of women in the branch and had blunted their efforts. His charismatic posturing was just the sort of male egotistical behavior that a strong woman could see right through. In January, Burroughs wrote Pickens that she had received another angry letter from Thomas, who felt undercut by the visiting national officers. "I just let him rant," she wrote, unimpressed. "He is as mad as a wet hen." Thomas died in 1930. Emma Merritt, the first woman branch president in Washington, replaced him.[24]

THE NAACP victory in the 1917 Louisville case did not stop other munici-
palities from trying to circumvent the ruling. In 1924, the Louisiana state
legislature passed a law permitting such measures in cities with over
twenty-five thousand people. The New Orleans Commission Council approved an ordinance on September 16, forbidding persons of either race
from building or renting homes in the other's districts. For each week that
a person violated the law, he was subject to a twenty-five dollar fine, a
thirty-day jail term, or both. The law did not apply to existing arrangements, and it had an escape clause: "the written consent of a majority of
persons of the opposite race" could exempt a petitioner from the restriction. Over time, the law might have a far-reaching effect.

Unlike most American cities, New Orleans was fairly integrated. As
NAACP branch president E. M. Dunn explained to John Shillady in 1920,
"The colored population of the city of New Orleans lives in every street or
locality and it is a difficult matter indeed to define white and Negro locality." The new law pleased Negrophobes but infuriated black home owners
and community leaders. The police enforced the law selectively against
them. Because of the city's relatively tolerant atmosphere, a considerable
number of blacks owned homes in "white" neighborhoods and often
rented a floor of their building. If those tenants moved out, the black home
owner would have a real problem: blacks could not move in, and whites
did not rent from blacks. The home owner typically depended on the
rental income to meet his mortgage payment. Even some white mortgage
holders were upset by the law. In a flat market, if the mortgagee defaulted,
the mortgagor's building might remain vacant in an integrated neighborhood. Black people began to organize against the law soon after it passed.[25]

The New Orleans segregation ruling was rooted deep in the city's historic past. In the same month that the ruling was approved, The *New Orleans Times-Picayune* reminded its readers with a banner headline that
September 1924 marked the fiftieth anniversary of the defeat of Reconstruction in Louisiana. "Uprising of New Orleans' Citizenry Put End to
Carpetbaggers' Reign of Terror," a banner headline announced. Aged veterans of the Confederacy stood with their grandchildren before a new
granite shaft at the foot of Canal Street to commemorate the event.[26] To
understand the significance of the struggle against the residential segregation ordinance, we must step back into the city's unique past.

As historians Gwendolyn Midlo Hall, Arnold R. Hirsch, and Joseph Logsdon have pointed out, New Orleans is more easily understood as a "hinge"
between the Caribbean and the American South. Race relations developed
differently there than in Anglophone America. The French founded New
Orleans in 1718, but slave importation lasted only thirteen years. French-

men kept their African slave mistresses openly, frequently acknowledged their offspring, and freed them. By the time of the Louisiana Purchase in 1803, New Orleans had more free people of color than any other American city.[27]

When the Civil War broke out, New Orleans was a busy port inhabited by a variety of ethnic and racial groups: white Americans living in an "uptown" or commercial zone on one side of Canal Street with a Francophone old city on the other side; free creoles of color, often Francophone; American-born Negro slaves; and European-born immigrant workingmen. The Francophones practiced Catholicism; the Anglophones worshipped at a variety of Protestant churches. Nevertheless, the lines between these ethnic and racial groups were not always tightly drawn. Each had become more like the "other" than many cared to admit.[28]

New Orleans was the first major Confederate city to fall to Union forces in 1862. Creoles of color and freedpeople made common cause to demand that all male citizens be treated equally before the law. They worked together while they retained separate identities and mutual suspicions of each other. Negro American freedpeople knew that some creoles had owned slaves themselves. Yet, Francophone intellectuals looked to the French Revolution as their political model. During Reconstruction, Francophone intellectuals played a vanguard role in arguing for what became the Fourteenth and Fifteenth Amendments. Negro American freedpeople had a more pragmatic view of what might be possible in racist America. As the historians Joseph Logsdon and Caryn Cosse Bell have shown, the paradigm of a light-skinned assimilationist elite betraying more radical darker-skinned freedpeople does not necessarily apply to the unique conditions of New Orleans.[29]

In 1875, the White Leagues overthrew the Reconstruction government and disbanded the legitimate state legislature. In 1891, Democrats drew up a new constitution that effectively disfranchised the state's black voters. They passed a series of Jim Crow laws, including one mandating segregation on intrastate railways. The creoles took the lead in the struggle against these developments, launching the only black daily newspaper in America, the *Crusader*, as a propaganda organ. They challenged the railroad segregation law in court, losing what would become the landmark case of *Plessy v. Ferguson* in the Supreme Court in 1896. In defeat, the separate identities of the two colored groups reasserted themselves, leaving a mutually suspicious divide.[30]

When the New Orleans NAACP branch began in 1915, many creoles lived in the "downtown" Seventh Ward, and Anglophone Negroes lived mostly on the other side of Canal Street. The old Catholic and Protestant divide continued, meaning that the two groups prayed, socialized, and generally married separately. But both groups contributed to the new NAACP. The Association established its headquarters in the Pythian Temple, an "American" lodge building. The members chose as their president Dr. George W. Lucas, a Baptist from Texas, for most of the 1920s. Lucas, an upbeat and sympathetic man, graduated from Flint Medical College and joined the Scottish Rite Masons. Among the Association's creole supporters was Constant C. DeJoie, founder in 1925 of the militant *Louisiana Weekly*. The NAACP leadership in New Orleans was thoroughly middle class, bringing together on the executive committee three doctors, three ministers, a lawyer, and two professors. The leadership reflected business and professional links between the two communities, which shared interests in insurance companies, banking, education, and professional services.

Like most branches, New Orleans lived fitfully until a crisis sparked mobilization. After some initial isolated protest, black New Orleanians came together under the NAACP umbrella to challenge the residential segregation law. Robert Bagnall visited New Orleans during the fall of 1924 and helped forge unity between the two groups. "[T]he people are quite stirred up over the matter," he wrote Johnson. Bagnall convinced Walter Cohen, the most famous New Orleans creole politician, to work with the Association. Cohen served as the comptroller of customs at the Port of New Orleans, the lone African-American Republican appointee in the South. As such he attracted enmity from white politicians of both parties, and his Jewish name, Roman Catholic faith, and slightly African blood attracted more attention. "I went down into the creole district and held conferences at two of their clubs and succeeded in arousing them," Bagnall wrote. "They realize that this affects them as well as the Americans." Throughout the campaign, both groups were self-consciously aware of their coming together. A poster for an NAACP meeting at the creole Autocrat Club on St. Bernard Avenue declared, "The people of the lower section of the city are to be complimented for the part they are playing and we trust that the people of the uptown section will be aroused to the sense of their duty."[31]

The stakes in New Orleans were quite high. Anna Beck was prosecuted under the law when she moved into a house on Milton Street in a "white" neighborhood. Beck worked as a schoolteacher and preferred not to pursue the matter for fear of losing her job. Benjamin Harmon was less vulnerable. He had purchased a cottage on Anderson Street thirty years ago when the district lay in swampy land. Now the land was filled in and the neighborhood built up. Shortly after the law passed, Harmon obtained a permit to add on to his home. A white man named John Tyler got an injunction blocking the project on the grounds that Harmon, an African-American man, might be expected to rent to a black family. The neighborhood was evenly divided racially, and Tyler wanted it to be white.[32]

The NAACP hired attorneys Loys Charbonnet, a white man, and Frank B. Smith, an African American, to represent Harmon. They argued the case before Judge Hugh S. Cage in civil district court, and to everyone's surprise, they won. Judge Cage found that despite his personal belief that the New Orleans ordinance should stand, he could not ignore the Louisville ruling. He expressed the hope that his own ruling would be overturned in the Supreme Court.[33]

Segregationists commenced an extralegal campaign to have their way. In October, terrorists shot up a Negro home, and the occupants fled. The next month, some New Orleans real estate men organized a consortium to enforce segregation through sales and lending practices. The "Louisiana Club for Segregation" sponsored a public meeting, whose poster fulminated against Negro home buyers: "They Want to be Your Next Door Neighbor! They Demand Social and Political Equality! Is White Civilization a Broken Thing? Protect the Value of Your Property!" Economic realities lent some irony to the last injunction, because some white sellers received better offers from blacks than whites. The realtors' campaign foundered on the rock of the profit motive.[34]

The NAACP, by contrast, gained momentum. A newly organized women's auxiliary sponsored a fund-raising dance at the Pythian Temple's Roof Garden and recruited new members at weekly meetings. The United Front Committee raised eighteen hundred dollars for the defense effort, and more people came to meetings than ever before. By the end of the month, the defense fund had received pledges of over six thousand dollars, and James E. Gayle, the chairman, felt disappointed that more had not been raised. The Association's letterhead showed seventeen different outreach committees.[35]

The Louisiana Supreme Court ruled on Tyler's appeal in March 1925. Writing for a unanimous court, Chief Justice C. J. O' Neill found that since equal restrictions had been placed on both races, the law did not discriminate. Tyler had argued that the Louisville decision did not apply to the Louisiana law, but that *Plessy* was more relevant. This must have carried some weight in Louisiana. The *Times-Picayune* praised the decision and noted that it would promote community peace and keep real estate values high. The *New Orleans States* played the decision as the second lead story. NAACP leaders in New York were naturally disappointed, but Lucas remained undaunted. "Our people are still encouraged and we mean never to stop until we win," he vowed.[36]

An aggressive city attorney now began prosecuting suspected African-

American violators with a vengeance. Lucas claimed that several hundred were arrested under the law. A typical example was Jessie Guinn, "found guilty of living in his own home in a so-called white neighborhood," Lucas wrote. Even the *Times-Picayune* worried that only colored people were penalized. By early July, the NAACP lawyers worked out a deal with city attorneys to desist until the case was heard at the U.S. Supreme Court. When the police continued making arrests anyway, black community leaders James A. Hardin, S. W. Green, some white realtors, and others met again with city officials to press their demands. Finally they won a restraining order staying further arrests.[37]

Spurred by the residential segregation fight, the New Orleans African-American community mobilized around a wide range of issues throughout the 1920s. Blacks complained that the school board underfunded the lone Negro high school, which had only seventeen rooms to serve a total Negro population of over one hundred thousand. When the ferry service across the Mississippi to Algiers was segregated, five hundred came to a protest meeting. In court, Comptroller of Customs Walter Cohen was exonerated on corruption charges brought by white rivals. Next the Charity Hospital opened a separate entrance for Negro patients. One of the major donors to the Charity Hospital had been Thomy Lafon, a creole philanthropist, and black residents were disgusted by the hospital's misuse of his bequest; three hundred came to a protest rally at the Pythian Temple. Many more signed a petition, but the board remained intransigent. African Americans launched a fund to build their own hospital. Throughout all this activity, terrorists bombed black-owned buildings and homes. The police made no arrests.[38]

The NAACP announced a recruitment drive for five thousand new members in 1926. William Pickens traveled sixteen hours by train from Little Rock to speak for the branch. Descending wearily from the train, he flew into a rage when he learned that the white lawyer, Loys Charbonnet, had been evasive about his commitment to file his brief at the Supreme Court. "[W]e are likely to be double-crossed by the white lawyer," Pickens alerted New York. The local NAACPers were less worried, but, perhaps motivated by Pickens's suspicions, they accompanied Charbonnet to the depot "to see that he really left." Charbonnet worked well with James A. Cobb in Washington and returned the following January to make final trial preparations.[39]

The Supreme Court heard *Harmon v. Tyler* on March 11, 1927. Charbonnet and Smith appeared for the NAACP, and the gallery was filled with prominent African Americans. Both New Orleans and the state of Louisiana sent leading attorneys to argue. They claimed that the ordinance's escape clause separated the New Orleans law from the Louisville law, but their protestation of race neutrality was undercut by their use of the word *darky* and reference to biracial people as "degenerate." Chief Justice William Howard Taft and Justice James C. McReynolds questioned the Louisiana officials sharply regarding the Louisville decision. Dissatisfied with what they heard, the Court overturned the state law, and with it the municipal ordinance fell. Predictably, the *Times-Picayune* deplored the decision, and the *Louisiana Weekly* applauded it. The New Orleans NAACP held a rally to celebrate, at which Lucas read a congratulatory telegram from Johnson.[40]

Lucas remained at the head of the New Orleans branch until his untimely death in 1931. His consistent civil rights activity during the Jazz Age prepared the way for activists such as Alexander Pierre Tureaud, who helped guide the branch for the next forty-five years. The New Orleans victory in the municipal ordinance case settled the issues raised in the Louisville decision. The New Orleans victory was defensive to be sure, but it put in place legal precedents that would help undermine Jim Crow.[41]

WHEN RESTRICTIVE COVENANTS or municipal ordinances failed to keep neighborhoods all white, some bigots turned to violence and intimidation. Many black families quickly sold out or moved away in the face of threats. Some stayed and fought back by mobilizing public pressure. On Staten Island, the New York City borough that looks out at the Statue of Liberty, one courageous family, aided by the NAACP, stared the bigots down and forced them to surrender.

Staten Island was the whitest New York borough. In 1930, only 2,576 African Americans lived there, making up less than 2 percent of the population. The Bronx and Queens had similar percentages of black residents, but their total populations were so much larger that black communities were forming in those boroughs. Brooklyn, while only 2.7 percent African-American, had almost 70,000 black residents and its own active NAACP branch, headed by Dr. Vernina Morton Jones, one of only a few black women doctors and NAACP board members. Staten Island's black community, by contrast, was scattered and leaderless.[42]

Samuel A. Browne, a Spanish-American War veteran who worked as a letter carrier, and his wife, Catherine, a teacher at Public School 11, bought a home at 67 Fairview Avenue in the West Brighton Section in February 1924. Six weeks later they received an offer to buy the house, and when they turned it down, the Brownes received a letter from the Ku Klux Klan. It promised that an army veteran would shoot Mrs. Browne from long range and kill Mr. Browne next. Undaunted, the Brownes and two children moved into their home on the Fourth of July. Racists formed a "protective association," and forty of them demonstrated outside the house a few weeks later. They pressured the postmaster to fire Browne. Ominously, the insurance company canceled their fire insurance. Rocks smashed the windows before dawn. The Brownes stayed. Sam kept his job. They fixed the windows and reinstated the insurance. Sam bought a revolver and called the NAACP.[43]

Walter White told the Brownes to contact the Justice Department. White called the New York City police, who posted a guard at the home. By the fall, a grand jury investigation was under way. It did not take long to discover that Browne's neighbor, a southern-born realtor, was behind the trouble. In August 1925 the man was indicted, and the Association paid for a civil suit against him. New York's African-American press made the case a *cause célèbre*. In September the NAACP and Reverend Adam Clayton Powell organized a defense rally at Harlem's Abyssinisan Baptist Church. Robert Bagnall spoke at a meeting on Staten Island and formed a new NAACP branch. Faced with this pressure, the white defendant settled out of court and never bothered Browne again. The postman, who had not flinched under serious pressure, became a vigorous NAACP activist and spoke about his case on several occasions.[44]

IF AMERICAN NEIGHBORHOODS were not completely segregated during the 1920s, it was only only because of efforts by families like the Curtises in Washington, the Harmons in New Orleans, and the Brownes on Staten Island. They mustered their own personal courage and turned to the wider black community for support. The NAACP won two of these three struggles, and although the Curtis case was lost in court, the whites in that neighborhood sold to African-American buyers. The biggest test of the issue would come in Detroit. Sam Browne never had to discharge his revolver. In Detroit, a white man would die trying to force a black family from their home.

20

Home Sweet Home

WHEN Ossian Sweet was a boy, he saw a mob burn to death a Negro named Fred Rochelle. This occurred in his hometown of Bartow, Florida, near Orlando. Ossian hid on the fringes of the throng, and the image of what he saw haunted him to the end of his days.

This experience may have contributed to Ossian's relentless desire to succeed in life. The son of a Methodist minister, he left home at age twelve and worked as a bellhop, a waiter, and even a Pullman porter. By age fourteen he was studying at Wilberforce College in Ohio, earning money by working at any menial job. Despite his poverty, he went on to study medicine at Howard University in Washington, D.C. There he witnessed another atrocity during the 1919 riot: he saw a black man dragged from a streetcar and beaten to death. After completing his studies in gynecology, Ossian married a beautiful music teacher named Gladys Mitchell. They raised enough money for Ossian to continue his studies in Vienna and Paris, where he worked with the famous radiologist Marie Curie. He even contributed three hundred francs to the American Hospital in Paris—only to find that when Gladys was ready to deliver their first child, she would not be admitted on account of her color.

Gladys was born in Pittsburgh, but she came to Detroit with her family at age seven, probably in 1909. Her father taught piano and performed, earning a good living. Gladys became a musician, too, finished high school, and went on to Teachers' College. She married Ossian in 1922. Marcet Haldeman-Julius, a magazine writer, described her as "a striking woman . . . creamy tan in tone," and her hair, when loosened, hung below her waist. She was "slender, graceful, finely wrought, sensitive, aloof." Ossian, this writer thought, was a "well-set up, broad shouldered, quiet, firm-jawed dignified man." He was race-proud and naturally extroverted, while Gladys, by contrast, seemed hardly to think about racial issues. They must have made a remarkable impression in Paris. When the Sweets returned to the United States in 1925, they settled in Detroit. Despite the obstacles

Dr. Ossian Sweet. Courtesy of Walter P. Reuther Library, Wayne State University.

faced by black doctors (they could not practice in all-white hospitals, and so were often limited to accepting only black patients), Ossian developed a busy practice.

Then they decided to buy a house. After the usual search, they purchased a yellow brick home on Detroit's East Side at 2905 Garland Avenue, near the corner of Charlevoix. The house was in a white working-class neighborhood, with a population of old stock Protestants and new immigrants. Ossian Sweet conducted the negotiations openly, by himself. He bought the house from an African-American man who passed for white, paying $18,500, his life savings. New home owners, the Sweets had bought into the American dream.[1]

Henry Ford's mass production of automobiles turned Detroit from a city that was 1 percent African-American to a central destination for black migrants. A racial determinist, Ford saw black workers as loyal men who shunned the strikes and radical ideas that lured European immigrants. After the World War, middle-class Americans could buy automobiles, and black and white workers from the South streamed into Detroit to build them. African Americans even sang a blues song about the migration:

I'm goin' to Detroit, get myself a good job
Tired of stayin round here with the starvation mob
I'm goin' to get me a job, up there in Mr. Ford's place
Stop these eatless days from starin' me in the face

Detroit ranked as the thirteenth largest American city in 1900 but registered fourth by 1920. In that year, almost forty thousand African Americans
lived in a city of about one million people, and a decade later the black
population had tripled. It showed the fastest rate of black population
growth of any major American city in the 1920s. These rural black southerners now became urban proletarians. They worked in the aluminum and
steel industries that fed the auto plants. They worked for other auto manu-
facturers besides Ford, such as Dodge and Packard, but Ford was the giant.
By 1926 ten thousand Detroit African Americans worked at the sprawling
River Rouge plant alone. They labored at the hottest, toughest, most dangerous jobs—spraying paint, grinding steel, sanding metal. Some worked
at the more skilled trades on the assembly line. To get a job at Ford, an
applicant went to his minister or the Urban League, and these community
leaders, men such as Father Everard Daniel, Don Marshall, or John Dancy,
spoke to the Ford people on his behalf. Thus an alliance was forged between the black community and Detroit's capitalists.[2]

The new black workers had to live somewhere, and they crowded into
many different sections of the city, forming pockets of black settlement.
The historic black community was located where Greektown and Lafayette
Park now are, downtown near the Detroit River. Later, African Americans
clustered around St. Antoine Street, farther north up Woodward Avenue on
the East Side. Some workers could afford homes, and they tended to buy
near the factories on the West Side along Epworth Boulevard. A new black
business district grew up along Milford Avenue. A separate African-American district appeared in the north West Side around Tireman Avenue,
forming "Gold Coast" and "Indian Village" communities. There was, thus,
no red-lined, socially marked, single black ghetto taking shape in Detroit,
as did happen in Manhattan's Harlem or Chicago's South Side.[3]

Detroit's demographic explosion made the once overwhelmingly northern-born white Protestant city a complicated place. Arriving alongside
southern blacks were southern whites, who joined Catholic European immigrants, old stock Americans, Greeks, Jews, and others in a rapidly ex-
panding urban area. The white southerners brought with them their
segregationist principles and its organizational expression, the Ku Klux
Klan. Beginning in 1917 in Detroit, the Klan recruited openly and tried to
solidify white Protestants along ethnic and religious lines. During the early

1920s, the Detroit Klan sponsored mass rallies, but its activity lacked a focus. In 1924 the Klan campaigned for a mayoral write-in candidate, Charles S. Bowles, who garnered over 106,000 votes and finished a close second to the victor, John W. Smith. Smith won the 1924 contest with a combined Catholic, liberal Protestant, African-American, and immigrant vote. Next the Klan fastened upon the issue of residential segregation. Here was an issue that could mobilize the very broadest support, although it diluted the Klan's anti-Catholic message. Klansmen sponsored various "neighborhood improvement associations," urging laws to mandate residential segregation and direct action against interlopers in white neighborhoods.[4]

The first victim of this campaign was Flita Mathis, a woman who lived at 5913 Northfield Street. In April 1925, a gang stoned her house and shattered some windows. Mrs. Mathis fired a revolver at the crowd but hit only her neighbor's house. The neighbor filed a criminal complaint, but the judge dismissed the suit.[5] A second case drew more attention. Dr. Alexander Turner, a prosperous physician with a mostly white clientele, purchased a home on Spokane Avenue in Detroit's northwest section. In June a mob of five thousand stoned his home, and he had to be evacuated by the police. He quickly sold the home. Dr. Ossian Sweet bought his home, far away on the East Side, shortly before Turner was attacked.[6]

Two more incidents erupted in July. On Tireman Avenue on the West Side, Vollington Bristol, an undertaker, refused to move after three nights of disturbances at his home. Next, John W. Fletcher, an African American living on Stoepel Avenue, fired into a crowd around his house. This time the volley struck home, wounding a white youth in the thigh. Every window of Fletcher's house had been broken, and his lawn was filled with bricks, coal, and other missiles. Fletcher and four others in his home were arrested, and although the charges were dropped, he, too, decided to move out. But Fletcher had drawn white blood, and now the Klan rose to the challenge. On Saturday night, July 11, they rallied ten thousand strong on West Fort Street. There a Tennessee Klansman, speaking before fiery crosses, demanded that Detroit enact residential segregation laws. Mayor Smith issued a statement denouncing agitators and defending Detroit's reputation as a peaceful city where "the law recognizes no distinction in color or race."[7]

After word spread on the East Side that a Negro had purchased a home nearby, the Waterworks Improvement Association held an angry meeting at the Howe School across the street from the unoccupied Sweet home. A speaker from the Tireman Avenue group warned that the new neighbors posed a threat to property values, and boasted of how his group had driven out the Turner family. Not long after, on September 8, the Sweets moved in. They anticipated some trouble. They left their two small children with friends and brought with them sacks of food, suspecting that the grocer might refuse them service. For reassurance, two of Ossian's brothers, Otis and Henry, and a few of Henry's friends joined them. For protection, they brought guns and ammunition along with the furniture.

On the first night, menacing whites appeared, shouting threats. The next evening, three insurance men stopped by on business, and Gladys prepared a roast pork dinner for the men and herself. While she was cooking, she heard Henry cry out, "My God! Look at the people!" A crowd of hundreds overflowed the street, with cars double-parked on both sides. After a while, stones thudded against the brick walls. Suddenly a taxi pulled up bearing Otis Sweet and a friend, and they dashed into the house under a hail of stones and shouts of, "Get the niggers!"

Later, Ossian remembered, "When I opened that door to let them in, I realized for the first time in my life I stood face to face with that same mob that has haunted my people throughout its entire history." He felt "a fear that no one could comprehend but a Negro." Henry recalled that "it looked like death if we tried to hide, and it looked like death if we tried to get out. We didn't know what to do." They pulled the blind and waited. Stones pounded against the house, and windows shattered. The men inside scattered, and some of them took up guns. Henry fired into the crowd from upstairs, and others did as well. They heard some screams, and finally a squad of police, who had been standing idly by thus far, demanded to be let in. They arrested all eleven people in the house, including the terrified twenty-three-year-old Gladys Sweet.

In the police van, the frightened detainees resolved to say as little as possible if they were interrogated separately. This the police did and refused to allow them a lawyer. The first question a sergeant asked Ossian Sweet was, "Why did you buy a house in a white neighborhood?" Only after a while did they each learn that they would be charged with the murder of Leon Breiner and assault with intent to kill another man who was wounded. They all faced life in prison. The Sweet's American dream had turned into the ultimate Kafkaesque nightmare.[8]

THE DETROIT NAACP had proudly hosted the national convention in 1921, but by 1925, it was virtually moribund. Its president, Fred H. Williams, scarcely answered his mail. Almost its entire income came from white contributors; black members gave only fifty or sixty dollars a year. This was a "disgrace," an angry Robert Bagnall wrote the president of the branch he himself had built up from the ground. Under national pressure, Detroit reorganized, making the Reverend Robert Bradby its new president. Bagnall congratulated the new leader, declaring that he was "gratified beyond words."[9]

Bradby and his colleagues turned the Detroit branch around. The new president was also pastor of the oldest, largest, and most prestigious African-American church in the city, Second Baptist, which had a congregation of three thousand. Bradby, a light-skinned Canadian-born man, had married into the wealthy Cole family. He had come to Detroit fifteen years earlier, when Second Baptist had only two hundred members. After a fire destroyed the building, he raised eighty thousand dollars and won a grand following. "He could make you cry," remembered longtime Detroit resident Bernard Coker. "During the altar calls people came down in droves. Women in elegant church clothes and white gloves . . . he'd have them laid out."[10] Bradby filled a railroad car full of Detroiters for the 1925 Denver NAACP convention. The invigorated branch won a string of small victories during the Klan mobilizations as well. The black community newspaper, the *Independent*, observed that the NAACP had won an acquittal for Flita Mathis, who had shot at the first mob. When Highland Park High School barred three African-American children from the class trip to Washington, D.C., the NAACP reversed the school authorities. During the spate of Klan violence, a black employee wounded three white attackers at work. Cecil Rowlette, an African-American attorney, represented Lee Sullivan in the court of Judge Ira W. Jayne, a white NAACP board member, and won an acquittal from an all-white jury. The New York headquarters was so impressed that it issued a national press release on these victories. Meanwhile, four hundred to five hundred people were attending the NAACP monthly meetings, and despite Bradby's personal rivalry with Mrs. Beulah Young, the adult leader of the junior division, that was growing as well.[11]

As soon as James Weldon Johnson read about the events in Detroit, he wired the branch for more information. W. Hayes McKinney, the branch counsel, and Mose Walker, first vice president, wrote back immediately with an abbreviated version of the facts. The branch was calling a mass meeting on Sunday, and they wanted Walter White to come out right away. When the NAACP board of directors assembled for its regular monthly meeting on September 14, the Sweet case was the main item on the agenda, and the legal brain trust attended in force: partners Arthur Spingarn and Charles Studin were there, and James A. Cobb came up from Washington to join eight others. Johnson reported on the recent developments, and the board members immediately recognized that the Detroit case had national implications. They would need the best available counsel and would have to raise a significant defense fund. The energetic assistant secretary boarded the first train out after the meeting, and by Wednesday, September 16, he reported his first impressions to Johnson.[12]

The Sweets were in big trouble. Judge Jayne told White that the police were "honeycombed" with Klansmen, who were recruited directly out of the South. Jayne was a tall and lanky gentleman farmer, one of the few honest judges in a sometimes crooked town. He could be sarcastic and sharp-tongued, and many lawyers were afraid of him, but he was fair. Jayne told the assistant secretary that even anti-Klan whites were opposed to integration. The prosecutor would probably exclude blacks from the jury. Finally, one of Sweet's brothers had admitted to shooting at the mob. This would not be an easy case to win. On the positive side, Detroit boasted a strong branch. Judge Jayne closely advised the mayor. Mayor Smith had appointed an interracial committee to look into racial tensions, and its chairman was a contributor to the Association. At its Sunday rally, the branch had launched a Special Sweet Defense Fund, and the three signers of the account were NAACP activists with reputations for integrity. At this meeting, the crowd overflowed Second Baptist and volunteered $676, and later a medical committee pledged another $500.

From his own observation, White quickly grasped that the biggest problem would be to secure appropriate legal representation. Ossian Sweet's personal attorney, Julian Perry, "commands no respect," White wrote, and Cecil Rowlette, whom Perry had called in, was "blustery, noisy and pompous." Charles Mahoney, who represented the three insurance salesmen, was capable, but, like the other two, was not up to a case of national significance.[13] The next day, White and the local NAACP leaders met with the defendants and forged an agreement giving the Association full control of the legal and financial conduct of the case, in cooperation with the attorneys already engaged. As if to demonstrate the obstacles in the way, the local attorneys failed to make any progress at the preliminary hearing while White was in town. A stream of police officers testified that only fifteen or twenty people were in the vicinity of the Sweet home at the time of the shooting. One officer, a recent arrival from Tennessee, bridled under Rowlette's examination, undoubtedly answering to a black man for the first time in his life. At the end, however, the judge bound over all eleven defendants on first degree murder charges and denied bail for all of them.[14]

This must have been the lowest moment for all the defendants, but most especially for Ossian and Gladys Sweet. Both must have regretted the decision to buy the house a thousand times. They had two small children, who could not possibly understand where their parents were. Ossian may have felt especially guilty for placing his wife, children, brothers, and their friends in such mortal peril. Sweet later told Marcet Haldeman-Julius, the magazine writer, "If I had known how bitter that neighborhood was going to be, I wouldn't have taken that house as a gift. But after I had bought it, I felt that I could never again respect myself if I allowed a gang of hoodlums to keep me out of it."[15] When White met Sweet in jail, this must have been a deeply moving moment for him as well. As a thirteen-year-old in 1906, he had crouched beside his father, rifle in hand, as the mob advanced on his own house during the Atlanta race riot. White was a fair judge of character, and he must have sensed Sweet's resolve. He probably estimated that Sweet would be the perfect representative of aspiring colored America.

The Sweets would need an attorney who commanded the respect of the Detroit legal community. White took Judge Jayne's advice that this attorney had to be a white man. The harsh reality was that a black attorney simply did not stand a chance with an all-white Detroit jury. Perry and Rowlette accepted this, but Rowlette wanted to direct the case from behind the scenes, and he favored employing Thomas W. Chawke, who, Rowlette said, "would take my instruction." Chawke was an outstanding criminal lawyer, but he had made a reputation for springing local gangsters who were probably guilty. The NAACP leaders saw the case in political context: they wanted to win, and they wanted the moral high ground. Rowlette figured Chawke would ask about five thousand dollars, and he proposed that the three colored attorneys would split the same amount among themselves. White favored securing the president of the Detroit Bar Association, but the man declined. This left the NAACP in a bind.[16]

After White returned to New York, the situation grew even more complicated. A rival defense committee, led by the Reverend Joseph Gomez, announced that it was forming a citywide group to raise funds locally. Its list of sponsors included several Methodist Episcopal denominations, which suggests that some old local church rivalries were at play.[17] Ultimately, the defendants could dictate the shape of the defense committee, but they were probably divided over this among themselves. On September 29, four of them—Otis Sweet and the three insurance men—sent emphatic letters to McKinney, the Detroit NAACP counsel, and Du Bois, insisting that the Association take full charge of the case. They protested the "sordid efforts of narrow self seekers for material gain or personal glory," referring to the unnamed Gomez group.[18] The absence of Ossian Sweet's name suggested disharmony on the part of the prisoners themselves. In time, the NAACP and the Gomez group established a *modus vivendi*.

On the Sunday, July 12, that the *Detroit Free Press* reported the big Klan rally, its lead story was the opening of the John Scopes trial in Tennessee. Scopes had violated state law by teaching evolution to his Central High School science class. William Jennings Bryan, the thrice-defeated Democratic candidate for president, volunteered his renowned oratorical skills to the prosecution. Speaking for the defense was the most prominent civil liberties lawyer in the country, Clarence Darrow. Now sixty-eight years old, the legendary Darrow battled the Great Commoner in a trial that riveted the nation. Americans sat glued to their radios as Bryan argued for fundamentalism and local control, and Darrow for free speech and science. Scopes was found guilty and fined one hundred dollars, but later got off on a technicality before the state supreme court. Darrow became an even bigger media celebrity and a hero to all progressives.[19]

While the effort to secure adequate representation for the Sweets drifted, an unsolicited letter came across Walter White's desk on October 6. This was from one N. K. McGill, assistant Illinois secretary of state and general counsel to the *Chicago Defender*. "I have free access to such minds as Mr. Darrow's," the correspondent offered. White wrote a perfunctory reply, but the very next day a flurry of telegrams passed between the New York NAACP office and its Chicago branch. Darrow, it turned out, was on his way to New York. After he arrived, Arthur Spingarn, Charles Studin, Johnson, and White met Darrow at the apartment of his colleague Arthur Garfield Hays.[20] Spingarn quietly explained the details of the Sweet case, and the famous attorney told the swarthy, tanned Spingarn that he sympathized with his people. Spingarn replied that he was a white man. Truly puzzled, Darrow haltingly asked the fair-skinned Walter White about his ethnicity, and he assured him that he was a Negro. Having resolved this humorous confusion, Darrow expressed interest in the case but declined to commit himself.[21]

Two days later White and Spingarn boarded the Wolverine for Detroit, bearing a five hundred dollar check for the defense committee. They met with Frank Murphy, the trial judge, and then with the local attorneys, who arranged a postponement. The possibility that the mighty Clarence Darrow might enter the case now put the NAACP in a commanding position. Murphy was then in his early thirties, a graduate of Ann Arbor, Harvard, and Trinity College, Dublin. Rumored to be a Sinn Fein sympathizer, he was a handsome bachelor and was often seen on the courthouse steps with beautiful women. White and Spingarn became convinced that Murphy would handle the case fairly. Spingarn returned to New York, while White and Judge Jayne decided to hire Walter Nelson as the local white attorney once Darrow agreed to enter the case. They would pay Nelson twenty-five hundred dollars and the three African-American attorneys fifteen hundred dollars each.[22]

Then White took the train across the flat Michigan landscape to meet Darrow in his Chicago office. Darrow tried to pin White down as to whether or not the Sweets had actually fired into the mob. White hedged until Darrow got him to admit that he thought they did shoot. Satisfied, Darrow agreed to take the case. "If they had not the courage to shoot back in defense of their own lives, I wouldn't think they were worth defending," White remembered Darrow saying. He would charge only five thousand dollars, far below his usual fee, and would bring Arthur Garfield Hays into the case with him. Along with Herbert J. Friedman of Chicago, they formed a powerful team of tough, highly regarded lawyers.[23]

Darrow went to Detroit himself. He met with Murphy and they set a court date for October 30. Next he conferred with the defendants and the local attorneys. "I have seldom seen such joy in the faces of any persons as appeared in those of the defendants when I introduced Mr. Darrow to them," White wrote. A wave of relief seemed to sweep through everyone connected with the case, and the African-American press nationally hailed Darrow's entry into the case as well.[24]

By hiring Clarence Darrow, the NAACP once again showed the value of a nationally organized civil rights movement. The Reverend Gomez and other local critics now had to take a back seat. When White returned to New York, William Pickens assumed his role, trying to smooth over lingering resentments. "This Detroit job is working my tongue out," he advised the New York office. Pickens reported that he and Gomez were getting along, "but he is unreasonable in that he hates Du Bois and does not like the leadership of the NAACP, which might possibly include me of course but I did not notice it," the puckish field secretary reported.[25]

Meanwhile, White and Johnson viewed the opening of the trial with optimism. Mose Walker, emerging as the real leader of the branch, reported that the Detroit legal community thought there was no case against the Sweets. Further, Judge Murphy was well disposed toward the defendants and was planning to run for mayor at the next election. He planned to use his popularity in the black community as a tiebreaker to win a majority. He had already granted bail to Gladys Sweet, which the Association took as an augury of his attitude.[26]

IN COURT, White was dazzled by their lead attorney's ability. "Darrow is the most amazing figure I have ever seen," he gushed to Johnson. "He's got the court . . . all with him. Most of the jurors are eager, too eager in view of the strength of the Klan here, to serve, and he ever so often makes some droll remark that sets the courtroom to laughing." The courthouse scuttlebutt said that Darrow would win an acquittal, but White was not that optimistic. Jury selection took a week.[27] For his part, Darrow pondered, as he questioned the panelists, the deep-seated, unconscious prejudices of his fellow Americans. "I kept wondering what a white man would think of his chances for getting a fair trial in Africa if he had killed a negro and was placed on trial before twelve men with black faces," he wrote in his autobiography.[28]

With a jury finally in place, prosecutor Robert Toms paraded scores of witnesses before them for the next three weeks. These were primarily neighborhood residents and policemen, who all swore that only fifteen or twenty people were near the Sweet house. Unfortunately for the prosecution, some of them first blurted out that there were many people and then corrected themselves. The deputy superintendent of police said there were no people around the house, and Inspector Norton Schuknecht, rumored to be a Klansman, saw seventy-five people. He admitted he had a squad of sixteen men under his command. The problem for the prosecution was that no one saw a particular individual fire a fatal shot. By charging all eleven defendants with conspiracy and equal culpability, the prosecution was in a precarious position unless naked race prejudice carried the day. By the end of the cross-examinations, Darrow and his colleagues poked fun at the notion that the total number of witnesses exceeded the number of alleged protesters in the street.[29]

On weekends, Walter White made lightning trips to midwestern cities, giving his account of the trial and raising funds. At a Chicago church, nine hundred people came out, but the fund appeal was bungled when the minister took a collection first for his own building. White raised twice as much in the Twin Cities, which had a much smaller black population. In Cleveland, a big meeting pledged twelve hundred dollars, and Toledo promised five hundred dollars more. African-American doctors in Chicago volunteered another two hundred dollars. Church meetings in Detroit kicked in over thirty-two hundred dollars. Mary McLeod Bethune, leader of the National Association of Colored Women's Clubs, spoke at one meeting. Meanwhile, Detroit's black community was packing into the courtroom, hanging on every word.[30]

After three weeks, the prosecution closed its case. Now it was Darrow's turn. He began with several African-American witnesses who had stumbled onto the edge of the crowd and had to flee for their lives under a barrage of stones. A few white witnesses told the court that an enraged

mob had been at the scene. At last, Ossian Sweet testified in his own defense. Under Hays's questioning, the dignified doctor told his life story,
from his Florida boyhood, through college, to Europe, and finally his decision to buy his home. He told how all the racial violence during his lifetime
had influenced his judgment, and by the time he was done, the courtroom
was hushed. Walter White wrote to Johnson that the Detroit newspapers,
which had at first disdained the defendants, now wrote that public opinion
was more favorably disposed toward them.[31]

A reporter for the *Nation* magazine described the scene as Darrow commenced his summation the next day. "A deep silence fell over the crowded
noisy courtroom. The old man with the unutterably sad face and the great
stooped shoulders seemed no mere lawyer pleading for hire. He seemed,
instead, a patriarch out of another age. . . . His voice was a low rumble; in
it resounded all the misery his tired eyes had seen." Then he changed key,
arguing briskly that the prosecution had failed to prove a conspiracy and
that a man had the right to defend his home. The courtroom was jammed
with spectators, scanning the jury's reaction for some sign of their inclination.[32]

Jury deliberations began the day before Thanksgiving. African Americans thronged the halls of the court building, hoping for an acquittal. Outside the jury room, court officers heard angry shouts from within and
fueled the rumor mill. The word was that some defendants would be convicted but most acquitted. At two in the morning, with the crowds still
waiting, Murphy sent the jury to bed. On Thanksgiving Day, the crowds
returned, munching sandwiches for their holiday meal. Finally the exasperated jury made its report. They could not reach a verdict on any defendant. In his autobiography, White recorded that one juror asserted during
the deliberations that "I don't give a God damn what the facts are. A nigger
has killed a white man and I'll be burned in hell before I will ever vote to
acquit a nigger who has killed a white man!" The prosecution now had to
decide whether or not to retry the case.[33]

Darrow was disappointed by the verdict. He knew that right was on the
defendants' side, and he declared that race prejudice alone kept the jurors
from returning acquittals. Most of the African-American press praised Darrow's handling of the case. The jury's failure to reach a verdict "denies the
right of a citizen to protect his home" the *Atlanta Independent* asserted.
The *Cleveland Call* praised the colored witnesses and summarized:
"[T]hank God that the NAACP had the inspiration and the influence to get
Darrow for Dr. Sweet." African-American papers generally reported the
incident, the opening of the trial, and the verdict on their front pages, but

not the proceedings of the trial. The national white press relegated the story to the back pages.[34]

As Oscar Baker, the Bay City NAACP leader, saw it, the Sweets had certainly won a "moral victory." The fact that the sympathetic Judge Murphy did not direct a verdict of acquittal made the outcome even better. While not the outright victory the defendants deserved, Baker rightly saw the result as a serious blow to further prosecution. Undoubtedly, Klan elements in Detroit would exert powerful influences in the other direction. Nevertheless, for the Sweets, being released on bail felt deeply liberating. Black Detroiters put up their homes as collateral, posting ten thousand dollars each for the Sweet brothers and fifty-five hundred dollars for the others.[35]

The defense had spent over $20,000, but more would have to be raised as it became clear that there would be a second trial for at least some defendants. The NAACP kicked its field work into high gear to raise the money. Pickens effected a greater degree of working unity among Detroit's various factions, who packed the Ebenezer AME Church to hear Ossian Sweet speak two days after his release on bail. Pickens then took off for Kentucky, speaking in the obscure small towns where the NAACP did its most overlooked, but perhaps most important, work. He raised $178 in Lexington, $35 in Owensboro, $30 in Maysville, and more in Frankfort. Then he was off to Indianapolis; Richmond, Indiana; and Cincinnati. James Weldon Johnson appeared in Philadelphia, which gave $1,000, and even the long-slumbering Chicago branch sprang to life, sending $500. Robert Bagnall toured the tristate New York City area, where the big event was a meeting for Detroit's Reverend Bradby at Harlem's Mother Zion AME Church, which garnered $800.[36]

Money poured in like never before. Clarence Darrow spoke at Harlem's Salem Methodist Episcopal on December 13 at "easily the largest" NAACP event in New York. Four thousand people jammed the building, and thousands more could not get in. Darrow spoke first in the main hall, and then to another assembly in a second room. The famous atheist shocked a score of ministers when he advised the audience not to rely on the Lord. "I have a suspicion that He is a Nordic anyway," Darrow declared. Johnson, White, and Reverend Bagnall especially must have cringed. The people contributed thousands of dollars. Meanwhile, Mary McMurtrie, a wealthy friend of Mary White Ovington's, contributed ten thousand dollars to the Association's general fund, the highest individual contribution the Association ever received.[37]

In January, Bagnall took the Sweets on a tour of Philadelphia, Baltimore, Pittsburgh, Cleveland, and Chicago. They raised almost three thousand dollars and spoke to thousands of people. In Chicago, the branch booked the armory but did little to attract an audience. "The five hundred present seemed a handful in that vast space," Bagnall mourned to Johnson. Moreover, the strain of events was telling on the Sweets. "I averted no fewer than four scenes; [and] aborted five quarrels between the Sweets." Bagnall tried to coach Ossian as a public speaker, "but as soon as he saw a big crowd his ego would burst through. The Sweets silent would have been much better. . . . When I saw them off this morning it was a relief beyond description. Tell Walter—never again!"[38]

Bagnall scored some significant public relations victories on his own. On February 14 he spoke at a meeting sponsored by Detroit's labor federation to 1,200 unionists. A few days later, 300 people came out for the monthly NAACP branch meeting. They were trying to sign up 10,000 members—a ridiculously high goal—but indicative of the spirit running through the city's black community. Bagnall next spoke to 250 people in Toledo and to 1,500 in Lima, Columbus, Chillicothe, and Dayton. In Akron in late February, Bagnall "had the queerest experience . . . I have ever undergone." When he arrived at the meeting house, he found 250 "hard looking whites" sitting in stony silence. Without doubt, this was the Ku Klux Klan. Gradually, a hundred colored people entered cautiously, and the room filled with anxious expectation. Undaunted, Bagnall gave his usual earnest NAACP pitch, and luckily there was no trouble.[39]

A remaining problem was the jockeying for influence by the three African-American attorneys on the case. White had arranged that their fifteen hundred dollar fee would be paid out of money raised locally, but the Gomez group and the local committee gave up after paying each eleven hundred dollars. The attorneys wrote a letter of protest to the *Detroit Independent*, the black community newspaper, but Mose Walker's brother-in-law was the editor, and he killed it. A drunken Cecil Rowlette threatened Bagnall that the attorneys would send the letter to the *Pittsburgh Courier* if they were not paid. From Detroit, Bagnall advised that although they had done nothing to earn the money, the twelve hundred dollars of blackmail was well worth the price. Further complicating the situation was mutual distrust among the three lawyers, as well as Bradby's opposition to Perry, who was Sweet's personal attorney. White regarded them all as bloodsuckers and advised first against paying a nickel, but ultimately the Legal Committee produced three four-hundred-dollar checks. The New Yorkers wanted the loyal Oscar Baker of Bay City to come in on the second trial, but he begged off, arguing that the case would be won without him. Darrow ultimately forged a team of assistants, consisting only of Thomas Chawke and Julian Perry, for the second trial.[40] The public saw none of this wrangling, but for the organizers, petty bickering characterized the Sweet trials from first to last. The NAACP faced the big issues in the case as national leaders of a political movement; their opponents were small-time opportunists looking to settle personal scores or win an easy buck.

Clarence Darrow steadfastly considered that the best scenario for the defendants would be if they were tried singly rather than in a group. He believed that if the prosecution lost the first case, they would quietly desist.[41] By mid-March, Darrow advised that Henry Sweet, Ossian's youngest brother, would be tried on April 1. Henry was the only one who had confessed to firing a shot. Marcet Haldeman-Julius described Henry, a mere twenty-two years old in 1926, as "a gentle soul, kindly and courteous, full of the bright, high hopes of youth, and miraculously unembittered" by his ordeal. A well-built man of medium height with "African features" and wearing a pencil mustache, he was a senior at Wilberforce when he faced charges of murder alone. On Monday, April 19, Judge Murphy opened his second trial.[42]

Again, the tedious jury selection slowed the calling of witnesses. The defense lawyers carefully admitted only northern-born men, seeking out the most open-minded and intelligent of the prospects. Prosecutor Robert Toms dismissed the only Negro panelist; the jury was again all white. The spectators were almost all black. The former U.S. minister to Liberia attended, and liberal white Detroiters came, too, such as the writer Anita Loos, the coauthor of *Gentlemen Prefer Blondes*. As opening arguments began, the court was packed and many had to be turned away.[43]

The same cavalcade of cops and neighbors testified that hardly anyone was on the street during the night of the shooting. One police witness testified that fifteen or twenty shots had come from the upper windows of the house, but no one saw Henry Sweet fire. On cross-examination, some teenage boys admitted throwing rocks at the home.[44]

The defense opened its case on May 6 and called fewer than a dozen witnesses. This time three white witnesses, including a *Detroit News* reporter, helped paint the picture of a large, stone-throwing mob gathering force as its numbers grew. John C. Dancy, the leader of Detroit's Urban League, detailed the explosive growth of the city's black population and explained that Negro home buyers did not mean to be "provocative" when they purchased homes in mostly white neighborhoods. Finally, Ossian Sweet told his own story to this second jury. Darrow, who probably believed, as he had told White months ago, that Henry Sweet fired the shot that killed Breiner, kept the young man off the stand.[45]

Darrow commenced his summation on Tuesday, May 11. Supporters of Henry Sweet packed the courtroom so tightly that there was scarcely room to breathe. The famous attorney did not disappoint. He spoke for seven hours, making one of the most direct, logical, and impassioned pleas of a storied career. He declared that he did not know who killed Breiner but that imprisoning Henry Sweet would be criminal. He easily picked apart the prosecution's story that the victim was killed by an unprovoked gunshot. Working on the jury's presumed distaste for residential integration, Darrow argued that the Sweets had to live somewhere and that they had a right to buy any home they chose. Then he lit into the spirit of the mob: "They had gathered as the Roman populace gathered at the Coliseum to see the slaves fed to the lions." The Sweets did fire, he agreed, as they had every right to do before their house crashed down around them. The members of the jury would do the same thing, wouldn't they? Throughout the summation, Darrow theatrically lowered and raised his voice, appealing by turns to intellect and emotion. Johnson reported that he "did not leave a dry eye in the courtroom." When Darrow finished, Johnson approached to offer his thanks and broke down in tears himself.[46]

The next day prosecutor Robert Toms summarized. Marcet Haldeman-Julius thought the speech "reminded one of the clatter of folding chairs after a symphony concert."[47] Toms made a simple appeal to find someone responsible for Breiner's death and made an insidious plea for white racial solidarity. The next morning, Judge Murphy charged the jury as to their duty, and the twelve men began their deliberations after lunch.

The crowd waited in the courtoom, worried and unsure what the outcome would be. After a few hours, the jury sent a note asking for further clarifications, and Murphy had the attorneys on both sides work on an answer to the questions. Johnson watched the lawyers scribble on their yellow pads, and as they did so, the court officer marched in to announce that there was a verdict after three and a half hours. Darrow and his colleagues showed alarm; this was a bad sign. "We for the defense, in spite of ourselves, were seized with apprehension," Johnson reported. "The probabilities were that a verdict so quickly reached was a compromise verdict. There was even a possibility of a verdict of guilty as charged." The prosecution team puffed itself up and began speaking magnanimously to the defense, trying on the role of gracious victors.

All returned to the court. Johnson sat next to Henry Sweet. "I put my hand on his arm and said, 'No matter what happens the National Association will stand by you to the end.' " With these anxious words of support, Johnson betrayed his forebodings to the youthful defendant. "I then began to live the most intense thirty seconds of my whole life," Johnson remembered. Everyone held their breath as the ritualized drama unfolded.

"Have you gentlemen in the course of your deliberations reached a verdict in the case of Henry Sweet? And if so, who will answer for you?"

"We have and I will. We find the defendant not guilty."

Johnson recorded: "The effect is electrical. We are transported in a flash from the depths to the heights. Someone starts to applaud but brings his hands together only once." Instead there were sobs of joy all around, and even the men showed tears upon their cheeks.[48]

For the NAACP, the victory in the trial of Henry Sweet was the dramatic high point of the 1920s. Unlike the Arkansas case, this did not drag on for years and conclude in a sober Supreme Court in the absence of the defendants. The Sweet case ended in public triumph and greatly enhanced the Association's authority before the African-American public.

There was still the matter of the remaining ten defendants, however. For the next few months, the defendants and the Association waited to see if prosecutor Toms would renew the other cases. He did not, and no one expected that he would. Early in September, Walter White went back to Detroit and met with new branch president Mose Walker and Reverend Bradby. The attacks on black families had stopped. Race relations had dramatically improved, as though the racist wave had crested and smashed upon the rock of black determination.

Nevertheless, there was bitterness for the Sweet family. Their two-year-old daughter had died. Gladys Sweet was in Arizona, attempting to recuperate from tuberculosis, which she may have contracted while held in jail.[49] She did not recover, however, and Henry Sweet died of the same disease as well. Their old home had long since been padlocked and put up for sale.

Many years later, Ossian Sweet, who once had been young, gifted, and black, who should have had a limitless and secure future before him, in the privacy of his own home committed suicide. He did to himself what no mob could do, but showed by his act that its shadow had never left him.

21

"I Can't Go Back to Aiken County"

ARLY in May 1925, Walter White received a disturbing news clipping from a correspondent in Orangeburg, South Carolina. The story told of a gunfight in Aiken County between a sheriff and his deputies with members of a family named Lowman on April 25. The sheriff's men had approached the Lowman farm because they suspected the tenants of bootlegging. In the ensuing altercation, the sheriff was killed. The deputies killed Mrs. Annie Lowman, fifty-five, and wounded her children, Bertha and Demon, and their cousin Clarence. The three wounded young people had all been charged with murder, tried, and convicted. Demon and Clarence were sentenced to death, Bertha to life in prison.[1]

White wrote to a contact in Aiken, a Masonic leader named C. C. Johnson. He didn't think there was much the NAACP could do about it. "Some of our people testified against the individuals convicted and that fact it seems to me sealed their fate," Johnson replied. The dead sheriff, H. H. Howard, was "a real friend," and the Lowmans were probably bootleggers. With that discouraging news, White wrote back that the Lowman affair might not be a case the Association could enter.[2]

In April and May, White was preoccupied with other matters, including the preparations for the upcoming Denver conference. The Lowman affair seemed distressing but insignificant at the time. The story was not reported at the April, May, or June NAACP board meetings. But when the Lowmans were lynched in October 1926, Walter White's exposure of the facts about Aiken County would help contribute to the decline of lynching as a part of American life.[3]

IN THE HISTORY of lynching, South Carolina ranked as one of the least offensive Deep South states. Since 1882, ten states had lynched more people than the Palmetto State, even though South Carolina ranked sixth in black population. Between 1882 and 1927, South Carolina had lynched 174 people, and only 14 of those occurred after 1919.[4] Further to the state's credit, Charleston had acted swiftly to put down white rioters in 1919 and dealt more sternly with those it caught than did Chicago.

The state had one corner, however, that was particularly violent. Along the Georgia border, north of Augusta, lay Edgefield County, which originally included the territory near Aiken. In this region, wealthy Low Country planters, usually of English descent and Anglican in religion, had long clashed with up-country Scotch-Irish hardscrabble farmers. During the eighteenth century, whites of both sorts massacred Indians. Later, plantation-owning "regulators" fought a hard war against outlaw gangs. During the Revolution, patriots and Tories killed each other without mercy there. Murder became the accepted manner of solving disputes, and the district became known as "bloody Edgefield." Preston Brooks, the South Carolina congressman who in 1855 assaulted Charles Sumner on the Senate floor, came from Edgefield County. In 1876 a gang executed an African-American state senator from neighboring Barnwell County. One of the participants was a young Edgefield farmer named Ben Tillman; fourteen years later this unapologetic racist would be the state's governor.[5]

"Pitchfork Ben" Tillman, riding a powerful wave of resentment against the old patrician "Redeemers," brought with him to Columbia the Edgefield County way of doing things. "Four members of the state's congressional delegation in the 1890s had killed someone," historian Walter Edgar noted. Charleston moved up to second place on the list of cities in murders relative to population. In 1903, Tillman's nephew gunned down the editor of the *Carolina State*, and despite the presence of eyewitnesses, he was acquitted.[6] Tillman's lieutenant, Cole Blease, later served as governor and senator, just as he had. Blease openly justified lynching with his famous declaration, "Whenever the Constitution comes between me and the virtue of the white women of South Carolina, then I say, 'to hell with the Constitution!' "[7]

Under these difficult circumstances, South Carolina African Americans could make little social progress. Despite the near balance in population between blacks and whites, total earnings of Negro teachers equaled one-eighth that of their white counterparts in 1923–1924. Almost three-fourths of the state's 109,000 African-American farmers lived as tenants on the land of whites. Independent farmers had little access to credit, markets, or knowledge about modern farming. The black urban population was small, and black businesses stagnated.[8]

This bad situation became radically worse during the 1920s when the price of cotton collapsed. Later the boll weevil killed the crop, dropping cotton production in half. Many white farmers sold out and became workers in newly developing mill towns like those of the Horse Creek Valley in Aiken County, Edgefield's neighbor to the southeast. Black farmers mostly left the state. After the 1922 harvest, fifty thousand left. Five counties, including Edgefield and three of its neighbors, lost more than 15 per cent of their total population during the 1920s. Some black farmers simply moved from one stricken county to the next, hoping to take advantage of the exodus to improve their situation.[9]

Sam Lowman was one of these farmers. He moved from Saluda County onto the land of William Hartley. Lowman brought with him his wife, Annie, their son, Demon, and his wife, Rosa, two daughters named Bertha and Bridle, and their cousin Clarence, fifteen. Sam Lowman worked hard, practiced his religion, and stayed out of trouble. Farmer Hartley had survived the hard times, and the Lowmans were the kind of tenants he wanted. Hartley had prospered, but he had a problem with his neighbors. They were Klansmen, and they didn't like him. To undermine Hartley's authority with his tenants, they showed up on his property in early April, dressed in robes, seized Demon Lowman, and whipped him. Apparently there was nothing Hartley or the Lowmans could do about it.

Two weeks later Sheriff H. H. Howard and three deputies, all in plainclothes, drove to the Lowman place in two cars. They stopped to ask directions from Clarence and Demon, who were working in a field. Sam was away grinding meal at the mill. The four unknown men found four Lowman women alone. Walter White told what happened next in the *Crisis*:

> The white men saw them. They drew their revolvers and started running towards the house to surround it. Sheriff Howard and Bertha Lowman reached the back steps at the same time. Pistol in right hand, the sheriff struck Bertha Lowman in the mouth with the back of his left and ordered her to "stand back!" Mrs. Lowman saw her daughter being struck and heard her scream. Older and slower, she had not had time to escape into the house. She picked up an ax and started to her daughter's assistance. Deputy Sheriff Nollie Robinson emptied his gun into her body and she crumbled into an inert and lifeless heap.
>
> Demon and Clarence Lowman heard their sister's cry of pain and fright and ran towards the house. Demon got a revolver and Clarence a shotgun. The two deputies at the front of the house started firing at Demon and he returned the fire. No one ever knew exactly what Clarence did. In a few seconds, however, the sheriff was dead, Bertha was shot twice . . . Clarence was gravely wounded, and Demon was shot in a less vital spot.[10]

The next day two hundred robed Klansmen attended Howard's funeral. Later they approached the jail, but Nollie Robinson, now the new sheriff, appealed for calm and dispersed the crowd. They came back and packed the courtroom on May 12 when all five Lowmans began their trial for first degree murder. Bertha and Clarence were still badly wounded. Bridle and Rosa had neither fired a shot nor been near Sheriff Howard, and Judge H. F. Rice directed a not guilty verdict for them. For Clarence, Demon, and Bertha, however, the verdicts were never in doubt. Their court-appointed attorneys barely went through the motions on their behalf. In his charge to the jury, Judge Rice eulogized the dead sheriff and even had to explain to the jurors not to hold a grudge against the defense lawyers, who had to do an unpleasant job. When the jury returned the expected verdicts, Rice sentenced the two young men to death and Bertha to life in prison. The executions were set for June 12. Sam Lowman, meanwhile, had been sentenced to two years on the chain gang for violating the Prohibition law, an unheard-of sentence. Three days after Lowman's wife was murdered, his children shot and accused of a capital crime, the sheriff claimed to have dug up a jug of whiskey on Sam Lowman's farm. That had been the purpose of the sheriff's visit on April 25—he had a tip about illicit liquor.[11]

AT THE END of the World War, the leading African-American organization in Columbia was the inoffensively named Capital City Civic League. The league hoped to achieve progress in a "quiet, legal, peaceful manner," working through the churches to register voters. Its leader was an attorney named Butler W. Nance, who kept an office on Sumter Street. In 1919, Nance helped transform the civic league into a branch of the NAACP.[12] Other civic league leaders who joined included Mrs. R. F. Brooks; R. W. Jackson, a postal employee; and Isaac Samuel Leevy, a merchant tailor. Later Dr. Matilda Evans, an initiator of public health projects; Modjeska Montieth Simkins; and Matilda Griffin also helped develop the NAACP branch.[13]

The new branch's first campaign continued the old civic league's activity. In early 1919, the branch registered 324 African-American voters. The following year, the branch organized women to register and had some success before the registrars turned them away. By the fall, Columbia had enrolled almost seven hundred NAACP members.[14]

After a few years, during which the branch defended a black youth against capital charges for "molesting" an unharmed white girl, Butler Nance died abruptly of apoplexy. The branch went into a funk from which it did not recover for a few years. "We had a fine branch there," Robert

Bagnall recounted to N. J. Frederick a few years later, but "it went to pieces" after Nance died. Frederick was born in Orangeburg and attended Claflin College and the University of Wisconsin. He became the principal of the Howard School in Columbia and later read law and was admitted to the bar. In January of 1925 he launched the *Palmetto Leader*, a weekly. Three months later the shootings at the Lowman farm occurred.[15]

Frederick wrote a letter to the NAACP office also, but he did not sign it. The anonymous Frederick reported that the sheriff's men had never identified themselves and that the deceased Mrs. Lowman may have shot Sheriff Howard. The Lowmans had been singled out because they were prosperous, and the sheriff resented their success. Whiskey found on the Lowman place three days later may have been planted, Frederick implied. Finally, there was the matter of the defendants' age. The newspapers had recently carried the spectacular story of Leopold and Loeb, who escaped the death penalty because of their age. The unknown correspondent felt it was his "duty" especially to save the youngest defendant.[16]

Frederick reviewed the record of the trial and filed seven exceptions with the state supreme court. The court stayed the executions, and in November it heard Frederick's argument. The court waited five months before ruling that the original trial was flawed. On April 25, 1926, the anniversary of the shootings and the day before the supreme court decision, over a thousand Klansmen held a memorial for the slain sheriff at Aiken. This was the first sign of a serious split between the environs of "bloody Edgefield" and the state's judicial elite.[17]

The second trial opened in October 1926. Frederick appeared on behalf of the Lowmans along with L. G. Southard of Spartanburg, the descendant of a Confederate general. Confronted with a real defense team that was not afraid of them, the prosecution had a difficult time showing that all three defendants were guilty of murder. Sheriff Howard had been killed at the rear of the house. Demon was in the front of the house. Bertha was unarmed, and Clarence, the only one who might have killed Howard, was a juvenile. The prosecution argued that all three were guilty by reason of conspiracy, but Frederick and Southard insisted that the supreme court had ruled that possibility out during the appeal.

In his summation, Southard argued that Howard and his men had wrongfully attempted to search the Lowman place, and the family members had legally defended themselves. This particularly upset the white spectators. Judge S. T. Lanham disregarded local sentiment and directed a verdict of not guilty for Demon, but the local authorities arrested Demon again and charged him with assault and battery with intent to kill. This was a clear case of double jeopardy. Bertha, Clarence, and Demon were locked up again.

When Judge Lanham cleared Demon of the accusation, a group of white men attending the trial got up in a group and left. Colonel Claude Sawyer, an elderly attorney, former aide to Governor Wade Hampton, and an opponent of the Klan, observed them file into the office of Edwin Stansfield. Stansfield was a newly elected member of the state legislature, the phony attorney for Bertha Lowman at the first trial, and a Klansman. Colonel Sawyer warned Aiken County solicitor Berte Carter that a lynching was being planned in Stansfield's office. Yet, only the jailer guarded the prison that night. As Walter White later learned, the meeting first considered whether to tar and feather or castrate the defense attorneys as well. From Stansfield's office, calls went out to Klansmen all over Aiken, Edgefield, and Barnwell Counties.[18]

On October 9, the national press reported that all three defendants had been taken from the prison and killed. The *New York Times* front-page story said that a masked mob of 100 to 150 men overpowered the jailer and sheriff at 3:45 in the morning. Four men broke into the jail through a screen, and the jailer summoned the sheriff, who was at first confronted by 20 men. Sheriff Robinson vowed that he would not release the prisoners, but he was outnumbered and jumped from behind. The mob seized its victims, drove them two miles beyond the city limits, and shot them. By the time Sheriff Robinson caught up, all he found at the Crosland Woods were the three corpses. Judge Lanham called the killings "a disgrace to civilization and to the white race." He ordered a coroner's inquest and convened a grand jury to investigate. Governor Thomas G. McLeod wired the coroner that his office would assist in its inquiry. The *Times* editorialized that the mob had committed "a wanton act of savagery. The victims were released in a wood, and, in Mexican style, shot down as they ran." James Weldon Johnson sent President Calvin Coolidge an angry message, asking him to "make forceful pronouncement on the situation to the people of the country," but as usual, Silent Cal did nothing.[19]

The next day, the coroner's jury convened and ruled that the victims had died at the hands of unknown parties. Sheriff Robinson and the jailer testified that they had not recognized any member of the mob. A brief notice of this appeared at the bottom of page 28 in the *New York Times*.[20] If not for the NAACP, that would have been the last anyone would have heard of Bertha, Demon, or Clarence Lowman.

AFTER WRITING to President Coolidge, James Weldon Johnson sent a letter to Governor Thomas McLeod, who replied ten days later that he would "do everything in my power" to arrest and prosecute the guilty. But the NAACP soon learned from three informants that the grand jury had been discharged, and the governor, who could recall it to a special session, seemed to be doing nothing. The first informant was N. J. Frederick, who had read the NAACP telegram to President Coolidge in the Columbia newspapers. Frederick, identifying himself this time as the lead attorney for the Lowmans, believed that Bertha and Clarence might have been cleared along with Demon. He wanted now to put himself at the service of the NAACP and revive sentiment for the antilynching bill. The next day, a white man named James L. Quinby of Graniteville, a mill town outside Aiken, sent the NAACP an astonishing letter. Quinby claimed to know the identity of the lynchers. He wrote that the whole law enforcement apparatus of the county, including the sheriff, was "honey combed" with Klansmen. Three lynchers, Quinby continued, were cousins of the governor. The mob leaders were bootleggers themselves, and the federal agents in the area knew all about them and looked the other way. The strange correspondent concluded in a dramatic postscript, "If I should be killed, you have my full permission to publish this letter." Then a third missive arrived from nearby Warrenville, signed by Austin H. Johnson, an agent for the Southern Railway. "The guilty parties . . . could be caught if you care to investigate," he wrote, and promised to point an investigator in the right direction.[21]

Walter White set out by train to investigate a lynching one more time, again in journalistic guise. He arrived at Spartanburg where he spoke with attorney Southard. At Columbia, White met with Frederick and Bishop John Hurst, an NAACP board member then teaching at Allen University. From Columbia, he traveled to Aiken, where he met with Colonel Claude Sawyer, the man who had warned about the lynching. Then White drove on to Graniteville to meet Quinby at his lonely hillside home. As White recalled in the *Crisis*, he told the man that his newspaper was particularly interested in linking the Klan to the crime. Quinby left the room, and "[t]wo minutes later, the door through which he had gone opened again. . . . I looked up. . . . There stood a man in the full regalia of the Ku Klux Klan!" For a panicked moment White thought he was in the hands of the enemy, but Quinby assured him that he was just demonstrating his authenticity as a former Kleagle. Quinby would become White's main informant over the next few months, banging out lengthy letters on a rickety typewriter and detailing the connections among the mill owners, lynchers, county officers, and moonshiners. Some viewed him as an unreliable eccentric, which he perhaps was, but he nevertheless wanted to return Aiken County to the way of the Lord, whose hand he saw in all human events.

After a few more interviews, White met at 9 P.M. with Austin H. Johnson at the train station. The railroad man gave White a list of twenty-one local lawmen who he claimed were at the scene of the crime. White then took the next train to Atlanta.[22]

The following day White wrote Governor McLeod a six-page bombshell of a letter, implying that he had forty-eight hours in which to act before a version of his letter wound up in the *New York World*. He recounted for the governor a different version of events from that which had appeared in the *New York Times*, one which showed the complicity of Aiken County law enforcement with the lynchers from the beginning. Then White wrote another letter to the *New York World*, naming his sources and boasting that "I unearthed in South Carolina a story which seems to be one of the most startling I have ever run across," telling of child labor, bootlegging, and a reign of terror in the county. "It will be darn nice to get back to civilization," White concluded.

In his letter to the governor and in an October 29 news release, White charged that the lynchers entered the jail without a struggle. Sheriff Robinson and three deputies, who he named, unlocked Bertha's cell. Bertha screamed and cried for mercy, knowing what was going to happen. Outside the jail, Clarence Lowman jumped from the car, was shot, and was tied to the fender of the vehicle. At the lynching site, two hundred automobiles had brought one thousand spectators. Among the leading actors there were Eugene Buckingham, three-term member of the legislature and a Cole Blease loyalist, and J. Crosslene Bush, now a member of the grand jury that was investigating the crime. White named twenty-four participants, including the governor's cousin, policemen, and county and town officials. James E. Kerr, reporter for the Aiken newspaper, saw it all. Managers of the Aiken mills watched also. The prisoners were told to run, and all were shot in the back. Bertha did not die at once and begged for her life again. The executioners raked her with gunfire so many times that her clothes burned. After committing this deed of unspeakable barbarity, ringleader Stansfield blithely complained to one of White's informants that his wife had "given him hell" for being out all night.

White even offered the governor an explanation for the decayed social relations that lay behind the crime. Here he relied especially on James Quinby, who knew the situation from the inside. The Ku Klux Klan began in Aiken, as in most places, as a Christian crusade against sin, attracting teetotalers and churchgoers. In Aiken, the solid citizens soon quit, and the organization fell into the hands of the bootleggers. They in turn recruited the law enforcement officials, who now controlled the lucrative illicit liquor market. This Klan-police cabal mixed easily with the managers of the

Walter White. Courtesy of Library of Congress.

new mills in the Horse Creek Valley, who routinely violated the child labor laws. White men who stood up to them were flogged, and only a few had dared to protest. "In all my experience, I have never before seen such a reign of lawlessness as exists in and near Aiken," White concluded.[23]

Upon his return to New York, White issued his own news release, which was picked up by some African-American papers, and turned his notes over to the *New York World*. That paper, which had run the anti-Klan series a few years earlier as a result of White's tip, now sent its star reporter, Oliver H. P. Garrett, to Aiken. For the first few weeks of November, the *World* ran his stories on the front page. These created a sensation in South Carolina, and in turn they were commented upon by the state's newspapers, which had fallen silent in October because the grand jury investigation gave out very little information. The NAACP was pleased by this development, but was distressed that the *World* gave them no credit for breaking the story. Nonetheless, Garrett's stories changed the landscape in South Carolina regarding lynching.[24]

Garrett's biggest coup was to report the testimony of Lucy Mooney, a white teenager whose cell across from Bertha Lowman's let her see and hear exactly what had happened. Mooney and Charles Lee, another white prisoner, gave affidavits to Quinby. They supplied realistic detail that reinforced Walter White's version of the events at the jail. Mooney and Lee swore that they heard the lynchers enter the jail in a jovial mood and chat with the jailer. They identified five men who came to the cell, including Sheriff Robinson and his deputy. While she was in jail, several people warned Lucy Mooney not to talk. Charles Lee also swore that he was threatened with lynching if he talked. Mooney was an illiterate eighteen-year-old who had been married off by her father to an old man who treated her like a slave and from whom she had run away. Despite being warned not to talk, the plucky white girl did exactly that. The *World* ran her picture on the front page several times, showing a smiling young woman adorned with a ladylike hat.[25]

South Carolina now had the worst possible public relations nightmare on its hands. Lynching could usually be explained away by blaming the victim, the anonymity of the lynchers, and the helplessness of the authorities. The ever-reliable image of the black brute and outraged white womanhood could in some cases quiet northern criticism. Lynching could often be hushed up by northern indifference. South Carolina now faced a scenario in which every element of the usual drama was inverted. Here were three dead Negro prisoners. One had been declared innocent; another was an unarmed woman who had previously been sentenced only to life in prison; a third was fifteen years old. In short, the victims of the lynching were not criminals. Walter White and Oliver Garrett showed that everyone knew who the lynchers were and that the authorities had joined them. Now, to make matters worse, the only outraged woman risked her life to refute the lies of Aiken County's lawmen. Her own life story revealed the way that South Carolina really treated its poor white women. Finally, the New York press was crying for action on its front pages.

Garrett's early stories had stressed that the investigation of the Lowman killings was at a standstill. After a week, his headline read "South Carolina Governor Moved by Girl's Story . . . But Doubts Convictions Can Be Obtained." The governor interviewed Lucy Mooney himself and was impressed by her "childlike simplicity." Garrett portrayed McLeod as being genuinely unhappy about the lynchings but unwilling to believe that people in his own entourage might have had something to do with it. Moreover, he lacked the will to proceed against law enforcement officials and refused to suspend Sheriff Robinson, as he had the power to do. The governor's photograph revealed a moonfaced, owlish countenance with a weak chin, peering at the world from spectacles perched under a balding dome. He took his first step against the miscreants by assigning a trusted constable named Will Rogers to launch his own investigation. With Garrett's accusations now in print, the formerly complacent lawmen began to issue their own self-serving denials. James P. Hart, one of the men Mooney identified, branded Quinby as a "crank," Austin Johnson as a criminal, and the *World* as an outside interloper. Lucy Mooney, he asserted, couldn't have seen what she claimed to have seen anyway. He himself, Hart averred, had been home in Edgefield County that night. But no sooner was the ink dry on this statement than a local reporter found that Hart had stayed at an Aiken hotel.[26]

Under the cover of the *World* investigation, the South Carolina press now wrote more regarding the Lowman lynching. R. Charlton Wright, publisher of the *Columbia Record*, launched a relentless attack on the governor's inaction and the county's cover-up. Wright went to Aiken the day after the lynching and learned that Hart had been put in charge of the investigation. Now that Hart looked like a perpetrator, the *Record* began to editorialize and report the story almost like the *World*. The *Record* printed a detailed map of the jail accompanied by a lengthy story that explained that Lucy Mooney's account made perfect sense. "The Aiken lynchings stand out as the most ferocious and abhorrent crimes committed in South Carolina during the many years of my residence here," Wright wrote in an editorial.[27]

Around the state, most newspapers demanded action against the lynchers. Spartanburg's two newspapers joined R. Charlton Wright's crusade.

The *Charleston News and Courier* wrote, "The people who have brought this ill fame upon Aiken County and upon South Carolina have struck their county and the state a vicious blow. . . . They deserve to be fully punished." The *State*, published at Columbia, noted that no doors had been broken down at the jail and that the sheriff and jailer had been armed. Some small town newspapers raised the old bugbear of northern interference, but it was clear that public opinion had swung against the Aiken gang.[28]

In mid-November came other encouraging signs of the times. Across the border in Georgia, nine men were convicted of lynching a prisoner in Coffee County. One was sentenced to life in prison, the others to terms of four to twenty years. The difference in this case was that the victim was a white man. Another surprising development from Georgia was the case of Silas Parmore, extradited from New Jersey to Georgia on a charge of murder. The NAACP had protested Parmore's extradition because of Georgia's lynching record. But Parmore got a fair trial and was acquitted. In Mississippi, a sheriff was deposed for permitting a lynching, and the state bar association issued an antilynching tract.[29]

Perhaps encouraged by these developments, Sam Lowman, as the surviving relative of the victims, threatened to sue Aiken County under the state's antilynching law. The county would be liable for restitution of two thousand dollars for each victim. Senator Cole Blease promised to defend his Aiken friends for free if the case came to court, which it apparently did not. Walter Duncan, a Klansman who published the *South Carolina Gazette* and the *Aiken Standard,* announced in his newspapers that the instigator of the entire publicity campaign had been Walter White, a Negro who passed as white. Astonished, Claude Sawyer asked White if Duncan's charge was true. "I had on amber colored glasses and did not take the trouble to scrutinize your color," Sawyer apologized. White replied that he wasn't sure what his race was, but that he was proud to have Negro blood in his veins.[30]

Meanwhile Governor McLeod finally removed several other prisoner eyewitnesses from the Aiken jail to Columbia, and his detective interviewed them. In Aiken itself a new mayor and the town's leading banker declared that the perpetrators ought to be caught. Garrett quoted an unidentified farmer who asked him, "What is the law for if you can shoot a man down whenever you want to?" Garrett's stories often referred to a "famous seventeen" whom he never named, although he claimed everyone in Aiken knew that these were the ringleaders. The momentum was turning against the lynchers, and it appeared they might be exposed. At the end of the month, the *Record* reported that three ex-governors and nine of fourteen circuit court judges responded to their inquiry that they hoped the killers of the Lowmans would be caught.[31]

Walter White remained unconvinced about Governor McLeod's intentions. His December *Crisis* article stated that the governor had never taken the one step that would have led to an indictment: posting a reward for testimony leading to arrest. White had, after all, written a letter to the governor containing the names of the lynchers and McLeod had not acknowledged the letter until the press started complaining. Moreover, a member of the mob was still on the grand jury itself. The governor was a "pussyfooter" who, White concluded, "will do nothing."[32]

White proved to be right. At the end of the month, McLeod conferred with his attorney general and the court solicitor for Aiken. They counseled him not to call a special term of the grand jury. The governor's own term was expiring on January 18, and the new governor would inherit the problem. McLeod vowed to work every day on the case and assured the public that the incoming governor would bring the guilty to justice. "My God I wish this was over," McLeod moaned. "Cole Blease Adherent Succeeds Him January 18" ran the next *World* headline.[33]

Walter White was disgusted by the state's failure to prosecute the lynchers. When the NAACP convened its annual meeting at St. Mark's Church in Harlem, it passed a resolution condemning the outgoing governor's appointment to the Federal Trade Commission. The NAACP statement upset attorney Southard, who advised White that "the Governor has done his utmost to bring the guilty to justice." Even Frederick concurred in part, on technical legal grounds.[34]

Built-in tension exists between movement activists and their attorneys. The activists generally view legal technicalities with impatience; the lawyers anticipate their opponents' objections and plan defensive strategies to meet them. The narrower part of this dispute, over whether or not the governor should have called the grand jury, reflected this typical division. Yet the deeper difference lay between NAACP political strategy and that of southern racial liberals. The NAACP had deliberately kept a low profile in the Arkansas case. Now, sensing a change in the national mood, the NAACP thrust itself forward by attacking a southern governor during an unresolved investigation. The Lowman lynching was now important enough that the *New York Times* covered this public exchange between Southard and White on two successive days. McLeod was at least publicly denouncing the lynching, while two Arkansas governors had justified mass murder in the Elaine cases. Even R. Charlton Wright thought that northern intervention did not help matters. The NAACP begged to differ. White replied to Southard that the governor should have convinced his prosecutors to see the business through to the end. He reminded Frederick that northern intervention had exposed the lynching in the first place.[35]

At the end of January, the new grand jury heard thirteen witnesses in the Lowman case. Seven of them had heard or seen what happened in the Aiken jail. The grand jury visited the jail itself. Judge J. Henry Johnson implored them to find a true bill against someone. "The time for words is past," he said. "It is time for action. . . . And God help Aiken County and South Carolina if you fail to do something." Grand juries only have to agree that a prosecutor has reasonable cause to act against an individual. The Aiken County grand jury deliberated for an afternoon and found that it did not have sufficient evidence to bring an indictment.[36]

Judge Johnson expressed bitter "regret" at the grand jury's inaction. New governor John G. Richards blasted it as "a miserable miscarriage of justice." He called on the legislature to appropriate twenty-five thousand dollars to continue the investigation. The major state newspapers condemned the grand jury and praised the governor. Meeting in Atlanta, the Commission on Interracial Cooperation hailed the governor for his strong stand. The state senate voted unanimously to back the governor, and the house later approved the resolution, calling the Lowman lynchings "a heinous crime." Apparently neither chamber considered the special appropriation for which he had asked. The house heard a new antilynching measure that would make it easier for the governor to remove a sheriff in a lynching case, but representative Stansfield, from whose office the Lowman lynching had been planned, mustered six votes against it in a heated committee meeting, and the bill apparently failed.[37]

Aiken County had fallen behind the times, even in South Carolina. The old spirit of bloody Edgefield County had never really departed from its soil. Reporters from Columbia noticed an eerie quiet in Aiken during the three days that the grand jury met and the lack of interest in, or surprise at, its verdict.[38] In Columbia and Charleston, moderate leaders of a New South, in journalism and politics, asserted the modern value of government by law. Aiken County whites lived by the premodern codes: whites killed by blacks must be avenged by blood. Racial solidarity trumped all other values. A white man did not indict his neighbor for killing Negroes. The Aiken County grand jury issued a disclaimer to its finding, saying that it disapproved of lynching and hoped that others would note its statement. But the final verdict is passed by history, which can only find that Aiken County covered up a crime of enormous proportions.

In the last week of February 1927, Sam Lowman was released from the Aiken County Jail after serving probably the lengthiest term in state history for possessing liquor. He had served seventeen months on the chain gang and three months in the penitentiary, at a time when the "real McCoy," as good smuggled liquor was called, flowed through Charleston virtually unchecked. Sam Lowman went directly to Columbia to see lawyer Frederick. The next day the two elderly black men went over to R. Charlton Wright's office, where they spoke for half an hour. The *Record* told Sam's story the next day. The paper showed a picture of the tall, balding old man, wearing a jacket and tie, a mustache, and a look of weary, inexpressible sadness. Wright may have shocked his readers; newspapers rarely ran sympathetic stories or photographs of Negroes in the 1920s.

The newspapers had entirely forgotten that Sam Lowman had been in the same building as his children and nephew on the night they were murdered. He heard their abduction and could do nothing about it. "I can't go back to Aiken County," Sam said. "I can't live among them people." Lowman broke down in tears in Wright's office. "It's pretty hard," he said. "It's awful to think that one man could treat another so bad, just because he had the upper hand." Old Sam Lowman was going north to Philadelphia, where he had two other sons, both veterans, and where Bridle and Rosa had gone.[39]

A month later Walter White came to Philadelphia to speak about the Lowman lynching. Twelve hundred people filled Gibson's Theater on a Sunday afternoon. With White and Lowman on the stage sat two Negro state representatives, a bishop of the AME Church, the city's leading lawyers, and the Shiloh Baptist Choir. White introduced Lowman. "This is the man the crackers said was a desperado, a moonshiner, a menace to the community. Can you look at him and see any of those criminal traits?" Sam Lowman, overcome with emotion, choked out a few words of gratitude and sat down. It is difficult to imagine a more moving scene than the sight of this farmer, whose family had been massacred, standing almost mute before a crowd of strangers who understood him.[40]

Lowman found his tongue in May at Harlem's Manhattan Casino. He had his own theory about the death of Sheriff Howard. Sam Lowman declared that one of the deputies killed Howard and that he did it deliberately to get his job. The *Amsterdam News*, which reported his speech, feared it would be sued for libel if it printed the name of the man who Lowman accused, but it could only have been Sheriff Robinson.[41]

N. J. Frederick, the attorney who feared to sign his name on a letter to the NAACP after the April 25, 1925, incident, learned the value of a nationally organized civil rights movement through his experience with the Lowman case. He wrote the Association a ringing endorsement, which it proudly sent out as a press release: "Every Negro with two grains of common sense ought to thank God for the NAACP and its courageous and efficient officers." He had his law practice, and he edited the *Palmetto Leader*, but he and his colleagues now decided to revive the Columbia branch. "Since the importance of this Association has been demonstrated right at our front door," he wrote, "a determined spirit to have a branch worth while has taken a hold on the leading people of this city."[42]

Church leaders joined the secular activists, and Reverend S. B. Wallace organized a membership drive. Robert Bagnall came to speak and fired the city up. Seventy-five people paid their one dollar dues, another nine gave ten dollars, and Matilda Griffin pledged one hundred dollars. By the summer of 1927, new president Dr. Julia Stuart reported that Columbia had over five hundred members, a women's auxiliary, a junior division, and a strong base at Benedict College and Allen University.[43]

The Lowman lynching generated a great deal of publicity in the African-American press. Most papers credited the NAACP and Walter White, but the *Pittsburgh Courier*, whose attack on the Association appeared in the same week as the lynching, downplayed the NAACP's investigation. After the *New York World* articles began, Sheriff Robinson accused White of suborning false testimony through bribery. He threatened to extradite White to South Carolina, and Southard volunteered to defend the New Yorker in this eventuality. Many African-American newspapers covered this development as well. The liberal weekly the *Nation* wrote an editorial titled "South Carolina's Shame," which credited White "for unearthing one of the ghastliest stories in American history," and several African-American papers reprinted this also. The *Baltimore Afro-American* even ran a cartoon series, showing White "taking his life in his hands" on his mission to South Carolina.[44]

The outcome of the investigation into the Lowman lynching mocked justice. The lynchers got away. Sheriff Robinson kept his job. Sam Lowman recovered nothing from Aiken County. Yet, the political and journalistic reaction to the Lowman lynching changed race relations in the South. It is a truism among historians that coincidence in time does not necessarily indicate causality between related events. The likelihood in this case is that South Carolina's ruling elite signaled a noticeable change from the days of Ben Tillman. Cole Blease sounded a lone note of hate amid a chorus of condemnation in the state.

Thirty people were lynched in the United States in 1926, and in 1927 the number dropped in half to sixteen, then eleven in 1928 and ten in 1929. The numbers spiked upward again during the depression years but never reached thirty. It is true that seven of the thirty lynched in 1926 were white, and in 1934, a year of intense economic strife, one more black man was lynched than in 1926.[45] Yet, the Lowman lynching generated more national publicity and condemnation at the highest level of the state than almost any similar event before or since.

Many factors caused the decline of lynching, but the steepest drop in a chronological decade occurred during the 1920s, falling from seventy-six in 1919 to seven in 1929. Prosperity, modernity, and the Great Migration played the largest roles in the decline of lynching. It is also certain that no political organization played a more important role in ending that social plague than the NAACP. Walter White's exposure of the Lowman lynching shone a spotlight on a part of America that would increasingly have to hide under a rock.

22

"The Supreme Court Will Some Day . . ."

BLACK communities and African-American individuals often feel ambivalent about school integration. No one advocates segregation, but many question the value of sending their children among whites who may want to destroy them psychologically, either by hostility or by assimilation. Children represent everything for adults: innocence, hope, the future. African Americans are especially torn between their hopes to participate in American life and their fears about the unpredictable people among whom they have been cast.

During the 1920s, the NAACP confronted the issue of segregated education in a number of complicated settings. In one case, African-American students at Harvard refused to be barred from the dormitories. Later the board of directors began what would be a thirty-year-long campaign to reverse the "separate but equal doctrine" that justified segregation. The *Crisis* ran a series of articles showing that southern states deprived black children of an equal education. When school segregation reared its head in the North, the NAACP fought in Gary, Indiana, to turn it back.

IN SEPTEMBER OF 1921, William J. Knox, an African-American student from New Bedford, began his career at Harvard University. Knox was assigned a dormitory room at Standish Hall, but a short time later he received a letter from an administrator, asking that he surrender his key. Apparently there had been some misunderstanding. When Knox inquired further about where he would be rooming, the administrator was compelled to disclose that the misunderstanding had to do with the color of Knox's skin. Harvard would no longer admit freshmen Negroes to its dormitories.

The Knox family was prominent in the New Bedford NAACP, and young Knox knew how to honor the family tradition. Accompanied by Harvard track star Edward Jourdain Jr., a fellow New Bedford African American, Knox called upon Harvard president A. Lawrence Lowell. Lowell explained, disingenuously, that the only change in Harvard's dormitory policy was that freshman residency was now obligatory. Harvard was not discriminating against colored students. It had not, however, compelled white students to live with colored students in the past, and it would not be placed in the position of doing so now. Southern students previously had the option of living off campus, but they no longer did, and Harvard wanted to be fair to everyone.

As Boston NAACP leader Butler Wilson found out from his own son, also a Harvardian, the southern whites knew to respect northern norms in Boston, and the segregation idea was probably Lowell's own. The Harvard president was more concerned about other challenges to the school's traditions, especially about the growing numbers of Jews accepted at Harvard, now nearing 15 percent of the student body. He and his Brahmin friends were also peeved at the political takeover of Boston by raffish Irishmen such as former mayor James Michael Curley and his ilk. Immigration bothered Lowell, and presidents Harding and Coolidge would soon sign immigration restriction legislation that conservative Bostonians were promoting. To Lowell, the problem of a few Negro students in the dormitories was a minor irritant among many problems that needed correcting.

Boston and Harvard University (located across the Charles River from Boston in Cambridge) stood in the American imagination, and rightly so, as bastions of racial liberalism. Massachusetts was the first state to outlaw slavery and permit black men to vote. It had been home to the abolitionist movement of William Lloyd Garrison, Wendell Phillips, and Frederick Douglass. The state had provided the first regiment of colored troops in the Civil War, and a magnificent monument to their heroism stood on the Boston Common across from the State House. The public schools were integrated, and discrimination in public accommodations was forbidden by law. As an article in the *Colored American Magazine* put it, Boston was "the paradise of the Negro."

This racial liberalism was real in relation to that of other cities, but there was one important exception to this picture. While the industries of most cities boomed during the 1920s, Boston's were in relative decline as shoe factories and textile mills moved south. Irish-American labor leaders and new immigrants made sure that the remaining jobs went to their people. Black Bostonians rarely held good-paying factory jobs, and migrants from the South generally headed elsewhere. While other black communities in the North grew significantly, Boston's black population remained small and economically marginalized.

Nevertheless, African-American activists still regarded Boston as a locus of twentieth-century militance. Harvard-educated William Monroe Trotter, son of a prominent Civil War veteran, launched the *Guardian* newspaper in 1901 specifically to attack the policies of Booker T. Washington. Trotter respected Boston's white racial liberals, but he discouraged his personal followers from joining an interracial movement in which he would not have the last word.

This peculiar local history produced a unique NAACP branch in Boston. Founded by the descendants of abolitionists, the branch was, along with Chicago, rare in having a predominantly white leadership in the 1920s. Its first president had been Francis Jackson Garrison, who as a boy had set the type on the *Liberator* with his famous father. Attorneys Moorfield Storey; Albert E. Pillsbury, the nephew of abolitionist Parker Pillsbury; former Atlanta University president Horace Bumstead; architect Joseph Prince Loud; and businessman George G. Bradford contributed to the branch leadership. The most prominent African-American leaders were Butler Roland Wilson and his wife, Mary Evans Wilson. In its earliest years, even the membership was probably mostly white, until Mary Wilson led a membership drive that signed up 2,553 people, making the Boston branch the largest in 1918. The Boston branch of the 1920s thus was an interracial group led mostly by white reformers. As the only branch so composed, it reminds us of how completely white racial liberalism had collapsed by the 1920s.

When the word about Lowell's discriminatory action got out among liberal Harvard alumni, they decided to take discreet action. In 1922, Lewis Gannett of the *Nation*, in concert with the NAACP, circulated a protest petition signed by 143 prominent alumni. George Bradford distributed the petition for the Boston branch. The petition called for an end to all discrimination at Harvard, and it appealed to the antislavery tradition of former Harvardians such as John Quincy Adams and Civil War colonel Robert Gould Shaw. All of Shaw's surviving classmates signed it.

The NAACP issued a news release on the Harvard policy in June, but the affair did not break into the national press until the winter of 1923. Lowell wrote to Roscoe Conkling Bruce, whose father had been Mississippi senator Blanche K. Bruce, that his son, too, would be barred from the dormitory. The NAACP solicited letters of protest from prominent African-American alumni, including Archibald Grimké and Washington, D.C., municipal court judge Robert H. Terrell. "Is the stock of the Puritans indeed dead?" asked W. E. B. Du Bois, Harvard's most distinguished African-American graduate. "The day has come when the grandson of a slave had to teach democracy to a president of Harvard." Johnson wrote to Lowell: "Harvard's surrender of its tradition and the tradition of liberal America to the slaveholder's prejudice intensifies the very problem which you as Harvard's spokesman are professing to meet."

Harvard's board of overseers came to the same conclusion. In April they issued a clear statement, without directly repudiating Lowell, that Harvard would admit all applicants according to merit and treat its students equally. The NAACP and its liberal allies had reversed what might have become a precedent for further discrimination at Harvard and other institutions of higher learning around the country. While the affair directly affected only a handful of elite students, the symbolic weight of this victory, which was covered widely in the press, was heavy indeed.

The victory at Harvard would be the Boston branch's last significant action for many years. The branch stumbled into a financial dispute with the national office involving the principle of how local contributions should be shared with the national office, each side suspecting the other of acting in bad faith. What should have been a tempest in a teapot finally had to be resolved by Ovington, Storey, and Johnson, the Association's three highest officers. At some unspoken level, the *contretemps* had something to do with the racial makeup of the Boston leadership. A later incident illuminated the problem. In 1926, Boston branch president Joseph Prince Loud complained that the "favorite colored baby" fund-raiser was a segregated activity in which his branch would not participate. Field secretary William Pickens, who organized the contests, replied with disdain that no one else had objected in the several years since the fund-raiser began. The last white liberals of the Boston NAACP could not quite accept the moderately nationalist character of the movement they had helped to found.[1]

ONE OF THE MOST important actions taken by the NAACP during the 1920s was its decision to address the inequality of African-American education in the South. This reorientation constituted the first step along the road to the 1954 Supreme Court victory that desegregated the nation's schools. The issue of southern education never dominated the Association's concerns during the 1920s. It launched no petition drives to the president, sponsored no legislation, and brought no suits. Yet the origins of *Brown v. Board of Education* lay in a series of discussions among the NAACP board of directors beginning in 1923.

The person most responsible for this reorientation was the indefatigable Florence Kelley, a sixty-two-year-old *doyenne* of American reform. Kelley was the daughter of a Quaker mother and Pennsylvania's antislavery congressman William "Pig Iron" Kelley. Her long career in American radical reform had been truly spectacular. After an early flirtation with Marxism, Kelley learned how to accomplish concrete reform. In Chicago she worked closely with Jane Addams and was appointed chief factory inspector for Illinois, a position she used to crack down on child labor and the exploitation of women workers. Later she moved to New York and became general secretary of the National Consumers' League, which organized boycotts of goods produced by child labor. She supplied Louis Brandeis with information leading to the vindication before the Supreme Court of Oregon's ten-hour workday for women.[2] Along with Du Bois and Ovington, Kelley represented the left wing of the NAACP board of directors.

Kelley's focus on the rights of children drew her attention to a seemingly benevolent bill that appeared in the U.S. Congress under several guises in the early 1920s. By 1923, the proposed Sterling-Towner bill would establish a Department of Education and Welfare and spend $100 million annually to promote literacy, especially in rural areas where illiteracy flourished. In effect, the bill would funnel tax revenue from the North and spend it disproportionately in the South. Literacy tests of soldiers during the war showed what everyone knew: the South suffered from an epidemic of educational deficiency.[3]

At the February and April 1923 meetings, Kelley led the board of directors through discussions that staked out a position of opposition to this bill. In the October *Crisis*, Kelley outlined that argument. The problem with the bill was that the southern states expended their education budgets on their separate systems in a grossly unequal fashion, often by factors of ten to one. The bill explicitly forbade the new department from monitoring its distributions to see that its grants were fairly spent. The money could not be used for capital improvements, which meant that in counties that provided no money for Negro education, no federal money at all would go to Negroes. Kelley did note guidelines that allotted money only to states whose laws mandated compulsory education, but there was no mechanism to police this requirement. The southern states were likely to spend the federal money only on white students.[4]

This analysis sparked controversy among some progressives and highlighted again the NAACP's radical position. The National Education Association lobbied hard for the bill. Du Bois published the anonymous letter of one progressive critic in the *Crisis*. The writer argued that any money spent on education was money well spent. Education of southern whites could only wear away race prejudice, which was based on ignorance. Finally, the bill was national in scope, and it did not make sense to hold the whole country hostage to southern race prejudice. In reply, Du Bois demonstrated by statistics the extent of the South's malevolence, and he argued that southern education was false to the core and untrustworthy.[5] Yet, he did not fairly meet the critical reader's objections. This was a complicated problem, and good points could be made on both sides of the specific tactical issue.

Ultimately, the United States did establish a federal department and expended funds in the South, which persisted in cheating African-American students out of their education. The wider importance of the Sterling-Towner legislation was that it focused the NAACP's attention on this seemingly intractable problem. Beyond opposing Sterling-Towner, what should the NAACP do about southern education?

Mary White Ovington noted a strategic possibility in the education issue. At the February 1923 board meeting, she abandoned the chair in order to point out that education demands could be advanced by southern branches where it might be dangerous to advocate desegregation or voting rights. A new agenda, less directly threatening to white supremacy, might revitalize some dormant southern branches. The board voted to form an education committee, which reported in April that it would issue a pamphlet on the Sterling-Towner bill.[6]

Most significantly, the board secured five thousand dollars from the Garland Fund to study education in the South. The grant paid for detailed reports on five states. A preview of these studies appeared in the November 1924 *Crisis*, which reprinted a map of South Carolina's counties, showing the average salary of white and Negro teachers in each. These varied by a factor of two to one in Greenville, the best place, and four to one in Orangeburg, more typical but not the worst place. The magazine noted some progress in Georgia, which was just completing a Negro high school in Atlanta, but the rest of the state was spending ten dollars on white education for every dollar spent on Negroes. In September 1926 the *Crisis* published its first detailed report, on Georgia, which piled up statistics and concluded "that there is great hostility towards Negro education." Mississippi came out the worst in these analyses, North Carolina the best of a bad lot.

Over the next few years, the Garland Fund would allocate more money to this pathbreaking project. With it, the Association hired Nathan Margold, a recent Harvard Law School graduate, to advance a legal strategy that would further a broad civil rights agenda. In May 1931 Margold submitted a 218-page preliminary report that called for a bold attack on the constitutionality of separate and unequal education. In the following years, a new team of African-American attorneys, headed by Charles Hamilton Houston, William Hastie, Leon Ransom, and Thurgood Marshall, would begin the process that would bring segregated education to an end.[7]

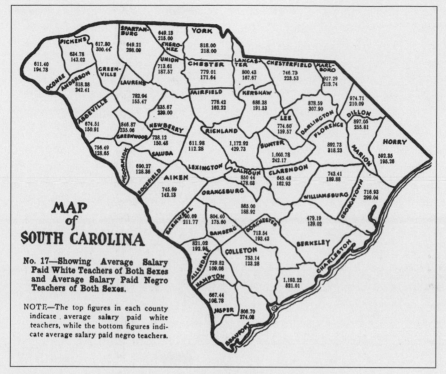

Separate and unequal education, South Carolina. Courtesy of NAACP.

ON MONDAY, September 26, 1927, hundreds of white students at Emerson High in Gary, Indiana, walked out of school. They marched down Broadway in a spontaneous demonstration, shouting slogans and carrying signs. Their grievance was simple: twenty-four black students had been assigned to the school of three thousand students, and they wanted them out. "We won't go back till Emerson's white" their signs read. The next day the students held a meeting in the school auditorium. Alberta Cheeks, one of the African-American students, decided she would see what the whites were up to. At the auditorium door she ran into principal E. A. Spaulding. The meeting "will not interest you," he assured her, blocking the way. Undaunted, Cheeks responded that it would and pushed her way past. "Of course it was very hard to stay in the meeting," she wrote later, "but I stayed in just the same."[8]

In the auditorium, Alberta Cheeks heard school superintendent William A. Wirt explain that integration was a fact of modern life and that the students may as well get used to it. Wirt was one of the most famous progressive educators of his day, and he was shocked when the students interrupted him with jeers and catcalls. School board member Henry G.

Hay told the students that to achieve segregation, the city would have to build a separate high school for the Negro students and that this was impractical. As one Gary historian wrote, "Wirt and Hay argued that [integration] was a regrettable necessity." None of the school officials enforced truancy laws against the strikers, who stayed out of school another two days as the strike spread.

On Friday, a joint meeting of the school board, city council, and Mayor Floyd E. Williams acceded to the white students' demands. The city council would appropriate fifteen thousand dollars to enhance the temporary Negro school building on Virginia Street and would allocate six hundred thousand dollars for a new high school. No strikers would be punished for truancy. All black students, except for six seniors, would leave Emerson High School. It was now up to Alberta Cheeks, her fellow black students, and the Gary African-American community to decide what they wanted to do about it.[9]

Gary, Indiana, was a company town, sprung up from the shores of Lake Michigan by the grand design of the United States Steel Corporation. The company created one of the largest steel mills in the world on the vast, empty space beside the lake. New immigrants flocked to the Steel City from eastern and southern Europe. When the flow of immigrants was cut off by the World War and the immigration restriction acts of the 1920s, U.S. Steel labor agents encouraged African Americans to come north. Only 383 African Americans inhabited Gary in 1910, but their number jumped 1,283 percent to 5,299 in 1920 and by 238 percent to almost 18,000 by 1930. No other city's rate of black population increase remotely approached Gary's.[10]

Besides the chance to work for U.S. Steel, Gary also promised a superior education system. By 1927, school superintendent Wirt had gained national attention as a progressive innovator. Wirt created "unit" schools that included students from kindergarten to high school age. The school day lasted eight hours; the curriculum was stimulating and the facilities outstanding. So when the school strike broke out in Gary, it made headlines around the nation.[11]

Three of Gary's schools extended to the high school grades. Emerson was the academic and college preparatory school. The big vocational school was Froebel, attended by 3,000 students, of whom 800 were African-American. Horace Mann had 1,773 students, all white. At Froebel, three African-American teachers instructed recent migrants from the South, most of whom had received little education. The other black students at Froebel were mostly segregated within the school also, but in some areas, notably sports, they participated together. The three schools in total included 3,000 high school grade students, of whom 352 were African-American. Of the lower grade schools, some were all African-American, such as the Virginia Street school, but Pulaski, two blocks away, had 700 white and 200 African-American students. The Roosevelt school had 600 white and 200 African-American students, but the Roosevelt annex had 1,530 segregated black students. They were taught by forty African-American teachers. Thus Gary schools were mostly segregated, with patches of integration.

The strike started at Emerson because eighteen sophomores had been transferred there from the Virginia school. With the black population growing at an explosive rate, white parents feared that its population would become like that at Froebel. Both schools were located on the north side of town. Black students lived in the south side, integrated residentially among immigrants. Emerson students were middle class, of old-stock Protestant heritage. Froebel's whites were largely immigrant, Catholic or Eastern Orthodox, and working class. Thus the transfer of African-American students to Emerson raised class as well as race issues.[12]

If Gary was a modern city, it still lay within the state of Indiana, northern bastion of the Ku Klux Klan. The Klan claimed three thousand members in Lake County in 1921, but its anti-Catholic propaganda met opposition in this immigrant city. Almost half of Gary's 102,000 residents were foreign-born. When the Klan tried to hold a parade in 1923, Mayor R. O. Johnson refused to issue it a permit. In 1925 Floyd E. Williams succeeded Johnson as mayor. He was not a Klan member, but he did not disavow Klan support. Williams probably expressed the prejudices of most Gary whites, but he was by no means a strident racist. Three African-American members were elected to the city council in a loose alliance with Williams, and he in turn dispensed jobs to the black community in typical patron-client fashion. Both mayors were Republicans, Democrats being a negligible force in Gary.[13]

The Gary NAACP branch, founded in 1917, faced some of the same problems that the Chicago branch developed. Many of its members worked in the steel mills, and the branch had to arrange its meeting times to accommodate day and night shift workers. At first it elected a prominent white president, Judge William Dunn, but it replaced him after he sentenced Chicago black men to prison for buying guns in Gary during the 1919 riot. Like their Chicago colleagues, Gary NAACPers had to define themselves against the National Equal Rights League, led by Ida B. Wells-Barnett in the Windy City. When branch president James Duncan collected money for an Arkansas defense fund organized by Wells-Barnett, Louis Campbell protested that the Association had its own fund. "Mr. Campbell is a very earnest and well-meaning gentleman," branch secretary Elizabeth Lytle advised the national office, "but he is a most erratic and strongly opinionated person. Things must go as he says or not all." This sort of conflict afflicted many branches, but it particularly hindered Gary in the early 1920s. Campbell wrote long letters to New York "that are about as clear as a London fog," Robert Bagnall complained.[14]

Despite his apparently undiplomatic personality, Campbell saw early on that the branch should fight for integrated schools and classrooms. He wrote an article for the *Gary Dispatch*, an African-American weekly, titled "Segregation Means Neglect," showing that the segregated grade schools suffered in comparison to white and integrated schools. Colored students had few books, could not take them home, and were overcrowded in their classrooms. Campbell was probably instrumental in arranging a public meeting for Wirt and William Pickens at the Froebel school. He organized a petition drive calling for an investigation of the segregated schools. But when Campbell confronted the principal at the Twenty-third Avenue school, the man threatened to fire the colored teachers. Under this pressure, the branch retreated and stripped Campbell of his authority. Campbell charged, unfairly, that Garveyites had taken over the branch. Three years later, Campbell gave up and moved to Chicago. "When every member of the Gary branch ought to be bending their energies working to have segregation in the Gary schools abolished," Campbell protested, the members had instead acquiesced to a dangerous trend.[15] The following year, just as Campbell predicted, the problem exploded in the branch's face.

The national NAACP immediately recognized that the Gary school strike posed a major threat to all African Americans. If the Gary students were segregated by law, school segregation could spread throughout the North. James Weldon Johnson issued a press release headlined "Gary Student Race Strike Laid to Klan Propaganda." The release called attention to the prosecution of Indiana Klan leaders, and it tried to link the strike to the morally bankrupt Klansmen. "The NAACP will back to the limit the right of young colored students of Gary to obtain an education without being segregated like pariahs," it declared. Two days later, Johnson sharpened the attack. "The issue is a simple one. Is the school system of Gary to be run for all Americans? Or is it to be dominated by a group of fanatics in what they conceive to be their own interests?" The Association sent a telegram to Superintendent Wirt, urging him to face down the segregationists, and released it to the press.[16]

In Gary, the local branch, acting in concert with the national office, entered into a whirlwind of activity. The national office dispatched its leading attorney in the state, Robert L. Bailey of Indianapolis, to help. On Friday night, September 30, seven hundred to eight hundred people packed

Rosemont Hall at Nineteenth and Broadway for a mass meeting. Bailey gave a fiery speech, calling on Gary black people to sue for their rights and defeat the mayor at the next election. The meeting formed a committee of leading Negro citizens, including two of the three African-American aldermen, to visit city officials. The next day Bailey conferred with local lawyers to get their opinions and assess their abilities. He heard from students and parents at another mass meeting. The Emerson youngsters were ready to stand up, Bailey reported to Johnson, adding that "the Cheeks girl . . . is a real heroine."

From this meeting the leadership delegation proceeded to the mayor's office, minus the aldermen, who were antisegregation but allied with the mayor. This turned into a tense confrontation. Williams angrily demanded to know who had given the speech against him the night before. Bailey identified himself at once.

"Do I look like a damn fool to you?" Williams expostulated.

"No, Mr. Mayor," Bailey replied, "but I fear that you played one in this school affair."

Williams then boasted of his achievements in Gary, which were not inconsiderable. He had hired Negro teachers, firemen, and police, and assigned a Negro foreman (over white objections) to supervise white men in the sanitation department. He had helped the Negro Masons build their meeting hall and smoothed the way for union recognition of the colored hod carriers union. Bailey reminded him that the present issue was the city's intervention in school matters, which he, Bailey, could assure the mayor was illegal. NAACP branch president John W. Russell and attorney Edward McKinley Bacoyn spoke up, too. Mayor Williams turned to Russell, asking him if he was not on the city payroll. "Don't you for a moment think that because I have a city contract you have bought me politically," Russell declared. "I am a Negro first." Mayor Williams was meeting New Negroes of the NAACP for the first time in his career.

The African-American leaders then repaired to Superintendent Wirt's office. The progressive educator, who, Bailey observed, had the disconcerting habit of wiggling his ears when he made a point, offered some hope for at least a compromise. He assured his visitors that he personally opposed segregation and believed that Klan sentiment flowed from fears bred of ignorance. The Froebel school remained a success, Wirt said, noting the lack of friction there and the popularity of colored athletes. Gary's elementary schools were more integrated than those of most other cities. At Emerson the problem lay with a weak principal, who should have suppressed the strike. The school board, he reassured the delegation, had opposed the strike. Bailey suggested that the African-American attorneys might file a "friendly suit" that would give him and the mayor a diplomatic rationale for keeping Emerson integrated. This meeting apparently ended on an upbeat note because Bailey's report emphasized the culpability of the mayor. What Bailey missed in Wirt's remarks was that white opposition to the strike focused on the students' usurpation of adult authority, not on a principled defense of African-American rights.[17]

Over the next few days, the Gary leaders crafted a political and legal response to the challenge of segregation. On Monday, October 3, concerned African Americans packed the city council chamber, intent on blocking an ordinance that would transfer fifteen thousand dollars in city funds to the school budget for the purpose of building a Negro school. The council chairman, a U.S. Steel official, made a paternalistic appeal to the African-American councilmen to vote "aye": Gary wanted to help its black people but not on a socially equal basis. The audience hissed, and the three black councilmen cast the only votes against. The segregationists won round one, but they had united the black community against them. Much liberal white editorial opinion outside Gary, including the *Chicago Tribune* and *New York Evening World*, opposed the Gary school strike and the council's action. The London *Times* picked up NAACP news releases, and the *Nation* magazine suggested sarcastically that the school's name should be changed from Emerson to Hiram Wesley Evans, after the Ku Klux Klan leader.[18]

On the legal front, African-American attorneys argued that the city council's action probably violated its own parameters. City money could not be transferred to the public schools, which had their own budget. Therefore the NAACP sought an injunction against the city on behalf of an African-American contractor and a leading Baptist minister. The judge changed the venue to neighboring Porter County, where another judge stayed the city's hand in late October. Early in December he permanently enjoined the city from transferring the funds, and the council repealed its ordinance of October 3. The city agreed to pay court costs. Round two went to the black community, but everyone realized that the fight had just begun.[19]

While the issue was before the court, the NAACP called several mass meetings. Religious and fraternal organizations joined in, and the people pledged twelve hundred dollars to cover the legal costs. In New York, the NAACP board of directors appropriated five hundred dollars to retain Bailey as chief attorney for the ensuing battle. Field organizer Pickens came out to speak in October and, surveying white opinion, warned against "foolish optimism" over the long haul. By early November the branch had sponsored four mass meetings, including one for Chicago politician Oscar

De Priest. James Weldon Johnson came out to speak later in the month. In the first two months, 267 Gary African Americans contributed financially to the school fight. The *Gary Colored American* praised the new black unity in the Steel City and the leading role of the NAACP.[20]

Under the surface, however, ambivalence about integration gathered some steam. An Elks leader bearing an old grudge against the NAACP hired a Chicago detective to throw mud at the integrationists. The gumshoe told the African-American press that a "Bow Tie Amalgamation" or a "Black Ku Klux Klan," an unholy crew of gamblers, Negro politicians, and the mayor, was operating in Gary. The mayor had Klan support, the black councilmen and NAACP met with the mayor, and the whole combination was corrupt. Several African-American newspapers reported these charges late in 1927, retailing this tissue of rumor, gossip, half-truths, and irrelevant truths for its scandal value.[21]

A more serious problem developed within Gary's African-American legal community. The attorneys competed among themselves for the NAACP's fee, and the branch divided over the question of whom to retain. The branch chose Edward McKinley Bacoyn, a talented twenty-eight-year-old with a gift for antagonizing friend and foe alike. Bacoyn worked hard and believed in the cause, but his rivals resented him and fueled discontent within the community. Bacoyn in turn was jealous of Bailey's favored relation with the national office.[22]

A third disruptive force in the antisegregation struggle came from those who honestly opposed it. Never a strong force anywhere by the late 1920s, Garveyism did have more backers in Gary than in most places. The Gary UNIA, led by two West Indians, stayed quiet during the first phase of the struggle. The local Garveyites probably were backed by African-American schoolteachers, because white parents emphatically opposed allowing them to teach their children. When enthusiasm for the struggle waned after the first few months, arguments along nationalist lines began to sound more convincing to waverers in the black community.[23]

While the NAACP won an easy court victory at first, it rested on narrow grounds. The state had in 1877 passed legislation enabling cities to segregate their schools. Gary had just done it illegally. The proper way to do so was for the school board to pay out of its own budget and to change the school assignments of Negro pupils by redistricting. The school committee and Wirt did this in December, after the court decision. Wirt meanwhile spoke at a black church, dangling before the congregation the prospect of greatly enhanced spending on separate Negro schools. Attorney Bacoyn concluded that a "cunning" white leadership had devised "to pull wool over the eyes of unsuspecting Negroes."[24]

Later in December and early in January 1928, Wirt met in small groups with the eighteen African-American students who were attending Emerson for the first time. He told them that they would be transferred back to the Virginia Street school, because "the officials of Gary wanted the schools to be like those of Birmingham." Young Ruth Kelly asked, "Then why don't they go back down South?" She met Wirt's glum response by asking, "What was the point of having a constitution if we wasn't going to keep it?" Alberta Cheeks was also bitter at the news that they were going to be transferred. "Now I want to know if my people are going to let us be put in this school and let the School Board break the law," she later wrote.[25] The sophomores had a lesson to teach their elders.

By January 9, only six graduating Negro seniors were left at Emerson. Bacoyn went to court, seeking writs of mandamus on behalf of the parents of the transferred students and the NAACP. Wirt and the school board would have to show cause for their actions. Bacoyn argued that the students had been transferred twice in one year, a violation of school policy. Moreover, they had been transferred from an accredited high school facility to the unaccredited Virginia Street school. The former was full of facilities that the latter lacked. The court again changed the venue of the hearing to the Valparaiso court of Judge Grant Crumpacker, who had ruled for the NAACP in December.[26]

Crumpacker heard the arguments in early May. Bailey came over to Valparaiso, working with Bacoyn as his assistant. Alberta Cheeks and her sister Earlene gave powerful testimony. They were now forced to attend school in Chicago to get a college preparatory education. Wirt maintained that the school assignments had been changed because of overcrowding at Emerson and that Virginia Street was an excellent school. Bacoyn felt confident that he and Bailey had won their case and that the school officials would have no grounds for appeal. Much to Bacoyn's dismay, the judge delayed his ruling until July, when he declared verbally in favor of the school board, putting off a written decision until September.[27]

This setback emboldened those within the black community who had been skeptical of the NAACP's strategy. The *Gary American*, a community weekly, ran a story headlined "Ridicule Showing in School Case." It argued that the suit might have been won had an alternative legal strategy of seeking an injunction against the redistricting been deployed. The tone of the article showed not constructive criticism but the snickering of an attorney spurned by the NAACP branch. A student plaintiff, Alberteen Marsh, hit right back against the author's defeatism. One need not be a lawyer, Marsh responded, to see that "a prejudiced board of education, encouraged by a weakling superintendent," had "changed an imaginary boundary line" to keep the black students out while wrongly proclaiming that race had nothing to do with the issue. The integrationists had lost on a narrow technicality, but they would not give up. "[T]he Supreme Court will some day hand down a decision," the prescient teenager wrote, that would vindicate the tenacity of the Gary students.[28]

That day was still twenty-six years away. In 1928, Judge Crumpacker ruled that Gary students would have to wait. Disgusted, Bacoyn wrote the national office that "the honorable judge says by his decision that he will leave these Negro children where the Nordic mob placed them." When the last black seniors graduated Emerson High in June, Emerson became an all-white school.[29]

Bacoyn was ready to soldier on, and *Cheeks v. Wirt* was argued in the state supreme court. But the fight had gone out of the Gary black community, and little money was raised locally for the suit. As Bacoyn observed, the local Negro ministry and press abandoned ship and accommodated to the new segregated reality.[30] Froebel High remained integrated, but the African-American students there were increasingly segregated within the school. Attorneys Bacoyn and Bailey renewed their rivalry until the national office smoothed over relations between them, but the *Cheeks* case lost in the 1930s.

The remnants of the Garveyite movement assumed leadership of the new Roosevelt High School. F. C. McFarland, principal of Roosevelt during the 1920s, argued the merits of a segregated education: black students would properly learn their own history and develop pride in their race. According to two students of the Gary black community, the majority of the African-American youth "overwhelmingly supported the school's establishment."[31] Given the widespread white hostility, this is not surprising. Only eighteen African-American students had attended the Emerson school, and their experience of it had been bitter. It surely must have been a relief for them to abandon the place.

If Gary African Americans showed ambivalence toward integration, they nonetheless resented being segregated. At the next mayoral primary they overwhelmingly rejected Mayor Williams, despite the support for him by Negro ministers, schoolteachers, the women's federation, and the UNIA. NAACPers campaigned for Williams's rival, who carried the African-American vote by 4,100–900.[32] The ambivalence toward integration in Gary's black community during the 1920s is still at the heart of the American dilemma at the opening of the twenty-first century.

23

"I Forgive You All and Hope to Meet You in Heaven"

NTERRACIAL sex lay at the center of white America's nightmare. White people shrouded the subject in a haze of hypocrisy and hysteria. For decades, the census had carefully counted mulattoes because white Americans feared the dilution of their supposedly superior racial stock. Everyone knew that mulattoes were produced by white men forcing themselves on slave women, but no one discussed this aloud. After the end of slavery, segregation was justified by fear that black men and white women would copulate. Many states passed laws prohibiting interracial marriage. Whites invented the myth of the Negro as rapist; the popular 1915 film *Birth of a Nation* wrote this story large. The D. W. Griffith movie depicted a heroic Ku Klux Klan riding to the rescue of a white woman about to be ravished by her Negro captor.

The myth was simple: WE are different from THEM. We are civilized; they are barbarian. We place our women on a pedestal; they are animals, creatures of lust. Of course, the myth was a projection of white impulses upon the Other. Behind closed doors white men beat their wives if they accused them of infidelity. Young women, who were expected to be virgins at marriage, sometimes consented to sex with their lovers and sometimes were raped by their boyfriends. Afterward, they might have regrets. How could a young woman explain her fallen state or a feared pregnancy? Time and again, they cried that an unknown Negro had raped them.

The results were always horrific. The word of a white person had to be taken as valid against the word of an African American. Because the cry of interracial rape threatened their manhood, white men had to show their virility by capturing someone. Once the culprit was caught, the community had to find the accused guilty. Naturally, this crime of crimes demanded the ultimate punishment. The Other was a Beast and had to be taught.

Western civilization would sink into a morass of mongrelization if interracial rape did not end with an execution.

As postwar race relations stabilized, lynching declined. More such alleged crimes were brought before courts of law. These threatened legal lynchings promoted a facade of justice, behind which lurked the old impulses. In their own way, legal lynchings were more sinister than extralegal mob action: they implicated law, justice, and reason in the madness that characterized race relations. A black man had to be insane to rape a white woman, and every African American knew it. If he wanted to satisfy his lust, whites didn't care if he raped a black woman. Few black men were prosecuted for raping black women in the 1920s; in fact, very few white men were prosecuted for raping white women. This chapter will describe how NAACP branches defended innocent men during the 1920s (and one case in which there was no NAACP). It will also examine statistics about the punishment of rape and the exclusion of African Americans from juries.

SERIOUS TROUBLE broke out in Knoxville, Tennessee, when an intruder murdered Bertie Lindsey in her bed on August 29, 1919. A Knoxville policeman went immediately to the home of Maurice Mays, an African American he knew, roused him from his slumber, and brought him before Lindsey's distraught roommate, her cousin. She glanced briefly through her tears and identified Mays as the murderer. Mays proclaimed his innocence, but was arrested and removed to Chattanooga for his protection.

Knoxville was a gritty industrial city in the northeastern part of Tennessee, inhabited by seventy-seven thousand residents, 15 percent of whom were African-American. In the spirit of the Red Summer, a Ku Klux Klan–inspired mob gathered at the jail where Mays was initially held. They stormed the building and tore through the prison. When they did not find Mays, they freed white prisoners, including convicted murderers. The governor called out the National Guard. The next morning armed whites attacked the black community, wounding four defenders. The guardsmen did little against the whites, but the county sheriff's men arrested fifty whites and no blacks during the fighting.[1]

Knoxville was then in the midst of a mayoral election, and Mays had been campaigning for the incumbent, John E. McMillan, who opposed the Klan. Mays apparently had incurred the wrath of the arresting officer, either for political reasons, or because of Mays's reputation for sleeping with white women, or both. He arrested Mays even before a description of the assailant was given out as a heavily built "yellow Negro" wearing overalls. Mays was a slender man who did not own overalls.[2]

On the day of the murder, Mays had canvased Knoxville's black section for Mayor McMillan, distributing handbills until late at night. Afterward he spent some time in the company of women friends and went to bed alone just after midnight. A few hours later, two policemen knocked on Mays's door, and he admitted them. The officers searched for a flashlight, revolver, and muddy pants, all of which identified the murderer. Mays had been a deputy sheriff, and he willingly surrendered his own gun, which had not been fired. The officers found neither flashlight nor muddy pants. Yet, they insisted on dragging Mays before the reluctant eyewitness, who, after being told he was the criminal, identified him. Mays insisted that she examine him more carefully, but the police whisked him away. Within a few days, in the tense atmosphere generated by the riot, Maurice Mays was brought to trial. The judge barred the testimony of defense witnesses, and Mays was convicted of first degree murder and sentenced to death.

The Knoxville and Chattanooga NAACP branches set out to raise money for Mays's appeal. The young man's poor and aged parents, who had adopted him, wrote letters to the NAACP in New York, begging for help. So did Mays, who also wrote plaintive poems from his cell. A five-stanza poem entitled "Help Me Please" began: "Doomed to die without a crime / My hope is public aid / Who will volunteer and help / To save me from the grave?" If this lacked the subtlety of Paul Laurence Dunbar, it wanted nothing for directness and pathos. Within two months, the Mays family and their allies raised $525. With it they hired Reuben L. Cates, a prominent white attorney, to represent Mays on appeal.[3]

If there were any doubts regarding Mays's innocence, subsequent events should have dispelled them for any fair-minded observer. Housebreaks and rapes similar to the Lindsey case had occurred prior to that crime. Afterward they continued. Only a few weeks later, a man brandishing a revolver and a flashlight broke into the home of a woman and raped her, threatening to kill her just as he had Bertie Lindsey. By September 1920 there had been a dozen similar crimes—some victims were raped, some escaped, some were murdered. Surviving victims described a swarthy white man as the perpetrator. The newspapers hushed up these crimes. Knoxville would rather permit a psychotic serial rapist/killer to go loose than admit that it had wrongly convicted a black man.[4]

The local NAACP branch, led by James L. Carey of Knoxville College and Reverend J. H. Henderson, moved aggressively to raise funds for a defense team that included Cates and two others. Yet the national office dragged its feet on the Mays case. National secretary John Shillady, demoralized by his beating in Austin, wrote in a memo that the national office should not contribute financially because, although Mays might be a frame-up victim,

Maurice Mays. Courtesy of NAACP.

he was not necessarily being framed up because he was a Negro. Soon to leave the Association, Shillady was losing his bearings. Yet the *Crisis* gave the case little coverage, and James Weldon Johnson, in a rare display of stinginess, suggested sending money "if only to make the record." When Knoxville sent a fund appeal on its own to some other branches nationally, New York reminded them politely that it could not do so; national fund appeals must come from the center. Walter White, to whom most correspondence on criminal matters was directed, argued in a series of internal memos that the national office should intervene more forcefully on Mays's behalf. The hard-pressed Association forwarded one hundred dollars, sent its own appeal to the Tennessee branches at least, and wrote more about Mays in the *Crisis*.[5]

By the end of 1920, the state supreme court ordered a new trial on the grounds that the jury, rather than the judge, should have issued sentence. The second trial opened and closed in late April 1921. Reverend Henderson wrote that lawyer Cates "could not have done better for one who was kin to him." Over the objection of the prosecution, Cates introduced the continuing crime spree into the record, probably while the jury was absent. Mays took the stand in his own defense, clearly described his movements about the city on the day of the crime, and declared that he had never met the victim, been to her house, or killed her. But the eyewitness identified Mays again, and a jury almost always convicted on such testimony. Mays showed no emotion when this jury found him guilty. The court again sentenced Mays to die, this time on June 26, and after some more maneuvering, postponed the date to December 15, 1921.[6]

Throughout, attorney Cates, Reverend Henderson, and Mays himself did not seem to believe that there would be an execution. At the worst, they expected that the governor would commute the sentence to life in prison, and that later the actual perpetrator would be caught in the act and confess to the Lindsey murder. Mays wrote an impassioned letter to the governor a month before the scheduled execution, restating his testimony in court and emphasizing that he had neither the motive for such a crime nor the bad character necessary to commit it. "I am innocent and God is a witness to my innocence," he concluded. African Americans flooded the governor's office with appeals for clemency. Nashville NAACP leader Reverend S. L. McDowell joined Mays's parents in a personal interview with the governor, who seemed visibly moved. The mood in the NAACP national office turned grim as the execution date approached. A few minutes before the scheduled execution, the governor granted Mays a ninety-day "respite" but not a reprieve. The miracle never came. Maurice Mays was electrocuted ninety days later for a crime he did not commit.[7]

The world forgot about Maurice Mays until five years later, when a white woman confessed to killing Bertie Lindsey. Sadie Mendil walked into the police station at Lima, Ohio, and told the authorities that she had spotted her then-husband strolling about Knoxville with Lindsey and had exacted her revenge by donning men's clothes, blackening her face, and killing Lindsey. African-American newspapers carried this story, and the NAACP national office sent journalist Helen Boardman to interview Mendil in Knoxville. The police discounted her story, and Mendil was not arrested. Boardman doubted Mendil's story, too, but learned about the authorities' suspicions regarding the real perpetrator.

Boardman met a Dr. H. M. Green, who had a contact in the police department. After Mays's execution, he said, the police developed another suspect, a swarthy white man who matched the description given by several victims. One of the victims, who was raped before the Lindsey murder, suspected that Mays was innocent because he was clean-shaven, while the new suspect (her assailant) had a mustache. Dr. Green claimed that the prosecutors suspected that Mays was innocent all along, but for political reasons did not want to appear to be protecting Mays.[8]

The Knoxville and Chattanooga NAACP branches did their best to defend Maurice Mays and failed. They also failed to unite the black community around the case. More conservative Tennessee African Americans did not speak out on Mays's behalf. Henderson, in Knoxville, noted that some black leaders were "as silent as lobsters" on the matter. Once again, the NAACP showed itself to be in the vanguard on a defense case. But the Tennessee branches could not sustain themselves; gradually most of them weakened as the decade wore on, and the more conservative Commission on Interracial Cooperation took the leadership role in the state's race relations.[9]

ROSEWOOD, FLORIDA, an all-black town that no longer exists, lay forty miles from Gainesville in the forest of Levy County. The area made its living by turning the red cedar trees, for which the town was named, into pencils. The men worked at the sawmill, three miles away in Sumner, and the women worked there as maids. The residents built twenty-five modest homes, three churches, and a Masonic lodge building. A white man ran the town's store.

On New Year's Day, 1923, a white woman, Mrs. Fannie Taylor, ran out of her home in Sumner, screaming that she had been raped by an unknown black man. The bruises on her face showed that she had been beaten. The sheriff knew that a Negro convict had recently escaped from the chain gang, and it was reasonable to believe that he was the perpetrator. The sheriff sent for bloodhounds and a posse, and the dogs followed a scent down the railroad tracks to Rosewood. They stopped at the home of Aaron Carrier. The sheriff demanded to know if Carrier had helped the convict to escape, which Carrier denied. Under torture, he changed his story. He had helped someone to escape: a white man, who had found Carrier in the Masonic hall. The white man was a Mason, too, and a Mason was sworn to help his fellows. Carrier had fetched a friend, Sam Carter, who owned a wagon, and they drove the man through the swamp, where he ran off.

A white mob would be disinclined to believe such a story. They made Sam Carter drive again to the place where the fugitive had been released, as the mob followed behind. But the hounds could not pick up the scent, and the mob reinterrogated Carter, hanging him by the neck and lowering him to the ground to get the truth out of him. Carter probably was telling the truth, but this was not what the mob wanted to hear, so they shot him.

Seventy years later, the granddaughter of Fannie Taylor's maid, Sarah Carrier, told a reporter that she and her grandmother had seen the white man enter and leave the house. He was a railroad man they had seen before: Fannie Taylor's secret lover. Sarah Carrier heard the lovers quarrel and then fight. Half an hour after the white man left, Fannie Taylor emerged from the house crying that she had been raped. How else could she explain her bruises? Telling the truth would only earn her another beating and a reputation as an adulteress.

The vigilante mob, however, was back to square one in its effort to catch the presumed Negro rapist. A few days later, the whites returned to Rosewood, presumably to interrogate Aaron Carrier again. This time they found Sarah, Aaron's mother, standing in the doorway, perhaps trying to tell what she had seen. Someone gunned her down where she stood. After seeing his mother murdered, Sarah's son Sylvester and other Rosewood African Americans shot into the mob and drove them off in a gunfight, killing two. The whites retreated but returned later to an eerie silence and entered the house, where they discovered Sylvester's corpse. The vigilantes burned Rosewood to the ground, killed several residents, and massacred even the farm animals. When Governor Cary Hardee wired the sheriff for information, he replied that everything was under control, even as the mob was doing its work.

The town's children and surviving adults fled into the woods, spending the night out-of-doors. The town's white storekeeper, the mill superintendent, and two railroad conductors arranged for a train to rescue Rosewood's former inhabitants. Some newspapers reported a death toll of eight, but many years later an unapologetic white murderer claimed that seventeen bodies had been buried in a mass grave. The black families, now homeless, dispersed to the homes of relatives and tried to forget the senseless violence that had claimed their neighbors and loved ones. Newspaper articles appeared in African-American weeklies and white dailies but quickly dropped from the pages. Two contemporaneous race stories got much more extensive coverage: the murder of renegade Garveyite James Eason and the trial of the Ku Klux Klan killers at Mer Rouge, Louisiana.

James Weldon Johnson wrote a bitter obituary for the town in his weekly *New York Age* column. "The boast of the South . . . is that the South may occasionally lynch a Negro for having committed a terrible crime but that it never wreaks vengeance upon the innocent and unoffending." Here an entire black community had been wiped off the map, giving the lie to all the other supposedly justifiable violence. His column the following week called on southern African Americans to swell their exodus from the South and take advantage of the opportunities in the North.

The mysterious convict and the elusive railroad man were never discovered, and the story was forgotten. Rosewood showed every naked evil of American society in the 1920s: it is a tale of lying, cowardice, race hatred, gratuitous violence, and hypocrisy. Some remarkable nobility shines through, of course: the loyalty of the two black men who died to help an unknown white man; the courage of the Carriers, who gave their lives trying to stop the violence; and the precious handful of whites who aided in the escape.

Seventy years later, the *St. Petersburg Times* ran a series on the Rosewood story. Around the same time, in a grand irony of history, a filmmaker dramatized the story in a movie, converting this obscure event of the 1920s into a better-known story. The Florida legislature passed a bill granting the survivors $150,000 each and establishing a college scholarship fund for their descendants, making Florida the first state to address the legacy of horror to which the nation as a whole is heir.[10]

LUTHER COLLINS's nightmare began on January 24, 1922, when Myrtle Davis told the Houston police that she had been raped by a Negro. She said that the man approached her and a male companion on a busy thoroughfare, pulled a gun on them, and forced both to walk 250 yards to a woodshed, in which he raped her while holding the gun on her companion. Instead of laughing off this story as fiction, the police matched the woman's description to Luther Collins, even though he claimed to be miles away from the scene of the crime. Tried in Harris County right after the alleged rape, Collins was convicted and sentenced to hang.[11]

E. O. Smith took charge of Collins's case for the Houston NAACP. The Houston Court of Criminal Appeals reversed the lower court because it had excluded from the record affidavits showing Collins's whereabouts at the time of the crime. Houston African Americans held special prayer services and packed the court when the decision was announced in a second trial: the jury could not reach a verdict. That should have resulted in Collins's freedom, but prosecutors sought a third trial. In the changed venue of Fort Bend County, Collins was found guilty and sentenced to ninety-nine years in prison. According to Walter White's Texas informants, Myrtle Davis described the alleged incident differently at each trial.[12]

The Houston NAACP appealed this decision also, and the higher court ruled to exclude unreliable testimony brought by the police. Another change of venue brought Collins's case to Washington County. The prosecutor there reviewed the evidence, declined to charge Collins, and announced that he was joining the NAACP. Collins walked out of jail in 1926, having lost four years of his life to a ridiculous frame-up.[13]

Texas African Americans contributed all two thousand dollars of the total defense bill. Houston's tenacious defense of Collins showed that African Americans could wage a long fight through the courts, pay for it themselves, and, with luck, win.[14] Had Collins's defenders given up at any point along the way and left his pleading to a public defender, he would have forfeited his life.

"On various occasions we have been attacked saying that we were alarmists and that we purposely distorted facts," White wrote to E. O. Smith. "The Luther Collins case is without doubt one of the clearest cut demonstrations of what a southern jury will do when a Negro, no matter how worthy, is charged with a crime by a white woman, no matter how worthless."[15]

AFRICAN AMERICANS faced much less persecution in the North than they faced in the South, but many innocent black men in the North also went

to prison for crimes they did not commit. Despite the fact that the Philadelphia NAACP was one of the best organized in the country, it could not
save Walter Rounds from such a fate. Like Luther Collins, he was convicted
of a crime that could not have happened and that his "victim" did not
even allege.

Walter White learned of Rounds's predicament late in February 1925.
He sought more information from Raymond Price Alexander, head of the
National Bar Association (the segregated version of the American Bar Association). Alexander had been Rounds's lawyer. "The idea that a man would
attempt rape in a public elevator seems so preposterous," White wrote.[16]
White had investigated the Tulsa riot in 1921, and he perhaps remembered
how the spurious charge of "assault" in an elevator had precipitated the
violence there.

Walter Rounds was operating his elevator in Jacquert's store on Thirteenth Street when the elevator came to a sudden stop between the fourth
and fifth floor. His solitary passenger, Margaret McPherson Stoddard,
stumbled as she bent over to fasten her galoshes. Stoddard screamed,
"[Y]ou nigger, you hit me," and ran for the police when she alighted. The
authorities handcuffed the young man and, back at the police station, gave
Rounds "the third degree." One policeman told Rounds he would kill him
if he didn't confess, so Rounds signed a confession. As Alexander pointed
out, Rounds was almost illiterate, and the confession was "written in the
King's English."

In fact, Rounds confessed to even more than Stoddard had accused him
of. On her way out of the store, she told Rounds's fellow employees that
the operator was "a dirty rotten nigger. They would tear him to pieces in
the South." Stoddard claimed that Rounds tried to rob her; the prosecutor
turned this into four counts of assault, one of them being "with intent to
ravish," an intent to which Rounds confessed while his arms were being
twisted. In court, four of Rounds's coworkers testified to his good character. Rounds took the stand in his own behalf, but the jury took only forty-
five minutes to find him guilty of several charges. The judge sentenced him
to thirteen years in prison.[17] Philadelphia was making Houston look good.

White thought the case could be won easily on appeal. Alexander advised him that the trial was "the most perfect frame-up in the annals of
Philadelphia criminal law," characterized by "the most vile sort of race
prejudice." After consulting with Arthur B. Spingarn, White realized that
Alexander had made some basic mistakes at trial. He had not challenged
Rounds's confession by grilling the policeman who had extracted it from
him. He had not made a summary speech, which, Spingarn thought, most
juries took as a sign that an attorney believed his client was guilty. An

appeal would have to be based on the trial record, and Alexander had not got all the facts on record. The NAACP apparently did not appeal Rounds's case, and the last reference to him in the correspondence shows him languishing in Moyamensing Prison.[18]

Failures like the Rounds case made the NAACP national office more cautious in matters of criminal defense. Rounds was not defended by the NAACP, but Alexander was a friend of the Association and a competent lawyer. This experience may have helped convince the Legal Committee that it could come to the aid of a defendant only if the branch had consulted with the national office at some point early in the process. The Philadelphia branch was loyal to the national leadership, but even in this case the national office felt stymied.

The Philadelphia branch had had a troubled first decade. By 1920, 134,229 African Americans lived in the city, making it the third largest community in African America. Despite Philadelphia's importance, early efforts to reconcile squabbling factions among members of the Constitution League (a white-initiated civil rights group), African-American doctors at Douglass Hospital, Quakers, and Unitarians met little success. By mid-decade J. Max Barber, the former editor of Atlanta's *The Voice of the Negro*, was branch president. Driven out of journalism, he became a dentist. Barber bore an old grudge against Du Bois, and he didn't like Walter White either. "I have a bit of white blood in me, but somehow I never warmed up to trust a half-white Negro," he confided to William Pickens. Within a few years, Barber had burned out and did not respond aggressively when Philadelphia experienced a race riot in 1918. A Colored Protective Association sprang up outside the branch to defend victims of police brutality.[19]

Barber at first promoted his replacement, Isadore Martin, but later came to resent him, too. Martin regularly attended board meetings in New York and cultivated a relationship with White and others there. In Philadelphia he developed a team leadership that worked more efficiently than that of most branches. When the board of education tried to segregate some schools, the branch formed an education committee led by Reverend William Lloyd Imes to fight for integration and employment of Negro teachers. This committee sponsored mass meetings to protest segregation, which agitated the community in the late 1920s. Millie Brinkley, Katherine H. Brown, and Fielding A. Ford organized membership drives that recruited several thousand people over the course of the decade. As usual, female leaders such as Brinkley and Brown did the hard work behind the scenes while males garnered the credit. When some women wanted to form a women's auxiliary, branch leader Julian St. George White worried that it might "shunt them aside" rather than encourage women to partici-

pate actively in the branch. "We count your branch the best in the Association," Bagnall reassured Isadore Martin, but it could not save the
unfortunate Walter Rounds.[20]

ON MARCH 18, 1927, police in Coffeyville, Kansas, were called to the home
of Julia Mooney, who claimed that she and her friend Margaret Akers were
"attacked" by three black men. Mooney was a high school senior and
Akers was younger. The police brought in bloodhounds and after a search
arrested three African Americans. The alleged incident occurred after midnight in a dark room, and the girls did not get a good look at their attackers.
All three accused men declared their innocence.

News of the alleged attack spread around Coffeyville, and a mob of over
a thousand men stormed the city hall where the culprits were supposed to
be. National guardsmen and sheriff's deputies drove the crowd away, but
not before they broke all the windows in the building. The angry mass
headed toward the black community, which the authorities did not defend. The mob beat two unlucky victims almost to death. From the vicinity
of Anderson's pool hall, black men shot into the crowd, wounding enough
invaders to disperse them. Two black men were wounded and also arrested; twelve whites were arrested, but the charges against all save one
were dropped.[21]

About twenty thousand people lived in Coffeyville, which lay 140 miles
south of Topeka on the Oklahoma border. About four thousand of the city's
residents were African-American, and some of them had organized an
NAACP branch, which had earlier tried but failed to stop Coffeyville from
segregating its schools. In this new emergency, black community leaders
offered a reward leading to the arrest of the real rapists. Few Coffeyville
African Americans believed that black men had raped the girls.[22]

It did not take long for the girls' story to break down. The older girl, it
turned out, had arranged a party in the absence of her parents. A Wichita
auto salesman named Ira Kennedy and, the newspapers hinted, two more
socially prominent young men presumably had consensual sex with the
older girl, and someone may have had sex with the younger. The older girl
kept insisting for a week that they "stick to the Negro story." Akers was
afraid of Mooney and feared that Kennedy would kill her if she talked.[23]

William Pickens visited Coffeyville in June, after most of the facts were
out but the cases not adjudicated. He was ripping mad. The white cavort-
ers, he raged, "knew exactly what to do: Have a good time and then go out
and cry 'Nigger!' " to divert attention. They had almost gotten away with
it, and he wanted the national office to back the local people to the finish.[24]

What made the aftermath unique was that the Coffeyville authorities prosecuted Ira Kennedy and Julia Mooney, and dropped the charges against the black men. The state attorney general even appointed an NAACP lawyer as a special assistant for the grand jury investigation. He was Elisha Scott, a colorful thirty-seven-year-old who had advised the Coffeyville NAACP on its desegregation work. Scott, a dark-skinned, bespectacled man with a deep voice and dramatic courtroom style, practiced criminal law in Topeka. He also defended Oklahoma Negroes driven off their land by oil speculators. Ultimately Kennedy and Mooney were acquitted, and the other two white men were never prosecuted, but the unusual aspect of this story is that they were charged at all.[25]

Scott next came to the defense of Napoleon Anderson and Hershel Ford, charged with shooting into the crowd and wounding two individuals. Both men were themselves wounded, and prosecuting them seemed unfair to Coffeyville African Americans. Anderson and Ford had made the unforgivable error of suing the city for twenty thousand dollars in damages to themselves and their property; they apparently believed that the police were supposed to protect them, just as they did white people. In September, Scott wrote that all major charges had been dropped against these two clients. The NAACP recruited forty new members during this period, and Scott reported that "the spirit is high and great praise [sounds] for the NAACP."[26]

Coffeyville represented a different national mood from that displayed in Knoxville (1919), Duluth (1920), Tulsa (1921), and Rosewood (1923). The same false cry of rape had called a mob into the street in these places. Different degrees of African-American resistance, based on the particular histories and relations of forces, emerged, but mobs and prosecutors wreaked horrible damage earlier in the decade. At Coffeyville, the mob was driven off relatively easily, and no one was wrongly convicted. This outcome had much to do with contingent circumstances and the pure unpredictability of human life, but it also reflected the gradually changing tenor of race relations in the 1920s.

FEW ASPECTS of their oppression hurt African Americans as much as bald disparate treatment in criminal justice cases. In the winter and spring of 1926, rape trials in Kentucky left black people in the Bluegrass State feeling angry and bitter. The Kentucky NAACP branches worked to insure that accused men received fair trials and that whites were punished for raping black women.

"Kentucky and West Virginia are a 'borderland' for us," field secretary

William Pickens wrote in a June 1923 memo, "and just as important to our success, perhaps, as they were to Lincoln's victory." On his Kentucky tour that year, he visited five cities, all facing different situations. On May 20 at Frankfort, the state capital, five hundred people came out to hear him at the AME Church. But the next day, at Maysville, on the Ohio border, a city where the Klan had been active, conservative Negroes tried to stop Pickens from speaking. The plucky organizer arranged a meeting at the courthouse, where a judge introduced him to an audience of three hundred. Hardly anyone contributed any money or signed up—Pickens thought the people came to see if the Klan would run him out of town—but the speech proved uneventful. At Louisville, all the ministers sided with the NAACP. Pickens observed that they quarreled among themselves but remained positive in their outlook. Then Pickens was off to Bowling Green, in southwestern Kentucky, where a Negro told him that they had no trouble with their white folks, except for an occasional lynching. Pickens was aghast at the man's acceptance of this state of affairs. In nearby Hopkinsville, the same sensibility prevailed. The state was a battleground, Pickens mused, "and let no man dream that [the right to organize] cannot be lost, even in Kentucky."[27]

Early in 1926, a series of highway robberies and rapes took place near Madisonville in southwest Kentucky, one hundred miles from Louisville. In one incident, three white girls claimed that three black men raped them after their vehicle broke down. The Ku Klux Klan staged a demonstration, demanding arrests. A short time later, another woman, Neil Catherine Breithaupt, claimed that three black men had raped her. She said that a male friend had parked their car after nightfall when the incident, whose details remained murky, occurred. The police were provided with a suitable Negro suspect when the client of a prostitute discovered a photograph of the woman with a black man. Armed with the photograph, the police confronted the prostitute, who identified Columbus Hollis as the man in the picture. In exchange for a promised reduction of sentence, Hollis identified Bunyan Fleming and Nathan Bard, colored patrons of another prostitute, as his more guilty accomplices, and on April 7 they were arrested.

On their own, Bard and Fleming secured the services of a white lawyer named Roscoe Conkling. William Warley, editor of the African-American *Louisville News*, also served as NAACP president in 1926, and he feared that Bard and Fleming were being framed. Along with an attorney friend, he journeyed to Madisonville, interviewed the accused men, and became convinced that they were innocent. Feeling against Bard and Fleming ran high in Madisonville, and troops had to be called in to forestall trouble. The local whites resented Warley and his friend as outside agitators, and warned them to get out of town, which they did. So cowed was the local black community that its leaders released a statement declaring that they did not hire the defense attorneys and had been content with the court-appointed man. Warley was compelled to cover the trial by culling the white dailies. He thought that Conkling, who also believed in the men's innocence, had proved that there was a reasonable doubt about the men's guilt. The trial lasted seven to eight days. Only Hollis, an interested party, named the defendants as being present at the scene. Neither the victim nor her male friend identified them. But Fleming's alibi witnesses, members of Hollis's family, testified against him. Bard and Fleming were convicted and sentenced to death, the jury deliberating for about fifteen minutes in each case. This was southern justice at its best when a black man was accused of raping a white woman.

In the few weeks between the arrest and trial, Warley and his fellow editor I. Willis Cole of the *Louisville Leader* expressed skepticism about the upcoming trial. On April 17 Warley's banner headline read "Lynching Coming? Madisonville Men Apparently Being Rushed to the Gallows by Farcical Trial." Afterward, he led with "The Expected Happens—Fleming and Bard Get Death Sentence." He reported lawyer Conkling's feeling that the trial was "fair" but the verdict "disappointing." The likelihood is that Warley's visit signaled the judge that the NAACP would appeal and that he should conduct the trial with a modicum of fairness.[28]

However, the length of the trial and the presence of a real defense attorney were not enough to convince a prejudiced jury. Conkling had wanted to move for a change of venue, but he mistakenly thought that Kentucky law required that two county residents sign for the motion. He could not find two people to come forward.[29] Madisonville lay in the same Klan-infested corner of Kentucky that had intimidated the black communities at nearby Bowling Green and Hopkinsville when Pickens visited in 1923.

With the verdict in, the county prosecutor made good on a threat he had issued during Warley's visit to Madisonville. Warley and fellow editor Cole had violated Kentucky's criminal syndicalism statute with their rabble-rousing editorials, he alleged. He soon learned that the statute had been repealed. Undaunted by this gaffe, he secured from a grand jury an indictment for libeling the judge. The indictment specified a few lines written by each editor—a ridiculous charge not even brought by its supposed victim. "Read it, laugh, then join the NAACP," Warley wrote. Yet, it represented a serious threat to freedom of the press. In November, a county court found the editors guilty and fined them $250 each.[30]

Meanwhile, Bard and Fleming moved for a retrial in the Hopkins County Circuit Court. Conkling argued that evidence had been wrongly admitted; that the judge had not explained "reasonable doubt" in his charge to the jury; and that the jurors had disregarded the law and the evidence. This appeal failed, and Warley wired New York that a third court "has decided that Fleming and Bard must die." Execution was set for April 8, 1927.[31]

Warley would not give up. He convinced a Judge O'Doherty to try to get the case before a federal court. The legal expenses mounted into several thousand dollars, but people who believed in the men's innocence accepted those costs. Fleming wrote new NAACP branch president G. P. Hughes a bitter, pleading letter: "We haven't had a dog's chance for our lives and as God is my judge, I am innocent and don't know anything about the crime. . . . They [the authorities] have Hollis believing that he will be turned a loose and paid for every day that he has been here, just as soon as they kill us." Yet it was not really clear to the various Louisville lawyers whether to press first for executive clemency or seek a federal lawsuit. Johnson vowed that the National Association would fight all the way to the Supreme Court, and White suggested that the case might be appealed under the precedent established in the *Moore* decision.[32]

Twenty-four hours before the scheduled execution, the last Kentucky Court of Appeals decided it lacked jurisdiction in the case. But federal judge Charles I. Dawson granted a writ of *habeas corpus*, staying the execution. Dawson issued a mixed opinion, reflecting the complicated status of the case. His ruling acknowledged that an intimidating atmosphere existed in the town of Madisonville and that the trial date had been rushed to accommodate local sentiment. Yet the failure of the defense to move for a change of venue was telling. He rejected the defense notion that local signatures were necessary; a defendant could move for a change on his own. Dawson upheld the sentences but allowed thirty days to craft a new appeal. With this time, defense lawyers won further stays from U.S. Supreme Court justice Oliver Wendell Holmes and from the governor, who postponed the execution.[33]

The NAACP turned the case file over to Louis Marshall, who ever since the Frank trial had maintained his interest in mob-dominated courtrooms. After a long delay, he reluctantly concluded that there was "a wide difference between this case and the Frank and Dempsey cases." He noted that Conkling, the original trial lawyer, had declared after the trial that it had been fair. The presence of troops at the courthouse could be used against the defendants as well as for them. Hostile newspaper articles were no worse than those sometimes seen in the North. Most damaging would be the defense's failure to seek a change of venue. Marshall recommended that the defense lawyers, who knew local conditions best, try to extend their clients' lives through state remedies, but he saw little hope for relief from the federal courts. Johnson had the unhappy task of forwarding Marshall's letter to Louisville, along with a check for $250 and his recognition of the branch's "heroic work and sacrifice."[34]

Throughout the appeals, some tension had existed between the national office and Louisville leaders over how much money New York should commit to the case. Late in October, with the execution less than a month away, Pickens met with the branch executive committee, which vented its frustration over the situation on the New York office. They realized that they might have erred in committing themselves so thoroughly at the beginning, because they had not hired the trial lawyer. The branch had one thousand members, but it had now spent eight thousand dollars and owed four thousand dollars more. Moreover, they felt that the Legal Committee had "almost lost the lives of the men because of the delay in our office." Pickens explained the relation between the national office, the Legal Committee, and the branches, feeling he had mollified local concerns. Johnson thanked Pickens for his work, explaining that the branch had put them in a difficult situation by agreeing to "extortionate lawyers' fees" without first consulting New York. With pressing demands from the Detroit Sweet case, the board had to husband its resources. In June 1928, branch leader Hughes wrote Johnson a conciliatory letter, easing some of the pressure under which everyone was placed by a capital case.[35]

Unfortunately, Louis Marshall proved correct about the federal courts: the Supreme Court refused to hear the case. Further appeals in Kentucky were exhausted. The state still employed the pre-Enlightenment method of public execution. On the morning of November 25, 1927, Bunyan Fleming and Nathan Bard were led before a crowd of seven thousand spectators. Two hundred national guardsmen with fixed bayonets insured order, but the audience was in a solemn mood. Bunyan Fleming, his soul somehow at peace in the face of his horrible fate, addressed the crowd. "Friends, I want to say you are looking into the face of an innocent man. . . . I forgive you all and hope to meet you in heaven." Nathan Bard attempted the same brave words but broke down. A Baptist minister said a prayer; the crowd fell silent and bared their heads; the executioner did his work.[36] Fleming's last words, combined with the testimony at trial, strongly suggest that the two men were innocent.

I. Willis Cole, in the *Louisville Leader*, forgave no one. "[T]here is no use of any person or newspaper making any attempt to appease Negroes' feeling over it. This cannot be done, absolutely not," he wrote. As new branch president he was earnestly resolved to go on fighting. He wrote Johnson of his sadness at the loss of Bard and Fleming, but insisted that "we won a moral victory and taught white Kentucky a lesson they will not forget." To show its determination, the branch planned an Emancipation Day demonstration on January 1.[37]

Cole and Warley had also appealed their own libel conviction. They secured Allen Dodd, a white leader of the Kentucky bar, to represent them. The national office contributed five hundred dollars to this case, and the editors raised money by speaking in the Midwest. African-American newspapers had been greatly alarmed by the decision and editorialized against it. New York liberals at the American Civil Liberties Union, the *Nation*, and the *New York Evening World* expressed concern. Yet a few weeks after the executions, the Kentucky Court of Appeals sustained their conviction.[38]

More insult followed the injury of the Bard and Fleming executions. At the end of 1926, the Louisville branch had urged the vigorous prosecution of Charles Falone, a white career criminal who beat and raped a young black woman. Kentucky white men who did this were usually charged only with "detaining a female." At a second trial, Falone was convicted of rape and sentenced to five years of hard labor and a one thousand dollar fine. "Had not the Louisville branch prosecuted the case it probably would have been dismissed," branch secretary Bessie Etherly wrote New York. But in February 1928, after serving a year of his sentence, Falone was paroled. "Colored people have reason to be disturbed, disappointed, and indignant over the release of Charles Falone," Cole wrote in the *Louisville Leader*.[39] African Americans had been given an object lesson in Kentucky justice: the innocent Bard and Fleming were hanged, the guilty Falone slapped on the wrist.

AT AGE SIXTY, Maude Collins of Florence County, South Carolina, learned from her doctor that she had a fatal disease. The news fell more heavily on her than it would upon most mortals, for Maude Collins had a guilty conscience. On May 3, 1928, she swore out an affidavit that said in part: "I, Maude Collins . . . realizing that I have not much longer to live, hereby desire . . . to undo the wrong I have done this Negro, the said Ben Bess, and I hereby declare that my testimony upon the trial of this case was untrue and that Ben Bess should not be serving any sentence therefore."[40]

Ben Bess had already served thirteen years of a thirty-year sentence for raping Mrs. Collins. In 1915 Bess had been a successful farmer in Florence County. He defied all convention by taking Mr. and Mrs. Collins, a white couple, as tenants. After a while, Ben Bess and Maude Collins began an affair, apparently without the objection of the now-deceased Frank Collins. Then, perhaps at the prompting of Bess's wife, the landlord declined

to renew his tenants' lease. Frank Collins thereupon accused Bess of raping his wife, to which Maude testified at trial. Their account must have
sounded unconvincing, because the jury deadlocked and Bess was released on a one thousand dollar bond. The prosecution won a conviction
at a second trial. Only a recommendation of mercy saved Bess from capital
punishment. His attorney wrote the governor that the jury believed him
innocent, but that one member spoke for them all when he said, "[T]he
black scoundrel should serve time for having relations with a white
woman." After Bess's conviction, blacks and whites who knew him appealed to the governor for clemency. Bess addressed humble letters to suc-
ceeding governors, but no one gave him a hearing. Bess seemed certain to
die a hard labor convict until Maude Collins's conversion.[41]

Governor John G. Richards, the official whom Walter White derided in
the Lowman case, immediately suspended Bess's sentence, and on May 12
he issued Bess a full pardon. The startling development caused a sensation
in the state's press. The *Columbia State* wrote, "As Governor Richards says,
'A grave injustice has been done this man.' " The *State* urged the legislature to compensate Bess for his four thousand days of hard labor and
raised six hundred dollars from its readers for him, a remarkable testimony
to the limits of racial hatred in South Carolina and perhaps a guilty reaction to the Lowman lynching. State officials even intimated they would
prosecute Maude Collins for perjury.[42]

Learning of this possibility, Maude Collins swore out a second affidavit
before an investigating detective. She had not committed perjury, she declared. She meant not to exonerate Ben Bess of guilt but only to forgive
him. According to the detective, Bess's friends had rewarded Collins upon
her first affidavit with a small sum of money. Faced with this surprising
turn of events, Governor Richards's agents persuaded Bess to return to
state prison until the matter could be sorted out. In July, Governor Richards revoked Bess's pardon. Bess was suddenly plunged back into the Kafkaesque nightmare from which he had fleetingly been released.[43]

At this point, attorney N. J. Frederick, who had defended the Lowman
family, appeared on behalf of Bess, seeking a writ of *habeas corpus.* He
collaborated with Bess's wife, who, despite her husband's infidelity, had
protested his earlier imprisonment and sought his release now as well.
Frederick thought he had an easy case and was confident of victory. An
unconditional pardon such as that issued by Governor Richards was irrev-
ocable. Bess had not consulted a lawyer before returning to prison, and his
detention was illegal. When a special master appointed by the governor
issued a report favorable to Bess, Frederick felt even more confident.[44]

So that he, a Negro, would not have to cross-examine Mrs. Collins personally, Frederick hired a white lawyer to do that job at the hearing. Despite this diplomatic tactic, Frederick lost the argument before Judge W. H. Townsend. He ruled that Collins did not fully understand her own statement in the first affidavit, that her statement had been induced by a fifty dollar payment from Bess's wife, and that the affidavit therefore had been obtained by fraud. Under that circumstance, the pardon could be revoked. The ruling, Frederick angrily related to NAACP headquarters, stood as "one of the most outrageous decisions I have ever read." If Collins had lied in the first deposition, Frederick fumed, why did the judge not conclude the second to be fraudulent also?[45]

In September, the NAACP board appropriated $250 to take Bess's case before the state supreme court. Condemned by Judge Townsend, the prisoner was remanded to state prison to serve out his sentence. A photograph after his defeat showed Bess under guard, dressed in a dark jacket and necktie, staring with a dazed look into the camera. At his side, Frederick, thin, earnest, and ebony-toned, wore a straw hat, glasses, a bow tie, and seersucker jacket. The papers clutched in his hand would need little revision when the case went to the South Carolina Supreme Court a year later.[46]

Ex parte Sallie Bess reversed the ruling of Judge Townsend. The supreme court met in a special "en banc" session in which the circuit court justices joined the court, voting 10–7 for Bess. "The general rule is that a pardon . . . cannot be revoked after its issuance, delivery and acceptance," the majority ruled. The exception was only if the pardon had been obtained by fraud, but that must be proven by a court, and the lower court had not ruled on that question; Townsend's sitting had been merely a *habeas corpus* decision. Ben Bess walked out of prison for a second time. As he had done with Sam Lowman, Frederick hustled his client out of state right away; Ben Bess went to Homestead, Pennsylvania.[47]

The Ben Bess case revived the Columbia branch, which slumped after the rush of energy generated by the Lowman lynching. Columbia signed up 129 new members in May 1929 and met its regular financial apportionment of $150. "I am sure that the NAACP will rejoice over the fact that again it has given real aid to one who has stood in need of its intelligent and vigorous assistance," Frederick wrote.[48] Without his and the branch's intervention, Ben Bess might have stayed in prison. The vote by the South Carolina Supreme Court reversed the lower court judge and the governor. It showed that in rare cases, respect for the law could trump the lie of a white woman falsely crying rape against an African American.

THE preceding narratives may strike the reader as a series of anecdotes showing that NAACP branches defended men falsely accused of rape. Taken alone, they prove nothing regarding the wider questions they inform. How pervasive was race discrimination in criminal justice during the 1920s? While a thorough examination of that issue is beyond the scope of this book, a closer examination is worthwhile. Because this chapter has discussed southern African Americans accused of rape in capital cases, let us turn to the available statistics on this problem.

The federal government did not compile statistics on capital punishment until 1930. Some states did, and some scholars have reconstructed the records of other states, adding in the number and race of people executed for rape. The following table shows data for twelve southern and border states and the District of Columbia. It indicates that African Americans were executed far out of proportion to their numbers. The numbers also demonstrate that rape was a capital offense only rarely for whites.

CAPITAL PUNISHMENT IN SOUTHERN AND BORDER STATES, 1920–1929 (NUMBER EXECUTED IN PARENTHESES)

State	Executions	White (rape)	African-American (rape)	African-American (% of population)	African-American (% executed)
Arkansas	36	10	26	26	72
Washington, D.C.	15	4	11 (1)	27	73
Florida	26	6 (1)	20 (4)	30	77
Georgia (1924–1929)	54	14 (1)	40 (5)	37	74
Kentucky	36	18	18 (3)	9	50
Maryland (1923–1929)	12	4	8 (3)	17	67
North Carolina	55	9 (2)	46 (12)	29	84
Oklahoma	14	8	6	7	43
South Carolina	37	9	26 (3)	46	72
Tennessee	27	11 (1)	16 (3)	18	59
Texas (1924–1929)	56	12 (3)	44 (10)	15	79
Virginia	45	4	41 (6)	27	91
West Virginia	24	13	11 (7)	7	46
TOTAL	437	122 (8)	313 (57)	≈ 25	72

SOURCE: Compiled from listings in William Bowers, *Legal Homicide: Death as Punishment in America* (1974; rept. Boston: Northeastern University Press, 1984), from appendix A, 399–523; U.S. Bureau of the Census, *Negroes in the United States, 1920–1932* (Washington, D.C.: Government Printing Office, 1935), 14, table 3. I have counted five men listed as "other" for race (probably Native Americans) as African-American.

The bottom line is unsettling. Of 437 executions in southern and border states, 313 of the executed were African-American. African Americans made up about 25 percent of the population and 72 percent of those executed. Almost three times as many blacks as whites were executed, but whites were four times as numerous, which means that blacks were executed about twelve times more often than whites. Damning as these statistics are, they probably understate the problem, because the states for which no statistics are available are Mississippi, Louisiana, and Alabama, which more closely resembled Georgia than West Virginia.

The table further shows that of the 122 white men executed, 8, or 7 percent of the total, were convicted rapists. Yet 57 of the 313 African Americans were charged with rape, or 18 percent of the total. Seven times as many African Americans were executed for rape as whites; whites were four times as numerous; thus blacks were executed for rape twenty-eight times more often than whites. Fewer than one white man a year was executed in the South for rape; five to six African Americans were executed annually in the South for rape.

How many of those African Americans executed were guilty? This is a subject for another volume. Yet, the narratives here suggest that many African Americans accused of rape were innocent and that many accused murderers acted in self-defense or were innocent. A study of death sentences imposed on convicted rapists in the South between 1945 and 1965 showed that 13 percent of black rapists were executed, and 2 percent of whites were. But the study also showed that the race of the alleged victim was the determining factor in who received the death penalty. Thirty-six percent of blacks convicted of raping whites got the death penalty; in only 2 percent of the other possible variants was the convicted man executed. The statistic strongly suggests that an African-American rapist of a white woman had to be insane to commit such a crime. Many others who were executed besides Maurice Mays, Bunyan Fleming, and Nathan Bard must have been innocent, too.[49]

IN A NOVEMBER 1929 article for the *Crisis*, NAACP special legal assistant William T. Andrews noted that Negroes suffered discrimination at every juncture of the legal system. They were more likely than whites to be arrested and had more charges brought against them. They were convicted on much less evidence. In southern states they were always excluded from juries, with rare exceptions, and in the North they were underrepresented. Once convicted, Negroes were less likely to be paroled or receive a suspended sentence. In prison, they were treated more harshly. The case of

Floridian Abe Washington showed the Association's determination to see that African Americans served on southern juries.[50]

Abe Washington committed a murder in December 1922 in Jacksonville, Florida. He was convicted and sentenced to hang the following year. Fortunately for Washington, Florida shortly afterward changed its method of execution to electrocution. His attorney protested that because Washington had been sentenced to hang, the state could not electrocute him. This diversionary tactic gained attorney S. D. McGill the time he needed to address the real problem that bothered him. Washington had been convicted by an all-white jury, like every other African American in the South.[51]

McGill wanted to change that, and he knew he would have to go to the U.S. Supreme Court to do so. He had no trouble convincing the NAACP Legal Committee and board of directors that he was raising a very important problem. James Weldon Johnson, Jacksonville native and one-time attorney, presented the matter to Louis Marshall. Marshall agreed to write Washington's reply brief to the Florida Supreme Court.[52]

McGill secured affidavits from two Duval County officials who affirmed that they had never summoned a Negro juror. The county's population was divided evenly between blacks and whites; many Negroes voted in Duval County, and many were qualified to serve on a jury. Yet, no Negroes had served for fifteen years on a jury in Duval County. These facts were not enough for the Florida State Supreme Court, which acknowledged their veracity but denied that they constituted race discrimination in Washington's specific case. Moreover, the issue had not been raised at trial. Marshall thought the language of the ruling was narrowly phrased, clearing the way for appeal to the U.S. high court on the substantive question.[53]

As the appeal made its way through the court, Duval County tacitly admitted that McGill had a point. The county called an African American to sit on a jury, but the prosecution promptly excluded him. Shortly afterward, a second African American was called and actually served. Change inched forward in Florida, step by step. Duval County yielded in practice if not in principle.[54]

The U.S. Supreme Court turned a blind eye to the problem, refusing to hear the NAACP appeal from the Florida court and giving no reason. Marshall and McGill both believed that public opinion drove judicial sentiment. Marshall's appeal to the Florida court arrived shortly after the execution of Massachusetts Italian-American anarchists Nicola Saco and Bartolomeo Vanzetti. Their case had taken seven years to reach its grim conclusion, and conservative public opinion was outraged by the delay.

Abe Washington's case was five years old, and twenty Florida men had gone to the electric chair since Washington was first convicted. Marshall thought it "extraordinary" that a southern Negro had avoided execution for five years. S. D. McGill appealed on his behalf for executive clemency, and Washington's sentence was commuted to a life term.[55]

24

"Never Let a Nigger Pick Up a Tool"

ON his way home from Haiti in 1920, James Weldon Johnson had to travel as a deck passenger with neither cabin nor bed. He was compelled to sleep on a bench in the smoking room, but even that was unavailable until midnight, when the white crewmen finished their dice game. Johnson unobtrusively overheard the conversation of the electricians and plumbers, an opportunity he had never previously enjoyed. He heard the same phrase repeated like a litany: "Never let a nigger pick up a tool. Never let a nigger pick up a tool."[1]

The phrase provides the Rosetta Stone of American working-class history. Several aspects of that history make it different from that of its European cousins: the presence of unlimited land along the frontier; the absence of a hereditary aristocracy; the immigrant sensibility of workmen who gradually assimililated their European identity into an American identity in two generations. But the most important difference between the American working class and the European working classes is that white American workers regarded themselves as a racial caste above benighted Negro slaves or workers. The outcasts were forever condemned to perform the menial chores, while they and their posterity would operate the machinery. This fundamental divide separates American history from European history. It explains why American workers never formed a labor party or were attracted to socialism, why they achieved a welfare state generations after Europeans did, and why they have weaker unions than those of European workers. White American workers are race-conscious first and class-conscious second.

Ever since Emancipation, millions of African Americans have had to deal with this conundrum. In 1920 they were overwhelmingly agricultural laborer or working class in their social composition, yet remained an undercaste within a class. White workers regarded black laborers as unfit to join their unions or otherwise associate with them. Herbert Hill, historian and NAACP labor director from 1948–1977, concluded in an essay on the racial policies of the American Federation of Labor (AFL) that "the great historic failure of organized labor lies in its tradition of racial discrimination."[2]

NAACP leaders grappled with this problem throughout the 1920s. They could do very little about it, but they were aware of its importance. Johnson, Du Bois, White, and Pickens had all raised themselves up from either poverty or working-class respectability. Their fathers had been, respectively, a headwaiter, unknown, a mailman, and a track laborer. None of them turned their back on their class background, no matter how well they dressed or how sophisticated they had become. The NAACP itself was born with the middle-class progressive movement and its critique of untrammeled corporate power. The whites on its board of directors were largely middle-class reformers oriented toward the working class: Mary White Ovington, Jane Addams, Florence Kelley, Clarence Darrow, John Haynes Holmes, Charles Edward Russell, and William English Walling all answered to this description. It is certainly true that local NAACP leaders, especially in industrial centers such as Detroit or Birmingham where capitalists hired African-American workers, favored cooperation with those employers rather than an impossible orientation to the white workers. Yet the Association's long-range orientation (which would not be realized until the birth of the Congress of Industrial Organizations in the 1930s) was toward the solidarity of black and white workers.

The NAACP worked toward this goal in the 1920s but achieved little success. Along with the Urban League and other leaders, they tried to hold the American Federation of Labor to their fraternal rhetoric. The NAACP supported A. Philip Randolph's Brotherhood of Sleeping Car Porters (BSCP), organized in 1925. Because few African-American workers had a union to represent them, the NAACP intervened on behalf of scores of workers who faced discrimination on the job. Finally, the NAACP contributed to the struggle for economic equality through the *Crisis*, in which Du Bois pondered the relation of black and white labor in the light of Marxist ideology.

DURING THE 1920s, African America began transforming itself from a rural southern agricultural population to a nationally distributed urban industrial one. By the end of the decade, 80 percent of the African-American population still lived in the South, but everyone noticed the new trend. From 1910 to 1930 the number of northern black workers more than doubled. There were half a million more black men working in the North in 1930 than in 1910. In 1930 African Americans had a higher employment rate than whites—59 percent to 47 percent for whites. More black women worked than did white women, and black people started work younger and kept working older than white people did.[3]

A survey of African-American nonagricultural occupations in order of the total employed shows that they worked at the most menial and lowest-paid jobs in 1930. By far the largest job category was domestic service, at which 1,174,000 black people, 84 percent of them women, were employed. Next came 228,000 hotel and restaurant workers, mostly porters, cleaners, and kitchen help, evenly divided by gender. In third place were 192,000 warehouse and retail employees: truck drivers, delivery men, and laborers. Other occupations were divided as follows: 181,000 men in the building trades; 177,000 in the iron, steel, and auto industries; 163,000 on the railroads; and 141,000 in miscellaneous manufacturing jobs. In ten fields, black workers predominated as a total percentage of the workforce: laundries, domestic service, turpentine industry, and fertilizer factories headed the list. In some southern states, African-American workers made up a majority of the longshoremen. Other industries that employed significant numbers of black workers included tobacco, coal, and meatpacking.[4]

The relation between black and white workers became a growing concern of the NAACP in the 1920s. The Association did not provide direct services to these workers because its ally, the Urban League, did. Founded in 1911 as part of the same progressive impulse as the NAACP, the Urban League was more the project of white philanthropists and social workers. It set for itself the task of educating newly urban migrants to the ways of the city, helping them secure housing, employment, and social services. Especially in the pre–New Deal era, the Urban League provided valuable services to thousands of African-American city dwellers. With a few exceptions, the Urban League's board members had had some connection to Booker T. Washington.

By the 1920s, the old tension between these former accommodationists and the militants was gone. Each group supported the other's goals. The Urban League depended almost entirely on philanthropists for money, and it did not seek to build a broad membership base, so the groups did not feel that they were rivals for money or members. The Urban League's African-American leaders included sociologists Eugene Kinckle Jones and Ira de Augustine Reid; Charles S. Johnson, who edited its monthly magazine, *Opportunity*; and T. Arnold Hill, director of industrial relations. NAACP leaders enjoyed collegial relations with them, especially in economic matters.

The Urban League's most important work in the 1920s was to convince employers to hire black workers. This was especially the task of T. Arnold Hill, who reminded employers that Negroes were hardworking employees, that it was in the national interest to ameliorate racial tensions by employing Negroes, and that a fair employment policy would yield a company more Negro consumers. The Urban League claimed it found jobs for forty thousand colored people annually in the 1920s, an impressive achievement.[5]

THE AMERICAN FEDERATION OF LABOR posed a big obstacle for African-American job seekers. The AFL organized skilled workers along narrow craft lines that did not represent all the employees in one industry. This meant that very few black workers enjoyed a contract arrived at by collective bargaining. At its origin, the AFL did adopt the racially inclusive policy of its predecessor, the Knights of Labor. However, as historian Herbert Hill concluded, "At the turn of the century, the American Federation of Labor had fully capitulated to a policy of chauvinism and discrimination against Negroes. . . ." The AFL had made its pact with the devil of race hatred.[6]

During the war and postwar years, African-American trade unionists and a few radical whites stepped into the vacuum left by the AFL. The Industrial Workers of the World (IWW) backed an organizing drive among black longshoremen on the East Coast, beginning in 1917. Ben Fletcher organized dockworkers in Baltimore and Philadelphia until he and other Wobblies were convicted and jailed under repressive wartime laws; Fletcher sat in the penitentiary until 1923. A. Philip Randolph, editor of the socialist *Messenger* magazine, agitated for Fletcher's release, and Du Bois hailed the effort in the *Crisis*.[7]

IWW workers struck the Great Southern Lumber Company in Bogalusa, Louisiana, in 1919. The company fired 250 men who signed union cards and sent a goon squad after Sol Dakus, an African-American organizer. In a gunfight, the thugs killed four white men who protected Dakus. Although the NAACP had nothing to do with these events, it published a pamphlet by Mary White Ovington, who wrote that the "white men who died in protecting a Negro in that lumber town, marked, let us dare to hope, the turning point in the history of southern labor."[8]

This hope was premature. The IWW men represented a small vanguard, soon to disappear. But militant black workers a few months later took their case to the floor of the AFL convention in Atlantic City. Twenty-three delegates representing segregated labor organizations put forward five resolutions decrying the federation's failure to represent black workers. The resolutions did not even challenge the lily-white practices of most white unions. The convention referred the resolutions to a committee that met their spirit halfway by recommending organizing drives among black workers. In the floor discussion, John Lacey, the African-American secretary of the Norfolk, Virginia, Labor Council, called on the delegates to remember the wartime contributions of Negro soldiers. He triggered an emotional response by white delegates. Swept away by Lacey's speech, forty delegates rose, one by one, pledging to open their rolls to black workers.[9]

The NAACP greeted this development with a cautiously optimistic statement. While noting the prior hostility toward black workers, the Association welcomed the new opening offered by AFL leaders. It urged Negroes to join AFL unions whenever possible and pointed out that equal treatment was the only way to preserve a fair standard of living for all workers. Colored labor should "go hundreds strong to the next meeting of the Federation."[10]

The convention's resolution on the matter was widely hailed in the African-American press, but the editors did not notice that the wording left wiggle room for lily-whites to keep to their old ways. For the next year, inertia reigned, and black delegates returned to the 1920 convention in Montreal determined to close the loopholes. This time debate focused on a challenge by Richmond freight handlers to the constitution of the railway clerks union. The organization committee tried to water down the freight handlers' resolution, but in floor debate the delegates voted to request the railway clerks to drop the "white-only" clause from their constitution. As historian Philip Foner noted, what lay behind the concerns of the white delegates was a fear that black workers might launch their own unions outside the AFL, accept lower wages than whites would, and drive them out of work. The AFL never made good on the resolutions of 1919 and 1920.[11]

In fact the railway clerks continued to keep the black freight handlers out of their union. By 1924, only fifty-one African-American locals were affiliated with the AFL, and most of these were small railroad lodges. The NAACP appealed to the federation to acknowledge the existing problem and take some action again that year. This initiative was probably motivated by the intransigence of the railroad brotherhoods at the Progressive Party convention and the ascension of William Green to the AFL presidency. Green had been a leader of the United Mine Workers, one of the few unions to accept black workers as members. The Association addressed an open letter to the federation, calling on it to match action to its rhetoric: "Is it not time for white unions to stop bluffing and for black workers to stop cutting off their noses to spite their faces?" it asked. The NAACP called for a meeting with the AFL and the railroad brotherhoods, but the entreaty fell upon deaf ears.[12]

IN the Jazz Age, the automobile was still an innovation and highways were poor. Most people and freight traveled on the rails; the national economy depended upon stable labor relations on the railroad. This gave railroad men bargaining power out of proportion to their numbers. White railroad men had very good jobs and expected to pass them on to their sons.

The most intransigent race exclusionists were to be found in the skilled trades among these aristocrats of labor. Historian Eric Arneson, in an essay on the racial attitudes of white railroad workers from 1880 to 1920, showed that these men believed Negroes incapable of operating railroad trains, because the work required mental skills and mechanical abilities that Negroes lacked. Arneson demonstrated that skilled white railroad men benefited economically by keeping black men in unskilled jobs, and psychologically by regarding themselves as a higher caste.[13] African-American railroad workers fought to maintain their slender foothold in the operating crafts, in the face of racist strikes, proposed changes in seniority rules, and new national legislation.

The census recorded that 163,000 African Americans worked on the railroad in 1930, 105,000 of whom worked in the South. These men worked overwhelmingly as track laborers (96,000) and Pullman porters (20,000), but 11,000 worked in the skilled operating crafts as firemen, brakemen, and even a few engineers. Others worked in the yards as switchmen.[14] Railroad firemen were essentially coal shovelers and engineer's assistants. Brakemen and switchmen held the most dangerous jobs, suffering crushed limbs or death if they miscalculated while coupling cars. Both these jobs were subordinate positions of indeterminate racial category, but they became more attractive to white railroaders during the postwar years.

In January 1919, two hundred white Memphis switchmen struck rather than work alongside African Americans, tying up freight and passenger service on the Illinois Central. The black workers were organized in a separate Colored Association of Railway Employees, led by J. H. Eiland. The whites insisted upon imposing a single seniority list for black and white workers, across crafts. The effect of this policy would be to drive the black workers from their jobs, because they would not be able to "bump" junior white men when work was reassigned. Eiland protested vigorously against this scheme to the Federal Railroad Administration (FRA). Memphis NAACP leader Robert Church Jr. and national secretary John Shillady joined him. The whites tied up the rail line for four days until the FRA agreed to adjudicate the dispute. A year later Eiland and Walter White argued the black workers' cause before the FRA and won a partial victory, including back pay for lost wages.[15]

Two years later a gang of white Mississippi railroad workers tried to drive African-American brakemen off their jobs by murdering them. One by one, four corpses turned up alongside the railroad tracks, one bearing a note that read, "Let this be a warning to all Negro brakemen." Others were beaten by armed whites who boarded their trains in the yards. Walter White demanded that the Interstate Commerce Commission or Justice Department investigate these crimes that the state authorities were ignoring. Bureacrats in both departments passed the buck on jurisdictional grounds. Eiland was not discouraged. The Illinois Central wanted to retain the Negro brakemen, and it set its own detectives to work. A few months later, U.S. marshals arrested two men and charged them with an assortment of crimes. Du Bois, disgusted by the boldness of the murderers, unleashed his anger in the *Crisis*. "In the fight against predatory capital, the railroad unions richly deserve defeat. They have been head and foot of a contemptible monopoly of labor. . . . They deserve to have their unions smashed."[16]

The railroad brotherhoods next tried to establish themselves as sole bargaining agents for all railroad workers in arbitration and mediation. They attempted to pass the Howell-Barkley bill, which would replace the wartime Railroad Labor Board with a board of adjustment composed of seven industry and seven labor representatives appointed by the president. Twenty-six African-American railroad labor leaders met in Chicago and issued a joint declaration against the bill. They pointed out that the lily-white brotherhoods did not represent them and would sell out their interests immediately; the black leaders wanted no change in a system that allowed them an appeal to federal authorities. Thomas D. Redd of Louisville and Thomas W. Driver of Little Rock, both NAACPers and railroad men, kept the national office abreast of the workers' protest.[17]

Southern African Americans lost five thousand laboring jobs on the railroads in the 1920s and a significant proportion of jobs in the operating crafts. They gained sixteen thousand laborer's jobs in the North, reflecting the general population trends and the greater track mileage in the North.[18] The efforts of black railroad workers in the early part of the decade helped set the stage for the first significant African-American trade union organization, A. Philip Randolph's Brotherhood of Sleeping Car Porters.

A. Philip Randolph was one of the most important African-American leaders of the mid–twentieth century. More than anyone else, Randolph understood that African Americans were an integral part of the working class and that to advance they must fight their way into the labor movement. He won the first contract for a major black union, caused President Franklin D. Roosevelt to establish the Equal Employment Opportunities Commission by threatening a march on Washington, and inspired the 1963 March on Washington.

Born in 1889, Randolph grew up the son of a poor preacher in Jacksonville, Florida. He came to New York in 1911, following in the footsteps of locally famous brothers James Weldon and Rosamond Johnson. Randolph booked passage on a steamboat with a friend, defraying the trip's expenses by washing dishes "until I got cramps on my fingers."[19]

In New York he got a job as a switchboard operator while attending City College at night. There he fell in with the campus radicals who championed the IWW strikes at the textile mills in Lawrence, Massachusetts, and Paterson, New Jersey. He became a Socialist; married Lucille Green, who had connections to the wealthy cosmetics queen C. J. Walker; and met Chandler Owen. In 1917 Randolph and Owen, who had been agitating on Harlem street corners, were asked by a leader of the New York Negro waiters' union to edit their magazine, the *Hotel Messenger*. The journal attracted to them a group of Harlem radicals, including Lovett Fort-Whiteman, Cyril V. Briggs, W. A. Domingo, Hubert Harrison, and Claude McKay. When the editors exposed internal union corruption, they were fired, and they rechristened the magazine as simply the *Messenger*.[20]

From 1917 until about 1924, the *Messenger* promoted racial equality, labor militance, political radicalism, and socialism. It welcomed the migration to the North, opposed World War I, and championed the Bolshevik revolution. Randolph and Owen became known around Harlem as "Lenin and Trotsky" and attacked the NAACP from the left.

As the wave of postwar radicalism subsided, the *Messenger* moderated its political stance. It moved away from IWW positions and toward the left wing of the organized labor movement. Randolph's attack on Garvey brought him into collaboration with the NAACP. The repressive nature of Lenin's Russia kept him from endorsing it with a blank check. After Coolidge won the election in 1924, Randolph realized how placid the public had become. He was maturing, but into a world that seemed to have no place for him.[21]

Then, everything changed for Randolph in a single day. On his way to the *Messenger* office at 2311 Seventh Avenue, an immigrant from St. Croix named Ashley Totten approached him. Totten was a Pullman porter. He had heard Randolph speak and had read the *Messenger*. Would Randolph give a speech to the porters? Randolph agreed; afterward Totten and his associates asked him to lead an organizing drive among the men. An employee in that role, Totten assured him, would be fired, as some already had been, and they needed an outsider to take charge.

Almost all the porters were African-American. They earned only $60 a month, and more in tips, but they regarded the tips as degrading. Porters often worked 100 hours a week, rarely qualified for overtime pay, had to buy their own uniforms, received inadequate pensions, and had a fake company union to represent them in shop floor disputes. The Brotherhood of Sleeping Car Porters called a meeting for August 25, 1925, at the Elks Hall on 129th Street in Harlem. To protect the five hundred participants from company spies, Randolph ran the meeting himself. The union would demand a monthly wage of $150, an end to tipping, a 240-hour work month, and compensation for work performed off the clock. The next day, two hundred porters joined the union.[22]

Randolph, Milton Webster in Chicago, C. L. Dellums in Oakland, and other organizers would have to work for twelve years before the Pullman Company signed a contract with them. The struggle tested the worth of every African-American institution. The Pullman Company bought off a number of African-American newspapers with advertising. The *Chicago Whip*, *Chicago Defender*, *St. Louis Argus*, and *Pittsburgh Courier*, among others, came down on the wrong side of the issue. Machine politicians such as Perry Howard and many prominent ministers joined the antiunion chorus, undercutting morale. When Randolph decided a strike would be risky in 1928, the Communists, who had done nothing to build the union, attacked him from the left.[23]

The NAACP, the National Association of Colored Women's Clubs, the Urban League, and the Pythian lodge stood with the union. The Garland Fund contributed ten thousand dollars to the cause. Robert Bagnall, in his travels around the country, gave inspiring speeches to the men. At the 1926 NAACP convention in Chicago, Pullman headquarters, the Association bestowed its Spingarn Medal on Randolph. The Brotherhood's "Committee of One Hundred" prominent supporters included Du Bois, Johnson, White, and board member Florence Kelley. When the porters first approached the company for negotiations, the NAACP acted as intermediary. The NAACP offered the Brotherhood steady support during its organizing drive.[24]

The *Crisis* gave the BSCP drive little coverage. This may have been because a long organizing drive generates little news, or because of a possible lingering antipathy between Randolph and Du Bois. They were passing each other heading in opposite ideological directions: Randolph, driven by the logic of his new responsibilities, had to moderate his political views and forge a relationship with leaders of the AFL. Du Bois was becoming more radical and would soon visit the Soviet Union. Yet, the important point about the relationship between the NAACP and the BSCP is that it was mutually supportive.[25]

Pullman porters marching. Courtesy of Chicago Historical Society.

THE TENSION between organized labor and black workers emerged again in Cleveland in 1927. During the summer, a suburban restaurateur hired about a dozen African-American workers to staff his modest establishment. Apparently a fair employer, he paid union scale and was willing to have the workers represented by the Hotel and Restaurant Employees Union. This white-only outfit not only refused to issue the workers a charter but also picketed the restaurant. The owner obtained an injunction barring the pickets, presumably on the grounds that neither he nor the employees were party to a dispute.[26]

Labor retaliated by proposing federal anti-injunction legislation. The Shipstead–La Guardia bill stipulated that "no court of the United States . . . shall have jurisdiction to issue any restraining order or injunction in a case involving . . . a labor dispute." The following March, Cleveland NAACP leader Harry E. Davis and novelist Charles Chesnutt testified against the bill before a Senate committee. While only federal employees would be affected by Shipstead–La Guardia, Davis protested that it would encourage states to pass similar legislation. With broader authority, state laws would leave Negro workers helpless against white pickets; employers therefore would be loathe to hire them. Davis and Chesnutt adduced as evidence for their claim the restaurant dispute and an affidavit by an electrician driven from his job by white union men.[27]

Davis and the Cleveland Chamber of Commerce prevailed upon the NAACP board to enter the fray. Davis came to New York to attend the April meeting, and set off a rare controversy. A few members, probably Charles Edward Russell and William English Walling, who worked with the AFL, objected that the bill would significantly aid the labor movement without unduly hurting colored workers. The board scheduled a special session to consider what stance to adopt. Moorfield Storey and Louis Marshall opposed the bill, and the Association issued a generally negative statement. As if to symbolize the relevance of this discussion, the Association received a complaint around this time from a New York Negro pipe fitter whose white union brother had punched him in the face without provocation. The Association called upon the heads of the state and national federation to discipline the man.[28]

This series of events caused Walling to seek a rapprochement between the AFL and the NAACP. He prevailed upon Green to meet Johnson, but nothing came of the proposal except a cordial exchange of letters. Instead, an AFL leader named John P. Frey delivered a provocative speech before a meeting of the Commission on Interracial Cooperation in Washington. Frey blamed the low Negro membership in the AFL on antiunion colored leaders. This brought an angry reply from Walter White in the *Nation*. White placed the blame on anti-Negro union leaders. Again playing conciliator, Walling reassured Frey and urged White to abjure public controversy with this strategic ally. White would not back down. Privately White wrote to a colleague that the "dishonesty, cowardice and downright viciousness of the AFL so far as Negro labor is concerned" had caused the feud. Du Bois blasted Frey in the *Crisis* as well. The AFL and the NAACP entered the depression at sword's point.[29]

IN THE ABSENCE OF trade union representation, the role of shop steward fell to the NAACP in African America. Annually, about a dozen or a score of appeals for help from workers suffering job discrimination came to the NAACP from postal employees. Because it was a federal job, they probably felt their employer might listen. White, the son of a mailman, addressed many letters to local postmasters on their behalf. In one typical incident, a Utica, New York, NAACPer wrote on behalf of her husband, who was ordered to work thirty-six hours straight at Christmastime; consequently he fell ill and was suspended for missing work. White went right to the top on this case, but Postmaster General Will Hayes accepted the Utica postmaster's decision. In another matter, Johnson interceded for an acquaintance, a twenty-five-year veteran of the Jacksonville post office, fired for collecting an unnecessary four cents "postage due" on a letter. The man got his job back but had to pay a one hundred dollar fine. Johnson was so incensed he issued a national press release on this obscure problem.[30]

The NAACP helped maritime stewards win a rare victory. Boats departing New York had once employed five hundred Negro stewards, but after the war the management replaced all but fifty of them with white men. Washington, D.C., NAACP leader Shelby Davidson joined a leader of the stewards in a protest before the U.S. Shipping Board. The agency ordered an end to race discrimination, and the men apparently regained their jobs.[31]

Sometimes the problems came from unions rather than employers. Late in 1929, an African-American upholsterer was kicked off a job when the union complained that the man didn't hold a union card. That was because the lily-white union didn't accept Negroes. When White wrote a polite letter of inquiry to an international vice president, the official wrote a bristling reply that each local admitted whomever it wished. White went over the bureaucrat's head to the state and national federation, threatening a lawsuit. The upholsterers' local quickly changed its tune. The Association cooperated in this matter with Frank Crosswaith, a leading African-American socialist.[32]

THE COUNTRY'S most serious natural disaster since the San Francisco earthquake struck the lower Mississippi Delta in the spring of 1927. After a rainy winter, the river rose, breaking down levees and overflowing its banks with the force of Niagara Falls. Over five hundred people were killed, a half million were left homeless, and a billion dollars' worth of property was destroyed. Rather than declare an emergency, President Coolidge and Congress left the relief effort to the Red Cross and the states.[33]

Most of those affected were African-American sharecroppers and tenant farmers. Reports varied about how they were treated in the refugee camps. The poet Langston Hughes, traveling in Louisiana, observed grossly unequal treatment of Negro refugees at Baton Rouge. Journalist Helen Boardman found similar circumstances at Vicksburg. By contrast, the treasurer of the Pine Bluff, Arkansas, NAACP reported that "never before have I seen the color line obliterated to the same extent." An African-American educator wrote that whites "had risked their lives in order to save colored people." In a disaster of such magnitude, which brings out the best and worst in people, both responses might be expected.[34]

Several African-American weeklies reported that one malicious practice in particular characterized the relief effort. State oficials, especially in Mississippi, posted armed guards around the African-American camps. Sharecroppers could leave only when the landlord came calling for his tenants.[35]

Late in May, White visited the Mississippi Delta to see if these rumors were true, and reported his findings in the *Nation*. White thought the treatment of Negroes was better than he expected in the relief camps. However, he verified the complaints about armed guards imprisoning tenant farmers. Moreover, while in the camps, black men were conscripted at gunpoint to rebuild the levees. White people did none of that work. Walter White complained to the Red Cross and Interior Secretary Herbert Hoover. Both promised to investigate and insure freedom of movement for the refugees. NAACP branches, like African Americans all over the country, contributed money to aid the flood victims. Many of the displaced sharecroppers left the South forever when the waters receded.[36]

A WORLD AWAY from the Mississippi Valley or the streets of Harlem, the Bolshevik Revolution was reshaping not only Russia but also the ideology of international socialism. By promising "Peace, Land, and Bread," the Bolsheviks gained popularity and in October 1917 seized power in a daring coup. Their revolution inspired radical socialists the world over to leave the Second International of mass parliamentary parties to follow their example.

Russian Communists also taught the world's radicals a lesson about oppressed nationalities. Unlike British or French socialists, who accepted their nation's imperialism, the Russians would grant self-determination to the peoples formerly oppressed by the czar. The Bolsheviks recruited Tatars, Latvians, Uzbeks, Armenians, Jews, and other non-Russians into their party. In Vladimir Ilyich Lenin's phrase, the revolution would liberate the "prison-house of nations" that was the old czarist empire.

Encouraged by the Russian Revolution, American Communists organized their new movement in 1919. These leftists could not agree among themselves on a variety of questions, so they formed two parties at first. Immigrant groups with their own foreign language newspapers made up a big disproportion of the American Communists. With Russian help, the squabbling radicals finally formed one party.[37]

The Communists inherited from the old Socialist Party a backward attitude toward what they called the "Negro question." At best, even radical socialist Eugene V. Debs argued that "there is no 'Negro problem' apart from the general labor problem." At worst, Victor Berger editorialized that "[t]here can be no doubt that the Negroes and mulattoes constitute a lower race." That was the range of opinion among American socialists.[38]

Like Communists in other lands, Americans journeyed to Moscow to meet with their new comrades and discuss the problems of their own country. The International established commissions to prepare resolutions on these issues, comprising delegates from several countries. At the Fourth Comintern Congress in 1922, Russian leaders forcefully called the attention of the Americans to the Negro question. The Negro commission included a Russian Jew; a Japanese; Otto Huiswood, a black man born in Suriname, now living in Harlem, and the first black American Communist; and Claude McKay, a Jamaican-born poet, now a Harlemite, and friend of James Weldon Johnson, who had helped pay his way to Moscow. The commission hammered out a broad resolution whose main purpose was to get the Americans to change their attitude and see the "Negro question" as central to the American Communist revolution.[39]

Meanwhile, other black activists began to consider Communism as their own ideology. Cyril Briggs, born on the island of Nevis but a Harlemite since 1905, launched the radical *Crusader* magazine and an organization, the African Blood Brotherhood, which fused black nationalism, socialism, and African diaspora themes. Most of its three thousand members existed only on paper, and it quickly dissolved. Briggs and his colleagues joined the Communists. With the exception of Lovett Fort-Whiteman, the new recruits were Caribbean-born.[40]

These black Communists saw the failure of the AFL to organize African-American workers and took that heroic task upon themselves. They launched an American Negro Labor Congress in 1925 in Chicago, with Fort-Whiteman at its head. Unfortunately, a majority-white audience showed up for the meeting. Just back from the Soviet Union, Fort-Whiteman appeared in a Russian outfit, and one of the speakers let the cat out of the bag by crying, "Long Live Communism!" from the podium. In the *Crisis*, Howard University economist Abram L. Harris Jr. raised a skeptical eye over the meeting's premise that black and white proletarian solidarity was on the American agenda. According to historian Mark Naison, this first clumsy effort to reach black workers "had something to offend virtually everyone in the black community." The organization stagnated, and the Communists let it drift into oblivion.[41]

For its part, the NAACP did not have an economic policy. It was a civil rights organization, and its members embraced widely varying economic ideas. Had it attempted to pronounce itself on the side of labor or capital, hard money or soft, protective tariffs or free trade, the organization would have broken apart. Communist critics of the NAACP, especially during the depression, failed to see that the NAACP was a united front of civil rights activists who differed on economic, political, religious, and other matters. The NAACP fought for an end to racial oppression, not class oppression. It was not a trade union, a producer's cooperative, or a benevolent society, but it did cooperate with these institutions of the African-American community.

The *Crisis* under Du Bois's editorship respected the limits of the organization's goals but nonetheless wrote about a wide range of matters. The *Crisis* was the organ of the NAACP, but it was also the expression of the Promethean mind of Dr. W. E. B. Du Bois, citizen of the world. Du Bois had regarded himself as a socialist since his student days in Germany. Russian Communism presented a new challenge. There was much about it that offended him. First, Du Bois had championed the Allied war effort, which radical socialists had opposed. Moreover, he was uncongenial to the anti-intellectual strictures of Lenin's democratic centralism. Du Bois was not religious, but he had a spiritual side that balked at the rigidly scientific dialectical materialism of Marxism. Beyond all that, he questioned Marxism's theory that the industrial proletariat was revolutionary. Du Bois knew white workers as a lynch mob waiting to happen.[42]

Du Bois was relentlessly curious and he reserved his judgments, but he expressed deep skepticism about another matter. The Negro group, he wrote, must reject class struggle within its own ranks. Negroes needed to develop their own banks, real estate companies, and insurance firms, or they would be left to the mercy of white exploiters. From time to time, the *Crisis* reported the accomplishments of Negro entrepreneurs, but it did this only spottily. Appearing favorably in its pages were a New Orleans baseball park owner, Chicago taxi fleet owners and bankers, Madame C. J. Walker's cosmetics empire, and North Carolina insurance men. In truth, the *Crisis* did not show much enthusiasm for these ventures. Du Bois was too much of a middle-class progressive to get excited about the achievements of businesspeople.[43]

Du Bois's skepticism about Communism did not prevent him from visiting the Soviet Union in 1926. He was approached that year by two Russians, "probably clandestine agents of the communist dictatorship," he later wrote. Their assignment was to interest liberal reformers in the USSR, and they paid for Du Bois's trip.[44]

The visit changed Du Bois's life forever. "I stand in astonishment and wonder at the revelation of Russia that has come to me," he wrote in the *Crisis*. "I may be partially deceived and half informed but if what I have seen with my eyes and heard with my ears is Bolshevism, I am a Bolshevik." It was Saul on the road to Damascus with the critical intelligence left intact. He visited five major cities and saw backwardness, desolation, and hope all mixed together. He began to take Marxism seriously. Like other African-American visitors, he must have been impressed by the meaninglessness of his skin color in this brave new world.[45] To Bolsheviks, black people were comrades, not outsiders.

Back in the United States, Du Bois spoke on "Russia and the Race Problem." He praised the Soviet nationalities policy, telling how he had seen books in thirty or forty languages roll off the presses for the country's newly literate readers. Communists did not force the Russian language on non-Russian speakers, and he contrasted this policy to the insensitive "Americanization" campaigns in postwar America, designed to strip immigrants of their heritage. Further, he was impressed by the anticolonial policy of Russia toward African and Asia, and the seriousness with which it regarded the struggles of Negro Americans. "The attitude of Russia on the race question within and without her boundaries is of tremendous significance to us," he concluded.[46]

William Pickens visited the USSR shortly after Du Bois returned. Lovett Fort-Whiteman invited Pickens to attend an anti-imperialist conference in Belgium, and the NAACP consented to this trip. The conference was postponed, and Pickens journeyed eastward through Germany and Russia. There he gave many speeches and met Leon Trotsky, hero of the October Revolution and enemy of Stalin. Although Pickens, too, wrote favorably of Russia on his return, he kept his distance from the Communist Party.[47]

From 1927 to 1929, the Russian situation changed. News of terrible famine and harsh repression made skeptics out of some wavering sympathizers. The situation in the Communist International changed, too. It was no longer the hotbed of ideas that was Lenin's international movement but the sinister instrument of Stalin that dictated policy to foreign sections.

At the Sixth Congress of the International, another Negro commission was established. The International leaders pressed forward the idea that black liberation was central to the tasks of American Communists. But the congress met in the context of the fight within the Russian party against "right deviation," and this faction fight carried over into the discussion on Negro work. The International theoreticians applied Soviet concepts on oppressed nationalities in a mechanical fashion to the United States. They concocted a schema that emphasized the right of southern Negroes to separate from the United States, as though Black Belt Alabama were Armenia. Among the American delegates, only Harry Haywood accepted this view with enthusiasm; four other African-American Communists, including Haywood's brother Otto Hall, wanted a more concrete civil rights agenda. The final draft also concluded that "Negro communists must explain to the Negro workers and peasants that only their close union with the white proletariat and joint struggle with them . . . can lead to their liberation. . . ." As one exasperated opponent of this idea observed, the mere fifty Negro American Communists would find it impossible to sell this back home. Ultimately, not even the American Communists could make much sense of this confusing document, and they largely ignored it. As the Trotskyist leader James P. Cannon wrote, the Communist Party made gains in the black community during the 1930s despite being yoked with this line, not because of it.[48]

Around the same time, Stalin decided that world capitalism had entered a fatal "Third Period" and had only a few more years to live. The depression that struck the United States gave some force to this idea. But Stalin adduced to it the notion that Communists must now strike out for power on their own. All non-Communist reformers were denounced as enemies and traitors. In the United States, the Communist Party lashed out at the NAACP as a bourgeois agent of imperialism. Following this line, they grabbed control of the Scottsboro boys case from the NAACP in 1931, and imposed ultraleft slogans and a sectarian defense policy on the case that almost got the defendants executed until the Communists changed their line. Du Bois saw this clearly in the early 1930s and attacked the Communists in the *Crisis*.[49]

It would be easy to dismiss the obscure polemics of the Communist Party regarding African Americans during the 1920s. Everything it did was disconnected from the real-life struggles of black Americans, and a tinge of the ridiculous infected all its activities. Yet, the Communist Party made one very important achievement between 1919 and 1929. It fundamentally and forever changed the attitude of white radicals toward African-American rights. They could now disregard the issue only at their peril. In the radical 1930s, the Communists marched boldly, if clumsily, into African America and won thousands of new converts where fifty had been before. Living African Americans had not seen its like; the attitude of white Communists had been matched previously only by the abolitionists. Meanwhile, the white pioneers of the NAACP began to die out as the Communists gathered strength and no new generation of white liberals joined them. After 1929, African Americans who wanted to belong to a militant interracial group now looked toward the Communist Party.

25

Poems and Novels; Jazz and Baseball

NEW stirrings of national consciousness give birth to new national cultures. A regeneration of commerce in Italy's Po Valley led to a Renaissance of classical Western civilization; the consolidation of the English nation produced a London audience that could understand Shakespeare; America declared its cultural independence from England in Ralph Waldo Emerson's Boston. For the emerging free nation of African America, Harlem was its Florence, London, and Boston. White modernists such as Ernest Hemingway or T. S. Eliot might feel disillusion after the World War and choose expatriation, but many African Americans felt the exuberance of their new, free black community in northern Manhattan and proudly called it their home. Like James Joyce's Stephen Dedalus in *A Portrait of the Artist as a Young Man*, African-American writers went forth to forge in the smithy of their souls the unrecreated conscience of their race. The *Crisis* published and encouraged these young writers. By doing so, the NAACP helped to create a common culture for the newly conscious nation of African America.

This chapter will examine the NAACP's relation to the new cultural movement. The *Crisis* played a central role in the early stage of the literary movement. It published, among others, the poets Claude McKay, Langston Hughes, Gwendolyn Bennett, and Countee Cullen, and prose writers Jean Toomer, Wallace Thurman, Arna Bontemps, and Zora Neale Hurston. W. E. B. Du Bois, James Weldon Johnson, Walter White, and *Crisis* literary editor Jessie Redmon Fauset all believed that the new writers would dismantle the stereotyped negative images of black people by creating mature, fully realized characters. Later in the decade, the *Crisis* criticized writers who portrayed a stereotyped Harlem full of cabarets and sin. The magazine's main cultural failure during the 1920s was to disregard jazz and the emerging Negro baseball leagues.

THE *Crisis* peaked in circulation and influence just after the World War. The monthly had begun as a modest venture that might have collapsed without NAACP backing. At its zenith in 1919, the magazine sold one hundred thousand subscriptions and in 1920 earned seventy-seven thousand dollars. Riding the crest of postwar radicalism, the *Crisis* became the political and literary voice of African America. The magazine functioned both as the Association's official organ and as Du Bois's personal magazine. As the editor put it in his autobiography *Dusk of Dawn*, "The Crisis would state openly the opinion of its editor, so long, of course, as that opinion was in general agreement with that of the organization."[1] The story of the Association's first decade is to a certain extent the working out of that compromise. So that it would not become an internal bulletin or news service, the NAACP established for a while a "branch bulletin" with suggestions on organizational matters, and a separate news service.

The *Crisis* was in part a literary magazine in its early years. Few African Americans had written prose with distinction by 1920, but the *Crisis* published stories by Charles Chesnutt, the leading black novelist of his day. In poetry, African Americans had a longer tradition, going back to Phillis Wheatley of Boston's Revolutionary War period, and recent practitioners such as Paul Laurence Dunbar and James Weldon Johnson had written lasting works. William Stanley Braithwaite, another Bostonian, edited the *Crisis*'s poetry selections. He favored writing that emphasized the commonality of human experience, preferring poems that reached for the timeless and universal.[2]

In 1919 Jessie Redmon Fauset came to New York to edit the magazine's literature. She wrote poetry, short stories, and novels and had a finely developed sense of each form. Fauset was born in 1882 in Camden, New Jersey; her father was a minister. The large family lived in genteel poverty, and Fauset persevered through the Philadelphia public schools to graduate from Girls' High. As an undergraduate at Cornell, she sent Du Bois a fan letter upon his publication of *The Souls of Black Folk*, thus initiating a literary correspondence. Because the Philadelphia public schools did not hire Negro teachers, she taught French at Washington's segregated but prestigious M Street High School. Her language skills and reliability were invaluable to Du Bois during the Pan-African Congress, upon which she ably reported in the *Crisis*.[3]

As editors, Fauset and Du Bois wanted to create a new Negro literature that they hoped would break down the stereotypes of the Negro created by white novelists. The Negro had thus far appeared either as a saint (Uncle Tom), a foil (Jim in *Huckleberry Finn*), a buffoon (Jim Crow, or Tambo and Bones in minstrelsy) or, more recently, as a beast (the rapist in

Birth of a Nation). The *Crisis* editors wanted a new literature featuring accomplished, literate, middle-class people like themselves. No such writing had yet crossed over to find a white readership. At first, they eschewed propaganda, but later in the decade Du Bois, perhaps under the impact of the Russian Revolution, began to insist upon it.

Fauset and Du Bois chose literary contributors who created out of their experience as African Americans. With its leading role in African America, the *Crisis* began forging a canon of work that reflected the New Negro's pride and national consciousness. Yet, Du Bois and Fauset insisted upon the essential Americanness of their identity. As Fauset put it, the middle-class characters she invented were "not so vastly different from any other American, just distinctive." That is, she was a cultural pluralist, not an assimilationist. Du Bois had expressed this point of view as early as *The Souls of Black Folk* in 1903. As the literary critic George Hutchinson argued, "In its cultural criticism, [the *Crisis*] continually hammered home the point that whatever was most American, culturally speaking, had an African-American origin." Indeed, African Americans, except for the native peoples, are the only Americans who have no particular place to go "home" to; in this sense they are more American than Anglo-Saxons.[4]

Using these cultural guidelines, Fauset published a stunning array of emerging poets and writers. As Langston Hughes noted, Fauset and a few others "midwifed the so-called New Negro literature into being. Kind and critical—but not too critical for the young—they nursed us along until our books were born." The Missouri-born Hughes dedicated "The Negro Speaks of Rivers" to Du Bois; it appeared during 1921 in the *Crisis*. Hughes linked the Negro who "heard the singing of the Mississippi when Abe Lincoln went down to New Orleans" with the Negro who "built my hut near the Congo." Countee Cullen was the adopted son of Reverend Frederick Asbury Cullen, a Harlem minister and New York NAACP partisan. His thematic material was less self-consciously African-American than that of Hughes; much of it did not reveal the race of the author. There was no mistaking the nationalism of Claude McKay, whose "If We Must Die" called his people to violent self-defense during the Red Summer of 1919. Although it was first published in Max Eastman's *Liberator*, Fauset would recognize it as a carefully crafted sonnet in the best English tradition, and she published other McKay poems. Another Renaissance standout to appear in the *Crisis* was Fauset's friend Gwendolyn Bennett, who exclaimed in "To Usward": "We claim no part with racial dearth / We want to sing the songs of birth!" As editor, Fauset introduced these New Negro writers to a national audience.[5]

As a group, the short story writers who appeared in the *Crisis* were less

Crisis cover celebrating the 20th anniversary of the NAACP. Courtesy of NAACP.

distinguished than the poets. In separate, thoughtful discussions of the magazine's contributions to literature, critics Arnold Rampersad and George Hutchinson ignore the short stories, with the exception of Fauset's own. The magazine did award Rudolph Fisher its prize in 1925 for "City of Refuge." This monitory tale tells of King Solomon Gillis, who runs away to Harlem after shooting a white man in North Carolina. King Solomon speaks in dialect, naively takes Harlem to be a safe haven, and is tricked in a confidence game that costs him his freedom. There is nothing uplifting about this story, and its selection shows that NAACP literary mandarins were less than strict in their standards.[6]

In 1925, the literary movement took a new turn as the young writers coaxed by the *Crisis* began to find their own voices and new venues for publication. The most important of these was *Opportunity*, the Urban League's monthly, edited by Charles S. Johnson. *Opportunity* sponsored an awards banquet in May 1925 and thereafter attracted the leading writers. Its distinguished interracial panels judged literary works in five different categories and awarded a $470 prize to each winner. Three hundred and sixteen hopefuls and their guests attended the banquet. The winners made up the roster of stars for the next few years and included Hughes and Cullen in poetry; E. Franklin Frazier and Sterling Brown in essay; and Zora Neale Hurston and Eric Walrond in short story. Hughes's poem "The Weary Blues" was an ode to an archetypal jazz pianist—a subject out of the range of acceptability for the uptight Du Bois. The *Crisis* had lost leadership of the movement to a younger, hipper, less "politically correct" crowd.[7]

That same year *Survey Graphic*, edited by Paul U. Kellogg, brought out a special number titled "Harlem: Mecca of the New Negro." Kellogg secured Alain Locke, a Howard University philosophy professor, to edit the special edition, which was later expanded and published as a book titled *The New Negro*. Locke was a latter-day Du Bois—twenty years younger as well as Harvard-, Oxford-, and Berlin-educated—but he had an aesthetic sensibility where Du Bois had an ethical sensibility. He shared, however, the NAACP view that art was important in shaping a new nation. His introductory essay declared that "Harlem has the same role to play for the New Negro as Dublin has had for the New Ireland or Prague for the New Czechoslovakia." Like Du Bois and Fauset, he was a cultural pluralist who saw the distinctive contribution African Americans could make to American life and letters. The classic collection chose the outstanding and representative writers who make up the first African-American canon. James Weldon Johnson, Fauset, White, and Du Bois all contributed to this inclusive volume that fairly represented the diverse panoply of New Negro writers.[8]

Taken together, these two events—the *Opportunity* awards banquet and the publication of *The New Negro*—showed the emergence of the new writers before a wider and whiter reading public. Yet, they also signaled that the *Crisis* and elder statesman Du Bois would not be able to dictate cultural tastes to the younger generation. New intellectual centers—the Urban League and Howard University—would also have their say. Meanwhile, the *Crisis* reported in May 1925 that its priorities would shift to labor, politics, education, art, and other matters. Next month the magazine featured a Du Bois–inspired little theater group, the Krigwa Players, and announced its own literary awards, underwritten by Amy Spingarn, Joel's wife. Du Bois reported neither the *Opportunity* banquet nor *The New Negro*'s publication. Literary Harlem threatened to polarize into two camps, each viewing the other with skepticism or contempt.[9]

In 1926 the *Crisis* ran a symposium on "The Negro in Art," asking writers to respond to seven questions regarding the relation between literature and propaganda. The final query defined the nub of the controversy. "Is there not a real danger that young colored writers will be tempted to follow the popular trend in portraying Negro characters in the underworld rather than seeking to paint the truth about themselves and their own social class?" Most respondents did not entertain the same worries that preoccupied the *Crisis* editors. Carl Van Vechten, in fact, was ready to celebrate the "underworld." "The squalor of Negro life," he enthused, "the vice of Negro life, offer a wealth of erotic, picturesque material to the artist." The next month Langston Hughes offered the most characteristic response— that writers should write as they pleased without regard to the concerns of others. Only the prim Jessie Fauset responded affirmatively, citing "the grave danger making for a literary insincerity both insidious and abominable."[10]

The publication of Van Vechten's *Nigger Heaven* the following year threw a bombshell onto the literary battlefield. Van Vechten, a former *New York Times* music critic and writer, had been the most enthusiastic white promoter of Negro writers, including White and James Weldon Johnson. White and wife Gladys had shepherded him about the Harlem party scene, and Van Vechten soon brought along his friends. His novel's provocative title referred to the segregated balcony section of movie theaters; the story suggested that Harlem was to Manhattan what the balcony was to the main floor. Here Van Vechten unfolded a plot of lust, avarice, jealousy, and revenge—in effect, a prose Italian opera. According to historian David Levering Lewis, NAACP staff member Richetta Randolph spoke for 90 percent of the race when she reacted to the sordid tale with disgust. The novel purported to show that the happy inhabitants of *Nigger Heaven* were the pimps, gamblers, and drinkers who remained true to their inner selves, while the pretenders to respectability suffered the same discontents as the repressed denizens of "civilization" everywhere.[11]

Van Vechten's almost forgotten melodrama is more important for the critical reaction to it than for its content. Du Bois's review was unsparing. "Carl Van Vechten's *Nigger Heaven* is a blow in the face," he began and concluded that "life to him is just one damned orgy after another, with hate, hurt, gin and sadism." He condemned it as trashy detective fiction. Walter White and James Weldon Johnson defended their literary friend; Johnson later called it a "fine novel." Novelists Nella Larsen, Charles Chesnutt, Charles Johnson, Langston Hughes, and *Messenger* writer George Schuyler accepted it as a naturalistic slice of life. Most white critics liked it; *Nigger Heaven* confirmed their image of Harlem as a jungle. But the real problem with the book, from Du Bois's point of view, was that it sold so well. This fact was not lost on the aspiring African-American poets and novelists who thought they could do better. If they did not all share Van Vechten's perspective on Negro life, they at least were determined to write about the common people, who had their vices, spoke in dialect, and sometimes acted on foolish impulses.[12]

The younger writers declared their independence in a new quarterly called *Fire!*, edited by Wallace Thurman and inspired by Van Vechten. Thurman had come to Harlem after a stint working alongside Arna Bontemps in the Los Angeles post office; in New York he worked at the *Messenger* and then at a liberal white monthly. Hughes, Zora Neale Hurston, Richard Bruce Nugent, and even Fauset's friend Gwendolyn Bennett contributed to the new but short-lived journal. One of Thurman's short stories, "Cordelia the Crude," featured a prostitute as a main character; Richard Bruce Nugent's "Smoke, Lilies, and Jade" celebrated homosexual lust. Du Bois restrained his contempt for the baser instincts so provocatively displayed on its pages.[13]

After his trip to Russia, Du Bois became more convinced that Negro literature should adhere to his standards. He gave a speech at the Chicago NAACP convention that he printed in the *Crisis*, calling on the young artists to paint positive images of their people. He justified the attention the *Crisis* paid to literature because good literature was part of the struggle to transform the country. Negroes were not just fighting for their rights, he asserted, but they also wanted to be themselves in a better country. Thus, he concluded, "all art is propaganda and ever must be, despite the wailing of the purists." Two years later, when Claude McKay's naturalistic *Home to*

Harlem appeared, Du Bois damned it as a product of Van Vechten's influence. The book "nauseates me," he wrote, "and after the dirtier parts of its filth I feel distinctly like taking a bath." Yet, he acknowledged McKay's earlier work and urged him to return to the higher self that he felt Van Vechten had corrupted. A wide-ranging essay on "Our Negro Intellectuals" by Allison Davis in the August 1928 issue attacked George Schuyler, Eugene Gordon, and even James Weldon Johnson and Langston Hughes for introducing jazz themes into their poetry.[14]

The younger writers struck back. Where Du Bois saw the evil influence of the white libertine Van Vechten, they saw the influence of the puritanical, minister-laden NAACP board of directors. The devilishly tongued Zora Neale Hurston, one of the best writers of the period, whose stories and novels recreated the lives of the poor, rural, and illiterate, joked about the restraining influence of white "Negrotarians" and "Niggerati" in the camp of the prudes. Hughes continued to publish in the *Crisis*, but he viewed the enforcement of a party line with disdain.

The debates of the Jazz Age continued among later generations of scholars. They discussed interracialism among the 1920s writers and the significance of the Renaissance itself. Because several African-American writers protested the influence of whites in their rivals' camp, some critics concluded that the literary movement failed because of white influence. Scholars Harold Cruse, Nathan Irvin Huggins, and to a lesser extent David Levering Lewis stress the movement's limitations. In contrast, George Hutchinson argues that the debates of the 1920s mask the essential dynamic of the literary movement. Both African-American writers and their white colleagues, Hutchinson submits, felt themselves to be part of the modernist movement that owed much to John Dewey's pragmatism and to the American cultural nationalism of Ralph Waldo Emerson and Walt Whitman. The Harlem Renaissance was concentrated in New York, he insists, not solely because of the predominance of Harlem in African America but also because New York's ethnically heterogeneous literary scene was receptive to black writers. Without the synergy between Greenwich Village and Harlem, the literary Renaissance would have been less geographically concentrated. The white writers, Hutchinson argues, mostly urged their African-American colleagues to write from their own experience, which was the same advice they gave everyone. By setting the Harlem Renaissance in a wider context and longer time frame, Hutchinson concludes that the achievements of the period lasted longer and had greater influence than the skeptics admit.[15]

While the literary historians' observations are intriguing, they take us beyond the bounds of the current investigation. There do remain some wider questions regarding the NAACP and the cultural movement. How useful was all the interracial socializing in Harlem and downtown? To what extent were the NAACP leaders wise to vest so much hope in culture as a tool to break down racial prejudice? Should the *Crisis* have participated so vigorously on one side of a cultural debate? What about the omission of popular culture, especially jazz and baseball, from its pages?

The NAACP leaders consciously encouraged interracial socializing as a way to break down stereotypes and secure more access to publishing houses for aspiring African-American writers. For them, this was an important aspect of their strategy to further the civil rights movement by promoting Negro culture. Walter White in particular played the role of go-between for blacks and whites, a role for which he was uniquely qualified. In bipolar American race calibrations, he was a "white" man, yet Negroes accepted him as one of their own because he felt himself to be Negro. Thus the apartment he and wife Gladys shared at 409 Edgecombe Avenue atop Sugar Hill in Harlem became the scene of frequent integrated cocktail parties. Writers newly arrived in town came to the Whites for aid and comfort; their friends included Countee Cullen, Rudolph Fisher, Nella Larsen, Claude McKay, Dorothy West, and Hale Woodruff, according to Lewis. His connections among white editors and intellectuals included Heywood Broun, V. F. Calverton, John Dewey, Sinclair Lewis, Dorothy Parker, and Van Vechten.[16]

From the perspective of the twenty-first century, it might be easy to dismiss the image of White and Johnson sipping cocktails with the literati as evidence of their disloyalty to African-American authenticity. Such a view would be ahistorical. American social mores prohibited such mixing in the 1920s, and it did not occur in a noticeable fashion until the NAACP-ers initiated it. As late as 1908, southern newspapers scandalized liberal New York society by publicizing a private interracial dinner at the Cosmopolitan Club. Mary White Ovington later titled one of her memoirs *Black and White Sat Down Together.* If the title sounds a little patronizing to the twenty-first-century ear, it is only because enough has changed in a hundred years so that Americans have forgotten how subversive that dinner was. Certainly, Jim Crow practices in America were not about to succumb to a round of literary banquets, but it is also true that broader social changes begin with the actions of vanguards.

How important was art to the civil rights movement? The answer to this question is a bit more complicated. On one hand, the *Crisis* editors showed that they were committed to bringing African Americans together through the medium of literature. Classic stories do produce a common cultural language through which a people find and identify themselves—every people needs its Dante, Shakespeare, Hugo, Goethe, or Twain to make itself into a nation. In this sense, the *Crisis* contributed to the moderate black nationalism that characterized the 1920s and the NAACP itself. Yet, editor Du Bois overestimated the role of literature in changing society. During the 1920s, the *Crisis* increasingly became a literary magazine. The covers became more artistic, imaginative, and universal than focused on concrete problems. African art and African-American beauties appeared on the covers, but neither Pullman porters, sharecroppers, nor unjustly accused criminal defendants graced the front page. As the decade wore on, the covers and content suggested that the NAACP's magazine had become a journal of the arts, not of a political movement.

Du Bois's visibility in the literary debates is also worth reconsideration. It did make sense that he as an individual intellectual would have something to say about the direction of the Negro arts. Yet, the political wisdom of lending the NAACP's imprimatur to one side of a literary debate is doubtful. The Association's purpose might have been better served if the *Crisis* had commented more dispassionately on the inclinations of the new writers, and courted them as political allies rather than engaged them as literary adversaries. The *Crisis* literary symposium showed that Du Boisian notions of "uplift" propaganda were in a distinct minority. None of the respondents, African-American or white, fell into line.[17] The effect of its loaded questioning was to drive away from the NAACP an individualistic aggregation of writers whose friendship might have benefited the movement.

Finally, it is worth noting that the literary Renaissance was not the only significant cultural activity of African America during the 1920s. In fact, far larger crowds were flocking to hear the new jazz music that African Americans created in the 1920s; its sound and spirit gave the decade a name that stuck: the Jazz Age. Black people were also filling the grandstands at baseball parks across the country to cheer on their favorite athletes of the Negro leagues. Du Bois, wedded to High Art principles of culture, did not report these developments. This was his most significant omission as *Crisis* editor, and it was fraught with irony: the very phenomenon he wished the Harlem Renaissance would produce—a distinctively African-American art that would help transform white American attitudes toward Negroes—unfolded before his eyes and he did not see it.

Moreover, the omission of jazz and baseball from the *Crisis* contributed to a later historiographic problem. Partly because the *Crisis* is such a source of knowledge about the 1920s, historians have focused on the Harlem-based writers, and downplayed the musicians and athletes who had a much wider following. The Harlem Renaissance drew writers from around the country to the big city. In contrast, jazz and baseball could be played everywhere. The *Crisis* focused attention on Harlem to the detriment of jazz centers such as New Orleans and Chicago, or baseball meccas such as Kansas City and Pittsburgh.

PREDICTABLY, the younger African-American writers never cashed in on Harlem's notoriety as Carl Van Vechten did. In fact, the Harlem prose writers of the 1920s did not create a character who lasted in the American imagination. Yet, it is hard to imagine the characters who came later and *did* last—Richard Wright's Bigger Thomas, James Baldwin's Rufus and Ida Scott, Ralph Ellison's unidentified Invisible Man, Toni Morrison's "Beloved," or Alice Walker's Celie—without the writers of the 1920s. They all owe something to the encouragement given by the NAACP to the young writers of the Harlem Renaissance.

The NAACP writers were neither assimilationist nor white-oriented. They helped fashion a self-conscious New Negro nation by imagining what it might look like in their prose, and by showing how white hostility stifled its potential. Whatever their personal failings as creative writers, they, along with their contemporaries, such as Langston Hughes or Zora Neale Hurston, prepared the way for later writers from Richard Wright to Toni Morrison and others yet to come.

Despite the *Crisis*'s shortcomings in reporting popular culture, the NAACP made important contributions to creating the new African-American nationalism of the 1920s. This sentiment was neither separatist nor assimilationist but pluralist: African Americans would define themselves in their own way, insisting on their distinct nationality in cultural expression, but on their fundamental Americanism as well. NAACP leaders asserted their moderate nationalism as writers themselves, and through the *Crisis*. The territory that they staked out corresponded to what most African Americans felt; that is why their organization survived while others collapsed. Moreover, their orientation has lasted and shaped mainstream American culture down to the present. Americans of the twenty-first century are all proud of their ethnic heritage in part because of the stand taken by NAACP leaders of the 1920s.

26

"The Hounds of God Howling in His Hills"

N June of 1928, Johnson, White, Du Bois, and other New York NAACP leaders set out by train for their annual convention, this time in the major city farthest from their headquarters: Los Angeles. Pickens had already spent the month before the convention in southern California, speaking at sixty meetings attended by thousands of people, many of them students.[1] "Nowhere else in the world is there such a stretch of endless avenue bordered with flowers and palms and doll houses," Du Bois exulted in the *Crisis*. Despite the enticements of the California sun, the delegates actually showed up for the daytime sessions, and at night six thousand supporters packed the Shrine Temple. Conventioneers were domiciled at the Somerville Hotel, owned by the NAACP leaders of the same name. Du Bois, expecting a fleabag, was overjoyed to discover a magnificent modern lobby and dining room adorned with Moorish arches.[2] The convention site and preponderance of California delegates showed that the NAACP had become a national organization. "In 1921, there was not a [California] town with fifty adult Negroes that did not have a branch," Mary White Ovington reminisced about a trip through the San Joaquin Valley that took her from El Centro to Stockton and down the coast from the Bay Area to San Diego.[3] By 1928, many of those branches had come and gone, but Los Angeles was now among the most vigorous in the nation. Los Angeles raised over four thousand dollars for the national office in 1926 and canvassed for five thousand members the following year. Branch president Dr. Claude Hudson, Beatrice Thompson, Mrs. J. M. Scott (who won the branch-building award in 1926), and attorney E. Burton Ceruti had fought for years to integrate the city's beaches, pools, and public facilities.[4]

As in Los Angeles, the northern California branch consistently carried out national campaigns under the leadership of its female activists. Mrs. Hattie H. E. De Hart mobilized the women to sign up twelve hundred members in the East Bay in 1924 and raised two thousand dollars in 1925 from a relatively small black population. A few years later, a self-interested out-group maneuvered to take over the leadership and caused a spate of factionalism. De Hart accused two attorneys of doing nothing to build the branch for years and then bringing in their allies to contest an election. The attorneys proved sore losers and wrangled over the balloting, but Reverend David R. Wallace defeated what De Hart called a "mean, selfish plot" by the attorneys to enhance their legal practice through NAACP leadership.[5]

Across the Bay, San Francisco African Americans insisted on forming their own branch. Only four thousand of them inhabited a city of six hundred thousand, yet landlords often refused to rent them apartments. The new NAACPers put a stop to a familiar plan by realtors to seal black renters off in a ghetto. Later in the decade they raised five hundred dollars to defend Edward Glass against extradition to Oklahoma. As in Oakland, the women raised money through the "popular baby" contest, and San Francisco maintained a spot on the branch honor roll throughout the decade.[6]

African Americans made up only about 2 percent of San Diego's one hundred thousand people. In the early 1920s, the branch divided over whether to purchase a separate recreational facility for young people when whites refused to rent them a building. Johnson wrote that he did not object to Negro groups securing their own property for Negro use only, but that this was not a proper use of money or time for a civil rights organization. The branch split, and national office loyalists objected when Du Bois gave a private lecture on Russia to the split-off group. Afterward, Viola Johnson led the loyal group in an energetic action campaign. They got the San Diego police to remove "white-only" signs from businesses and a YMCA pool, they ended the singing of insulting songs at the Logan School, and they saw to the prosecution of whites who abused Negro maids financially or sexually. As in other California branches, female leaders played an important role at the local level.[7]

ONE OF THE MAJOR TOPICS at Los Angeles was the upcoming presidential election. This time the energy that had followed La Follette in 1924 flowed around New York governor Al Smith. A Catholic and a "wet" of polyglot immigrant descent who was perceived as an Irishman, his very candidacy struck a blow at intolerance. NAACP leaders had already taken a serious look at Smith. Board member Charles Studin had enticed White to return from his European fellowship to join Smith's campaign. New York social worker Belle Moskowitz, an early NAACP supporter, arranged an interview for White at the governor's mansion with the Happy Warrior. White drafted a statement on civil rights for Smith, but he failed to issue it. The same failure of liberal nerve that had transpired with La Follette repeated itself with Smith. Once again, a southern vice presidential candidate warned against losing the Solid South, already in rebellion over Smith's religion and liberalism. The negotiations between Smith and White broke down.[8]

Beyond the disinterest of Smith and Republican candidate Herbert Hoover in civil rights matters lay the fundamental question of Negro disfranchisement and its wider effect on American democracy. Du Bois spoke on this subject at Los Angeles, and the *Crisis* ran two articles on it subsequently. Du Bois showed that southern states, in their determination to disfranchise Negroes, inevitably disfranchised poor whites as well. In the worst five southern states, 82 to 92 percent of age-eligible voters did not vote. In South Carolina, the worst state, fewer than 10,000 voters cast a ballot for each congressman, but in New Mexico, over 105,000 votes were cast in each congressional district. In Louisiana, a state with almost a million potential voters, 274,592 whites and 980 Negroes registered to vote in 1924.[9] Faced with this situation, the NAACP worked with Massachusetts congressman George Tinkham during 1929 to pass a bill that would reduce the representation of states that disfranchised its voters, in accordance with the provisions of the Fourteenth Amendment. As everyone knew, such gestures were merely symbolic.

James Weldon Johnson told the *Chicago Whip* that Smith had promised nothing to them and that Negro voters would probably choose Republican Herbert Hoover out of inertia.[10] Smith did cobble together a group of black supporters who campaigned for him in Boston, New York, and Chicago. Some African-American weeklies shifted over to Smith, among them the *Chicago Defender, Baltimore Afro-American, Boston Guardian,* and *Norfolk Journal and Guide.* Both candidates pandered to the white South, and Du Bois joined a group who called on both candidates to appoint southern Negroes to office if elected. In the October *Crisis,* Du Bois, his rapier wit undiminished with age, printed a blank space under a heading that promised to tell what Smith and Hoover said about Negro rights. He called for a vote for socialist Norman Thomas. On election day, Smith won an estimated 17 percent of the Negro vote in Philadelphia and 25 percent in Cleveland, Chicago, and Harlem. Predictably, Du Bois concluded in the *Crisis* about Smith and rival Herbert Hoover that "it does not matter a tinker's damn which of these gentlemen succeed." The trend of 1924 had continued, but the majority of Negro voters, as Johnson had predicted, stayed Republican.[11]

AT ITS TWENTIETH ANNIVERSARY convention in Cleveland, the Association's veteran leaders put the movement's accomplishments in perspective. No civil rights progress appeared imminent, and the NAACP was in a reactive rather than proactive mode. The founding leaders emphasized that long-term changes are not accomplished quickly. In the summer of 1929, stock market prices and volume trading rose spectacularly, and no NAACPer could imagine the depression that would change the landscape of American politics, and especially its racial politics, in the coming decade.[12]

In fact, Edwin R. Embree, the president of the Julius Rosenwald Fund, recounted the not insubstantial gains made by African Americans over the preceding decades. Negroes owned two billion dollars' worth of property, and seven hundred thousand owned their own homes. Over two hundred thousand Negroes owned farms and another seventy thousand ran a business. Seventy-three Negro-owned banks handled over one hundred million dollars in business. In education, black Americans now boasted four genuine universities in Howard, Fisk, Atlanta, and the merged New Orleans colleges. Over forty-eight thousand Negroes worked as teachers. This, Embree could rightly say, was unthinkable fifty years earlier.

Mary White Ovington pointed out that the NAACP's progress was due in large part to the work of its women. For twenty years she had encouraged female leaders to step forward, and that work was beginning to bear fruit. Mary Talbert, she reminded the audience, had started the work of women within the movement in a big way. "Mrs. Talbert laid down her life for us," she declared. "There is no question that her illness came because of her untiring efforts against lynching." In the next decade, Pittsburgh's Daisy Lampkin would pick up where Talbert and Addie Hunton had left off in the 1920s.

Du Bois also cast a retrospective glance in a speech titled "What the NAACP Has Meant in American Life." At its founding, the NAACP was denounced by its conservative opponents as a "bitter" and "radical" group. Now, its very respectability testified to its progress. There had been seventy-eight lynchings in the year of its birth and eleven in the last year. Only one school in the world, Atlanta, offered a course on the Negro in 1909. It was still a question in 1909 whether Negroes would vote at all; but now they were beginning to vote in the South and were getting elected in the North. The main task, he concluded, still lay ahead. "The significance of what we have done is not so much the advancement made as the foundation we have begun to lay." While the NAACP did not claim all the credit for Negro advancement, it could certainly be proud of its record. "[W]e started it," he insisted. "We kept it up. We were the hounds of God howling in His hills, and we had to be heard."[13]

The 1929 convention did indeed mark a milestone for the Association, just as 1929 did in American life. An era of prosperity and irresponsibility came to a close with the October stock market crash, and over the following decade Americans would learn that prosperity did not depend solely on an unchecked market. The NAACP began a complicated leadership transition that would bring it into alliance with liberal New Dealers and militant labor activists.

By some cosmic magic, the old leaders of the NAACP began to die off in the fall. Before 1929 was out, the board of directors would note the passing of journalist Paul Kennaday, who had faithfully attended board meetings for years, and Charles Bentley, the Chicago dentist and founding member of the Niagara movement. The most notable deaths, occurring in quick succession, were those of Moorfield Storey and Louis Marshall. Along with the brothers Spingarn, Marshall had symbolized the special relationship between African Americans and Jews during the 1920s. White and Ovington went to Boston for Storey's memorial meeting in King's Chapel; it was a gathering of old reformers and the pride of the city's legal community. Du Bois penned a fitting tribute to the man who had crafted the Association's first legal victories and given the movement his wisdom, prestige and money. "The inheritor of the finest abolitionist traditions, Mr. Storey throughout his long life held faithfully to the high ideals that justice and opportunity should know no color line. . . . The name of Moorfield Storey for this and generations to come will be treasured and revered by all men of all races who love liberty."[14]

Unfortunately, Storey's name, like those of other civil rights pioneers of the early twentieth century, was quickly forgotten as a new generation of radicals raised broader questions about American life, government, and race relations. A background question for the NAACP in the 1920s—how African-Americans were oppressed economically—was pushed to the foreground as the economy collapsed. Communists under the ideological sway of Stalin's Comintern stepped onto the stage that the NAACP had occupied and attempted to shove the old reformers off. In the Scottsboro case of nine African-American youths falsely accused of rape, the Communists wrested the defense away from the NAACP. By noisily linking their anticapitalist rhetoric to a defense case that had nothing to do with the politics of the accused, by postulating a nonexistent alliance between black and white workers, and by denouncing the NAACP and other supporters of the defendants as bourgeois obstructionists, the Communists bungled a case that the NAACP knew how to win. The NAACP had already brought to a successful conclusion the Arkansas, Ossian Sweet, Luther Collins, Ben Bess, and other cases similar to Scottsboro, but in the new radical world of the depression, the NAACP was caught off guard. The real line of the civil rights movement naturally flowed through an organization devoted solely to civil rights, not through a Communist Party whose repressive Stalinist baggage had little purchase on African Americans. The radicalism of the 1930s has caused the NAACP leaders of the 1920s—Johnson, White, Ovington, Storey, Pickens, Bagnall, Talbert, Hunton, and the others—with the exception of Du Bois, to be wrongly forgotten.

Further reasons for the lapse of historical memory include the accident of Du Bois's longevity and the messy leadership transition that the NAACP effected in 1929. The Association had been held together at the very top during the 1920s by the relation among Johnson, Du Bois, and White. Johnson was one of the few men whom Du Bois respected as an equal. By the end of the twenties, Johnson's political focus began to fade. His health had been poor, he had to take leaves of absence more and more frequently, and in 1929 the board gave him a year off to fulfill a Rosenwald Fund grant for creative writing. In September, the board assigned White as acting secretary. Johnson never returned, taking a teaching position at Fisk, which he held until his untimely death in a 1938 automobile accident.

That left White and Du Bois as the leading figures in the Association. Ovington later retired as chairman of the board, to be replaced by Joel Spingarn, but the real leadership had long been exercised by the staff. Du Bois and White had had little contact with each other because Johnson's solid figure restrained their mutual distrust. White saw Du Bois as a gifted but flawed freelancer whose restless intellect made him unsuitable to edit the organization's magazine. Du Bois saw White as a bureaucrat lacking the intellectual depth to think about the complicated new problems posed by changing times.

While there was surely some truth to each man's perception of the other, each seriously underestimated the other's enduring strengths. Du Bois's developing perception that the Association's goals would not be met in the short run led him to argue that Negroes should put more effort into building their own separate institutions. Also, his study of Marxism convinced him that the NAACP was ill equipped to address the broader problem of the Negro's oppression as part of the working class. For the rest of his career he would juggle the ideas of black nationalism and socialism. After airing them in the *Crisis* in the early 1930s, Du Bois left the Association in 1934 for Atlanta University. He wrote for the next twenty-nine years as an independent gadfly and as a figure in the Communist Party orbit. His uncompromising stance led him to the margin of American politics, an inspired prophet always out of step with the mainstream. Hounded by witch-hunters during the 1950s, he died in Ghana on the eve of the 1963 March on Washington, a forgotten figure whose rightful place in American history is only now being recovered.[15]

Walter White led the Association until his death in 1955. He lived long enough to see the 1954 Supreme Court decision that overturned school segregation. White gave a lifetime in pursuit of this triumph, yet no one in American life associates his name with it. The NAACP fought a series of rearguard actions during the 1930s, during which time its influence receded. But White maneuvered the Association toward the strategic alliance that underlies American liberalism to this day. With the emergence of the Congress of Industrial Organizations in the 1930s, White forged an agreement with progressive labor leaders such as Walter Reuther of the United Auto Workers, literally calling African-American strikebreakers out of the auto plants through a bullhorn. In politics he made special friends of Eleanor Roosevelt and Harry Truman. The labor–African American–liberal alliance, so consistently sought by the NAACP during its early years, began to take shape during the New Deal and triumphed with the modern civil rights movement. In part because this new alliance was compromised by the cold war witch-hunt, its centrality has been downplayed in popular memory. And Walter White—a man of mixed "racial" identity whose "blackness" he constructed as a boy during the Atlanta race riot—has served poorly as a historical protagonist in an American society overly concerned with racial authenticity.

If their names have been forgotten, the work of the early NAACPers endured. Whatever their strategic disagreements or personal failings, they all shared a vision of a desegregated America in which African Americans retained their unique identity and participated fully in American life. A new generation of leaders came forward in the 1950s and 1960s to realize their dream. Between the Los Angeles and Cleveland NAACP conventions, in January 1929, the first Atlanta NAACP branch president, A. D. Williams, became a grandfather. His daughter had given birth to the child who would become Dr. Martin Luther King Jr. We will all profit by learning not only his story but also that of his political antecedents.

Abbreviations

All correspondence is from the Papers of the NAACP, microfilm edition, unless otherwise noted. The collection is divided into Parts, each of which contains many reels. Researchers may consult the excellent finding aid to this collection for the approximate frame number. The minutes of the NAACP board of directors are in Part 1, reel 1, up to 1925, and continue on reel 2. I have not repeated this location in the endnotes.

Correspondence in the Papers of the NAACP, Library of Congress (LC), Washington, is noted by box number and file name. Branch files are arranged alphabetically and by date within each box.

ABS	Arthur B. Spingarn
JWJ	James Weldon Johnson
MWO	Mary White Ovington
RWB	Robert Wellington Bagnall
WEBD	William Edward Burghardt Du Bois
WFW	Walter Francis White
WP	William Pickens

Notes

NOTES TO CHAPTER 1

1. James Weldon Johnson, *Along This Way: The Autobiography of James Weldon Johnson*, (1933; rept. New York: Viking Press, 1968), 337–38.

2. David Levering Lewis, *W. E. B. Du Bois: Biography of a Race 1868–1919* (New York: Henry Holt, 1993), 552–57.

3. John Hope Franklin, *From Slavery to Freedom: A History of Negro Americans, 3d ed.* (New York: Alfred A. Knopf, 1967), 456–76.

4. Lewis, *Biography of a Race*, 564.

5. *Crisis*, December 1918, 61; *Crisis*, January 1919, 110–12; Lewis, *Biography of a Race*, 569–74. Unless noted otherwise, all subsequent note citations for this chapter are from 1919.

6. *Crisis*, May, 18–23; June, 63–67; W. E. B. Du Bois, *Dusk of Dawn* (1940; rept. New Brunswick, N.J.: Transaction Publishers, 1994), 262–63.

7. *New York Age*, February 22, 1; *New York Times*, February 18, 1; Lewis, *When Harlem Was in Vogue* (New York: Oxford University Press, 1979), 3–5.

8. *Crisis*, January, 119–21; *Crisis*, February, 163–65; Lewis, *Biography of a Race*, 574–76.

9. Minutes, Board of Directors, February, Part 1, reel 1 Papers of the NAACP (microfilm). Further citations from NAACP Papers are microfilm edition unless otherwise noted. Board of directors meetings are on this reel through 1924, and on reel 2 from 1925 through 1929. Dickson D. Bruce Jr., *Archibald H. Grimké: Portrait of a Black Independent* (Baton Rouge: Louisiana State University Press, 1993), 235.

10. *Crisis*, May, 7–9; NAACP board minutes, May, NAACP Papers.

11. *Crisis*, May, 13–14.

12. Robert L. Zangrando, *The NAACP Crusade against Lynching, 1909–1950* (Philadelphia: Temple University Press, 1980), 35.

13. Charles Flint Kellogg, *NAACP: A History of the National Association for the Advancement of Colored People*, vol. I, *1909–1920* (Baltimore: Johns Hopkins University Press, 1967), 234.

14. William B. Hixson, *Moorfield Storey and the Abolitionist Tradition* (New York: Oxford University Press, 1972), is the best biography of Storey. Zangrando, *Lynching*, 41, 46–50.

15. Storey to Shillady, January 10, Part 1, reel 24, NAACP Papers.

16. Storey to Shillady, March 15, 29, April 26, Part 1, reel 24, NAACP Papers.

17. *New York Age*, May 10, 1; *New York Times*, May 6, 15; Shillady to Storey, March 18, 21, 28, Part 1, reel 26, NAACP Papers.

18. Storey to George W. Wickersham, March 21, 1921, Part 1, reel 26, NAACP Papers.

19. *New York Age*, May 10, 2.

20. Mary White Ovington, "Early Impressions," in *Black and White Sat Down To-*

gether: The Reminiscences of an NAACP Founder, ed. Ralph E. Luker (New York: Feminist Press, 1995), 3–6.

21. NAACP convention proceedings, June 1919, Part 1, reel 8, NAACP Papers.

22. MWO, "How Texas Mobbed John Shillady," in *Black and White*, 90.

NOTES TO CHAPTER 2

1. Among some recent studies of the new migrant communities are Peter Gottlieb, *Making Their Own Way: Southern Blacks' Migration to Pittsburgh, 1916–1930* (Urbana: University of Illinois Press, 1987); James R. Grossman, *Land of Hope: Chicago, Black Southerners, and the Great Migration* (Chicago: University of Chicago Press, 1991); Florette Henri, *Black Migration: Movement North, 1900–1920: The Road from Myth to Man* (Garden City, N.Y.: Anchor Books, 1976, direct quote 63; Kenneth L. Kusmer, *A Ghetto Takes Shape: Black Cleveland, 1870–1930* (Urbana: University of Illinois Press, 1978); Joe William Trotter Jr., *Black Milwaukee: The Making of an Industrial Proletariat, 1915–1945* (Urbana: University of Illinois Press, 1988); Trotter, *The Great Migration in Historical Perspective* (Bloomington: Indiana University Press, 1991).

2. Henri, *Black Migration*, quotes 56, 58; Roi Ottley, *The Lonely Warrior: The Life and Times of Robert S. Abbott* (Chicago: Henry Regnery, 1955).

3. Henri, *Black Migration*, 69–80; U.S. Bureau of the Census, *Negroes in the United States, 1920–1932* (Washington, D.C.: Government Printing Office, 1935), chapter II, 3, 55.

4. Earl Lewis, "Expectations, Economic Opportunities, and Life in the Industrial Age: Black Migration to Norfolk, Virginia 1910–1945," in Trotter, *Great Migration*, 22–23; Bureau of the Census, *Negroes*, 55.

5. In addition to works cited earlier, see also Trotter, "Introduction: Black Migration in Historical Perspective, A Review of the Literature," in Henri, *Black Migration*, 1–21; and such works as Robin D. G. Kelley, *Hammer and Hoe: Alabama Communists during the Great Depression* (Chapel Hill, N.C.: University of North Carolina Press, 1990).

6. Bureau of the Census, *Negroes*, 3.

7. Arthur I. Waskow, *From Race Riot to Sit-In, 1919 and the 1960s: A Study in the Connections between Conflict and Violence* (Garden City, N.Y.: Doubleday, 1967), 13–16.

8. JWJ, *Along This Way*, 338–41; JWJ to Shillady, May 18; JWJ to MWO, May 23, Part 1, reel 16, NAACP Papers.

9. Constance McLaughlin Green, *The Secret City: A History of Race Relations in the Nation's Capital* (Princeton: Princeton University Press, 1967), 184–98.

10. *Crisis*, September, 241–43; JWJ to MWO, August 20, Part 1, reel 16, NAACP Papers.

11. JWJ, *Along This Way*, 343; JWJ to MWO, August 20, Part 1, reel 16, NAACP Papers.

12. Walter Francis White to JWJ, January 17 and 20; WFW to Shillady, January 17 and 21, Part 1, reel 25, NAACP Papers.

13. Typescript report by WFW, February 3, Part 1, reel 25, NAACP Papers.

14. Memorandum from WFW, March 18; WFW to Shillady, May 22, May 29; WFW to MWO, July 30, Part 1, reel 25, NAACP Papers.

15. William L. Tuttle Jr., *Race Riot: Chicago in the Red Summer of 1919* (1970; rept. Urbana: University of Illinois Press, 1996), 3–11, 32–65.

16. WFW to MWO, August 7, 11, 13, Part 1, reel 25, NAACP Papers; WFW, "Chicago and Its Eight Reasons," *Crisis*, October 293–95.

17. Tuttle, *Race Riot*, 108–56; WFW, "Chicago," *Crisis*, 293.

18. Tuttle, *Race Riot*, 184–207; WFW to MWO, August 7, Part 1, reel 25, NAACP Papers.

19. Tuttle, *Race Riot*, 157–83; WFW, "Chicago," *Crisis*, 293–95.

20. WFW to MWO, August 11, 13, Part 1, reel 25; WFW, *A Man Called White: The Autobiography of Walter White* (New York: Viking Press, 1948), 45–46.

21. Board minutes, September 1919, NAACP Papers; *Crisis*, October, 297–98.

22. MWO, *The Walls Came Tumbling Down* (New York: Arno Press, 1969), 166; Waskow, *From Race Riot to Sit-In*, 17–20; *Topeka Plaindealer*, July 25, in NAACP anti-lynching file, Part 7 A, reel 19.

23. Stephen A. Reich, "Soldiers of Democracy: Black Texans and the Fight for Citizenship, 1917–1921," *Journal of American History* 82, no. 4 (March 1996): 1,478–1,504.

24. June 5 deposition of Mrs. Carrie B. Barrett; P. A. Williams to Shillady, June 6; Austin branch charter; Austin branch file, NAACP Papers, Library of Congress, Washington, D.C.

25. MWO, *Walls*, 171–75; MWO, "How Texas Mobbed John Shillady," 88–93; *New York Age*, August 30, 1.

26. *New York Age*, August 30, 1; *New York Times*, August 23, 10; Herbert J. Seligmann, "The Press Abets the Mob," *Nation*, October 4, 460.

27. *New York Times*, August 23, 10, August 25, 2; *New York Age*, September 6; MWO, *Walls*, 174.

28. MWO, "How Texas Mobbed John R. Shillady," *New York Times*, August 23, 10 and August 25, 2.

29. MWO, *Walls*, 175; JWJ, *Along This Way*, 343.

30. *New York Age*, September 6 and 13.

31. Storey to MWO, September 6, Part 1, reel 25, NAACP Papers; Reich, "Soldiers of Democracy," 1,500–1,501.

32. Arthur B. Spingarn, "Oral History Interview," Oral History Collection, Butler Library, Columbia University, 62–63; MWO, *Walls*, 147.

33. David R. McMahon, "The Origins of the NAACP in Omaha and Lincoln, Nebraska, 1913–1926" (master's thesis, Creighton University, 1993).

34. Waskow, *From Race Riot to Sit-In*, 110–20; *Chicago Defender*, October 4, 1919, 1.

35. Board minutes, March 10, 1919, NAACP Papers.

36. *New York Age*, June 14, 1; Ralph Ginsburg, *One Hundred Years of Lynching* (Baltimore: Black Classic Press, 1988), 120–21.

37. *New York Age*, July 5, 1919.

38. *New York Age*, June 4, 1; *Chicago Defender*, April 5, 1919; *Chicago Defender*, January 3, 1920, 1.

39. *New York Age*, June 4, 1919, 4; *Chicago Defender*, August 2, 1919, 20.

NOTES TO CHAPTER 3

1. Louis R. Harlan, *Booker T. Washington: The Making of a Black Leader, 1856–1901* (London: Oxford University Press, 1972), quotes 218; August Meier, *Negro Thought in America 1880–1915: Racial Ideologies in the Age of Booker T. Washington* (Ann Arbor: University of Michigan Press, 1968).

2. Harlan, *Booker T. Washington: The Wizard of Tuskegee, 1901–1915* (London: Oxford University Press, 1983); Ann J. Lane, *The Brownsville Affair: National Crisis and Black Reaction* (Port Washington, N.Y.: National University Publications, Kennikat Press, 1971).

3. Stephen R. Fox, *The Guardian of Boston: William Monroe Trotter* (New York: Atheneum, 1970); for an earlier civil rights organization, see Emma Lou Thornbrough, "The National Afro-American League, 1887–1908," *Journal of Southern History* (November 1961): 494–512.

4. James M. McPherson, *The Abolitionist Legacy: From Reconstruction to the NAACP* (Princeton: Princeton University Press, 1975); Kellogg, *NAACP*, 9–19.

5. MWO, "The NAACP Begins," in *Black and White*, 3–55, direct quote 55.

6. Carolyn Wedin, *Inheritors of the Spirit: Mary White Ovington and the Founding of the NAACP* (New York: John Wiley and Sons, 1998).

7. Daniel Walter Cryer, "Mary White Ovington and the Rise of the NAACP" (Ph.D. diss., University of Minnesota, 1977), 367.

8. Kellogg, *NAACP*, 19–44.

9. WEBD, *The Autobiography of W. E. B. Du Bois* (1968; rept. New York: International Publishers, 1988), 257. A good deal of Kellogg's *NAACP* covers the intramural struggles within the board over the *Crisis*. The indispensable work now is Lewis, *Biography of a Race*, 466–500, for the early years of the *Crisis*.

10. Kellogg, *NAACP*, 44–51; Lewis, *Biography of a Race*, 408–24.

11. Kellogg, *NAACP*.

12. Ibid., 18–19.

13. WEBD to JWJ, December 18, 1914, February 1, 1915, April 2, 1915, in Series I, Box 6, File 136, JWJ Papers, Beinecke Library, Yale University; Oswald Garrison Villard to Robert Lansing, September 3, 1915, Part 11 B, reel 8, NAACP Papers.

14. JWJ, *Along This Way*, 308–9; WEBD to JWJ, November 1, 1916, Series I, Box 6, File 136, JWJ Papers.

15. Bernard Eisenberg, "James Weldon Johnson and the NAACP 1916–1934" (Ph.D. diss., Columbia University, 1968), 30–34.

16. JWJ, *Along This Way*, 317–44.

17. Elliott Rudwick, *Race Riot at East St. Louis, July 2, 1917* (New York: Atheneum, 1972); NAACP statement, "To the People of New York," in Herbert Aptheker, *A Documentary History of the Negro People in the United States*, vol. III (New York: Carol Publishing Group, 1993), 181–83.

18. Robert V. Haynes, *A Night of Violence: The Houston Riot of 1917* (Baton Rouge: Louisiana State University Press, 1976).

19. Liva Baker, *The Justice from Beacon Hill: The Life and Times of Oliver Wendell Holmes* (New York: Harper Collins, 1991), 482–83.

20. Baker, *Holmes*, 497–500; Kellogg, *NAACP*, 183–85.

21. Kellogg, *NAACP*, 89–92.

22. Derived from board attendance, 1920, in board minutes, Part 1, reel 1, NAACP Papers.

23. Lewis, *W. E. B. Du Bois: The Fight for Equality and the American Century, 1919–1963* (New York: Henry Holt, 2000), 35–36 for Du Bois; A. Lee Beaty et al. to NAACP, May 6, 1920, Box G-155, NAACP-LC; Board minutes, October 1921, and WEBD to William Pickens, March 28, 1921, in reel 1, William Pickens Papers, Schomburg Institute.

24. Arthur B. Spingarn, "Reminiscences of Arthur B. Spingarn," interview by Thomas F. Hogan, in Columbia Oral History Collection, Butler Library, Columbia University.

25. B. Joyce Ross, *J. E. Spingarn and the Rise of the NAACP, 1911–1939*, (New York: Atheneum, 1972), esp. 104–20; *Crisis*, February 1930, 63.

26. Branch secretary's report, April 1924, Part 1, reel 1, NAACP Papers; Hasia R. Diner, *In the Almost Promised Land: American Jews and Blacks, 1915–1935* (1977; rept. Baltimore: Johns Hopkins University Press, 1995); Lewis, "Shortcuts to the Mainstream: Afro-American and Jewish Notables in the 1920s and 1930s," in *Jews in Black Perspectives: A Dialogue*, ed. by Joseph R. Washington Jr. (Lanham, Md.: University Press of America, 1989), 83–97.

NOTES TO CHAPTER 4

1. Robert Wellington Bagnall to JWJ, February 6, 1919, Part 1, reel 15, NAACP Papers; Kellogg, *NAACP*, 202.

2. Theodore Kornweibel, "Robert W. Bagnall," in *Dictionary of American Negro Biography*, ed. Rayford W. Logan and Michael R. Winston (New York: W. W. Norton, 1983),

20–21; Bernice Dutrieulle Shelton, "Robert Wellington Bagnall," *Crisis* 50, no. 11 (November 1943): 334.

3. Undated correspondence, "Suggestions Concerning a Fuller Organization of the NAACP," by RWB; RWB to MWO, November 11, 1919, Part 1, reel 16, NAACP Papers.

4. RWB to JWJ, July 31, August 20, 1919, Part 1, reel 16, NAACP Papers.

5. RWB to JWJ, August 20, September 4, 1919; RWB to MWO, December 27, 1919, Part 1, reel 16, NAACP Papers.

6. Lillian S. Williams, "Mary Morris Talbert," in *Dictionary of American Negro Biography*, 1,095–99.

7. Mary B. Talbert to John R. Shillady, December 23, 1918; Talbert to JWJ, December 29, 1918, Part 1, reel 24, NAACP Papers; Steven A. Reich, "Soldiers of Democracy," 1,478–1,504.

8. Reich, "Soldiers of Democracy," 1,490.

9. Reich, "Soldiers of Democracy," 1,490; Mary Talbert to RWB, September 22, 1921, Part 1, reel 25, NAACP Papers.

10. Mary Talbert to JWJ, March 14, May 16, June 10, 1919, Part 1, reel 25, NAACP Papers; New York *Age*, October 11, 1919, 1.

11. Addie W. Hunton and Kathryn M. Johnson, *Two Colored Women with the American Expeditionary Forces*, ed. Adele Logan Alexander (1920; rept. New York: Simon and Schuster Macmillan, 1997); Susie King Taylor, *Reminiscences of My Life in Camp* (1902; rept. New York: Arno Press, 1968).

12. Jessie Carney Smith, ed., "Addie W. Hunton," in *Notable Black American Women*, Detroit: Gale Research, 1992, 536–40; MWO, *Portraits in Color* (New York: Viking Press, 1927).

13. Emmett J. Scott, *Scott's Official History of the American Negro in the World War* (1919; rept. New York: Arno Press and the New York Times, 1969), Alice Dunbar-Nelson quoted on 375.

14. Hunton and Johnson, *Two Colored Women*, 9–17.

15. Hunton and Johnson, *Two Colored Women*, 28–85, quote 153; *New York Age*, July 5, 1919, 1.

16. Adele Logan Alexander, introduction to *Two Colored Women*, by Hunton and Johnson, xvii.

17. Rudy McEnglish to Addie Waite Hunton, July 4, 1921, Part 1, reel 16, NAACP Papers.

18. Secretary's report, June 1920, Part 1, reel 4; Addie Hunton to MWO, October 22, 1920; Report of January 3 to February 7, 1923, by Addie Hunton, Part 1, reel 16, NAACP Papers.

19. Direct quote in secretary's report, June 1923, Part 1, reel 4; Report for February 1923, Part 1, reel 16, NAACP Papers.

20. WP, *Bursting Bonds: The Heir of Slaves: The Autobiography of a "New Negro"* (1923; rept. Bloomington: Indiana University Press, 1991), 3–17.

21. Ibid., 49–75.

22. Ibid., 79–95.

23. Ibid., 121–41.

24. Pickens, *Bursting Bonds*, 121–41; Sheldon Avery, *Up From Washington: William Pickens and the Negro Struggle for Equality 1900–1954* (Newark, Del: University of Delaware Press, 1988).

25. Pickens, *Bursting Bonds*, 215–25; James Weldon Johnson, "Views and Reviews," *New York Age*, May 17, 1919, 4.

26. Secretary's reports, April, May, June 1923, Part 1, reel 4, NAACP Papers.

27. Herbert Hill, interview by author, December 9, 1997.

28. Avery, *Pickens*, 9.

NOTES TO CHAPTER 5

1. *Boston Globe*, October 2 and 3, 1919, 1; *New York Times*, October 2, 1919, 1, October 3, 1919, 6; *Louisville Courier*, October 2, 1919, 2, October 3 and 4, 1919, 1; *Birmingham Age Herald*, October 2, 3, and 4, 1919, 1.; *New Orleans Times-Picayune*, October 2 and 3, 1919, 1. Unless noted otherwise, all subsequent note citations for this chapter are from 1919.

2. *Boston Globe*, October 6 and 7, 1.; *Louisville Courier*, October 6 and 7, 1; *New Orleans Times-Picayune*, October 6 and 7, 1; *Birmingham Age Herald*, October 6, 1; *New York Times*, October 4, 5, and 8, 1.

3. Richard C. Cortner, *A Mob Intent on Death: The NAACP and the Arkansas Riot Cases* (Middletown, Conn.: Wesleyan University Press, 1988), 25–26; WFW, *A Man Called White*, 47.

4. Bob Church to WFW, October 6, Accessions Box M76-358, Arthur I. Waskow Papers, Wisconsin State Historical Society. Hereafter, material in this collection is from the accessions box unless otherwise noted. Branch Charter; O. H. McGowan to Oswald Garrison Villard, July 20, 1918; George Johnson to NAACP, August 21, 1918; WFW to O. H. McGowan, September 3, 1918; WFW to J. H. McConico, October 8, 1918, all in Little Rock branch file, Part 12 A, reel 4, NAACP Papers (microfilm).

5. Cortner, *Mob Intent*, 25–28.

6. Joey McCary, "The Red Scare in Arkansas," *Arkansas Historical Quarterly* (Autumn 1978): 264–78.

7. Unnamed secretary for Governor Brough to W. A. McElroy, October 7, Box 19, Helena file, Waskow Papers.

8. WFW, *A Man Called White*, 49–50.

9. Telegram from WFW to JWJ, October 13, Waskow Papers; WFW, *A Man Called White*, 50–51; Herbert Hill, interview by author, December 9, 1997.

10. WFW, " 'Massacring Whites' in Arkansas," *Nation*, December 6, 715–16; Unsigned article (probably WFW), "The Real Causes of Two Race Riots," *Crisis*, December 1919; Unmarked typescript pages from pamphlet, *The Arkansas Rioters*, in Waskow Papers.

11. O. A. Rogers Jr., "The Elaine Race Riots of 1919," *Arkansas Historical Quarterly* (Summer 1960): 142–50.

12. J. W. Butts and Dorothy James, "The Underlying Causes of the Elaine Race Riots of 1919," *Arkansas Historical Quarterly* (Spring 1961): 95–105; Cortner, *Mob Intent*, 3–7.

13. WFW, " 'Massacring Whites' "; "Two Race Riots."

14. Waskow, *From Race Riot to Sit-In*; Cortner, *Mob Intent*.

15. S. H. Tarbet to *Crisis*, July 4, 1920, Waskow Papers.

16. Cortner, *Mob Intent*, 122.

17. S. H. Tarbet to *Crisis*, July 4, 1920. In an E-mail to the author on March 2, 2000, Griffin Stockley, an Arkansas student of the Phillips County events who has carefully reviewed the extant trial transcripts, pointed out that Scipio Jones was aware of Tarbet's letter and never raised this theory in court. He is therefore skeptical of my interpretation, and he and other Arkansas scholars are researching the incident in more depth than this overview allows.

18. Greenfield Quarles to David Thomas, January 5, 1920, Box 19, Helena file, Waskow Papers.

19. For Nat Turner, see Franklin, *From Slavery to Freedom*, 212–13. Arkansas historians, having organized a conference on this subject in 2000, are pursuing this matter.

20. Statement by George Washington Davis, November 30, 1920, Waskow Papers.

21. Cortner, *Mob Intent*, 124–25, based on affidavit of H. F. Smiddy, September 21, 1921, in Record, *Moore v. Dempsey*.

22. *Memphis Press*, October 4, in Army File, Waskow Papers.

23. Undated memorandum from Colonel Isaac Jenks, Army file, Waskow Papers.

24. WFW to Thomas Mufson, December 9, 1921, NAACP: Probe File, Waskow Papers.

25. Unsigned article (probably WFW), *Crisis*, December 1919.

26. Georges LeFebvre, *The Great Fear of 1789: Rural Panic in Revolutionary France*, trans. Joan White (Princeton University Press, 1973), is a classic account of this type of phenomenon.

27. Cortner, *Mob Intent*, 14–18.

28. NAACP board minutes, November 10, 1919, NAACP Papers; Cortner, *Mob Intent*, 39–43.

29. Special meeting, NAACP board of directors, November 24, 1919; Cortner, *Mob Intent*, 43.

30. MWO to branches, November 26; MWO to Edith Wharton Dallas, December 9, Waskow Papers.

31. Helen A. Holman to NAACP, November 27; MWO to John A. Milholland, December 17, Waskow Papers.

32. Cortner, *Mob Intent*, 39–54.

33. Cortner, *Mob Intent*, 84–105; Waskow, *From Race Riot to Sit-In*, 154–60.

34. Cortner, *Mob Intent*, 100–105, direct quote 93.

35. *The Capper Papers* (brochure); Julia B. Roundtree to Mary C. Nerney, January 12, 1914; Roundtree to Roy Nash, March 17, 1917; "A Protest by the Topeka Branch of the NAACP," in Topeka branch file, Part 12 D, reel 6; for the *Brown* decision, see Richard Kluger, *Simple Justice* (New York: Vintage Books, 1975).

36. Report by James H. Guy, October 12, 1920, Topeka file, Part 12 D, reel 6.

37. Robert Hill to Thomas Price, November 26; Hill to U. S. Bratton, December 4; Waskow Papers.

38. John R. Shillady to Hugh Fisher, January 23, 1920; Fisher to Shillady, January 26, Waskow Papers; for a good discussion of African-American and white attorneys in the civil rights movement, see Jack Greenberg, *Crusaders in the Courts* (New York: Basic Books, 1994), 26–42.

39. Hugh Fisher to George W. Murphy, January 27, 1920; Fisher to John R. Shillady, January 30, 1920, Waskow Papers; Cortner, *Mob Intent*, 55–61.

40. Topeka *Daily Capital*, February 2, 1920; Hugh Fisher to John R. Shillady, February 3, 1920; Waskow Papers.

41. John R. Shillady to Hugh Fisher, February 6, 1920; Shillady to NAACP branches, February 6, 1920; Fisher to Shillady, February 10, 1920; Shillady to Fisher, February 16, 1920; Telegram from JWJ to Shillady, February 16, 1920, Waskow Papers.

42. WP to J. M. Cox, February 6, February 24, 1920; WP to J. A. Booker, February 24, 1920; Cox to WP, February 19, 1920, Waskow Papers.

43. *Crisis*, March 1920, 235; for a discussion of the Ku Klux Klan in Arkansas, see Charles C. Alexander, *The Ku Klux Klan in the Southwest* (Norman: University of Oklahoma Press, 1995), 21–35.

44. NAACP to Hugh Fisher, February 25, 1920; Fisher to John Shillady, February 25, 1920; J. W. Ross to JWJ, February 14, 1921, Waskow Papers.

45. Cortner, *Mob Intent*, 70–71.

46. Ibid., 76–83.

47. Ibid., 74–76.

NOTES TO CHAPTER 6

1. Brenda Gayle Plummer, *Haiti and the Great Powers, 1902–1915* (Baton Rouge: Louisiana State University Press, 1988), 219–20.

2. Hans Schmidt, *The United States Occupation of Haiti, 1915–1934* (Rutgers University Press, 1971), 66–70, direct quote 68.

3. Schmidt, *Haiti*, 70–84, direct quotes 84 and 78.

4. JWJ, "Self-Determining Haiti," *Nation*, September 4, 1920, 265–67.

5. JWJ, "Self-Determining Haiti"; photograph in Schmidt, *Haiti*.

6. Peter William November, "Unite with Our Brothers: The NAACP and the U.S. Occupation of Haiti, 1915–1936" (paper, Harvard University Archives). James Weldon Johnson, in his autobiography *Along This Way*, incorrectly remembers the date as February (345).

7. JWJ to Moorfield Storey, December 17, 1919, and January 24, 1920, Part 1, reel 17; JWJ diary; Field secretary report, March 1920, Part 1, reel 4, NAACP Papers.

8. JWJ, *Along This Way*, 3.

9. JWJ, *Along This Way*, 344–45; Magdaline W. Shannon, *Jean Price-Mars, the Haitian Elite, and the American Occupation, 1915–1935* (New York: St. Martin's, 1996), 20–22; Arthur C. Holly to JWJ, December 20, 1920, Box 8, File 180, JWJ Papers, Beinecke Library, Yale University.

10. Appointment card, Box 8, File 180, JWJ Papers; JWJ, "Self-Determining Haiti," August 20, 1920; JWJ, *Along This Way*, 347; JWJ to Louis Borno, December 3, 1920, File 180, JWJ Papers.

11. JWJ, *Along This Way*, 347–48; JWJ, "Self-Determining Haiti," September 25, 1920, 346; Shannon, *Price-Mars*, 35, 54–55; JWJ to Pauleas Sannon, November 5, 1920, Box 8, File 185; JWJ to Perceval Thoby, August 11, 1921, Box 8, File 181, JWJ papers.

12. JWJ, *Along This Way*, 348–49.

13. JWJ, *Along This Way*, 350–52.

14. JWJ, *Along This Way*, 350–60, quote 359.

15. Herbert J. Seligmann, "The Conquest of Haiti," *Nation*, July 10, 1920, 35–36.

16. JWJ, "Self-Determining Haiti," August 28, 1920, 236–38.

17. JWJ, "Self-Determining Haiti," *Nation*, September 4, 1920, 265–67, September 11, 1920, 295–97, September 25, 345–47.

18. Undated press release, Part 11 B, reel 8, NAACP Papers; *New York Times*, September 21, 1920, 16.

19. *New York Times*, September 21, 1920, 16, September 22, 1920, 14.

20. WFW to Calvin Chase; JWJ to Coleman Du Pont; JWJ to Warren G. Harding, all September 22, 1920; Part 11 B, reel 8, NAACP Papers.

21. Alfred Henriquez to JWJ, September 27, 1920; Arthur Holly to JWJ, December 10, 1920; JWJ to Louis Borno, November 5, 1920; all Box 8, File 180; JWJ to Etienne Mathon, September 23, 1920, Box 8, File 181, JWJ Papers, Beinecke Library, Yale University.

22. WFW to Ernest Gruening, October 1, 1920; Memo by WFW, October 5, 1920, Part 11 B, reel 8, NAACP Papers; Robert L. Beisner, *Twelve against the Empire: The Anti-Imperialists, 1898–1900* (New York: McGraw-Hill, 1971).

23. JWJ to Warren G. Harding, October 14, 1920 (telegram), and October 27, 1920 (letter); NAACP press release, October 16, 1920; JWJ to Bob Church, October 16, 1920; Joel E. Spingarn to JWJ, October 17, 1920; JWJ to Senator Henry Cabot Lodge and four other senators, October 18, 1920; Part 11 B, reel 8; NAACP board minutes, March 1920, Part 1, reel 1, NAACP Papers.

24. JWJ to Emmett J. Scott, October 13, 1920, Part 11 B, reel 8, NAACP Papers; JWJ to Arthur Holly, December 22, Box 8, File 180, JWJ Papers; NAACP board minutes, February 1921, Part 1, reel 1; Herbert J. Seligmann to Georges Sylvain, April 25, 1921 Part 11 B reel 8, NAACP Papers.

25. Schmidt, *Haiti*, 121–23; November, "Unite with Our Brothers," 53–55.

26. November, "Unite with Our Brothers," 58–64; Robert Dallek, *Franklin Delano Roosevelt and American Foreign Policy, 1932–1945* (New York: Oxford University Press, 1979), 86–87.

NOTES TO CHAPTER 7

1. *Crisis*, March 1920, 240. Unless noted otherwise, all subsequent note citations for this chapter are from 1920.

2. *New York Times*, February 10, 1; *Chicago Defender*, February 14, 1; Lowell U. Harrison and James C. Klotter, *A New History of Kentucky* (University of Kentucky Press, 1997), 348–51; George C. Wright, *Racial Violence in Kentucky, 1865–1940: Lynchings, Mob Rule, and "Legal Lynchings"* (Baton Rouge: Louisiana State University Press, 1990), 194–96.

3. NAACP board minutes, February 1920, NAACP Papers.

4. Patrick Shaheen McElhone, "The Civil Rights Activities of the Louisville Branch of the NAACP: 1914–1960" (master's thesis, University of Louisville, 1976).

5. R. R. Williams to Oswald Garrison Villard, December 24, 1918, Part 8 A, reel 4, NAACP Papers; further correspondence re: Alabama on same reel.

6. Grace Hooten Gates, *The Model City of the New South, Anniston Alabama, 1872–1900* (University of Alabama Press, 1996), 3–33.

7. John R. Shillady to R. R. Williams, December 27, 1918.

8. R. R. Williams to John R. Shillady, January 10, 1919.

9. R. R. Williams to John R. Shillady, January 17, 1919.

10. R. R. Williams to John R. Shillady, May 16, 1919; Shillady to Williams and to A. Mitchell Palmer, both May 17, 1919.

11. R. R. Williams to Moorfield Storey, May 25, 1919.

12. Shillady to Archibald H. Grimké, May 28, 1919; R. R. Williams to Emmett J. Scott, June 7, 1919; R. R. Williams to Shillady, July 7, 1919; Williams to Shillady, July 10, 1919.

13. James R. Ballard et al. to Shillady, July 12, 1919.

14. WFW to James A. Cobb, July 18, 1919.

15. James A. Cobb to JWJ, July 21, 1919.

16. JWJ to Cobb, August 2, 1919; Cobb to JWJ, August 28, 1919.

17. Williams to Shillady, October 24, 1919; JWJ to Newton Baker, November 14, 1919; Cobb to JWJ, November 21, 1919.

18. Cobb to JWJ, November 21, 1919.

19. Telegram from Cobb to MWO, December 3, 1919; R. P. Stewart to Kline, January 30, 1920; Cobb to Shillady, February 14, 1920.

20. Cobb to Shillady, February 21, March 6; Baker, *Holmes*, 438–39; *Caldwell v. W. E. Parker*, 636 (1920); Cobb to Shillady, April 24.

21. *Crisis*, March 1920; Edgar Caldwell to JWJ, March 26; JWJ to Caldwell, April 1.

22. *Birmingham Age-Herald*, July 31, 6; *Crisis*, October, 282.

23. *Crisis*, October 1920, 282.

24. Williams to Shillady, May 5.

25. Sidney D. Redmond to WEBD, April 17, Series 8 A, reel 8, NAACP Papers; further correspondence this section from same reel.

26. James C. Cobb, *The Most Southern Place on Earth: The Mississippi Delta and the Roots of Regional Identity* (Oxford University Press, 1992), 3, 121.

27. Sidney Redmond to Du Bois, April 17; *Crisis*, June 1920, 69–70.

28. Telegram from NAACP to Governor Lee M. Russell, April 20; H. H. Casteel to NAACP, April 20.

29. NAACP to Governor Russell, April 21; NAACP press release, April 22; Russell to NAACP, April 26; Albert D. Kirwan, *Revolt of the Rednecks: Mississippi Politics, 1876–1925* (Gloucester, Mass.: Peter Smith, 1964), 294–98; *Boston Chronicle*, May 1, and *New York Age*, May 8, NAACP Papers.

30. Shillady to Redmond, April 28.

31. Shillady to Robert Church, April 16; Lawrence C. Jones to WEBD, April 28; Redmond to Shillady, April 28.

32. Redmond to Shillady, April 28.

33. Redmond to Shillady, May 1.

34. Acting secretary's report, September, Part 1, reel 4, NAACP Papers; Telegram from Franklin to WFW, September 2; WFW to M. S. Stuart, September 7.

35. *Crisis*, May, 5.

36. NAACP convention proceedings, June 1919, Part 1, reel 8; NAACP board minutes, December 1919, NAACP Papers.

37. W. Fitzhugh Brundage, *Lynching in the New South: Georgia and Virginia, 1880–1930* (Urbana: University of Illinois Press, 1993), 208–15; Kenneth Coleman, ed., *A History of Georgia* (Athens: University of Georgia Press, 1977), 290; John Dittmer, *Black Georgia in the Progressive Era, 1900–1920* (Urbana: University of Illinois Press, 1980), 208–9; Ronald H. Bayor, *Race and the Shaping of Twentieth-Century Atlanta* (University of North Carolina Press, 1996), 17, 19.

38. Brundage, *Lynching New South*, 263, table 3; Coleman, *Georgia*, 292–3; George B. Tindall, *The Emergence of the New South, 1913–1945* (Baton Rouge: Louisiana State University Press, 1967, 1991), 185–86.

39. Dittmer, *Black Georgia*, 201.

40. Brundage, *Lynching New South*, 231–32.

41. Bureau of the Census, *Negroes*, 55, table 10; Coleman, *Georgia*, 413.

42. Dittmer, *Black Georgia*, 12–13.

43. Clifford M. Kuhn et al., *Living Atlanta: An Oral History of the City, 1914–1948* (Athens: University of Georgia Press, 1990), 37–44; A. D. Williams to John R. Shillady, July 9, 1919, Atlanta branch file, Part 12 A, reel 9, NAACP Papers.

44. Taylor Branch, *Parting the Waters* (New York: Simon and Schuster, 1988), 30–37.

45. WFW to JWJ, February 22, 1917, Part 12 A, reel 9, NAACP Papers.

46. Truman K. Gibson to JWJ, March 7, 1919; Harry Pace to JWJ, March 21, 1919; L. C. Crogman to Shillady, April 18, Part 12 A, reel 9; NAACP convention report, 1919, Part 1, reel 8, NAACP Papers.

47. Brundage, *Lynching New South*, 230–31; Dittmer, *Black Georgia*, 206–7; A. D. Williams to Shillady, July 9, 1919, Atlanta branch files, Part 12 A, reel 9, NAACP Papers; JWJ, *Along This Way*, 354.

48. NAACP convention report, 1920, Part 1, reel 8, NAACP Papers; for Harry Pace, see Lewis, *Biography of a Race*, 217.

49. Edward L. Bernays, *Biography of an Idea: Memoirs of a Public Relations Counsel* (New York: Simon and Schuster, 1965), 208–16; *Atlanta Constitution*, May 29, 1.

50. JWJ, *Along This Way*, 356–57.

51. *Atlanta Constitution*, May 31, 1; NAACP convention report, 1920, Part 1, reel 8, NAACP Papers.

52. *Atlanta Constitution*, June 1, 11; NAACP convention report, 1920, Part 1, reel 8, NAACP Papers.

53. *Atlanta Constitution*, June 2, 4, June 3, 9; NAACP convention report, 1920, Part 1, reel 8, NAACP Papers.

54. NAACP convention report, 1920, Part 1, reel 8, NAACP Papers; JWJ, "Views and Reviews," *New York Age*, June 12, 4.

55. NAACP convention report, 1920, Part 1, reel 8, NAACP Papers.

56. Undated synopsis of legal cases, Atlanta branch file, Part 12 A, reel 9; NAACP convention report, 1921, Part 1, reel 8, NAACP Papers.

57. RWB to E. Franklin Frazier, January 21, 1925; Frazier to RWB, February 3, 1925; RWB to A. T. Walden, March 15, 1929; Atlanta branch file, Part 12 A, reel 9, NAACP Papers.

58. Brundage, *Lynching New South*, 227, direct quote 234–35, 242–43.

NOTES TO CHAPTER 8

1. Statement by Warren Greene, St. Louis County attorney; Unsigned investigator's report; both 7 A, reel 13; NAACP pamphlet, *Mob Violence*, 12 C, reel 15, Duluth branch file,

NAACP Papers; Roy Wilkins, *Standing Fast: The Autobiography of Roy Wilkins* (1982; rept. New York: Da Capo Press, 1994), 41–45; Bureau of the Census, *Negroes,* 7, table 6.

2. Telegram from JWJ to Grace Lealtad; Telegram from JWJ to Charles S. Smith; NAACP to Governor J. A. Burnquist, all June 16, 1920; Telegram from JWJ to Burnquist June 17; MWO to Burnquist, June 18; Telegram from Charles Sumner Smith to JWJ, June 21, 7A, reel 13, NAACP Papers. Unless noted otherwise, all subsequent note citations for this chapter are from 1920.

3. JWJ, "Views and Reviews," *New York Age,* July 3, 4; JWJ to Valdo Turner, June 26, Part 7 A, reel 13; JWJ to George B. Kelley June 30, Part 12 C, reel 15, NAACP Papers.

4. Undated newspaper articles in Part 12 C, reel 15; *Nation,* June 26, 841; Telegram from Charles Sumner Smith to JWJ, June 21, 7 A, reel 13, NAACP Papers.

5. Ethel Ray to WEBD, July 19; W. H. Ray to Moorfield Storey, July 20; George B. Kelley to NAACP, June 24; JWJ to Rosamond Johnson, August 25; Kathryn Lealtad to NAACP, August 27, 1920; see e.g., William Francis to Kelley, July 1; Kelley to Francis, July 6, all 12 C, reel 15, NAACP Papers.

6. Wilkins, *Standing Fast,* 34; Duluth branch charter in Duluth branch file, Part 12 C, reel 15, NAACP Papers.

7. Undated fund appeal, Charles W. Scrutchins to William Francis, July 2, both in Duluth branch file, Part 12 C, reel 15, NAACP Papers.

8. "In Re Duluth Assault," investigator's report, June 28; Charles S. Smith to JWJ, June 29, both Part 7 A, reel 13, NAACP Papers.

9. George B. Kelley to William Francis, July 6; Charles S. Scrutchins to JWJ, July 15, Duluth branch file, Part 12 C, reel 15, NAACP Papers.

10. Affidavit of Max Mason; Charles S. Smith to JWJ, July 15 and 22; H. R. Merry to NAACP, December 16; Undated memo, WFW, Part 7 A, reel 13, NAACP Papers; Wilkins, *Standing Fast,* 42–44.

11. Charles M. Blackburn to NAACP, October 9, Part 7 A, reel 13, NAACP Papers.

12. MWO to Burnquist, July 6, Part 7 A, reel 13; Charles Sumner Smith to Burnquist, July 15; George B. Kelley to NAACP, October 8, Duluth branch file, Part 12 C, reel 15, NAACP Papers.

13. Fund appeal, August 3; George B. Kelley to NAACP, July 10, Duluth branch file, Part 12 C, reel 15; St. Louis County grand jury report, Part 7 A, reel 13, NAACP Papers.

14. Wilkins, *Standing Fast,* 44.

15. Randolph C. Downes, *The Rise of Warren G. Harding* (Ohio State University Press, 1970), 402–26.

16. J. H. Eiland to JWJ, May 29; JWJ to Eiland, June 16; Part 11 B, reel 18, NAACP Papers; JWJ, "Views and Reviews," *New York Age,* June 12, 4.

17. JWJ, "Views and Reviews," *New York Age,* June 19, 4; JWJ to Bob Church, June 16; Telegram from JWJ to Mrs. W. Spencer Murray, July 1, part 11 B, reel 18, NAACP Papers; JWJ, *Along the Way,* 357.

18. *New York Age,* June 19, 1.

19. Telegram from JWJ to Walter A. Butler, July 1; Part 11 B, reel 18, NAACP Papers; *Crisis,* September 1920, 230.

20. Richard B. Sherman, "The Harding Administration and the Negro: An Opportunity Lost," *Journal of Negro History* 49, no. 3 (July 1964): 151–68, quote 153.

21. JWJ to Warren G. Harding, July 23; George B. Christian to JWJ, July 27, Part 11 B, reel 18, NAACP Papers.

22. WP to JWJ, July 29; Harry E. Davis to JWJ, July 27, August 5, Part 11 B, reel 18, NAACP Papers.

23. JWJ to George B. Christian, August 28, Part 11 B, reel 18, NAACP Papers.

24. Downes, *Harding,* 539–46.

25. George B. Christian to JWJ, September 22, Part 11 B, reel 19, NAACP Papers.

26. Downs, *Harding,* 546–48, direct quote 546.

27. *New York Age*, September 11, 1; September 25, 4; JWJ quote, October 30, 4.

28. Downes, *Harding*, 552–60.

29. Downes, *Harding*, 622–23; *New York Age*, November 13, 1, 4; JWJ to Harry E. Davis, November 6, Part 11 B, reel 19, NAACP Papers.

30. *Crisis*, September, 215; Ernest R. McKinney, "The Election Comes," *Crisis*, October, 274–76; *Crisis*, December, 57.

31. Unsigned article, *Nation*, November 10, 517; *Nation*, "The Defeat of Wilsonism," November 10, 520; *Nation*, "The Triumph of Reaction," November 17, 548. A review of Moorfield Storey's book *Problems of Today* in the November 17 *Nation* (568) praises his high-mindedness and civil rights commitment but condemns his attacks on American Federation of Labor leader Samuel Gompers, thus neatly encapsulating the split between pro-labor and pro–civil rights activists.

32. Marjorie Spruill Wheeler, "A Short History of the Woman Suffrage Movement in America," 9–19, and Linda G. Ford, "Alice Paul and the Triumph of Militancy," 277–294, in Wheeler, *One Woman, One Vote: Rediscovering the Woman Suffrage Movement* (Troutdale, Oreg.: Newsage Press, 1995).

33. Robert Booth Fowler, "Carrie Chapman Catt, Strategist," 295–314, in Wheeler, "Woman Suffrage"; Cryer, "Ovington," 383–85.

34. MWO to Vida Milholland, February 26, 1919; Milholland to MWO, March 25, 1919; MWO to Milholland, April 8, 1919, Part 1, reel 20, NAACP Papers; Rosalyn Terborg-Penn, "Discontented Black Feminists: Prelude and Postscript to the Passage of the Nineteenth Amendment," 261–78, in *Decades of Discontent: The Women's Movement, 1920–1940*, ed. Lois Scharf and Joan M. Jensen (Westport, Conn.: Greenwood Publishing Group, 1983), 261–78.

35. Anastasia Sims, "Armageddon in Tennessee," 333–50; Rosalyn Terborg-Penn, "African-American Women and the Suffrage Movement," 150–51, in Wheeler, *One Woman*.

36. *New York Times*, September 19, 1920, 12.

37. WP, "The Woman Voter Hits the Color Line," *Nation*, October 6, 1920, 372–73.

38. Terborg-Penn, "African-American Women," 152–53; *Crisis*, November, 1920, 23; JWJ, "The Colored Woman Voter," *New York Age*, 4.

39. Mary Church Terrell, *A Colored Woman in a White World* (New York: Arno Press, 1980), 308–17; Dorothy Salem, *To Better Our World: Black Women in Organized Reform, 1890–1920*, (Brooklyn: Carlson Press, 1990), 238.

40. Cryer, "Ovington," 387–88.

41. Florence Kelley to MWO, December 22, 1920; MWO to Mary Talbert, December 30, 1920, Part 11 B, reel 17, NAACP Papers.

42. November 8, 1920, fund letter signed MWO, Part 1, reel 25; J. C. Merriman to MWO, December 13, 1920; Mary Talbert to Catherine Lealtad, January 3, 1921; Talbert to MWO, January 5, 1921, Part 11 B, reel 17, NAACP Papers.

43. MWO to Alice Paul, January 4, 1921, Part 11 B, reel 17; Addie Hunton to MWO, March 25, 1921; Part 1 reel 16, NAACP Papers; Cryer, "Ovington," 389–90. The statue of Susan B. Anthony, Elizabeth Cady Stanton, and Lucretia Mott now sits, after seventy-five years in storage, in the Capitol Rotunda, its all-white characters still a sore spot for African-American feminists.

44. *New York Times*, November 4, 1920, 1.

45. Application for Klan membership, WFW, September 21, 1920, Part 11, reel 4, NAACP Papers. All subsequent note citations for this chapter are from this reel unless otherwise noted.

46. Undated report from WFW; Statement by WFW to Justice Department, December 17; WFW, "Election by Terror in Florida," *New Republic*, January 12, 1921, 195–97.

47. *New York Age*, December 18, 1920, 1; For land boom, see George B. Tindall, *The*

Emergence of the New South, 1913–1945 (1967; rept. Baton Rouge: Louisiana State University Press, 1991), 104–10.

48. *Crisis*, February 1921, 165; Secretary's report, January 1921, Part 1, reel 4, NAACP Papers.

49. Unidentified clippings, Part 11 B, reel 4; NAACP board of directors, January 1921, Part 1, reel 1, NAACP Papers.

50. *Sentinel*, January 7, 1921; N. B. Young to WFW, January 5, 10, and 27, 1921; J. G. Singletary et al. to NAACP, December 31, 1920; "A woman friend" to NAACP, December 30, 1920; "Colored teacher" to JWJ, January 5, 1921; Unidentified article; all in Part 11 B, reel 4, NAACP Papers.

51. WFW to Nathan Young, January 7, 1921.

NOTES TO CHAPTER 9

1. E. David Cronon, *Black Moses: The Story of Marcus Garvey and the Universal Negro Improvement Association* (1955; rept. Madison, Wis.: University of Wisconsin Press, 1969), 63–70; *New York Age*, August 21, 1920, 1.

2. Cronon, *Black Moses*, 3–10.

3. Gilbert Osofsky, *Harlem: The Making of a Ghetto: Negro New York, 1890–1930* (1963; rept. New York: Harper Torchbooks, 1966), 122–23, 128–29.

4. Ibid., 87–117.

5. Ibid., 113–17, 120.

6. JWJ, *Black Manhattan* (1930; rept. New York: Da Capo Press, 1991), 3.

7. *Crisis*, May 1916, 9; Marcus Garvey to WEBD, April 25, 1916; WEBD to secretary to Garvey, April 29, 1916, in *Marcus Garvey and Universal Negro Improvement Association Papers*, vol. I, ed. Robert A. Hill (Berkeley: University of California Press, 1983), 187; Cronon, *Black Moses*, 39–63; Judith Stein, *The World of Marcus Garvey: Race and Class in Modern Society* (Baton Rouge: Louisiana State University Press, 1986), 38–50.

8. Cronon, *Black Moses*, 73–102; Stein, *Race and Class*, 89–107.

9. For African-American sailors, see W. Jeffrey Bolster, *African American Seamen in the Age of Sail* (Cambridge, Mass.: Harvard University Press, 1997).

10. W. A. Domingo to editors, *Messenger*, January 15, 1923; Flyer in Part 11 A, reel 35, NAACP Papers.

11. Osofsky, *Harlem*, 131–35.

12. Hill, *Garvey Papers*, vol. I, xxxv.

13. Cronon, *Black Moses*, 81–93; Stein, *Race and Class*, 89–107.

14. Fred Moore, interview by Hill, *Garvey Papers*, vol. II, 622–23.

15. Wilford H. Smith to ABS, January 27, 1921; ABS to Smith, February 10, 1921; Hill, *Garvey Papers*, vol. III, 41; Cronon, *Black Moses*, 130; NAACP board minutes, February 1921, Part 11A, reel 15; NAACP Papers; WEBD, *Autobiography*, 273–74.

16. *Negro World*, March 29 and April 5, 1919, in Hill, *Garvey Papers*, vol. I, 392–94; *Crisis*, December 1920, 58–60.

17. Garvey to WEBD, July 16, 1920, vol. II, 426; Marcus Garvey, interview by Hill, August 18, 1920; WEBD, interview by Hill, August 22, 1920, *Garvey Papers*, vol. II, 602–3, 620–21.

18. WEBD in *Crisis*, December 1920, 58–60, and January 1921, 112–15.

19. Stein, *Race and Class*, 108–27; Cronon, *Black Moses*, 124–32.

20. "Open Letter from the President of Liberia," *Crisis*, June 1921, 53.

21. Stein, *Race and Class*, 213–22.

22. *New York Dispatch*, April 22, 1921; *Negro World*, December 17, 1921, in Hill, *Garvey Papers*, vol. III, 361, 283–84; WP to Ernest Gruening, October 11, 1921; WP to Dr. H. Claude Hudson, June 4, 1922, reel 1, Pickens Papers.

23. Cronon, *Black Moses*, 90–92; Hill, *Garvey Papers*, vol. I, lxxix–lxxx.

24. Stein, *Race and Class*, 128–51.

25. JWJ, *New York Age*, September 24, 1921, 4; Garvey in Hill, *Garvey Papers*, vol. IV, October 1, 1921.

26. NAACP press release, January 20, 1922; Garvey to JWJ, January 21, 1922, Part 11 A, reel 35, NAACP Papers.

27. Stein, *Race and Class*, 153–60, direct quote 154. Stein's perceptive interpretation of Klan-Garvey relations emphasizes that both movements represented maneuvers by elitist outsiders to capture the mainstream of their respective polity.

28. Garvey to WP, May 5, 1922; WP to Garvey July [?] 1922, Part 11 A, reel 35, NAACP Papers.

29. Theodore Kornweibel Jr., *No Crystal Stair: Black Life and the Messenger, 1917–1928* (Westport, Conn.: Greenwood Press, 1975), 134–40; Johnson, *New York Age*, August 19, 1922, 4.

30. *New York Times*, August 7, 1922, in Hill, *Garvey Papers*, vol. IV, 816–17; *New York Age*, August 28, 1920, 1; Cronon, *Black Moses*, 108.

31. Jervis Anderson, *A. Philip Randolph: A Biographical Portrait* (1972; rept. Berkeley: University of California Press, 1986), 130–32.

32. Stein, *Race and Class*, 171–85.

33. Bagnall et al. to attorney general, Part 11 A, reel 35, NAACP Papers.

34. Kornweibel, *No Crystal Stair*, 134–75; W. A. Domingo to editors, *Messenger*, January 15, 1923; JWJ to W. A. Domingo, January 23, 1923, Part 11 A, reel 35, NAACP Papers; WP, "Garvey and the Rest of Us," *New York Dispatch*, April 22, 1921, in Hill, *Garvey Papers*, vol. III, 361.

35. Anderson, *Randolph*, 137.

36. Osofsky, *Harlem*, 133.

37. WEBD, "The UNIA," *Crisis*, January 1923, 120–22.

38. Stein, *Race and Class*, 223–47. Stein, a careful researcher, does not share my view of the NAACP's orientation.

39. Cronon, *Black Moses*, 110–18.

40. Ibid., 120–24.

41. WEBD, "A Lunatic or a Traitor," *Crisis*, May 1924, 8–9; Manning Marable, *W. E. B. Du Bois: Black Radical Democrat* (Boston: Twayne Publishers, 1986), 118–19.

42. Cronon, *Black Moses*, 136–37.

NOTES TO CHAPTER 10

1. *New York Times*, January 1921, 1. All subsequent note citations for this chapter are from 1921 unless otherwise noted.

2. *New York Times*, January 28, 10.

3. *Boston Globe*, January 27, 6.

4. *Crisis*, February, 160; Undated memo by WP, Part 7 A, reel 8, NAACP Papers.

5. WP, "The American Congo—Burning of Henry Lowry," *Nation*, March 23, 426–27.

6. Frederick Knollenberg to Governor Thomas McCrae, L. W. Washington to E. C. Morris, Helena, Arkansas, both January 20; Telegram from McCrae to Knollenberg, January 23, Part 7 A, reel 8, NAACP Papers.

7. WP, "The American Congo."

8. Kenneth T. Jackson, *The Ku Klux Klan in the City, 1915–1930* (1967; rept. Chicago: Ivan R. Dee, 1992), 45–48.

9. JWJ, *New York Age*, February 4, 4.

10. Editorials, all January 28, 1921; NAACP circular letter, February 9, Part 7 A, reel 8, NAACP Papers.

11. Lester C. Lamon, *Black Tennesseans, 1900–1930* (Knoxville: University of Tennessee Press, 1977), 265; Memorandum from WP, Part 7 A, reel 8, NAACP Papers.

12. *Atlanta Constitution*, March 25, 1.

13. Pete Daniel, *The Shadow of Slavery: Peonage in the South, 1901–1969* (Urbana: University of Illinois Press, 1972), 110–16.

14. *Atlanta Constitution*, January 17, *New York Tribune*, January 14, Part 10, reel 16, NAACP Papers; NAACP board minutes, October 1920, Part 1, reel 1.

15. Daniel, *Shadow of Slavery*, 110–11.

16. *Atlanta Constitution*, March 25–April 8, 1921; Daniel, *Shadow of Slavery*, 117–18.

17. *Atlanta Constitution*, April 7; *New York World*, April 7, Part 10, reel 16, NAACP Papers.

18. *Atlanta Constitution*, March 26, April 7.

19. *Atlanta Constitution*, April 8–10; Daniel, *Shadow of Slavery*, 126.

20. Daniel, *Shadow of Slavery*, 19–25, 113.

21. Ibid., 19–42.

22. Ibid., ix–xii, 3–18.

23. Telegrams from JWJ to Harding, Daugherty, and Dorsey, March 28; JWJ to J. C. Banks, April 1; JWJ to John Fitzpatrick, April 6; Secretary's report to board of directors, April 9; WFW to A. H. Shaw, April 2; Telegram from Dorsey to JWJ, April 14; all in Part 10, reel 17, NAACP Papers.

24. *Atlanta Constitution*, March 28, 4; *Knoxville Sentinel*, March 28; *Asheville Citizen*, *Chattanooga Times*, *Spartanburg Herald*, April 11, 1921; all in Part 10, reel 17, NAACP Papers.

25. *New York Times*, March 29, April 11; *Chicago Herald and Examiner*, n.d.; *Buffalo Express* and *Hartford Courant*, April 13; all in Part 10, reel 16, NAACP Papers.

26. *Atlanta Constitution*, April 1, 12; *Macon Telegraph*, March 31, April 15; *Atlanta Journal*, March 31; *Zebulon Journal*, n.d.; *Sylvania Telephone*, April 15; *Dublin Herald*, April 18; *Savannah News*, April 29; all in Part 10, reel 16, NAACP Papers.

27. Atlanta branch annual report, 1921; "Synopsis of Legal Cases"; both in Atlanta branch file, Part 12 A reel 9, NAACP Papers; Herbert J. Seligmann, "Slavery in Georgia, A.D. 1921," *Nation*, April 20, 591–92.

28. *New York World*, April 27, 1921, Part 10 A, reel 16, NAACP Papers; JWJ in *New York Age*, May 7, 1921, 4.

29. Daniel, *Shadow of Slavery*, 130–31.

30. Scott Ellsworth, *Death in a Promised Land: The Tulsa Race Riot of 1921* (Baton Rouge: Louisiana State University Press, 1982), 45–49.

31. Ellsworth, *Tulsa*, 8–16; Buck Colbert Franklin, *My Life and an Era: The Autobiography of Buck Colbert Franklin*, ed. John Hope Franklin and John Whittington Franklin (Baton Rouge: Louisiana State University Press), 1997, 199–200.

32. Ellsworth, *Tulsa*, 17–44.

33. Ibid., 48–53.

34. Ibid., 53–66; WFW, "The Eruption of Tulsa," *Nation*, June 29, 909–10.

35. Franklin, *Autobiography*, 196.

36. "Tulsa," *Nation*, June 15, 1921, 839; Ellsworth, *Tulsa*, 89–94.

37. Ellsworth, *Tulsa*, 78–89.

38. Ibid., 94–97.

39. WFW, "The Eruption of Tulsa."

40. *Crisis*, April 1926, 268–69; John Hope Franklin, interview by author, March 29, 1996.

NOTES TO CHAPTER 11

1. Harold Isaacs, *The New World of Negro Americans* (London: Phoenix House, 1963); Francis L. Broderick, *W. E. B. Du Bois: Negro Leader in a Time of Crisis* (Stanford: Stan-

ford University Press, 1959); Henry Lee Moon, *The Emerging Thought of W.E.B. Du Bois* (New York: Simon and Schuster, 1972); all stress Du Bois's elitist tendencies.

2. Memorandum from WEBD, October 27 1920; for responses, see, for example, Harry Pace to WEBD, November 5, 1920; George Cook to WEBD, November 6, 1920; all in reel 9, WEBD Papers (microfilm).

3. NAACP board minutes, November and December 1920, NAACP Papers.

4. Bulletin 1 for the Second Pan-African Congress, in Aptheker, *Documentary History*, 335–36; NAACP news release, April 23, 1921, Part 11 B, reel 18, NAACP Papers; NAACP board minutes, July 1921.

5. NAACP news release, August 4, 1921, Part 11 B, reel 18, NAACP Papers.

6. "To The World" (Manifesto of the Second Pan-African Congress), in Aptheker, *Documentary History*, 337–42, direct quote 342.

7. Jessie Fauset, "Impressions of the Second Pan-African Congress," *Crisis*, November 1921, 12–18.

8. WEBD, "The Negro Mind Reaches Out," *Foreign Affairs* 3, no. 3 (1924); rept. in Alain Locke, ed., *The New Negro: Voices of the Harlem Renaissance* (New York: Atheneum, 1992), 389–91.

9. Fauset, "Impressions of the Second Pan-African Congress," 15.

10. Marable, *Black Radical Democrat*, 101; WFW, *A Man Called White*, 62.

11. Fauset, "Impressions of the Second Pan-African Congress"; Du Bois, "A Second Journey to Pan-Africa," *New Republic*, December 7, 1921, 39–42; rept. in David Levering Lewis, ed., *W. E. B Du Bois: A Reader* (New York: Henry Holt, 1995), 662–67.

12. C. W. Dennis to WFW, April 9, 1921, Part 11 B, reel 18, NAACP Papers; Herbert J. Seligmann to WEBD, May 27, reel 10, Du Bois Papers; Claude E. Barnett to WFW, July 30, Part 11 B, reel 18, NAACP Papers; *Chicago Defender*, September 10, 1, and October 1, 1; all 1921.

13. Resolution of the Third Pan-African Congress, in Aptheker, *Documentary History*, 430–32.

14. Marable, *Black Radical Democrat*, 106–7; WEBD, *Crisis*, February 1924.

15. "The Fourth Pan-African Congress," in Aptheker, *Documentary History*, 544–49.

NOTES TO CHAPTER 12

1. Zangrando, *NAACP Crusade*, 1–31; Claudine L. Ferrell, *Nightmare and Dream: Anti-Lynching in Congress, 1917–1922* (New York: Garland Publishing, 1986), 111–19.

2. Zangrando, *NAACP Crusade*, 42–43; Ferrell, *Nightmare*, 120–22.

3. Zangrando, *NAACP Crusade*, 55–56; Ferrell, *Nightmare*, 138–49; Storey to Shillady, November 9, 1920, Part 1, reel 24, NAACP Papers; further Storey letters this section from same reel unless otherwise noted.

4. *New York Age*, December 18, 1920, 1.

5. Storey to George Wickersham, January 15 and 22; Wickersham to Storey, January 20, 1921.

6. JWJ, *Along This Way*, 362; NAACP board minutes, January and April 1921; JWJ NAACP diary, 1921, Part 2, reel 2, NAACP Papers.

7. JWJ diary, March 23–25, 1921, Part 2, reel 2; JWJ, *Along This Way*, 362; Zangrando, *NAACP Crusade*, 57; Memorandum from JWJ to President Warren G. Harding, April 4, 1921; Telegram from JWJ to WFW, April 4, 1921, Part 2, reel 2, NAACP Papers.

8. JWJ to President Harding, April 13 and 20, 1921, Part 2, reel 2, NAACP Papers; JWJ, *Along This Way*, 362.

9. Ferrell, *Nightmare*, 163–72.

10. Zangrando, *NAACP Crusade*, 60; Ferrell, *Nightmare*, 173–78.

11. Text of bill in Ferrell, *Nightmare*, 314–15; see also 179–87.

12. JWJ to Storey, October 21 and 28, 1921, Part 2, reel 2, NAACP Papers; Ferrell, *Nightmare*, 188–90, JWJ, *Along This Way*, 363.

13. Richard B. Sherman, "The Harding Administration and The Negro: An Opportunity Lost," *Journal of Negro History* 49, no. 3 (July 1964): 161–68, direct quote 158; *New York Age*, October 29, 1, and November 5, 4, 1921.

14. Secretary's report, November 1921, Part 1, reel 4, NAACP Papers; Zangrando, *NAACP Crusade*, 62.

15. Circular letter from JWJ, January 2, 1922, Part 2, reel 2, NAACP Papers. At least one such international incident had taken place. During the Benjamin Harrison administration, two American sailors were killed in a tavern brawl in Chile, and the administration insisted upon prosecution and reparations. See Walter LaFeber, *The New Empire: An Interpretation of American Expansion* (Ithaca: Cornell University Press, 1963), 130–36.

16. JWJ to national office, January 4, 1922, Part 2, reel 2; Secretary's report, January 6, 1922, Part 1, reel 4, NAACP Papers.

17. Ferrell, *Nightmare*, 195–98.

18. Ibid., 201, 234; JWJ, *Along This Way*, 366.

19. Zangrando, *NAACP Crusade*, 64; Ferrell, *Nightmare*, 191–93, JWJ, *Along This Way*, 366. Both Zangrando and Ferrell record 231 votes in favor.

20. Secretary's report, February 1922, Part 1, reel 4, NAACP Papers.

21. JWJ, *Along This Way*, 367.

22. Ferrell, *Nightmare*, 241–43.

23. Secretary's report, March and April 1922, Part 1, reel 4, NAACP Papers; *New York Age*, January 7, 1, and June 10, 8, 1922; *Baltimore Afro-American*, June 9, 1; Zangrando, *NAACP Crusade*, 64–65.

24. Zangrando, *NAACP Crusade*, 64; Clarence G. Contee, "Butler R. Wilson and the Boston NAACP Branch," *Crisis*, (December 1974), 346–48.

25. John A. Garraty, *Henry Cabot Lodge: A Biography* (New York: Knopf, 1983); Borah speech on Haiti, *New York Age*, May 6, 1922, 1.

26. NAACP board minutes, May 1922, NAACP Papers.

27. *New York Times*, May 7, 1922, 1.

28. NAACP board minutes, May 1922; Telegram from JWJ to *San Antonio Express* and *Houston Post*, May 8, 1922, Part 7 A, reel 19, NAACP Papers.

29. JWJ to President Warren G. Harding, May 9, 1922, Part 2, reel 2, NAACP Papers.

30. Dan Kelly to JWJ, May 18, 1922, Part 7 A, reel 19, NAACP Papers.

31. Monte Akers, *Flames after Midnight: Murder, Vengeance, and the Desolation of a Texas Community* (Austin: University of Texas Press, 1999).

32. Kelly's speech in report on Newark convention, 1922, Part 1, reel 8; J. W. H. Crim to JWJ, June 20, 1922, Part 7 A, reel 19, NAACP Papers.

33. Secretary's report, June 1922, Part 1, reel 4, NAACP Papers; JWJ to "Herb" [Seligmann? Stockton?], May 21, 1922, Box 24, JWJ Papers, Beinecke Library, Yale University; *New York Age*, June 3, 1922, 4.

34. Herbert Stockton to WFW, April 6, 1922; Louis Marshall to Herbert Stockton, July 17, 1922; Herbert Stockton to Louis Marshall, July 21, 1922; Part 1, reel 24, NAACP Papers; Ferrell, *Nightmare*, 254–65.

35. Ferrell, *Nightmare*, 262–67; ABS to Herbert Stockton, July 6, 1922, Box 7, July–December 1922 file, ABS Papers, LC.

36. Newark convention reports, Part 1, reel 8, NAACP Papers.

37. Gloria T. Hull, ed., *Works of Alice Dunbar-Nelson* (New York: Oxford University Press, 1988), xxix–xxx.

38. Alice Dunbar-Nelson to JWJ, August 23, 29, and October 12, 1922; Alice Dunbar-Nelson to WFW, September 8, 1922, Part 11 B, reel 9, NAACP Papers.

39. George Cannon to MWO, October 4; Cannon to JWJ, October 17; NAACP news release, November 9; all 1922, Part 11 B, reel 9, NAACP Papers.

40. Oscar Baker to RWB, March 9, 1922; Oscar Baker to JWJ, March 17 and 25, 1922; Oscar Baker to WFW, September 14, 1922; Charles Townsend to WFW, September 28, 1922; Oscar Baker to national office, November 8, 1922; NAACP news release, October 9, 1922; Norman McCrae and Bernard Coker, interview by author, December 12, 1997.

41. W. T. Nutter to WFW, July 22 and August 9, 1922; George L. Vaughn to JWJ, November 13, 1922; George de Reef to JWJ, October 16, 1922, Part 11 B, reel 9, NAACP Papers.

42. Ida B. Wells-Barnett, *Ida B. Wells-Barnett on Lynchings* (1892; rept. New York: Arno Press and New York Times, 1969).

43. Jacquelyn Dowd Hall, *Revolt against Chivalry: Jessie Daniel Ames and the Women's Campaign against Lynching* (New York: Columbia University Press, 1979).

44. NAACP board minutes, July 1922.

45. NAACP board minutes, December 1922, January and February 1923; Lillian S. Williams, "Mary Morris [Burnett] Talbert," in *Notable Black American Women*, 1,095–99.

46. JWJ to MWO, August 4, 1922; JWJ to George B. Christian, September 9, 1922; Telegram from JWJ to President Warren G. Harding, August 22, 1922, Part 2, reel 2; Secretary's report, September 1922, Part 1, reel 4, NAACP Papers.

47. JWJ to Richetta Randolph, September 17, 1922, Part 2, reel 2; JWJ, *Along This Way*, 369–70; Secretary's report, October 1922, Part 1, reel 4, NAACP Papers; Zangrando, *NAACP Crusade*, 235, note 84.

48. Moorfield Storey to JWJ, July 12, 1922; JWJ to Storey, October 11, 1922; Zangrando, *NAACP Crusade*, 67–68.

49. Edward Bernays to ABS, September 11, JWJ to ABS, September 15, Roger Baldwin to ABS, October 13, Box 7, July–December 1922 file, ABS Papers, LC; JWJ to WFW, November 23, 1922, Box 24, JWJ Papers, Beinecke Library, Yale University.

50. JWJ, *Along This Way*, 371.

51. Telegram from JWJ to President Warren G. Harding, December 3, 1922, Part 2 reel 2, NAACP Papers; Zangrando, *NAACP Crusade*, 69–70.

52. JWJ, "Views and Reviews," *New York Age*, December 16, 1922, 4; JWJ, "Memorandum from Mr. Johnson to Du Bois: Re: *Crisis* Editorial," in Sandra K. Wilson, ed., *Selected Writings of James Weldon Johnson*, (New York: Oxford University Press, 1995), 40–45.

53. JWJ, "Views and Reviews," *New York Age*, December 23 and 30, 1922, 4.

54. Zangrando, *NAACP Crusade*, 75; Undated letter signed "Perry Howard," JWJ correspondence, Part 2, reel 2, NAACP Papers.

55. JWJ, *Along This Way*, 373–74.

56. Zangrando, *NAACP Crusade*, table 2, 6. There is a growing literature on this subject. Especially useful is W. Fitzhugh Brundage, *Lynching in the New South: Georgia and Virginia, 1880–1930* (Urbana: University of Illinois Press, 1993).

57. JWJ to Joel E. Spingarn, December 15, 1922, JWJ Correspondence, Part 2 reel 2.

NOTES TO CHAPTER 13

1. Zora Neale Hurston, "Jonah's Gourd Vine," in *The Portable Harlem Renaissance Reader*, ed. David Levering Lewis (New York: Viking Penguin, 1995), 719–28.

2. Unidentified Canadian newspaper, January 12, 1922, Part 8 A, reel 1, NAACP Papers. All subsequent note citations are from this reel unless otherwise noted.

3. NAACP news release, January 23, 1922.

4. J. D. Howell to NAACP, January 12, 1922; "Aunt Ab" to "Violet," January 16, 1922.

5. NAACP news release, January 23, 1922; *New York Times*, January 17, 1922, 9.

6. Lillian S. Williams, "Afro-Americans in Buffalo, 1900–1930: A Study in Community Formation," in *Afro-Americans in New York Life and History* 8, no. 2 (July 1984): 7–32; Amelia G. Anderson to MWO, January 18, 1922.

7. WFW to MWO, January 19, 1922; Amelia Anderson to MWO, January 24, 1922, Part 12 B, reel 2.

8. NAACP news release, February 1, 1922; Unsigned telegram to NAACP, February 17, 1922; R. B. Andrews to WFW, February 20, 1922.

9. WFW to Reverend William E. Guy, February 17, 1922; *New York Times*, January 18, 1922, 16.

10. WFW to F. F. Treleaven, February 23, 1922; *New York Times*, February 25, 1922, 8; Reverend J. D. Howell to WFW, March [?] 1922.

11. Williams, "Afro-Americans in Buffalo."

12. "Statement of Facts Pertaining to the Case of Thomas Ray"; June 22 [1919?] *Milledgeville News*.

13. "Statement of Thomas Ray," Wayne County Jail, October 5, 1920; "Decision of Governor Groesbeck," n.d.

14. "Statement of Facts Pertaining to the Case of Thomas Ray"; WFW to JWJ, October 13, 1920.

15. "Statement of Facts Pertaining to the Case of Thomas Ray"; WFW to W. Hayes McKinney, October 21, 1920; *Crisis*, January 1921, 116–17, and July 1921, 218–19.

16. *Detroit Free Press*, June 22, 1921; "Decision of Governor Groesbeck."

17. *Atlanta Constitution*, July 31, 1921.

18. Untitled statement, February 3, 1921; *Charleston Gazette*, February 1, 1921.

19. Branch charter, Part 12 C, reel 26, NAACP Papers.

20. Joe William Trotter, *Blacks in Southern West Virginia, 1915–1932* (Urbana: University of Illinois Press, 1990), 246–48.

21. MWO, *Portraits in Color*, 47–51.

22. Quote in Trotter, *Blacks in Southern West Virginia*, 248; NAACP reports, November 1919 and December 1921, Part 12 C, reel 26, NAACP Papers.

23. R. C. McIver to NAACP, January 7, 1921; Mordecai Johnson to NAACP, January 21, 1921, Part 12 C, reel 26; Trotter, *Blacks in Southern West Virginia*, 255–56.

24. Memorandum February 3, 1921, Part 8 A, reel 2.

NOTES TO CHAPTER 14

1. Tom Dillard, "Scipio Africanus Jones," *Arkansas Historical Quarterly* 31 (1972): 201–19, direct quotes 212.

2. Scipio A. Jones to JWJ, February 16, 1921; Jones to WFW, March 25, April 29, April 30, 1921; Part 7 A, reel 8, NAACP Papers.

3. Cortner, *Mob Intent*, 108; Kerlin letter in *Nation*, June 15, 1921, 847.

4. Cortner, *Mob Intent*, 108–14.

5. Ibid., 115–16.

6. Ibid., 116–21.

7. Ibid., 121–25, direct quote 123–24.

8. *Ex Parte Frank Moore*, U.S. District Court, Western Division, Eastern District of Arkansas, in Box 19, Arthur I. Waskow Papers, Wisconsin State Historical Society, Madison, Wisconsin.

9. Cortner, *Mob Intent*, 130.

10. NAACP board minutes, September 1921; JWJ to Jones, September 20, 1921; Jones to JWJ, September 23, 1921, Part 7 A, reel 8 NAACP Papers. Arkansas historians and activists convened a conference early in 2000 to consider the Elaine events. Attorney and novelist Griffin Stockley, in an unpublished paper titled "The Elaine Race Massacre of 1919—the Legal Perspective," argues that McHaney was legitimately concerned about the disposition of the cases, that he argued the *Ware* cases and made a crucial appearance later on behalf of the *Moore* defendants. Stockley has read the trial records, which I have not, and

he may have a more accurate picture of McHaney's motivations than I have presented in the text. The Arkansas researchers are making a vital contribution to this neglected story.

11. Jones to NAACP, September 30; Jones to ABS, October 8 and 30, Part 7 A, reel 8, NAACP Papers; ABS to Jones, October 8, Box 6, July–December 1921 file, ABS Papers, LC.

12. Storey to MWO, November 21, 1922, July–December 1922 file, ABS Papers, LC.

13. Cortner, *Mob Intent*, 136–43.

14. Storey to WFW, November 16, 1922, Box 6, July–December 1922 file, ABS Papers, LC.

15. WFW to U. S. Bratton, November 15; Bratton to WFW, November 28; Jones to WFW, November 25 and December 13; WFW to Jones, December 4; all 1922, Box 6, July–December 1922 file, ABS Papers, LC.

16. Cortner, *Mob Intent*, 147–52.

17. U. S. Bratton to WFW, January 11, 1923; WFW to Jones, January 12, 1923, Box 19, NAACP Appeals file, Waskow Papers.

18. *Moore v. Dempsey*, 261 U.S. 86 (1923).

19. Cortner, *Mob Intent*, 160–65.

20. Ibid., 166–84.

21. Ibid., 185.

22. Ibid., 185–92, Marshall quote 158.

23. *New York Age, Chicago Defender*, and *Baltimore Afro-American* for February 1923 and January 1925.

24. WFW to Jones, February 2, 1925, Part 7 A, reel 8, NAACP Papers; *Crisis*, December 1921, 72–76, and January 1922, 115–18, for example, printed Jones's brief, with only a three-line appeal for funds appended. *Crisis*, March 1923, 220–21; WFW, "The Arkansas Cases," April 1923, 259–61; "The Arkansas Cases Nearly Ended," January 1924, 124–25; "The End of the Arkansas Cases," April 1925, 272–73.

25. J. F. McConico to NAACP, April 7, 1920; J. M. Conner to NAACP, August 28, 1920, Box 19, NAACP Appeals file, Waskow Papers; *Crisis*, April 1921, 254; Cortner, *Mob Intent*, 107.

26. "NAACP Administrative File: New York Foundation," December 7, 1919–December 12, 1921, Part 11 B, reel 17; Arkansas Special Fund file, Part 7 A, reel 21, NAACP Papers.

27. "Arkansas Riot Cases, Resume, and expenses, October 4, 1929," Box 19, NAACP Appeals file, Waskow Papers.

28. W. A. Singfield to NAACP, July 19, 1920; Singfield to RWB, September 24, 1921, Part 12 A, reel 4, NAACP Papers.

29. Judith Ann Still, "Carrie Still Shepperson: The Hollows of Her Footsteps," *Arkansas Historical Quarterly* (Spring 1983): 37–46.

30. Carrie L. Shepperson to RWB, June 2, 1924, October 4, 1926; Shepperson to WFW, June 15, 1924; *Amsterdam News* article, n.d., in Part 12 A, reel 4, NAACP Papers.

31. WP to Shepperson, January 5, 1925, and March 21, 1927; NAACP news release, April 16, 1926; RWB to L. A. Hyatt, May 23, 1927; *Arkansas Survey*, June 18, 1927, in Part 12 A, reel 4, NAACP Papers.

32. Charles C. Alexander, *The Ku Klux Klan in the Southwest* (1965; rept. Norman: University of Oklahoma Press, 1995), 185–93.

33. *New York American*, November 19, 1921; *Memphis Commercial Appeal*, November 26, 1921; *Little Rock Gazette*, February 4, 1922; *New York Times*, August 2, 1922, Part 7 A, reel 8, NAACP Papers.

34. *Arkansas Survey*, January 17, 1925, Part 7 A, reel 21, NAACP Papers.

35. Unsigned article (probably WEBD), "The Arkansas Cases Nearly Ended," *Crisis*, January 1924, 124–25; WFW, "The Defeat of Arkansas Mob Law," April 1925, *Crisis*, 259.

NOTES TO CHAPTER 15

1. Robert V. Haynes, *A Night of Violence: The Houston Riot of 1917* (Baton Rouge: Louisiana State University Press, 1976), 8–46.

2. Haynes, *A Night of Violence*, 90–114.

3. Ibid., 115–39.

4. Ibid., 140–71.

5. Ibid., 171–207.

6. Ibid., 208–53.

7. Ibid., 254–71.

8. Ibid., 275–96.

9. WEBD, "Houston," *Crisis*, October 1917, 284–85.

10. JWJ, "Houston," *New York Age*, August 30, 1917, 4; *Baltimore Afro-American*, September 1, 1917, 1, 4.

11. Martha Gruening, "Houston: An Investigation," *Crisis*, November 1917, 14–19.

12. WEBD, "Thirteen," *Crisis*, February 1917, 187–89; *Baltimore Afro-American*, December 15, 1917, 1, 4.

13. Haynes, *A Night of Violence*, 280–83; JWJ, *Along This Way*, 321–26, direct quote 325.

14. Haynes, *A Night of Violence*, 297–301.

15. E. O. Smith to WFW, May 22, 1918; Clifton F. Richardson to NAACP, June 17, 1918; John Shillady to Henry V. Mims, July 28, 1918; Houston branch charter; H. M. Edwards to NAACP, June 28, 1919, Part 12 A, reel 19, NAACP Papers; Haynes, *A Night of Violence*, 305–7.

16. James R. Hawkins to JWJ, December 31, 1919, and February 22, 1920; Memorandum from WFW, February 26, 1920; Isaac A. Deyo to John Haynes Holmes, September 29, 1920; Holmes to JWJ, October 4, 1920; WEBD to JWJ, November 17, 1920, Part 9 A, reel 4, NAACP Papers.

17. NAACP board minutes, March 1921; Secretary's report, October 1921, Part 1, reel 4; NAACP news release, September 27, 1921; Charles Curtis to James H. Guy, October 14, 1921; Arthur Capper to Guy, October 15, 1921, Part 9 A, reel 4, NAACP Papers.

18. Secretary of War John W. Weeks to Julius Kahn, December 6, 1921, Part 9 A, reel 4, NAACP Papers.

19. William A. Burnett to JWJ, February 16, 1922; George Hobbes to JWJ, March 28, 1922; JWJ to Isaac Deyo, June 10, 1922; WFW to James A. Cobb, June 30, 1922; Cobb to WFW, July 27, 1922, Part 9 A, reel 4, NAACP Papers; Haynes, *A Night of Violence*, 311–13.

20. John Geter to WFW, November 20 and December 19, 1922; George Hobbes to JWJ, December 10, 1922; James R. Hawkins to JWJ, March 4, 1923, Part 9 A, reel 4, NAACP Papers.

21. WFW to L. F. Coles, November 6, 1922, Part 9 A, reel 4, NAACP Papers.

22. Wilkins, *Standing Fast*, direct quote 54, 55–70.

23. WFW to L. F. Coles, September 13, 1923; "Address of JWJ at Leavenworth," Part 9 A, reel 4, NAACP Papers.

24. Letters to NAACP from Joseph Thompson, October 9, 1923; S. A. Clark, n.d., Resolution of Delaware State Federation of Colored Women's Clubs, October 11, 1923; Robert E. Jones, October 16, 1923; Ernest Tidrington, October 16, 1923, Part 9 A, reel 4; Secretary's report, November 1923, Part 1, reel 4; John H. Colton, January 4, 1924, Part 9, reel 5, NAACP Papers; *Crisis*, January 1924, 125–26, and March 1924, 210–12.

25. "Statement of Henry J. Dannenbaum at NAACP Office in Washington"; *Houston Informer*, December 1, 1923, Part 9 A, reel 4; J. M. Adkins to RWB, November 9, 1923; E. O. Smith to NAACP, n.d., Part 12 A, reel 20, NAACP Papers.

26. Telegram from JWJ to Reverend L. K. Williams, January 23, 1924 (among others); List, "Delegation Presenting Petition for Twenty-fourth," William Monroe Trotter to JWJ, January 24, 1924; JWJ to Trotter, January 25, 1924, Part 9 A, reel 5, NAACP Papers.

27. WFW to Harry Davis, January 10, 1924; WFW to William Henry Lewis, January 15, 1924; *Pittsburgh Courier*, January 12, 1924; *New York Times*, February 8, 1924; *Indianapolis Ledger*, February 16, 1924; *Pittsburgh Courier*, n.d., Part 9 A, reel 5, NAACP Papers; *Crisis*, March 1924, 210–12.

28. John W. Weeks to JWJ, February 12, 1924; JWJ to Hamilton Fish, February 26, 1924; JWJ to Negro editors, February 27, 1924; Part 9 A, reel 5, NAACP Papers.

29. JWJ to John W. Weeks, April 19, 1924; JWJ to Robert L. Vann, April 24, 1924, Part 9 A, reel 5. An April 22 memorandum from WFW describes a meeting with the same Majors Ross and Stansfield that is entirely upbeat, promising the major reductions that would be announced in May. Memorandum from WFW, April 22, 1924, Part 1, reel 25, NAACP Papers.

30. John W. Weeks to WFW, May 13, 1924; NAACP news release, May 16, 1924; Carl Murphy to JWJ, May 24, 1924, Part 9 A, reel 5, NAACP Papers; *Baltimore Afro-American*, May 23, 1924, 1.

NOTES TO CHAPTER 16

1. Jackson, *Klan in the City*.

2. Eric Foner, *Reconstruction: America's Unfinished Revolution, 1863–1877* (New York: Harper and Row, 1988), 425–44.

3. David M. Chalmers, *Hooded Americanism: The History of the Ku Klux Klan*, 3d ed. (Durham, N.C.: Duke University Press, 1987) 22–31.

4. Chalmers, *Hooded Americanism*, 31–35.

5. WFW, *A Man Called White*, 53–56; NAACP news release, September 16, 1921, Part 11 B, reel 5, NAACP Papers. Subsequent note citations to NAACP material for this chapter are from this reel unless otherwise noted.

6. NAACP news releases, March 23, July 18, September 16, 1921; WFW to W. W. Lambert, April 21; WFW to Harry Sims, May 21; NAACP to Patrick Scanlan, August 24; all dates 1921.

7. WFW to B. F. Smith, n.d., NAACP to Harry Davis, August 3; JWJ to members of Congress, October 4; JWJ to L. M. Hershaw, October 11; NAACP news release, October 13; all dates 1921.

8. Chalmers, *Hooded Americanism*, 254–55, 270–72; WFW to New York City Bomb Squad; M. J. Lahey to JWJ, August 25; MWO to Roy Turner, August 25; all dates 1921. For estimates of Klan strength, see Jackson, *Klan in the City*, 235–40.

9. NAACP news release, September 16, 1921; Jackson, *Klan in the City*, 11; Alexander, *Southwest*, 41–54.

10. JWJ to Mrs. Franham Bishop, October 16, 1921.

11. Chalmers, *Hooded Americanism*, 36–38.

12. Frederick Lewis Allen, *Only Yesterday* (1931; rept. New York: Harper and Row, 1959), 124–25; John W. Love to JWJ, October 30, 1921; JWJ to Love, November 3, 1921; Veterans' Bureau field letter, February 3, 1923; Albon Holsey to JWJ, April 2, 1923; "Notes on Tuskegee Hospital Situation," April 11, 1923, Part 11 B, reel 30, NAACP Papers. Subsequent note citations to NAACP material for this chapter are from this reel unless otherwise noted.

13. Pete Daniel, "Black Power in the 1920s: The Case of the Tuskegee Veterans' Hospital," *Journal of Southern History* 36, no. 3 (1970): 368–88; Quote in Albon Holsey to B. J. Davis, May 30, 1923.

14. Robert Moton to Warren G. Harding, February 14; Veterans' Bureau field letter, February 3; George B. Christian to Colonel George E. Ijams, February 23; all dates 1923.

15. Melvin Chisum to Robert Moton, March 21, 1923.

16. Moton to JWJ, February 19; Albon L. Holsey to JWJ, April 2; George B. Christian to

Herbert J. Seligmann, April 28; NAACP news release, May 1; Holsey to WFW, May 4; Holsey to George E. Cannon, May 4; all dates 1923.

17. Shelby Davidson to WFW, May 12, 1923; JWJ to Warren G. Harding, May 16, 1923.

18. Daniel, "Black Power in the 1920s," 376–77; William A. Porter to WFW, June 5, 1923.

19. Daniel, "Black Power in the 1920s," 377–78; Albon Holsey to WFW, July 7, 1923; *Crisis*, September 1923, 216–17.

20. JWJ to Warren G. Harding, July 5, 1923; Memorandum from WFW to JWJ, July 7[?], 1923; NAACP news release, July 13, 1923.

21. Daniel, "Black Power in the 1920s," 380–88; *New York World*, July 6; *New York Herald*, July 10; Shelby Davidson to WFW, August 6; NAACP news release, August 10; all dates 1923.

22. *Jackson Daily News*, n.d.; *Birmingham Age-Herald*, July 11, 1923; *New Orleans Item*, July 11, 1923, Part 11 B, reel 30, NAACP Papers.

23. Albon Holsey to James A. Cobb, May 10, 1924; WFW, *Man Called White*, 69–71.

24. Clement Wood, "Alabama: A Study in Ultra-Violet," *Nation*, January 10, 1923, 33–34.

25. Chalmers, *Hooded Americanism*, 78–84.

26. Dorothy A. Autrey, "The NAACP in Alabama, 1913–1952" (Ph.D. diss., University of Notre Dame, 1985), 48–78.

27. Robert Bagnall, "Report on Southern Trip," December 1921, Part 1, reel 15; Addie Hunton, Report February 7–March 7, 1923, Part 1, reel 16; Autrey, "NAACP in Alabama," 64–68.

28. Autrey, "NAACP in Alabama," 90–110; Hunton, Report for February 7–March 7, 1923, Part 1, reel 16.

29. Autrey, "NAACP in Alabama," 78–90; Hunton, Report of February 7–March 7, 1923, Part 1, reel 16.

30. Autrey, "NAACP in Alabama," 38–42. An alternative analysis, which sees the NAACP as an obstacle to black proletarian advancement, is in Robin D. G. Kelley, *Hammer and Hoe: Alabama Communists during the Great Depression* (Chapel Hill: University of North Carolina Press, 1990), 7–9.

31. Jackson, *Klan in the City*, 144–46.

32. Jackson, *Klan in the City*, 146–51; Richard E. Tucker, *The Dragon and the Cross: The Rise and Fall of the Ku Klux Klan in Middle America* (Hamden, Conn.: Shoestring Press, 1991), 43–49.

33. Tucker, *The Dragon and the Cross*, 88–96.

34. Ibid.; Chalmers, *Hooded Americanism*, 168–69.

35. Tucker, *The Dragon and the Cross*, 101–24.

36. NAACP news releases, May 12, May 14, May 23; JWJ to Ransom, May 14; Random to JWJ, May 16; all dates 1924, Part 11 B, reel 19. The national political implications of Klan power will be developed in the next chapter.

37. Bureau of the Census, *Negroes*, 7, Table II, 6; Report of Robert Bagnall, October 27, 1924, Part 1, reel 15.

38. December 23, 1921, *Indianapolis News;* Harry D. Evans to WFW, March 18, 1922; R. B. H. Smith to NAACP, March 1, 1924; O. W. Langston to WP, April 12, 1924, Part 12 C, reel 9.

39. Tucker, *The Dragon and the Cross*, 113–14; Eulalia Proctor to WFW, October 11, 1924, Part 11 B, reel 19.

40. Eulalia Proctor to WFW, October 11; *Shining Star*, October 25; *Indianapolis Leader*, October 25; all dates 1924 in Part 11 B, reel 19; O. W. Langston to NAACP, September 25, 1924, Part 12 C, reel 9.

41. Memorandum from WFW to WEBD, November 6, 1924, Part 11 B, reel 19; Tucker, *The Dragon and the Cross*, 122–25.

42. Tucker, *The Dragon and the Cross*, 136–81.

43. Jackson, *Klan in the City*, 215–34.

44. *The Crisis*, August 1925, 181–83.

45. Jackson, *Klan in the City*, 232–34.

46. *Crisis*, June 1927, 119; July 1927, 203.

47. WEBD, "The Shape of Fear," in *New American Review* (June 1926), in Eric J. Sundquist, ed., *The Oxford W. E. B. Du Bois Reader* (New York: Oxford University Press, 1996), 385–94, quote 394.

48. WEBD, "The Shape of Fear."

49. Speech by Herbert Adolphus Miller, in *Crisis*, October 1925, 287–91; WEBD, "Cultural Equality," in Sundquist, *Oxford Du Bois Reader*, 394–400, quote 398. For WEBD's earlier views, see, for example, "The Conservation of Races" (1897 paper), in David Levering Lewis, ed., *W. E. B. Du Bois: A Reader* (New York: Henry Holt, 1995), 20–27.

50. Horace Mann Bond, "Intelligence Testing and Propaganda," *Crisis*, June 1924, 61–64; Untitled articles by WEBD, *Crisis*, July 1920, 118–19, and February 1927, 179.

51. Du Bois, "Cultural Equality," in Sundquist, *Oxford Du Bois Reader*. A dramatic account of the Stoddard debate is in Lewis, *Fight for Equality*, 235–37.

NOTES TO CHAPTER 17

1. August Meier, *Negro Thought in America, 1880–1915* (Ann Arbor: University of Michigan Press, 1963), 26–42.

2. Martin Kilson, "Political Change in the Negro Ghetto, 1900–1940s," in Nathan I. Huggins et al., eds., *Key Issues in the Afro-American Experience* (New York: Harcourt, Brace 1971), 167–92.

3. For Coolidge, see Robert H. Ferrell, *The Presidency of Calvin Coolidge* (Lawrence: University of Kansas Press, 1998), and Donald R. McCoy, *Calvin Coolidge: The Quiet President* (Lawrence: University of Kansas Press, 1967). *Baltimore Afro-American*, February 3, 1921, 1; JWJ, *Along This Way*, 374.

4. Chalmers, *Hooded Americanism*, 203, 214; NAACP press releases, May 31, June 9, and September 16, 1924, Part 11 B, reel 20, NAACP Papers. Subsequent note citations to correspondence for this chapter are from this reel unless otherwise noted.

5. Chalmers, *Hooded Americanism*, 202–12; Geoffrey Perrett, *America in the 1920s: A History* (New York: Simon and Schuster, 1982), 186–88; NAACP press release, June 24, 1924.

6. *Crisis*, September 1924, 221–24; JWJ to *New York World*, Part 11 B, reel 19.

7. Page Smith, *Redeeming the Time: A People's History of the 1920s and the New Deal* (New York: McGraw-Hill, 1987), 112–14, quote 112.

8. WP to JWJ, July 6, 1924; Walter J. Bilder to JWJ, July 8, 1924.

9. JWJ to Edgar Parks, September 30, 1924.

10. NAACP press release, July 11, 1924; *Nation*, July 23, 1924, 8.

11. La Follette news release, August 6; WFW to G. Victor Cools, August 8, 14; Cools to JWJ, August 11; Cools to WFW, August 15, 19; WFW to Arthur Warner, August 15; all dates 1924.

12. JWJ, "The Gentlemen's Agreement and the Negro Vote," *Crisis*, October 1924, 260–64.

13. "Symposium," *Crisis*, November 1924, 12–14; NAACP board minutes, November 1924.

14. Harry Nelson to JWJ, September 24, 1924; *Crisis*, December 1924, 55.

15. C. C. Galloway to JWJ, October 21, 1924; Du Bois, "Opinion," *Crisis*, December

1924, 55; A. Dorsey Clayton to JWJ, October 23, 1924; Chalmers, *Hooded Americanism*, 143–48.

16. *Crisis*, December 1924, 55.

17. St. Clair Drake and Horace R. Cayton, *Black Metropolis: A Study of Negro Life in a Northern City* (1945; rept. New York: Harcourt, Brace, 1970), 8, table 1; 9, table 2; 3–27.

18. Christopher Reed, *The Chicago NAACP and the Rise of Black Professional Leadership* (Bloomington: Indiana University Press, 1998), 1–25.

19. Roi Ottley, *The Lonely Warrior: The Life and Times of Robert S. Abbott* (Chicago: Henry Regnery, 1955); Arvarh E. Strickland, *History of the Chicago Urban League* (Urbana: University of Illinois Press, 1966), esp. 1–55; James R. Grossman, *Land of Hope: Chicago, Black Southerners, and the Great Migration* (University of Chicago Press, 1991).

20. Reed, *Chicago NAACP*, 51–53.

21. Undated memorandum from RWB to JWJ; Morris Lewis to WFW, January 21, 1922; RWB to JWJ, March 11, 1922; RWB to Charles E. Bentley, September 25, 1922; MWO to Jane Addams, October 23, 1922, Part 12 C, reel 1. Subsequent note citations to Chicago correspondence for this chapter are from this reel unless otherwise noted.

22. RWB to Morris Lewis, January 11, June 27; Lewis to RWB, March 17, May 29, December 8; JWJ to Lewis, March 27; all dates 1923; Unsigned 1924 annual report; NAACP board minutes, February 1, 1923.

23. RWB to Carl G. Roberts, March 21, 1925.

24. Reed, *Chicago NAACP*, 66–72; Lewis to WFW, December 2, 1925; Archie L. Weaver to JWJ, January 4, 1927.

25. *Crisis*, July 1926, 120–21; *Crisis*, August 1926, 178–80.

26. Reed, *Chicago NAACP*, 70; Archie L. Weaver to WFW, November 30, 1926; Lewis to WP, September 19, 1927.

27. Reed, *Chicago NAACP*, 74–78.

28. Kenneth L. Kusmer, *A Ghetto Takes Shape: Black Cleveland, 1870–1930* (Urbana: University of Illinois Press, 1978), 10, 46–52.

29. Ibid., 145–48.

30. Russell H. Davis, "Harry E. Davis," in *Dictionary of American Negro Biography*, 161–62.

31. WFW to Samuel Mather, n.d., 1920; Harry Davis to JWJ, September 15, 1920; Branch bulletin, October 1920, Part 12 C, reel 22. Subsequent note citations to Cleveland material for this chapter are from this reel unless otherwise noted.

32. NAACP news releases, April 25, June 13, 1924; Kusmer, *Ghetto Takes Shape*, 263.

33. "Resume of Facts Regarding Intimidation of Mr. and Mrs. Hill, July 14, 1924"; NAACP press release, October 24, 1924; J. A. Logan to RWB, October 25, 1924.

34. Harry E. Davis to WFW, February 5, 8, 1926; *Cleveland Plain Dealer*, July 7, 1926, 1; NAACP news release, July 30, 1926.

35. Harry E. Davis to WFW, November 15, 1922; Clayborne George to NAACP, March 19, April 28, and May 20, 1926; Unidentified article, April 28, 1926. I cannot determine how this case was resolved.

36. NAACP news release, November 18, 1928.

37. Osofsky, *Harlem*, 161–68.

38. Ibid., 159–61, 168–78.

39. *Crisis*, December 1924, 105; NAACP board minutes, November 1924.

40. Osofsky, *Harlem*, 170–72; *Crisis*, April 1929, 118, 135.

41. NAACP board minutes, November, December 1921; January, March 1922.

42. M. Waller French to MWO; May 7, 1920, branch minutes; *New York Globe*, April 20, 1921; *New York Dispatch*, May 6, 1921, Part 12 B, reel 4.

43. Osofsky, *Harlem*, 116–17.

NOTES TO CHAPTER 18

1. Conrey Bryson, *Dr. Lawrence A. Nixon and the White Primary* (1974; rept. University of Texas at El Paso, 1992), 1, 18.

2. George B. Tindall, *The Emergence of the New South, 1913–1945* (Baton Rouge: Louisiana State University Press, 1967), 94, 101–2, 165, 167; Bureau of the Census, *Negroes*, 14, table 3.

3. T. R. Fehrenbach, *Lone Star: A History of Texas and the Texans* (New York: American Legacy Press, 1983), 633–48.

4. Darlene Clark Hine, *Black Victory: The NAACP and the Destruction of the Democratic White Primary, 1924–1944* (Millwood, N.Y.: KTO Press, 1979), 25–41; Bryson, *Dr. Lawrence A. Nixon*, 3–4.

5. Hine, *Black Victory*, 54–60.

6. Ibid., 45–50, 72–73; Quintard Taylor, *In Search of the Racial Frontier: African-Americans in the American West* (New York: W. W. Norton, 1999), 232; J. R. Morriss to JWJ, July 3, 1928, Part G-I, Box 204, San Antonio branch file, LC.

7. Bryson, *Dr. Lawrence A. Nixon*, 73–74.

8. Ibid., 19–28.

9. Ibid., 29–34.

10. NAACP board minutes, February 1925; NAACP to Knollenberg, February 16, 1925, Part 4, reel 4, NAACP Papers. Subsequent note citations to correspondence for this chapter are from this reel unless otherwise noted.

11. Washington to WFW, March 4; NAACP news release, April 3; Circular letter, April 14; *Dallas Express*, April 18; all dates 1925.

12. NAACP board minutes, November 1925; Secretary's report, December 1925, Part 1, reel 4; Hine, *Black Victory*, 81–83.

13. Andrew Buni, *Robert L. Vann of the Pittsburgh Courier: Politics and Black Journalism* (Pittsburgh: University of Pittsburgh Press, 1974), 149.

14. Ibid., 148–61, Johnson quote 152.

15. Budget in board minutes, beginning 1927.

16. J. C. Austin to NAACP, February 11, 1921; RWB to J. C. Austin, April 11, 1922; WP to JWJ, December 11, 1924; RWB to Homer S. Brown, January 7, 1926; RWB to JWJ, February 15, 1929; Jeanne S. Scott to RWB, May 4, 1929; Part G-I, Box 190, Pittsburgh branch Files in annually dated folders, LC.

17. Bryson, *Dr. Lawrence A. Nixon*, 38–39; Hine, *Black Victory*, 77–79; Cobb to JWJ, January 11, 1927.

18. Hine, *Black Victory*, 79; NAACP news release, January 5, 1927.

19. "Louis Marshall," *Dictionary of American Negro Biography*, vol. I, 326–28.

20. NAACP news release, February 21, 1927.

21. Holmes Decision #117 October 1926; Telegram from WFW to JWJ, March 7, 1927, NAACP Papers.

22. NAACP news release, March 8, 11, 1927; N. B. Young to JWJ, March 9, 1927; Twelve editorials in African-American press, e.g., *Palmetto Leader*, Columbia, South Carolina; *New York Times*, March 8, 1927.

23. Lawrence A. Nixon to JWJ, March 12, 1927; Bryson, *Dr. Lawrence A. Nixon*, 45; L. W. Washington to JWJ, March 18, 1927, Part 4, reel 5.

24. Bryson, *Dr. Lawrence A. Nixon*, 49–50.

25. NAACP news release, July 27, 1928, Part 4, reel 5.

26. Bryson, *Dr. Lawrence A. Nixon*, 57–66. A good one-page summary of all five cases may be found in Paul Brest and Sanford Levinson, *Processes of Constitutional Decision-making Cases and Materials* (Boston: Little, Brown, 1983), 855.

27. Hine, *Black Victory*, 83.

28. Norman L. Crockett, *The Black Towns* (Lawrence: Regents Press of Kansas, 1979), 81–113; Bureau of the Census, *Negroes*, 6, table 4; 14, table 3.

29. Leaflet for Simmons speech; *Oklahoma City Black Dispatch*, April 1, 1921; Rusk charter, in Part I, Box G-72, Boley file; NAACP news release, February 29, 1924, in Box 172, Chickasaw file, all LC.

30. Jimmy Lee Franklin, *Journey Toward Hope: A History of Blacks in Oklahoma* (Norman: University of Oklahoma Press, 1982), 116.

31. A. Baxter Whitby to JWJ, August 30, 1920: Whitby to WFW, January 1, 1921, and January 23, 1922; Box G-174, NAACP Papers-LC.

32. Alexander, *Klan Southwest*, 131–155.

33. Alexander, *Klan Southwest*, 199; A. Baxter Whitby to JWJ, September 29, 1923, Box G-174, Oklahoma City file, NAACP Papers-LC; NAACP news release, December 12, 1924, Part 11, reel 19.

34. W. H. Twine to WFW, October [?] and 24; JWJ to Harlan Stone, October 17; NAACP news release, October 22; Unidentified article (probably *Muskogee Cimeter*) October 24; Carter Wesley to WFW, October 27; all dates 1924, Part 11, reel 19.

35. Franklin, *Journey Toward Hope*, 117; *New York Sun*, October 24, 1924; Unidentified Associated Press story, January 1925; *Muskogee Times-Democrat*, June [?] 1925, Part 11, reel 19.

36. Franklin, *Journey Toward Hope*, 119–27.

37. Bureau of the Census, *Negroes*, 6, table 5; 55, table 10; Hine, *Black Victory*, 90–91; Hine cites Kousser.

38. Brundage, *Lynching New South*, 184–89.

39. William Andrews to Louis Marshall, October 30, 1928, February 28, 1929, Part 1, reel 15; Andrews to Joseph Pollard, May 6 and 17, 1929, Part 4, reel 4; Hine, *Black Victory*, 93–94.

40. Alfred E. Cohen to William Andrews, October 10, 1929; Reid to WFW in Hine, *Black Victory*, 94.

41. Andrew Buni, *The Negro in Virginia Politics, 1902–1965* (University of Virginia Press, 1967), 96–105, direct quote 105.

42. Memorandum from WFW, "Visit to Richmond, Virginia," February 26, 1929, Part 4, reel 4.

43. Dorothy Salem, "Maggie L. Walker," in *African American Women, A Biographical Dictionary* (New York: Garland Publishing, 1993), 530–32.

NOTES TO CHAPTER 19

1. Green, *Secret City*, esp. 54, table 9; 203.

2. Lewis Newton Walker Jr., "The Struggles and Attempts to Establish Branch Autonomy and Hegemony: A History of the District of Columbia Branch NAACP, 1912–1942" (Ph.D. diss., University of Delaware, 1979), 10–98.

3. Bruce, *Archibald Grimké*.

4. *Corrigan and Curtis v. Buckley*, District of Columbia Court of Appeals 4059 (1924); *Chicago Whip*, May 3, 1925, both in Part 5, reel 4, NAACP Papers. Subsequent note citations to Washington correspondence for this chapter are from this reel unless otherwise noted.

5. NAACP press release, February 15, 1924.

6. Rayford Logan, "James A. Cobb," in *Dictionary of American Negro Biography*, 119–20; *Corrigan and Curtis v. Buckley*, District of Columbia Court of Appeals 4059 (1924); NAACP press release, June 13, 1924.

7. NAACP news release, October 31, 1925; Marshall to JWJ, September 25, 1925; Marshall to Moorfield Storey, May 28, 1926.

8. *North Capitol Citizen*, January 9, 16, 1925; NAACP press release, September 12, 1924, and February 27, 1925.

9. JWJ to Cobb, October 27; Cobb to JWJ, October 28, November 12, all dates 1925; NAACP leaflet, Part 12 A, reel 6.

10. NAACP news release, January 8, 1926; Cobb to JWJ, January 13, 1926.

11. Walker, "History of D.C. Branch NAACP," 101. My impression of Thomas flows from the events that follow.

12. Louis Pinkett to RWB, December 27, 1925; Jennie McGuire to WFW, March 16, 1926; Part 12 A, reel 6.

13. MWO to Laura B. Glenn, January 12; Glenn to MWO, January 14; Neval Thomas to MWO, January 14; JWJ to A. S. Pinkett, February 11; all dates 1926; Part 12 A, reel 6.

14. *Corrigan v. Buckley*, 271 U.S. 323 (1926); Marshall to Storey, May 28, 1926; JWJ to Cobb, May 26, 1926; NAACP news release, May 27, 1926. An excellent account of restrictive covenant cases is Clement E. Vose, *Caucasians Only: The Supreme Court, the NAACP, and the Restrictive Covenant Cases* (Berkeley: University of California, 1967). For *Corrigan v. Buckley*, see 17–19, 52–54.

15. *Baltimore Afro-American*, n.d.; Cobb to JWJ, March 28, 1927, Part 12 A, reel 6; Green, *Secret City*, 204–5, quote 205.

16. *Washington Sentinel*, January 23, 1926; Neval Thomas to JWJ, March 27, 1927; Thomas to Calvin Coolidge, August 8, 1927; *Philadelphia Tribune*, November 3, 1927; *Baltimore Afro-American*, October 20, 1928; Washington, D.C., annual report, 1927, Part 12 A, reel 6.

17. Washington, D.C., branch record, 1919–1928; WFW to Neval Thomas, April 5; A. S. Pinkett to RWB, October 4, 8; RWB to Pinkett, October 7, 14; Pinkett to JWJ, November 10; MWO to Pinkett, November 21; all dates 1927, Part 12 A, reel 6.

18. *New York Age*, May 12, 1928; WP, "The Neval Thomas Banquet and NAACP Sabotage," unidentified paper, June 16, 1928, Part 12 A, reel 6.

19. NAACP board minutes, April 1928; Thomas to WP, June 19, 1928, Part 12 A, reel 6.

20. NAACP board minutes, July 3, 1928; July 16, 1928.

21. "Charges by Neval Thomas sent to Board of Directors"; NAACP board minutes, November and December 1928.

22. NAACP board minutes, December 1928.

23. Evelyn Brooks Barnett, "Nannie Burroughs," *Dictionary of American Negro Biography*, 81–82; NAACP board minutes, December 1928; MWO to Nannie Burroughs, December 14, 1928; JWJ to A. S. Pinkett, December 15 and 26, 1928; Nannie Burroughs to NAACP, n.d.; all Part 12 A, reel 6; WEBD to Carl Murphy, n.d., Part 12 A, reel 7.

24. Nannie Burroughs to WP, January 12, 1929, Part 12 A, reel 7.

25. Donald E. De Vore, "The Rise from the Nadir: Black New Orleans between the Wars, 1920–1940 (master's thesis, University of New Orleans, 1983), 62–66; E. M. Dunn to John Shillady, April 12, 1920, Part 5, reel 4.

26. *New Orleans Times-Picayune*, September 14, 19, 1924, 1.

27. Gwendolyn Midlo Hall, "The Formation of Afro-Creole Culture," in *Creole New Orleans: Race and Americanization*, ed. Arnold R. Hirsch and Joseph Logsdon (Baton Rouge: Louisiana State University Press, 1992), 58–87; and Hirsch and Logsdon, introduction to Part III, *Creole New Orleans*, 189–200.

28. Joseph G. Treagle Jr., "Creoles and Americans," in Hirsch and Logsdon, *Creole New Orleans*, 131–85.

29. Joseph Logsdon and Caryn Cosse Bell, "The Americanization of Black New Orleans, 1850–1900," in Hirsch and Logsdon, *Creole New Orleans*, 201–61.

30. Ibid., 245–61.

31. De Vore, "Rise from the Nadir," 21–26; RWB to JWJ, September 24 and n.d.; Leaflet for November 30 meeting, Part 5, reel 2.

32. George Lucas to RWB, October 24, 1924, Part 5, reel 4.

33. RWB to George Lucas, October 30, 1924; Lucas to RWB, November 1, 1924; Unidentified clipping; Part 5, reel 2.

34. NAACP news release, October 10; *New Orleans Times-Picayune*, November 23, 1924, Part 5, reel 2; George Lucas to RWB, February 7, 1925; Poster, December 9, 1924, meeting, Part 5, reel 4.

35. George Lucas to RWB, November 9, 1924, Part 5, reel 2; Lucas to RWB, November 19, 1924, Part 5, reel 4; James E. Gayle to RWB, November 27, 1924, Part 5, reel 4.

36. "Decision of Louisiana Supreme Court"; "Brief for Benjamin Harmon"; *New Orleans Times-Picayune*, March 5, 1925; *New Orleans States*, March 2; WFW to George Lucas, March 4; RWB to Lucas, March 5; Lucas to WFW, March 14; all dates 1925; Part 5, reel 4.

37. George Lucas to WFW, April 1, 1925; *New Orleans Times-Picayune*, May 15, 1925, Part 5, reel 2; *Louisiana Weekly*, October 24, 1925, November 14, 1925, February 20, 1926 (viewed at Amistad Research Center, New Orleans); De Vore, "Rise from the Nadir," 66.

38. *Louisiana Weekly*, November 14, December 12, December 26, 1925; February 6, May 1, May 15, October 2, October 9, 1926; all page 1; De Vore, "Rise from the Nadir," 70–71.

39. WP to NAACP, April 11, 1926; George Lucas to WP, April 26, 1926; James A. Cobb to JWJ, April 28, 1926; Cobb to JWJ, January 29, 1927; Part 5, reel 2; *Louisiana Weekly*, April 3, 1926.

40. George Lucas to WFW, February 26, 1927, Part 5, reel 4; NAACP news release, Part 5, reel 2; De Vore, "Rise from the Nadir," 72; *Louisiana Weekly*, March 19, 1927.

41. For Tureaud, see the introductory biography in the Alexander Pierre Tureaud Papers, Amistad Research Center, New Orleans; for Lucas, *Louisiana Weekly*, January 17, 1931.

42. Bureau of the Census, *Negroes*, 54, table 9.

43. "Chronology [Browne case] 1924"; Memorandum from O. D. Williams to JWJ, July 26, 1924; Part 5, reel 2.

44. Memorandum from Herbert J. Seligmann, n.d.; NAACP news releases, September 25, November 10, November 25, 1925; Part 5, reel 2.

NOTES TO CHAPTER 20

1. Marcet Haldeman-Julius, "The Defendants in the Sweet Trial," *Haldeman-Julius Monthly* vol. 4, no. 1 (June 1926), direct quotes 3, 11, in MWO Papers, Box 11, File 4, Walter Reuther Library, Wayne State University, Detroit; WFW, "The Sweet Trial," *Crisis*, January 1926, 125–29.

2. Richard W. Thomas, *Life for Us Is What We Make It: Building Black Community in Detroit, 1915–1945* (Bloomington: Indiana University Press, 1992), 17–26; August Meier and Elliott Rudwick, *Black Detroit and the Rise of the United Auto Workers* (New York: Oxford University Press, 1979), 3–33, blues song, 5.

3. Bernard Coker and Norman McCrae, interview by author, December 12, 1997.

4. Jackson, *Klan in the City*, 127–43.

5. "Statement of Facts: People v. Flita Mathis," Part 12 C, reel 12, NAACP Papers.

6. Thomas, *Life for Us*, 136–40; WFW, "Negro Segregation Comes North," *Nation* October 21, 1925, 458–59.

7. David Allen Levine, *Internal Combustion: The Races in Detroit, 1915–1926* (Westport, Conn.: Greenwood Press, 1976), 153–58; *Detroit Free Press*, July 12, 1925, 1.

8. Haldeman-Julius, "The Defendants in the Sweet Trial" and "Clarence Darrow's Defense of a Negro," *Haldeman-Julius Monthly* (July 1926) in MWO Papers.

9. RWB to Fred H. Williams, February 6, 1925; RWB to Robert Bradby, March 4, 1925, Part 12 C, reel 12, NAACP Papers. Subsequent note citations for this chapter are 1925 unless otherwise noted.

10. Bernard Coker and Norman McCrae, interview by author, December 12, 1997.

11. *Detroit Independent*, May 30; NAACP press release, June 3; Robert Bradby to JWJ, July 27; Part 5, reel 2.

12. Telegram from JWJ to Bradby, September 11; Mose Walker and W. H. McKinney to JWJ, September 12; Part 12 C, reel 12; NAACP board minutes, September 14, 1925.

13. WFW to JWJ, September 17[?], Part 5, reel 2.

14. For Jayne, telephone interview by author with Nathan Milstein, February 11, 1998; "Agreement Entered into on September 17, 1925, between Dr. O. H. Sweet and His Ten Co-defendants and the Detroit NAACP," Part 5, reel 2; WFW, "Negro Segregation Comes North," *Nation*, 459.

15. Haldeman-Julius, "Defendants in the Sweet Trial," 8.

16. WFW to Oscar Baker, October 5, Part 5, reel 2.

17. "City-wide Committee for Sweet Fund Is Organized," *Detroit Independent*, October 2, Part 5, reel 2.

18. O[tis] O. Sweet et al. to W. H. McKinney, September 29; O[tis] O. Sweet et al. to WEBD, September 29, Part 5, reel 2.

19. *Detroit Free Press*, July 12, 1; Clarence Darrow, *The Story of My Life* (New York: Charles Scribner's Sons, 1960), 244–78; Frederick Lewis Allen, *Only Yesterday* (New York: Harper and Row, 1950), 167–71.

20. WFW to Oscar Baker, October 5; N. K. McGill to WFW, October 6; Telegram from JWJ to Charles Bentley, October 7; JWJ to Clarence Darrow, October 7, Part 5, reel 2; NAACP board minutes, October 13, 1925.

21. WFW, *A Man Called White*, 76–77. The problem with this anecdote is that White says James Weldon Johnson, an unmistakably black man, was also in the room. Nevertheless, Arthur Garfield Hays remembers it the same way in his autobiography, *City Lawyer* (New York: Simon and Schuster, 1942), 207.

22. For Murphy, telephone interview by author with Nathan Milstein, February 11, 1998; Memorandum on Detroit situation, October 8; RWB to Frank Murphy, October 8, Part 5, reel 2; Haldeman-Julius, "Clarence Darrow's Defense."

23. WFW, *A Man Called White*, 76–77.

24. Memorandum from WFW to Herbert J. Seligmann, October 22; WFW to Clarence Darrow, October 24, Part 5, reel 3; *Washington Daily American*, October 21; *Pittsburgh Courier*, October 24 and 31; *Detroit Independent*, October 23; *Baltimore Afro-American*, October 24, Part 5, reel 2.

25. WFW to Ira W. Jayne, October 22; WP to WFW and JWJ, October 25, Part 5, reel 3.

26. Mose Walker to WFW, October 22, Part 5, reel 3.

27. WFW to JWJ, n.d., Part 5, reel 3.

28. Darrow, *Story*, 307.

29. WFW, "The Sweet Trial," *Crisis*, January 26, 1926, 125–29; David E. Lilienthal, "Has the Negro the Right of Self-Defense?" *Nation*, December 23, 1925, 724–25; WFW to JWJ, November 13, Part 5, reel 3.

30. WFW to JWJ, November 7, 9, 16, 17, 18, Part 5, reel 3; Secretary and field secretary reports, November 25, Part 1, reel 4.

31. WFW, "The Sweet Trial"; WFW to JWJ, November 20, Part 5, reel 3.

32. Lilienthal, "Has the Negro the Right?"; White, *A Man Called White*, 78.

33. WFW, *A Man Called White*, 78–79 (the source of this quote is unclear and may be a WFW invention); NAACP press release, November 28; WFW to Harry E. Davis, November 30, Part 5, reel 3.

34. *Atlanta Independent*, December 3; *Cleveland Call*, December 5, 4; *Boston Chronicle*, December 5; *Pittsburgh Courier*, December 5, Part 5, reel 4.

35. Oscar Baker to WFW, December 1; "Memo: Sweet Case," December 8, Part 5, reel 3.

36. Secretary and field secretary reports, November 25, Part 1, reel 4; Archie L. Weaver to NAACP, November 18, Part 12 C, reel 1.

37. *New York Age*, December 19, 1; Field secretary report, January 1926, Part 1, reel 5; NAACP board minutes, December 1925.

38. RWB to JWJ, n.d., Part 1, reel 15; *Chicago Whip*, January 16, 1926, Part 5, reel 4.

39. Field secretary report, February 14–16, 1926; RWB to national office, received February 25, 1926, Part 1, reel 15.

40. RWB to JWJ, February 17, 1926, Part 1, reel 14; Memorandum from WFW to JWJ, February 1; Memorandum from WFW, February 18; WFW to Mose Walker, February 20; WFW to Oscar Baker, March 5, 1926; Report of WFW on trip to Detroit, March 21–24, 1926, Part 5, reel 3.

41. Memorandum from WFW and JWJ on interview with Darrow at Belmont Hotel, New York, February 2, 1926, Part 5, reel 3.

42. Haldeman-Julius, "Defendants in the Sweet Trial."

43. *Detroit Free Press*, April 20, 8; April 22, 4, 1926; Haldeman-Julius, "Clarence Darrow's Defense."

44. *Detroit Free Press*, May 5, 1926, 4.

45. *Detroit Free Press*, May 6, 1926; Haldeman-Julius, "Clarence Darrow's Defense."

46. *Detroit Free Press*, May 12, 1; JWJ, "Detroit," *Crisis*, July 1926, 117–20.

47. Haldeman-Julius, "Clarence Darrow's Defense."

48. Johnson, "Detroit."

49. NAACP board minutes, September 13, 1926.

NOTES TO CHAPTER 21

1. WFW to B. F. Wiley, May 14, 1925, Part 7 A, reel 16, NAACP Papers. Subsequent note citations to correspondence for this chapter are from this reel unless otherwise noted.

2. WFW to C. C. Johnson, May 14; C. C. Johnson to WFW, May 16; WFW to Johnson, May 19; all dates 1925.

3. NAACP board minutes, April, May, June 1925; Secretary's reports, April, May, June 1925, Part 1, reel 4.

4. WFW, *Rope and Faggot: The Biography of Judge Lynch* (1929; rept. New York: Arno Press, 1969), 258, table VII.

5. Fox Butterfield, *All God's Children: The Bosket Family and the American Tradition of Violence* (New York: Alfred A. Knopf, 1997), 3–18, 40–42.

6. Walter Edgar, *South Carolina: A History* (Columbia: University of South Carolina Press, 1998), 468.

7. Franklin, *From Slavery to Freedom*, 339–40; George B. Tindall, *Emergence of the New South*, 171.

8. Asa H. Gordon, *Sketches of Negro Life and History in South Carolina*, 2d ed. (1929; rept. University of South Carolina Press, 1971).

9. Edgar, *South Carolina*, 483–88.

10. WFW, "The Shambles of South Carolina," *Crisis*, December 1926, 72–75.

11. WFW, "Shambles of South Carolina." White reported the source of this tip as a letter from an African-American Baptist minister, but the letter was never produced, and the reason for the raid remains unclear.

12. "An Address to the People of South Carolina"; Butler Nance to MWO, February 5, 1919; Nance to JWJ, July 19, 1919, Part 12 A, reel 8.

13. Columbia branch charter, membership lists, Part 12 A, reel 18; Moore, *Columbia*, 380–81.

14. Butler Nance to MWO, February 5, 1919; Nance to NAACP, May 20, 1919; Mrs. R. F. Brooks to John Shillady, November 6, 1919; Nance to WFW, September 12, 1920, Part 12 A, reel 18.

15. Postcard from R. W. Jackson to RWB, February 1923; RWB to N. J. Frederick, December 4, 1926, Part 12 A, reel 18. Moore, *Columbia*, 380.

16. Unsigned, [N. J. Frederick] to WFW, May 18, 1925.

17. WFW, "Shambles of South Carolina."

18. WFW, "Shambles of South Carolina"; WFW to Governor Thomas McLeod, October 26, 1926.

19. *New York Times*, October 9, 1926, 1.

20. *New York Times*, October 10, 1926, 28.

21. JWJ to Governor Thomas McLeod, October 10; McLeod to JWJ, October 18; N. J. Frederick to JWJ, October 11; James Quinby to JWJ, October 12; A. H. Johnson to JWJ, October 12; all dates 1926.

22. WFW to N. J. Frederick, October 22, 1926; WFW to Bishop John Hurst, October 22, 1926; WFW to Mr. Swope or Mr. Beazell, *New York World*, October 26, 1926; WFW, "Shambles of South Carolina"; WFW, *A Man Called White*, 56–59. White's *Crisis* article and autobiographical account differ in some details. For Quinby, see, for example, letters to WFW, November 15 and December 1, 1926, or *New York World*, November 4, 1926.

23. WFW to Governor Thomas McLeod, October 26, 1926; WFW to Mr. Swope or Mr. Beazell, October 26, 1926.

24. WFW to Mr. Beazell, October 17, 1926; Memorandum from JWJ to Mr. Seligmann, January 25, 1927; WFW, "Shambles of South Carolina"; WFW to N. J. Frederick, February 24, 1927, Part 7 A, reel 17.

25. *New York World*, November 5, 1926; Affidavit of Lucy Mooney, affidavit of Charles Lee, both November 2, 1926.

26. *New York World*, November 8 and 9, 1926, 1.

27. *Columbia Record*, November 15, 1926; *Columbia Record* article reprinted in *New York World*, November 10, 1926; Wright editorial quoted in *New York World*, November 19, 1926.

28. *Columbia State*, November 15, 1926; *New York World*, November 13 and 19, 1926 (summaries of South Carolina press); *Charleston News and Courier*, November 18, 1926.

29. *New York Times*, November 18, 1926, 2, and November 19, 1926, in NAACP Papers, Part 7 A, reel 16.

30. *Columbia State*, November 13; *Columbia Record*, November 18; *Philadelphia Public Journal*, November 21; Claude Sawyer to WFW, November 23; WFW to R. Charlton Wright, December 1; WFW to Sawyer, December 2; all dates 1926.

31. *New York World*, November 11 and 12, 1926; *Columbia Record*, November 30, 1926.

32. White, "Shambles of South Carolina."

33. *Columbia State*, December 1, 1926; *New York World*, December 1, 1926.

34. NAACP news release, January 3; WFW to L. G. Southard, January 3; Southard to WFW, January 5; N. J. Frederick to WFW, January 8; all dates 1927.

35. WFW to Southard, January 17, Part 7 A, reel 16; *New York Times*, January 3 and 4; Wright to WFW, February 6; WFW to Frederick, February 24, Part 7 A, reel 17; all dates 1927.

36. *Columbia Record*, January 25, 1927; *Columbia State*, January 29 and 31, 1927, Part 7 A, reel 17.

37. *Spartanburg Herald*, January 31, February 1 and 3; *Charleston News and Courier*, February 1, 1927; WFW to South Carolina secretary of state, March 25, Part 7 A, reel 17; all dates 1927.

38. *Columbia State*, January 29, 1927, Part 7 A, reel 17.

39. N. J. Frederick to WFW, February 26, 1927, Part 7 A, reel 17; WFW to Isadore Martin, February 28, 1927, Part 12 B, reel 6.

40. Julian St. George White to WFW, March 30, 1927, Part 12 B, reel 6; *Pittsburgh Courier*, April 2, 1927, Part 7 A, reel 16.

41. *New York Amsterdam News*, June 1, 1927, in Ralph Ginzburg, *One Hundred Years of Lynchings*, 175–78. Walter White's *Crisis* article has Howard killed by a pistol, and Clar-

ence Lowman, the only defendant who might have killed him, holding a shotgun. James Edwin Kerr, a reporter with ties to Sheriff Robinson, has Howard killed by buckshot. Kerr letter to *Columbia State,* October 13, 1926, in letter from WFW to Louis Marshall, November 15, 1926, Part 7 A, reel 16.

42. N. J. Frederick to WFW, November 8, 1926, Part 7 A, reel 16, and December 11, 1926, Part 12 A, reel 18.

43. R. W. Jackson to RWB, January 31; Julia Stuart to NAACP, July 31; Jackson to RWB, August 8, Part 12 A, reel 18; all dates 1927.

44. *St. Luke's Herald,* November 8; *Baltimore Afro-American,* November 13 and 20; *Philadelphia Tribune,* November 8 and 20; *Dallas Express,* November 20; *Amsterdam News,* November 17 and 24; *St. Paul Echo,* November 8; *St. Louis Argus,* November 19, are some of the clippings in part 7 A, reel 17; all dates 1927.

45. Zangrando, *NAACP Crusade,* 6, table 2.

NOTES TO CHAPTER 22

1. Mark Schneider, "The Boston NAACP and the Decline of the Abolitionist Impulse," *Massachusetts Historical Review* I (1999): 95–110. Note citations for this section rely especially on NAACP Papers, LC, Box I C-270, Harvard University file. For the branch's first decade, see Schneider, *Boston Confronts Jim Crow, 1890–1920* (Boston: Northeastern University Press, 1997), 133–59.

2. "Florence Kelley," *Notable Black American Women,* vol. II, 316–19.

3. Florence Kelley, "The Sterling-Towner Bill," *Crisis,* October 1923, 252–55.

4. NAACP board minutes, February and April, 1923; Kelley, "Sterling-Towner."

5. WEBD, "Opinion," *Crisis,* March 1924, 199–201.

6. NAACP board minutes, February, March, April 1923.

7. Mark V. Tushnet, *The NAACP's Legal Strategy against Segregated Education, 1925–1950* (Chapel Hill, N.C.: University of North Carolina Press, 1987), 4–6, 21–33; "Education," *Crisis,* November 1924, 8–9, and "The Negro Common School in Georgia," *Crisis,* September 1926, 248–49, 262–65.

8. Deposition of Alberta Cheeks, Part 3, reel 8, NAACP Papers. Subsequent note citations to NAACP material for this chapter are from this reel unless otherwise noted.

9. James B. Lane, *City of the Century: A History of Gary, Indiana* (Bloomington: Indiana University Press, 1978), 142–44, direct quote 143.

10. Lane, *City of the Century,* 28–52; Bureau of the Census, *Negroes,* 55, table 10.

11. Lane, *City of the Century,* 62–63.

12. Report of Robert L. Bailey, October 1, 1927.

13. Jackson, *Klan in the City,* 97; Lane, *City of the Century,* 93–95; Bailey report, October 1, 1927.

14. Elizabeth Lytle to Roy Nash, March 13, 1917; John Shillady to Gary branch, July 31, 1918; Gary to national office, June 11, 1919; Louis Campbell to MWO, May 25, 1920; Lytle to Shillady, n.d.; Branch minutes, March 26, 1920, all Part 12 C, reel 8. RWB quote is in RWB to Morris Lewis, February 14, 1923, Part 12 C, reel 1.

15. Louis Campbell, "Segregation Means Neglect," *Gary Dispatch,* n.d., in 1921 file; *Gary Daily Tribune,* April 11, 1921; Petition in 1922 file; Campbell to RWB, August 4, 1922; Thomas J. Wilson to RWB, August 7, 1922; JWJ to Campbell, February 14, 1923; JWJ to Wilson, February 14, 1923; Campbell to JWJ, September 30, 1926, Part 12 C, reel 8.

16. NAACP news releases, September 27, 29, 1927.

17. Bailey report, October 1, 1927.

18. NAACP news releases, October 7, 14, 1927; Lane, *City of the Century,* 145.

19. Telegram from Robert L. Bailey to JWJ, October 25; Bailey to WP, November 11; NAACP news release, November 25, December 16; all dates 1927.

20. Memorandums from JWJ, October 11, 13, 1927; NAACP news release, October 21, 1927; Edward McKinley Bacoyn to JWJ, November 8, 1927; "Report of Gary branch," n.d.; *Gary Colored American*, December 15, 1927.

21. *Chicago Whip*, November 5, 1927; *Norfolk Journal and Guide*, n.d.; *Gary Colored American*, December 15, 1927; John Russell to JWJ, December 14, 1927; Robert Bailey to JWJ, December 17, 1927.

22. Milo Murray to Bill Andrews, March 15, 1929, Part 3, reel 9.

23. Stein, *Race and Class*, 242–47.

24. Unsigned documents (probably Edward McKinley Bacoyn), "Conference with Mr. Wirt" and "Propaganda."

25. Statements by Ruth Kelly and Alberta Cheeks.

26. Edward McKinley Bacoyn to Bill Andrews, January 18, 1928; NAACP news release, January 19, 1928; Bacoyn to Robert Bailey, February 17, 1928; Brief, *Edwards v. Wirt and School City of Gary*.

27. Robert Bailey to JWJ, April 10, 1928; *Valparaiso Didette Messenger*, May 1, 1928; *Gary American*, July 11, 1928.

28. Alberteen Marsh letter to *Gary American*, July 16, 1928; William Andrews to Marsh, July 19, 1928.

29. Edward McKinley Bacoyn to Bill Andrews, July 11, August 13, September 14, 1928.

30. Edward McKinley Bacoyn to Bagnall, October 2, 1928.

31. Neil Betten and Raymond A. Mohl, "The Evolution of Racism in an Industrial City, 1906–1940: A Case Study of Gary, Indiana," in *Politics in Black America: Crisis and Change in the Negro Ghetto* (New York: St. Martin's Press, 1973), ed. Martin Kilson, 283–96, direct quote 295.

32. Edward McKinley Bacoyn, "Meet Gary 1929"; Milo Murray to Bill Andrews, May 13, 1929, Part 3, reel 9.

NOTES TO CHAPTER 23

1. Lester C. Lamon, *Black Tennesseans, 1900–1930* (Knoxville: University of Tennessee Press, 1977); Waskow, *From Race Riot to Sit-In*, 13–16.

2. "Maurice Mays and the Lindsey Murder Mystery," n.d., probably the *Knoxville Herald*, Part 8 A, reel 9, NAACP Papers. Subsequent note citations to source material for Mays for this chapter are from this reel unless otherwise noted.

3. Typescript, "Maurice F. Mays"; Mays to Governor A. A. Taylor, November 10, 1921.

4. Circular fund appeal from Reverend J. H. Henderson, September 6, 1920; NAACP news release, August 10, 1921.

5. J. H. Henderson to Catherine Lealtad, September 18, 1920; Memorandum from WFW to Shillady, May 10, 1920; Memorandum from WFW to JWJ, April 19, 1921; *Crisis*, January 1921, 118.

6. Reverend J. H. Henderson to WFW, November 23, 1920, April 30, 1921; Knoxville *Sentinel*, April 19, 20, 21, 1921.

7. Maurice Mays to Governor A. A. Taylor, November 10, 1921; Reverend S. L. McDowell to WFW, December 6, 1921; WFW to McDowell, December 12, 1921.

8. Dr. H. M. Green to JWJ, September 10, 1927; "Investigation of Mrs. Sadie Mendil's Confession," by Helen Boardman.

9. Reverend J. H. Henderson to WFW, March 30, 1921; Dr. H. M. Green to JWJ, September 12, 1927; Lamon, *Black Tennesseans*, 264–73.

10. John Taylor, "The Rosewood Massacre," *Esquire*, July 1994; *New York Age*, January 13, 1923, 1, JWJ quote 4, January 20, 4; *New York Times*, January 6, 1923. The film *Rosewood* invents a nonhistorical character played by Ving Rhames, a returned war veteran who

wreaks vengeance on the white attackers, but in many other respects is generally accurate.

11. E. O. Smith to WFW, June 13, 1923, April 23, 1924, Part 12 A reel 19.

12. E. O. Smith to WFW, June 13, 1923; E. O. Adkins to WFW, March 20, 1924; NAACP news release, November 7, 1924, Part 12 A, reel 19.

13. NAACP news release, March 19, 1926, Part 12 A, reel 20.

14. Memorandum from C. P. De Walt, September 8, 1926, Part 12 A, reel 20.

15. WFW to E. O. Smith, February 20, 1925, Part 12 A, reel 19.

16. WFW to Raymond Price Alexander, March 10, 1925, Part 12 B, reel 6, NAACP Papers. Subsequent notes citations to correspondence for this chapter are from this reel unless otherwise noted.

17. Raymond Price Alexander to WFW, March 20, 1925; Typescript, "Commonwealth v. Walter Rounds, March 4, 1925; *Washington Daily American,* n.d.

18. Raymond Price Alexander to WFW, March 20, 1925; WFW to Isadore Martin, April 28, 1925, May 4, 1925.

19. Kellogg, *NAACP,* 124–26; Vincent P. Franklin, "The Philadelphia Race Riot of 1918," in Kilson, *Crisis and Change,* 336–50; J. Max Barber to WP, June 18, 192[3?]; Barber to WP, April 18, 1929; in Box 1, "J. Max Barber" file, WP Papers, Schomburg Institute, New York Public Library.

20. William Lloyd Imes to WFW, January 20, 1923; Isadore Martin to RWB, March 29, 1923; RWB to Fielding A. Ford, July 31, 1923; Julian St. George White to RWB, October 15, 1926; RWB to Martin, January 5, 1925.

21. *New York Times, New York Telegraph,* March 19, 1927; Elisha Scott to WFW, May 15, 1927, Part 7 A, reel 11.

22. Elisha Scott to WFW, May 15, 1927; *New York Evening Post,* May 31, 1927; Part 7 A, reel 11.

23. *New York Evening Post,* May 31, 1927; *Coffeyville Daily Journal,* June 20, 1927; NAACP news release, June 3, 1927; Part 7 A, reel 11.

24. WP to NAACP, June 5, 1927, Part 2, reel 20.

25. D. G. Whitecker and D. M. Hunigan to WFW, May 9, 1927; Elisha Scott to WFW, May 18, July 16, July 20, 1927; Part 7 A, reel 11; Richard Kluger, *Simple Justice* (New York: Random House, 1997), 384–86.

26. Elisha Scott to WFW, June 27, September 24, 1927, Part 7 A, reel 11.

27. Memorandum from WP, June 1, 1923, Part 2, reel 20.

28. *Louisville News,* April 17, April 24, May 1, 1926, Part 12 A, reel 11, NAACP Papers. Subsequent note citations for this chapter are from this reel unless otherwise noted. Wright, 263–64.

29. *Louisville News,* May 1, 1926.

30. Typescript, n.d., from *Louisville Leader; Louisville News,* May 22; *New York World,* September 27; Memorandum from JWJ, November 27; all dates 1926.

31. Typescript, "Commonwealth of Kentucky v. Bunyan Fleming"; Telegram from William Warley to NAACP, December 1, 1926.

32. Bunyan Fleming to G. P. Hughes, December 6; O'Doherty to Hughes, December 11; William Warley to JWJ, December 11; JWJ to Robert L. Bradby, December 20; all dates 1926; WFW to Hughes, January 28, 1927.

33. Wright, *Kentucky,* 264–65; Telegram from G. P. Hughes to WFW, July 15, 1927.

34. Louis Marshall to JWJ, July 14, 1927; JWJ to G. P. Hughes, July 19, 1927; Part 12 A, reel 12.

35. WP to JWJ, October 27, 1927, Part 2, reel 20; JWJ to WP, October 31, 1927; Hughes to JWJ, June 20, 1928, Part 2, reel 2.

36. *St. Louis Argus,* December 2, 1927, Part 12 A, reel 12.

37. *Louisville Leader,* n.d.; I. Willis Cole to JWJ, December 3, 1927; Part 12 A, reel 12.

38. Forrest Bailey to JWJ, September 28; *Louisville Leader,* n.d.; NAACP news release,

November 5; *New York World*, September 27; *St. Paul Echo*, October 2; *Pittsburgh Courier*, October 9; all dates 1926, Part 12 A, reel 11.

39. Wright, *Kentucky*, 300–1; Bessie Etherly to RWB, December 22, 1926; *Louisville Leader*, February 5, 1928, Part 12 A, reel 12.

40. *New York World*, May 31, 1928; Affidavit quoted in unidentified news article, Part 12 A, reel 19. Subsequent note citations to Bess material for this chapter are from this reel unless otherwise noted.

41. *New York World*, May 31, 1928.

42. *New York Times*, June 10, 1928; WFW to William P. Beazell, (*New York World*), July 31, 1928.

43. *Columbia Record*, June 21, July 17, 1928; Typescript, "Chronology of Ben Bess Case."

44. N. J. Frederick to William T. Andrews, July 21, 1928; Frederick to WFW, July 30, 1928.

45. N. J. Frederick to RWB, August 24, 1928.

46. RWB to N. J. Frederick, September 19, 1928; *Chicago Defender*, September 22, 1928.

47. *Ex Parte Sallie Bess*, Case 385; N. J. Frederick to Bill Andrews, October 8, 1928; Frederick to WFW, October 16, 1928.

48. RWB to R. W. Jackson, June 24, 1929; N. J. Frederick to WFW, October 16, 1929.

49. David Lester, *The Death Penalty: Issues and Answers, 1608–1985* (Springfield, Ill.: Charles Thomas, 1998), 56.

50. William T. Andrews, "The Negro in Law," *Crisis*, November 1929, 369, 390.

51. Washington's crime was variously reported as "slaying a negress during a dance hall brawl," unidentified news article, and "defending his daughters from the advances of a white man as he advanced on the Washington house," NAACP news release, September 30, 1927; November 8, 1929, Part 8, reel 11. Subsequent note citations to Washington material for this chapter are from this reel.

52. S. D. McGill to JWJ, April 1; JWJ to McGill, April 4; NAACP release, October 7; NAACP board minutes, September; all dates 1927.

53. Louis Marshall to JWJ, November 12, 1927; Marshall to S. D. McGill, February 27, 1928; Memorandum from NAACP, March 6, 1928; Typescript, "Opinion Florida Supreme Court," January 1928.

54. S. D. McGill to JWJ, December 27, 1927.

55. S. D. McGill to JWJ, October 24, 1928; Louis Marshall to JWJ, November 12, 1927; NAACP news release, November 8, 1929.

NOTES TO CHAPTER 24

1. JWJ, *Along This Way*, 355.

2. Herbert Hill, *The Racial Practices of Organized Labor in the Age of Gompers and After*, ed. Hill and Arthur M. Ross (New York: Harcourt, Brace and World), 365–402. See also Hill, *Black Labor and the American Legal System* (Madison: University of Wisconsin Press, 1985).

3. Gunnar Myrdal, *An American Dilemma: The Negro Problem and Modern Democracy* (1944; rept. New York: Harper and Row, 1962), 294; Bureau of the Census, *Negroes*, 287.

4. Myrdal, *An American Dilemma*, appendix 6, 1,079–1,124.

5. Nancy J. Weiss, *The National Urban League, 1910–1940* (New York: Oxford University Press, 1974).

6. Phillip Foner, *Organized Labor and the Black Worker, 1619–1981* (1974; rept. New York: International Publishers, 1982), 64–73, Gompers quote 68; Hill, "Racial Practices," 15.

7. Foner, *Organized Labor*, 158–59; *Crisis*, June 1919.

8. MWO, "Bogalusa," Part 10, reel 10, NAACP Papers. Subsequent note citations to NAACP material for this chapter are from Part 10 unless otherwise noted.

9. Foner, *Organized Labor*, 151–59.

10. *Crisis*, September 1919, 239–41.

11. Foner, *Organized Labor*, 160–68.

12. Foner, *Organized Labor*, 168–70; *Crisis*, August 1924, 53–54.

13. Eric Arneson, "Like Banquo's Ghost It Will Not Down: The Race Question and the American Railroad Brotherhoods, 1880–1920," *American Historical Review* 99, no. 5 (December 1994): 1,601–33.

14. Arthur B. Hill to WFW, December 13, 1924, reel 4, table 2.

15. NAACP news release, January 21; J. H. Eiland to W. S. Carter, January 26; Carter to Eiland, February 7; all dates 1919; Memorandum from WFW, January 4–5, 1920; NAACP news release, April 10, 1920, reel 22.

16. WFW to Interstate Commerce Commission (ICC), May 25; WFW to U.S. attorney general, May 25; ICC to WFW, May 27; R. P. Stewart to WFW, May 31; *New York World*, August 1, reel 22; *Crisis*, September; all dates 1921.

17. Senate bill 2646; Typescript, "Protest against the Adoption of Howell-Barkely Bill," April 7, 1924; Thomas Redd to WFW, June 10, September 19, 1924; Thomas Driver to WFW, November 21, 1924, reel 22.

18. Myrdal, *An American Dilemma*, 1,105.

19. Anderson, *Randolph*, 23–52, quote 52. There are many fine books on Randolph; a good introduction is Benjamin Quarles, "A. Philip Randolph," in *Black Leaders of the Twentieth Century*, ed. John Hope Franklin and August Meier (Urbana: University of Illinois Press, 1982) 139–65.

20. Anderson, *Randolph*, 53–61.

21. Anderson, *Randolph*, 138–50; *Messenger*, November 1924, 369–71.

22. Anderson, *Randolph*, 153–69.

23. Ibid., 168–86.

24. BSCP news release, August 12, 1926; RWB to Frank Crosswaith, April 15, 1926; A. Philip Randolph to WP, July 1, 1926; NAACP to S. C. Hungerford, (Pullman Co.), n.d.; NAACP board minutes, November and December, 1927; Foner, *Organized Labor*, 177–87.

25. Marable, in *Black Radical Democrat*, 110, credits the *Crisis* as the union's best supporter and cites Du Bois's willingness to put personal feelings aside. The second point may be true, but the *Crisis* ran only two or three brief articles on the union during the 1920s and never featured its struggle. See *Crisis*, January 1926, 115, and January 1927, 131. The correspondence between the BSCP and Du Bois is small and formal in tone. See A. Philip Randolph to WEBD, December 28, 1927, reel 21; Frank Crosswaith to WEBD, January 11, 1928, reel 24; Randolph to WEBD, April 29, 1929, reel 27, in WEBD Papers.

26. Typescript, *Wills v. Local 106*, July 12, 1927, reel 4.

27. Senate bill 1482; *Cleveland Press*, March 16, 1928; Affidavit of Charles E. West, reel 4.

28. Clark L. Mock to JWJ, March 12; Harry E. Davis to JWJ, April 5 and May 2; Memorandum from JWJ, April 28, reel 11; NAACP board minutes, April and special meeting April 13; all dates 1927.

29. William English Walling to William Green, May 29, Green to Walling, May 31; Green to JWJ, November 20; all dates 1928; WFW to Walling, January 18, 1929; WFW to Benjamin Stollberg, January 26, 1929, reel 11; *Nation*, January 9, 1929; *Crisis*, July 1929, 241; Foner, *Organized Labor*, 175–76.

30. Mrs. B. A. Sannicks to JWJ, March 1, 1921; WFW to Will Hayes, March 8, 1921; J. C. Koons to WFW, May 25, 1921, reel 7; NAACP news release, February 3, 1928, reel 11.

31. NAACP news release, February 24, 1922, reel 10.

32. NAACP news release, October 29, 1929; Typescript, "With Regard to J. H. Jones";

WFW to William Green, February 14, 1930; William Kohn to WFW, February 28, 1930, reel 7.

33. Geoffrey Perrett, *America in the Twenties: A History* (New York: Simon and Schuster, 1982), 246-47.

34. Helen Boardman[?] typescript article, "Vicksburg: A Victory for the South"; L. M. Moon to JWJ, May 14, 1927; R. E. Malone to Mrs. Black, May 19, 1927, reel 13.

35. Anonymous to *Chicago Defender*, May 2; *Pittsburgh Courier*, May 14; William H. Gill to NAACP, May 18; all dates 1927, reel 13.

36. WFW, "The Negro and the Flood," *Nation*, June 22, 1927, 688; Typescript, "The NAACP Makes Suggestions to the Red Cross"; WFW to Herbert Hoover, June 14, 1927; Will Irwin to WFW, June 11, 1927; "Report of the Colored Advisory Commission on the Mississippi Valley Flood Disaster," chaired by Robert R. Moton, is quite favorable to government relief efforts, reel 13.

37. Theodore Draper, *The Roots of American Communism* (New York: Viking Press, 1957).

38. Ray Ginger, *Eugene V. Debs: A Biography* (New York: Collier Books, 1949), 275-78; Irving Howe, *Socialism and America* (New York: Harcourt, Brace, Jovanovich, 1985), 21.

39. Mark Solomon, *The Cry Was Unity: Communists and African-Americans, 1917-1936* (Jackson: University of Mississippi Press, 1998), 38-43; Wayne F. Cooper, *Claude McKay: Rebel Sojourner in the Harlem Renaissance* (Baton Rouge: Louisiana State University Press, 1987), 171-92.

40. Mark Naison, *Communists in Harlem during the Depression* (Urbana: University of Illinois Press, 1983), 3-25; Solomon, *Cry Was Unity*, 3-21.

41. Solomon, *Cry Was Unity*, 52-59; Naison, *Communists in Harlem*, 13-14; Abram L. Harris Jr., "Lenin Casts His Shadow over Africa," *Crisis*, April 1926, 272-75.

42. This passage owes much to Marable, *Black Radical Democrat*, 108-13.

43. *Crisis*, August 1921, 154; November 1921, 20; February 1927, 184-88; March 1927, 4-5; September 1928, 306-7; WEBD to Bishop John Hurst, May 17, 1927, reel 22, WEBD Papers.

44. WEBD, *Dusk of Dawn*, 285-88. Du Bois apparently gets the date wrong, and the words "communist dictatorship" probably show his feelings in 1940 during the Stalin-Hitler pact, not in 1927 or at the end of his life.

45. *Crisis*, November 1926, 9-10, February 1927, 189-90; WEBD, *Dusk*, 287; see Cooper, *Claude McKay*, 174-75, for an account of the positive response McKay got in the streets of Moscow.

46. WEBD, "Russia and the Race Problem," reel 22, WEBD Papers. The best account of Du Bois's trip is in Lewis, *Fight for Equality*, 194-204.

47. Lovett Fort-Whiteman to WP, August 20, 31, September 1, 1926, Box 1, in WP Papers, Schomburg Library; Avery, 110-25; NAACP board minutes, January 1927.

48. Solomon, *Cry Was Unity*, 68-91, gives a detailed and sympathetic account of this discussion; Harry Haywood, *Black Bolshevik: Autobiography of an Afro-American Communist* (Chicago: Liberator Press, 1978), 256-69, gives a participant's account; James P. Cannon, "The Russian Revolution and the American Negro Movement," in *The First Ten Years of American Communism* (New York: Lyle Stuart), 229-43.

49. WEBD, "The Negro and Communism," *Crisis*, September 1931.

NOTES TO CHAPTER 25

1. WEBD, *Dusk*, 293.

2. Arnold Rampersad, *The Art and Imagination of W. E. B. Du Bois* (1976; rept. New York: Schocken Books, 1990), 184-89.

3. Carolyn Wedin Sylvander, "Jessie Redmon Fauset," *Dictionary of Literary Biogra-*

phy, vol. 51 (Detroit: Bruccoli Clark Layman, 1987), 76–86; Lewis, *When Harlem Was in Vogue*, 121–25.

4. Fauset quoted in Rampersad, 187; George Hutchinson, *The Harlem Renaissance in Black and White* (Cambridge, Mass.: Belknap Press of Harvard University Press, 1995), 142.

5. For Hughes, See Rampersad, *Art and Imagination*, 187; other references in Sondra Kathryn Wilson, ed., *The Crisis Reader* (New York: Random House, 1999); Hughes, 24–25; Cullen, 11–12; McKay, 37; Bennett, 3.

6. Rudolph Fisher, "City of Refuge," in Locke, *The New Negro*, 57–75.

7. Lewis, *When Harlem Was in Vogue*, 113–15.

8. Locke, *The New Negro*.

9. Lewis, *When Harlem Was in Vogue*, 95–97, 115–18; Hutchinson, *Harlem Renaissance*, 170–209, 390.

10. *Crisis*, March 1926; April 1926, 278; June 1926, 72.

11. Lewis, *When Harlem Was in Vogue*, 188.

12. *Crisis*, December 1926; Lewis, *When Harlem Was in Vogue*, 109 (JWJ quote), 186; Langston Hughes, *The Big Sea* (1940; rept. New York: Hill and Wang, 1996), 268–72, gives a sympathetic reading.

13. Lewis, *When Harlem Was in Vogue*, 193–97; For Nugent, see Lewis, *Harlem Renaissance Reader*, 762–63.

14. WEBD, "Criteria of Negro Art," October 1926, 290; June 1928, 202; Allison Davis, "Our Negro Intellectuals," August 1928, 268–69, both in *Crisis*.

15. Hutchinson, *Harlem Renaissance*, 16–17. It does not escape me that Hutchinson and I, both white writers, emphasize the positive contributions of progressive whites, while African-American critics remain more skeptical.

16. Lewis, *When Harlem Was in Vogue*, 139.

17. Rampersad, *Art and Imagination*, 194–96.

NOTES TO CHAPTER 26

1. NAACP Board minutes, May 1928.

2. *Crisis*, September 1928, 311.

3. MWO, *Black and White*, 115.

4. RWB to WEBD, January 20, 1927; WP to Mrs. J. M. Scott, March 19, 1927; *California Eagle*, March 25, 1927, Box G-16, Los Angeles file, LC.

5. Northern California NAACP to fraternal societies, November 1, 1924; Hattie de Hart to RWB, November 3, 1926, January 13, March 9, 1927, Part 12 D, reel 2, NAACP Papers.

6. Edward D. Mabson to RWB, April 9, 1923, October 7, 1924; RWB to Tabytha Anderson, August 6, 1925; San Francisco NAACP to fraternal orders, October 26, 1928, Part 12 D, reel 2, NAACP Papers.

7. JWJ to Mrs. Dodge, April 18, 1924; Viola Johnson to WEBD, January 19, 1927; Vila Johnson to JWJ, February 11, 1927, Part 12 D, reel 2, NAACP Papers.

8. WFW, *A Man Called White*, 99–101.

9. *Crisis*, August 1928, 265, September 1928, 295–96.

10. WFW, *A Man Called White*, 99–101; *Chicago Whip*, August 11, 1928, Part 11 B, reel 20, NAACP Papers.

11. Nancy J. Weiss, *Farewell to the Party of Lincoln: Black Politics in the Age of Franklin D. Roosevelt* (Princeton: Princeton University Press, 1983), 3–12; *Crisis*, October 1928, 346.

12. For the stock market, see John Kenneth Galbraith, *The Great Crash of 1929* (1954; rept. Boston: Houghton Mifflin, 1961), 71–92.

13. Cleveland convention, Part 1, reel 8, NAACP Papers.

14. NAACP board minutes, May, October 14, October 28, 1929.

15. For WEBD's departure from the NAACP, see Lewis, *Fight for Equality*, 275–301. I also have the benefit of Herbert Hill's thoughts on the White–Du Bois relationship: Herbert Hill, interview by author, December 1997.

Selected Bibliography

Manuscript Collections

Alexander Pierre Tureaud Papers, Amistad Center, Tulane University

Arthur B. Spingarn Papers, Manuscript Division, Library of Congress

Arthur I. Waskow Papers, Wisconsin State Historical Society

James Weldon Johnson Papers, Beinecke Library, Yale University

Mary White Ovington Papers, Walter Reuther Library, Wayne State University, Detroit

NAACP Papers, Manuscript Division, Library of Congress

NAACP Papers, microfilm edition

W. E. B. Du Bois Papers, microfilm edition

William Pickens Papers, Schomburg Institute, New York Public Library

Newspapers

Baltimore Afro-American
Chicago Defender
Louisiana Weekly
New York Age

Books

Akers, Monte. *Flames after Midnight: Murder, Vengeance, and the Desolation of a Texas Community.* Austin: University of Texas Press, 1999.

Alexander, Charles C. *The Ku Klux Klan in the Southwest.* 1965. Rept. Norman: University of Oklahoma Press, 1995.

Anderson, James D. *The Education of Blacks in the South, 1860–1935.* Chapel Hill: University of North Carolina Press, 1988.

Anderson, Jervis. *A. Philip Randolph: A Biographical Portrait.* 1972. Rept. Berkeley: University of California Press, 1986.

Aptheker, Herbert. *A Documentary History of the Negro People in the United States.* Vol. III. New York: Carol Publishing Group, 1993.

Avery, Sheldon. *Up From Washington: William Pickens and the Negro Struggle for Equality, 1900–1954.* Newark, Del.: University of Delaware Press, 1988.

Ayers, Edward L. *The Promise of the New South: Life after Reconstruction.* New York: Oxford University Press, 1992.

Baker, Ray Stannard. *Following the Color Line: American Negro Citizenship in the Progressive Era.* 1908. Rept. New York: Harper Torchbooks, 1964.

Bontemps, Arna. *One Hundred Years of Negro Freedom.* New York: Dodd, Mead, 1961.

Broderick, Francis L. *W. E. B. Du Bois: Negro Leader in a Time of Crisis.* Stanford: Stanford University Press, 1959.

Bruce, Dickson D. Jr. *Archibald Grimké: Portrait of a Black Independent.* Baton Rouge: Louisiana State University Press, 1993.

Brundage, W. Fitzhugh. *Lynching in the New South: Georgia and Virginia, 1880–1930.* Urbana: University of Illinois Press, 1993.

Bryson, Conrey. *Dr. Lawrence A. Nixon and the White Primary.* 1974. Rept. El Paso: University of Texas at El Paso, 1992.

Cannon, Poppy. *A Gentle Knight: My Husband, Walter White.* New York: Rinehart Publishing, 1956.

Chalmers, David M. *Hooded Americanism: The History of the Ku Klux Klan.* 3d ed. Durham: Duke University Press, 1987.

Cooper, Wayne F. *Claude McKay: Rebel Sojourner in the Harlem Renaissance.* Baton Rouge: Louisiana State University Press, 1987.

Cortner, Richard C. *A Mob Intent on Death: The NAACP and the Arkansas Riot Cases.* Middletown, Conn.: Wesleyan University Press, 1988.

Cronon, Edmund David. *Black Moses: The Story of Marcus Garvey and the Universal Negro Improvement Association.* Madison, Wis.: University of Wisconsin Press, 1969.

Cryer, Daniel Walter. "Mary White Ovington and the Rise of the NAACP," Ph.D. diss., University of Minnesota, 1977.

Daniel, Pete. *The Shadow of Slavery: Peonage in the South, 1901–1969.* Urbana: University of Illinois Press, 1972.

Diner, Hasia R. *In the Almost Promised Land: American Jews and Blacks, 1915–1935.* 1977. Rept. Baltimore: Johns Hopkins University Press, 1995.

Dittmer, John. *Black Georgia in the Progressive Era, 1900–1920.* Urbana: University of Illinois Press, 1980.

Du Bois, William Edward Burghardt. *The Autobiography of W. E. B. Du Bois: A Soliloquy on Viewing My Life from the Last Decade of Its First Century.* 1968. Rept. New York: International Publishers, 1988.

———. *Dusk of Dawn.* 1940. Rept. New Brunswick, N.J.: Transaction Publishers, 1994.

Edgar, Walter. *South Carolina: A History.* Columbia: University of South Carolina Press, 1998.

Ellsworth, Scott. *Death in a Promised Land: The Tulsa Race Riot of 1921.* Baton Rouge: Louisiana State University Press, 1982.

Ferrell, Claudine. *Nightmare and Dream: Anti-Lynching in Congress, 1917–1922.* New York: Garland Publishing, 1986.

Foner, Phillip S. *American Socialism and Black Americans: From the Age of Jackson to World War II.* Westport, Conn.: Greenwood Press, 1977.

Fox, Stephen R. *The Guardian of Boston: William Monroe Trotter.* New York: Atheneum, 1970.

Franklin, Jimmy Lee. *Journey Toward Hope: A History of Blacks in Oklahoma.* Norman: University of Oklahoma Press, 1982.

Franklin, John Hope. *From Slavery to Freedom: A History of Negro Americans.* 3d ed. New York: Alfred A. Knopf, 1967.

Franklin, John Hope, and August Meier, eds. *Black Leaders of the Twentieth Century.* Urbana: University of Illinois Press, 1982.

Gatewood, Willard B. *Aristocrats of Color: The Black Elite, 1880–1920.* Bloomington: Indiana University Press, 1990.

Giddings, Paula. *When and Where I Enter: The Impact of Black Women on Race and Sex in America.* New York: William Morrow, 1984.

Ginzburg, Ralph. *One Hundred Years of Lynchings.* Baltimore: Black Classic Press, 1988.

Goings, Kenneth W. *The NAACP Comes of Age: The Defeat of Judge John W. Parker.* Bloomington: Indiana University Press, 1990.

Gottlieb, Peter. *Making Their Own Way: Southern Blacks' Migration to Pittsburgh, 1916–1930.* Urbana: University of Illinois Press, 1987.

Grant, Donald L. *The Anti-Lynching Movement, 1883–1932.* San Francisco: RE/Search Publications, 1975.

Green, Constance McLaughlin. *The Secret City: A History of Race Relations in the Nation's Capital.* Princeton: Princeton University Press, 1967.

Grossman, James R. *Land of Hope: Chicago, Black Southerners, and the Great Migration.* Chicago: University of Chicago Press, 1991.

Hadlock, Richard. *Jazz Masters of the 20s.* 1972. Rept. New York: Da Capo Press, 1988.

Hall, Jacquelyn Dowd. *Revolt against Chivalry: Jessie Daniel Ames and the Women's Campaign against Lynching.* New York: Columbia University Press, 1979.

Haynes, Robert V. *A Night of Violence: The Houston Riot of 1917.* Baton Rouge: Louisiana State University Press, 1976.

Haywood, Harry. *Black Bolshevik: Autobiography of an Afro-American Communist.* Chicago: Liberator Press, 1978.

Henri, Florette. *Black Migration: Movement North, 1900–1920: The Road From Myth to Man.* Garden City, N.Y.: Anchor Books, 1976.

Hine, Darlene Clark. *Black Victory: The NAACP and the Destruction of the White Primary, 1924–1944.* Millwood, N.Y.: KTO Press, 1979.

Hirsch, Arnold R., and Joseph Logsdon. *Creole New Orleans: Race and Americanization.* Baton Rouge: Louisiana State University Press, 1992.

Hixson, William B. *Moorfield Storey and the Abolitionist Tradition.* New York: Oxford University Press, 1972.

Hughes, Langston. *Fight for Freedom: The Story of the NAACP.* New York: W. W. Norton, 1962.

Hutchinson, George. *The Harlem Renaissance in Black and White.* Cambridge, Mass.: Belknap Press of Harvard University Press, 1995.

Jackson, Kenneth T. *The Ku Klux Klan in the City, 1915–1930.* 1967. Rept. Chicago: Ivan R. Dee, 1992.

Johnson, James Weldon. *Black Manhattan.* 1930. Rept. New York: Da Capo Press, 1991.

———. *Along This Way: The Autobiography of James Weldon Johnson.* 1933. Rept. New York: Viking Press, 1968.

Kelley, Robin D. G. *Hammer and Hoe: Alabama Communists during the Great Depression.* Chapel Hill: University of North Carolina Press, 1990.

Kellogg, Charles Flint. *NAACP: A History of the National Association for the Advancement of Colored People.* Vol. I. *1909–1920.* Baltimore: Johns Hopkins University Press, 1967.

Kilson, Martin, ed. *Politics in Black America: Crisis and Change in the Negro Ghetto.* New York: St. Martin's Press, 1973.

Kluger, Richard. *Simple Justice.* New York: Random House, 1975.

Kornweibel, Theodore Jr. *No Crystal Stair: Black Life and the Messenger, 1917–1928.* Westport, Conn.: Greenwood Press, 1975.

Kusmer, Kenneth L. *A Ghetto Takes Shape: Black Cleveland, 1870–1930.* Urbana: University of Illinois Press, 1978.

Lane, James B. *City of the Century: A History of Gary, Indiana.* Bloomington: Indiana University Press, 1978.

Levy, Eugene. *James Weldon Johnson: Black Leader: Black Voice.* Chicago: University of Chicago Press, 1973.

Lewis, David Levering, ed. *The Portable Harlem Renaissance Reader.* New York: Penguin Books, 1994.

———. *W. E. B. Du Bois: A Reader.* New York: Henry Holt, 1995.

———. *W. E. B. Du Bois: Biography of a Race, 1868–1919.* New York: Henry Holt, 1993.

———. *W. E. B. Du Bois: The Fight for Equality and the American Century, 1919–1963.* New York: Henry Holt, 2000.

———. *When Harlem Was in Vogue.* New York: Oxford University Press, 1979.

Locke, Alain, ed. *The New Negro: Voices of the Harlem Renaissance.* 1925. Rept. New York: Atheneum, 1992.

Marable, Manning. *W. E. B. Du Bois: Black Radical Democrat.* Boston: Twayne Publishers, 1986.

McPherson, James. *The Abolitionist Legacy: From Reconstruction to the NAACP.* Princeton: Princeton University Press, 1975.

Miller, Loren. *The Petitioners: The Story of the Supreme Court of the United States and the Negro.* New York: Random House, 1966.

Myrdal, Gunnar. *An American Dilemma: The Negro Problem and Modern Democracy.* 1944. Rept. New York: Harper and Row, 1962.

Naison, Mark. *Communists in Harlem during the Depression.* Urbana: University of Illinois Press, 1983.

Osofsky, Gilbert. *Harlem: The Making of a Ghetto: Negro New York, 1890–1930.* New York: Harper Torchbooks, 1966.

Ottley, Roi. *The Lonely Warrior: The Life and Times of Robert S. Abbott.* Chicago: Henry Regnery, 1955.

Ovington, Mary White. *Black and White Sat Down Together: The Reminiscences of an NAACP Founder.* Edited by Ralph E. Luker. New York: Feminist Press, 1995.

———. *The Walls Came Tumbling Down.* New York: Arno Press and the *New York Times,* 1969.

———. *Portraits in Color.* New York: Viking Press, 1927.

Pickens, William. *Bursting Bonds: The Heir of Slaves: The Autobiography of a "New Negro."* 1923. Rept. Bloomington: Indiana University Press, 1991.

Rampersad, Arnold. *The Art and Imagination of W. E. B. Du Bois.* 1976. Rept. New York: Schocken Books, 1990.

Raper, Arthur F. *The Tragedy of Lynching.* 1933. Rept. Montclair, N.J.: Patterson Smith, 1969.

Record, Wilson. *Race and Radicalism: The NAACP and the Communist Party in Conflict.* Ithaca: Cornell University Press, 1964.

Reed, Christopher. *The Chicago NAACP and the Rise of Black Professional Leadership.* Bloomington: Indiana University Press, 1998.

Ross, B. Joyce. *J. E. Spingarn and the Rise of the NAACP, 1911–1939.* New York: Atheneum, 1972.

Salem, Dorothy. *To Better Our World: Black Women in Organized Reform, 1890–1920.* Brooklyn: Carlson Press, 1990.

Solomon, Mark. *The Cry Was Unity: Communists and African-Americans, 1917–1936.* Jackson: University Press of Mississippi, 1998.

Spear, Allan H. *Black Chicago: The Making of a Negro Ghetto, 1890–1920.* Chicago: University of Chicago Press, 1967.

Stein, Judith. *The World of Marcus Garvey: Race and Class in Modern Society.* Baton Rouge: Louisiana State University Press, 1986.

Taylor, Quintard. *In Search of the Racial Frontier: African Americans in the American West, 1528–1990.* New York: W. W. Norton, 1999.

Thomas, Richard Walter. *Life for Us Is What We Make It: Building Black Community in Detroit, 1915–1945.* Bloomington: Indiana University Press, 1992.

Thornbrough, Emma Lou. *T. Thomas Fortune: Militant Journalist.* Chicago: University of Chicago Press, 1972.

Trotter, Joe William Jr. *Black Milwaukee: The Making of an Industrial Proletariat, 1915–1945.* Urbana: University of Illinois Press, 1988.

———. *Blacks in Southern West Virginia, 1915–1932.* Urbana: University of Illinois Press, 1990.

———. *The Great Migration in Historical Perspective.* Bloomington: Indiana University Press, 1991.

Tucker, Richard E. *The Dragon and the Cross: The Rise and Fall of the Ku Klux Klan in Middle America.* Hamden, Conn.: Shoestring Press, 1991.

Tushnet, Mark V. *The NAACP's Legal Strategy against Segregated Education, 1925–1950.* Chapel Hill: University of North Carolina Press, 1987.

Tuttle, William L. Jr. *Race Riot: Chicago in the Red Summer of 1919.* 1970. Rept. Urbana: University of Illinois Press, 1996.

Villard, Oswald Garrison. *Fighting Years: Memoirs of a Liberal Editor.* New York: Harcourt, Brace, 1939.

Waskow, Arthur I. *From Race Riot to Sit-In, 1919 and the 1960s: A Study in the Connections between Conflict and Violence.* Garden City, N.Y.: Doubleday, 1967.

Wedin, Carolyn. *Inheritors of the Spirit: Mary White Ovington and the Founding of the NAACP.* New York: John Wiley and Sons, 1998.

Weiss, Nancy J. *The National Urban League, 1910–1940.* New York: Oxford University Press, 1974.

Wells-Barnett, Ida B. *Crusade for Justice: The Autobiography of Ida B. Wells.* Edited by Alfreda Duster. Chicago: University of Chicago Press, 1970.

White, Walter. *A Man Called White: The Autobiography of Walter White.* New York: Viking Press, 1948.

———. *Rope and Faggot: The Biography of Judge Lynch.* 1929. Rept. New York: Arno Press and the *New York Times,* 1969.

Wilkins, Roy, with Tom Mathews. *Standing Fast: The Autobiography of Roy Wilkins.* 1982. Rept. New York: Da Capo Press, 1994.

Wilson, Sandra K., ed. *Selected Writings of James Weldon Johnson.* New York: Oxford University Press, 1995.

Wright, George C. *Racial Violence in Kentucky, 1865–1940: Lynchings, Mob Rule, and "Legal Lynchings."* Baton Rouge: Louisiana State University Press, 1990.

Zangrando, Robert L. *The NAACP Crusade against Lynching, 1909–1950.* Philadelphia: Temple University Press, 1980.

Periodicals

Daniel, Pete. "Black Power in the 1920s: The Case of Tuskegee Veterans Hospital." *Journal of Southern History* 36, no. 3 (1970): 368–88.

Meier, August, and John H. Bracey Jr. "The NAACP as a Reform Movement, 1909–1965: To Reach the Conscience of America." *Journal of Southern History* 59, no. 1 (February 1993): 3–30.

Meier, August, and Elliot Rudwick. "Early Boycotts of Segregated Schools: The Case of Springfield, Ohio." *American Quarterly* 20, no. 4 (1968): 744–58.

Sherman, Richard B. "The Harding Administration and the Negro: An Opportunity Lost." *Journal of Negro History* 49, no. 3 (July 1964): 151–68.

Dissertations

Autrey, Dorothy A. "The NAACP in Alabama, 1913–1952," Ph.D. diss., University of Notre Dame, 1985.

Index